THE LABOURING CLASSES IN EARLY INDUSTRIAL ENGLAND, 1750–1850

THEMES IN BRITISH SOCIAL HISTORY

edited by Dr J. Stevenson

This series covers the most important aspects of British social history from the renaissance to the present day. Topics include education, poverty, health, religion, leisure, crime and popular protest, some of which are treated in more than one volume. The books are written for undergraduates, postgraduates and the general reader, and each volume combines a general approach to the subject with the primary research of the author.

THE LABOURING CLASSES
IN EARLY INDUSTRIAL
ENGLAND, 1750–1850

John Rule

LONGMAN
London and New York

LONGMAN GROUP LIMITED
Longman House, Burnt Mill, Harlow
Essex CM20 2JE, England
Associated companies throughout the world

*Published in the United States of America
by Longman Inc., New York*

©Longman Group Limited 1986

First published 1986

BRITISH LIBRARY CATALOGUING IN PUBLICATION DATA

Rule, John
  The labouring classes in early industrial
  england, 1750–1850.—(Themes in British
  social history)
  1. Labor and laboring classes—Great Britain
  —History
  I. Title   II. Series
  305.5'62'0941   HD8389

ISBN 0-582-49172-X

LIBRARY OF CONGRESS CATALOGING IN PUBLICATION DATA

Rule, John, 1944–
  The labouring classes in early industrial England,
1750–1850.

  (Themes in British social history)
  Bibliography: p.
  Includes index.
  1. Labor and laboring classes—England—History.
2. England—Social conditions.   I. Title.   II. Series.
HD8389.R85 1986   305.5'62'0942   85–16665
ISBN 0-582-49172-X (pbk.)

Set in 10/11pt Linoterm Times
Produced by Longman Group (FE) Limited
Printed in Hong Kong

CONTENTS

v

Contents

ACKNOWLEDGEMENTS

We are indebted to the following for permission to reproduce copyright material: Edward Arnold Ltd and the Author, Professor S. Pollard for Table 6 from Table p222 *Genesis of Modern Management*; Adam & Charles Black Ltd for Table 4 from Table p108 *Consumption and Standards of Living* by C. Zimmerman, pub. Williams & Norgate 1936.

LIST OF TABLES

PREFACE

This book appears in a series aimed at students and, hopefully, at the 'general reader'. My object has been to offer a synthesis of the vast amount of work which has been done in recent years on the material condition, culture and responses of the working classes during a period of exceptional upheaval. I have given much space to updating familiar debates, such as that over the 'standard of living', but have also attempted to bring in subjects not so well covered in older textbooks: the family, leisure, popular culture and the work experience. This last has been especially neglected until recent years despite the centrality of the workplace and its social relations in the lives of working people. Some explanation is necessary for a slighter treatment of several important topics. This is a volume in a series in which other titles have already become established as authorities on some areas of the wide canvas attempted here. The impact of the New Poor Law and the development of factory legislation have been covered by Ursula Henriques in *Before the Welfare State: Social administration in early industrial Britain*, 1979. John Stevenson, *Popular Disturbances in England 1700–1870*, 1981, has allowed me to give less space to unstructured forms of popular protest than their frequency would seem to require. A. D. Gilbert, *Religion and Society in Industrial England: Church, chapel and social change 1740–1914*, 1976, and J. Weeks, *Sex, Politics and Society: The regulation of sexuality since 1800*, 1981, offer fuller treatment of subjects underexplored here. Crime will be the subject of other volumes which will have appeared by the time this book does.

I have also been influenced by the availability of up-to-date student texts. The pre-1850 history of trade unionism has not seen a substantial general treatment since the Webbs' classic was published nearly a century ago. This would seem to justify the space allowed in this book. I am well aware that most labouring people were not members of trade unions, but English trade unionism is perhaps more conditioned by its historical past than in any other country. It is important that this history be presented.

It would be impossible to thank as many scholars as those whose work has been drawn upon in such a wide-ranging work as this. Any author has as great a debt to those scholars with whom he has, in places, disagreed as perhaps to those whose opinions most closely approach his own. Among those whose contribution to the economic and social history of this period is substantial and indispensable, but with *some* of whose conclusions I differ, are A. E. Musson, S. D. Chapman, E. H. Hunt and R. M. Hartwell. Readers can consult their writings in the course of coming to their own judgements.

I have always enjoyed working with my Southampton colleagues. I single out Frederick Mather and Adrian Vinson because their interests as scholars, being related to my own, have made their comments especially welcome. Viv Luffman has coped yet again with a much amended draft and translated it into good copy, while Bryan Luffman was able to use his knowledge of social history to advise her what my typescript probably meant to say: a bonus benefit on top of many hours of discussion of most of the subject area of this book.

My wife has, as ever, been prepared to undertake much of the tedious but demanding tasks associated with book-making: proof reading, indexing and even counting pages. Most of the writing was done in 1984 so the only really appropriate dedication can be to the memory of the six men of Tolpuddle.

Among the very many useful things which my editor, John Stevenson, advised was to give some help to a younger generation of readers over the matter of money. I have accordingly given decimal equivalents throughout. But not only decimalisation separates today's students from the wage and price data of 1750–1850: even more of a problem is the exceptional inflation of recent times. I was once offered in 1962 employment as a clerk at £3.00 for a five-and-a-half-day week. Between me and the skilled wages of, perhaps, £1.50p a week of a craftsman in the early nineteenth century yawns no gap of comprehension equal to that of a modern student on an inadequate grant of perhaps £30 a week. The family budget below gives some idea of prices in the middle of our period (1795) when a farm labourer could expect to earn no more than 8s. (40p) in the south of England (shillings=s./ old pence (denarii) = d.):

Bread (or flour)	6s. 8d.	(33p)
Yeast and salt	4d.	(1.67p)
Meat	8d.	(3.33p)
Tea, sugar and butter	1s. 0d.	(5p)
Soap, starch	2½d.	(1.04p)
Candles	3d.	(1.25p)
Thread	3d.	(1.25p)

Preface

This was for a very bad time when food prices were *high* and the labourer would have needed to spend more than his usual income on food alone. Another 20p to 30p a *week* would have very substantially relieved him: a further 80p would have placed him among the well-paid workers.

JOHN RULE
Southampton 1985

INTRODUCTION:
PERSPECTIVES AND PROBLEMS

Describing a period of economic and social history as one of 'change', or as an 'age of transition', has become a cliché from which few periods of modern history have escaped. More urgency is conveyed by 'age of transformation' and even greater by 'age of revolution' with its dramatic conveyance of ideas of major structural change and social upheaval. The period 1750–1850 has attracted more such labels than most. To offer a social history of those years is to suggest to the intending reader that the 'great discontinuity' of modern times, the industrial revolution, will be central to its discussion and fill most of its pages. If a wider perspective is indicated, then coverage of those changes in rural society commonly short-handed the 'agricultural revolution' will be anticipated. (Although most recent specialists deny the validity of such a phenomenon as a near contemporaneous accompaniment of the industrial revolution.) Images of new turnpike roads, of canals and of the railway steaming into the last twenty years of the period come together as the 'transport revolution' and, most dramatic of all, the fact that about 1740 there began a sustained rise which took a 1700 population of around 5 million (England and Wales) to almost 18 million by 1851 justifies the use of 'demographic revolution'. With little fundamental change in its sex and age structure, the growing population produced an unprecedented increase in the supply of labour (an estimated 143 per cent between 1780 and 1850), as well as in mouths to feed and bodies to clothe and house.[1]

Remarkably, these revolutions interacted to result over the period as a whole in an output of goods and services which outpaced the increase in population. This growth was neither consistent nor even. The eighteenth century saw two distinct spurts: one beginning around 1740 and the other, more dramatic, around 1780 and associated with the 'take-off' of the industrial economy. Growth was also uneven over the first half of the nineteenth century and there was no significant improvement in consumption levels per head before 1820. Taking the period as a whole, national income per capita rose from £11 a year in

1

1780 to £28 in 1860.[2] Such an abstraction is of course hardly even an approximation to actual distribution, which involves a much more vexed discussion, but undeniably over the century under discussion the national output available for the population increased hugely and, in contrast to previous eras, growth was not only rapid, but sustained. Since agricultural output increased steadily rather than dramatically, and since little measurable extra productivity could have come from the overwhelmingly domestic service sector, it must be presumed that the increase in manufacturing and mining was spectacular. To most people the essense of an industrial revolution lies in the transformation through technology of manufacturing and in its re-organisation into a new factory mode of production characteristic of industrial capitalism – 'machinofacture' Marx termed it. The textile mills of Lancashire and the West Riding, labelled 'dark and satanic' as much in romantic literature as in socialist critique, stand in a sharply delineated foreground, their image, like that of the railway, inseparable from smoke and steam.

Factories had existed before 1750 but as isolated examples, visited in wonderment as novel presences in a world of manufacturing dominated by smaller-scale production and using manual power and techniques. Only from the closing years of the eighteenth century does it make any sense to talk of a factory *system* of production and to recognise, just, that one is standing in the foothills of a system destined in time to assume a heavy predominance in the nation's manufacturing and, over an even longer period, to absorb the energies of the greater proportion of the manufacturing labour force. Like most dramatic concepts, that of 'industrial revolution' in conveying a major truth, exaggerates the suddenness and completeness of actual happenings. Historians label retrospectively, and only a perceptive few of the people who lived through the years they describe can have anticipated fully the outcome which they assume. To travel hopefully, it is suggested, is better than to arrive. The working people of England in those years were travelling to a destination which they had not preselected and very many of them without much hope.

In the pages which follow, the 'hardy perennial' questions addressed to the social condition of the English working people of the period will be discussed alongside some posed by more recent interests and research findings. The factory children who persist in plucking the sleeve of the reader of history, imploring large-eyed and bent-bodied from Blue Book pages will continue to receive compassion no matter how much a 'harder' school of modern historians seeks to justify their employment and excuse the conditions in which they lived and laboured. So too will the working wives and mothers unable to find the time or money to meet the domestic needs of their families. No less evident was the appalling health-destroying environment of the new towns, or the strains of accommodation to the machine-dictated rhythms of factory production. No recent research has gone very far towards denying the depression and degradation of the southern farm labourer denied a living wage and forced into servile dependence on the poor law. The destruction of the handloom weavers is no less tragic for being presumed inevitable. The story is one of resistance as well as of endurance and adaptation: of trade unionism forged in a hostile environment, of the desperate 'Captain Swing' protest of farm labourers seeking the right to work for a living wage, and of Chartism, the world's first national labour movement.

In a short introduction there is little point in rehearsing the arguments and the presentation of events and experiences which fill the succeeding chapters. Space can be allowed only to set out some of the more fundamental indicators of change. Those who suggest that the very notion of an industrial revolution is misleading are usually implying that the transformation of the economy was more drawn out than the usual dates of demarkation suggest. The 'modern' economy began a long time before the second half of the eighteenth century, especially in what might be described as the 'evolution of capitalism' and its accompaniment the growth of a wage-dependent labour force. Most 'revolutions' have both short- and long-term causes. Without some broad and time-absorbing process of 'preconditioning' the final culmination of dramatic industrialisation would be unthinkable. Seventy years ago the Hammonds remarked: 'So much attention has been bestowed on the development of capitalism before the Industrial Revolution, that there is perhaps a tendency to underestimate the importance of the changes that accompanied the Revolution.'

Accepting that the 'fate of the worker at the Industrial Revolution was predetermined . . . by the social changes' which preceded it, they still ascribed to it the destruction of the 'last vestige' of initiative and choice in the daily lives of working people.[3] Simplistic notions of a pre-industrial 'Golden age' have been rightly scorned, notably by Dorothy George: 'Many of the evils which have been regarded as the direct result of the industrial revolution were as characteristic of the domestic system as of the factory system which gradually superseded it'.[4] Yet even to present the domestic modes of production as necessarily antecedents to 'machinofacture' is to mislead. Increasing output by hand workers outside the factory not only accompanied the birth and development of the factory system, but in several cases their numbers were expanded or even brought into being as a consequence of that development. Weavers, knitters, cutlers, shoemakers and the like were down to the 1840s the largest grouping of workers engaged in manufacture. Cotton handloom weavers on their own were probably still the largest single grouping of any specialised group into the 1820s. Numbers had increased substantially as a result of the early industrial revolution and within a short time the trade was overstocked with labour and degraded in status. Steam and the factory were the main cause of this increase between 1780 and 1830 for it was the mill-spun yarn, ahead by half a generation of the mechanisation of weaving, which had called for it and conferred a brief era of prosperity before the power loom completed a decline into oblivion. This means that they, in their very large numbers, must as much as the new factory proletariat be thought of as characteristic workers of a phase of the industrial revolution. There were other paradoxes. The new machines were to be turned and fitted by a new class of skilled craftsman, the engineer, but the factories which housed them, as well as the houses of those workers whose rhythms of labour they dictated, were built by one of the oldest of labour processes: the laying of one brick upon the top of another. The cloth, once weaving had been mechanised, poured from these factories yet was destined for another generation to be made into garments by the 'sweated' hordes who lived by the needle. With so much work still technologically untransformed in the middle years of the nineteenth century, it has been argued that for the bulk of the labouring population real changes in the work process did not take place until after the various terminal dates commonly assigned to the industrial revolution.[5]

But even if not technologically transformed, many of the hand trades were organisationally restructured. The spread of the 'sweating system' was as much a part of the labour exploitation which supported the 'workshop of the world' as was the emergence of the factory system. Perhaps throughout the period the only group of workers able to maintain – or at least able to put up a struggle to maintain – their status and well-being were the male-dominated skilled craft trades of the 'workshop' with their long traditions, exclusivity and dependence on skill to give them some protection in the labour market.

POLITICAL DIMENSIONS: THE FRENCH REVOLUTION

One other 'revolution' is part of the picture, although it did not take place in England: the French Revolutionary upheavals of 1789–1815. This is both because the French example with its challenging jacobin ideology stirred and fed the popular radicalism of English artisans and also because the wars with revolutionary and Napoleonic France lasting from 1793 to Waterloo had an enormous impact on the country. For more than twenty years, in the very midst of demographic explosion and economic and social upheaval, England was involved in a long war with extraordinarily high levels of participation. Dr Emsley has suggested: 'if there was a common experience shared by all Britons in the last decade of the eighteenth century and the early years of the nineteenth century it is to be found less in the changes resulting from the industrial revolution and more in the demands of war'. Invasion fears provided a constant threat and sense of insecurity and although some sectors of the economy such as the royal dockyards benefited from increased activity, disruption from the closing of overseas markets slumped manufacturing areas like the East Midlands into unemployment, misery and Luddism. High food prices, fundamentally because of bad harvests but seriously aggravated by the war situation, produced food crises of exceptional severity in 1795–6 and 1800–01 accompanied by rioting of alarming proportions. Price and wage inflation distorted both commodity and labour markets and in the outcome produced a severe post-war dislocation and deflation. On top of all this came the mobilisation of the able-bodied men. According to Emsley, government plans in 1794 for regulars, militia men and sailors suggest that is was planning to put about one in every ten men of military age under arms.[6]

E. P. Thompson's presentation of English radicalism and jacobinism in these years has hardly met with uncritical acceptance, but even if he has overstressed and overestimated the strength of the popular revolutionary societies, there is no doubt that the very evident apprehension of the government on this score reflected the fact that the 'new' radicalism professed the ideology of an enemy and recruited its followers from a more 'dangerous' population than had the radicalism of the 1760s and 1780s. If some historians quibble at describing an English government as 'counter-revolutionary', it must at least be acknowledged that it reacted to a perceived threat of revolution with a policy of repression. It is this which gives to the period 1793–1815 its unique configuration in bringing together economic exploitation and political repression.[7] Among the Hammonds' merits is that, unlike some of their critics, they understood the political context within which economic transformation was taking place; the 'shock of the French Revolution' had led government to a new way of looking at the mass of the nation:

> The poorer classes no longer seemed a passive power: they were dreaded as a Leviathan that was fast learning his strength. Regarded before as naturally contented, they were now regarded as naturally discontented. The art of politics was not the art of keeping the attachment of people who cherished their customs, religion, and the general setting of their lives, by moderation, foresight, and forbearance: it was the art of preserving discipline among a vast population destitute of the traditions and restraints of a settled and conservative society, dissatisfied with its inevitable lot and ready for disorder and blind violence. For two revolutions had come together. The French Revolution had transformed the minds of the ruling classes, and the Industrial Revolution had convulsed the world of the working classes.

The central message of their book *The Skilled Labourer* is a political one. The changes which go to make up the industrial revolution were not produced by some objective 'natural' force which can be conveniently neutered by such a term as 'industrialism'. For good or ill they were the products of a strong ideology: industrial capitalism. In so far as governments in coming to accept the premises of that ideology made it an 'official' one and ensured its success, then *laissez-faire* became as much a political as an economic ideology. The Hammonds saw a struggle between labour and capital in these terms: 'The upper classes divided their world into capital and labour, and they held that the struggle was between custom and initiative, between the prejudices of the poor which hampered industry, and the spirit of acquisition and adventure in the rich which encouraged it'.[8] In *The Rise of Modern Industry* (1925) they argued that necessary for the triumph of modern capitalist industry was the destruction of those regulating controls which had been operated first by the guilds and then by a paternalist government. In repealing the wage-fixing clauses of the Elizabethan Statute of Artificers in 1813 and those relating to apprenticeship in 1814, Parliament was finally registering the 'defeat of the workman and small master'. In this context they explicitly placed Luddism, as did Thompson, at 'the crisis point in the abrogation of paternalist legislation and in the imposition of the political economy of *laissez-faire* upon and against the will and conscience of the working people'.[9] However, some critics have suggested that the transition to a *laissez-faire* economy had substantially taken place well before the second decade of the nineteenth century so that only the bare bones of protective regulation remained and these were ill-regarded. The fact that, for example, the Statute of Artificers had only a symbolic rather than an actual importance well before the repeals of 1813 and 1814 does not mean that it had not retained a special significance in the consciousness of artisans. They continued to act at the crisis points of their trades as if regulatory redress of their grievances was obtainable. The statute had an important reality in the sense of what *ought* to be, based on a powerful vision of a past when well-being had been preserved by custom and by protective legislation. In this sense the struggles of artisans against capitalist innovations which threatened their livelihood and status do mark a special crisis: a moment of conflict between triumphing *laissez-faire* capitalism and older notions of a social or 'moral' economy. The series of disappointments suffered by framework knitters, handloom weavers and calico printers was the outcome of the last era in which oppressed sections of the artisan classes hoped in the first instance for redress from a Parliament prepared to curb the activities of capital. Each trade seems to record anew its disillusionment as the cotton workers did in 1811 after failing to secure an act for a minimum wage:

> We are only mechanics, of course ill acquainted with the reason why
> some measures are frequently opposed at one time, by the same argu-
> ments by which at other times they are vindicated and supported . . .
> This committee are utterly at a loss to conceive on what fair ground
> legislative interference can be improper under circumstances so neces-
> sitous.[10]

Few modern historians would paint a picture of political oppression in
terms as extreme as the Hammonds did. Of Lord Liverpool's post-war
government they wrote: 'Probably no English Government has ever
been quite so near, in spirit and licence, to the atmosphere that we
associate with the Tsar's government of Russia.'[11] It is not perhaps a
particularly apt analogy, but this government did suspend habeas
corpus, operate through a network of police spies and informers, and
censure the press. The working people of the period of the industrial
revolution had not only to face painful adjustments but had to do so in
an atmosphere of implacable and sustained hostility from government
towards any defensive organisation they attempted to form. The
government of 'liberal toryism' headed by Liverpool was no more
oppressive than the wartime governments which had preceded it, and
the Reform Act of 1832 had been already passed when a Whig government assisted a tyrannical local magistrate and a revengeful judiciary
to transport, in 1834, six poor labourers from Tolpuddle for forming a
trade union.

THE LABOUR FORCE: CHANGES IN STRUCTURE AND IN SCALE

To detail the changes taking place in the deployment and organisation
of the labour force and to assess how many labour processes were
subjected to serious reformation would need another book fully as
long as this one, and there are textbooks available for the student.[12]
Here we can only indicate outlines and suggest trends. If the idea of
industrial revolution has a validity, it is as the shorthand expression of
a marked shift in the labour force away from agriculture and into
manufacturing. This shift was especially rapid in the early decades of
the nineteenth century after being gradual but definite over much of
the eighteenth. Around 1700, perhaps somewhere between a quarter
and a half of the occupied population were in manufacturing and
mining and their output was roughly equal to that of agriculture in
value. By mid-century, trade and manufacturing together may have
employed more workers than did agriculture although the problem of

'mixed' occupations makes precise measurement impossible. By 1801 the 29.7% recorded as occupied in agriculture, if added to the 11.2% in trade, clearly outweighed the 35.9% primarily engaged in agriculture. Between 1801 and 1811 there was little movement, but between 1811 and 1821, while agriculture fell by 4.6%, manufacturing rose by 8.2%. By 1851 manufacturing and mining accounted for the employment of 42.9% of the labour force. Thereafter there was little shift towards manufacturing which in 1881 was only 0.65% higher than it had been thirty years before. The continued decline in agriculture had been increasingly taken up by the tertiary sector (Table 1). Share of the labour force is not a measure of absolute numbers. Those engaged in agriculture continued to form the largest single category in 1851 with more than 2 million workers (Table 2). Before 1851 it is not possible to make a systematic classification of the manufacturing and mining labour force. The majority of those employed in manufacturing in 1851 still did not work in factories, nor in any form of establishment which employed a large number of workers under one roof or on one site.

TABLE 1   Estimated percentage distribution of the British labour force, 1811–1911

	Agriculture, forestry, fishing	Manufacture mining, industry	Trade and transport	Domestic & personal	Public, Pro-fessional & all other
1811	33.0	30.2	11.6	11.8	13.3
1821	28.4	38.4	12.1	12.7	8.5
1851	21.7	42.9	15.8	13.0	6.7
1881	12.6	43.5	21.3	15.4	7.3
1911	8.3	46.4	21.5	13.9	9.9

However, increasing numbers did do so, for the change in scale from the eighteenth to the nineteenth century is unmistakeable. Large establishments were not unknown before 1800. Portsmouth dockyard with 2,228 workers on its establishment in 1772 was large by any standard. Plymouth was not much smaller and the other royal dock-yards too were significant employers. Several copper mines in Cornwall approached such levels, with Wheal Alfred employing more than a thousand in 1790. A few ironmasters also stood out: Arthur Young in 1776 thought Darby employed 1,000 in Shropshire and Crawley 'several hundreds' near Newcastle. There were, of course, large employers under the domestic modes of production, putting out yarn or nail-iron to hundreds of homes. One Black Country nailor did so to more than a thousand homes.[13]

In the nineteenth century it was an increasing experience to work as part of a large workforce on a single site. Coal mines in the eighteenth century were thought large if they employed more than 100 miners and

TABLE 2 British occupational distribution, 1851 (in thousands)

	Males	Females	Total
Agriculture, horticulture and forestry	1,788	229	2,017
Fishing	36	1	37
Domestic offices and personal services	193	1,135	1,328
Textiles	661	635	1,296
Clothing (including boot- and shoe-making and repairing)	418	491	909
Metal manufacture, machines, implements, vehicles, etc.	536	36	572
Building and construction	496	1	497
Transport (roads, railways, canals, docks, sea, including domestic coachmen and grooms)	433	13	446
Food, drink and tobacco	348	53	401
Mining and quarrying, and workers in their products	383	11	394
Wood, furniture, etc.	152	8	160
Bricks, cement, pottery and glass	75	15	90
Paper, printing, books and stationery	62	16	78
Skins, leather, hair, etc.	55	5	60
Chemicals, oil, soap, etc.	42	4	46
Commercial occupations	91	—	91
Professional occupations and subordinate services	162	103	265
Public administration	64	3	67
Armed forces	63	—	63
All others occupied	445	75	513
Total occupied	6,545	2,832	9,377

the norm was around 40. There was no technological revolution in the techniques of coal-getting, and the heavy increase in demand which accompanied the industrial revolution had to be met very largely by increasing the labour force. In the first quarter of the nineteenth century, underground workforces of 200 to 300 became quite usual on most of the major coalfields, while by the 1840s the largest collieries in the north-east were employing between 500 and 1,000. At the end of the eighteenth century the number of coalminers in England and Wales can hardly have numbered less than 50,000, but even from this significant base their increase was spectacular through 118,000 in 1841 to 219,000 by 1851.[14]

Employment statistics for the tin and copper mines of Cornwall are unusually good. An enumeration made for Boulton and Watt in 1787 put the total number of employees at copper mines at 7,196 of whom 2,684 were women and children. To this count must be added around 2,000 workers at tin mines. An estimate of 5,000 to 6,000 men and 4,000 to 5,000 women in 1799 seems a reasonable figure, and the very considerable expansion in copper mining over the first decades of the nineteenth century is reflected in a figure of 29,166 (male and female) for 1837 and an 1851 census count of 36,284 (including 5,916 females). A careful survey of 159 mines in 1837 allows very precise knowledge of the characteristic scale of enterprise. Sixty-four of these mines which included a large number of very small operations employed more than 100 workers, ten more than 500 and five of these more than 1,000. In fact more than 60% of the mining labour force was employed at mines with more than 250 persons and just over 30% in the five largest concerns with over 1,000 workers.[15]

By the mid-nineteenth century the factory system was the predominant mode of production only in the manufacture of woollen and cotton cloth. By the early 1830s seven Manchester cotton firms each employed more than 1,000 workers, a further thirty more than 500 and forty-six more between 200 and 499. The late mechanisation of weaving meant that even by 1815 cotton mills counted for only 114,000 employees, predominantly women and children, but the advent of the power loom reduced handloom weavers from around 240,000 in 1820 to only 50,000 by 1850 as the factory labour force in cotton increased to 331,000, of whom 57% were female. Wool production changed its mode more slowly. Its factory labour force was very largely confined to the West Riding and in 1850 numbered around 74,000, but the persistence of handloom weaving – there were still only 9,500 power looms in the woollen and worsted manufacture in 1850 – meant that *overall* male workers still marginally predominated. By 1833 eleven Yorkshire spinning mills employed more than 200 workers, which seems also to have been the typical size of the small number of silk factories in Derby and Macclesfield operating within an industry still numerically dominated in the early nineteenth century by the outworkers of Spitalfields (London) and of Coventry.[16]

The stocking-knitting and lace-making trades of the East Midlands remained outside the factory until the second half of the nineteenth century. There had already been 4,650 frames at work in the district in 1727, and by the time of the Luddite disturbances of 1811 around 20,000 frames employed perhaps 50,000 people. The 1851 census gives a labour force of 65,000. Although for the most part the hosiers who put out the work were operating on a small or middling scale, a few put out yarn to a hundred or more knitters. The cutlery trades of Sheffield were similarly untouched by the factory system; the 6,000 cutlery and file makers around 1800 had increased to more than 14,000 by 1851 making Sheffield one of the growth towns of the industrial revolution. Its 1801 population of 46,000 made it a very large town by the standards of that time, yet by 1851 had reached 135,000. This growth in employment was almost entirely accounted for by the persistence of small-scale artisanal production where, as in the various metal-working trades of Birmingham, small masters employing a few journeymen and apprentices in specialist branches of the very heterogeneous manufacture of small metal goods were typical. Many of them still bought their own raw materials although they were very much dependent upon selling their product to merchant capitalists and very rarely marketed directly. Birmingham was to William Hutton, who first went there in 1741, already 'large and full of inhabitants, and those inhabitants full of industry'. Its 1801 population of 73,000 amounted to a nine-fold increase over its 1700 figure, and by mid-century it was approaching a quarter of a million inhabitants.[17]

With Black Country nail-making likewise dominated by hand production, around 29,000 workers in 1851, it is clear that the small forge was prevalent in metal goods manufacture throughout the period. There were, however, within metal manufacture some very large enterprises, even before the end of the eighteenth century usually concerned with the production of the iron itself and with the heavier forgings and castings such as ploughshares, boilers and other machine parts.

In general, it is hardly much of a distortion to suggest that the manufacture of finished consumer goods in England down to the mid-nineteenth century was for the most part small-scale and un-mechanised. The cloth-producing mill workers were swamped by those who worked by hand in one branch or another of the clothing trade. There were 10,991 master tailors in England and Wales in 1851 and only 4% of them employed more than 10 workers out of the very large labour force of 151,000 tailors. To their number can be added 72,000 seamstresses, 296,000 milliners, 17,000 hatters and 30,000 glovers, as well as several smaller groupings, to make up the vast number of garment makers. Shoe-making was similarly structured, although showing increasing tendencies to concentrate, especially in and around Northampton. Its 241,000 male and 31,000 female workers in 1851 outnumbered those employed in coal mines.

Small masters predominated in the building trades despite the appearance in some towns of 'general contracting'. Direct and sub-contracting by the various tradesmen was common with self-employment known everywhere, and prevalent outside the bigger towns. Typically a master craftsman worked with one or two permanent employees, journeymen and apprentices, and hired unskilled labour from time to time. Seventy of England and Wales' 26,360 masters in the building trades in 1851 employed 100 or more men, but three-fifths of them employed only one or two each of the half a million or so who filled the ranks of the various trades of brick-laying, joining, slating, masonry, etc. Perhaps a further 60,000 workers supported them in making bricks, burning lime or quarrying stone or slate.

Through the eighteenth century the manufacture of pottery had rapidly been concentrating on the 'five towns' around Burslem. By

1762 Burslem's 150 potteries were employing 7,000 people and in 1781 John Wesley remarked on the town's continuing growth with inhabitants flowing in from every side. By 1851, 36,000 potters were employed (11,000 of them female). The eighteenth-century dominance of Wedgwood declined and by the 1830s several large firms exceeded his Etruria in employment and output. Thirty-six firms employed more than 100 workers, seven of them more than 350. Two-thirds of the firms, however, employed less than ten, and so pottery manufacture was only a partial exception to the norm of hand production of consumer goods. Printing too should be accounted a consumer industry for its output of books and newspapers. Its expansion, especially in the provinces, was rapid in the third and fourth decades of the nineteenth century with a workforce of 9,000 in 1831 more than doubling by 1851. The typical shop outside of London remained very small.

Shipyards, we have noted, were among the largest of enterprises in the eighteenth-century economy. In sheer size, the naval dockyards dwarfed most private yards, which remained for the most part small in the mid-nineteenth century. Only thirteen of 327 firms making returns in 1851 employed more than 100 workers, while at mid-century Portsmouth employed 2,000 and Chatham around 2,500. The bulk of these workers were craftsmen in wood: shipwrights, mast and block makers, caulkers, who were supported by sail and rope-makers. In the second half of the century ship-building was to be transformed, bringing into being new kinds of workers: plate makers, riveters and boilermakers. The provisioning of the ships was a significant element in the demand for casks and barrels which employed 20,000 coopers in 1851. The official figure of 446,000 transport workers included the merchant seamen, although not the 37,000 fishermen. The importance of the railway was beginning to show now in operating staff, rather than in the gangs of navvies who had dominated the construction phase. Railworkers in the major companies numbered 182,963 in 1848 and the railwayman was to become the best known representative of a new kind of worker in the Victorian economy: the 'uniformed working class', sharing security and conditions of employment, as well as deferential attitudes, with other groups like post-office workers.

This necessarily sketchy and impressionistic map of employment seems to confirm the point insisted upon by recent historians that factory employment was untypical. Professor Musson states: 'It is evident that the typical British worker in the mid-nineteenth century was not a machine-operator in a factory but still a traditional craftsmen or labourer or domestic servant.'[18] The problem lies, however, not so much in accepting the relative proportions (Hopkins' calculations from the 1851 census give 1.75 million employed in 'mechanised industry and mining' against 5.5 million in non-mechanised industry)[19] but in the way 'traditional' conveys an image of *unchanging* craft production. Neither the level of skill, the possibility of taking pride in craft, control over the labour process nor the intensity and remuneration of labour remain unchanged simply because manual modes persist. This argument is central in the discussion of labour processes, remuneration and trade unionism discussed below. Here we need only to insist that the 'sweated' tailor or shoemaker and the 'scamping' carpenter or cabinet-maker had little in common with the traditional form of their craft. Merchant capitalism, especially in the form of the 'readymade' warehouse, had resulted in a structural transformation of their trades as significant and serious in its implications and as evidently 'exploitative' in its character as was the factory system.[20] In addition, as Raphael Samuel has pointed out, the industrial revolution was not simply a matter of machine minding. It brought into being new demands for heavy manual labour:

> The industrial revolution, so far from abridging human labour, created a whole new world of labour-intensive jobs: railway navvying is a prime example, but one could consider too the puddlers and shinglers in the rolling mills, turning pig-iron into bars, the alkali workers stirring vats of caustic soda, and a whole spectrum of occupations in what the Factory Legislation of the 1890s was belatedly to recognise as dangerous trades.[21]

FEMALE AND CHILD LABOUR

Throughout the period of this book the employment of women and children was usual and important. Although the industrial revolution is very often given especial significance in calling out women and children into the labour force, it is clear that the percentage of the occupied population accounted for by them was rather consistent until the rapid decline in the employment of married women after 1851 and the growth of schooling for children in the second half of the nineteenth century.[22]

In the eighteenth century, women and children for the most part formed a hidden labour force in manufacturing. Hidden because their work was commonly done in the home and was in very many cases, especially cloth making, performed as part of a family unit of production rather than separately waged. Not all female outwork, however, was undertaken as part of a family work unit. Dr Berg has indicated that several putting-out trades moved to absorb the available labour of women in the home and developed modes of production and organisation appropriate to that end. Lace-making and straw-plaiting are only the best known examples.[23] In addition, there were some specifically female trades such as millinery, stay-making and mantua-making. In the mid-eighteenth century such trades were so low paid as to be commonly regarede as recruiting centres for prostitution. The process by which, in the first half of the nineteenth-century, the sweating system exploited the labour of female outworkers in the 'needle trades' has often been described. The *Song of the Shirt* is in its way almost as powerful an image of capitalist exploitation as any mill-town Gradgrind.[24]

Despite the coming of the mill with its predominantly female workforce, there is little hard evidence to support the view that the industrial revolution actually increased female participation in waged work. Accurate levels for the eighteenth century are unattainable: it is necessary only to assume that, among the labouring population, women, wives and daughters were expected to work both in manufacturing and in agriculture. Industrialisation only increased and changed the nature of employment available to some women in some districts. Changes in agriculture associated with the decline in the family farm, the growth of a landless labour class and a switch into cereal production probably decreased female employment by making it much more seasonal. (see below, p. 41).

Women could be found in many sectors of the manufacturing economy, although excluded by the frontier of apprenticeship and the organisations of skilled male workers from the workshop craft trades. Legislative exclusion, other than indirectly through apprenticeship, only came with the Mines Act of 1842. It is impossible to know what percentage of the labour force women made up in the eighteenth century, but the 30% of the 'official' working population in 1811 remained constant until 1851. In that year the number of females occupied amounted to 39% of the total female population. This is certainly an underestimate for so much of women's work was part-time, 'unofficial', concealed in the home or so submerged within a husband's employment as to escape enumeration. Of the classes enumerated, the preponderance of domestic service is striking, accounting for 37.3% of occupied women, while textile production and garment manufacture together accounted for about the same percentage. Agriculture came next, but a long way behind, with 7.7%. Of 128,418 female agricultural employees sufficiently fully employed to be listed in agriculture, 64,000 were dairywomen which, in contrast to its gentle and pretty image, involved heavy labour in the churning and turning of butter and huge cheeses. The inability of agrarian England to afford sufficient female employment is directly reflected in the fact that it was largely from the villages that young girls were drawn into urban domestic service.[25]

Relatively few women worked in heavy industry, though nail-making was an exception, and they were becoming increasingly important in several of the workshop metal trades of Birmingham. Female labour underground in coal mines was ended by the Act of 1842, but it had never been known in some districts, nor had it in the tin and copper mines of Cornwall. Women were far more significant as surface workers picking, breaking and sorting coals and ores. Dr John has suggested that the 1841 occupational statistics seriously underestimate women mineworkers at 2,350 and that on the eve of the 1842 Act there were perhaps around 5,000–6,000 employed above and underground. Opportunities above ground did not expand in the short run after the exclusion from underground, and the 1851 census records only 2,649 females in coal mining in England and Wales.[26] Proportionately, the metal mines of Cornwall, especially copper, which was very demanding in its call on female surface labour, were much heavier users. In 1851, 5,922 females worked at Cornish mines with twice as many working on copper ores as on tin.[27]

Defenders of Britain's capitalist industrialisation are prone to point out that child labour was an integral and essential input into the economy well before the factory system. It is a superfluous insistence for no one ever supposed otherwise: arguments having always been about the *form* and intensity of child labour. Like female labour, the labour of children was often hidden within the producing household. While it is indeed true that Daniel Defoe, in his tours of the early eighteenth century, was especially delighted to find that in the clothing counties, 'the very children after four or five years of age, could everyone earn their own bread', he is in fact pointing out what a great blessing, to his mind, manufacturing conferred in so providing employment. The inference is that the degree of underemployment in rural districts *generally* meant that children were only casually and intermittently employed. The selection for comment of this aspect of manufacturing certainly shows that eighteenth-century opinion approved of child labour; it might also confirm that children were expected to work, but it does also suggest that the economy *as a whole* was considered to afford insufficient employment for children. It is difficult to accept Dr Hunt's view that child labour in 1851 was probably less extensive than it had been before the industrial revolution: that is to confuse acceptance with availability; desire with opportunity. At mid-century around a third of children under fifteen were working. However, there is good reason to think this figure based on the 1851 census is a serious underestimate. The census cannot be presumed to have been very effective in listing children working within household production or in other ways assisting adult workers. Dr Hunt suggests that an increased valuing of education was also responsible for a decline in child employment. In fact, as will be established below, the common pattern of attendance, for those who did attend, was to do so for only two or three years. It is misleading to consider schooling without pointing out that there was no association of school attendance with a specific and required number of childhood years. If around a third of children were recorded as working, then to their number must be added all those who were not at that moment working, but who

15

were, after a brief schooling, to work for the rest of their childhood years. Legislation in factory and mine had only an insignificant effect after 1833, denying (although there was some evasion) admission to the cotton and woollen mills to those under eight, and underground labour to those under ten. However important for the future, legislation on child employment was selective in application and attempted only to safeguard it from specific abuses not to seriously reduce its extent. In so far as an increasing birth rate and a fall in child mortality are generally accepted as key explanations of the demographic revolution, then it seems likely that the proportion of children in the population was increasing so that by 1851 more than a third was fifteen or less. It seems unlikely that child labour should have shown any tendency to decrease. In fact, factory and mine employment, the areas most seized upon by contemporaries and by historians, did not in 1840 account for more than a quarter of child employees, while agriculture accounted for 28.4% of all boys under fifteen and 17% of all girls listed in 1851.[28]

URBANISATION

The connection between industrialisation and urbanisation is not a necessary one. The shanty towns peopled by underemployed rural migrants surrounding the cities of the present-day underdeveloped economies testify to this. For nineteenth-century Europe it was, however, a usual connection and for Britain 1750–1850 an exceptionally close one. Labour in manufacturing, despite the persistence of industrial villages of miners, weavers, knitters, nailors and the like, increasingly concentrated in towns. The figures speak dramatically for themselves. In 1750 London was the only English town with a population of more than 50,000; by 1801 there were eight and in 1851 twenty-nine, nine of which exceeded 100,000. In this census year Britain became officially a nation in which more of the populace were classified as urban than as rural. More than a third of these urban inhabitants lived by then in cities with 50,000 or more inhabitants. Manchester grew from 27,000 to 180,000 between 1770 and 1830, and yet the emergence of the factory town had been delayed by the dependence of the first mills on water power. With the coming of the steam mill, textile towns grew especially rapidly but no more so than some centres of metal manufacturing. Manchester, Birmingham, Sheffield and Leeds all increased by more than 40% over the third decade of the nineteenth century. By this time, with high birth rates and marginally improved death rates, cities were able to grow from natural increase as well as from migration.[29]

The link between manufacturing growth and urbanisation was

evident even in the eighteenth century, and was as significant as the growth of the spas, like Bath, which have been allowed to assume too much of the foreground of eighteenth-century urbanisation. Dr Corfield has shown that specialised manufacturing towns were among the most rapidly growing. It is not simply a matter of Defoe noting 'Black Barnsley' or writing of the 'dark and black streets' of Sheffield, or that Burslem was so smoke-filled by 1750 that people groped their way in daytime. These were exceptions for comment, but there was a more general increase in the size of urban manufacturing centres. Five of the ten largest provincial towns in 1775 owed their size chiefly to manufacturing: Birmingham, Norwich, Manchester, Sheffield and Leeds. Of the other five only Bath had no considerable manufacturing whereas Liverpool, Newcastle, Plymouth and Bristol did. Not far behind them were others like Nottingham, Coventry, Exeter and Portsmouth. Manufacturing or mining was also the *raison d'être* of a host of smaller towns of 3,000–5,000 inhabitants. From a very long list we can pick our clothing towns like Bury, Bradford, Tiverton, Wigan or Oldham; centres of mining like Camborne; or of manufacture like Wolverhampton. It is doubtful whether towns of 5,000 or fewer inhabitants can be said to provide a true urban experience, and in 1700 only around 16% of England's population lived in towns even of that size while by 1801 perhaps only a third lived in settlements of more than 1,000 inhabitants. In the chapters which follow the impact of this change on the working and non-working lives of the English labouring people and their adaptation to urban ways of life will be considered inseparably from that of industrialisation. The problems of the new modes of production and those of urban living cannot be reasonably segregated even if not inconsiderable numbers experienced the one without the other.[30]

London is a special case. Its population of 675,000 in 1750 represented 11% of the population of England. By 1800 its population was approaching a million and by 1851 two and a half million. Throughout this period it remained a great manufacturing centre. In the eighteenth century it had been the major location of the artisanal trades with its tailors, printers, watchmakers, silkweavers, hatters and literally dozens of other crafts from house painting through to surgical-instrument making. In the first half of the nineteenth century it still predominated in the manufacture of a range of consumer goods, increasingly 'sweated' from the exploited labour of men and women.

PROLETARIANISATION: THE GROWTH OF WAGE LABOUR

'The proletariat originated in the industrial revolution which took place in England in the last half of the [eighteenth] century, and which has since then been repeated in all the civilized countries of the world', wrote Engels, and Professor Hobsbawm has stressed in a well-established textbook that labour in an industrialised economy is 'overwhelmingly the labour of proletarians [who] have no source of income worth mentioning except a cash wage which they receive for their work'. In a strict sense the *industrial* proletariat is the special creation of industrial capitalism and the factory system. According to Engels, 'the manufacturing worker of the sixteenth to the eighteenth centuries, still had, with but few exceptions an instrument of production in his own possession – his loom, the family spinning wheel, a little plot of land'. He lived 'almost always' in a 'more or less patriarchal relationship' to his employer rather than in that of the proletariat to his employer which was 'purely a cash relation'.[31] Dr Stedman Jones has pointed to two conditions of exploitation of labour by capital: the *expropriation of the product* whereby the workman ceases to own the materials upon which he works or the finished product of his labour: he sells, in effect, not a product but labour power; and the *expropriation of nature*, that process of alienation through which the worker loses any control of the labour process working under supervision to the dictated rhythms of modern industry.[32] It seems clear that the second of these is essentially the outcome of 'machinofacture' and the factory system, but the first may have become the normal condition of a large section of the labour force well before the industrial revolution. It is evident that to Marx and Engels, urban proximity of work and living is an important pre-condition for the emergence of a conscious proletariat capable of class action on a wide scale, but if we use 'proletariat' more generally to describe those of the labouring people who depend upon selling their labour power, then in England proletarianisation had already proceeded a long way by 1750. England by then possessed a wage-dependent population and a consequent form of labour market which distinguished it from other European countries. Over a substantial part of the country wage labour had become, or was becoming, an agrarian as well as a manufacturing norm, creating the 'farm labourer' so unfamiliar to the peasant-dominated social structures of other countries. Dr Clarkson has pointed out that if the suggestions of some early modern historians are correct, then the suggested two-thirds both of the urban and rural population as wage dependent for the sixteenth and seventeenth centuries would leave little room for any substantial shift over the eighteenth century when the calculations of Deane and Cole seem to point to a two-thirds fraction for 1800. The early figure has been inflated both by the inclusion of family members who would not have been officially listed in later enumerations and by including 'peasant-labourers' to whom wage labour was supplementary as well as clothing workers like those of the West Riding who were really self-employed. Nevertheless, this, together with the more recent insistence by a seventeenth-century historian that riots in the West Country can best be understood as the protests of a wage-dependent artisan class with only collateral farming interests,[33] reminds us how very widespread and normal wage labour was in England well before the industrial revolution.

West Country weavers or East Midlands knitters might work in their own cottages or even on their own looms or (less likely) frames but they were fully dependent upon work put out by a capitalist clothier or hosier who collected and marketed the product of their labour, paying what, even if termed a 'price', was effectively a piece rate. A weaver might be 'master' of his trade, and if the institution was still kept up, of his apprentice, but he was also, though 'master of his time' working in his own cottage, the employee of the master clothier. The early development of trade unionism in the West Country clothing districts clearly reflects that separation of interest between labour and capital which Adam Smith took for granted in *Wealth of Nations* (1773). In the farm labourers of the southern counties and of East Anglia, in the rural clothworkers and metalworkers of many districts and in those urban crafts like printing, tailoring and hat-making where a class of *permanent* journeymen provided the labour, a 'proletariat' in an important sense of the word already existed by the end of the eighteenth century. 'A journeyman', wrote a pamphleteer in support of protesting London tailors in 1745, 'is understood to be one, who has by apprenticeship or other contract, served such a portion of his time . . . as rendered him capable to execute every branch or part of the trade, whereby he is at full liberty . . . to set up in the world as a master of his profession; and is only called a Journeyman while he continues to serve under the direction of others at certain wages'. Setting up was hardly possible for the vast majority who, 'common as locusts' and 'poor as rats', were permanently the 'artificers as well as labourers in that trade'. The printers, representing themselves in 1809 as unusual among London trades in having little hope of affording to set themselves up as independent masters, were in fact very far from being so.[34]

In an important sense such artisans cannot present a *fully* proletarian consciousness, for tradition, assumption and customary expectations tied their consciousness in part to the world they were losing in a lingering continuity of values, although they were wage dependent, and even though paradoxically from their ranks came the vanguard of the early labour movements. Their prominence in late-eighteenth- and early nineteenth-century protest movements had led some historians to deny the reality of class-consciousness. The gulf between the skilled

19

artisan and the common labourer is, they argue, a yawning manifestation of the differences in material well-being, status perception, self and other esteem and value systems which deny the existence of a single working class even by the mid-nineteenth century. There was no homogeneity of condition, experience or response. The vexed and involved questions of class formation and consciousness will be treated at the end of this book, but here it is appropriate to point out that many strands of consciousness stemming from differing experiences of exploitation and levels of expectation went into the 'making' of a working class. Trade unionism, the most apparent and fundamental of the defences of labour, clearly pre-dates industrialisation and the factory system. Perhaps in the eighteenth century it was more effectively entrenched among many groups of male skilled workers than it was in the first half of the nineteenth century. There is a tendency to complain that labour historians devote too much space and attention to a trade unionism which was, as an elite phenomenon, irrelevant to the experiences of the unskilled bulk of the male labour force and to practically all working women. As a corrective this has point, and doubtless the space given to trade unionism in this book will be criticised. Yet it can be defended, not only because no general synthesis of work on early trade unionism of any length has appeared since the Webbs' classic study, but also because trade unionism was much more significant than can be suggested by 'official' membership statistics, being formative in the development of a discourse of labour and of a labour consciousness. Trade unionism should not be considered as much in terms of formal and permanent organisations as it has traditionally been. For thousands more workers than can be counted in membership statistics, a collective labour experience and response was central even if amounting, on most occasions, to no more than a tacit insistence that the customs and norms of the workplace be regarded, and was only episodically dramatic. When trade unionism did spread beyond the ranks of the skilled, the labourers neither discovered nor invented it: they absorbed it and with it methods, including strike action, which had been well tested. The 'Martyrs of Tolpuddle', it will be recalled, did not conceive of 'union' out of the blue Dorset skies; they had heard of it and, thinking it offered something appropriate to the circumstances in which they found themselves, attached themselves to it.

The impact of the century of social and economic transformation 1750 to 1850 on the labouring people cannot be analysed only in terms of conditions of work or material well-being. It falls, as E. P. Thompson has remarked, upon 'the whole culture' from which both assent and resistance to change arise.[35] In the following chapters a broad canvas is attempted and in considering so many questions much coverage will be judged superficial; some omissions regrettable; some inclusions misguided and some interpretations misleading. I hope the reader will find an attempt to synthesise the work of so many historians on so many aspects of working-class history useful, but some degree of generalisation is inevitable while compression is inescapable. Whether or not an English working class was 'made' by 1830 or even by 1850 is hotly debated, as is the extent to which it participated in and conditioned its own 'making'. One thing does seem certain: there can be no presumption of a uniform and wholly homogeneous experience.

REFERENCES AND NOTES

1. The main sources for the statistics used in this chapter are: **B. R. Mitchell** and **P. Deane**, *Abstract of British Historical Statistics*, Cambridge U.P., 1962 and **A. E. Musson**, *The Growth of British Industry*, Batsford, 1978. The labour supply is usefully discussed in **N. L. Tranter**, 'The labour supply 1780–1860', in **R. Floud** & **D. McCloskey**, (eds) *The Economic History of Britain since 1700*, 1981, I, pp. 204–26.

2. **D. N. McCloskey**, 'The Industrial Revolution 1780–1860: a survey', in Floud & McCloskey, *Economic History of Britain*, I, p. 106. For eighteenth-century trends see **N. C. R. Crafts**, 'The eighteenth century: a survey', ibid., pp. 1–16.

3. **J. L.** and **B. Hammond**, *The Skilled Labourer*, ed. J. G. Rule, Longman, 1979, pp. 1–2.

4. **M. D. George**, *England in Transition*, Penguin, 1953, p. 136.

5. For an important discussion see **R. Samuel**, 'Workshop of the world: steam power and hand technology in mid-Victorian Britain', *History Workshop Journal*, 3, 1977, pp. 6–72.

6. **C. Emsley**, *British Society and the French Wars 1793–1815*, Macmillan, 1979, pp. 4, 33.

7. **E. P. Thompson**, *The Making of the English Working Class*, Penguin, 1968, p. 217.

8. **J. L.** and **B. Hammond**, *The Town Labourer*, ed. J. Lovell, Longman, 1978, pp. 64–5; and *Skilled Labourer*, pp. 211–12; see also their *The Rise of Modern Industry*, 1972 edn, p. 108.

9. Ibid, pp. 104, 108–9.

10. Hammonds, *Skilled Labourer*, pp. 64–5.

11. Ibid, p. 299.

12. For a useful survey see **E. H. Hunt**, *British Labour History 1815–1914*, Weidenfeld & Nicolson, 1981, Ch. 1 and 2.

13. For eighteenth-century manufacturing see **J. G. Rule**, *The Experience of Labour in Eighteenth-century Industry*, Croom Helm, 1981, Ch. 1.

14. Coal industry figures have been taken mainly from Musson, *Growth of British Industry*, pp.95–6.

15. The sources for tin and copper mining are cited in **J. G. Rule**, 'The labouring miner in Cornwall *c.*1740–1870: a study in social history', Ph.D. University of Warwick, 1971, pp. 8–14.

16. Figures from Musson, *Growth of British Industry*, pp. 82–3 and **S. Pollard**, *The Genesis of Modern Management*, Penguin, 1968, p. 114.

17. **William Hutton**, *Life of William Hutton F.A.S.S.*, 1817, p. 110.

18. Musson, *Growth of British Industry*, pp. 130–41.

19. **E. Hopkins**, *A Social History of the English Working Classes 1815–1945*, Arnold, 1979, p. 3.

20. For a discussion of this structural change on a wider basis see **J. G. Rule**, 'Artisan attitudes: skilled labour and proletarianisation in Western Europe before 1848', *Bulletin of Society for Study of Labour History*, 1985.

21. Samuel, 'Workshop of the world', pp. 8–9.

22. See **E. Richards**, 'Women in the British economy since about 1700: an interpretation', *History*, vol. 59, no. 197, 1974, pp. 337–57.

23. **M. Berg**, 'Domestic industry, women and community in eighteenth-century England', in **P. Joyce** (ed), *Historical Meanings of Work*, Cambridge U.P., 1986 (forthcoming) and *The Age of Manufactures 1700–1820*, Fontana, 1985.

24. **R. Campbell**, *The London Tradesman*, 1747, repr. David & Charles, 1969, pp. 206–9, 225–8; and for the continuing link with prostitution in the middle nineteenth century see Mayhew's report, 'Prostitution among needlewomen', in **E. P. Thompson** and **E. Yeo** (eds), *The Unknown Mayhew*, Penguin, 1973, pp. 175–7.

25. Apart from **I. Pinchbeck's** standard work, *Women Workers and the Industrial Revolution 1750–1850*, Cass, 1969, see the contemporary article by Harriet Martineau on the findings of the 1851 census, in *Edinburgh Review*, vol. 109, 1859, pp. 293–336, reprinted in **J. Saville** (ed.), *Working Conditions in the Victorian Age*, Gregg, 1973.

26. **A. V. John**, *By the Sweat of Their Brow: Women workers at Victorian coal mines*, Croom Helm, 1980, pp. 24–5.

27. Rule, 'Labouring miner in Cornwall', pp. 8–11.

28. Hunt, *British Labour History*, pp. 9–13; Rule, *Experience of Labour*, pp. 42–3.

29. Figures for the growth of towns in the nineteenth century are from Mitchell and Deane, *British Historical Statistics*, pp. 24–6. For the eighteenth century see **P. J. Corfield**, *The Impact of English Towns 1700–1800*, Oxford U.P., 1982.

30. Ibid., pp. 22–33; Rule, *Experience of Labour*, pp. 18–21.

31. **F. Engels**, *Principles of Communism*, 1847, repr. Pluto Press, n.d., pp. 7–8; **E. J. Hobsbawm**, *Industry and Empire*, Weidenfeld & Nicolson, 1968, p. 66.

32. **G. Stedman Jones**, 'England's first proletariat', *New Left Review*, 90, 1975, p. 49.

33. **L. A. Clarkson**, 'Wage-labour, 1500–1800', in **K. D. Brown**, *The English Labour Movement 1700–1951*, Gill and Macmillan, Dublin, 1982, pp. 1–3; **Buchanan Sharp**, *In Contempt of all Authority: Rural Artisans and Riot in the West of England 1586–1660*, University of California Press, 1980.

34. For these and further examples see Rule, *Experience of Labour*, pp. 33–7.

35. See **J. G. Rule**, 'The property of skill in the period of manufacture' in **P. Joyce** (ed.), *Historical Meanings of Work*, 1986 (forthcoming); **E. P.**

Thompson, 'Time, work-discipline and industrial capitalism', *Past and Present*, no. 38, 1977, p. 80.

Part One

MATERIAL CONDITIONS

Chapter 1

THE STANDARD OF LIVING

Reviewing a polemic of Robert Southey's against the 'manufacturing system' in 1830, Lord Macaulay asserted: 'In the old world we must confess ourselves unable to find any satisfactory record of any great nation, past or present, in which the working classes have been in a more comfortable situation than in England during the last thirty years.'

Southey had made it easy for the great propagandist. By presenting his critique in the form of a dialogue with the ghost of the Tudor statesman Sir Thomas More, he allowed Macaulay to make scathing comparisons between the condition of the peasantry of the reign of Henry VIII and that of the English labouring people of 1830 and to avoid more difficult comparisons with the middle years of the eighteenth century. Macaulay presented as matters of fact assertions on health, longevity and general material comfort. People lived longer, a gradual lengthening of life span over several generations was 'as certain as any fact in statistics': 'We might with some plausibility maintain that the people live longer because they are better fed, better attended in sickness, and that these improvements are owing to that increase of national wealth which the manufacturing system has produced.'[1]

In linking the growth of a larger and more prosperous population to an improvement in mortality, he was presenting a view which was popular enough in its time and, indeed, subscribed to by many demographic historians since. However, recently the vast advance in the techniques of population measurement and reconstruction has established that increasing fertility, due especially to a lowering of the age of women at marriage, was more significant. Momentarily in the late eighteenth century it has been suggested that falling real incomes threatened a return to an old demographic pattern of late marriage and decreased nuptiality, but industrialisation revitalised employment so that from the early nineteenth century both population and income grew together to a unique extent.[2]

Macaulay's case for a substantial mortality improvement was in any case hardly based on factors which can be attributed to the growth of the 'manufacturing system'. He stressed the decline of the great epidemics, notably the bubonic plague, before which the people of Europe had been 'swept away by myriads'. Inoculation and vaccination certainly reduced the impact of smallpox; indeed, Dr Razzell attributes a crucial demographic effect to this. In general, however, the passing of the great epidemics which had visited the pre-industrial world with such devastation seems to have had little to do with the increase in the consumption of wheaten bread and the greater availability of cotton clothing. Even in pre-industrial society, Professor Chambers clearly established the ability of disease to check population growth independently of levels of nutrition.[3]

Those who stress the generally beneficial effect of the industrial revolution upon the living standards of the population are usually labelled 'optimists', and if their assertion was simply that the support of an astonishing increase in population was the critical factor, or perhaps, with Ireland in mind, the avoidance of demographic catastrophe, then, even allowing for the fact that industrialisation was productive of a larger and more dense population as well as supportive of it, their position would be hard to dispute. It would be no easier to dispute that, relative to the experience of the labouring people of most countries, that of the English was distinctly favourable. What, however, cannot be accepted without *severe* qualification is the 'optimist' argument for a significant *improvement* in the standard of living in general (excepting only a few 'casualties') as an *accompaniment* of the industrial revolution. That position is no more tenable than the extreme 'pessimist' one of widespread and increasing immiseration. It is upon this debate, not upon sweeping and simple contrasts between 'pre-industrial' – a term of dubious precision – and industrial England that this chapter will concentrate.

The modern debate over the standard of living began in 1926 when Sir John Clapham took up arms against a critique of industrialisation running from Arnold Toynbee through the Webbs to the Hammonds which had presented a pessimistic view of its impact on the working classes. Clapham, anti-Bolshevik and committed upholder of conservative values and the free market, sought to defend the industrial revolution and its capitalist nature from 'the legend' that for the working man, 'everything was getting worse' down to some 'unspecified date between the drafting of the People's Charter and the Great Exhibition'. From his intervention, the still persisting labelling of two sides of disputants 'optimists' and 'pessimists' developed. The early 'pessimists' certainly made statements extreme enough to provoke anyone who thought the market economy and the capitalist form of production had something to be said for them. Toynbee had written of a period 'as disastrous and terrible as any through which a nation ever passed' – a sweeping judgement even allowing for the fact that he could have had no foreknowledge of the coming twentieth century's darker moments. Side by side, he argued, with a great increase in wealth and in material production had come, as a result of free competition, increasing pauperism, a rapid alienation of the classes and 'the degradation of large bodies of producers'. The Webbs argued that if a Chartist in 1837 had looked back over fifty years he would have noticed a 'positive decline in the standard of living of large classes of the population'. Even more influential in forming popular conceptions of the industrial revolution was the trilogy of volumes on the condition of the labourer produced between 1911 and 1919 by J. L. and Barbara Hammond. Their persuasive and lively prose, with copious quotations from contemporary sources, popularised a critique of individualist industrial society. Their verdict was unequivocal: the industrial revolution had brought 'a great extension of material power and of the opportunities that such power bestows, yet the final result had been deplorable'.[4]

The debate among historians has been much drawn upon ideological lines, as had been the contemporary one. Nowadays, however, it is as likely to be representatives of the 'optimists' who make bold assertions about the impact of the industrial revolution: R. M. Hartwell's claim, for example, of 'an unambiguous' increase in the workers' standard of living or that of Professor Gash that this increase has been 'substantially confirmed by the recent research'. The misleading presumption of such statements should no more deceive the serious student than should that other proclivity of the 'optimists' to present themselves as objective and bias-free while at the same time deploring the unhistorical, ideological motivations of the 'pessimists'. The debate is far from concluded by recent research. Indeed, re-assessments of the rate of economic growth before 1830 have suggested that the optimistic assumption of a national product rapidly and consistently outpacing the growth of population has assumed rather too fast a growth rate. Given the nature of the evidence and the lack of conclusive data, it is unlikely that the debate is capable of clear resolution in favour of either side.[5]

Clapham urged a rigorous approach, cutting through sentiment with statistics. The 'literary', romantic Hammonds could be devastated with a few telling blows from a cost of living index. Linking a price index for 1779 to 1850 devised by N. J. Silberling to wage data, he pronounced that between 1795 and 1824 'that rather vague figure the average English (with Welsh) labourer appeared to have improved his gross earnings 15 to 20 per cent'. Faced with this new quantitative confidence, the Hammonds made a rather premature retreat to the non-quantifiable reaches of the subject and asserted that it was in the 'quality of life' than in the narrower, more measurable 'standard' of living that the most evident deterioration took place. In fact Clapham was wielding a paper sword. Ironically it was Professor R. S. Ashton, from 1949 the 'optimists' leading soldier, who destroyed the essential prop of his argument. With derision he dismissed the value of indices based on Silberling which, though of use as an index of wholesale price trends, was not so for the devising of retail price indices. Rent was omitted altogether, and the 'basket of commodities' used so different from eighteenth-century consumption habits that Ashton suggested 'Silberling man' must have been a diabetic: 'The ordinary Englishman of the eighteenth century would have been puzzled by him.' He was hardly less sceptical of the value of another much used data source, Gilboy's indices of eighteenth-century wages and prices. She took little account of regional diet variations and based her data on contract prices paid by institutions: 'Mrs Gilboy's bricklayers dressed up as bluecoat boys would hardly have been recognised as brothers by the pitmen of Northumberland or the weavers of Lancashire or Somerset.'[6]

Ashton did not stress the obvious inference: if the Silberling index was of little value then so too was the argument of Clapham which had rested on it. Clapham's case has a further weakness. He claimed that improvement was evident by 1824, yet most recent research seems to agree that any rise in real wages in the early nineteenth century owed more to price deflation than increasing earnings, and had only just about begun by 1820. Subsequent research has not only criticised Clapham's sources; it has disputed his dating. Ashton's favoured dates for the industrial revolution are 1760 to 1830 and so his 'optimist' conclusions have also been weakened by the emerging consensus of the historians of economic growth (usually seen as the 'natural allies' of the optimists) that real improvement only began towards the end of that period. He once expressed surprise at finding students in the 1950s still believing in the Hammonds' pessimism. This university teacher of the present day is surprised to find so many students under the impression that the 'hard' empirical approaches of Clapham and Ashton have effectively refuted the woolly, romantic impressionism of the Hammonds. Clapham was a fine economic historian whose contribution had been immense, but in the context of the standard of living debate he would now seem to be of only historiographical interest.[7]

In the cold-war atmosphere of the years following the Second World War, Ashton dominated what, starting as an important corrective, became a new orthodoxy. On the pessimist side a few scholars, notably Professor Hobsbawm, struggled to keep the debate alive until a later growth of interest in social history continued and refreshed it by investigating the wider impact of industrialisation. This revived concern for the broader canvas of experience has brought the works of the Hammonds back into the arena as something other than 'Aunt Sallies'. Ashton was more cautious in the claims he made for amelioration than some of his followers have been. At times he wrote as if overwhelmed by the complexities of the evidence and the deficiencies of the data: 'We must restrict our ambitions, realise the limitations of our bag of tricks, and refrain from generalisations. We cannot measure changes in real wages by means of an index of wholesale or institutional prices.'[8] Nevertheless he steadfastly advanced the conclusion that by 1830 the industrial revolution had materially benefited more people than it had disadvantaged. The 'optimists' have succeeded in disproving statements of extreme immiseration and of an absolute and widespread deterioration in standards of living. However, modern 'pessimists' do not usually stress an absolute material decline, but rather a relative one during a period in which the condition of the working classes improved at best only marginally while national income per head increased impressively. They stress too the long delay before the increase in material production brought significant and sustained rewards to the generality of the people. Further, they maintain that the costs of social dislocation and the effects of environmental deterioration on the health and quality of life of the working classes weigh heavily in the balance against a marginal and selective material improvement. As Thompson has put it, the record is unremarkable: 'More potatoes, a few articles of cotton clothing for his family, soap and candles, some tea and sugar, and a great many articles in the *Economic History Review*.'[9]

Not surprisingly a group of moderate interpretations has emerged around the growing consensus of no decline to 'asiatic standards' but of only modest and uneven improvement. Professor Mathias suggests that the continuing debate is in itself suggestive that no *marked* change either way took place and that there was no general movement towards deterioration although wartime shortages and inflation tended in that direction between 1795 and 1815. Professor Deane saw 'no firm evidence' for an overall improvement between 1780 and 1820 with on balance a tendency for earnings to fall rather than rise. Between 1820 and 1840 she thinks the balance of evidence shifts to the 'optimist' side. Either way the net change was slight. More recently, Dr Hunt has argued that despite 'bold and contradicting claims', there was no dramatic change in the course of real wages either way. Such a conclusion is, he suggests, acceptable to 'most reasonable men', and recent research offers comfort for neither 'gloomy Marxists' or 'light-hearted optimists.'[10]

THE PROBLEM

Both sides tend to begin from particular macro-economic perspectives. Optimists argue that given rising national income per capita it is logical to assume an improvement in average living standards unless there is evidence of a significant redistribution of income away from the working classes. On the other hand, some pessimists assert that the nature of an industrial revolution with its emphasis on fixed capital is to increase the share of investment relative to that of consumption. The model is a simple one: the investment needs of industrialisation are met at the expense of consumption. Abstractions like per capita income convey nothing of the facts of income distribution. At times of increasing national income it is perfectly possible both for workers' incomes to increase absolutely *and* at the same time to decline relatively to the position of middle- and upper-class incomes. An increment to national income could simultaneously reward some groups significantly, marginally benefit others and produce a deterioration in the standards of a third.

It is largely accepted that the investment needs of the British industrial revolution, given its early stage of technological development, were historically low. The 10–15% of GNP postulated as necessary for 'take-off' by Professor Rostow was not reached until the railway age. Nevertheless, even if from levels of around 5% at the beginning, investment reached around 10% by 1840, that still means a relative decline in the percentage of national income available for consumption which would have increased the effect of any trend towards a more uneven distribution of the consumption share. However, it must be accepted that the rate of economic growth was sufficiently rapid and the investment needs of the early industrial economy sufficiently low to make the idea of an improvement in living standards a reasonable hypothesis at the level of theory, and to suggest that a simple version of the 'sacrifice of the first generation' view of industrialisation would be less true of the British experience than it might have been in later industrialisations which began from lower income levels and which had greater investment needs. Professor Hobsbawm has argued that the large share of investable funds held by large landowners and financiers meant that capital did not find its way readily into industrial uses, and therefore manufacturers were forced to press more heavily on their workers and to use the cheaper labour of women and children. Undoubtedly the early factory masters and mine owners got their labour cheaply. Perhaps this was mostly due to the tendency of population increase towards an over-supply of labour which helped keep wages down to near subsistence level until the labour surplus was absorbed.[11]

We have too little knowledge of actual income distribution to expect conclusive results from macro-economic perspectives. In the absence of hard data, we should not too readily assume that because post-1860 studies suggest a constant share in national income for wages, they necessarily increased in proportion to national income before 1860, or that because growth economists have associated increases in national income with a more equal distribution that this was necessarily so in the specific historical case of Britain before 1850. Indeed, there is reason to suppose that this latter association is not generally true of the early years of industrialisation but *becomes* true with its development. In the specific case of Britain, Professor Perkin has argued from an analysis of income tax returns from 1801, compared with estimates from official sources from 1848 and 1867, that there was a considerable shift over the nineteenth century towards the rich and well-to-do.[12]

It is difficult to isolate an average in a situation of varied experiences. It is as difficult to identify trends over a period marked by extreme fluctuations in prices. Such attempts could even prove mischievous if they produced an average to which few workers approximated or a 'constant' which never held good for more than a year or two at a time. It is generally agreed that in this period movements in real wages were more determined by changes in the price level than by changes in money wages. This presents serious problems. Several years within the period showed spectacular increases in food prices over those of the preceding year, and were followed by years in which food prices fell. Years of food rioting like 1795/6, 1800/01, 1812 and 1847 stand out. Professor Flinn has valiantly attempted to iron out these maverick years by using moving averages to produce trends, but we are still left with the vexed matter of selection of starting and finishing dates. Among the 'optimists', Clapham chose 1794–1824, Ashton 1790–1830 and Hartwell 1800–50. Among the 'pessimists', Hobsbawm chose 1790–1850, while in his reconsideration of the debate, Professor Taylor chose 1780–1850.[13] Clearly no analysis of trends should start or finish with an aberrant year. Professor Flinn remarked that although 1800 might mark the beginning of the century, it is 'a most unwise choice' as a starting date as it was the most exceptional in the price-history of the century 1750 to 1850. It was a year which with acute food shortages and massive price increases brought starvation very near for many of the lower orders. By dating his case for an improvement in real wages over the period 1800 to 1850 from that year, Professor Hartwell brings a double bias. He starts from an abysmally poor year and argues to a rather good one. By extending his period to 1850 rather than the 1830 preferred by earlier 'optimists', he conceals the fact revealed by recent research that improvement was very largely confined to the period after 1820. Professor Perkin has tested several different starting and finishing dates against commonly used indices and his results are striking. Hartwell's dates would produce an increase of 85% in real wages whereas if the more normal year of 1790 were used with the baddish one of 1840, the improvement is reduced to a range of 17–24%. A comparison of two normal years, 1790 to 1845, produces an increase range of 33 to 50%.[14]

Professor Flinn attempted a more systematic analysis drawing upon a wide sample of indices and seeking to level out the price peaks. He was less disparaging than some have been of the value of the available price indices and noted a 'quite remarkable degree of agreement' between them in their reflection of trends. Using them together with the Bowley and Wood and the Gilboy wage series, he believed some degree of generalisation was possible. Rather than select a period within it, he chose to use the century 1750 to 1850 and sub-divided it into trend periods by measuring between quinquennia located at selected turning points. Those chosen were: 1750/4, 1788/92, 1809/15, 1820/6 and 1846/50. To level the distorting effect of 1813, which was both a long- and a short-run peak, he substituted the averages of 1809–11 and of 1814–15 for 1812 and 1813. His findings were that up to 1788/92 four of six indices showed an improvement in real wages over a range from 13–21%. From 1788/92 to 1810/14, nine of twelve indices available showed a fall of 50–100% (six being within 65–86%). Apart from two series which remained level from 1810/14 to 1820/4, the others fell by up to 35% (ten of thirteen less than 20% and eight by less than 12%). After the early 1820s, money wages seem to have changed little, except in the case of tragic groups like the handloom weavers, and there is little change indicated from the indices 1820/4 to 1846/50, their range being +5 to −5%. In general in the second quarter of the nineteenth century, for most groups a slower rate of price deflation did not erode the gains of the post-1815 decade, for wages did not decline by much and in some cases even rose. However, gains in the second quarter were of the order of less than 1% per annum compared with a more rapid 2–3% in the short period 1813–25. His conclusions that in the French War years marginal gainers balanced marginal losers, and that the really significant improvement was concentrated in the post-war decade, has not been universally accepted. It has been pointed out that by using different five-year averages on the same data a 10–15% higher price rise in the French War years could be produced followed by a 5% bigger fall to the mid-1820s. On these figures, Flinn's pro-position that wages kept up with inflating prices in the war years is less than firm. Dr Gourvish is not as convinced of the value of indices based on averages which take no account of regional variations: 'Far from venturing a definite opinion on real wage experience; therefore my stress would be on regional and occupational variations over the crucial period together with a healthy scepticism about real wage improvement . . . a wide variety of working-class experience, set against a backcloth of general pessimism, for the period c 1790–1830'.[15]

A more recent measurement (1983), carried out by two scholars familiar with macro-economic theory and econometric methods, supports Flinn's view that there was little significant change in real wages either way before 1810/14, but does not agree that real wage improvement began with the deflation turning point of 1813. Instead, a decline between 1815 and 1819 is suggested with a concentration of the real improvement between 1820 and 1850, which saw a near doubling of real wages. This case rests on the assumption that real *full time* adult male wages are the most appropriate indicator. We shall see below that this is not an unquestionable assumption.[16]

Francis Place wrote that when people spoke of the working classes: 'We shall find them all jumbled together as the 'lower orders', the most skilled and the most prudent workman, with the most ignorant and imprudent labourers and paupers, though the difference is great indeed, and indeed in many cases will scarce admit of comparison.'[17] That, along with social manners, the standard of living experiences of different groups within the working classes varied considerably is well known. Ashton recognised two groups whose divergent experiences explain why contemporary opinions differed. His 'guess' was that the group which benefited was larger than the one which did not. The suggestion of two groups is an oversimplification. Ashton described a disadvantaged group 'whose incomes were almost wholly absorbed in paying for the bare necessaries of life' as consisting of 'masses of unskilled or poorly skilled workers – seasonally employed agricultural workers and handloom weavers in particular'.[18] Leaving aside the question of the skill level of handloom weavers, it is seriously misleading to imply that the losers were essentially the un- or less skilled. Not only were skilled farm workers, like shepherds and carters in the south, even if better off than ordinary farm labourers, among the poorly paid, while farmhands in the north were not, but there were groups of skilled workers like calico printers who suffered very considerably from competition with machinery, while others like tailors did so from the 'sweating' of unskilled handworkers. As Sir John Hicks has remarked, machines *do* very often replace skilled labour and it was for precisely that reason that their use was advocated. The block-making machinery introduced into Portsmouth dockyard in 1801 enabled ten unskilled men to do the work of 110 skilled ones. Economic history confirms that there is no quick and painless process by which displaced labour can move to growth sectors of the economy. The problems of geographical mobility, the transferability of skill and physical suitability are immense. Yet one anticipates an article by an 'optimist' which will blame all the problems of displaced and de-skilled labour in the industrial revolution on the fact that the bicycle was not soon enough invented! The difficulty of implying that skill was a protection against a falling living standard can be illustrated from the experiences of London's artisans. Tucker in 1936 based a much-used index on the ability of 'a typical regularly employed London artisan' to make his customary purchases.[19] But which artisans? The growth of the 'sweating system', especially in garment manufacture, was as much a part of the nineteenth-century capitalist economy as was the factory system. Through its extension the gap between the 'honourable' (bespoke) and 'dishonourable' (ready-made) sections of the trade, which had already existed in the late eighteenth century, widened into a gulf. The 'honourable' end could usually employ only around one in seven of London's tailors in 1849. It is all too evident from the investigations of Mayhew and others that although the warehouse-supplying sweated end of the trade drew in female and unskilled labour in increasing quantities, a very large number of skilled men were also drawn down into it. As Mathias has remarked, for many London artisans the hungry thirties preceded the hungry forties. In the process, casual replaced regular employment and ever-falling piece rates replaced steady time-wages. If, as E. P. Thompson has remarked, we were concerned only with the skilled 'society men' in regular employment, the controversy as to artisan living standards would long ago have been resolved in favour of the 'optimists'. But we cannot be so confined in our concerns. For the most part skilled artisans were neither so regularly employed nor so well paid as Clapham, Ashton and Chaloner have suggested. An index based on the assumption of steady employment at 'honourable' wages has only a partial application.[20]

It is sometimes argued that the handloom weavers cannot be properly regarded as 'victims' of the industrial revolution: rather that they were sufferers because they stayed outside the factory. Weavers and knitters formed the largest occupational group after farm labourers, with cotton handloom weavers the most numerous single group of workers in manufacturing in the 1820s. However, their fate after the advent of power weaving cannot be regarded other than as an effect of the industrial revolution. That they existed in such numbers was because they had multiplied as a consequence of the early mechanisation of spinning. It was the mill-spun yarn which brought about the increase in their numbers, and which gave them their period of prosperity before an inherent over-stocking of the trade began a slow decline in standards accelerated by the advent of machinery into a disaster. They cannot therefore be conveniently explained away as belonging, along with such groups as nailors, to an older pre-industrial sector rather than being 'an authentic feature of the new capitalist order which . . . may be seen where there are steam factory operatives, and meat-eating engineers. It was the mills which spun the yarn and the foundries which made the nailrod upon which the outworkers were employed.'[21]

If, despite such difficulties, the standard of living controversy is to be reduced to a balance sheet of gainers and losers, how acceptable is Ashton's 'guess' that the former outnumbered the latter? (Since his terminal date was 1830, we shall in fact be asssisting his case if we examine the balance at mid-century, for not only is there a strong case for believing that significant improvement in living standards was concentrated into the second quarter of the nineteenth century, but also those groups like engineers, railway servants and printers who are generally accepted to have done well were more numerous in 1850 than they would have been twenty years earlier.) Two aspects need to be considered: the performance of particular groups and their weight within the working class. Perkin has attempted an analysis. Best of all in improving their living standards were not the male adult factory workers who did not start high enough up the earnings scale to have a large surplus over the purchase of necessaries, but the group which came later to be known as the 'aristocracy of labour'. Mostly they were craftsmen: printers, joiners, cabinet-makers, cutlers, blacksmiths, wheelwrights, building craftsmen and the like. From their ranks dropped those artisans like woolcombers, calico printers and shearmen, technologically displaced from previously advantageous positions, and those artisans who slipped into the 'dishonourable' section of their trade. Into their ranks came the new skilled: iron puddlers, engine drivers, engineers and fitters and fine cotton spinners. Such men were paid from 50 to 100% above the level of unskilled labourers. At most, they accounted for 15% of the labour force, and with their real wage levels at least keeping up, it was they who: 'ate meat, vegetables, fruit and dairy produce, lived in the best and newest cottages and filled them with furniture and knick-knacks, bought books and newspapers, supported mechanics' institutes and friendly societies, and paid the heavy subscriptions to the craft trade unions.'[22]

Below them came the male factory workers. Cotton workers could earn from 1.3 to 3 times the average of the northern farm labourer: 14s. 6d. (72½p) for card room operators and as much as 33s. 3d. (£1.66¼p) for fine spinners. But it must be remembered that these men were an elite minority even in their own industry in which they were heavily outnumbered by women and child workers. In 1835 only about a quarter of cotton workers were adult males, and the much lower earnings of women and children meant that average wages for *all* operatives were among the lowest for any industry. For the male spinners, wages improved sharply up to 1830 and after a relative fall-back rose by 1850 to around three times their 1800 level. They could, except at unfavourable points in their family cycle, afford a satisfactory diet, decent clothing and household goods. A minority within their own industries, male factory workers were an even smaller one within the larger labouring population. Even if comparable groups like miners, transport workers and iron-ship builders are added, those below them in the earnings scale still clearly outnumbered them. Among these were the handloom weavers and knitters whose 25s. (£1.25) a week or more in their late eighteenth-century 'golden ages' had fallen to truly desperate levels of 5s. (25p) or less by the 1830s. Their numbers fell from around 250,000 in 1831 to 23,000 by 1856. Outside the main textile branches, the number of outworkers did not fall. In nail and chair-making, in tailoring and boot-making, in cabinet-making and in dress-making, assessment of the wage levels of the greater number is pointless. Simply they struggled to exist alongside the unskilled casual labourers, the street sellers and the vagrants, many of whom are hardly among the 'waged' population at all. As the later researches of Booth and Rowntree were to reveal, here was a large section of the lower orders who were not to benefit from industrialisation before the twentieth century.

That the average wages of farm labourers rose between 1795 and 1850 from 8s. 11d. to 9s. 6d. (45p to 47½p) – 15% in real terms – is due to the improving condition of the northern labourer. In East Anglia and in the southern and western counties, farm labourers and their families lived in unbelievable poverty and squalor. Comparisons with the eighteenth century are complicated because of the evident movement away from living-in farm service, where bed and board were provided, to living-out wage employment, and because of the loss of significant perquisite advantages from the diminishing commons. Even propagandists of the agricultural revolution like Arthur Young came eventually to recognise the extent to which the enclosure of common land had disadvantaged the rural poor. It has been suggested by Professors Chambers and Mingay in a frankly admiring textbook on the agricultural revolution that a postwar fall in wages ended in 1824 with most labourers still earning higher money wages than they had been before the war and that although prices had not fallen back to prewar levels and taxes were higher, the majority of labourers were better off than they had been in 1790. For the quarter of a century after 1824 there was no very large increase in money wages, nor until the fall in prices of the 1840s in real earnings. Few historians would be so complacent in asserting even such a qualified improvement for 'most' labourers. Since the gap between the better-paid north and the desperate south was widening, conditions in the latter (except around London) were such as to make it more to the point to wonder how the labourers managed to live than to speculate about a penny or two on their standard of living. In the worst area, south Wiltshire, winter rates of 6–7s. (30–35p) in 1794 rose through 8s. (40p) in 1804 to reach 12s. (60p) by 1814. By 1817 they had slipped back to 7s. or 8s., and through to 1844 were never much above 7s. For the long summer days wages were better and specialised workers like carters and shepherds could expect around 23s. (£1.15) a week or more. On one side of the famous wage line drawn by Caird in 1851 from Shropshire to the Wash, a Lincolnshire labourer could earn 11s. (55p) a week and one in the West Riding 14s. (70p). On the southern side, Gloucestershire and Suffolk labourers joined Wiltshire on 7s. (35p).

Dr. Horne's assessment is that by the 1790s the standard of living had fallen for thirty to forty years as food prices and population rose. Movement in money wages in the south where the lack of manufacturing offered little alternative employment could be negligible. In Herefordshire in 1805 wages were said to have been stagnant for forty years. Similar findings have come from a recent study of East Anglia and the Home Counties. Here male real wages, after rising for thirty years after 1740, stabilised but then in the war years lost any gain and showed no consistent recovery after 1825, a slight improvement 1811 to 1825 giving way to another period of decline. As significant as the fall in wages after the war was the increasing resort to temporary labour or Poor Law subsidy so that in the south and east a full week's wages at any level was scarcely obtainable.[23]

Two further matters need to be considered: whether adult male money earnings are an appropriate basis for measuring trends in the standard of living, unless an allowance can be made for periods of unemployment, and whether in an age when women and children worked the movement of *family* earnings would be a better measure.

If industrialisation with its greater vulnerability to the trade cycle brought greater risk and incidence of unemployment to a larger proportion of the population, then it is dangerous to assume that higher weekly earnings necessarily produced a commensurate improvement in material living standards. Data on unemployment is especially scarce. All acknowledge its importance but conclude there is no fully satisfactory measure of its impact. As industrialisation developed, the impact of a cyclical pattern of boom and slump can be perceived. In bad years such as 1816, 1819, 1826–7, 1830–1 and 1842–3 there were dramatic short-term increases in unemployment among industrial workers of a kind not usually found in the pre-industrial economy. Unemployment in Bolton in 1842 was 60% among mill workers and even higher among building workers. Hobsbawm has pointed to the very high levels of unemployment in this year all over industrial Britain and concludes that no discussion which 'overlooks the massive waves of destitution which swamped large sections of the labouring poor every depression, can claim to be realistic'. How far should unemployment reduce the real wage increase claims of the 'optimists'? Hobsbawm feels that at least they throw doubt upon the 'less critical' statements, but on present levels of research are not sufficiently confirmed to establish an alternative view. The undoubted high levels of depression years stand out as creating short-term peaks as depressions came and went with a new speed. In this sense, as Mathias has suggested, a form of unemployment developed which was 'almost the economic antithesis of the chronic disease of underemployment on the land', although Flinn has argued that this change to short-term unemployment from the inherently irregular working or underemployment of agriculture or domestic industry was a gain for the factory system.[24]

It is at least debatable whether a situation in which under hand-manufacture problems of the market leading to less work being put out lead to reductions in the piece-rate earnings of artisans and other domestic workers is not preferable to one in which sudden redundancy from a reasonably remunerated occupation reduces income to nil and throws the worker on to poor relief. In 1842, 15–20% of the population of Leeds had a weekly income of less than 1s. a head.[25] Certainly the traumatic experience of outright redundancy must be placed among the harmful psychological experiences which industrial society brought with it.

If factory employment can be credited with being, except in short-term depressions, more regular than artisan or domestic modes of production, then this was not a benefit which had reached most of the working population within the period of our concern. Manufacturing artisans, building workers and others all continued to experience long periods of inactivity. Figures from Leeds for 1839 illustrate the level of correction necessary to allow for this. Among trades generally inactive for one month, the tailor's 16s. (80p) becomes 14s. 8d. (72.5p), the joiner's 19s. 6d. (97.5p), 17s. 11d. (89.6p) and the printer's 21s. (£1.05p), 19s. 3d. (96.25p). Among those commonly inactive for two months, shoemakers reduce from 14s. to 11s. 8d. (70p to 58.33p), hatters from 24s. to 2s. (£1.20p to £1) and masons from 22s. to 18s. 4d. £1.10p to 91.7p). A number of trades worked only nine months and the 25% correction needed here would reduce sawyers to 15s. from 20s. (75p from £1), bricklayers to 17s. 3d. from 23s. (86.25p from £1.15p) and painters to 15s. from 20s. (75p from £1).[26] The need for such corrections was well known. They are fully accounted for in a description of the London trades published in 1747 and taken into account by Adam Smith in his discussion of wage differentials. The largely seasonal factors which determine this continued to operate in the nineteenth century as they had done in the eighteenth, although the problem of demand fluctuations caused by the 'London Season' was peculiar to that city. Finally, it should be noted that the increasing impact of cyclical peaks in unemployment adds yet another variable to the problem of measuring trends in real wages. For example in 1825 industrial prosperity lessened the impact of high food prices, whereas in 1835 manufacturing prosperity and a good harvest reinforced each other positively, while in 1847 high prices and industrial depression did so negatively.[27]

Unemployment in agriculture has recently been investigated by Dr Snell. Using Poor Law settlement examinations he has presented a serious challenge to the view of Professor Chambers put forward in 1953 that farming improvements increased rather than decreased agricultural employment. Chambers had been concerned to challenge the view that there was in Marx's terms an 'expropriation' of the peasantry, which through the agency of parliamentary enclosure created a new proletariat for the industrial revolution. That extreme view is no longer seriously held, but Chambers' argument (taken up by many since) that improved agriculture was labour-intensive in the absence of significant new machinery before 1880 has become something of an orthodoxy. Snell's findings differ. His examination of nine

East Anglian and Home Counties found that agrarian changes were already by the second half of the eighteenth century bringing about a marked increase in winter unemployment for men, and in summer unemployment for women, once men increasingly dominated the harvest. A switch to cereal production brought increasingly acute seasonal unemployment especially between 1814 and 1834, which seriously questions the presumed capacity of the new 'improved' agriculture to generate greater and more regular employment throughout the year for the growing male labour force. Indeed, male seasonal unemployment would have been even more acute if there had not been a fall-off since the eighteenth century in the levels of female employment in agriculture. Chambers had been concerned with the Midlands, but at the very least his findings can no longer be extended to support a *general* view of the effects of improved agriculture.[28]

The impact of the industrial revolution on the family is discussed below (pp 168–89) but here we must consider the direct relevance of family earnings to the standard of living. Engels made out an extreme case against the factory system in writing of instances in which demoralised fathers saw their role as breadwinners eroded as family support came to depend increasingly on the labour of women and children. From this perspective it is argued that if the factory system offered increased opportunities for women and children to contribute to family support, then it did so at the expense of adult males. The young women who began to operate power looms in the 1820s represented the final stage in the extinction of the handloom weaver, while the factory's early dependence on skilled male mule spinners created a new male skill, but not one to which the declining adult hand weavers could transfer, nor which needed the number of hands weaving had employed at its height. The most immediate effects of the development of factory spinning towards the end of the eighteenth century were felt by the rural districts. The number of hand-spinners needed to keep a weaver in yarn was such that for surprising distances around the great cloth-making centres, countless women, farmers' wives and daughters, among others, supplemented the family income by taking in wool to spin. If in the factory towns increasing opportunities for family employment came into being, then it was at the expense of the very widespread loss of earning opportunities from spinning in the rural households; something which was much commented on in the late eighteenth century.

Of direct relevance to the understanding of working-class living standards is the family cycle. Even at cotton spinners' wages it was most likely that families would experience poverty during the years when their children were mostly too young to work. The studies of Preston by Anderson and of Oldham by Foster confirm this.[29] It was during this period that wives in the mill towns would make every effort to return to work. Anderson has noted that in the vast majority of families where a mother worked, there would have been considerable distress had she not done so. In this respect the textile areas were not unique. From brief data given for a Cornish mining family in 1842 it is possible to construct, by making a few reasonable demographic suppositions, a model of a family economy passing through its cycle.

TABLE 3   A family earnings cycle 1827–47

Year	No. in household	Earnings per head per month (new pence)
1827	6	46
1832	8	38
1837	10	52.5
1842	9	83
1847	7	117

(Age of miner in 1842 was 47)

From Table 3 it can be seen that income per head was at its low point, only 32.5% of its highest one which came when two grown lads as well as the father were working. This fully supports the comment of a contemporary investigator that the period when it was most difficult for the married miner to make ends meet came before his children were old enough to work. During this period the degree of embarrassment increased with their number. Since miners' brides were commonly pregnant at marriage, this embarrassment came very soon after marriage.[30]

It is fair to conclude that even at the better end of adult male earnings most working-class families could expect to live through a period of poverty. When sickness or redundancy intervened, as they so often did, then even the best-favoured groups of workers could slip into destitution. This clearly stresses the importance for the earlier nineteenth century too of the classic cycle of poverty found by Seebohm Rowntree and others at the end of the century. Rowntree also drew attention to 'secondary poverty', i.e. that caused by misspending of income on 'luxuries', especially drink. We shall be considering below similar suggestions resting on the poor housekeeping of working-class wives. Exact quantification in this area is hardly possible, but there can be little doubt that drinking was a problem of sufficient dimension to have been a contributor to the poverty of very many families, and to the destitution of not a few. Such were, however, individual cases even if not uncommon (witness the remarkable growth of temperance and teetotal movements) and would not seem to generally affect conclusions drawn from the movements of wages and prices and the availability of employment which were the determinants of real income levels.

REFERENCES AND NOTES

1. **T. B. Macaulay**, 'Southey's colloquies', *Critical and Historical Essays*, Vol. II, Everyman, 1907, pp. 197, 219.
2. **E. A. Wrigley** and **R. S. Schofield**, *The Population History of England 1541–1871: a reconstruction*, Edward Arnold, 1981. Some students may find this work difficult. They could approach through the review article by **Professor M. W. Flinn** in *Economic History Review*, XXXV, no. 3, 1982, pp. 443–57 and through **Dr Wrigley**'s article 'The growth of population in eighteenth-century England: a conundrum resolved', *Past and Present*, no. 98, 1983, pp. 121–50.
3. **P. E. Razzell**, 'Population change in eighteenth-century England: a re-interpretation', *Economic History Review*, XVIII, 1965, pp. 312–32; **J. D. Chambers**, *Population, Economy and Society in Pre-Industrial England*, Oxford, 1972. Ch. 4.
4. The most convenient summary of the debate on the standard of living is the foreword to the Panther edition (1972) of **B. Inglis**, *Poverty and the Industrial Revolution* which also appeared as an article in *Encounter* in September 1971. Also valuable is the introduction to **Arthur J. Taylor** (ed.), *The Standard of Living in Britain in the Industrial Revolution*, Methuen, 1975. The direct quotations used in the opening paragraphs have been taken from these two reviews. For bibliographical details of the major contributions, see the bibliography.
5. Quoted in Inglis, p. 21; **N. Gash**, 'The state of the debate', in *The Long Debate on Poverty*, Institute of Economic Affairs, Second Impression, 1974, pp. xxiii–xiv.
6. Quoted in Inglis, p. 23; **T. S. Ashton**, 'The standard of life of the workers in England, 1790–1830', repr. in Taylor (ed.), pp. 47–50.
7. See **P. H. Lindert** and **J. C. Williamson**, 'English workers' living standards during the Industrial Revolution: a new look', *Economic History Review* (second series), XXXVI, no. 1, Feb. 1983, pp. 1–25.
8. Ashton, 'Standard of life', Taylor (ed.), p. 52.
9. **E. P. Thompson**, *The Making of the English Working Class*, Penguin, 1968, p. 351.
10. **P. Mathias**, *The First Industrial Nation*, Methuen, 1969, p. 222; **P. Deane**, *The First Industrial Revolution*, Cambridge U.P., 1965, pp. 268–69; **E. H. Hunt**, *British Labour History 1815–1914*, Weidenfeld & Nicolson, 1981, pp. 58–60, 63.
11. **F. Crouzet** (ed.), *Capital Formation in the Industrial Revolution*, Methuen, 1972, Intro. p. 63.
12. **H. Perkin**, *The Origins of Modern English Society 1780–1880*, Routledge & Kegan Paul, 1969, pp. 135–6.
13. For the varying dates see Taylor (ed.), Intro. pp. xx–xxii; M. W. Flinn, 'Trends in real wages, 1750–1850', *Economic History Review* (second

series), XXVII, 3, 1974, pp. 395–413.
14. Perkin, *Origins*, pp. 137–8.
15. Flinn, 'Trends in real wages'; **T. R. Gourvish**, 'Flinn and real wage trends in Britain, 1750–1850', *Economic History Review* (second series), XXIX, 1, 1976, pp. 141–2.
16. Lindert and Williamson, 'Workers' living standards'; see also **G. N. Von Tunzelmann**, 'Trends in real wages, 1750–1850, revisited', *Economic History Review*, XXXII, no. 1, 1979, p. 41.
17. Quoted in Thompson, *Making*, p. 212.
18. Ashton, 'Standard of life', in Taylor (ed.), p. 57.
19. **J. Hicks**, *A Theory of Economic History*, Oxford U. P., 1969, p. 149; **P. Linebaugh**, 'Labour history without the labour process: a note on John Gast and his times', *Social History*, vol. 7, no. 3, pp. 322–31 for examples of labour-saving machinery in the dockyards; **R. S. Tucker**, 'Real wages of artisans in London, 1729–1935' (1936), repr. in Taylor, (ed.), p. 27. The unpublished thesis of **Dr L. D. Schwatz** suggests little significant movement in living standards in East London between 1770 and 1820. ('Conditions of life and work in London *c.*1770–1820, with special reference to East London', D.Phil., Oxford, 1967, Intro.).
20. Mathias, *First Industrial Nation*, p. 221; Thompson, *Making*, p. 268; **A. Musson**, *British Trade Unions, 1800–1875*, Macmillan, 1972, p. 18.
21. Thompson, *Making*, p. 288.
22. Perkin, *Origins*, pp. 143–9. For a critique see Taylor (ed.), pp. xlviii–xlix.
23. For farm labourers' wages see **J. D. Chambers** and **G. E. Mingay**, *The Agricultural Revolution 1750–1880*, Batsford, 1966, Ch. 5, 'Prosperity and depression, 1750–1846'; **R. W. Malcolmson**, *Life and Labour in England 1700–1780*, Hutchinson, 1981, pp. 145–6; **P. Horn**, *The Rural World 1780–1850*, Hutchinson, 1980, pp. 31–5, 46–7 and 242–8; and **K. D. M. Snell**, 'Agricultural seasonal unemployment, the standard of living, and women's work in the south and east: 1690–1860', *Economic History Review* (second series), XXXIV, no. 3, 1981, pp. 407–37.
24. **E. J. Hobsbawm**, 'The British standard of living, 1790–1850' (1957), repr. in Taylor (ed.), pp. 70–5; Mathias, *First Industrial Nation*, p. 22; Flinn, 'Trends in real wages', pp. 410–11.
25. Hobsbawm, 'British standard of living', p. 71.
26. Ibid., p. 75.
27. **R. Campbell**, *The London Tradesman*, 1747, repr. David & Charles, Newton Abbot, 1969. For a discussion see **J. G. Rule**, *The Experience of Labour in Eighteenth-century Industry*, Croom Helm, 1981, Ch. 2; Taylor (ed.), Intro., p. xlvii.
28. Snell, 'Agricultural seasonal unemployment', pp. 430–1; **J. D. Chambers**, 'Enclosure and labour supply in the Industrial Revolution', first published in the *Economic History Review* (second series), vol. V, 1953, is reprinted in **E. L. Jones** (ed.), *Agriculture and Economic Growth in England 1650–1815*, Methuen, 1967, pp. 94–127.
29. **John Foster**, *Class Struggle and the Industrial Revolution: Early industrial capitalism in three English towns*, Methuen Paperbacks, 1977, esp. pp. 91–8 and Appendix 1; **Michael Anderson**, *Family Structure in Nineteenth-Century Lancashire*, Cambridge U.P., 1971, pp. 29–32.
30. *Report of the Royal Commission on Child Employment*, BPP, 1842, xvi,

p. 757. See discussion in **J. G. Rule**, 'The labouring miner in Cornwall 1740–1870: a study in social history', Ph.D. thesis, University of Warwick, 1971, pp. 100–3.

Chapter 2

WORKING-CLASS CONSUMPTION

DIET

Historians who specialise in the analysis of working-class dietaries after 1870 work on a period when transport improvement and retailing developments were producing a degree of national uniformity. In addition, the larger number of budgets available allows for generalisation without too much fear of overlooking significant regional variations. For an earlier period no such confidence is possible: for regional variations were of great importance and specimen budgets are scarce and scattered. Generalisation before 1870 is fraught with difficulties.[1] Various supply factors determined diet at the local level. Soil and climate dictated the crops which could be grown. Northern areas were more suited to other cereals than wheat. The mild climate of Cornwall allowed the taking of two potato crops a year. In some areas ground given over to crops, such as hops in Kent, reduced the land available for the cultivation of potatoes or other vegetables. Counties on the coast could make good use of sea fish which was scarcely available inland. Eden, in 1797, noted that around Yarmouth and parts of the Norfolk coast the poor 'lived much on fish, which is generally very cheap'. Fish was also much consumed around Hull, in Lancashire and in Devon. In Cornwall, pilchards especially were a very significant food.[2] Some sources of food were very local, as at Calne in Wiltshire, where pigs' entrails were cheap as a by-product of the bacon trade. Despite the present-day rush of the well-heeled middle classes to fill their freezers from the hedgerows, 'free foods' contributed in only a supplementary manner, but blackberries and nuts were gathered in season, especially by children, while shore dwellers did not overlook limpets, mussels and the like. Eden found that the poor around Ecclesfield in Yorkshire not uncommonly dined on boiled and seasoned nettles. Gleaning and poaching were capable of providing free food in more significant quantities than hedgerow picking.[3]

Supply of things other than food was also important. In Cornwall it was the availability of salt rather than of the fish itself which limited the ability of the poor to preserve pilchards for the winter. Fuel was crucial. Eden's well-known distinction between the dietary practices of the north and those of the south was essentially based on this: 'The cheapness of fuel is, perhaps, another reason why the meals of the Northern peasant are so much diversified, and his table supplied with hot dishes.' It was not just that the high cost and scant availability of fuel restricted the cooking methods available to the southern labourer, but also that they forced him into a higher expenditure pattern. He had to resort largely to ready-made bread, a fact still being emphasised by Seebohm Rowntree in 1913.[4]

Obviously cooking methods varied in a direct relationship to the availability of fuel, but they were influenced by other factors as well. Some of these were mere matters of taste and preference, but others had dietary significance. Eden stressed the value of soups and broths in the north and regretted that dear fuel prevented their wider use in the south where labourers could not 'eke out their scanty portions by culinary contrivances'. Cheaper cuts of meat require longer cooking. One of Jonas Hanway's well-intentioned recipes, for ox-head soup, certainly used ingredients at give-away prices (much in line with those miracle prescriptions for hunger which ladies of fashion devised from inputs which would have made the five loaves and two fishes seem veritable abundance to feed all the poor of their villages), but it required three and a half hours of boiling. Eden was perhaps inclined to be carried away by the wonderful efficacy of 'culinary contrivance' for as Rowntree was to point out: 'A pound of beef, for instance with a thrifty family may serve three dinners and provide three separate entries – roast beef, cold beef and Irish stew, which suggests a liberal dietary. But when all is said and done, it is only a pound of beef.'[5]

Methods of cooking which required the use of fat increased the nutrition content of the food so cooked, but fat was in itself an additional item which had to be budgeted for against other items. However, cabbage was often cooked in fat (dripping) as a main meal. Some regional specialities were not always as nutritious as they have since become: cornish pasties only infrequently contained meat and were in poor years only a palatable way of eating turnips.[6]

Despite Eden's belief that labourers were in many areas of moderate wages better off than those in high wage ones, it is unwise to ignore the obvious connection, especially for farm labourers, between varied diet and the higher wages of the north and parts of the Midlands. More than sixty years after Eden's survey, Smith, who only ventured conclusions after great deliberation, picked out Cornwall, Devon, Somerset, Dorset, Wiltshire, Staffordshire, Oxford, Berkshire and Hertfordshire as counties where carbohydrate and protein consumption was seriously below average and where agricultural wages were on the low side. However, in relation to the standard of living controversy in respect of poorer groups, we are in an area of such marginality that the famous law of Ernst Engels that when income increases, the proportion spent on food normally declines, can hardly be said to have operated (Table 4).[7] However, Engels accepted that this ratio did not necessarily hold good in times of dearth, when the proportion spent on food was necessarily increased in most groups.

TABLE 4   Eden's budgets: 64 cases. Percentage of expenditures for food

Income groups in $ (1936) p.a.	No. of families	% for food
75	1	68.3
100	19	73.9
125	23	80.0
150	13	82.0
175	5	85.8
200	1	95.7
225	2	73.0

Source: From Zimmerman (see note 6)

Sir James Caird's famous line drawn in 1851 through the middle of Shropshire to the Wash separated the two areas of southern low and northern high agricultural wages. Only in pockets in the south, such as Kent, where proximity to London and some well-paid work connected with hop cultivation kept up wages, was there no evident co-existence of poor wages with poor diet. There was hardly any offsetting of low wages by spatial differences in the cost of food. Dr Hunt has shown that, even after 1850, regionally low food prices did not compensate significantly for low wages, and this certainly holds equally good for the first half of the nineteenth century. It was in the high wage areas that the cheaper bread cereals, oats and barley, were largely grown. As an investigator in 1850 remarked, the fact that the availability of potatoes and other vegetables enabled the Dorset labourer to support his family more cheaply than could the better-paid Kentish labourer did not make the condition of the two comparable. The much higher Kentish wages enabled the labourer there to enjoy a more varied diet and to be 'a stronger and healthier man'.[8]

The percentage of income spent on food can never be simply a function of its level. In marginal situations it has to increase if food prices rise faster than wages. In less marginal situations there may be some room for manoeuvre by switching from dearer to cheaper foods. In some districts wages were partly paid in kind and it would be tempting to assume that where this prevailed it resulted in a better and more constant diet. The hinds of Northumberland and Durham received substantial food allowances as well as a free cottage in addition to 10–12s. (50–60p) a week in 1850 and were certainly the best fed of all the rural labourers whose condition was described in the *Morning Chronicle*. However, although they were an elite among northern farm labourers, the day labourers who were not paid in kind were *still* better fed than their low-waged southern counterparts. In some areas, part-payment in food could actually depress standards of living: in Cornwall some farm labourers were obliged to accept inferior grain at a valuation frequently above market levels. So poor in general was the living of the southern farm labourer in 1850 that the *Morning Chronicle* reporter in the end concluded that the variations in local practices which he discovered within that region between counties were not of great significance: 'When I was informed that in Wiltshire, proverbial for the low scale of its wages, the labourers were better off as a class than some of their neighbours, I could not avoid ejaculating – God help them elsewhere.'[9] The first official detailed survey of labourers' diets was undertaken in 1863 by Dr Edward Smith and confirms the persistence of significant regional variations. On his extensive and detailed evidence it is surprising that any serious historian could ever have suggested anything other than the most slight and selective improvement in working-class food consumption before the 1850s. Concentration at first on the 576 rural labourers' budgets examined by Smith will remove the possibility of confusion from intra-regional variations between town and country. Smith estimated that 30% of the families were dependent upon ready-baked bread and 50% made some use of it. The counties where ready-baked bread was general included most where the diet was especially poor: the five south-western counties, parts of the South Midlands, the eastern and the south-eastern counties. In part, dear fuel still explained this. Wheat flour was the principal in 60% of the families and partly used in 90%. White bread was everywhere preferred as it could be eaten with little or no butter, while brown bread was commonly thought to purge the children. Outside the north, oatmeal was used only in small quantities. Barley bread was still used a little in parts of the north and in the far south-west, but its use was diminishing. The average weekly intake of flour per adult was 12¼ lb, but the extremes were 15 lb in Shropshire and the northern counties and 10 lb in Cornwall.[10]

For foodstuffs other than cereals, regional variations were also marked. No clear pattern in the use of vegetables emerged. Smith noted the universality of the potato and the savings on bread which it permitted, but still thought of it as largely a seasonal food useful from the end of summer to the beginning of winter. Green vegetables were even more seasonal: at times they could be used daily, and at other times perhaps only once or twice a week. Where fat was available, cabbage was usually cooked in it. Onions were much used in season. Turnips were a symbol of poverty, the lowest form of human food, but

Smith thought that by 1863 their use had declined even in poorer districts. Sugar consumption averaged 7½ oz per adult a week, treacle was in part substituted in 52% of the families. Some favoured northern counties averaged 14 oz or more, while in southern and western counties it was below 6 oz. Smith thought the use of sugar was linked to tea consumption, and that the low use of it in Devon was because of the availability of milk as an alternative, but it also seems to have been heavily used in some northern counties where milk was equally available. Butter was used, primarily in the summer, in 97% of the families and some form of separated fat in 99%. Extremes around the average of 5½ oz were marked, with more than 10 oz per adult weekly in Kent, Durham, Lancashire and Surrey, and only 3 oz or less in Norfolk, Somerset and Hertfordshire. Less than 4 oz were consumed in Devon: a warning against assumptions that the labourers shared in commodities which were produced for the market.[11]

Compared with the *Morning Chronicle* evidence of 1849/50, meat consumption seems to have become more general. It was now eaten in 99% of the families; butchers' meat in 70% and bacon in 74%, 46% using both. Intake was in fact still very low. Almost a third of the families never tasted butchers' meat or else too infrequently for it to be averaged in ounces per week. Such families were especially to be found in Devon, Somerset, Wiltshire, Gloucestershire, Shropshire and, more surprisingly, in Cumberland. Only in Somerset and Wiltshire were families found who ate no meat at all. The average (including bacon) was 16 oz per adult, but the extremes were a group of northern counties and Surrey where levels exceeded 24 oz (35 in Northumberland), and Shropshire, Essex, Somerset and Wiltshire where weekly adult intakes were below 7 oz. Fish hardly entered into rural diets outside of Cornwall.

Milk was much less used than townspeople might have expected. Whole milk was used only by a minority. In some counties like Devon, skimmed milk was cheap as a by-product of butter making, but where cheese was made only whey was available. The trend towards livestock farming was leading farmers to retain milk for feeding calves, while in arable districts it was hardly available. The average of all kinds of milk was a low 1.6 pints per adult a week. The heaviest user was Westmoreland with 6 pints, while Northumberland, Lancashire, Yorkshire, Cornwall, Devon, Worcestershire, Shropshire, Lincolnshire, Cheshire, Nottinghamshire, Durham and Cumberland all consumed between 2 and 4½ pints. Surrey consumed less than 2 pints, Gloucestershire less than ¾ pint and Essex and Cambridgeshire less than half a pint per adult per week.

Cheese ranged in price from 8d. to 10d. (3½p to 4p) a pound. In some counties it was regarded as an inferior substitute for meat; while in others, like Yorkshire with a generally good dietary, it was regarded as a luxury not commonly purchased by the poor. There were high users like Dorset with 12½ oz per adult per week, and others like Cumberland, Kent, Surrey, Wiltshire, Gloucestershire and Sussex who all used about 5 oz. However, despite its place as the traditional lunch of the ploughman in half of all counties, rural labourers' families did not exceed the level of 2 oz per adult a week. In Cornwall it was less than an ounce. Eggs were hardly used anywhere. Where wives kept hens, then the 'egg money' was much too valuable to forgo and was used to replace clothing. Tea was used in 99% of the households at an average of 2½ oz per family a week with hardly any regional variation. It was already the most universal item in the English diet.

Smith's findings both confirm the persistence of regional variations and deny any real validity for claims of dietary improvement before 1850, for a comparison of his figures with the findings of the *Morning Chronicle* reporters suggests strongly that any advances in the food consumption of farm labourers and their families was slight and took place after mid-century. Dr Hunt has shown the persistence of wage variations which in 1867–70 still retained much of their early pattern. Cumberland labourers with 18s. 6d. (92½p) a week still earned much more than the 12s. 6d. (62½p) commonly paid in Devon. Smith gave the average expenditure on food per week per adult as 2s. 11d. (14½p), but if any of the investigators of 1849/50 read his report, they would hardly have been surprised to find the value of food consumed uniformly below average in the south-western and some south-eastern counties and that parts of Kent and Surrey stood higher than the other southern counties. They would have expected the northern labourer to fare much better. The Somerset labourer with his 10 lb of bread and less than 5 oz of meat a week was still a long way behind his Northumberland counterpart who ate 15 lb of bread and 35 oz of meat. If he tried to lift his spirits with a *good* cup of tea, then his 4 oz of sugar a week and half a pint of milk fell well behind the other's 12 oz of sugar and 4½ pints of milk.[12]

CHANGES IN THE CONSUMPTION OF CEREALS, MEAT, FISH AND TEA

Consumption changes in these commodities are the most frequently commented on in the standard of living debate. Hartwell, for the 'optimists', has argued for a substantial increase in working-class consumption of all these commodities by 1850. So far as cereals are concerned, historians have tended to accept the view that wheat bread was in very general use even in the north by the end of the eighteenth century. Some see this as clear evidence of dietary improvement and others stress the status connotations, especially for the southern labourer who, it is argued, regarded any suggestion that he might switch to cheaper bread grains, or even worse to potatoes, as an attempt to degrade his diet: a resented attempt to reduce him to near 'Irish' levels. There is some truth in this, but the matter is more complex. In the first place, since there is no firm evidence that wheat production outpaced population growth, while some groups may have experienced this 'improvement', others may even have increased their dependence on non-wheat cereals. The evidence which is cited in support of the idea of a general extension of wheaten bread by the late eighteenth century is of an impressionistic nature. McCulloch, for example, was completely wrong in his assertion that wheat bread had replaced barley bread in Cornwall. It is more likely to have been the case that even in the early nineteenth century in some areas (with intra-regional variations as important as inter-regional ones) any change to wheaten bread was so recent and co-conditional that a switch to cheaper grains in times of scarcity and high prices is unlikely to have produced deep resentment. Wheat bread in such areas was perhaps a preference but it was not yet an expectation. Dr Collins has researched this matter much more thoroughly than have most participants in the standard of living debate. He suggests that even by 1800 wheat bread consumption in normal times probably did not account for the consumption of more than 70% of the population of England and Wales. It was by then consumed regularly in that part of the kingdom roughly south-east of a line through Hull–Shrewsbury–Cardiff–Taunton, and even then cheaper grains were often substituted in dear years, and barley bread continued to be eaten in villages long after it had been given up in towns. Rye was mainly used in Yorkshire and the north-east; oats north of a line from Liverpool to Filey Bay and in upland Wales, peas and beans in the border counties, and barley in Wales, Welsh border counties, parts of the Midlands and in south-western England. The Midlands may have been a mixed area with a sizeable proportion of the population, especially the rural poor, persisting in using barley or oat bread. Collins suggests that by the 1830s barley bread mostly went out of fashion even in these areas, but an examination of two remote mining districts shows that non-wheat bread could persist beyond this. In eighteenth-century Cornwall, barley was largely consumed, and as late as 1831 barley bread was described as the 'staff of life' in a petition against the Beer Shop Act. By 1836 there was a 'partial' adoption of wheat by the labouring classes, but a specimen miner's budget of 1842 shows a weekly consumption of 20 lb of barley compared with 5lb of wheat. The lead miners of the northern Pennines used mostly rye bread throughout the eighteenth century and only seem to have foresaken it around 1840. Interestingly they did not change directly to wheaten bread but to barley bread at the very time when it had largely disappeared elsewhere, and the superiority of barley bread over wheaten was still being asserted locally in the 1870s.[13]

The most obvious substitute for cereals in the diet of the poor was the potato. In his well-known study, Salaman placed great stress on the role of the bread crises of 1795/6 and 1800/1 in overcoming popular resistance to the 'Irish' root. In fact, contemporaries remained uncertain about its future. Southey, in 1815, thought potatoes could assist in diminishing poverty, if they came to be as much used in the south as they were in the north, while in the 1790s Davies and Eden had expressed opposite views. Davies thought the potato 'an excellent root' which deserved to be generally used but was not likely to become so. In most districts there was neither sufficient ground available for its cultivation nor a sufficient availability of the milk, which he considered essential for their cooking. Eden was of very different opinion: 'In the course of very few years, the consumption of potatoes in this kingdom will be almost as general and universal as that of corn.' He drew attention to their use in Cumberland, Devon, Dorset, Kent, Lancashire, Westmoreland, Yorkshire and Pembroke among other places. His prediction was to prove the more accurate. The increasing numbers of Irish who came to work in the expanding British economy relied upon it, and spread its use in the new industrial towns. By the 1840s, in both rural and urban England the potato was familiar in every home and essential in most. In Lancashire and in Cornwall it had been in regular use from the mid-eighteenth century, the mild climate of the latter allowing two crops a year. Suitable for eating with preserved pilchards, it meant that by the end of the eighteenth century fish and potatoes had become the 'usual fare' of Cornwall's labouring population.[14]

The *Morning Chronicle* reports of 1849/50 reveal that it was by then essential for the survival of the labourer's family in most southern counties. Those favoured with a garden or allotment could grow at least part of their needs. In Suffolk and Norfolk, bread and potatoes were reported the 'general diet' of the labourer, as they were in Dorset and in the south-west generally. Only Kent was a noted exception: here, even by mid-century, the potato was little used. Land which might have been used for its cultivation was instead used for hops. The reporter was struck with the contrast of Kent with Dorset in respect of the poor man's larder:

> In the latter county I found it generally to contain (when there was anything in it) a quantity of turnips and cabbages, a few potatoes and perhaps a solitary loaf – with, now and then, certainly not always a bit of cheese, and, rarely, a piece of butter. In Kent, on the other hand, I found in it, when the family were at work, several loaves and almost invariably some butter and cheese, and occasionally a piece of bacon or animal food of some kind, but very few vegetables of any description.[15]

The potato may have been generally accepted by the early nineteenth century, but what did stick in the labourer's throat was the turnip. In times of real hardship, when prices soared beyond reach or when sickness or unemployment reduced a household to a truly desperate condition, then this root, thought of as more appropriate for livestock, was the food of last resort: often begged or stolen from the fields. To be so reduced was to reach the depths of dietary deprivation and degradation. In 1849 those whose more usual fare was bread and potatoes were sometimes forced to substitute turnips, and they were much used in Cornwall and in Dorset. One Fenland woman desperately feeding her family on turnips was herself unable to stomach them: 'I can't eat the turmots, they perish my insides so.'[16]

Wheaten bread may have been regarded as a standard by some groups of southern labourers, but it was meat which was the most potent of all dietary symbols. Meat on his table had distinguished John Bull from less fortunate foreigners in the eighteenth century. Nostalgia for the 'days of meat' was among the most frequent sentiments of regret expressed by 'degraded' workers looking back from the middle years of the nineteenth century. The assessment of trends in working-class meat consumption is a speculative venture in the absence of any widespread dietary survey between Eden's of 1797 and the middle years of the nineteenth century. Lack of data perhaps explains why both 'optimists' and 'pessimists' have argued that trends in meat consumption favour their cases. The problem needs a separate consideration of rural and urban experiences, or rather of those of farm labourers and manufacturing workers.

The evidence of 1849/50 strongly indicates that levels of meat consumption by farm labourers and their families in the south had sunk to negligible proportions by the end of the eighteenth century and remained at these very low levels to the middle years of the nineteenth. The proportion of meat expenditure of the Kentish labourer declined by 20% between 1793 and 1812 while expenditure on bread increased by 26%. This shift was no short-lasting effect of the French Wars. Comparison of a budget of 1837 with one from seventy years earlier shows a drop over the period in the share of income spent on meat from 24.3 to 15.2%. Eden reported that the Kentish labourers had eaten meat daily into the 1780s but by the time of his investigation of 1797 was hardly tasting it in winter. The *Morning Chronicle* reported only the occasional use of bacon or fresh meat. The evidence from Kent certainly supports Hobsbawm's view that meat consumption by the working classes had most probably peaked before the last decade of the eighteenth century.[17]

Kentish farm labourers were the best paid in the south, and if meat contributed little to their diet, then it could hardly have done more in the other poorer counties. The superiority of Kentish diet lay rather in a significantly higher consumption of cheese. The evidence of 1849/50 confirms Eden's findings of fifty years before that southern farm labourers neither expected nor got meat. If the degraded artisan of the 1830s looked back through the misty eyes of nostalgia to the time of daily meat, by 1850 the southern farm labourer had not even a sustaining memory of its regular consumption. At best he knew its taste from a small amount weekly. In Devon and Somerset it was hardly ever tasted. In the former, a county where Eden supposed meat to have been eaten twice a week before the wars, a woman told the investigator:

> Lord, bless you, sir, we wouldn't know ourselves if we did. We never have a taste of it, but we get a bit from the lady [vicar's wife]. Sometimes I get a bone which I boil, or a bit of mate [sic] from her, which I take home in my hand or in my pocket. At other times I get a bit of grease, and but for this we wouldn't taste meat.[18]

Fish made Cornwall a special case, but in Dorset one family afforded only half a pound of meat a month between ten, while another had only its pig killed at Christmas for the winter. Perhaps one in twelve of labouring families in the south-west kept a pig, but the better cuts – like eggs – were kept for sale to provide for clothing, shoes or rent: 'even such of them as do feed a pig, seldom participate in the eating of it'. A Wiltshire family bought half a pound of bacon for Sundays: 'It is but a mere taste, but we have not even that the rest of the week.' Very many families in that and in neighbouring counties tasted it even less frequently. In Norfolk and Suffolk, farmers frowned on their labourers keeping pigs or poultry, claiming that they stole grain to feed them. In these eastern districts, meat was hardly more known to rural labourers than it was in the south. 'Last Sunday', said a Suffolk woman, 'we had a bit of pork that I gave 9d. (3½p) for; it was the first bit that we'd had for many a long week.' The reporter never saw a piece of fresh meat in any of the cottages which he visited in the three counties of Norfolk, Suffolk and Essex: 'that it may be occasionally had there can be no doubt, but it is certainly at very rare and long intervals.' In Cambridgeshire he suspected that only poaching supplied meat for many labourers.[19]

As in Eden's time, the evident contrast was with the north. In Durham the reporter met with a labourer who had read the previously published accounts of the condition of his southern counterparts: 'He seemed to think the lot of men who hardly tasted meat from one year's end to the other a very pitiable one, and assured me that he had it every day.'[20]

Rural manufacturing workers, like weavers and knitters, may be presumed to have spent strongly on meat during their 'golden years'. At such times they were daily consumers of meat before going into their catastrophic income declines in the nineteenth century. Trends are hardly relevant when wages fell to levels at which meat could not have been afforded at any price. Memories of better days were of a fuller and better existence: a different quality of life, work and leisure – but among such memories the eating of meat figures prominently. By the 1830s the weavers of Pudsey thought to eat meat other than on Sunday was 'a luxury fitter for the rich than for them'. Framework knitters in their petition of 1819, when they earned only from 4s. to 8s. (20p to 35p) a week, bemoaned the necessity of substituting 'meal and water or potatoes and salt for that more wholesome food an Englishman's table used to abound with'. Macclesfield's silk weavers didn't eat much meat by 1849, although some 'would have it' and struggled to afford it: 'They would think the world wouldn't go on if they hadn't flesh meat to dinner.' Their fellows in Middleton, former cotton weavers now employed on silk by an entrepreneur from Spitalfields, still expected to eat meat, but had nevertheless a feeling of relative dietary decline. Two or three pounds of meat were bought weekly for the family and made into as many dinners 'as we can scheme' at half a pound a time: 'But what's that for eating? Why my share at meal times is not bigger nor my thumb. So I often throw it in, and take a fried ingan [sic] and two or three drops of vinegar to relish the potatoes. That's about our general way of living.' A Yorkshire woollen weaver spoke in similar manner: meat was certainly dearer, although she generally ate some meat for dinner, people filled up with plenty of porridge and potatoes, and so lived as well as forty years previously.[21]

Pitmen when earning good wages were among the biggest meat eaters. One stated in 1850 that although they could not get as much meat as they could eat, a miner must have meat, a man needing 2 to 3 lb a week for himself. Wages varied within the mining districts and between them. In some areas the truck system distorted prices, but when they could afford it colliers gave a high priority to purchasing meat – a food they thought essential for sustaining hard underground labour. Staffordshire colliers were reported to live well when times were good: 'Their pleasures are essentially animal, and if they had £4–5 per week it would go on food and drink.' Their custom kept a flourishing poultry market at Bilston afloat. Metal miners seem to have fared less well in general: in the 1860s the low meat content of the Cornish miner's dietary was still being associated with his poor health.[22]

Town workers had generally a higher per capita meat consumption than farm labourers. Caird remarked in 1852 that whereas bread still formed the chief article of consumption in farming districts, in the manufacturing ones where wages were good: 'the use of butchers' meat and cheese is enormously on the increase'. Town levels per head, however, conceal a great range of experiences between groups and for individuals. For factory workers a family's consumption level was determined by its stage in its own cycle, the ratio of earning hands to consuming mouths. The years of very young children were likely to be those in which diet was least adequate. Diet, too, was inevitably

affected by the new cyclical pattern of unemployment which industrialisation brought. Between groups, standards varied enormously.
Gaskell in 1836 wrote of a 'town mill artisan's diet' as a staple of
potatoes and wheat bread washed down with coffee. Meat was in most
cases a very small part of his diet and when purchased was usually of
poor quality. Below this 'norm' were the Irish who subsisted mainly on
potatoes, and well above it were the fine spinners, the aristocrats of
cotton manufacture, whose standards were comparable to those of the
rising artisan groups like printers and engineers.[23] Engels too noted
that the better-paid, especially at favourable points in their family
cycle, had good food when in full employment: they ate meat daily for
lunch and supped off bacon and cheese. Where wages were less, meat
was consumed only two or three times a week, and the proportion of
bread and potatoes increased. 'Descending gradually', he found meat
consumption steadily reducing to a low level of a small piece of bacon
once a week. Beneath this were the families who had only bread,
cheese, porridge and potatoes, and lowest of all the Irish with only
potatoes.[24]

In older artisan centres like Birmingham and Sheffield where the
metal workers were not de-skilled by 1850, wages remained comparatively high, and levels of meat consumption on a par with the
better-paid workers in the factory towns. Even so the specimen budget
of a Sheffield cutler in 1855, described as one of the better off, gave an
annual adult consumption of only 81 lb. A well-paid London artisan
secure in the 'honourable' section of his trade was said in 1841 to buy
from an income of 30s. (£1.50p) per week 2.8 lb per head for his family
(4 lb adult equivalent). Artisans on £1 a week were consuming an adult
equivalent of 1.4 lb and those on 15s. (75p) only 1 lb. Similar levels are
suggested by an inquiry of 1834. An artisan on £2 a week would
provide his family with meat at least twice a week, to lift their diet of
soup, bread, potatoes and herrings. But £2 a week was a good wage.
Figures for Manchester and Dukinfield in 1836 and 1841 give a mode
per capita expenditure of 3d.–4d. (1.25–1.67p) per head per week,
which at prevailing prices would hardly have bought a pound. When
we note that in 1936/7 the poorest class on less than £2 10s. (£2.50p)
ate 30.4 oz of meat per head, a perspective is clearly put on the low
levels of meat consumption of even middling income groups among the
working classes in the first half of the nineteenth century.[25]

Other indices seem to suggest little which contradicts the evidence of
the scattered surviving budget data. Hobsbawm has pointed out that
Smithfield statistics for the number of livestock sold (1,800 = 100)
show a rise to only 146 for beef cattle and 176 for sheep against a
population increase for London of 202 and, until the railway, there was
no great increase in country-killed meat reaching London. His use of
these statistics has been criticised. The number of beasts slaughtered is
clearly not a direct indicator of the weight of meat available. Hobs-

bawm has pointed out, however, that the average carcass weight would have had to have increased by around 40% for beef and 15% for cattle between 1801 and 1841 for meat supply to have kept pace with population. Dead meat sales could affect his argument, for dead meat was sold mainly at Newgate, but in important years, for example from 1818 to 1830 when its supply almost halved, its sales actually declined. Evidence from provincial markets and for home killing is lacking, but there really seems on the present state of the evidence no reason to suppose that the Smithfield trend is other than indicative of a failure of meat supply to keep up with population. In any event there seems little likelihood that working-class meat consumption could have risen without a strong distribution shift in its favour, and on the evidence of surviving budgets a shift seems, if anything, more likely to have been the other way.[26]

Budgets reveal expenditure by families on meat, but they do not reveal how it was shared within the family. Certainly children consumed less than adults, but there was also a 'sexual division of consumption'. Husbands were commonly favoured as the breadwinner and received a disproportionate share of the meat, or perhaps got it when the rest of the family made do without. This inequality persisted through to Edwardian times – the only one of Rowntree's rural families to buy no meat in 1813 was one in which the father took lunch at work, and the wife did not think it necessary to purchase meat for the rest of the family. Smith in 1863 described husband-favouring as an almost universal practice: 'The important fact is that the labourer eats meat or bacon almost daily, whilst his wife and children may eat it once a week.' Men commonly took left-over meat to work, or else they lunched at work while wives and children made do with bread and tea. Professor Burnett has wondered how men could have managed the 'immensely long hours they worked without a diet considerably richer in proteins than that received by the rest of the family'. But did not wives (and children too) in many cases work 'immensely long hours'? In so far as women in the middle years of the nineteenth century retreated increasingly into the role of wives and mothers, perhaps they became conditioned to this kind of sacrifice.[27] Arguably the small amounts of meat which are indicated in many budgets should not be regarded as dietary components but rather as relish. Dr Hunt has suggested that 'non-farinaceous' food in such minute quantities is 'hardly more than flavouring to help the bread go down'. For this reason the strong flavour of bacon was as much a recommendation as its price and the usefulness of its fat. Spitalfields silk weavers had a taste for several such 'relishes', according to Mayhew and Smith.[28]

All in all, Professor Hartwell's assertion that in the first half of the nineteenth century 'The English working class came to expect meat as part of the normal diet' is not a convincing one. There is a good deal of evidence to the contrary. His use of 'came to' furthermore conceals the fact that whatever the level of expectation was in 1850, between 1795 and that date many groups including southern farm labourers and many of London's artisans, as well as those he describes as living in 'pockets of technological underemployment', experienced a marked decline in their expectations of meat consumption: 'I should like a piece of roast beef, with the potatoes done under it, but I shall never taste that again', a London silk weaver told Mayhew in 1849. Professor Burnett seems nearer the truth in regarding 1848 as marking the end of a 'hungry half-century' during which the diet of the majority of town dwellers was at best stodgy and monotonous and at worst hopelessly deficient in quantity and in nutriment.[29]

Hartwell also suggested that an increasing consumption of fish made an important contribution to working-class diets after 1815. There seems little evidence to support his view that 1815 was a turning point before which, apart from gluts, fish was a luxury for the well-to-do. Southey in that year pronounced it 'disgraceful' that fish were so expensive and in such short supply in great cities and towns. He blamed collusion between Billingsgate's merchants and the smacksmen for artificially limiting London's supply. But did this situation change rapidly after 1815? A review of London's supply in 1842 thought plaice had only recently become plentiful and that, with the seasonal exceptions of sprats, mackerel and herrings, fish was still looked upon as a luxury by most classes, while in the inland counties, 'the peasantry know not the taste of fresh sea fish'.[30]

It is true that the great expansion of trawling after 1830 was a major development, but before 1850, trawlermen sought chiefly the 'up market' varieties of sole and turbot and still thought of plaice as offal. It is true that London's poor made a much greater seasonal use of fish than many contemporaries thought. Herring was most popular, but mackerel was also valued. Three-quarters of these fish were sold by the costermongers, usually in a preserved form, but mackerel was sold and eaten fresh. Two-thirds of the 23,250,000 of them sold at Billingsgate in 1850 reached customers through costermongers and hawkers. Their season was, however, a very short one: shorter even than it might have been, for the hawkers turned instead to summer soft fruits at the very time the mackerel shoals were in the Channel. Early season fresh mackerel were eagerly sought after in London as early as 1800, when fast-sailing smacks from Torbay awaited the arrival of the Cornish luggers in Mounts Bay and sailed up Channel to land them at Portsmouth for overland carriage. Such early season fish were high priced, but for most of the year it paid only to send the expensive varieties like turbot or sole from the south-west to London before the coming of the railway, and even then it was the prospect of sending soles rather than plaice which produced a fishing boom at Brixham. Plymouth was not reached by the railway until 1849 and the Tamar not bridged for ten years after that. The fishing activities of the great Humber ports did not begin until the 1840s with the discovery of the North Sea banks (beginning with the Great Silver Pits in 1843). The number of fishermen in England and Wales in 1841 was 24,000, by 1881 it was 58,000. Such evidence suggests strongly that the great expansion of fish-catching began after 1840 and had not before mid-century added significantly to the dietaries of urban England. As for rural districts, it had still not touched them by the time of Smith's survey of 1863.[31] The coming of the railway, the use of ice at sea and the development of the ruthlessly efficient trawling method of fish-taking were the agents of the spectacular growth in sea fish supply and distribution. By about 1850 London was seeing the results in the ousting of mackerel by plaice from the top of the fresh sea fish league, but no real trend was evident before 1840. Hartwell's turning point of 1815 is a red herring. In other cities and towns sea fish were an inconsiderable dietary component before 1860.

Fish entered working-class dietaries only as a regional speciality before 1850. Some *few* areas were heavy consumers. Pilchards in Cornwall were a dietary staple – a *distinguishing* characteristic according to Smith in 1863. But this was no indicator of dietary improvement, for it had long been the case. Pilchards, in fact, were caught in quantities far beyond the consuming power of the local mining population. The surplus had been exported since the sixteenth century, for no home market for the salted pilchard outside of Cornwall and south Devon ever developed. Contemporaries most probably did underestimate the extent and volume of the pre-railway fish trade, but it was overwhelmingly seasonal, and the prime markets for sea fish remained Bath in the south-west and Scarborough in the north.[32]

Contemporaries exhibited a distinctly ambivalent attitude towards tea consumption. Some cursed its increase as a sign of 'luxury'; others, like Cobbett, saw tea drinking as evidence of a sad decline from beer-drinking old England. Even moderate opinion recognised that hot tea was, especially for women and children, a necessity to complement cold and scanty fare. Tea and bread was described in 1836 as the staple diet of all millhands except for the fine spinners. It was the mainstay of the smuggling trade and so statistics of its availability are necessarily vague. Consumption most probably did increase over the period, although at a rate which was not sustained. McCulloch noted that by the 1830s consumption had increased 'greatly' since the time of Adam Smith, even allowing for the distorting effect of smuggling before Pitt's duty reduction of 1783 produced a three-fold increase in legal imports in two years. The increase had, he thought, been sharp up to about 1800, but thereafter had become 'comparatively slow and inconsiderable'. In fact, import statistics show UK consumption at 1.41 lb a head in 1800, did not reach that average again until 1841/50 and had been stagnant at the lower levels of 1.28/1.27 from 1811 to 1830.[33]

Budgets show that only small amounts were bought even by those labouring families who used it daily. A well-paid London compositor in 1810 purchased only a quarter pound weekly for a family of four and a northern pitman on the same wage of 30s. (£1.50p) a week bought only 2 oz for a family of five. In 1841 a skilled London worker on the same wage bought the same amount for a family of the same size, while one earning 15s. (75p) bought 3 oz. At the bottom of the pile in 1839, a widow with four young children, scraping a living, spent daily on tea a halfpenny or a penny which at 6d. (2½p) an ounce would have produced less than half an ounce a week. Nield's budgets show the better-off working-class families buying around 3 oz a week in 1841 and the poorer ones often an ounce or less. Such amounts hardly produced daily the traditional 'good, strong cup of tea': 'Tea!' proclaimed a weaver in 1849, 'more like hot water and sugar!' while at the end of the eighteenth century the tea taken by the miners of west Cornwall was described as: 'Little better than warm water without milk or sugar.'[34]

It is doubtful whether tea is as good an indicator of consumption changes as G. R. Porter suggested when plotting the *Progress of the Nation* in 1847:

> The consumption of this class of articles affords a very useful test of the comparative conditions at different periods of the labouring classes. If by reason of the cheapness of provisions, the wages of the labourer afford means for indulgence, sugar, tea and coffee are the articles to which he earliest has recourse.[35]

Rather, tea had become by 1800 a near universal essential and its per capita decline in the 1820s and 1830s suggests real pressure on consumption standards. Porter, using 'indulgence' in 1847 with reference to tea, was a century out of date. Of his other indicators coffee, though far from unknown, was not primarily a working-class drink despite the confident assertion of Mr Bounderby that Coketown's factory operatives *insisted* on Mocha coffee in the same manner as they rejected all but the prime cuts of meat! Sugar may be a better indicator than either tea or coffee. Its consumption levels were closely related to those of tea because much more than milk, it was the 'necessary' accompaniment. Since tea was itself no longer an indulgence, and can be plausibly viewed as increasing in importance as dietary standards declined, then it is clear that sugar cannot be properly regarded as a luxury even though two right-wing commentators on Engels have suggested that increasing sugar consumption in the 1840s was an 'indication of rising living standards'. In 1801 (excluding Ireland) the average per capita consumption was 30.6 lb; by 1811 it had declined slightly to 29.3. Except in 1831, it did reach 20 lb again between 1824 and 1845 with a low of 15.3 in 1840; consumption between 1839 and 1845 was the lowest of the first half of the century, although by 1848 the level was at 24.9.[36]

In so far as weak tea was substituted for beer, then it meant a decline in nutritional intake even allowing for the poor quality and adulteration of much urban beer. Beer drinking per head from public brewing fell from the beginning of the century to 1851 from 33.9 to 19.6 gallons per capita, a trend which was only slightly interrupted in 1834/6 with the passing of the Beer Act. It is a reasonable conjecture that it fell more sharply among women and children than among men. For, apart from the greater likelihood of men drinking outside the home, they frequently took beer during the course of their work and were, as we have seen, favoured at home. All in all there seems little evidence that tea consumption points towards an improvement in consumption standards from 1815 to 1850, while the decline in per capita consumption of the more elastic commodities of beer and sugar seems to suggest a fall in standards.

GENERAL CONCLUSION

It has been suggested by a leading optimist that by 1850 'the Londoner' was consuming each week 5 oz of butter, 30 oz of meat, 56 oz of potatoes and 16 oz of fruit, compared with 1959 figures of 5 oz of butter, 35 oz of meat, 54 oz of potatoes and 32 oz of fruit. He concludes 'the consumption of basic foods in 1850 London was not wildly inferior to that of modern England'.[37] This seems seriously misleading. Who, one wonders, were these 'Londoners'? Certainly Henry Mayhew never met them. These calculations are, in any case, rough countings from poor data, and London was very much the best supplied urban market, often at the expense of provincial ones. Professor Burnett is nearer the truth when he suggests that any improvement by 1850 had come about only in the previous five years. The findings of the first systematic survey of working-class budgets carried out officially in 1864 by Dr Edwin Smith shows conclusively that significant dietary gains were largely confined to the second half of the nineteenth century, and that regional variations in standards of food consumption were still very evident in the 1860s.

THE EXPERIENCE OF THE WORKING-CLASS CUSTOMER

Indices of food prices are often based on wholesale prices and as such are seriously biased in favour of 'optimist' conclusions. In fact there was a widespread contemporary agreement that the poorer classes paid significantly more for their food than did the better-off and bought inferior goods. It was suggested that the excess paid by the small-quantity purchasing poor was in the order of 30%. Markets were not the purveyors of wholesome food at fair prices to allcomers which they are sometimes romanticised as. Gaskell in 1836 described the Saturday markets in the cotton districts. Saturday was both market and pay day. The markets began the day well-equipped, with beef, mutton, veal and pork plentiful and in good quality; vegetables were similarly in supply, as were cheese and butter. In the morning the market was crowded with 'well dressed and respectable people'. But at noon a change took place. Out came the 'coarse, diseased animal food' and the 'deteriorated vegetables' as well as the refuse of the morning's supply; a congregation of small dealers bought in cheaper stuff for resale. If the afternoon session was markedly different from the morning, worse was to come in the evening: 'And what a scene is Saturday night's market – to a hubbub of discordant sounds – what jangling, swearing drunkenness, noisy vociferation, confusion, worse confounded riot and debauchery!'[38] Engels, too, presents the poor as being paid on Saturdays only in time to come late to the market (5 to 7 p.m.), to find the potatoes poor, the vegetables wilted, the cheese old and poor, the bacon rancid and the meat tough, old and often decayed. The sellers by that time of day were small hucksters, who bought in the poorer foodstuffs. Some of the poor postponed their marketing until 10 o'clock when they bought cheap food, perhaps past safe use. Food found unfit for sale at Liverpool was not unknown to re-appear next day in Manchester. Charles Kingsley gives a similar description of a London market in 1848:

> It was a foul, chilly, foggy Saturday night. From the butchers' and green-grocers' shops the gaslights flared and flickered, wild and ghastly over haggard groups of slipshod dirty women, bargaining for scraps of stale meat and frost-bitten vegetables, wrangling about shortweight and bad quality. Fish stalls and fruit stalls lined the edge of the greasy pavement, sending up odours as foul as the language of sellers and buyers. Blood and sewer water crawled from under doors and out of spouts, and reeked down the gutters among offal, animal and vegetable, in every stage of putrefaction.[39]

Varying weights and measures as well as justified suspicions of short measure caused resentment and confusion in the eighteenth century. The extent of the confusion was revealed by a parliamentary investigation in 1758 which recommended standardisation and the manufacture of metal rather than wooden weights and measures as the latter could be planed down. Sometimes, however, short measure was directly related to genuine confusion over weights, such as with the butter-market sellers at Winchester in 1797. But the poor consumers were correct to suspect deceit on not infrequent occasions:

Me thought I saw a red-nose Oast
As fat as he could wallow
Whose carcase, if it should be roast,
Would drop seven stone of tallow
He grows rich out of measure
With filling measure small
He lives in mirth and pleasure
But poor men pay for all.[40]

The level of prosecution for such offences depended upon the vigilance of local authorities, but local records of the eighteenth century reveal an incidence of fraud comparable with the ninety-six cases over three months in Manchester in 1844 noted by Engels.[41]

Buying from the lower class of shop did not provide immunity and came more expensive. In 1834, the capital's small tradesmen were described as a 'predatory, moving body who for the most part live in various ways by chicanery and plunder'. The poor were cheated as to weight and quality and often through already incurred debts were not free to go elsewhere. Two years later it was stated to be a 'well-known fact' that working men paid dearer for their provisions than did the other social classes. In part this was because they purchased in small quantities – meat by the single pound, potatoes by a meal's worth at a time, cheese and butter by the quarter pound, tea and sugar by the ounce – and because they depended upon credit. Taking the two together, they paid perhaps a third more for their food. As London's 'sweating' trades expanded, the warehouse capitalists, who put out the work, demanded security for the materials. The necessary sum was often advanced by grocers and bakers on condition that the poor tradesmen bought in their shops. Once 'tied', then second-rate articles at inflated prices had to be taken. Mayhew's informant told him that he had never heard of a butcher advancing money as slop workers did not buy meat. High shop prices were not confined to urban areas. Cornish fishermen in 1849 paid dear for tea, coffee and sugar, because they had no time to travel into Penzance and avoid the high prices of the village shop. In rural Hampshire in 1828 a paternalist squire opened a shop on his estate with the object of undercutting overcharging shopkeepers.[42]

Even more iniquitous was the truck system. Widespread in the eighteenth century – complaints are recorded from the weavers of Somerset (1726) and in neighbouring Gloucestershire in 1739, from Devonshire weavers in 1743 and Sheffield cutlers in 1756 – it became general in the nineteenth. An Act of 1831 seems to have had little effect. Gaskell commented on the prevalence of truck in Lancashire in 1836, while Engels claimed that by paying in cash but at the same time insisting employees purchased at specified shops, employers everywhere were able to evade the law. Dodd, in 1848, reported the practice to be common in agricultural districts, where paying in cheques on the village miller, often a relative of the farmer, ensured that the poor paid 25–30% more for their victuals: 'the highest price for the worse goods and dares not complain'. A savage indictment of its practice in mining districts appeared in the *Morning Chronicle* description of Staffordshire in 1849: 'A great flagrant social and industrial evil', the law on which was 'so habitually and grossly violated as to be all but a dead letter'. Employers of all kinds were guilty, the great ironmasters as well as the 'ignorant butties'. Capitalists employing hundreds of men milked them of 5–10% of their wages:

> I have not, indeed, been more startled by any phenomenon in the course of my researches than the constant and daring violation of the Truck Act in Staffordshire and the utter helplessness of the people under the oppression of the Tommy masters. I am told that not a few magistrates are themselves notorious truck shop keepers.

Such powerful men overawed the press in their 'notorious, flagrant and habitual violation of the law', workpeople, tradespeople, and the 'honourable masters' were alike made subservient and suffered together through 'the cupidity of men who ignore every consideration save that of profit'.[43]

Deliberate and often dangerous adulteration of foodstuffs was a commonplace in the eighteenth and nineteenth centuries. Alum was used to whiten bread, drugs were added to porter and ale, logwood to brandy, pepper to gin, water to milk, sand to sugar and earth to pepper. Additions were made to colour, to increase bulk or to strengthen flavour. Even smugglers who usually relied on the high quality of their product were reported to extend their supplies of tea with elder leaves which had been steeped in urine. Sugar bakers were discovered using ground glass to 'frost' their cakes. Indeed, Accum's *Treatise on the adulterations of food and culinary poisons* called attention to red lead as a colouring in cheese and lead and copper in confectionery thirty years before the *Lancet* investigations of the 1850s resulted in the Food and Drugs Act of 1860. Engels had devoted much attention to the problems of food adulteration in 1844, but his work was not translated into English for a further forty years. He quoted from the *Liverpool Mercury*: 'Salted butter is sold for fresh, the lumps being covered with a coating of fresh butter, or a pound of fresh being laid on top to taste while the salted article is sold after this test, or the whole mass is washed and then sold as fresh.' Sugar was mixed with ground rice and with the refuse of soap boiling, chicory with coffee, cocoa with fine brown earth and treated with fat. Tea with sloe leaves or re-roasted old leaves; pepper with powdered nutshells and port made by mixing alcohol and dye, so that more of that wine was consumed annually in England than was produced in Portugal. The poor were the victims because the rich could afford to patronise the shops with reputations to keep. The poor dealt where they could get credit and, in any event, if no Manchester customer trusted a grocer in Ancoats he could easily move to Chorlton or Hulme where no one knew him.[44]

It was to combat such practices as well as to obtain price advantages and lessen the bonds of credit that co-operative retailing gained working-class support in the nineteenth century. It was estimated that the labouring people of Stockport purchased 50% of their domestic commodities on credit in 1833 paying from 2–4s. (10–20p) in the pound for the privilege of getting bound to the huckster and thereby becoming unable to avoid short weight or poor quality. Robert Owen thought that by bulk buying for his workers in the early markets he had saved the larger families around 10s. (50p) a week out of their weekly £2: 'They had previously been necessitated to buy inferior articles, highly adulterated at enormous prices, making their purchases at small grocery and grog shops, chiefly on credit and their butchers meat was generally little better than skin and bones.'[45]

In short, wholesale price indices cannot accurately inform the historian either on the prices actually paid by working-class consumers or on the quality of the articles which they did purchase. The evidence may be scattered and inconclusive but it is difficult not to get the impression that the working classes could be as much exploited as consumers as they were as wage earners.

CLOTHING

Foreign observers frequently remarked that in England the common people wore no class-distinguishing dress, no peasant costume. It has been suggested that the fact that lower-class Englishmen dressed in no manner clearly different from their social superiors (servants aping their masters) indicates an urge to social emulation which was important as a demand-side explanation of the coming of an industrial revolution based upon textiles.[46] Contemporary observers from the early eighteenth century commented on the dress 'extravagances' of the lower orders, often in much the same tone of indignant condemnation used by many of the better-off do so on the life-styles of the unemployed in our own day: they *know* them to live better lives on the dole than do the hard-pressed middle classes on five-figure salaries. Defoe, in 1704, thought maidservants indistinguishable in matters of dress from their mistresses, while Henry Fielding, in 1751, thought that the emulation in style, which began when the nobleman copied the prince, progressed down through society until it reached the 'very dregs of the people'. By 1817 a 'fondness for dress' was lamented to have all but destroyed those 'becoming marks whereby the several classes of society were formerly distinguished' especially in the urban districts and above all in London.[47] Professor Perkin sees a 'desire to keep up with the Joneses' operating even in eighteenth-century England as much at the lower as at the upper levels of society: 'the common people, at work and especially at leisure, wore a conscious imitation of the dress of their immediate superiors'. He is too wise an historian, however, not to see this as an indicator of a *comparative* affluence, not the 'luxury' insisted upon by some contemporaries. It was comparative in two respects, as a Swiss visitor in the 1780s noted: inequality was just as marked but individuals of the lower classes were better clothed, fed and lodged than in other countries. Secondly, by the later eighteenth century they were more able to procure a range of cheaper consumer goods, which included cheap cotton clothing, than they had been before. There was no spectacular increase in working-class consumer demand. Perkin notes that it was the upper and middle classes who fuelled the expansion of Birmingham's metal industries, Staffordshire's potteries, and for the first muslins and printed cottons. Percolation downwards was a slow affair reaching first the lower middle classes and then the 'aristocracy' of skilled labour, and perhaps by the end of the period the factory operatives and similar better-paid groups like miners. The *aggregate* increase in working-class demand, especially for clothing, was clearly important in sustaining the output of the new factories. It would have increased in any event with the expansion of the waged economy. If a poor labourer buys a pair of cheap boots only once a year then, compared with societies in which peasants still fashioned their own wooden clogs, that is a not insignificant, in the outcome, demand-side factor: 'no excise – no wooden shoes!' shouted a London crowd besieging Parliament in 1733.[48]

At the level of actual rather than average experience, analysis becomes more difficult. The working-class experience in respect of real wage levels was, as we have seen, an immensely varied one. For most of the period with which we are concerned, that is to say up to *c*. 1830, the losers may well have outnumbered the gainers. It seems reasonable, therefore, to conjecture that whatever the case with aggregate demand levels, for very many labouring families their consumption of clothing showed as evident a deterioration as did their consumption of food. It was all very well for Ricardo to argue that the sacrifice of 'a very small quantity of his food' would, as technical change lowered the prices of manufactured goods relative to agricultural ones, enable a labourer to 'provide liberally for all his other wants', but that 'small' sacrifice was not to be made on the margins of subsistence.[49] Perhaps observers did not always see what they thought they saw. In London especially the working people they came into contact with would be domestic servants to whom the discarded clothes of their employers were a recognised perquisite. It would be entirely misleading to judge the appearance of the lower orders in general from that of those in domestic service or in the retail trades.

Few well-heeled visitors ventured into the outcast world of St Giles, or into the equivalent ragged quarter of other towns.

Country labourers' budgets often record *no expenditure at all* on clothing in the southern and eastern counties; an omission which is as evident from the late eighteenth-century ones supplied by Davies and Eden as from the mid-nineteenth-century ones in the *Morning Chronicle*. For these households, clothing had to be begged, received from charity, or purchased exceptionally from harvest earnings. For very many labouring people this was the 'cast-off' generation. True as it is that the textile industries were the 'leading sector' of the industrial revolution with their vastly increased output of cotton and wool cloth, the evidence which comes from poor households and which speaks from actual working-class experiences rather than from macro-economic inference suggests that spectacular increases in production had no very early or marked impact on lower-class clothing consumption except in respect of a shift to cotton, noted by Southey in 1815, which in itself was not an unmixed blessing for, while it offered superior hygiene, it afforded less warmth.

In the second quarter of the nineteenth century, allegations of working-class extravagance in matters of dress continued to be made. Young women from the quilting factories of Spitalfields in 1840 were said to display their affluence in 'bonnets with showy ribbons, and ear drops [and] red coral necklaces of four or five strings, bracelets and other finery' in which they appeared at Greenwich fair. Similarly the Cornish mine girls had a 'reprehensible taste for gaiety and display', while the mill lasses of Lancashire were constantly decried for similar offences. It is noticeable that such strictures were applied to young women independently employed. Doubtless their circumstances did allow a brief season of display before marriage brought sobriety in this, as in other areas. Young women silk workers in Macclesfield were said in 1849 to have 'their backs gay, although their bellies pinched for it'. In the case of young men, good clothes also formed part of the 'style' of eighteenth-century apprentices like Francis Place, or William Hutton, although in many cases they could hardly afford to keep up the desired appearance.[50] For the married with children to provide for, clothing was basically a matter of warmth and decency. It was saved for; its purchase put off as long as possible; passed on and mended to do as long as it could. In Mayhew's London, a whole section of poorer craftsmen 'translated' old boots to serve as new for the poor.[51]

Dress standards, like diet, obviously varied between the different layers of the working class. At the bottom of the pile the farm labourers of the south and east could often afford no change of clothing at all. Higher up, in times of full employment, the mule-spinners of the cotton towns could appear in 'comfortable and respectable velveteen jackets, with waistcoats and trousers of dark fustian cloth'. Usually well-shod, they gave an appearance of unostentatious comfort. Engels regarded fustian as the proverbial costume of the working man: they were known as 'fustian jackets' in contrast to the broadcloth-wearing gentlemen. Fergus O'Conner, the Chartist leader, made a point of dressing in fustian whenever he went to Manchester. Hats were universal for working men in England, 'round, high, broad brimmed, narrow brimmed'; only the younger factory operatives wore caps.[52]

Even new clothing in good condition was thought by Engels to have been ill-suited to the damp climate. Although the middle class afforded flannel next to the skin and flannel shirts and scarves, the working class were scarcely ever in a position to use woollen clothing and their cotton was less effective against the cold and rain. Should a workman buy a woollen coat for Sunday wear, then he would purchase from one of the cheap shops using 'devil's dust' cloth made for sale rather than for use. In a fortnight it would be threadbare. Or he would buy an old second-hand coat which had perhaps only a few weeks' more useful life: 'Working-men's clothing in most cases is in bad condition and the best pieces are often in the pawnshop.'[53] In bad times the pawnbroker received the wardrobe of his district. During the London shoemakers' strike of 1812, they were said to have been 'packed with clothes'.[54]

Contemporary propagandists for the factory system naturally emphasised the great benefit of cheap clothing. Nassau Senior stressed the great advantage to working-class consumption in general which came from the reduced cost of clothing, while some historians have followed contemporaries in suggesting that even the demographic revolution owed something to the mortality-decreasing effect of cheap, washable, cotton underclothing! Not all contemporaries were as impressed, being better able to distinguish the actual bounty of machine industry from its vaunted potential. Gaskell was scornful of Edward Baines' insistence on the 'advantage to the poor man that his wife can purchase a printed calico gown for 2s. 6d. (12½p). This is a fact he repeatedly insists upon. It seems to us a very poor compensation for poverty . . . or the workhouse.' The ragged farm labourers attacking threshing machines in the riots of 1830/1 could hardly have been receptive to the reasoning of Henry Brougham:

> Your clothes, your stockings, your shirts, are all made by Machines far more curiously contrived than the threshing machines. The calico which makes your shirts is woven by a machine, attended only by a girl, but in consequence of the little labour required to manage it, the shirt which formerly cost seven shillings [35p], now costs only eighteen pence [7½p].[55]

G. R. Porter's confident assertion of 1851 that 'Few indeed were so low' as to be unable to afford decent and appropriate clothing was very wide of the mark. The 65% fall in the price of cotton goods between 1820 and 1845 must have brought cotton goods within the range of increasing numbers of the population, but working-class budgets show, in very many cases, such a small margin over food and rent for purchases of any kind that to build an 'optimist' argument upon the availability of cotton clothing is less than convincing. Mayhew presented a tabulation showing that in towns clothing actually wore out more quickly than in the country and as a cost at the same original price was actually 50% more expensive.[56] At the levels of consumption to which some groups of the population had been reduced by the middle years of the nineteenth century, clothing beyond the necessary minimum was a luxury. Extravagance in this direction if affordable in the good times, at least allowed the possibility of pawning in bad ones: 'popping' the overcoat is the theme of one of our best-known nursery rhymes. A good coat worn other than on a Sunday could, as a Chartist missionary found to his embarrassment when attempting to agitate the mining districts of Cornwall in 1839, so mark a man that his 'brothers' would assume him to have come from a superior station in life: 'As I was walking ever so many of the working men lifted their hats to me in passing, it could only be because I had a good coat on. I cannot bear such servility to the appearance of wealth.'[57]

With characteristic irony, Shelley addressed 'the people of England who toil and groan' and 'who weave the clothes which your oppressors wear/And for your own take the inclement air'. If he had in mind the increasingly depressed handloom weavers, silk weavers or framework knitters, then it is fair comment. It is certainly one echoed in the poem of a Keighley weaver in 1834: '. . . for the weavers, a set of poor souls With clothes on their backs much like riddles for holes'.[58]

WATCHES

Evidence on diet is scanty, on clothing even more sparse, and on other goods which might have been consumed by the labouring people, very scarce. We can therefore offer only a brief comment. Furnishings are mentioned in the following chapter on housing and leisure consumption is the subject of another. But what of watches? These consumer symbols of the new time-conscious capitalist society were pawned as often as the proverbial suit. It has been suggested that by the mid-eighteenth century in London, labouring men as well as artisans frequently possessed silver watches. But the latter seem much more likely owners than the former when a watch would have cost around £2. Ownership may well have expanded significantly by the closing years of the century when Pitt expected a proposed tax in 1797/8 to raise £200,000 a year. Early in the nineteenth century imported watches were quoted as low as 5s. (25p) and by 1834 the price of an efficient British one could be as little as £1.[59]

Perhaps the watch was the marginal purchase of the working man by the early nineteenth century. Afforded in good times, in some towns through 'watch clubs', there was presumed to have been one in every

Lancashire handloom weaver's pocket during their 'golden age' of the 1790s, as there was in mule-spinners' pockets in the Manchester of fifty years later. In bad times, demand slumped. The Watchmakers of Clerkenwell in 1817 blamed their distress not only upon foreign competition, but also on a general depression in which a watch was the first purchase forgone by the labouring people. Ironically during this crisis, the watchmakers had to pawn what was the most essential and valued of their possessions: their tools.[60]

REFERENCES AND NOTES

1. **D. J. Oddy**, 'Working-class diets in late nineteenth-century Britain', *Economic History Review* (second series), XXIII, 1970, p. 314.
2. See **J. G. Rule**, 'Regional variations in food consumption among agricultural labourers, 1790–1860', in **W. Minchinton** (ed.), *Agricultural Improvements: Medieval and Modern*, Exeter University Press, 1981, pp. 112–37.
3. **John Burnett**, *Plenty and Want: a social history of diet in England from 1815 to the present day*, Penguin, 1968, p. 43; **F. M. Eden**, *The State of the Poor*, 1797, abridged **A. G. L. Rogers**, Routledge, 1928, p. 353.
4. Eden, *State of the Poor*, p. 104; **B. S. Rowntree** and **M. Kendall**, *How the Labourer Lives*, Nelson, 1913, p. 40. Much research still needs to be done on whether the rural poor bought grain, flour or bread. Recent work on Dorset, a very rural county, showing that even small villages had bakers by 1800, seems to support Eden's position: **K. D. Bawn**, 'Social protest, popular disturbances and public order', Ph.D. Thesis, University of Reading, 1984.
5. Quoted in **B. Inglis**, *Poverty and the Industrial Revolution*, Panther, 1972, p. 92; Rowntree, *How the Labourer Lives*, pp. 38–9.
6. *Morning Chronicle*, 14 November 1849.
7. 'Report by Dr Edwin Smith on the food of the poorer labouring classes in England', in *Sixth Report of the Medical Officer of the Committee of Council on Health*, BPP, 1864, XXVIII, App. 6, p. 238; table from **Carl C. Zimmerman**, *Consumption and Standards of Living*, Williams & Norgate, 1936, p. 108.
8. Reproduced in **J. D. Chambers** and **G. E. Mingay**, *The Agricultural Revolution 1750–1880*, Batsford, 1966, pp. 140–2; **E. H. Hunt**, *Regional Wage Variations in Britain 1850–1914*, Clarendon Press, 1973, p. 79; *Morning Chronicle*, 6 March 1849.
9. **T. L. Richardson**, 'Agricultural labourers' standard of living in Kent, 1790–1840' in **D. Oddy** and **D. S. Miller** (eds), *The Making of the Modern British Diet*, Croom Helm, 1976, p. 106; *Morning Chronicle*, 5 January 1850; 14 November 1849; 27 October 1849.
10. Smith, 'Report', pp. 239–41.
11. Ibid., pp. 242–3.
12. See the summary of Smith's findings in Rule, 'Regional variations', pp. 130–6.

13. **E. J. T. Collins**, 'Dietary change and cereal consumption in the nineteenth century', *Agricultural History Review*, XXIII, 1975, pp. 99–110; **J. G. Rule**, *The Labouring miner in Cornwall c1740–1860: A study in social history*, Ph.D. thesis, University of Warwick, 1971, pp. 109–12; **C. J. Hunt**, *The Lead Miners of the Northern Pennines in the Eighteenth and Nineteenth Centuries*, Manchester U.P., 1970, pp. 170–2. The Bedfordshire poor were 'all' said to eat barley bread in 1800, **P. Horne**, *The Rural World 1780–1850*, Hutchinson, 1980, p. 38.

14. **R. N. Salaman**, *The History and Social Influence of the Potato*, Cambridge U.P., 1949, pp. 459–66; **R. Southey**, 'Review of Colquhoun's *Treatise on the Wealth of the British Empire*', *Quarterly Review*, 1815; Eden, *State of the Poor*, p. 103; **D. Davies**, *The Case of the Labourers in Husbandry stated and considered*, London, 1795, p. 31; Rule, 'Labouring miner', pp. 109–12.

15. *Morning Chronicle*, 27 October, 5 December, 26 December, 10 November, 28 November, 14 November 1849; 6 March 1850.

16. Ibid., 14 November 1849; 18 October 1850.

17. The calculation is based on comparison of a budget in the *Morning Chronicle*, 6 March 1850 and in Eden, *State of the Poor*, p. 208; Richardson, 'Agricultural labourers' standard of living', p. 106; See **E. J. Hobsbawm's** discussion of meat consumption trends in an appendix to his article 'The British standard of living, 1790–1850' repr. in **A. J. Taylor** (ed.), *The Standard of Living in Britain in the Industrial Revolution*, Methuen, 1975, pp. 82–92.

18. Eden, *State of the Poor*, p. 173; *Morning Chronicle*, 10 November 1849.

19. Ibid., 14 November, 28 November, 27 October, 5 December, 26 December, 18 October 1849.

20. Ibid., 9 January 1850.

21. **J. Lawson**, *Progress in Pudsey* (1888), repr. Caliban Books, 1978, p. 26; Burnett, 'Plenty and Want', p. 63; **P. E. Razzell** and **R. W. Wainwright** (eds), *The Victorian Working Class: Selections from letters to the Morning Chronicle*, Cass, 1973, pp. 195, 202, 208.

22. Razzell and Wainwright, *Victorian Working Class*, pp. 223, 243; Rule, 'Labouring miner', p. 112.

23. Chambers and Mingay, *Agricultural Revolution*, p. 181; **P. Gaskell**, *Artisans and Machinery* (1836), repr. Cass, 1968, pp. 118–21.

24. **Frederick Engels**, *The Condition of the Working Class in England* (1845), Granada edn., 1982, p. 105.

25. Hobsbawm, 'British standard of living', pp. 85–6.

26. Ibid., pp. 85–92; **R. M. Hartwell**, 'The rising standard of living in England, 1800–50' (1961), repr. in Taylor (ed.), *Standard of Living*, p. 108 and also Taylor's introduction, pp. xxii to xxiii.

27. Rowntree, *How the Labourer Lives*, Budget no. 20; Smith, 'Report', p. 249; **M. Anderson**, *Family Structure in Nineteenth-Century Lancashire*, Cambridge U.P., 1971, p. 77; Burnett, *Plenty and Want*, p. 55.

28. **E. H. Hunt**, *British Labour History, 1815–1914*, Weidenfeld & Nicolson, 1981, p. 83; **J. Burnett**, *History of the Cost of Living*, Penguin, 1969, p. 210; Smith, 'Report', pp. 221–3.

29. Hartwell, 'Rising standard of living', pp. 112–13; **E. P. Thompson** & **E. Yeo** (eds), *The Unknown Mayhew*, Penguin, 1973, pp. 129–30; Burnett, *Plenty and Want*, p. 73.

30. Hartwell, 'Rising standard of living', p. 115; Southey, 'Review', p. 413; *Quarterly Review*, LXIX, 1842, pp. 231–2. See **J. G. Rule**, 'The home market and the sea fisheries of Devon and Cornwall in the nineteenth century', in **W. Minchinton** (ed.), *Population and Marketing: Two Studies in the History of the South-West*, Exeter U.P., 1976, pp. 123–39.

31. Rule, 'Sea fisheries', pp. 124–5.

32. Ibid., p. 131.

33. Gaskell, *Artisans and Machinery*, p. 118; J. R. McCulloch, Notes to 1812 Edition of Adam Smith, *Wealth of Nations*, pp. 773–4.

34. Based on specimen budgets in Burnett, *Plenty and Want*, pp. 62–72; Razzell and Wainwright, *Victorian Working Class*, p. 202; Rule, 'Labouring miner', p. 111.

35. Burnett, *Plenty and Want*, p. 25.

36. **Charles Dickens**, *Hard Times*, 1854; Burnett, *Plenty and Want*, p. 25, quoting **W. Chaloner** and **W. Henderson**.

37. Hartwell, 'Rising standard of living', pp. 116–17.

38. *Westminster Review*, 25, 1836, p. 458. Reprinted in **C. J. Wrigley** (ed.), *The Working Classes in the Victorian Age*, vol. I, Gregg, Farnborough, 1973. These are facsimile reproductions and pagination is as in originals. **William Dodd**, *The Labouring Classes of England*, Boston, 1848, repr. A. M. Kelly, New Jersey, 1976, p. 43; Gaskell, *Artisans and Machinery*, pp. 119–20.

39. Engels, *Working Class*, p. 101; **Charles Kingsley**, *Alton Locke*, 1850 edn, p. 75.

40. See **Avril M. Leadley**, 'Some villains of the eighteenth-century market place', in **J. G. Rule** (ed.), *Outside the Law; Studies in Crime and Order 1650–1850*, Exeter U.P., 1982, pp. 22–4.

41. Ibid., p. 26.

42. *Frazers Magazine*, 1834, pp. 574–5, in Wrigley (ed.); *Westminster Review*, 25, 1836, p. 458, in Wrigley (ed.), Thompson and Yeo, *Unknown Mayhew*, pp. 251–2; Razzell and Wainwright, *Victorian Working Class*, p. 19; *Report of the Select Committee on Increase in Criminal Convictions*, BPP, 1826/7, VI, Evidence of Sir Thomas Baring, p. 53.

43. For truck practices in the eighteenth century, see **J. G. Rule**, *The Experience of Labour in Eighteenth-Century Industry*, Croom Helm, 1981, pp. 138–9; Gaskell, *Artisans and Machinery*, p. 297; Dodd, *Labouring Classes*, p. 43; Razzell and Wainwright, *Victorian Working Class*, p. 247; Engels, *Working Class*, pp. 208–10.

44. For adulteration in the eighteenth century, see Leadley, 'Villains of the market place', pp. 30–32; Engels, *Working Class*, pp. 102–3.

45. Quoted in **R. Tames**, *Our Daily Bread*, Penguin Education, 1973, pp. 27–28.

46. This argument has been advanced by **E. W. Gilboy**, 'Demand as a factor in the Industrial Revolution', 1932, repr. in **R. M. Hartwell**, *The Causes of the Industrial Revolution in England*, Methuen, 1967, pp. 121–38. A more qualified presentation, which more clearly recognises the significant time-gap between a middle-class consumer effect and its spread to the working class can be found in **H. Perkin**, *The Origins of Modern English Society*, Routledge, 1969, pp. 89–97.

47. Gilboy, 'Demand', p. 135.

48. Perkin, *Origins*, pp. 90, 92–3, 97, 141–2; **G. Rudé**, *The Crowd in History*,

1730_1848, John Wiley, 1964, p. 51.

49. Quoted in **M. Berg**, *The Machinery Question and the Making of Political Economy 1815–1848,* Cambridge U.P., 1980, pp. 53–4.

50. **Sally Alexander**, 'Women's work in nineteenth-century London: a study of the years 1820–50', in **J**. **Mitchell** and **A**. **Oakley**, *The Rights and Wrongs of Women,* Penguin, 1976, p. 96; **R. Burt** (ed.), *Cornwall's Mines and Miners: Nineteenth-Century Studies by George Henwood,* Truro, 1972, p. 68; Razzell and Wainwright, *Victorian Working Class,* p. 195; **W. Hutton**, *Life,* 1817 edn, p. 96; **Francis Place**, *Autobiography,* ed. M. Thale, Cambridge U.P., 1972, p. 63.

51. Thompson and Yeo, *Unknown Mayhew,* pp. 334–6.

52. Engels, *Working Class,* p. 99; Razzell and Wainwright, *Victorian Working Class*, pp. 166.

53. Ibid., p. 100.

54. **N. Mansfield**, 'John Brown, a shoemaker in Place's London', *History Workshop,* no. 8, 1979, p. 131.

55. Gaskell, *Artisans and Machinery,* footnote to p. 325; Berg, *Machinery Question,* pp. 74, 241.

56. Quoted in Taylor (ed.), *Standard of Living,* p. xxxv.

57. *Weekly Record of the Temperance Movement,* 25 Oct. 1856, p. 250.

58. Berg, *Machinery Question,* p. 243.

59. For a discussion of the availability of watches, see **E. P. Thompson**, 'Time, work-discipline and industrial capitalism', *Past and Present,* no. 38, 1967, pp. 66–70.

60. Rule, *Experience of Labour,* p. 50.

Chapter 3

HOUSING

Britain was by the mid-nineteenth century recognised as the greatest manufacturing economy the world had seen and as the possessor of Europe's most extensive and squalid slums. Clearly the two are related. Only special pleading can suggest that industrialisation and the spread of urban civilisation were unrelated phenomena in the nineteenth century. They were linked both by the expansion and spread of the new factory towns and by the growth of the urban outworking 'sweating' trades. These Marx knew as the 'new domestic system', a form of home production which was not the precursor of the factory system but its complement. Not only were industrialisation and increasing urbanisation linked materially in resulting from changing modes of production, but they were also linked ideologically. For if *laissez-faire*, the unregulated operation of market forces, is held to be the dynamic philosophy which underlay Britain's surge in economic output, then, in housing – the provision of which is among the most speculative of trades – the market economy seems most evidently to have failed to meet the basic needs of the labouring people. Wherever housing is not heavily supplemented from public building, then the homeless and the inadequately housed, even in the most active of private economies, have formed embarrassingly large groups. According to the economists, 'demand' exists only among those with the means to pay. This definition seems especially inappropriate in the area of housing. Those without roofs over their heads could not 'demand' housing if they were unable to afford rents which would bring profit to the speculative builder and the private landlord. The old, the sick, the casually employed and the low-waged with large families struggled, and have continued to struggle, to find housing. Even today the idea of a 'property-owning democracy' is a dangerous myth which takes no account of the needs of that large minority of the population who can never aspire to house-ownership. In the early nineteenth century too, notions of 'self-help' in housing were irrelevant to the situations not only of the lower-waged workers, but grossly so to the 'bottom of the pile', those who got their living as they could: the unemployed, the widowed, the unemployables, the sick and the aged.

House-building, because of its speculative nature, moved in response not to the demographic cycles which determined need, but under the influence of economic considerations determined by the business cycle, levels of interest, and the price of available land. Houses are not built where there is no need, but need is not in itself a sufficient condition for increasing house-building in a market economy. Hence the building and the manufacturing sectors of the economy link in the direct sense that high rents can only be paid out of higher wages: 'The slums were part of . . . the economy of low wages, and one of their practical functions was therefore to underpin Victorian prosperity.'[1] Speculative builders were themselves increasingly attempting to force lower wages on their employees. Under the system of 'general contracting' they were forcing down the craftsmen and producing a new type of 'scamping' worker working with shoddy materials. Much new housing even as it sprang up could have been truly built under the slogan: 'We are building the slums of the near future.' Speculative builders, low wages, uncertain employment and high ground rents and prices were among the determining factors which make it quite unsatisfactory to attribute the Victorian slum solely to the housing problems posed by a rapidly increasing population: 'In terms of human values, the slums of Victorian London were three-dimensional obscenities as replete as any ever put out of sight by civilised man.'[2]

RURAL HOUSING

It is not contended that the urban housing of nineteenth-century England represented a deterioration over pre-existing rural housing in the quality of its construction. Much rural housing was in itself so bad that there was no margin for deterioration. Unlike food, clothing or other commodities which can be used to indicate trends in living standards, housing is as much a matter of existing stock as of production. This was especially true of rural districts where during most of the nineteenth century the greater part of the labouring and pauper populations did not live on the few 'improved' cottages built by a handful of paternalist landowners. They did not live in new cottages at all; they occupied the old homes built-up by their ancestors and repaired and extended over generations by the labourers themselves.[3] 'Cottage' conveys a distinctly more rosy image than many of the other words used by contemporaries. Cobden spoke of habitations in Dorset as 'worse than the wigwams of American indians', while Cobbett described cottages in Wiltshire as 'little better than pigsties' and as 'wretched hovels'. Some in Lincolnshire he described as 'miserable sheds'. Rural homes were described by Dodd in 1848 as 'mere hovels for shelter', while in the southern counties they were labelled 'cabins', rather than cottages by the *Morning Chronicle* in 1849.[4] Since most of the housing so described had been in existence from the eighteenth century or even longer, there is little reason to presume any significant change in the period under study in the physical quality of rural housing. Variations dependent upon the availability of materials such as slate, flint and timber gave clear local characteristics to much housing, but what separated most urban from most rural housing was the rarity of stone or brick in the countryside. Clay mixed with straw to bind it was the common constructional material and it went by different names: 'cob' in Cornwall, 'stud and mud' or 'wattle and daub' in the Home Counties, 'post and plaister' in the north, but this filling in of timber-frames with clay made 'mud-walled' the literal description of rural housing. The worst examples were roofed with turf and floored with earth. The processes of decay natural to such construction are well illustrated in a description from Buckinghamshire in 1842:

> The vegetable substances mixed with mud to make it bind rapidly decompose, leaving the walls porous. The earth of the floor is full of vegetable matter, and from there being nothing to cut off its contact with the surrounding mould, it is peculiarly liable to damp. The floor is frequently charged with animal matter thrown upon it by the inmates, and this rapidly decomposes by the alternate action of heat and moisture. Thatch placed in contact with such walls speedily decays yielding a gas of the most deleterious quality.[5]

New thatch had excellent qualities of waterproofing and insulation, but old thatch lost both and, in addition, harboured vermin. With no ceilings, the droppings from roofs fell directly upon the inhabitants. Renewed clay also has advantages: it must be thick to stand and was presumably warmer than the single-brick thickness of much urban housing. But again the problem was decay. Earth floors sometimes had springs bursting through, so that little channels had to be cut under the doorways to carry off the water.

Sanitary arrangements were primitive or non-existent. Often they consisted of a hole in the ground under a lean-to shed, emptied only when the garden needed manure. Where there was any waste removal at all, it was conducted by surface drains usually into the nearest ditch.[6]

Of course, there were better cottages for a fortunate few. *Some* farmers and landowners took a real interest in providing them. The 'model' buildings designed and erected by such men were truly 'cottages', reaching their most extreme and irrelevant expression in the 'cottage ornée', with its warmth-losing high eves and light-denying ornate windows. However, by mid-century, individuals and groups like the 'Cottage Improvement Society' began to evolve and propagate more suitable dwellings. Commonly designed in pairs with a main room 12–15 feet square, two bedrooms and often a cellar or pantry, increasingly as bricks became more available they were built in that material by landlords like the Duke of Bedford. Dorothea Brookes in George Elliot's *Middlemarch* is a literary representative of a fashionable concern, but most recent authorities agree that it made a quantifiably unimportant contribution to rural housing and that there was no part of the kingdom which did not have the majority of its rural inhabitants living in damp and squalor. However attractive they might look from a distance, for the most part country cottages could hardly survive closer inspection. As Professor Burnett has remarked: 'harmony with surroundings is after all an aesthetic consideration'.[7]

OVERCROWDING

If there was little evident change in the quality of rural housing between 1750 and 1850, there was a striking increase in overcrowding. Three factors were primarily responsible. The most crucial was the rapid growth of the rural labouring population and in family size. The population of Dorset increased 40% 1801–31 and that of other rural counties grew similarly: Suffolk 38%, Wiltshire 29%, Norfolk 43%, Berkshire 32%, for example. Overcrowding is revealed retrospectively in the findings of an inquiry of 1864. Eight hundred and twenty-one parishes in England were surveyed containing 69,225 cottages housing 305,567 persons, an average of 4.4 per cottage. Less than 5% had more than two bedrooms, while 40% had only one. Single-bedroomed cottages averaged four persons per bedroom and two-bedroomed ones 2.5. The amount of air space available at 156 cubic feet in the bedrooms was only about three-fifths of that required by law in common lodging houses. Typical was a 10 ft square bedroom with a 7 ft ceiling for 4.5 persons. As Edward Smith pointed out, 'the peasant lost the immunity of the open air' which he gained from his employment when he retired to his bedroom. A Dorset family of eleven occupied two rooms. The single bedroom contained three beds: one shared by four teenage sons, another by three daughters and the third by the husband, wife and two youngest children. The room had no curtain or partition and only one 15 inch square window.[8] The *Chronicle* reporter in 1849 found in the West Country a 'cabin', 'suddenly thrown up out of the ground', its mouldy imperfect sandstone walls, low thatched roof, two small windows and ill-fitting door enclosed two dark rooms. One of these served as a bedroom for a family of nine who slept on sacks filled with oatchaff. Such conditions, he learned, while not the condition of all labourers, were those of a 'very great number of Englishmen – not in the backwoods of a remote settlement, but in the heart of Anglo-Saxon civilisation in the year of grace 1849'.[9]

Such conditions conflicted with the 'holy family' puritan ideology of Victorian England. Indeed, the reporter more than hinted at the existence of incest as a rural as well as an urban problem. In a few instances, families seem to have made special efforts to overcome this risk: two families arranging for the females to sleep in one cottage and cottage and the males in another, but for the most part the mixing of the sexes was unavoidable and low wages and the shortage of accommodation forced rural families to intensify the problem by taking in lodgers.[10]

The second cause of rural overcrowding, after population growth, was the deliberate action of farmers and landlords in depleting the rural housing stock. Even model cottage builders like the Duke of Bedford used their power of eviction to keep a tight hold over those who lived on their lands. He claimed that the provision of model dwellings would do much to raise the social and moral condition of the labouring classes, but it is tempting to ask, with Dr Gauldie, what happened to those whom he found too unsuitable to remain on his estates? Those who were too poor or too improvident to pay their rent regularly, whose age or infirmity or whose large number of children might make them burdens on the poor rate, or those whose independence of spirit made them bridle at the restrictions of estate life, so that they seemed rebellious and dangerous? Nineteenth-century landed proprietors felt it no part of their duty to house the immoral, the undeserving or the socially undesirable. For reasons beyond their control, labourers could slide into such categories. During the high demand of the boom farming years of the French Wars, landowners had been happy to have a large supply of labour to hand. Then they had pulled down no cottages. When the good years ended, the falling demand for labour together with the gathering momentum of population growth rapidly began to show itself in the rising burden of the poor rates. Then began the attempts to decrease the numbers of actual and potential paupers living on their lands. With Malthusian theories offering a legitimation for their conduct, dehousing policies by rural landlords and farmers began to produce a stream of protest from many parts of the country. From Norfolk the estates for eight to ten miles around Norwich were reported 'entirely cleared of tenantry' as a consequence of the occupiers of land resorting to every expedient to prevent labourers from obtaining the settlement right to poor relief. In parts of Devon and Somerset, cottages were being demolished more quickly than they were being built, while the Bishop of Winchester spoke in 1829 of the want of cottages in Hampshire, instancing a parish where there had been left only 29 cottages for 110 inhabitants giving an average space of 12 by 10 ft for each cottage of 8–10 persons. *Blackwoods Edinburgh Magazine* in the following year strongly challenged the Malthusian assumptions which underlay such actions: 'destroying the comforts, degrading the character and deteriorating the morals of the poor'. It doubted whether destroying cottages would check improvident marriages: 'Somehow it would seem that the peasantry of Hampshire contrive to multiply in spite of the pains which have been taken to withhold from them the wicked encouragement of comfortable cottages'.[11]

One is inclined to agree with Dr Gauldie that such conditions and attitudes contributed substantially to the growth of towns, which filled up with country people searching for homes as well as for work. But in the first instance the rural homeless, for whom there was no work or room in the landlord-dominated 'closed' villages, would have been more likely to have moved to swell the populations of the 'open' villages, where no power of removal rested in proprietorial hands. Such villages could rapidly grow into shanty towns, like Castle Acre in Norfolk which, as a result of cottage-removing around Norwich, had become 'the coop of all the scrapings in the country, for if a man or a woman do anything wrong, they come here, and they think by getting among them they are safe'. At such times as the cottage-destroyers did require extra labour, then they reaped a second advantage from their evicting activities. From the crowded open settlements, labourers would walk five, ten or twelve miles for day-work in the fields. The parish of Northhill in Norfolk supplied around 500 labourers on this basis to farmers around Norwich. The worst abuse was that the separation of the labourer from the parish of his work led to the notorious 'gang system' by which farmers obtained sub-contract labour drawn from the 'open' parishes, as and when they wanted and without any direct responsibility as employers towards those who toiled in their fields. Others who did not remove to the 'open' parishes perhaps ended up in the slum quarters which were increasingly becoming a feature of country towns. Ipswich in 1850 had a district in which 106 courts contained 627 overcrowded houses in conditions of defective drainage, stagnant water and only one privy for every five houses.[12]

The third factor behind the overcrowding problem was also related to farmers' activities in seeking to avoid their Poor Law responsibilities. By not employing yearly-hired farm servants, they prevented their labourers from gaining a settlement. This motive, plus the rising cost of boarding, had, especially in the south and east, brought about a very marked decline in living-in farm service ever since the French War years. The historian of farm service has noted a 'wholesale extinction' of the institution rather than a gradual decay by the 1830s, outside of the north and one or two pockets elsewhere. The fact that children no longer left the family cottages in their early teens to live-in with farmers destroyed a centuries-old mechanism which had controlled household size and had allowed the nuclear family to 'export' some children to ease the burden of the worst years of the 'family cycle'.

Further, living-in service lasted for young people until around the age of twenty-four, and had the demographic effect of producing late marriages. Its decline into wage labour was a form of proletarianisation which was linked to a younger age at marriage and hence to increased family size. In families in which there were not only more births, but in which the teenage children continued to reside, there was bound to be an increase in overcrowding, especially in the south and east where the decline in living-in was most rapid and where the opportunities for employment outside agriculture were scarce.[13]

The northern farmworker with his higher pay and different hiring system in some respects fared better. This was mainly because he was much more likely to have a plot of land attached to his cottage, the provision of which was part of the contract of the 'hinds' see below, p. 109). Dodd noted that in Northumberland not only did most cottages have gardens, but without the pressure of an over-expanding agrarian proletariat, their supply was more adequate. However, the quality of the housing does not in itself seem to have been superior except in so far as walls were more likely to have been stone built. Earth floors were usual and unceilinged thatched roofs common, except where slate was easily available. A survey of 1842 found most agricultural labourers living in single-roomed cottages: a finding which was still valid in 1864 when 224 rural homes visited in Northumberland and Durham disclosed not a single example of a cottage with more than one bedroom: 'The majority of Northumbrian and Durham peasants, whether rich or poor, hind or collier, live in but one room, day and night with all the family.'[14] 'Whether rich or poor' is a significant remark. In rural districts, housing standards had no strong correlation with wage levels. Outside of the south and east it was the attached plot which mattered and, indeed, which was often the object of the lease. On the plot, the cottage itself was often self-built. If housing quality is measured in terms of healthy living, then it owed most to factors like low population density, a local geology which afforded good stone, and a hillside location which allowed reasonable drainage. As we shall see. the pitmen of the north-east in their rapidly-growing lowland villages, hurriedly built to meet new mining needs, were, for all their higher pay, less healthily housed than the lead miners of the same counties, who inhabited the remote Pennine hillsides. The higher pay of the pitmen showed itself instead in their diet and in the furniture and knick-knacks which filled their shoddily-constructed overcrowded homes.[15]

MINERS' HOUSING

As well as farmworkers, some manufacturing workers and miners were rural dwellers. The conditions of the former will be discussed below, but miners, who in some districts combined their mining with farming, will be considered next. The lead miners of the Northern Pennines lived higher than perhaps any other occupational group! Of their villages, Allenhead was 1,327 ft above sea level and Nenthead 1,411. In this remote area the villages were centres for a dispersed hamlet population of scattered houses. The eighteenth-century miners naturally mixed mining with farming and were able to continue to do so down to the middle years of the nineteenth century. A description of the 1840s describes their way of life: 'Their work is among lead ore, sealing pastures, waiting upon and feeding cattle, mowing, winning and stacking hay, and carting fuel against the winter season.' In 1834 the typical holding consisted of about three acres of meadow and three or four of enclosed upland pasture. In the eighteenth century before enclosure, the pasture would have been obtained from open-moor grazing. Dr Hunt has calculated that for the village of Coalcleugh, 56.8% of houses and small holdings in 1861 and in the Allenheads district 65.8% did. Many of these holdings were on land leased from the mining companies who favoured attaching their employees to their mines. Others were on land leased from local landowners who from the late eighteenth century were aware of the value of rent income from land-eager miners in areas where few alternative tenants were likely to present themselves.[16]

The houses erected on these plots were commonly built by the miners themselves using the local sandstone. They reflected the dual occupation of the miners and their extreme location. In the eighteenth century they were thatched with a steep rise to allow snow to fall off, although slate roofs had become widespread by the 1840s. Most were long two-storied buildings. The ground floor had a living room at one end and a cattle shed at the other. Over the living room were one or two bedrooms, and over the cattle shed, a hay loft. The system of pay, with balances being adjusted at six-monthly intervals, allowed many miners the opportunity of acquiring some land, although in bad times the small-holdings were frequently mortgaged.

Houses for supervisors and for smelters had always been built in the villages by the mining companies and, in this remote area, later pressure on suitable land as mining activities expanded forced a growing minority of miners to live in the villages. The Quaker-owned London Lead Company began to develop its village of Nenthead for residential purposes after 1820, providing gardens with cottages as a substitute for farming land. But over the district as a whole, even by the mid-nineteenth century probably more families had holdings than did not.[17]

The miners of Cornwall, despite the great copper boom which began in the mid-eighteenth century and expanded their numbers from around 9,000 in 1787 to more than 36,000 in 1851, were another group in which a plentiful availability of moor land gave an opportunity of small-holding. Although some of their number lived in the growing mining centres of Redruth and Camborne, they typically occupied cottages scattered over the western mining districts of the county. In picturesque locations, sometimes even on cliff tops with the rolling Atlantic for a backcloth, their white-washed walls suggested to many observers a state of comfort. Closer inspection, with nose as well as eye, would have swiftly dispelled such an impression. Close-up, the typical miner's cottage was small, usually of only two rooms. An indication of their size at that time is given by a late-eighteenth-century description of them as 'little huts'. An archaeological survey of surviving physical evidence produced this summary:

> Apparently charming cottages were often hideously overcrowded. The thick walls and comfortable-looking thatch hid floors of beaten earth or more usually a mixture of lime and ash which was little better . . . and continually damp. Moreover those solid cob walls often suffered badly from damp and rats. There were rarely any traces of a damp proof course, and usually no proper foundations.[18]

Windows were few and small, though some compensation was afforded by the use of the 'hepse' or half-door.

Any improvement by the early nineteenth century was marginal. A study of the typhus which was endemic in the mining districts contrasted the appearance of country cottages in west Cornwall with their 'spruce gardens' separated by low walls from 'green meadows adjoining' with the sanitary reality:

> . . . besides towns and villages much in want of sanitary regulations, there are extensive and barren downs and wet and dreary moors, over which are scattered groups of comfortless cob houses and numberless single cottages, wretchedly built and damp and dirty in the extreme. At their doors may be seen the usual mudpools, which in winter overflow . . . while in summer these semi-fluid accumulations of putrid slime, continue to exhale offensive and deleterious miasmata from their dark green surfaces.

The rapidly-growing mining settlement of Chacewater still lacked any underground drainage system in 1853, while town miners in Camborne in 1842 persisted in keeping pigs in their back gardens and carefully fostered their dung heaps. Structurally, there was some improvement. In 1842 miners were described as inhabiting for the most part 'decent cottages' often stone-built with four rooms, although two-roomed cob dwellings were still very common. It was estimated that a reasonable cottage might be built for £35 to £50, but clearly that was beyond many miners, for the same authority describes 'hovels of a very miserable description' built by miners of a 'less reputable class'. Some of these were built on sites excavated in the hillsides so that on one or even two sides, their roofs rose but little above the level of the adjoining ground.

If many of the cottages gave the appearance of being thrown up by amateurs, it was because many of them had been built by miners themselves. Several local landowners made a practice of granting leases on small plots of land on the abundant waste of the moors and downs. On these plots, miners erected cottages. The practice had begun in the eighteenth century, one landowner estimating in 1793 that over the previous few years fifty such cottages had been built on three to five acre plots leased by him, while his father had leased out a further sixty acres between 1756 and 1786. A mine steward for another landowner wrote at length to his employer in 1802 stressing how such grants contributed the moral bonus of keeping the miners, with their ample leisure time, out of the inns:

> I have often wished that the proprietors of wasteland would endeavour to direct and guide the industry of these people, to such efforts as would lessen their evils, by alloting each of them 3 or 4 acres for the term of three lives . . . under the small annual rent of about 2s. [10p] an acre. Whenever this has been tried around this neighbourhood the happy effects have soon been perceived. In the course of a few years they have been able to rear up little cottage houses . . . and instead of meeting them staggering from their former haunts, the Brandy Shops . . . you may now see them busily employed in cultivating their little fields . . . How great must be the satis faction of a humane, benevolent landlord in seeing so many little dwelling houses in green meadows arising year after year in dismal barren spots, where nothing grew before but useless heath.

The granting of such leases continued into the middle years of the nineteenth century, but became less common as the mining population expanded, so that by 1841 it was estimated that about a quarter of the miners inhabited such cottages built on small plots, while the rest rented cottages built, often in small terraces, by speculative landlords often neighbouring tradesmen or builders. There was very little provision of housing by the mine owners in contrast with the coal-mining districts. A house of his own was said, in 1838, to have been the 'grand desideratum' of the miner. Given the availability of heathland and the fact that the peculiar system of payment used in the mines, the tribute system, brought windfalls from time to time to a fair number of the miners, it was an ambition they perhaps more realistically held than did most working men of the time: 'If they have managed to live without getting into debt, when they get this start, the first thing they do is to build a house.' Perhaps once or twice in his working lifetime a tributer could have the chance of clearing a 'start' of £40–50 in a month or two. A description of the house on its plot of land which one such successful tributer built has survived:

> The place of my birth was a boulder-built cottage, with reedy roof, bare
> rafters, and clay floor . . . The rough house had no backdoor, nor any
> windows looking northward, except one about a foot square in the little
> pantry: but on the south side it had four windows, and a porch of primitive
> granite, literally small unpolished boulders. The woodwork of the roof was
> all visible, and sometimes the stars could be seen at night, though my father
> was sure to have a thick layer of reed put on as soon as winter approached.
> There was no partition in the sleeping room, which ran from one end of the
> building to the other . . . The eastern end wall was much injured in my
> grandmother's time, through the explosion of a bag of gunpowder, which
> my uncle Mathew was foolishly drying before the fire.[19]

In the eighteenth century the colliers of several districts were sometimes able to combine mining with a modicum of husbandry. Arthur
Young in 1770 gave a description of miners' holdings in Yorkshire
which is strikingly similar to the 1802 description of Cornwall:

> Now there is not a collier without his farm; each from three or four to 20
> acres of land. Most of them keep a cow or two, and a galloway: raise the
> corn etc. they eat; are well fed, well clothed, industrious and happy. Their
> time is spent at home instead of the alehouse.[20]

Young, however, presents this as something of an exception, believing
that in general the miners could not be prevailed upon to farm, even if
they had time and land available. The old mining centres of the
eighteenth century, Kingswood, near Bristol, and the Forest of Dean,
were communities of independently minded woodland people whose
exercise of common pasture and woodland rights was as essential to
their way of life as was the seeking of coal. Kingswood was an area of
little significance by the nineteenth century and although the Forest of
Dean expanded, its growing population threatened the traditional
livelihood of the free miners. As relatively large pits began to be
worked in the 1820s, their conditions of employment changed so that
the 'distinction between employer and employee came to mean more
than the distinction between native and stranger'. Equally threatening
to their customary livelihood was the growth of population, for where
there were 7,014 people competing for living space in 1831, there were
20,555 in 1871. The average area of freehold land per cottage fell as a
result from 1.25 acres in 1834 to half an acre by 1871, while their
common rights were increasingly invaded.[21]

Colliers in other districts, the ones which were to become the main
centres of supply in the nineteenth century, despite their higher than
average wages, lived by the mid-nineteenth century in some of the
worst housing described by sanitary-minded investigators. In the
north-east, housing was provided as part of the miner's bond of hiring.
Evictions from their company houses provided the most harrowing
scenes of the great pitmen's strikes of 1832 and 1844. The miners

regarded their homes as sanctioned by the custom of centuries and bitterly resented the power of the masters to turn them out.

The number of collieries in the north-east had been 62 in 1822: by 1850 it was 184. The miners increased in number (men and boys) from around 12,000 in 1800 through 21,000 in 1829 to 33,000 by 1844. This great expansion had largely been the result of extending the area of coal-getting eastwards and southwards. New colliery villages sprang up in East Durham and around Bishop Auckland in the south. One village, Thornley, had had a population of 50 in 1831 and 2,730 by 1851. It was these villages, springing up virtually overnight, dominated by men migrating ahead of families, which mostly earned the colliery districts their unsavoury housing reputation:

> The lodging which is obtained by the pitmen is perhaps on the whole the worst and dearest of which any large specimens can be found in England . . . (because of) the high number of men found in one room, in the smallness of the ground plot on which a great number of houses are thrust, the want of water, the absence of privies, and the frequent placing of one house on top of another.[22]

'Pit rows' in Durham were described in 1849 as unique, being 'neither country village nor meaner part of manufacturing town . . . (with) . . . more than the inconveniences of the one, and more than the ugliness of the other'. Houses were described as 'intolerably filthy and unwhole-some . . . foul, priviless, ill-watered, unscavenged, overcrowded lairs'. Such houses were provided by the mineowners, but were of poor quality, 'constructed wholesale they are the only houses in which these work-people can possibly live'. Whole villages were built without a single cess-pool or privy. The lowest class had only one room, rather better ones the addition of an attic, while only the third class had an extra room for sleeping besides an attic. Large families still commonly occupied two rooms. Housing was accounted part of wages and ap-portioned by the proprietor or his agents according to family size. A young couple went initially into a single-roomed back-to-back or lean-to and moved into the next class when they had a young family. If they had *sons*, as soon as they were able to work at the mine they moved up to the third class, but if they had only daughters, no matter how many, they remained in the second class, for parents with employable lads were given the preference in obtaining work and houses. Since the small attics were too small to be of use, perhaps around half of the mining families lived in virtually a single habitable room which served as kitchen, living room, bedroom, and for washing. This last gave special concern to middle-class investigators, for men and grown lads washed half-naked in front of wives, daughters and sisters. Ironically, the few decent houses provided for deputies and overmen were nick-named 'Quality Row'. As a group, miners married young and had large families, so overcrowding came early. For the majority of miners the only 'home comfort' was their virtually free coal, which at least gave them that rarity in working-class homes: a good fire.[23]

Living conditions in the Midlands were, if anything, worse: only about half as good according to one view in 1849. Here the miners ate well in good times, but lived in poor detached cottages, or else in rows or clusters sprinkled amid the rubbish waste. Overcrowding and insanitary conditions had meant that most of the pit villages around Wednesbury and Bilston had been ravaged by the cholera. Gardens were unknown because the constant smoke allowed nothing to grow for mile after mile. Shifting and sinking of the ground made the cracking of the house walls very noticeable.[24] It was around Wednesbury in 1776 that Arthur Young had remarked that there was 'not one farm house nothing that looked like the residence of a mere farmer'.[25] We are worlds away here from the double-occupation 'tinnerhusbandman' still being recorded in some west Cornish parish registers in the second half of the eighteenth century.

THE TOWNS

Even when poorly constructed, most town houses were built from superior materials to cob and thatch. It was not so much their individual deficiencies, but the collective environmental horror which they presented which shocked contemporaries and has led even those historians who take an optimistic view of the industrial revolution in general to pass strong judgements on the new manufacturing towns. Dr Chapman has remarked that the story of working-class housing is 'not one to give much comfort to optimist historians of the standard of living issue', while Professor Thomis states that a 'deteriorating urban environment' was one of the 'most disastrous and continuing consequences of industrialisation'. Professor Mathias pronounced 'environmental decline' as the 'most intense social problem resulting from industrialisation'. E. P. Thompson, in insisting on a marked decline in the 'total conditions' of town life, finds himself in company he has not always shared.[26]

In 1750, around a fifth of the population lived in towns of more than 5,000 inhabitants; by 1850 around three-fifths did. Urban problems had been foreshadowed in London and in some other cities well before the end of the eighteenth century. Compare Henry Fieldings's description of St Giles with that of Engels almost a century later:

> There are great numbers of houses set aside for the reception of idle persons and vagabonds, who have their lodgings there for two-pence a night; that in the above parish, and in St George, Bloomsbury, one woman alone occupies seven of these houses, all properly accommodated with miserable beds from the cellar to the garret . . . in these beds men and women, often

strangers to each other, lie promiscuously.

Engels, too, found the houses of St Giles 'occupied from cellar to garret, filthy within and without'. Their appearance was such that no human being could possibly have wished to have lived in them. But nothing could have compared with the dwellings in the narrow courts and alleys between the houses, in which:

> . . . the tottering filth and ruin surpass all description. Scarcely a whole window pane can be found, the walls are crumbling, door posts and window frames loose and broken doors of old boards nailed together, or wanting in this thieves quarter where no doors are needed, there being nothing to steal. Here live the poorest of the poor, the worst-paid workers with thieves and the victims of prostitution indiscriminately huddled together, the majority Irish or of Irish extraction, and those who have not yet sunk into the whirlpool of moral ruin which surrounds them, sinking daily deeper, losing daily more and more of their power to resist the demoralising influence of want, filth and evil surroundings.[27]

Urban problems were not new, but it was above all industrialisation which brought town living to increasing numbers of Britain's growing population. London also grew even faster in the nineteenth century for different reasons than it had in the eighteenth: from the 1820s especially, it grew from the expansion of sweated outwork. Industry was clearly a main source of urban growth, as Dr Corfield has recently stressed. Specialised manufacturing towns like Sheffield, Birmingham and Manchester were already expanding rapidly in the eighteenth century, well before the coming of the factory, but steam power freed factory masters from the need to locate their mills by country streams and brought the familiar topography of the mill town into being. The deteriorating environment already noted in Manchester before the end of the eighteenth century made it, in the first half of the nineteenth, a symbol to the world of the 'new civilisation' of the industrial revolution. Nearby Stockport was hardly better regarded. To Engels it was renowned as one of the 'duskiest, smokiest holes' and looked, 'excessively repellent'. Manchester and its environs he estimated as housing 350,000 working people: 'almost all of them in wretched, damp, filthy cottages'. In such dwellings, 'no cleanliness, no convenience, and consequently no comfortable family life' was possible. Especially notorious was the Ancoats district which, according to a visitor in 1849, was a 'wide-lying labyrinth of small dingy streets, narrow unsunned courts, terminating in gloomy cul-de-sacs and adorned with a central sloppy gutter'. It had been built by 'unchecked speculators' who ran up 'mobs of filthy and inconvenient streets and courts, utterly unheeding, or perhaps profoundly ignorant of the sanitary and social guilt of their doings'. Newer working-class districts like Cheetham had rather better housing, but it is instructive that the most striking difference which the observer noted was that whereas in Cheetham cellars were used for lumber or for coal, in Ancoats they were 'separably occupied' by an old person or even by a family.[28]

Across the Pennines, Leeds disclosed the seats of the woollen manufacture to be scarcely different from those of cotton:

> The low-lying districts along the river and its tributary becks are narrow, dirty and enough in themselves to shorten the lives of the inhabitants, especially of little children. Added to this, the disgusting state of the working-mens' districts about Kirkgate, Marsh Lane, Cross Street and Richmond Road, which is chiefly attributable to their unpaved, drainless streets, irregular architecture, numerous courts and alleys, and total lack of most ordinary means of cleanliness, all this taken together is explanation enough of the extreme mortality in these unhappy abodes of filthy misery.

This description by Engels hardly differs from that of the *Morning Chronicle* reporter six years later who found the town a perfect 'wilderness of foulness', so filthy as to give the impression of having been built in 'a slimy bog'.[29]

In the wake of the major cholera visitations came the great sanitary investigations of the 1840s, inspired by Edwin Chadwick, which provide the historian with so many indictments of England's ill-built, insanitary and overcrowded towns. There is little point in going in detail over such familiar ground. The comparative mortality statistics of the middle years of the nineteenth century speak eloquently enough of environmental deterioration. To move to a town was to move to a shorter life; To be born in one was to have a less than even chance of surviving infancy. In 1840, 57% of the working-class children of Manchester died before their fifth birthday, compared with 32% in rural districts. The death rate for all England and Wales 1839/40 was 1:45; in Manchester it was 1:32.72, while in the same county the miners of Prescott enjoyed a ratio of 1:47.54.[30] Chadwick produced age-at-death figures in 1842 which show how large a regional and class variation there was in the decline in the national death rate which most probably took place over the first four decades of the nineteenth century (Table 5).

TABLE 5 Average ages at death in 1842
(Arranged in reverse order of life-expectancy for labourers

	Gentry	Tradesmen	Labourers
Liverpool	35	22	15
Bethnal Green	45	26	16
Manchester	38	20	17
Leeds	44	27	19
Derby	49	38	21
Truro	40	33	28
Rutland	52	41	38

A survey of Halifax in 1851 conducted independently reveals the same disturbing pattern. There, 'operatives' were given an average age at death of 22, shopkeepers 24 and the gentry and manufacturers 55.[31]

Such figures, uncorrected for age structures or migration flows, are crude by present-day standards, but there is little doubting the reality of mortality differentials which confirm the wide differences in life expectation which distinguished urban from rural districts and the low life expectation of operatives in manufacturing towns. The figures for Liverpool, however, indicate that shortened working-class lives were not confined to manufacturing towns.

THE HOUSING OF MANUFACTURING AND SIMILAR WORKERS BEFORE THE INDUSTRIAL REVOLUTION

The high-density 'thrown-up' housing of the new industrial towns was foreshadowed in several eighteenth-century cases: 'The fastest expanding industrial centres and great seaports in particular were dramatic exemplars of the problems inherent in mass living on a large scale', being 'cramped, crowded, polluted, unhealthy, and often ugly'. Then, as later, there was no concept of town planning involving zoning of industrial away from residential areas. But as the poorer working-class districts began to display all too vividly an undesirable aspect, so the better-off segregated themselves and avoided by evasion the problems of modern urban living as they have ever since continued to do. The glass manufactories of Bristol were said to darken the city with continual outpourings of smoke and dirt and to almost suffocate the inhabitants with 'noxious effluvia'. In 1760, however, the hills around the city were said to offer to the 'industrious tradesmen', who had been breathing the 'impure air of a close street', the opportunity to 'open his air-pipes nigh chock'd with noisome exhalations', but the propertied classes were ever prone to privatise the open spaces of 'Old England' and by 1761 the 'delightful spot' of Kingsdown was being built upon:

> Each petty tradesmen here must have his seat,
> And vainly thinks the height will make him great:
> But little things look less the more they rise:
> So wrens may mount until they look flies.
> . . .
> Come hither pedlars quit your dusty stalls.
> Here build your seats, and rise your garden walls.
> And when you've built it o'er call it what you will
> 'Twill not be Kingsdown then, but Pedlars Hill.

As the dockyards growth brought a tremendous influx of workers into

Portsmouth, by 1775, on former common land outside the city, had appeared 'a very populous genteel town'.[32]

Even in the great town-building era of Georgian England, there was not an endless market for builders in satisfying the more spacious needs of the bourgeoisie, and profits had to be sought, especially by smaller builders, from constructing high-density, low-quality housing for the working classes. Liverpool's Toxteth has become in our time an infamous symbol of the problems of inner-city life, as even conservative politicians have received a new 'education' from the time-honoured English urban tradition of riot. In 1773/4 a local entrepreneur, Cuthbert Bisbrown, leased land with the idea of building a new town but, reflecting the way in which the building process then worked, had insufficient control over his sub-leasees, who departed from his dream by cramming in high-density cheap housing. There was not enough demand for every builder to construct for the middle class, and so what emerged was a 'maze of close and gloomy courts' with cramped housing and mean and narrow streets.[33]

Speculative building for working-class occupation reinforced existing patterns of high-density living in nucleated town centres. A characteristic approach was the infilling of the backland properties fronting on to the established street pattern. At Leeds, vastly increasing numbers were accommodated within the same area. At Kendal, growth over a century added no new street patterns, while Nottingham, notorious for its overcrowding, grew from intensification rather than by extension. True there was a ring of unenclosed fields surrounding the town, but growth outside was not impossible. There was only a very gradual realisation of the problems being built into this pattern of infilling, only exceptional men like John Wood in 1781 produced plans which could go to the extreme of suggesting separate privies for each household! If there was improvement it came from the increasing use of better materials, notably of brick rather than of timber, not from new approaches to urban housing.[34]

Eighteenth-century conditions which most forshadowed the killer-towns of the industrial revolution were likely to be found where the conditions which produced the industrial town were already in being. A 1791 description of Preston, growing with the new cotton manufacture, will serve to illustrate a late-eighteenth-century glimpse into a nineteenth-century urban future:

> . . . Sudden and great call and temptation for hands from the country, of this county and others, and many distant parts; crowded of course in their lodgings; tempted, by extra gain, to long continued application at sedentary work, in air contaminated both by the exhalation and breathing of many people together, and also by the effluvia of the material used, in confined places; and, though getting good wages, yet . . . provisions being dear . . . living but poorly in diet, these people are frequently visited, especially in autumn and the beginning of winter, with low and nervous fevers; in short

putrid and gaol distempers.[35]

The existence of such conditions does not mean that there was no general deterioration in the quality of urban life in the nineteenth century. First, new units of housing in the expanding towns of the late eighteenth century were for the most part still being supplied at a rate broadly equivalent to the overall rate of growth of population. Before 1801 the number of inhabitants per house actually fell in some towns, although not in exceptional cases like Liverpool where cellar dwellings were already notorious. It seems, too, that the expanding urban population was being accommodated in a multiplication of small dwellings rather than by the sub-division of larger properties into multi-occupied housing.[36] Secondly, there is some evidence that there was, even if limited in its effectiveness and confined in its concerns, some degree of interest in town improvement in the eighteenth century which was later overtaken in the rush to build the 'Coketowns' of the new manufacturing age. Some consideration is merited by the activities of the Pavement Commissions set up by private Acts of parliament to overcome the deficiencies of the parish vestry and the inefficiencies of municipal corporations. These Acts for improvements, such as street paving, removing 'nuisances', street lighting and the provision of a 'watch' to guard against crime, were sufficiently numerous to severally constitute, at least in intent, a reform of urban government. In the late eighteenth and in the early nineteenth centuries a total of more than 300 Acts had been passed, exclusive of those establishing commissioners of sewers. By 1830 only Leicester, Nottingham, Wenlock and Wigan among municipal boroughs of 11,000 or more inhabitants had obtained no such Act. By the late eighteenth century they were sufficiently numerous, according to Dr Corfield, to constitute a 'truly significant part of the system of administration'. In one town after another local powers were sought to deal with such matters as nuisances from animals, encroachments on to the roads and for paving or lighting. The Act of 1790 obtained for Honiton in Devon is a good example of intent. It required that 'streets and public passages were properly paved, or otherwise repaired, and cleansed and lighted, and all nuisances, annoyances and incroachments therein removed, and a regular watch established in the night time'.[37]

Acts give powers to statements of intent, but how effective were they? An historian of local government suggests that they made 'some elementary but important provision for public health'. Especially beneficial where it took place was the substitution of underground sewage from the open 'kennel' and the employment of scavengers to remove night soil and other filth and rubbish. There was, however, a tendency for the improvements to be concentrated other than in the working-class districts of towns, and some commissioners were notoriously inactive. At least they indicated an awareness of the need for communal responsibility over the basic conditions of town life.[38]

In the newer industrial towns of the nineteenth century, such a concern was largely absent before the cholera scares of the 1830s. It was this missing element of 'policing' to which the *Westminster Review* in 1833 attributed the environmental problems of the new manufacturing centres:

> In erecting towns, land was let by proprietors for the most part non-residents, to speculators who unrestrained by any police regulations built houses for the poorer inhabitants, often destitute of the conveniences which minister to comfort and cleanliness – huddled together in confined groups, separated only by narrow streets, and intersected by close courts, alleys and avenues, where filth was permitted to accumulate. The streets not being subjected to the influence of any police laws were permitted to remain unpaved were unscavenged, and consequently became the receptacles of the most disgusting offal.

In such circumstances, Kay noted the 'air of discomfort, if not of squalid and loathsome wretchedness' which pervaded the new towns.[39]

Thirdly, there is some evidence that superior artisan housing occupied by skilled workers did exist in some places in the eighteenth century and in towns noted for their artisan character persisted into the nineteenth. Workers in rural manufacture lived, as the name 'cottage' industry implies, in housing not always distinguishable from that of other rural workers. If they had extra space and, as an imperative of their occupations as weavers and the like, extra light, then this was offset by the disadvantages inherent in home working. The cottage of the rural outworker was often ill-ventilated, damp and cold, and the very fact that work was carried on in it could mean the invasion of living space by noxious fumes and smells as well as pressures on space by the clutter of the manufacturing activity. Nevertheless, rural manufacturing was in the countryside and accordingly allowed access to purer air and more open space.[40]

The homes of town workers were far from salubrious. Before 1770 much of the urban accommodation of groups like weavers and knitters was being provided in the infilling of courts and yards, with the poorest workers living in one-roomed dwellings slightly more comfortable than a stable, perhaps with a loft for sleeping. Slightly better-off workers occupied two-roomed dwellings. In Leeds the lowest class of housing was a single rented room three to six yards square occupied at 4d. (2p) a week mainly by widows and spinsters. Working-class families of four or five people commonly had two rooms, a living room with a sleeping chamber above. Such rooms were usually 14 ft square and rented at 6d. (2½p) a week. For 9d. (4p) a week, better-off artisans could rent a larger cottage with rooms 20 ft square. Taking one place with another, Dr Chapman has suggested that urban cloth workers in the eighteenth century rented houses of only one or two rooms, often single storied and valued between £10 and £30: £10 was the usual value of a stable.[41]

London's artisans tended to occupy tenements in larger buildings. Dr George described the standard dwelling of the artisan even in one of the better trades as a single furnished room, which was often workshop as well as domestic space. Differences in social grade among the workers was marked by the part of the house occupied, by the respectability of the street or court, and by the distinction between the lodger and the room-keeper rather than by the occupation of a greater number of rooms. Yet to Francis Place no advice was more important to offer to the aspiring young artisan than that he should by always trying to keep two rooms allow some differentiation between working and domestic space.[42]

Despite the prevalence of low-quality accommodation for large numbers of eighteenth-century artisans, there are indications that some artisan groups lived in rather better houses, which they sometimes owned themselves. Many trades had had 'good days' of relative prosperity and these periods produced their crop of better buildings. Representative of this were the three-storey buildings favoured by such as weavers or watchmakers where large attic windows, still recognisable in some towns today, provided the necessary light for an upper storey workroom. Lancashire's 'golden age' for weavers of 1788 to 1811 produced such purpose buildings. Samuel Bamford described an example:

> My uncle's domecile, like all the others consisted of one principal room called the 'house', on the same floor as this was a loomshop capable of holding four looms, and in the rear of the house on the same floor with this were a small kitchen and a buttery. Over the house and the loom shop were chambers; and over the kitchen and buttery was another apartment and a flight of stairs. The whole of the rooms were lighted by windows of small square pains, framed in lead.[43]

In such periods of prosperity, artisan earnings were sufficiently stable to allow subscription to building clubs as a means to home ownership. In Nottingham the periods of artisan prosperity saw a better class of housing built on the outskirts of the town, as in the cotton boom of 1784. These houses, with scullery, pantry, two upstairs bedrooms and 450 square yard gardens, contrasted with the one-room dwellings of poorer workers in the town and the survival of the rock-dwellings, the walled-up caves to the north-east. The better houses produced in this boom were essentially three boxes on top of each other for living, sleeping and working. The second floor had large workshop windows, and most had a cellar underneath: 'The houses of the working class at the present time, generally consist of a cellar, a room to dwell in, called the house-place, a chamber, a shop over it to work in, a room in the roof, called a cock-loft and a small pantry.'[44]

Frequently they were built back-to-back or 'blindback' because of the infilling of old frontages, especially during a second housing boom of the 1820s. Prosperous independent knitters and weavers could, by the standards of the time, then build substantial houses incorporating workshops, though in Leicester a garden workshop was more common. In Nottingham the 1820s boom produced a spread of three-storey houses with gardens into the green belt around the town, but the 'twist net' fever also produced slum housing as congestion resulted from the inflooding of workers. Houses were split, cellars used for residential purposes, and even stables used for habitation. By 1835 the typical urban framework knitter was as ill-lodged as he was fed and clothed, and the court in which he resided was described as 'an abundance of small tenements, let to many stockingers . . . and there being many families, and even lodgers in all, it swarmed with population. Maggots in carrion flesh, or mites in cheese, could not be huddled more closely together.'[45]

That well-paid artisans could live in better accommodation than most workers is also suggested by the reputation which artisan towns like Birmingham and Sheffield carried into the nineteenth century. In both places, clubs helped some to home-ownership. In Sheffield, although casual workers, mostly Irish, lived in worse conditions, some of the artisans managed through building clubs around 1830 to build houses on plots paid for over ten to fourteen years. The great centre of the cutlery manufacture was certainly growing through infilling into a compact mass as the open spaces were being swallowed up in the two or three decades before 1850. The population trebled between 1801 and 1850, twice the national average, but the standard artisan's cottage remained brick-built and slate-roofed. It had a cellar, living room, first-floor bedroom and second attic bedroom. The cellar was not usually lived in, while the living room was used for cooking and washing. The man, wife and smaller children slept in the chamber, while older children and perhaps a lodger slept in the attic. Houses were one room deep and built back-to-back, with a rear staircase against the partition with the backed-on house. Privies served from two to twelve households. At a rent of around 2s. 6d. (12½p) a week, landlords expected to make around 6–7%. Standards of housing began to deteriorate in the 1840s and 1850s under pressure of population, but for the first half of the nineteenth century had been above those of other industrial towns. Above all, Sheffield's skilled artisans continued to occupy *separate* houses with a low density per house: 'We have not yet', wrote an observer in 1833, 'got into the abominable way of cellars or of many families living in the same house.'[46]

Birmingham, England's other town famous for its 'independent' artisans through the first half of the nineteenth century, also showed substantial evidence of infilling from the early eighteenth century. By 1836 a survey revealed 2,030 courts containing 12,254 tenements. These varied in size, but the average number of tenements per court in 1841 was only six. It was usual for every Birmingham family to have its own dwelling, and cellar dwellings were unknown. Birmingham artisans had a proclivity for clubs formed for many purposes, and housing was prominent among them. Those of the 1780s and 1790s advanced £60 to £120 on shares of 5–10s. (25–50p) repayable over fourteen years. Such sums were capable of building artisan homes of two up and two down. What was true of Birmingham's artisan elite was not so of the rural outworking districts of the Black Country, where the nail-makers lived in one-roomed huts on the waste. Compared in 1832 to the 'miserable cabins of the wild Irish', they were made of fire clay mixed with straw and stubble and had thatched roofs and no windows. They seemed, by that date, to have changed little from 1753 when a visitor, allowing that Wolverhampton had 'good brick houses', found the artisans on the outskirts lived in 'many wretched hovels'.[47]

TYPES OF URBAN WORKING-CLASS HOUSING IN THE NINETEENTH CENTURY

It has recently been suggested that a snapshot should not be taken for a motion picture and that mortality cannot be inferred to have worsened for city-dwellers in general because it became higher in fast-growing cities. In fact mortality improved in the countryside *and* in most towns. The point can be accepted, but it does not change the fact that environmental deterioration meant that *despite* their lower wages and nutritional levels, the life-expectancy of farm labourers remained significantly above that of industrial workers: a difference still manifest in 1850. It has also been suggested that the bourgeoisie was the social group most concentrated in the unhealthy cities. Assuming such to have been the case, it is still consistent with Chadwick's tabulation which shows that tradesmen's expectations of life were also dependent on location: in Rutlandshire their expectation was *twice* that of Manchester. But in all cases they had measurably longer expectations of life than did labourers.

The new industrial towns of the north and Midlands have been associated with one particular ill-famed form of house: the back-to-back. Yet, however much modern opinion might look down upon a house which was totally deprived of through ventilation and, so light could penetrate, limited to one room deep, it was not looked upon with disfavour by contemporaries. Its best attribute was that it allowed scarce urban space to be used in a way which gave to each dwelling its own front door. It was a form of dwelling intended from the start for working-class occupation. Originating in the eighteenth century and although known in Bermondsey as early as 1706, they never became popular in London, but became characteristic of industrial towns further north. At best they can be represented as a crude attempt to allow a separation of living from sleeping, and the fact that they were not thought of as 'undesirable' is indicated by the numbers which were erected by artisan building societies, as well as by speculative builders. Ten per cent of housing in the borough of Leeds was of this form in 1801, which allowed builders the chance to secure minimum returns from the maximum number of houses per acre, having a typical floor area of five yards square. In such towns as Leeds, where infilling had increased from the eighteenth century, 'blindback' building was already common and there was no abrupt transition between building against a yard wall and building against a second house. In Nottingham in 1831 of 11,000 houses more than 7,000 were back-to-back. Concern with the absence of through ventilation led to their outlawing in Manchester in 1884 and in Sheffield in 1864. However, they continued to be built in Liverpool and in Bradford until 1881. In Leeds they totalled 60% of the total number of houses completed year by year until 1905 and some were still being built in 1937.[48]

Consideration of other types of working-class housing supports Professor Burnett's suggestion that the purpose-built back-to-back has a comparatively high rating.[49] At the bottom of the housing pile, floating and immigrant, especially Irish, communities filled the common lodging houses. 'What physical and moral atmosphere reigns in these holes', proclaimed Engels. They were in Manchester the focus of crime from their forced centralisation of vice. In the late 1840s around 90% of Liverpool's lodging housekeepers were of Irish extraction. Next up the housing ladder came the separately occupied cellar. In Liverpool, where they were especially notorious, large proportions of the population lived in semi-subterranean homes, which at best were unsatisfactory from every point of view, and at worst were 'disgusting and offensive insults to humanity'. In that city in 1790, 6,780 out of a population of 53,583 lived in cellars, which had, from the first been built for residential use. By 1797 they were being described as a major abuse extending even into the houses of the 'mediocrity' who were beginning to let their cellars for separate occupation. To describe such dwellings as 'damp' would be an understatement. A description of 1841 tells of a visit to the wife of a labouring man:

> She had been confined only a few days and herself and infant were lying on straw in a vault, through the outer cellar, with a clay floor impervious to water. There was no light or ventilation in it and the air was dreadful. I had to walk on bricks across the floor to reach her bedside, as the floor itself was flooded with stagnant water.

Such were not the extreme conditions of an unfortunate few. Gaskell in 1833 estimated Manchester's cellar population as around 20,000, which hardly seems impressionistic when it is related to a counting of 7,307 cellar dwellings in Liverpool with each containing an average of 3.29 persons.[50]

Above the cellar, in both senses, came the rented room or rooms in divided tenement buildings. In England, unlike on the Continent, purpose-built flats were not built for the working classes. Rooms were generally provided by the subdivision of larger houses originally occupied by middle-class families. The descent of such properties into multi-occupation is the clearest of indicators of the decline of an area into a slum. In Liverpool in the 1790s many hundreds of large houses which did not rent as a whole at more than £4-6 per annum were said to have crowded into them eighteen to twenty persons from cellar to garret, and from 1810 on the conversion of middle-class housing into working-class tenements gained momentum as the middle class moved out from the city centre. At the bottom, the line between the poorest single room and the lodging house is barely definable, but there was a range of quality and status. Subdivision into floors or rooms was often informal and unrecorded, and below ordinary letting sub-letting went on. In all large towns the poorer working classes occupied not houses but a room or rooms in a house. Above the poor, the artisan striving for decency would aspire to two rooms as the 'irreducible minimum . . . the difference between a home and a mere shelter: with two rooms one could begin to take pride, to cook and clean, furnish and decorate, comfort and cherish the family'. Many, perhaps most, of London's working classes aspired to no more than this, renting for around 2s. 6d. to 4s. (12½–20p) a week. Above this level only the more securely employed 'aristocrats of labour' could hope to occupy a whole floor of three or four rooms. Such a tenement, Mayhew estimated in the mid-nineteenth century, would have cost from 5s. to 7s. (25–35p) per week.[51]

The best kind of purpose-built working-class housing was the through terrace, where the back alley access for the night soil men gave a measure of superiority over the back-to-back which, however well built, was inseparable from the court system with its piled up filth. Where working-class housing was built in London, it was commonly of this type, which was also more common in Bristol and in parts of the Potteries. But in general, with respect to urban working-class housing and its place in the standard of living debate, it is difficult not to agree with Professor Burnett that there was simply a 'perpetuation of existing inadequacies and already low standards in a new environment in which their scale and intensity were further heightened'. The outcome of the new environment was that no aspect of life suffered such cumulative deterioration as a result of the industrial revolution than did public health.[52]

EMPLOYER-PROVIDED HOUSING

Some mention has already been made of employer-provided housing in mining and agricultural districts, and manufacturers too sometimes housed their own workers, especially in the period of water-powered mills in remote districts. Such housing could be among the best of its time. In 1849 a reporter found the village built around the mills of the Ashworth cotton firm near Bolton to be 'as sweet, wholesome, and smokeless as it could be were its denizens the most bucolic hinds of Devon'. Here were not squalid hovels, but 'good stone cottages', some with two or three bedrooms. Most of the town of Ashton-under-Lyne was new, having grown up with the advent of power-weaving and, in contrast with the squalor of the old part, the new districts were full of comfortable cottages provided by the factory owners: 'every mill surrounded with neat streets of perfectly uniform dwellings, clean and cheerful in appearance'. Rented at from 3–4s. (15–20p) a week with an extra few shillings a year for a garden, they represented around 10% of the wages of the highest paid, and 20% of the average for all workers. Not all colliery-owned houses deserved the bad reputation which mining cottages had in general; there were exceptions like those provided by the Fitzwilliam collieries in south Yorkshire which were described in 1842 as 'superior' with four rooms, pantry, pigsty and a long garden at the rear. With a convenience to every six or seven houses, they were let at 2s. (10p) a week.[53]

It would be quite misleading to regard such examples as representative of company housing in general. Modern views on factory villages are conditioned by two things: a tendency to associate them necessarily with community-building improvers like Robert Owen or the Strutts and, from an interest in vernacular architecture, to evaluate all from the few built strongly enough to survive to our age. As Dr Chapman has pointed out, widespread inferior accommodation has left no record or physical trace. Responses to the Factory Commissioners in 1833 – an investigation not usually thought of as biased against mill-owners – show that only a minority of mill-owners provided housing for their employees: that only a portion of these did so in any quantity, and a smaller one from motives of philanthropy or 'improving' idealism. Factory 'colonies' represented less than 10% of all English cotton concerns and had, in percentages, declined rapidly once steam power relocated the mill in the town. The few colonies which did remain at mid-century were often substantial. The Strutts at Belper housed 2,000 people in 500 houses, while the Arkwrights owned 266 houses at Cromford. Ashworth's Egerton works housed 1,200 hands in 1842. Such provision was equal to the better urban housing built at Manchester since a local act of 1844 had banned back-to-backs, but in Yorkshire the back-to-back tradition was continued in factory housing as it was in speculative building. In neither county did the large majority of mills make any housing provision. Of 881 large firms making returns in 1833, 299 gave no details, 414 stated no provision and of the 168 who provided some housing most only provided a few.[54] Outside of textile mills and mines, examples of company housing could be found in metal manufacture, in potteries and in engineering (for example by Boulton and Watt in Birmingham).

The association of factory 'colonies' with the rural era of water-powered mills reflects the need of entrepreneurs to create their own communities of labourers: the more especially since early mills depended more upon the labour of women and children than of men. Dr Chapman has suggested that housing was often provided at a second stage by an entrepreneur who had first taken advantage of pre-existing local labour. Arkwright's move to Cromford in 1770 was to the already available labour of the wives and children of lead miners, while Strutt moved to a major nail-making centre at Belper in 1778. Arkwright built no houses before 1777 and Strutt none before the 1790s.[55]

Standards of provided housing varied widely. The long gap in time between the factory mechanisation of spinning and that of weaving is interestingly revealed by the fact that Arkwright, Watson and Peel all built houses whose lower rooms were occupied by looms or frames: in such instances the separation of work from home was hardly complete. Nor was the ideal of one family to a dwelling necessarily adhered to. Davison and Hawksley, the Nottinghamshire pioneers of mechanised worsted spinning, built in 1788 a row of fifteen three-storey houses known as 'Cottage Row' in which each dwelling was converted into two-roomed flats. Single workpeople and apprentices were 'forced' on to families as lodgers. Oral tradition spoke of 1,000 apprentices living in one row of eighteen cottages![56]

Motives for housing provision varied, but the chance of profit was certainly among them. Rents as high as 3s. or 4s. (15p or 20p) a week offered reasonable returns on building costs, while the chance to operate 'company stores' meant that the exploitative truck system was especially associated with company villages. A strong desire to promote moral reformation or a crusading zeal to better the condition of the workers were possessed by only a few mill-owners. Many more could, however, appreciate the extra element of discipline which owning the houses of their labour force afforded: employee's habits could be regulated outside as well as inside working hours. At Ashton-under-Lyne the mill workers were even watched at weekends: 'If he does not mend his manners he may look out for other employment.' Ashworths so effectively discouraged married women with children from working that only four were employed. The sale of liquor could be controlled. Sunday School attendance enforced, or even, in one recorded case, membership of the Volunteers required. The ability to exclude trade unionism was especially useful. All those who joined the Miners' Association from the Fitzwilliam collieries in 1844 were told to leave their work and their houses, while the eviction of the striking Durham miners and their families in that year is a well-known black moment in English history. The difference between the village mill-owner and the town-owner was well expressed in the 1830s: the former 'commanded the population' while the latter were 'in some degree commanded by the customs of the people'. As the Hammonds put it, the employees who lived in the factory 'colonies' were not citizens of this or that town, but hands of this or that master.[57]

REFERENCES AND NOTES

1. **H. J. Dyos** and **D. A. Reeder**, 'Slums and suburbs', in **H. J. Dyos** & **M. Wolff** (eds), *The Victorian City: Images and Realities*, Routledge, 1978, vol. II, p. 361.
2. Ibid., loc. cit.
3. **E. Gauldie**, *Cruel Habitations. A History of Working Class Housing 1780–1918*, Unwin, 1974, p. 49.
4. Ibid., p. 22; **J. Burnett**, *A Social History of Housing 1815–1970*, Methuen edn, 1980, p. 36; **William Dodd**, *The Labouring Classes of England*, Boston, 1848, repr. A. M. Kelley, New Jersey, 1976, p. 38; **P. E. Razzell** and **R. W. Wainwright** (eds), *The Victorian Working Class: Selections from Letters to the Morning Chronicle*, Cass, 1973, p. 3.
5. Gauldie, *Cruel Habitations*, p. 23.
6. Ibid., pp. 54, 57.
7. Burnett, *History of Housing*, pp. 48–53, 36.
8. Ibid., pp. 43–4.
9. Razzell and Wainwright, *Victorian Working Class*, p. 3.
10. Dodd, *Labouring Classes*, pp. 38, 43.
11. Gauldie, *Cruel Habitations*, pp. 48, 34; Razzell and Wainwright, *Victorian Working Class*, pp. 12, 53; *Blackwoods Edinburgh Magazine*, XXVII, April 1830, p. 554.
12. Gauldie, *Cruel Habitations*, pp. 68, 74; Razzell and Wainwright, *Victorian Working Class*, pp. 3–4; quoted in **D. Rubinstein** (ed.), *Victorian Homes*, David and Charles, 1974, p. 113.
13. **A. Kussmaul**, *Servants in Husbandry in Early Modern England*, Cambridge U.P., 1981, pp. 23–4, 26–7.
14. Dodd, *Labouring Classes*, p. 55; **C. J. Hunt**, *The Lead Miners of the Northern Pennines*, Manchester U.P., 1970, p. 143.
15. Razzell and Wainwright, *Victorian Working Class*, pp. 226–7.
16. Hunt, *Lead Miners*, pp. 145–8.
17. Ibid., pp. 138–45.
18. **M. E. Weaver**, 'Industrial housing in west Cornwall', *Industrial Archaeology*, vol. 3, no. 1, p. 24.
19. The contemporary sources on which this account of Cornish miners' housing is based are fully documented in my unpublished thesis: 'The

labouring miner in Cornwall c.1740–1870: a study in social history', University of Warwick, Ph.D., 1971, pp. 103–9.

20. **Arthur Young**, *A Six Months Tour through the North of England*, 1771, II, p. 263.

21. **C. Fisher**, *Custom, Work and Market Capitalism: The Forest of Dean Colliers, 1788–1888*, Croom Helm, 1981, pp. x-xiii, 107. For an account of Kingswood in the eighteenth century, see **R. W. Malcolmson**, 'A set of ungovernable people: the Kingswood colliers in the eighteenth century', in **J. Brewer** & **J. Styles** (eds), *An Ungovernable People. The English and their Law in the seventeenth and eighteenth centuries*, Hutchinson, 1980, pp. 85–127.

22. Gauldie, *Cruel Habitations*, p. 65; Hunt, *Lead Miners*, p. 143.

23. Razzell and Wainwright, *Victorian Working Class*, pp. 225–7.

24. Ibid., pp. 245–6.

25. **Arthur Young**, *Tours in England and Wales selected from the Annals of Agriculture*, 1932, p. 142.

26. **S. D. Chapman**, (ed.), *The History of Working-Class Housing: a Symposium*, David and Charles, Newton Abbot, 1971, p. 12; **M. I. Thomis**, *The Town Labourer and the Industrial Revolution*, Batsford, 1974, p. 52; **P. Mathias**, *The First Industrial Nation*, Methuen, 1969, p. 208; **E. P. Thompson**, *The Making of the English Working Class*, Penguin, 1968, pp. 352–3.

27. **Henry Fielding**, Causes of the Late Increase in Robbers, 1751, p. 75; **F. I. Engels**, *The Condition of the Working Class in England*, Granada edn, 1982, pp. 60–1.

28. Ibid., pp. 76–7, 96; Razzell and Wainwright, *Victorian Working Class*, pp. 166–7, 170.

29. Engels, *Working Class*, pp. 72–3; Razzell and Wainwright, *Victorian Working Class*, pp. 213–14.

30. Engels, *Working Class*, pp. 136–8, quoting official statistics.

31. This table is reproduced in many places; it can be found, for example, in Thompson, *The Making*, p. 365.

32. **P. J. Corfield**, *The Impact of English Towns 1700–1800*, Oxford U.P., 1982, pp. 178–9; **P. T. Marcy**, *Eighteenth Century Views of Bristol and Bristolians*, Bristol Branch of the Historical Association, 1966, p. 14; **A. Geddes**, *Portsmouth during the Great French Wars 1770–1800*, Portsmouth City Council, 1970, p. 3.

33. Corfield, *English Towns*, pp. 179–80.

34. Ibid., pp. 180–1.

35. **J. L.** and **B. Hammond**, *The Town Labourer*, 1917, repr. Longmans, 1978, p. 30.

36. Corfield, *English Towns*, pp. 181–2.

37. **B. Keith-Lucas**, *The Unreformed Local Government System*, Croom Helm, 1980, pp. 108, 112; Corfield, *English Towns*, p. 157.

38. Keith-Lucas, *Local Government*, p. 116.

39. *Westminster Review*, no. 18, 1833, p. 386.

40. See the discussion in **J. G. Rule**, *The Experience of Labour in Eighteenth-century Industry*, Croom Helm, 1981, p. 90.

41. **S. D. Chapman**, intro. to *The Devon Cloth Industry in the Eighteenth Century*, Torquay, Devon and Cornwall Record Society, vol. 23, 1978, pp. xvi-xvii discusses these problems from the evidence of insurance

records. See also his article, 'Workers' housing in the cotton factory colonies, 1770–1850', *Textile History*, VII, 1976, pp. 113–16.

42. **M. D. George**, *London Life in the Eighteenth Century*, 1925, repr. Penguin, 1966, p. 104; **Francis Place**, *Autobiography*, ed. M. Thale, Cambridge U.P., 1972, p. 116.

43. **Samuel Bamford**, *Early Days*, repr. Cass, 1967, pp. 98–9.

44. **S. D. Chapman**, 'Working-class housing in Nottingham during the Industrial Revolution', in Chapman, *Working Class Housing*, p. 139.

45. Ibid., pp. 135–9, 143, 151.

46. This account of Sheffield housing is based on **S. Pollard**, *A History of Labour in Sheffield*, Liverpool U.P., 1959, pp. 4–21.

47. For Birmingham's housing, see **S. D. Chapman** and **J. N. Bartlett**, 'The contribution of building clubs and freehold land societies to working-class housing in Birmingham', in Chapman, *Working Class Housing*, pp. 223–44; Chapman, 'Workers' housing in the cotton factory colonies', p. 115; Razzell and Wainwright, *Victorian Working Class*, p. 288.

48. Burnett, *History of Housing*, pp. 71–72; **M. W. Beresford**, 'The back-to-back house in Leeds, 1787–1937', in Chapman, *Working Class Housing*, pp. 95–113; Pollard, *Labour in Sheffield*, p. 100; Chapman, 'Nottingham', p. 152; **J. H. Treble**, 'Liverpool working class housing, 1801–1851', in Chapman, *Working Class Housing*, p. 168.

49. Burnett, *History of Housing*, pp. 71–2.

50. Engels, *Working Class*, pp. 98–9; Treble, 'Liverpool', pp. 168, 179; Burnett, *History of Housing*, p. 61.

51. Treble, 'Liverpool', pp. 168–9; Burnett, *History of Housing*, p. 67. With the rapid nineteenth-century expansion of Newcastle, most of the poorer classes in Gateshead in 1850 lived in tenements: 'Few mechanics can afford to pay for more than one room', **R. Grace**, 'Tyneside housing in the nineteenth century', in **N. McCord** (ed.), *Essays in Tyneside Labour History*, Newcastle upon Tyne Polytechnic, 1977, p. 180.

52. Burnett, *History of Housing*, pp. 77, 93; Razzell and Wainwright, *Victorian Working Class*, pp. 248–9.

53. Ibid., p. 188, pp. 183–5; **G. Mee**, 'Employer–employee relationships in the Industrial Revolution: the FitzWilliam collieries', in **S. Pollard** and **C. Holmes** (eds), *Essays in the Economic and Social History of South Yorkshire*, South Yorks. C. C., 1976, p. 49.

54. **S. D. Chapman**, 'Workers' housing in the cotton factory colonies', pp. 134, 117–31; **S. Pollard**, 'The factory village in the Industrial Revolution', *Economic History Review* (second series), LXXIX, 1964, p. 518.

55. Chapman, 'Cotton factory colonies', pp. 118–20.

56. Ibid., p. 126.

57. Razzell and Wainwright, *Victorian Working Class*, pp. 184, 186; Mee, 'FitzWilliam collieries', p. 57; Pollard, 'Factory village', pp. 526–7, 514.

Part Two

WORK

Chapter 4

THE WAGE AND ITS FORM

In 1850 the stone quarrymen of Swanage in Dorset were 'discovered' by the correspondent of a national newspaper to be a distinctly peculiar group of workers. Conditioned by centuries of tradition, they were exclusive to the point of refusing to work with anyone whose father had not been a local quarryman or whose mother had not been the daughter of one. Even quarrymen from nearby Portland were not accepted. But most peculiar of all was the way in which they were paid for their labour:

> All such payments which are not made in actual money – those so made being very few – or in goods, are made either in stone or bread. The workers in the quarries are paid in stone, and it is for stone that they receive in exchange such articles as they consume. It is quite true that there is a money value put on everything but stone is almost the universal substitute for money.

Workmen were engaged at an agreed money value of so much per day or per week but at settlement received that value in stone. A class of merchants kept goods which they exchanged for the stone: but bread, not money, was the medium of exchange. Each kept a bakehouse and loaves from these constituted the 'small change' of the district. Expensive items such as a pair of new boots might be exchanged directly for their value in stone, and some publicans also accepted a quantity of stone against which quarrymen might drink, but for most ready money transactions *bread* was commonly used. 'If a woman wants a piece of ribbon she must take a loaf with her to the shop.' Various dealers subsequently converted the bread into money. These stages of discounting effectively reduced the daily wage of 3s. (15p) to 2s. (10p) and not surprisingly the men regarded the system as exploitative and wished the merchants would deal in money, but did not seem to expect that their employers would pay in anything other than stone. In an industry characterised by small-scale producers, the status of labourer was itself a fluid one. At times a quarryman might take a piece of ground and employ one or two others; at other times he might himself be so employed. Payment in stone rather than in money served to deny any real status difference between employer and employee.

This was, in 1850, an exceptional case and the reporter hardly expected his readers to readily believe that 'so rude and primitive a state of society is to be met with within a few hours ride of the Metropolis', but it reminds us that the social historian of the period can understand little of the complexities of the remuneration of labour if he carries back simple notions of a money wage offered in exchange for measured labour time or for piecework.[1]

Sub-contracting was widespread, and in many cases, for example in mining, increasing rather than decreasing in extent and replacing earlier forms of direct hiring. In metal mines especially, intricate forms of 'bargaining' linked remuneration both to the quantity and quality of the tin, lead or copper ore raised. Fishermen commonly worked, before the trawling era, on the 'share'. In Cornwall, of the profit of a lugger's catch, one-seventh went to the boat-owner, half of the remainder to the owners of the nets and from the residue the hands received equal shares with the boy taking half a share. Typically a crew consisted of six or seven men and the boy, but where the owner was able-bodied and male, he commonly sailed as skipper and took his crew share as well as the boat's. If he provided nets, then he added that share too, but other fishermen in the crew might have provided nets, and they too then took a part of the three-sevenths share going to the nets. Nets were expensive and easily lost or destroyed so it would frequently happen that a man who had sailed on one trip as a net-owner as well as share-hand might find himself only in the position of the latter on his next trip.[2]

Fully independent producers in agriculture and in manufacturing were a declining class throughout the period. Adam Smith in 1776 could roundly declare that in Europe twenty men worked for a master for each one who was his own. What was generally true of Europe was more especially so of England where proletarianisation had proceeded to the point where the great economist was able to assume throughout the *Wealth of Nations* that wages could be understood to be what 'they usually are', that is the contract between a worker, who was one person, with the owner of the stock which employed him, who was another. An investigation of London in 1800 has shown that in that great centre of the artisan trades the truly self-employed amounted to only around 5% or 6% of the working-class population.[3]

Proletarianisation in the general sense of a reduction of the bulk of the working population to living from the sale of their labour power was the dominant process of the age and it was very well advanced before the factory mode of production was at all widespread. The margins, however, remained blurred. As they struggled in the second quarter of the nineteenth century towards refining the language which described the growing divide between capital and labour, the early socialists found it impossible to insist upon the exclusion of *working* masters from the latter. But the defining conditions of owning no land, or of working on materials owned by another, or of having no involvement in the marketing of the product of one's labour did not lead quickly to a simple and single concept of the 'wage'.

In England, proletarianisation had given eighteenth-century agriculture a structure unique in Europe in being based not on a peasantry but on a class of landless labourers. Yet even within that class, variations were significant. In the first place there were status differentials reflected in the higher wages of such as carters or shepherds, and in the second place there were important differences in the form of hire. At one extreme the declining but still important class of farm servants were hired for the year and board was the basis of their remuneration. With regional variations in the rate of decline their numbers were shrinking as living-out labourers provided a more profitable source of labour, but there was some contrary movement as activities like dairying provided increasing demand for living-in female servants like Hardy's Tess in counties like Dorset.[4]

Farm labourers' wages were usually stated in the form of so many shillings per week, but that should not be taken to imply, especially in the southern counties, that they were normally hired and fired by the week. Increasingly through that bitter age which followed the ending of the French Wars and persisted through the hungry forties, labourers were taken on by the day and only for the number of days that their labour was needed. To say, wrote one writer in 1849, that wages in Suffolk were 8s. (40p) a week was a 'perfect delusion'. They were paid only when needed, got nothing when sick, or in bad weather, and the employers even stopped their wages on a nationally declared day of General Thanksgiving.[5] It is small wonder when 4–5s. (20–25p) was a more realistic figure that it should have been reckoned that living-in servants with £8–10 per year on top of their board were usually better off. Since, however, living-in was confined to the unmarried it was, even where it still existed, a stage in a man's life rather than a continuing alternative to underpaid and extremely casual day labour.

Between the living-in farm servant and the day labourer came another form of hiring, chiefly in the north. In Durham 'hinds', superior hands usually with authority over other labourers, had rent-free cottages, and on top of wages of 10–12s. (50–60p) a week, substantial allowances of potatoes, grain, butter and milk worth a further 4s. (20p); they had the security of a yearly hiring. A farm of 200 acres usually employed two hinds but drew the rest of its labour from day workers, who with a 'regular' 12s. 6d. (62½p) a week in the 1840s were much better off than their southern brothers. In Northumberland existed another form of the hind system where the hind was paid chiefly or even wholly in kind and which embraced most of the farm workers of the county.[6] Shepherds and drovers in the northern counties were given a number of beasts for every hundred they tended as well as being supplied with wheat, oats and potatoes. In the Lake District the predominant economy of small farms created a low demand for agriculture labour, but where it existed food was usually provided. In east Yorkshire 'the mode of paying wages' in 1842 was for farmers to make a deduction for the supply of a mid-day meal amounting to about half: leaving the equal amount to take home for rent and feeding the labourer's family. The farmers liked the hard labour performed by full-stomached men, but the system was considered a 'great evil' by those concerned with the welfare of women and children.[7]

Wages partly paid in kind existed elsewhere, for example in the form of cider and grain in parts of the West Country, but were in general of decreasing value. The extra labour of harvest time was almost always separately remunerated and those earnings were relied upon for the payment of rent and, if possible, the replacement of clothing. Agricultural employment for women and children was even more casual than for men. Although in parts of the north the supplying of the labour of a wife (or 'surrogate wife') was a condition of the hind's bond, for the most part female farm labour was task oriented. They were called in to work not only at harvest time, but for potato or pea planting, while children both helped at these tasks and were directly employed for stone-picking and bird-scaring:

> I do not remember the time when I did not earn my living. My first occupation was, driving the small birds from the turnip seed, and the rooks from the peas. When I trudged afield, with my wooden bottle and my satchell over my shoulders, I was hardly able to climb the gates and stiles, and, at the close of day, to reach home was a task of infinite labour. My next employment was weeding wheat, and leading a single horse at harrowing barley. Hoeing peas followed, and hence I arrived at the honour of joining the reapers in harvest, driving the team and holding the plough.[8]

The increasingly casual nature of female employment on the land, and its impact on the standard of living of rural families, has been discussed above. Truck payment has been less studied in agriculture than in manufacturing and mining, but its existence was widespread wherever extreme irregularity of employment did not make it inapplicable. Towards the middle of the nineteenth century, sub-contracting began to appear in a new form in parts of East Anglia. The 'gang system' involved men, women and children under 'gang masters' who contracted with the farmers to supply mixed labour groups:

> There is a complete disseverment between the farmer and the labourer; the farmer has no interest either in the character or condition of the latter; the whole power as well as responsibility is delegated to an ignorant and grasping gangsman, whose tyranny is the more oppressive in that he is little if at all superior either in intellect or station to the labourer.

Wages were pushed to the lowest levels, and the gang masters were notorious for truck-trading.[9]

MANUFACTURING AND MINING

Outside of agriculture the starting point for any discussion of wage forms is the distinction between those who sold simple labour power and those who sold *skilled* labour power. Common labourers could expect neither the level of remuneration nor the regularity of employment of the skilled labourer, though the latter was certainly not immune from uncertain levels of both. In both categories London wages tended to be higher than provincial ones, and everywhere women were largely excluded from the ranks of the skilled. Adam Smith thought the wages of masons and bricklayers in London to be from 50–100% above those of their associated labourers, being from 15–18s. (75–90p) compared with 9–10s. (45–50p) In the provinces they were respectively 7s. to 8s. (35–40p) and 4–5s. (20–25p). Dr George believed the wages of labourers in the building trades to have been generally around two-thirds of the level of craftsmen for the eighteenth century, while Professor Hobsbawm has suggested a twofold differential between skilled and ordinary labourers was one of 'great antiquity and persistence'. But this differential refers to rates rather than to actual earnings and for them a ration of 2:3 or 3:5 was usual.[10]

Unskilled labourers are the forgotten 'poor, bloody infantry' of the army of labour. While the connection between gender and the means of acquiring a skill has been given some attention, generally speaking the wage forms and levels of common labour are not easily recoverable by historians. From time to time groups like dockers emerge in greater detail, as do special eighteenth-century groups like coal-heavers. Usually this is because through a *de facto* control over entry they were able to secure some of the benefits of a restricted labour supply which the skilled man usually obtained through the institution of apprenticeship. Dockers were in general only slowly emerging, at most ports as a distinct labour group. To one observer of 1850, London's dockers were still the epitome of unskilled muscle power, 'a striking instance of mere brute force'. Every kind of man could be found at the docks from failed tradesmen through old soldiers and foreign refugees to discharged servants and, indeed, 'anyone who wants a loaf and is willing to work for it'. It was one of the few places in the Metropolis where men could get employment without 'either character or recommendation'. Hiring was casual in the extreme. The wind determined the arrival of ships and hence the work available, so earnings with overtime could reach 15s. (75p) a week or sink to nothing. The docker had already become the symbol of casual employment. Yet by the 1840s there were signs of forms of hiring which were to become characteristic. At St Katherine's dock a preference system was being worked whereby privileged workers could qualify for a 'ticket' giving them first chance of work. They formed the permanent core of the labour force and vacancies in their limited numbers were supplied from the best of the 'preferable' labourers, and in turn the gaps which they left from the residue. Proportions reveal the persisting casual nature of most dock labour: 250 permanent labourers were supplemented by only 150 preferable labourers on a dock where at the peak of activity 1,713 labourers could be engaged in a day with an average of 1,086 and a low point of 515. Of those who carried goods to and from the docks, we know even less than of those who laboured on them, but there were very many of them: Liverpool had an estimated 3,000 carters by 1849.[11]

Many of those who manufactured goods by hand methods belonged to some extent to the ranks of the skilled. Their degree of skill varied considerably, but even the most degraded outworking weaver of plain cloth was not thought of, nor regarded himself, as a common labourer even if his wages were at worst quite as low and his regularity of employment as uncertain. Historians who attempt to analyse the responses of groups such as handloom weavers and framework knitters even in their years of decline without reference to this, distort the self-image of such men; 'common weaver' was a humble enough ascription, but it was still of a different order from common labourer.

To note the existence of a differential in pay and conditions related to skill is a starting point, but to make sense of the 'wage' in eighteenth-century manufacturing and, indeed, into the nineteenth century, a myriad of forms have to be investigated. To know the wages of the shipwright, the historian needs to understand: 'treble days, double days, day-and-a-half, two for one, task, job, common hours, nights and tides' – not all of which mean what they seem to mean. Around 1800 the workers at papermills in the south of England were customarily paid for an eight-hour day, yet their standard day was twelve hours with overtime rates. In 1796 their employers had complained that because of this a demand for an increase of 3–4s. (15–20p) a week, which they were representing as modest, amounted in fact to a demand for an extra 7s. 6d. (37½p).[12]

The dominant mode of production before the factory, and for a long time unevenly alongside it, was the 'putting-out' system of home-working to which time wages were obviously inappropriate, but characteristic of this mode was the wide difference between the rate for the work and the final settlement. The usual piece rate was the basis of an agreement but actual remuneration depended upon a variety of adjustments. Dominant among these deductions were 'stoppages' made by employers on a variety of pretexts. Some were straightforward such as rent for premises or for looms, frames or similar equipment, but it must not be expected that they were fixed at appropriate market levels. Rather they frequently provided an opportunity for employers to lower wages without changing their nominal rate. The framework knitters of the East Midlands were a group whose employers were particularly notorious for such abuses. A stocking-frame cost around £50 and by 1800 few knitters owned their own, despite the fact that in times of slack trade a second-hand one could be very cheaply bought. Exploitation centred on the fact that even if a knitter did own his own frame, he still needed to take in work from the hosier, the merchant capitalist who controlled the trade. Nottingham masters either refused work to any but those who rented frames from them or, if times were brisk enough to call for increasing output, to charge a knitter half-rent for the privilege of using his own frame. Hosiers took care to keep their rented frames in sufficient work for the deduction to be covered. William Hutton bought his first frame in 1746 for £10 but found: 'the stocking frame being my own, and trade being dead, the hosiers would not employ me'. As the century wore on, rents became increasingly oppressive with the growth of a class of middle-men 'putting out' between the hosiers and the stockingers. These men drew their income from deducting higher rent from the latter than they paid to the former. There was no system of relating rents to the value of frames or to the expected income from working them. Rents increased after 1780 at a time when second-hand costs were low and earnings were declining. The hosier enjoyed a certain profit from the frame whether the knitter was in full work or not.

Rent was not the only deduction. If the seaming of the stockings was not done at home by a knitter's wife, that was deducted. For the journeyman knitter who used a corner of a master knitter's workroom, there was standing as well as frame rent and a charge made by the small master for taking in work as 'agent' for his journeyman. A list of 1811 shows the extent of deductions from a wage of 13s. 3¼d.:

Seaming	1s. 1d.	(5.42p)
Needles	3d.	(1.25p)
Oil	½d.	(0.21p)
Candles	3d.	(1.25p)
Coals	1½d.	(0.625p)
Frame standing	3d.	(1.25p)
Expenses taking in work	1s. 0d.	(5.00p)
Frame rent	1s. 0d.	(5.00p)

4s. 0d.   (20p) from a wage of
13s. 3¼d. (66.35p)

The deductions of this kind made for such necessary items as candles and oil were common to a great many trades, and although charac-teristic of the putting-out system were not confined to it. The London coal-heavers were under the employment control of 'undertakers', usually publicans who did the actual contracting with the masters of the collier boats. Apart from having to give a cut of their earnings to the undertakers, the heavers were forced to purchase their shovels and other supplies from them at excessive prices. So tight was the grip of the undertakers over the occupation that they evaded with ease an eighteenth-century Act passed to protect the men and triumphed over the competition of an alternative employment office set up in 1768 by a sympathetic magistrate to break their hold. In the early nineteenth century until some degree of protection was afforded by an Act in 1831, they took home around 11s. (55p) in every £1 they earned although constraint over entry kept their wages above those of common labour.[13] Cornish miners were required to purchase their candles from the mine, even though they were cheaper in village shops. The mine-owners explained that it was necessary to ensure that candles were of a sufficient quality, but one mine in 1864 recorded a profit of £531 from selling candles to the miners.[14]

Necessary items which piece-workers had to supply themselves were noted by Mayhew to reduce even the starvation wages of the 'sweated' needle workers of London in the mid-nineteenth century: 'In a day and a half', she continued with a deep sigh, 'deducting the cost of thread and candles for the suit (to say nothing of firing), I earns 3¾d. [1.56p] – not 2d. [0.83p] a day'. In some branches, 'trimmings' had also to be supplied.[15]

Even more contentious than deductions for goods or services supplied were 'abatements': imposed fines for claimed poor quality or short-weight work. Their imposition was widely accepted to have been aimed more at cutting wages than securing quality control:

> We'll make the poor weaver work at a low rate;
> We'll find fault where there's no fault, and so we will bate;
> . . .
> Then next for the spinner we shall ensue,
> We'll make them spin three pound instead of two,
> . . .
> But if that an ounce of weight they do lack,
> Then for to bate threepence we will not be slack

runs an early eighteenth-century poem on the practices of clothiers.[16] Such abatements continued wherever outwork persisted or increased. Mayhew provides London examples, while an investigator who met a weeping woman in Bedfordshire in 1850 found her to be a lace-maker who had been bated to the extent of 6s. (30p) out of a 15s. (75p) piece rate. Such practices were reducing what had been one of the few reasonably well-paid employments open to women to a supplement to husbands' earnings. The unmarried lace-makers had now to be helped by the parish, 'or else the're not virtuous, and goes on the streets'.[17]

Wherever piecework had to be presented for inspection, then excuses for deduction could be made. In the northern coalfield, fining miners for sending up 'corves' judged to be improperly filled was a running grievance throughout the period, while similar resentment was aroused in several trades, such as hat-making, wool cloth weaving, shoemaking and forging, when employers reduced wages on the pretext of the embezzlement of part of the raw material which had been put out.[18]

Employers were also able to impose extra work for the same pay. Avoiding the accusation of cutting the nominal rate for a job, they could instead increase the quantum in subtle ways. In textile manufacture, warping bars were lengthened to produce four or five more yards to the piece: a practice which produced complaints from weavers from, for example, Gloucestershire in 1756, Essex in 1758 and Wiltshire in 1801. In the last case the effect was that clothiers reduced the time they allowed in their calculations of rates for a piece of cloth from twenty-three hours to twenty.[19] A very clear illustration comes from the cutlery trade of Sheffield where in 1787 a master, Joseph Watkinson, demanded thirteen knives to the dozen. It produced a strike and the cutler songwriter Joseph Mather's most bitter denunciation:

> That offspring of tyranny, baseness and pride
> Our rights hath invaded and almost destroyed
> May that man be banished who villainry screens,
> Or sides with big W. . . . . . .n and his thirteens.
>
> And may the odd knife his great carcass dissect:
> Lay open his vitals for men to inspect
> A heart full as black as the infernal gulf
> In that, greedy, blood sucking, bone-scraping wolf.[20]

Birmingham's metal workers suffered effective reductions in the 1820s from the increasing expectation of manufacturers of a discount on the price of articles 'sold' to them by the artisans. The city's glass blowers struck in 1846 against an attempt to raise output without an accompanying increase in wages by increasing the number of articles to be made in a work period (the 'move') until it exceeded 'the usage and custom' of the trade.[21]

From the side of the workers came some counter expectations. Certain incidental, but necessary, labour processes such as 'stopping' (the repairing or edging of cloth), were paid for by the employer over and above the rate for the main labour. Such customary expectations were tenaciously clung to and attempts to disallow them figure frequently in the grievance catalogues of eighteenth-century workers. In so far as they represented time necessarily spent on other than the main task, their removal was in some ways analogous to later practices imposed on factory workers such as being required to change clothes or wash in their own time, or in mines in the change to counting a shift from the time a miner relieved his 'oppo' in place rather than from the time of his arrival at 'grass' – a very considerable difference when in the Cornish mines by the mid-nineteenth century, ladder climbs could easily take an hour. The loss of the right to relieve at surface was therefore in effect a significant cut in the wage.[22]

Alongside such allowances were certain expected perquisites usually involving the right to retain waste materials. These were commonly much more than 'little extras'. As Dr Linebaugh has pointed out, in the eighteenth century the idea of an exclusively money wage gained ground only very slowly and fitfully. 'Chips' (waste timber) to the shipwright 'cabbage' (waste cloth) to the tailor, 'sweepings' to the porter were among perquisites regarded as part of the 'wage' by those who expected to enjoy them. The more so because in many cases, for example 'chips', they were a by-product of the central labour process: to make ships was also to make 'chips'.[23] In woollen districts, weavers were allowed to retain the cut ends when a piece was removed from the loom ('thrums'). Attempts by clothiers to end this retention produced a bitter strike in Essex in 1757/8 despite an offer of 3d. (1.25p) a thrum compensation:

> They made a demand of our waste, without offering any allowance for the same: (and by degree did we tamely submit, we should be brought under a yoke, which would have some affinity to that of the Egyptian Bondage). Though we would not presume to deny, but that afterwards through the negotiation of the Right Hon. Robert Nugent Esq. they offered us 3d. per bay in lieu thereof. The waste is a small perquisite that hath been granted us for several hundred years past, which we were able to prove by our ancient Books of Record, which have been no less than 14 or 15 times ratified and confirmed at the General Quarter Sessions.

The sense of a legitimate right is deep here. The involvement of a member of parliament, the ratification by justices and the sanctioning of 'time immemorial' all strengthen the sense of legitimate right rather than employer concession. In the event 500 weavers struck to 'support our ancient custom' for four winter months before being starved back on the employers' terms.[24]

In the royal dockyards, 'chips' were originally waste scraps of timber allowed to the shipwrights for firewood. By the reign of Charles I they had developed into a valued part of the shipwright's remuneration, and to the government a costly loss of timber. An attempt to commute them into a wage increase of 1–3d. (0.42–1.25p) a day made in 1650 was one of several attempts made to control the amount of timber leaving the yard until the Admiralty temporarily gave up its attempts in 1677. In 1753 a rule was introduced restricting chips to no more than could be carried untied under one arm. This was no more successful than had been the decree of 1741 which declared only those 'chips' made with axe or adze to be lawful, excluding those made by sawing. Workers continued to carry out large amounts of timber and to take time in working hours to 'manufacture' chips by cutting up large pieces of timber! In 1792 each workman was said to carry home daily amounts of deliberately contrived 'chips' and to finish work early to allow time to produce lengths of sawn timber which could be sold outside for a shilling apiece. The practice died out in the nineteenth century. It was at long last replaced by an allowance in 1805 and even this was discontinued in 1830. Ropes, sail canvas and cordage were also taken from shipyards by other workers. Such practices must be seen within the context of the notoriously long arrears of pay from which yard workers suffered. Wages in 1762, for example, were fifteen months behind, and the fact that in 1766 they were only six months so at Plymouth was seen as a matter for congratulation testifying to 'the honour and humanity' of the Admiralty. In such a situation the clinging of the shipyard workers to customary perquisites which could be readily converted into cash rather than accept commutation into a money allowance is understandable.[25] In general the valuing of perquisites by workers is hardly surprising given long-delayed pay and, as we have seen, the variety of depredations which employers could make upon the money wage without changing its nominal level. It is clear that the customary rate for piecework in many trades was mediated by these practices. This may in part explain why wage rates persisted unchanged in many trades over periods so long that they became sanctioned by custom rather than by the labour market. Employers could in effect reduce wages in bad times by intensifying their abatements and by increasing the piece quantum or by attacking perquisites. Certainly nominal rates under the old putting-out system were hardly ever subjected to the direct cutting which was to become their continual fate under the 'sweating' practices of the 'new domestic system' in the second quarter of the nineteenth century. Here, cutting could be the more extreme because it involved the competitive exploitation of female labour.[26]

In many trades the relationship between the prime exponent of the skill and the subsidiary labour necessary for the complete manufacturing process was not that between a skilled craftsman and an unskilled assistant as it was, for example, in the building trades; the rapid take-over of labouring by Irish immigrants in many towns in the nineteenth century produced an ethnic divide between building craftsmen and their labourers. Unskilled subsidiary processes were often the temporary input of apprentices and regarded as part of their learning process. In cases such as this, what was meant by a wage for unskilled labour was hardly clear cut. Remuneration could range from nothing at all in the early months of a period of indentured service to an almost craftsmen's rates near its end. In the glass manufacture of Stourbridge, the product was produced by a group known as the 'chair' which consisted of the workman (gaffer), servitor, footmaker and taker-in. The last was a boy who took the finished glass to the oven. When, and if, he became an apprentice he would move up to the third position of footmaker.[27] In many places and trades, so-called apprentices were employed with no intention of providing proper training, but simply as a form of unskilled or semi-skilled labour at rates below those even of common labour.[28]

117

In cottage industry most evidently represented by the rural weaver, subsidiary labour was largely performed by members of the household and received no separate wage: the contribution of women and children being reckoned as part of the wage received by the weaver. As the 'sweating' outwork system developed in early nineteenth-century urban England it too could involve the family labour input into piece-good production. Even where work was done on the premises of the employer, wives could be taken in to perform subsidiary tasks. London's hatters took their wives to the workshops to pick coarse hairs out of their material, a task for which they would have had to pay an assistant from 6–9s. (30–45p) a week out of their 1824 wage of £2. 3s. (£2. 15p).[29] The carry-over of the view that women's earnings were either supplementary or incorporated into the wages of male heads of households produced, even in trades where women worked outside the home or at home with no direct connection with their husbands' trade, an expectation that women's wages, even where comparable levels of skill and effort were demanded, would be much lower than those of men. This is further discussed below, but a striking illustration comes from a guide to the trades of London published in 1747. Of the trades described, only three apprenticeship-entered trades for women are specified: milliners, mantau-makers, and stay and bodice-makers. Their weekly earnings when fully employed were 5–8s. (25–40p) a week compared with low-status trade wages of 12–15s. (60–75p) for painters and 10–15s. (50–75p) for tailors. Two of these three female trades were explicitly linked with prostitution.[30] No gap between man and man was so large, so widespread and so taken for granted as that between men and women.

Skilled workers as a group are clearly enough identified as making status claims and having wage expectations which separated them from common labourers, but within the ranks of the skilled there were many levels and distinctions both between and within trades. Such groups as masons, tilers and carpenters might commonly share expectations and status. The saddlers complained in 1777 that their 12–15s. (60–75p) a week was lower than the norm for a properly apprenticed trade. Printers, though, whom Dr Johnson thought had a very good number for a guinea (£1.05p) a week, would have felt hard done by if they had received no more than ordinary tailors and shoemakers.[31] *Within* the garment-producing trades the distinction beween the richer 'bespoke' West End trade and the piece-working East End making for ready-made warehouses was fundamental. It had been prefigured in the eighteenth century and forms one of the striking contrasts of Mayhew's mid-nineteenth-century survey which reveals an organised minority of society men at the quality end resisting the swamping of the unskilled majority. To their resistance, the form of the wage was crucial. By refusing to accept other than time wages and declining to work off the master's premises, they hoped to defend themselves against the downward spiralling piece rates of the home-working 'dungs'.[32]

Fine gradations within a trade can be illustrated from coach-making. In the 1820s the trade's workmen were divided into: body-makers, carriage-makers, trimmers, smiths and spring-makers and involved also wheelwrights, painters, platers and brace-makers. The body-makers were the best paid:

> a species of aristocracy to which the other workmen look up with feelings half of respect, half of jealousy. They feel their importance and treat the others with various consideration: carriage makers are entitled to a species of condescending familiarity, trimmers are considered too good to be despised; a foreman of painters they may treat with respect, but working painters can at most be favoured with a nod.[33]

Professor Hobsbawm has stressed the importance of customary expectations in wage determination before the mid-nineteenth century. Workers expected remuneration commensurate to their status assumptions and the need to support an expected quality of life. Piece rates could remain unchanged over very long periods. A West Country weaver in 1802 spoke of the rate for weaving a particular kind of woollen cloth as never altering 'nor yet in my father's memory'. London masons in 1775 complained that their usual 15s. (75p) a week had been fixed seventy years previously while fellmongers in 1800 were asking for an advance on a rate which had not been changed for forty years. Taunton serge weavers in 1764 received a rate which had persisted for thirty years while, according to Gravenor Henson, when the plain silk-stocking-makers struck in 1814, they believed they had had their rates raised only twice in 200 years. Such attitudes, Hobsbawm persuasively argues, continued among craftsmen through the first half of the nineteenth century, so that even new groups like engineers who, up to 1840 sold labour in a sellers' market, tended to fix their wage demands by customary references rather than by calculation of what the market would bear.[34]

Enough has been said to suggest that as late as the second quarter of the nineteenth century 'wages' can be related to no simple concept of the sale of labour power in a market. Certainly by the 1820s, groups of artisans like John Gast's London shipwrights had come to accept a wage form which in itself took away the distinction which divided the working day into necessary and surplus labour, and came to show a 'wage pride' in coming close to an acceptance of the Ricardian position that they were actually paid for their work. But such growing acceptance of the 'wage idea' among groups of superior artisans broke around 1820 the congruence of such groups with a broader working class which still clung to 'non-wage' expectations, including the self-appropriation of perquisites, and continued to pose problems for capitalist employers by remaining 'unalterably antipathetic to wage discipline' and insufficiently responsive to monetary incentives.[35]

THE FORM OF THE WAGE AND THE INTENSITY OF LABOUR

It seems a reasonable presumption that time wages were inappropriate to situations where work does not take place on premises where entry and exit cannot be logged. The mine or factory offers the opportunity for timed wage labour on a large scale, the workshop on a smaller one. The insistence on punctuality in the early mills with heavily disproportionate fines for lateness is well documented. But there is no necessary connection between work on an employer's premises and time rather than piece rates. So long as the indispensable skill of some workers allowed them a degree of control over the labour process, then traditional piece rates (prices) for labour could continue into the workshop. Employers could expect a 'fair day's work for a fair day's wage' based on customary expectations and workers could even take care that over-zealous comrades did not disturb notions of what was 'normal' and thereby not only obtain for themselves a disproportionate share of available work, but risk a lowering of the rate for all.[36]

London's hatters in the early nineteenth century worked by the piece on their employers' premises but, considering eight hats a day a fair day's output, came and went at no fixed hours. Work was not always available for the number of hours journeymen would have liked to have worked. Place recalled that if work had been constantly available piece-rate earning breeches-makers could have earned 18s. (90p) a week in the 1790s, but in many shops it was hardly ever possible to earn more than 14s. (70p). Print workers also regulated themselves to a particular number of pages rather than strictly to time, and although tailors' hours had since 1721 been regulated by Act of parliament, they were often called upon to work for only part of the day. Even the 'new' skilled men, the engineers, worked to a similar pattern. On the grounds that overwork harmed their health, they attempted to regulate their labour by a sanction known as 'chasing', i.e. jeering and intimidation, 'if a very active fellow got forward in that way'.[37]

The skilled male spinners in the early cotton mills were also accustomed to work for piece rates, but were themselves the employers of child assistants whom they paid by the week. As his own central labour made him the pacemaker, the spinner's response to the piece rate drew his assistants along with him. This was largely true also of the power loom weavers, although as many of these were female as were male when that process too entered the factory. However much the factory bell created the possibility of time wages, the impression that piece rates would induce a greater intensity of labour was carried into the workshop, having been gaining ground since the days of the *Wealth of Nations*. The shipwrights of Portsmouth had complained in 1775 that the introduction of a piecework scheme into the dockyard would 'occasion progressive suicide in our bodies'.[38] Employer concern with the form of the wage became especially evident from about 1830 with an increasing belief in the efficacy of systems of payment by results. Marx was of the view that capitalist employers took it for granted that piece rates were the system of wages best suited to capitalism.[39] Before 1830 it would be a mistake to read too much significance – other than in specific cases like tailoring where it drew a frontier between the skilled and the less skilled – into the distinction between time and piece rates. So long as craftsmen were not threatened with deskilling machinery, and were still capable of resisting the engulfing tide of unskilled labour; so long as customary notions of a 'fair day's work for a fair day's pay' were sustainable by powerful collective pressures and by the employer's continuing dependence upon essential manual skills, then time and piece rates could often be directly translated into each other: note the use of the word 'price', for example in the building trades, to denote the expected rate for a job. Workmen produced an accepted output for an accepted remuneration from an accepted working week.[40]

Yet processes of change can be observed in many instances. The new skill of engineering, so frequently pointed to by historians as the outstanding example of the industrial revolution's *creation* of a new class of skilled men, illustrates the changing intensity of labour consequent upon modifications in the form of the wage. Technical innovations like the slide-lathe and planer began, *c.*1840, to break down craft control in many branches of the industry as the trend towards the machine tool permitted the standardisation of many processes and accordingly allowed the expansion of piece-rate systems into machine shops. Further technical developments such as semi-automatic boring and slotting stepped up the pace of change. Not only piece rates but sub-contracting 'piecemasters' began to appear in some branches giving certain *skilled* workers the incentive to bring unskilled assistants into the industry. Against this background the ASE began its struggles in 1851 to restrict the operation of the new machines to 'fair' craftsmen. It was not a very successful campaign. According to Platts of Oldham, the union's main protagonist in the great strike of 1852, by 1863 apprenticeship had been generally abandoned in their works, and semi-automatic machines were by then altogether out of the hands of skilled men. The 'piecemaster' system was universal: 'As a general rule all work that is susceptible of measurement is paid by the piece. In such work the workman usually hires and pays the boys who assist him.'[41] Thomas Wood, the son of a Yorkshire weaver, served a full apprenticeship as an engineer in a plant making power looms (the irony of which did not escape the son of a handloom weaver). He realised that he would have, if he was to secure his future, to move away from the small country works: 'I heard about new tools, new machines, and new ways of working.' In 1845 he left for Oldham to join Platts with its

2,000 employees. He found the old differentials and habits of his small shop no longer existed. Instead of the 'country-made tools' there were standardised ones of 'Whitworth's make' and there was no gradation of payment: 'no favour was shown – no paying a man what he was worth, but the ostensible rule was a fixed standard of wage, and if the man was not worth it he must go'. He did, however, manage to accommodate himself to what was not just a new form of the wage, but a new work experience:

> Men in large shops are not troubled with a variety of work, but had one class of work and special tools. The men soon became expert and turned out a large quantity of work with the requisite exactness without a little of the thought required of those who work in small shops where fresh work continually turns up but always the same old tools. I learned quickness and accuracy, also that hard work and application were indispensable.

Laid-off in a period of slack trade with fifty others, he worked at Darlington, but it was a return to the past: 'It was a small engine shop with no proper order or economical method of working.' Yet after his experience at Platts, Wood himself had imbibed something of the ethic of his employers and could record his satisfaction at seeing those 'old' engineers who 'posed as good hands', 'clever', and gave themselves airs: 'I have seen the destruction of many of these windbags in my time. The improved method of working and supervision has been the death of them.'[42]

Under the new systems, as Professor Foster has noted, the skilled engineer was actively engaged as pacemaker and as technical supervisor and that this made the role of the new pacesetting craftsman significantly different from that of the old craft elite:

> While the self-imposed work routine of the craft worker served to insulate him from employer control, that imposed by the technological demands of the new industry equally firmly identified the skilled worker with management. For the new generation of engineers fulfillment was to be very much in terms of career achievement at work.[43]

Foster has extended this analysis of the 'new' kind of skilled man to the cotton mills. He suggests that in the 1840s and 1850s the survival of the male mule-spinner, despite attempts to deskill him and break his power through the self-acting mill, was the result of processes similar to those at work in engineering. Employers needed within their labour force a pacemaker grade whose response to piece-rate imperatives would force an intensification of labour from their time-paid assistants, juvenile and female. In this way the mule-spinners effectively enforced discipline on behalf of the management. From this development, he suggests, stems the lack of interest in the 1840s and 1850s of mule-spinners in the revived short-time movement compared with their marked involvement in the 1830s. In contrast, the time-paid piecers were active.[44]

In many instances the selection of working groups was determined by the skilled men. In 'shoaling' in the dockyards the shipwrights mixed the old with the young and fit, not only as a means of insuring against the discarding of the former, but a safeguard against a pace setting on the basis of the most youthful. In agriculture, the most traditional of industries, harvest time, the period of most intensive labour, had its pace determined without the direct intervention of the farmer. Terms with him were agreed by the 'lord of the harvest' elected from the ranks of the harvesters. He set the required pace of labour and made the rules which governed its rhythms. He imposed fines on those whose labour was shoddy or slow. After mock trials he ordered physical ritual punishments such as 'booting' with a leather boot. In pastoral areas at the annual shearing the shearers elected a captain, who not only agreed terms with the farmer but held in himself the power to discharge poor or unco-operative workers.[45]

In the printing trades the compositors had in the rules of their 'chapels' elaborate codes of behaviour which disciplined a considerable proportion of the labour process without recourse to the employer. Accounts of their customary practices date back to the late seventeenth century, insuring good, mutual work habits. Within each chapel the compositors were organised into a 'companionship' under a 'clicker' who apportioned the work among the men who earned a lump sum on the basis of the number of lines set. The 'fat', the half-printed pages which were customarily paid at the rate for a full page, was evenly distributed. If a chapel member had a complaint against another he called a meeting and, if his complaint was accepted, a fine was levied upon the offender. They were levied for swearing, drunkenness, fighting, dropping tools, leaving type dirty, or leaving a candle burning at night. Clearly they were intended to ensure harmonious relationships among the printers and to encourage work habits which promoted the collective good. The sense of belonging was emphasised by periodic 'treatings' on occasions such as the coming out of apprenticeship, the moving to a new process, or by elaborate initiation rituals (rites of passage) among not only printers, but among other skilled groups such as hatters, who had also an elaborate system of workshop courts, and coopers.[46]

Liverpool shipwrights resisted a piece-rate system which, although it would have allowed larger earnings to the young and fit, would have made it 'very hard to see the old men walking about, without being able to get a day's work'. Here the custom of the trade became enshrined in the rule book of the shipwrights' union. Such absorptions were common among skilled labour groups. Dr Behagg has documented it for Birmingham where within the city's matrix of workshops, the customs of the trades became the basis of the unions' regulated forms of defence.[47]

Adam Smith expressed concern over the effect of the intensity of labour induced by piece rates on the health of workers. Dismissing the deeply prevalent view that workers when they could earn in four days sufficient to maintain them for a week, would be idle the other three, he argued to the contrary; the greater part: 'when they were liberally paid by the piece, are very apt to overwork themselves, and to ruin their health and constitution in a few years'. Although he accepted that greater intensity of labour was achievable through piece-rate methods, 'a poor independent workman will generally be more industrious than even a journeyman who works by the piece', his belief in the dangers of overwork seem to have been deeply held.[48] To move from his guarded acceptance of piece rates to their use as the main means of increasing labour intensity in the middle years of the nineteenth century is to see the form of the wage as crucial in both factory and outwork. In Marxist terms the 'expropriation of the product' had long been achieved by the capitalist, but the increasing emphasis on the piece-rate system as well as the more obvious manifestations of imposed disciplines on labour must be seen as a means of the further expropriation: the expropriation of nature.[49]

In cotton mills, as we have seen, piece rates and time discipline combined to intensify labour. In 1833 around half of all cotton mill employees were on piece rates. In the second quarter of the nineteenth century the 'discovery' of the benefits of payment by results were propagated so widely as to be regarded as an innovation of major significance. Long-established systems like those in use in the tin and copper mines of Cornwall, previously described as quaint and peculiar, were now discussed as models for emulation. From the nature of supervising labour underground, time wages had always been rare in mining: payment by results being necessary to ensure that production was kept up rather than as an incentive for its increase. Cornish mining was discussed widely and influentially: Charles Babbage, J. S. Mill and Henry Mayhew were only the best known of those to draw approving attention towards tributing and tutwork. The principle of tributing was that the miner contracted with the mine company to work a measured part of the mine for an agreed percentage of the value of the ore which he raised. He 'bargained' at a form of 'dutch auction' in competition with his fellows, basing the price he would accept on his estimate of the potential of the part of the mine ('pitch') which was up for taking. Economists could thus present him as a kind of 'co-venturer' with the capitalist in the risks of enterprise, and therefore committed in a special way to hard work and disinclined to strike action.[50]

J. S. Mill in 1845 commented that the Cornish miners were invariably joint-adventurers in the mining concerns and, for 'intelligence, independence, and good conduct as well as prosperous circumstances, no labouring population in the island is understood to be comparable to the Cornish miners', and in his *Principles of Political Economy* again wrote highly of a system which raised the condition of the Cornish miner 'far above that of the generality of the labouring class'. Mill, like others who favoured the system, had no first-hand knowledge of it. They seem to have been quite ignorant of the extraordinary nature of the tributer's gamble which could reduce him to a position of destitution more often than it lifted him to a peak of prosperity. Underground conditions changed: veins which had seemed full of promise suddenly petered out:

> A month had nearly ended,
> And he severe had wrought
> Day after day in darkness,
> And it was all for nought.
> The mineral vein had faded
> And now all hope was fled,
> Tomorrow should be payday
> His children have no bread.

John Harris's poem *The Unsuccessful Tributer* was from a man who had known the despair he described, but who had also had a period of successful tributing which had enabled him to buy his own house.[51] On balance there is no doubt that the miners valued the sense of 'independence' which the tribute system gave them, but it was the mine-owners who gained most from a system under which miners competed to lower the price of their own labour.

So much was the superiority of piece-rate wages being asserted in the economic discourse of the 1830s that Marx's view of the system as the one best suited to capitalism is hardly surprising. However, the principle which increasingly underlay its practice, especially in overstocked sections of the labour market, was not, as Adam Smith seems to have assumed, the carrot but the stick. No one better illustrated this than Mayhew in his investigation of the 'sweated trades' of London. With the tailors, a strike defeat of 1834 marked the point of change for the better end of the trade from time to piece wages. In this respect those from the quality West End shops joined their already degenerated East End brothers. Very quickly piece rates established themselves at a level which implied one and a half days labour to earn what had been traditionally a day's pay. It was to become worse: not only were the best-skilled men of the West End now paid only for work actually done, but to keep their incomes up men working at home could take on other workmen, more distressed than themselves, as well as exploit their own wives and children. 'The regular tailor is being destroyed, a man's own children are being brought into competition against himself', complained one skilled hand to Mayhew. Carpenters faced similar problems: outside of a shrinking 'honourable' section who were paid either time rates or according to an agreed book of prices, the spread of piecework had produced 'scamping' and the bringing in of unskilled helpers.[52]

In the small workshops of Birmingham by 1830 employers of engineers and foundry workers were evidently using piece rates as stick rather than carrot. George Holyoake, who served his time as a whitesmith, remembered the pressures on the artisans of the 1830s. A man who could afford to dress decently would often choose not to do so for fear that his employer would take it as a sign that he was too highly paid. He commented on the ten years' transportation received by one workman for stealing a small file: 'The arbitrary and continual reduction of prices by the master was a far more serious theft of the earnings of all the men. That was the way in which employers behaved generally so far as I knew them.' In contrast to an image of a Birmingham of harmonious class relations which some historians like to present, Holyoake saw 'continual resentment, sullenness and disgust'.[53]

During the years after 1830 payment by results had become the managerial orthodoxy. It was at its most exploitative in the sweated outworking trades where it bore no resemblance to the customary price paid to the eighteenth-century worker for his piece over a generation or more without change. Things were very different by 1849 when a poor silk weaver lamented: 'Why, there's seven of us here . . . all dependent on the weaving here, nothing else. What was four shillings [20p] a yard is paid one and nine [8½p] now . . . They've lowered the wages so low, that one would hardly believe the people would take the work. But what's one to do! the children can't *quite* starve.' Female 'slopworkers' could tell similar tales. One, making waistcoats, told Mayhew:

> Prices have come down very much indeed since I first worked for the warehouse – *very much*. The prices when I was first employed there were as much as 1s. 9d. [8.75p] for what I now get 1s. 1d. [5.42p] for. Everyweek they have reduced something within these last few years. Work's falling very much. The work has not riz [sic], no! not since I worked at it. It's lower'd but its not riz.[54]

Home work must be paid by the piece, but what is significant is the deliberate adoption of piece-rate systems in the factory where the possibility of clocking in and out would seem to make time wages logical. Whether piece rates were general or whether, as we have seen, 'pacemakers' on the central labour process passed on their imperatives to time-paid subsidiary workers, their imposition was as much linked to the intensification of labour as was the new stress on time discipline and accommodation to the pace of machinery. Such things, as Professor Pollard has remarked, as well as the demographically caused increase in the supply of labour, are necessary to explain how the demand for labour in the early industrial revolution was met without an increase in its price.[55]

REFERENCES AND NOTES

1. **P. E. Razzell** and **R. W. Wainwright** (eds), *The Victorian Working Class: Selections from Letters to the Morning Chronicle*, Cass, 1973, p. 45.
2. Ibid., pp. 17–18.
3. **Adam Smith**, *The Wealth of Nations*, 1776 edn, E. Cannan 1904 pbk, 1961, I, pp. 73–4; **L. D. Schwarz**, 'Income distribution and social structure in London in the late eighteenth century', *Economic History Review*, XXXII, no. 2, 1979, pp. 256–7.
4. Razzell and Wainwright, *Victorian Working Class*, pp. 9, 15–16; **I. Pinchbeck**, *Women Workers and the Industrial Revolution 1750_1850*, Cass, repr. 1969, pp. 41–2, 91; the most recent account of farm service is **A. Kussmaul**, *Servants in Husbandry in early modern England*, Cambridge University Press, 1981, for its varying geographical incidence see the table on p. 15 for 1851.
5. Razzell and Wainwright, *Victorian Working Class*, pp. 49–50, 15–16.
6. Ibid., pp. 59–62, 66; **William Dodd**, *The Labouring Classes of England*, 1848, repr. Kelley, New York, 1976, pp. 54–5.
7. Razzell and Wainwright, *Victorian Working Class*, pp. 62, 66; Dodd, *Labouring Classes*, p. 54.
8. Ibid., p. 55; *The Autobiography of William Cobbett*, ed. W. Reitzel, Faber edn, 1967, p. 11.
9. Dodd, *Labouring Classes*, pp. 52–3.
10. For a fuller discussion, see **J. G. Rule**, *The Experience of Labour in Eighteenth-Century England*, Croom Helm, 1981, pp. 61–3; **M. D. George**, *London Life in the Eighteenth Century*, Penguin edn, 1966, pp. 168–9; **E. J. Hobsbawm**, 'Custom, wages and work-load in nineteenth-century industry' in *Labouring Men*, Weidenfeld & Nicolson, 1964, p. 346.
11. For coal-heavers, see Rule, *Experience of Labour*, pp. 40, 142; Razzell and Wainwright, *Victorian Working Class*, pp. 91, 270.
12. Rule, *Experience of Labour*, p. 63; *Commons Journals*, LI, 21 April 1796, p. 595.
13. For a useful discussion of some aspects of this problem, see **J. Styles**, 'Embezzlement, industry and the law in England, 1500–1800', in **M. Berg, P. Hudson** & **M. Sonenscher** (eds), *Manufacture in Town and Country before the Factory*, Cambridge U.P., esp. p. 182–8. Deductions from framework knitters' wages are fully discussed and documented in Rule, *Experience of Labour*, pp. 141–2 and coal-heavers p. 142, and in **M. D. George**, 'The London coalheavers', *Economic Journal: History Supplement*, 1927, pp. 214–28.
14. **J. G. Rule**, 'The labouring miner in Cornwall: a study in social history', Ph.D. thesis, University of Warwick, 1971, p. 48.
15. **E. P. Thompson** and **E. Yeo** (eds), *The Unknown Mayhew*, Penguin, 1973, p. 167.
16. The poem is printed in full in **P. Mantous**, *The Industrial Revolution in the Eighteenth Century*, 1961 edn, pp. 75–7.
17. Razzell and Wainwright, *Victorian Working Class*, pp. 67–8.

18. Rule, *Experience of Labour*, p. 134; **E. Welbourne**, *The Miners' Unions of Northumberland and Durham*, Cambridge U.P., 1923, p. 21.
19. Rule, *Experience of Labour*, pp. 137–8.
20. **G. I. H. Lloyd**, *The Cutlery Trades*, repr. Cass, 1963, pp. 241–2.
21. **C. Behagg**, 'Custom, class and change: the trade societies of Birmingham', *Social History*, vol. 4, no. 3, 1979, pp. 466–7, 469.
22. Rule, 'Labouring miner', pp. 32–4, 85–6 and **A. K. Hamilton Jenkin**, *The Cornish Miner*, Allen and Unwin, 1962, p. 221.
23. See **P. Linebaugh**, 'Labour History without the labour process: a note on John Gast and his times', *Social History*, vol. 7, no. 3, 1982, pp. 319–28.
24. The dispute is described in Rule, *Experience of Labour*, pp. 126–7.
25. Ibid., pp. 128–30 for a discussion of 'chips.'
26. Examples of rate cutting in the London trades in the mid-nineteenth century abound in the writings of Henry Mayhew. Two recent works on the 'sweating system' are: **D. Bythell**, *The Sweated Trades. Outwork in Nineteenth-Century Britain*, Batsford, 1978, esp. pp. 42–3 and **J. A. Schmiechen**, *Sweated Industries and Sweated Labor. The London Clothing Trades, 1860–1914*, Croom Helm, 1984, Ch. 1.
27. **E. Hopkins**, 'Working conditions in Victorian Stourbridge', *International Review of Social History*, XIX, 1974, pt. 3, p. 423.
28. Rule, *Experience of Labour*, pp. 100–1.
29. *Third Report from the Select Committee on Artisans and Machinery*, BPP, 1824, V, p. 97.
30. **R. Campbell**, *The London Tradesman*, 1747, repr. David and Charles, Newton Abbot, 1969, pp. 206–9, 226–8.
31. Rule, *Experience of Labour*, pp. 62–3; George, *London Life*, pp. 166–7.
32. Thompson and Yeo, *Unknown Mayhew*, pp. 218–24 and see below for the significance of the tailors' strike of 1834. For the division in the eighteenth and early nineteenth centuries see Rule, *Experience of Labour*, pp. 151–6.
33. Hobsbawm, 'Custom, wages and work-load', p. 347.
34. Ibid., p. 345; *Report from the Select Committee on the Combination Laws*, BPP, 1825, IV, p. 280; Rule, *Experience of Labour*, p. 61.
35. Linebaugh, 'Labour history without the labour process', pp. 322–5.
36. Hobsbawm, 'Custom, wages and work-load', p. 348.
37. *S.C. on Artisans and Machinery*, Third Report, pp. 96–7; Rule, *Experience of Labour*, p. 195; **M. Thale** (ed.), *Autobiography of Francis Place*, Cambridge U.P., 1972, pp. 105–6, 112; **M. Berg** (ed.), *Technology and Toil in Nineteenth Century Britain*, Humanities Press, 1979, p. 159.
38. **A. Geddes**, *Portsmouth during the Great French Wars 1770–1800*, Portsmouth City Council, 1970, p. 19.
39. Hobsbawm, 'Custom, wages and work-load', p. 357.
40. Ibid., p. 353.
41. **J. Foster**, *Class Struggle and the Industrial Revolution. Early industrial capitalism in three English towns*, Methuen, 1974, pp. 226–7,
42. **J. Burnett** (ed.), *Useful Toil. Autobiographies of Working People from the 1820s to the 1920s*, Allen Lane, 1974, pp. 304–12.
43. Foster, *Class Struggle*, p. 229.
44. Ibid., pp. 231–2.
45. Rule, *Experience of Labour*, p. 195; **Bob Bushaway**, *By Rite, Custom,*

Ceremony and Community in England 1700–1880, Junction Books, 1982, pp. 111–13.

46. **C. Manby Smith**, *The Working Man's Way in the World,* 1853, repr. Printing Historical Society, 1967, pp. 171, 184–6, 12–13; **E. Howe** (ed.), *The London Compositor: Documents relating to the Wages, Working Conditions and Customs of the London Printing Trade,* Oxford U.P., 1947, pp. 84–5; Rule, *Experience of Labour,* pp. 198–201.

47. Ibid., p. 197; **C. Behagg**, 'Secrecy, Ritual and Folk Violence: The Opacity of the Workplace in the First Half of the Nineteenth Century', in **R. D. Storch** (ed.), *Popular Culture and Custom in Nineteenth-Century England,* Croom Helm, 1982, pp. 154–79.

48. Smith, *Wealth of Nations,* I, pp. 91–2.

49. See the discussion of this distinction by **G. Stedman Jones**, 'England's first proletariat', *New Left Review,* 90, 1975, p. 55.

50. **S. Pollard**, *The Genesis of Modern Management,* Penguin, 1968, p. 222; the tribute system is discussed in detail in Rule, 'Labouring miner', pp. 34–71, 376–83.

51. **J. S. Mill**, *The Claims of Labour,* 1845, Toronto U.P., *Collected Works,* IV, 1967, p. 383; *Principles of Political Economy,* Toronto U.P., 1965, pp. 769–70; **J. Harris**, *Wayside Pictures, Hymns and Poems,* 1874, pp. 158–9; **J. H. Harris**, *John Harris, the Cornish Poet,* Partridge and Co., 1888, p. 46.

52. Thompson and Yeo, *Unknown Mayhew,* pp. 226, 403–9.

53. **G. J. Holyoake**, *Sixty Years of an Agitator's Life,* T. Fisher Unwin, 1907, pp. 21–2.

54. Thompson and Yeo, *Unknown Mayhew,* pp. 133, 148.

55. **S. Pollard**, 'Labour in Great Britain', in **P. Mathias** & **M. M. Postan** (eds), *Cambridge Economic History of Europe, Volume VII. The Industrial Economies: Capital, Labour, and Enterprise Part I, Britain, France, Germany and Scandinavia,* Cambridge U.P., 1978, p. 158.

Chapter 5

LABOUR INTENSITY, WORK DISCIPLINE AND HEALTH

The much commented on failure of workers to respond to the incentive of extra earnings by offering extra labour has been mentioned several times above. Behind it lay the contrast between traditional work rhythms and the labour expectations of a modern economy. E. P. Thompson summed this up in a seminal article in which he described the 'characteristic irregularity' of labour patterns before the coming of large-scale machine-based production. Wherever men were in control of their own working lives they tended to alternate bouts of intense labour with ones of idleness. This rhythm was typical of the home-based worker but it was equally true of the small workshop where men paid by the piece came and went with an irregularity which did not pose too many problems for employers whose fixed capital investment was low. A hatter's day in 1824 was said to have been long, but to have had no fixed hours, while before the coming of the de-skilling shearing frames, wool shearmen were said in 1802 to content themselves with earnings of 10s. (50p) a week, when by working longer hours they could have earned 25s. (£1.25p).[1]

So well did the Sheffield cutler songwriter Joseph Mather capture the customary week of that town's artisans in his song *The Jovial Cutlers* of 1793 that, like practically every other historian of the subject, we will quote from it. The cutler is described as sitting before his smithy fire on a Monday:

Brother workmen cease your labour,
Lay your files and hammers by,
Listen while a brother neighbour
Sings a cutler's destiny:
How upon a good Saint Monday,
Sitting by the smithy fire
Telling what's been done o' t' Sunday
And in cheerful mirth conspire.

His wife enters indicating her ragged and outmoded attire; she at least

130

would appreciate a little less idleness and a little more response to monetary incentives. Her nagging tongue is revealingly described by her husband as moving with a faster motion than his 'boring stick at a Friday's pace': the week's working rhythm is revealed to be that of a man controlling his own time. Monday he took as a holiday; Tuesday he slowly got into his stride but by Friday he was flat out in order to complete the number of pieces of cutlery needed to secure his normal income. Obviously the necessary input of labour was determined by piece rates and by food prices: adverse movement in either would increase the number of hours worked, but would still not indicate just what hours should be worked.[2]

'Saint Monday' was almost a universal observance among manufacturing workers and miners: weavers, woolcombers, shearmen, cobblers, printers, potters and several of the many trades censured for keeping it as a holiday. The longer calendar of the year, as well as the shorter one of the week, was punctuated by unofficial holidays in an age which commonly allowed only Christmas Day and Good Friday as official ones. Such occasions were local wakes and feast days: the day of the patron saint of the trade (St Crispin for shoemakers, Bishop Blaise for woolcombers, St Clement for workers in iron, St Piron for tin miners etc.); 'gaudy days', proclaimed by northern colliers on the hearing of the first cuckoo and, in the royal dockyards, the king's birthday. Adam Smith differed from many of his contemporaries in seeing artisans' bouts of drunken dissipation as the *result* of intense labour, although Francis Place could write with feeling of the desire for leisure which would come over even the most painstaking and industrious men after a period of hard work.[3] Such, however, were occasional imperatives: those commentators who described a deep-rooted leisure preference were closer to the general case in which, as Max Weber noted of the piece-rate receiving 'traditional' worker:

> He did not ask: how much can I earn in a day if I do as much work as possible? but: how much must I work in order to earn the wage which I earned before and which takes care of my traditional needs? . . . A man does not by nature wish to earn more and more money, but simply to live as he is accustomed to live and to earn as much as is necessary for that purpose.[4]

Throughout the eighteenth century abounding complaints produce a concurrent testimony that artisans, miners and outworkers who could support their customary expectations from five day's labour would not work six. 'Great earnings', claimed Arthur Young, caused all those 'the least inclined to idleness' to work only four or five days. This was a 'fact so well-known' in every manufacturing town that it hardly needed proving. Elsewhere in his writings, he returned to the same point:

> The master manufacturers of Manchester wish that prices might always be high enough to enforce a general industry; to keep the hands employed six

days for a week's work; as they find that even one idle day, in the chance of its being a drunken one, damages all the other five, or rather the work of them.

William Hutton who wrote a history of Birmingham in 1781 (and had himself been a framework knitter in Derbyshire before moving to that city) stated that manufactures tended to decay when 'plenty preponderates', for the generality of working men would perform no more than would produce maintenance, and hence high wages or low prices would decrease the supply of labour.[5]

Such responses must cast doubt on any attempt to measure the average working day of the eighteenth-century worker in manufacturing. Agricultural work was much more determined by the nature of the task to be performed and the hours of daylight available. In any case in the overstocked south in the first half of the nineteenth century, farm labourers would have welcomed the chance to have worked a good many more hours than were normally available to them. For artisans working outside the home, some information is available. The Act of 1721 required London's tailors to work from 6 a.m. to 8 p.m. with an hour's break for dinner. In 1752 the tailors petitioned for a reduction on the grounds that twelve hours from 6 a.m. was usual in 'most handicraft trades'. In fact, a comprehensive survey of 1747 suggests that fourteen hours was not that unusual except in the daylight-dependent trades such as building and shipbuilding. In 1768 the tailors got a reduction to thirteen hours, but how far this represented a general tendency for well-organised tradesmen is impossible to know, and although by the last years of the century some favoured groups *may* have gained something like a ten-hour day, a reference in 1827 to the 'English system' of working from six to six probably conforms to the usual expectation of the artisan.[6]

Eighteenth-century miners seem to have worked shorter shifts than became usual in the nineteenth. In the eighteenth they were frequently represented as working fewer hours than practically any other kind of worker. Young commented on the fact that lead miners in the Dales had often finished by one o'clock. Yorkshire pitmen commonly worked eight hours and sometimes only six. In the lead mines of the northern Pennines, men driving levels and sinking shafts worked a two-shift system of five eight-hour days, but in Yorkshire's lead mines did six six-hour shifts. Pitmen on the great Northern coalfield were working six to seven hours in the 1760s but perhaps eight to ten by the end of the century to equal those which Lancashire's colliers seem to have been working throughout the century. Around Leeds in 1787 the eight-hour shift still prevailed, but the twelve-hour one was common by 1842. It was a feature both of coal and metal mining that boys and females working on the surface tasks very often worked a longer day than the underground men, especially at busy times.[7]

In the copper and tin mines of Cornwall, the tutworkers who worked in opening up the 'dead' ground usually worked eight-hour shifts through the twenty-four hours, while tributers who raised the actual ore came and went with greater freedom. At the beginning of the seventeenth century, four hours underground was said to be about all that a miner could manage because of the badness of the air, but shifts of six and eight hours were usual in the eighteenth century. Longer shifts had been tried but were found to lead to poor productivity per man hour:

> they were nothing but an excuse for idleness; twelve hours being too many for a man to work without intermission. Accordingly when a pair of men went underground formerly, they made it a rule, to sleep, as long as a whole candle would continue burning; then rise up and work for two or three hours pretty briskly; after that, have a touch pipe . . . and so play and sleep away half their working time: but mining being more expensive than it formerly was, those idle customs were superseded by more labour and industry.

This was in 1776 and at this time the miners were also notorious for holidaying: 'This has been a broken time with the labourers – so many Holy-days as people call them but in fact they are idle, feasting days – have occasioned a great loss to every mine.'[8]

The hours of home-based workers can only be guessed at. In so far as a generalisation may be ventured, then they almost certainly, for many groups like handloom weavers, framework knitters and outworking tailors and shoemakers, moved in the opposite direction to those of the more privileged artisan groups. Competition from increasing labour supply as markets opened for lesser quality products and from, but only in some instances, machinery produced so rapid a decline in piece rates after 'the golden ages' of high labour demand came to an end that necessity became the driving imperative for reported hours of, for example, fifteen, sixteen or even twenty hours for cotton weavers in 1808. Now there was no choice. Leisure preference could not be indulged, and with it went the distinctive leisure culture of the artisan: degradation went beyond material conditions as 'Friday's pace' became the norm to offset falling rates. What was true of cotton weavers was so too of woollen weavers, silk weavers and of stock-ingers.[9]

Hours in the first cotton-spinning mills which began to appear in the last quarter of the eighteenth century varied. Mantoux, on the basis of the enquiry of 1816, instances fourteen, sixteen and even eighteen hours with a forty-minute dinner break as common for the largely child and female labour force. Around Manchester fourteen hours or a shift system with sixteen hours on and eight off was common. Samuel Oldknow, generally regarded as an humane employer, expected his apprentices to work for thirteen hours from 6 a.m.[10]

THE NEW DISCIPLINE

The spread of the factory system was slow and uneven. The first employees were at a frontier of labour: they experienced as innovation what coming generations internalised as normal. Those who did not enter the factory underwent no comparable cultural shock of adjustment to a newly dictated pace and rhythm of labour. Even where there was a shift in the scene of labour from home to non-mechanised workshop there was no necessary shift from casual to intensified labour. Groups of skilled workshop artisans were among the most devoted of worshippers of St Monday and continued to be so through the first two-thirds of the nineteenth century. New trades like engineering displayed the tendency as well as older trades. Thomas Wright, 'The Journeyman Engineer', devoted an entire chapter of his account of *The Habits and Customs of the Working Classes* of 1867 to the practice of keeping St Monday.[11] Wherever groups of well-organised artisans possessed a still essential skill, then they held the key to the control of the processes and pace of labour. To them, St Monday was a potent assertion of a special kind of independence. Dr Reid, in a study of the artisans who peopled the workshops of Birmingham, has shown its persistence in a city where 'the matrix of small workshops' formed a 'conducive environment for the survival of immemorial work rhythms'. In 1842 the employers were still stating that they had great difficulty in getting their men to work on Mondays: 'civilization' had substituted cricket for dog fights, but they still took place on Mondays. Of twenty-two railway excursions organised in 1846, only six did not leave on a Monday. As late as 1863/4 the 'general observance of St Monday' was said to lose more time than either late-coming to work or prolonged meal breaks. Eventually the chief agent of erosion was to be the Saturday half-holiday movement, but it came only gradually into specific work situations.[12] Sheffield was another town of metal-working artisans. There the employer Joseph Rogers, who by the mid-1840s had established extensive control over all processes of his manufacture, could not get his grinders to work on Tuesdays: 'Tuesday is a "natty day" with grinders when nothing will persuade them to work – not even a barrel of ale, and yet [we] have more control over this class of workmen than any other manufacturers.' Twenty years later the grinder was still showing a persistent independence; he was:

> not tied to any stated hours of labour; he has a key of the wheel, and enters it at his own time, working when he likes and playing when he likes . . . while . . . the factory hand is necessarily in a condition of . . . dependence on the manufacturer . . . this authority on the one side and the subjection on the other . . . scarcely exist in Sheffield. The relation of employer and

employed there has very little in it of the relation between master and servant.[13]

Where skilled workers controlled the work process their assistants were largely bound to their rhythms, even if at times preparation of materials etc. could continue in the absence of the craftsman. An old potter recalled Mondays in the potteries during his childhood of the 1840s when the potters still retained a 'devout regard for St. Monday'. Child and woman assistants came to work on Mondays and Tuesdays to prepare clay for the potters who were still absent drinking. Largely unsupervised, they worked at a relaxed pace and helped themselves to a shorter day. Towards the end of the week, however, they suffered as the piece-rate-earning potter demanded from them fourteen or even sixteen hours labour as he struggled to make up his wages: 'I have since thought that but for the reliefs at the beginning of the week for the women and boys all through the potworks the deadly stress of the last four days could not have been maintained.'[14] In pot-making, as in hatting, supplementary labour assisted an individual piece-rated craftsman; it is only where *chains* of production emerge that synchronisation of labour demands adjustment to a new time discipline. Such an imperative was evident in exceptional cases as early as 1700, in which year the well-known Law Book of the Crawley ironworks at Newcastle was produced. Here, where Arthur Young reported in 1771 an annual wage bill of £12,000 for 'several hundreds of labourers', the iron master Ambrose Crawley produced a written code of 100,000 words to regulate his labour force. Many of the orders concerned time-keeping. Order 103 followed a complaining preamble about a 'pretended' right to 'loyter' on the part of some 'thinking by their readiness and ability to do sufficient in less time than others', while others foolishly seemed to have thought that 'bare attendance without being imployed [sic] in business' was sufficient and some so 'villainous' as to glory in their idleness while upbraiding others for their diligence, with this edict:

> To the end that sloath and villany should be detected and the just and diligent rewarded, I have thought meet to create an account of time by a Monitor, and do order [that] from 5 to 8 and from 7 to 10 is fifteen hours, out of which take 1½ for breakfast, dinner etc. There will be thirteen hours and a half neat service . . .

This thirteen hours was to be calculated after all deductions for being at taverns, alehouses, coffee houses, breakfast, dinner, playing, sleeping, smoking, singing, reading of 'news history', quarrelling, contention, disputes or 'anything forreign [sic] to my business, any way loytering'. The monitor was to keep a time sheet for each employee and to go by one clock only 'which clock is never to be altered but by the clock-keeper'. A bell was to be rung every morning at 5 a.m. for beginning work, at eight for breakfast, at 8.30 for resumption of work, at twelve for dinner and at one for the restart and finally at 8 p.m. for leaving work.[15] Crawley, like Josiah Wedgwood, was a precocious eighteenth-century precursor of a concern with time-keeping which became central to the managerial concerns of the early factory masters. At his Etruria works, Wedgwood strove to impose a new discipline on pottery workers who, as we have seen, were notoriously irregular in their work habits. Here he introduced the first recorded instance of a clocking-in system, backed by the stiff fine of 2s. (10p) for any workman entering late. Although he turned Etruria into the apogee of a pre-machinery production unit by turning skilled workers into 'detail' workers by a specialisation designed to 'make such machines of men as cannot err', Etruria still fell short of the fully-fledged factory system. When one stage of production depends upon another, then synchronisation of labour is clearly indicated, but *manual* pace still determines the rhythms of labour. It is when human labour is teamed with power-driven machinery that a new and different pace is dictated.[16] Etruria was in no way typical of the potteries, nor had it become so by the mid-nineteenth century. An old potter, whose methodist soul decried the lax attitude of his fellow workers of that time, remarked:

> . . . how impossible economy was in a trade so loosely conducted. It would have been better for employers and workpeople if they had been in the disciplinary grip of machinery . . . A machine worked so many hours in the week would produce so much length of yarn or cloth. Minutes were felt to be factors in these results, whereas in the Potteries hours, or even days at times, were hardly felt to be such factors.[17]

In the 'Coketown' of Charles Dickens the mill workers 'all went in and out at the same hours, with the same sound upon the same pavements, to do the same work; the intensity of which was dictated by the 'piston of the steam engine' working up and down 'like the head of an elephant in a state of melancholy madness'. Something as obvious as the necessary accommodation of human labour to a new dimension of work when a power-driven machine switched on to a regular momentum, remains tireless until it is switched off, was as evident to contemporaries as it has been to later historians:

> Whilst the engine runs the people must work – men women and children are yoked together with iron and steam. The animal machine breakable in the best case, subject to a thousand sources of suffering . . . is chained fast to the iron machine, which knows no suffering and no weariness.[18]

The new intensification of labour is clear, but the switching on of a machine also represents a *moment of time* which human labour must be brought to accept: its switching off represents another and work time is demarked sharply from non-work time. Accepting this did not come easily to the first generation of factory workers. It has been suggested that one of the reasons for the use of child labour in the mills was that it reduced dependence on adult labour whose traditional work habits were too deeply ingrained. Certainly, privileged groups like adult male mule spinners did persist in exhibiting degrees of absenteeism which were comparable to those of their artisan brothers, and even Wedgwood had to acknowledge that little could be expected from his pottery hands during the local wakes. Ultimately, as in Lancashire, one answer was to legitimise the 'wakes' by making them formal holidays.[19]

Once in the factory, the need to ensure attendance gives way to the need to install notions of 'time thrift'. Bad time-keeping was punished by fines totally disproportionate to the value of the time lost; or else those only a minute or two late were locked out to lose a whole shift's pay. Pioneers like Arkwright had to 'train his workpeople to a precision and assiduity altogether unknown before, against which their listless and restive habits rose in continued rebellion.' In the factory, formal work rules replace custom as the order of the workplace. It was said in 1821 that so strict were the orders in a flax mill that if an overseer of a room was found talking to any person in mill hours he was summarily dismissed, as he was if he were found 'a yard out of his ground'. Another example of a mill order from 1830 is equally emphatic: 'Any person found from the usual place of work, except for necessary purposes, or talking with anyone out of their own Ally [sic] will be fined 2d. [1p] for each offence.'[20]

The 'stick' for both adult and child workers was evident in fines and in dismissal. Apprentice children could be sanctioned by neither, and here corporal punishment in a *general sense* was probably widespread even if serious beatings were the indulgence of atypical sadists. Quick cuffs, a hotly delivered blow or two from a strap were common enough methods of restoring the attention of a child when delivered by overseers or by the adult operatives whose labour they supplemented. Robert Owen was certainly not the only mill-owner to prohibit such acts outright. However, the apprentice era was a short-lived one. When steam power re-located the mill in the town by releasing it from dependence on water power, employers rejoiced in the return of an ample labour supply over which dismissal and its threat was the most dependable sanction. Less serious misconduct, even from children, could be dealt with by fines. Fines were high, ranging from 6d. to 2s. (2½p to 10p) for an ordinary offence which could mean anything from two hours to a day's pay. At one Stockport mill, swearing, singing or being drunk was punished by a fine of 5s. (25p).[21]

The 'carrot' was less widely used than the 'stick', although as we have already noted, the use of money incentives was being incorporated into wage systems. Professor Pollard[22] has tabulated the returns (see Table 6) on means of discipline used in 1833 and clearly demonstrates, from a source accepted as well-disposed towards the factory masters, the prevalence of punishment over incentive.

TABLE 6   No. of firms using different means to enforce discipline among factory children, 1833[22]

Negative		Positive	
Dismissal	353	Kindness	2
Threat of Dismissal	48	Promotion or higher wages	9
Fines, deductions	101	Reward or premium	23
Corporal punishment	55		
Complaint to parents	13		
Confined to mill	2		
Degrading dress, badge	3		
Total:	575		34

Not until the second half of the nineteenth century did the factory's routinised and regular day become generally accepted by a workforce in which children were a steadily shrinking element. This accommodation was based not only on a perception of what was necessary to subsist, but also on one which could relate the possibility of higher earnings to the enjoyment of non-work time. As a novelist of the 1950s was to vividly capture, the weekend with its conspicuous consumption of leisure goods and opportunities became the justification for the working week. An emphasis which seems especially pungent in that 'do it yourself' for the family man and working on cars or motorbikes for the young and unattached also display a displacement to non-work time of that pride in craft and in creation which have been increasingly eroded by the modern production line.[23]

WORK AND HEALTH: THE OCCUPATIONAL PATHOLOGY OF THE EIGHTEENTH CENTURY

Romantic notions of a 'rude' peasantry and artisanry romping healthily and robustly through the eighteenth century are easily dispelled. Many occupations were inherently unhealthy: something which stemmed from the nature of the materials worked upon or the labour process involved. The increasing division of labour and the growth of manufacturing in artisan and workshop modes produced a distinctive occupational pathology for the age. It was taken for granted by Adam Smith that each trade had its 'peculiar infirmity'. Indeed, medical concern with occupational health goes back as far as 1700 with the publication by the Italian physician Bernard Ramazzini of *De Morbis Artificum Diatriba*. In this work, well known in an English translation in the mid-eighteenth century, Ramazzini added to the diagnostic questions on diet and symptoms suggested by Hippocrates a further question: 'What occupation does he follow? . . . This should be particularly kept in mind when the patient to be treated belongs to the common people.'

Of workers in mining and manufacturing from the collier to the gilder, one English pamphleteer wrote in 1782: 'while they minister to our necessities, or please our tastes and fancies, [they] are impairing their health and shortening their days'. Manufactures were the equal of war in producing a mournful procession of the blind and lame, and of enfeebled, decrepit, asthmatic, consumptive wretches, 'crawling half alive upon the surface of the earth'. The language which gives us grinder's asthma (or consumption), grinder's rot, mason's disease, miner's asthma, miner's phthsis, potter's rot, rock tuberculosis, stonehewer's phthsis, stone worker's lung for the dust-produced disease of the lungs (silicosis); also offers at a lower level of seriousness, occupational bursitis in the varying forms of: bricklayer (or miner's) elbow, weaver's bottom, housemaid's knee, hod-carrier's shoulder and tailor's ankle. The hatter was 'mad' from the paranoia which was one of the several symptoms of mercury poisoning.

Any discussion of occupational health must take account of several qualifying factors. Environment, diet and indulgences such as drink also contributed to the destruction of workers. Hours of labour were a material factor. Sedentary occupations limited to a modern short working day and offset by good diet and healthy recreation may not seem especially dangerous to physical well-being, but in trades such as shoemaking or tailoring in the eighteenth and early nineteenth centuries such offsetting conditions did not exist. The overworked journeyman tailor could become the 'wretched emblem of death and hunger'. One of the greatest authorities, Charles Turner Thackrah, was convinced that shortening of hours was the most urgently needed of remedies. Vicious circles, especially in female trades like shirt-making, linked low wages – long hours – exaggerated infirmity (eye strain) – increasing disability – inability to work on better-paid work – still lower wages and so on.

Bad health could result from any one or a combination of several factors. It could stem directly from the harmful effects of materials used, e.g. lead poisoning; from a poor working environment, damp, cold, ill-ventilated, dust-laden or hot; from the physical deterioration which resulted from harmful postures or cramped conditions; or from the overstraining of particular muscles or organs. On top of these, in many occupations there was an ever-present danger of injury or death from accident.

Lead can be taken as illustrative of the effects of working with a noxious material: it was widely used by house painters, plumbers, glaziers and pottery workers. Ramazzini described the symptoms of it among the last named: 'First their hands become palsied, then they become paralytic, spenetic, lethargic, cachectic and toothless, so that one rarely sees a potter whose face is not cadaverous and the colour of lead.' One undoubtedly beneficial change introduced by Wedgwood into Eturia was a closely regulated hygiene practice to minimise contamination from the lead used in glazing. But in this respect as in others, Etruria was not typical of the pottery manufacture, and in 1831 the characteristic symptoms as described by Ramazzini were still being described in the English potteries. House painters, whose lead-affected condition was fully described in 1757, were also still being described in 1831 as unhealthy-looking and short-lived. As well as the proverbial madness, the mercury used in hat-making produced the palsy known as the 'hatter's shakes'. Arsenic, used in some glazes, was a further problem in the potteries, as it was in copper refining whose workers were said in 1794 to become emaciated in a matter of weeks and to die within a few years. Dyeing chemicals affected the health of the calico printer, and soot produced the well-known sweep's cancer which afflicted the climbing boys.

Malevolent effects from deleterious working conditions were even more widespread. The pale faces of miners from metal mines reflected bad air, extreme working temperatures and dampness. Such effects were hidden by the blackened faces of their coal-mining brothers; but the death-dealing dust was more evident. Dust was a real killer not only for miners, but for masons, bricklayers, coal-heavers, and even bakers and hairdressers. Few occupations were more deadly than that of the grinder in the cutlery trades whose life was dreadfully shortened. Woolcombers worked in the intense heat and fumes of charcoal stoves and few even in the mid-nineteenth century attained fifty years of age.

Cramped working postures were part of the miner's life, but they were not the only sufferers. Occupational cramps and 'craft palsies' were productive of deteriorating spasmodic muscular conditions in many trades affecting, for example, cotton-twisters, nailmakers, saddlers, sawyers and tailors. Eyestrain was widespread in most branches of the needle trades with tailors being beyond the higher-paid close-stitched work by the time they were forty, an age at which many watchmakers could no longer see well enough to keep up their earnings. Weavers complained of the effects of long hours of standing, while the working position of lockmakers led to a part of the Black Country being christened 'Humpshire'.

Indoor sedentary occupations involving long hours were commonly linked to consumption, a predisposition which was significantly increased by the cross-legged posture in which tailors traditionally worked. 'You rarely see a tailor live to a great age' wrote Campbell in 1747, an observation echoed eighty years later by Turner Thackrah:

> He is 19 years of age, wretchedly meagre and sallow. He came from the country six years ago blooming and healthy. But since this period he has

lived in Leeds, been confined to his baneful position from morning to night in a small low room.

We see, he remarked, 'no plump and rosy tailors'. Their susceptibility to stomach disorders and to pulmonary consumption was one which was the 'lamentable state of a great number of artisans'. Shoemakers suffered similarly and their faces marked them 'almost as well as a tailor'.

For many labourers, ruptures from heavy lifting were sufficiently common for a National Truss Society to be formed in 1786 for the support of the 'bursten' poor. Physical injury or even death was high in mining but inherent too in many trades where sharp tools were used in confined spaces. In mines there was the special danger from rock collapses and cave-ins and the risks associated with the use of explosives. In the coalfields, natural explosive potential was present in the 'firedamp' which would be ignited by a miner's candle. The dust-shortened life of the Sheffield grinder could be even more drastically curtailed if his rapidly spinning grindstone were to shatter into flying slivers of stone.

Such health problems were largely accepted. There was no notion of 'compensation' in wage rates. There did not have to be, for workers did not *choose* to run the risks of a particular employment. They accepted the short lives of the cutler or the miner, because they were born and grew up in Sheffield or Cornwall and were the sons of cutlers or miners. The comfortable classes could take it for granted that such conditions were the lot of the workers. Particularly unhealthy occupations such as working in the lead works of Whitechapel amounted to a virtual death sentence. Only the truly desperate would have undertaken them. Those who came from the bottom of the pile had no expectations of anything better; and there was no special claims to be considered from those who worked in 'dishonourable' trades and were badged by degeneracy and evident inferiority.[24]

If the pre-factory situation of manufacturing and mining workers is so dismal, why has the factory system been so loaded with opprobrium? Largely because it not only concentrated labour in a form which made it difficult to ignore, but relied so heavily on the labour of children and of women that is seemed especially exploitative of the labour of those who were weak by virtue of age or sex. So far as the conditions of adult male operatives were concerned, it would not be easy to make out a case for health deterioration. That the employment of women and children was widespread before the factory system hardly needs pointing out. The vivid illustrations of the Bluebooks of the 1840s showing small children drawing heavy loads of coal on all fours through narrow, dark levels, could as well have come from the mines of Shropshire in 1770, where a contemporary described children who 'with their hands and feet on the black, dusty ground and a chain about their body, creep and drag along like four footed beasts, heavy loads of the dirty mineral, through ways almost impassable to the curious observer'.[25]

Conditions in cottage industry where women and children worked as part of the family unit of production were hardly ideal. Small, damp and ill-ventilated habitations where living and working competed for space were no more healthy than were the conditions in many factories. Indeed, where harmful materials were worked on, fumes were present for a longer period than they were when work and home were separate. Nevertheless the cottage gave access to pure air and to space, while in many instances the mixing of manufacturing or mining with farming employment, and in general the lack of stress in the rhythms of domestic production, gave some opportunities of renewing the vigour which hard labour drained from the body. The extent and conditions of family work in the home are discussed below but it should be noted here that the child apprentice in craft or cottage industry was as vulnerable to corporal punishment or other forms of harsh treatment as the factory child – except in the important sense that none were as unprotected as the pauper child removed from home, friends and locality to a place where they knew no one. Defenders of the factory system are, however, apt to indulge in a special pleading which denies that there were *any* significant differences. In fact, to a greater and more systematic extent than pre-existing modes of production, the factory system separated child labour from the family economy and placed it in a more intolerable total environment. Long, regimented hours, more formal discipline and the danger of the mangling of tired limbs from unguarded machinery, all imply differences in both the form and pace of child labour. That child labour existed in eighteenth-century manufacturing and that the lot of these children was often a far from happy one does not permit us to regard the exploitation of child labour by the early factory masters as little more than a continuation of well-established practice. Observers of the few factories which existed before the end of the eighteenth century noticed the difference. Thomas Percival, a Manchester doctor, lived close to the early cotton mills and commented on the effect of a 'confinement' which 'either cut them off early in life' or rendered their constitutions sickly and feeble. In 1784 a critical report on the Manchester mills condemned their low ceilings and floors crowded with machinery. It noted that the adherence of cotton dust to friction-heated oil meant an offensive smell was always present. At night the situation was worsened by the lack of ventilation and the heat and smoke of great numbers of candles. Aiken, who wrote in 1797, was also a doctor. He described apprentices, brought in batches from distant workhouses, confined for long hours, often through the night, in 'injurious' air. Temperature changes from extremes of heat to cold predisposed them to sickness and disability, while epidemics were rife. The evidence produced in the several parliamentary inquiries which came between 1816 and the 1840s has been variously accepted or dismissed, but what little evidence survives on the early mills strongly points to a deleterious effect on the health of their mostly young employees.[26]

HEALTH IN FACTORY AND MINE

We have already noted the occupational pathology of the eighteenth century. In so far as many of the older trades continued throughout the first half of the next century to follow the same mode of production, then for the most part their associated health problems persisted. In so far as many of them underwent an intensification of labour as they became increasingly 'sweated', it is a reasonable assumption that their 'peculiar infirmities' became even more telling. It is this condition which was so well documented by observers of the 'sweated trades' like Henry Mayhew. Increasingly, too, the sewing trades employed women in outworking conditions of unbelievable squalor and hard and lengthy labour. Mayhew found one woman living over a coal shed who ate only dry bread and weak coffee. She made shirts at from 2–3d. (1–3p) each, had to find her own thread, and to make a living had to work from 6 a.m. to 9 p.m., and in summer from 4 a.m. to 10 p.m. – 'as long as I can see' – when there was a 'press of business' she sometimes began at 2 or 3 a.m., 'merely lying down in my clothes to take a nap of five or ten minutes'. At best she cleared 5s. (25p) a week, but more often, after paying for candles, only 2s. 6d. (12½p). Even more pathetic was the condition of another whose eyesight prevented her from taking the best work and who from want of nourishment, close confinement in a small room and over-work had been destroyed in health.[27]

In this section we are concerned with the health aspects of work in mill and mine in the first half of the nineteenth century. In whatever conditions adults worked, then alongside them worked their child assistants, usually for the same length of time. Unformed bodies and soft bones bent to strains an adult frame could have better resisted. Furthermore life and health expectancy were significantly affected by the fact of *having been* a child worker. Polluted air in mills, like deficient air in mines, took its toll slowly in proportion to the length of exposure. By the time a child piecer attained the age of eighteen, he or she would have already been absorbing the lint-laden air of the cotton mill for perhaps a decade. By the time a young copper miner reached manhood, he had subjected his lungs to six years of breathing the oxygen-deficient air of the level end.

Machinery, too, must be accounted very largely a new risk. The long catalogue of accidents is distressing, but without modern expectations of recording and inquest, the risk cannot be quantified. The record abounds with vivid illustrations of the dangers to which the factory children were exposed and to which far too many were sacrificed. This experience of a 'factory cripple' speaks for itself:

> At the age of 8 or 9, his limbs began to show symptoms of giving way, under the excessive fatigue to which he was subjected . . . Every precaution was taken that the humble means of his widowed mother would permit, to prevent her only boy from being made a cripple; but in vain. Oils, flannel bandages, strengthening plasters and mixtures, were incessantly applied; and every thing but the right one, (viz. taking him from the work), were one by one tried, rejected, and abandoned. In defiance of all these remedies, he became from excessive labour, a confirmed cripple for life. His knees gave way and gradually sunk inwards till they touched each other.

The frail child was still subject to beatings from the overseers or spinners. Moved into another part of the factory, his coat got entangled in machinery and he had a narrow escape from death.[28]

Children working underground in mines for coal and for metal ran the same risks from cave-ins and rockfalls as the adult miners, but as mines went deeper into worse air (the safety lamp of Sir Humphrey Davy enabled them to be sent into depths at which the traditional candle would not have burned), then the invisible death from bad air took inexorably a much larger toll than did the sudden explosion or collapse.

Given the conditions in which working people lived, it is not easy to attribute specifically to working conditions poor health which was in part a product of the total living environment. In some instances, evidence can be used retrospectively. When modern doctors have identified and labelled the pulmonary disease bysinosis as being caused by the inhalation of cotton dust, then it is probable that in the even more laden air of a cramped and unventilated early nineteenth-century mill, the lint was taking its toll. Care is needed in reaching such conclusions for not all subsequently identified conditions can be read back. The second occupational disease especially associated with working cotton, 'mule spinner's cancer' (of the hand), is associated with a change in use from animal to mineral oil which did not take place until 1870.

There were not wanting doctors to take the side of the factory owners: men prepared to be complacent about the effects of sixteen-hour standing shifts on young bodies of nine-year-old children, or even to suggest that factory labour was actually beneficial! Why, Sir Robert Peel asked his critics when he introduced his Act of 1816 to protect cotton mill apprentices, if conditions were so good, did they not take a holiday there? Professor Mathias would condemn the extreme apostles of *laissez-faire* 'who resisted every limitation imposed upon employers by statute in the name of individual liberty and the bogy of impending commercial disaster' to the 'lowest ledges of Dante's inferno'.[29] I would allow them the concession of taking their doctors.

A better advert for his profession was Turner Thakrah who, having thoroughly investigated in 1831 the health aspects of most trades, did not understate the problems of non-factory workers, but nevertheless regarded the factory system as having brought an evident deterioration:

> I stood in Oxford-row Manchester, and observed the streams of operatives as they left the mills at 12 o'clock. The children were almost universally ill-looking, small, sickly, barefoot, and ill-clad. Many *appeared* to be no older than seven. The men, generally from 16 to 24, and none aged were almost as pallid and thin as the children. The women were the most respectable in appearance, but I saw no fresh or fine-looking individuals among them . . . Here I saw, or thought I saw, a degenerate race – human beings stunted, enfeebled, and depraved – men and women that were not to be aged – children that were never to be healthy adults. It was a mournful spectacle.

He had listened to and considered the arguments which attributed the ill-health of the factory population to its dissipated habits and poor living conditions:

> Still, however, I feel convinced that independently of moral and domestic vices, the long confinement in mills, the want of rest, the shameful reduction of the intervals for meals, and especially the premature working of children, greatly reduce health and vigour, and account for the wretched appearance of the operatives.[30]

William Blake's imperishable image of 'dark, satanic mills' mingles with unforgettable pictures and descriptions from contemporary investigation to produce a persuasive vision of the factory child: thin and pale-faced dragging a stunted or even deformed body through an expenditure of labour appropriate to the unrelenting momentum of the machine, and doing so through long hours of the day and night. The indictment is persuasive. It is also polemic, but it is not a false picture however much some modern historians seek to 'correct' its emphasis. Rather few Englishmen had visited factories before 1800, but in the first half of the nineteenth century conditions in them became the subject of widespread and bitter debate as the aroused conscience of the nation overcame the resistance of the mill-owners, the political economists and their parliamentary allies. It is a debate which has continued among modern historians. Since few students enter this area of controversy without bringing with them at least half-remembered images of the overworked factory children as victims, it may come as a surprise for them to discover that there are some historians who seek to contradict any general condemnation of the era of the factory child. Would it not be more reasonable for them as defenders of the market economy to argue that child labour was a necessary but passing stage in the birth of the industrial economy: a concomitant of the formative stage of that great release of material productive power which allowed a few fortunate economies to banish the poverty of centuries of underemployment? They could point to the lesson of Ireland where population grew without an accompanying industrial revolution. Most moderate historians would follow this line of argument. But there are a few historians whose determination to excuse the 'heroic' early factory masters is usually presented under the flag of 'objectivity'. The student should not be confused by the label. The motivation is often to dispute any suggestion by historians of the 'left' that capitalism was exploitative. Milder collectivists like the Hammonds as well as Engels and later Marxists are alike labelled distorters. Taken together, such 're-assessments' do indeed add a degree of qualification to the more extreme moral indignation which found its best-known exponents in the Hammonds. Examined separately, they seem to display more of the features of special pleading than of objectivity.

The case for re-assessment has several strands. One is to insist that child labour was not a novelty introduced by the industrial revolution. This is perfectly proper: no serious historian suggests that it was, and we have discussed above the different *nature* of child labour in the pre-factory economy. More contentious is the debate over the quality of the evidence. The bulk of the evidence supporting the condemnation of child labour was assembled by those who were already committed on the issue, in many cases fanatically so. The student need not expect the evidence collected by Michael Sadler's committee of 1832 to do other than support the case for restricting child labour, being prepared by his committed colleague Richard Oastler and his Short-time Committees of factory workers. Extreme cases were presented as representative and 'better' cases ignored. The emphasised instances of overt brutality need not be taken as typical. But this does not mean that they did not happen. It is the inherent brutality of a system which was exploitative by its very nature in working children of very tender years for long and arduous hours in unhealthy conditions which is the real issue. In parading the worst possible examples culled from the 1832 report, the Hammonds in their much-read *Town Labourer* gave a decidedly impressionistic portrayal of the factory system. Their 'offence' was pointed out in a rather unexceptional article by W. H. Hutt in 1926 which has been since made to bear a major proportion of the 'optimist' case.[31] But it was not the Sadler Report which led to legislation. It led to the delaying tactic of appointing a second and further inquiry, the Factory Commission of 1833. It is true that the evidence collected by that investigation was much less condemnatory of the factory system, hardly surprising given its composition. 'Optimist' historians in expressing a preference for its findings should not fail to indicate two things. Firstly, most contemporary commentators regarded it as an over-corrective; secondly the evidence of 1832 may be unrepresentative, but it is neither untrue nor dishonest;

and thirdly that many important contemporary critics of the factory system deliberately based their critiques on the findings of 1833 to *avoid* the imputation of bias. This was true of both Peter Gaskell and of Frederick Engels. After all, the findings of 1833 were in the end quite sufficient to lead in an age of hide-bound *laissez-faire* to legislative intervention to protect the factory children from their masters.

What, then, were the findings of this second 'less biased' inquiry of 1833? The risk to life and limb from unfenced machinery was described as a great evil. Some factories were praised for their efforts to minimise this danger but: 'there are other factories . . . by no means few in number, nor confined to the smaller mills, in which serious accidents are continually occurring'. Not only was this so, but in many cases there seemed little concern for the victims of accidents: 'their wages are stopped, no medical attendance is provided, and whatever the extent of the injury no compensation is afforded'. Children everywhere were found to work the same number of hours as the adult operatives and that the effects of this were in a great number of cases:

> Permanent deterioration of the physical constitution. The production of disease often wholly irremediable, and the partial or entire exclusion (by reason of excessive fatigue) from the means of obtaining adequate education and acquiring useful habits, or of profiting by those means when afforded.[32]

Since children at the age when they suffered these injuries were not free agents, a case was made out for the intervention of the legislature on their behalf. The resulting Act of 1833 was a milestone in extending to 'free' children a degree of protection which, although limited to textile mills, still considerably extended the scope of the Acts of 1802 and 1816 which had covered only apprentices in cotton mills.

The problem of the enforcement of this Act has been well described elsewhere, most usefully by Dr Henriques in a volume in this series.[33] It remains for us to assess what softening of the standard image of exploited child labour in the factories of the industrial revolution is needed. Firstly it is important not to present a uniform unchanging picture of conditions throughout the first fifty or so years of the factory system. The most evidently exploitative period, that of the apprenticeship system, had virtually ended by 1820. In it the largely rural-sited mills had drawn on an unfree pauper labour despatched from Poor Law institutions. These uprooted unfortunates were lodged in dormitories and fed parsimoniously. Even here a modern champion of the factory master has employed the well-tried tactic of attacking the veracity of a much-cited contemporary source, John Brown's *A Memoir of Robert Blincoe* (1832). Poor Robert, the orphan victim of the brutality of the early mills has had his sufferings dismissed, and the *Memoir* described as a polemic. However, so 'over the top' is Dr Chapman's attack that it has been effectively rebutted by Professor Musson, himself no extreme historian of the 'left'. Blincoe was born in

1792 and sent from the St Pancras workhouse in 1799 with eighty other children to a Nottinghamshire cotton mill. His harrowing account describes bad food, hard work over a fourteen-hour day, beatings and frequent accidents from machinery. He once ran away and was flogged on his recapture. Yet he was to look back on this mill as having been tolerable compared with the Derbyshire mill of Elias Needham to which he was moved in 1803. Here, despite the Act of 1802, he suffered frightful cruelties, which he claims were deliberately hidden from the not very enquiring eyes of the local magistrates who were supposed to inspect the mill. Food was so poorly supplied that the apprentices raided refuse dumps. They had little clothing and worked a sixteen-hour day without breaks. Death from fever and other diseases was frequent. Treatment was horrific and punishment severe. Sadistic overseers practised what amounted to pathological cruelty. Blincoe openly indicts the factory owner Needham and his sons as not only being aware of the disgusting brutality being handed out in his mill, but of participating in it. The catalogue of suffering in the *Memoir* is extreme, but it can hardly be dismissed as invention. Blincoe recounted his experiences in a temperate tone, and his memories were confirmed by others who worked at the mill, and reaffirmed on oath by himself. The account must stand as an indictment of the apprentice era. Of course, such conditions were by no means universal. Blincoe himself expressed the view that in centres like Manchester, mills were more effectively inspected. It was in the isolated rural mills that such extreme treatment took place and by the end of the first decade of the nineteenth century the apprenticeship system had very much declined, so that in his evidence given in 1833, Blincoe himself stated such cruelties as he had suffered from were by then rare. Chapman, however, wants to defend Needham even in his own time. He admits that hours were long, diet monotonous and living conditions crowded, but states that in the reports of local magistrates there was no mention of cruelty, sickness or death. Quite so, but one of the strongest of Blincoe's complaints was of magistrates who came to the mill to wine and dine with the owner and could hardly have paid less attention to the conditions they were supposed to supervise. Why should the evidence of such men be regarded as 'unbiased' while the author of *The Memoir* is dismissed as a 'gullible sensationalist'? Blincoe himself became a small employing manufacturer, Chapman points out, but what of it? There is not the slightest suggestion that he was a bad one. As Professor Musson has pointed out, Blincoe in his evidence to the 1833 inquiry was denouncing exploitation, not condemning the factory per se. Perhaps it could be noted in passing that he gave his evidence to the Commission of 1833, not to the presumed biased inquiry of 1832. It is difficult to dispute the conclusion of Professor Musson that:

> There is no doubt whatever that many children were exploited and ill treated in the early textile mills, that they were used as cheap factory labour,

that their hours of work were far too long, that accident, ill-health and deformities were common, and that cruel punishments were often inflicted. There is no doubt that, as the *Memoir* asserts, the owner of Litton Mill [Needham], 'although perhaps the worst of his tribe, did not stand alone'.[34]

Of course the *Memoir* is biased: how could it have been otherwise? But unless it is suggested that it is deliberate prevarication from beginning to end, its impact remains staggering. Dr Chapman's defence of some of the employers of child labour is contained in *The Early Factory Masters*, in general an important and scholarly work on the Midlands spinning industry. But what are we to make of a 'defence' which records that at one mill more than a third of the apprentices recruited died, absconded or had to be returned? Out of 780 apprentices taken on by this firm, only *two* are recorded as later employed as adult workers. This was a 'good' firm. Dr Chapman is not prepared to condone the sadism of Needham and the overseers, but considers it important to 'relate it to the conscience of the period'. Of the accusation that children were suspended by their arms over machinery, he has this to say:

> Cruel punishments to children were not unusual in the eighteenth century, and two of those described . . . were in fact advocated by progressive educationalists . . . Lancaster worked out an elaborate code of rewards and punishments, among which was 'the log', a piece of wood weighing four to six pounds, which was fixed to the neck of the child guilty of his or her first talking offence. On the least motion one way or another the log operated as a dead weight on the neck. Needham clearly tried to copy this progressive idea of the age. More serious offences found their appropriate punishment in the Lancastrian code; handcuffs, the 'caravan', pillory and stocks, and the 'cage'. This latter was a sack or basket in which more serious offenders were suspended from the ceiling. Needham clearly borrowed this idea too, though his children are alleged to have been suspended by their arms over the machines.[35]

Students of the debate over the treatment of factory apprentices should remember that the objective position is presumed to be that of juryman, not counsel for the defence.

When the factory debate got under way in the 1820s, the age of pauper apprenticeship was practically over, and the child labour force largely recruited from children placed there by their parents and not uncommonly working alongside them. Even if the effectiveness of factory legislation after 1833 is debatable, there seems good reason to suppose that conditions improved in the later 1830s and in the 1840s. Engels too easily gives the impression to the less-than-careful reader that the conditions which he relates from the inquiry of 1833 were fully representative of conditions when he wrote in 1844. By then, favourably inclined commentators such as William Crooke Taylor could sneer at the 'burst of sentimental sympathy' which had been directed towards the child operatives and had 'frightened the isle from its propriety': 'I remember very well when first I visited a cotton-mill feeling something like disappointment at not discovering the hoppers into which the infants were thrown.' Yet it is clear that Crooke Taylor was mostly familiar with exceptionally well-conducted mills. He implied as much when he *singled out* the care taken to guard machinery at one of his favourite establishments. He was inclined to read the conditions of the 1840s back to the 1830s and it is not to be supposed that he would really have been as 'well contented' to exchange his 'little study' for the working space of the cotton spinner![36] That factory reform, once secured, should have been rapidly accepted to the extent that few could be found in the 1840s ready to admit to having opposed it was a matter of contemporary comment.

The language of the leaders of the factory movement was often extreme. It was *meant* to sway opinion, as when Richard Oastler invoked the image of 'Yorkshire slavery' in a letter to the *Leeds Mercury* in 1830: on conditions in the worsted mills of Bradford: 'Thousands of our fellow creatures and fellow subjects, both male and female, the miserable inhabitants of a Yorkshire town . . . are this very moment existing in a state of slavery more horrid than are the victims of that hellish system "colonial slavery".' He was charging the atmosphere with emotion, but he was also by analogy using one issue of contemporary concern to point to the existence of another. A leading 'optimist' historian seems to find the slavery image inappropriate, but it seems not to present the same difficulty to a recent historian of English children who is also a specialist in the history of slavery.[37] We should remind ourselves that the horror felt by present-day readers was shared by contemporaries, including Tory politicians, journalists, disinterested humanitarians, a disproportionate number of Anglican clergymen, as well as some enlightened factory owners in an age harsher than our own. If some modern historians, lacking their sensitivity, see them simply as agitators for factory reform, then that is a pity for our age.

REFERENCES AND NOTES

1. **E. P. Thompson**, 'Time, work-discipline and industrial capitalism', *Past & Present*, no. 38, 1967, pp. 56–97; **J. G. Rule**, *The Experience of Labour in Eighteenth-Century Industry*, Croom Helm, 1981, p. 55.
2. Rule, *Experience of Labour*, p. 56.
3. Ibid., pp. 56–7.
4. **Max Weber**, *The Protestant Ethic and the Spirit of Capitalism*, Unwin, 1965, p. 59.
5. **William Hutton**, *A History of Birmingham*, 1781, p. 69; **Arthur Young**, *A Six Months Tour through the North of England*, 2nd edn, 1771, p. 149.
6. Rule, *Experience of Labour*, pp. 57–8; Thompson, 'Time, work-

discipline', p. 85.

7. Rule, *Experience of Labour,* pp. 58–9 for miners' hours.
8. Ibid., pp. 59–60.
9. Ibid., p. 60.
10. Ibid., p. 61.
11. **Thomas Wright**, *Some Habits and Customs of the Working Classes,* repr. Kelly, New York, 1967, pp. 108–30.
12. **D. A. Reid**, 'The decline of St Monday, 1776–1876', *Past & Present,* no. 71, 1976, pp. 77, 81–2, 86.
13. **R. D. Storch**, 'The problem of working-class leisure. Some roots of middle-class moral reform in the industrial north: 1825–50', in **A. P. Donajgrodzki** (ed.), *Social Control in Nineteenth Century Britain,* Croom Helm, 1977, p. 146.
14. **Charles Shaw**, *When I Was a Child,* 1903, repr. Caliban, 1977, pp. 49–54.
15. Thompson, 'Time, work-discipline', pp. 81–2.
16. See **N. McKendrick**, 'Josiah Wedgwood and factory discipline', *Historical Journal,* IV, 1961, p. 56.
17. Shaw, *When I Was a Child,* pp. 185, 181.
18. **Charles Dickens**, *Hard Times,* 1854; **J. T. Ward**, *The Factory System. Volume 2. The Factory System and Society,* David & Charles, Newton Abbot, 1970, pp. 26–7 quoting Sir James Kay-Shuttleworth on Manchester.
19. **S. Pollard**, *The Genesis of Modern Management,* Penguin, 1968, p. 213.
20. Ibid., pp. 216–17.
21. Ibid., pp. 218–21.
22. Ibid., p. 222.
23. **Alan Sillitoe**, *Saturday Night and Sunday Morning,* W. H. Allen, 1958.
24. The sources for eighteenth-century manufacturing are fully documented in Rule, *Experience of Labour,* Ch. 3, 'Work and health'.
25. Quoted in **L. Moffit**, *England on the Eve of the Industrial Revolution,* 1923, repr. Cass, 1963, pp. 256–7.
26. Ibid., p. 259; in **W. Bowden**, *Industrial Society in England towards the End of the Eighteenth Century,* 1925, repr. Cass, 1965, pp. 267–8; **J. Aiken**, *A Description of the Country From Thirty to Forty Miles around Manchester,* 1795, repr. Kelly, New York, 1968, pp. 219–20.
27. **E. P. Thompson** and **E. Yeo** (eds), *The Unknown Mayhew,* Penguin, 1973, pp. 145, 148.
28. **William Dodd**, *The Laboring Classes of England,* 1848, repr. Kelly, New York, 1976, pp. 15–17.
29. **P. Mathias**, *The First Industrial Nation,* Methuen, 1969, pp. 205–6.
30. **C. Turner-Thackrah**, *The Effects of the Principal Arts Trades and Professions and of civic states and habits of living on Health and Longevity,* 1831, quoted in Ward, *Factory System,* 2, p. 29.
31. **J. L.** and **B. Hammond**, *The Town Labourer,* 1917, repr. Longmans, 1978, Ch. 8 & 9; **W. H. Hutt's** article, 'The factory system of the early nineteenth century' was repr. in **F. A. Hayek** (ed.), *Capitalism and the Historians,* University of Chicago, 1954, pp. 156–84.
32. Ward, *Factory System,* 2, pp. 106–7.
33. **Ursula R. Q. Henriques**, *Before the Welfare State. Social Administration in early industrial Britain,* Longman, 1979, Ch. 4 & 5.
34. *A Memoir of Robert Blincoe,* Manchester, 1832. Dr Chapman's attack

on the value of the *Memoir* as evidence is in: *The Early Factory Masters*, David and Charles, 1967, pp. 199–209. The worth of the *Memoir* was re-asserted by **Professor A. E. Musson**, *Trade Union and Social History*, Cass, 1974, ch. nine: 'Robert Blincoe and the early factory system'.
35. Chapman, *Early Factory Masters*, pp. 170–1, 203–4.
36. Quoted in Ward, *Factory System*, 2, pp. 63–4.
37. Ibid., p. 74; **R. M. Hartwell**, *The Industrial Revolution and Economic Growth*, Methuen, 1971, Ch. 17: 'Children as slaves', but see **J. Walvin**, *A Child's World*, Penguin, 1982, p. 62.

Part Three

COMMUNITY

Chapter 6

COMMUNITY

So far we have considered the material condition of the labouring people and their work processes and conditions. Work and its role in the creation of value and its share in the economic product is obviously central to the social history of working people: too many so-called histories of the 'working class' have far too little to say about the labour process. However, there are dimensions of experience which demand an extension of perspective. In the following pages such matters as family, sexual behaviour, the use of non-work time and popular culture will be discussed. As a preliminary to their discussion, the term *community* will be used as a convenient hold-all for those aspects of working-class life which in part at least transcend the workplace.

At least as much as 'class', 'community' eludes consensual definition. To a large degree it has been dominated by the dichotomy insisted upon by the German sociologist Ferdinand Tonnies in 1887, between *Gemeinschaft* (community) and *Gesellschaft* (society). The former was a subjective community existing *a priori*; one belonged to it, and belonging to it by its members was its essence. It was subconsciously rather than calculatively interactive in its social relations which depended upon a closeness, even inseparability, of locality, work and kinship links: 'In Gemeinschaft (community) with one's family, one lives from birth on, bound to it in weal and woe. One goes into Gesellschaft (society) as one goes into a strange country.'[1] As opposed to *being* a part of it, one *became* a part of *Gesellschaft* (the social form more characteristic of industrial civilisation, associated rather than 'organic', utilitarian rather than 'natural') in which there was less intimacy in a more public life and where the wholeness of community tends to be replaced by a more *conscious* recognition of reciprocal interest. The choices of relatively independent individuals reflect *Gesellschaft*, as does the emergence of special associations for special purposes. Such a dichotomy is related to a rural/urban division and is central to both contemporary and subsequent representations of the processes of social change at work in this period. It was between

1750 and 1850 that the fundamental proportional shift between rural and urban living took place in England with a balance at the 1851 census. Obviously the inhabitants of a village or small town (it was possible in 1795 for the vicar of Corfe in Dorset to list every household in that settlement with its inhabitants, relationships, ages and earnings)[2] could 'know' each other, both in the present and through the dimension of the generations. Marriage, overwhelmingly intra-parochial, intermingled in-law relationships with blood ones to cement the cohesion of locality. In Tonnies' terminology, *Gemeinschaft* is bound to have been stronger among a rural village people than among an urban one: a lasting and 'genuine' social form in contrast to which *Gesellschaft* is represented as transitory and superficial. The association of *Gemeinschaft* with 'organic' settled, small-scale, face-to-face rural communities rather than with uprooted and mobile larger urban populations is an obvious and, at a fundamental level, a useful one. Presenting the new industrial towns as the antithesis of communal cohesion and 'belonging' came easily to the critics of the early industrial revolution. Engels wrote: '. . . here the morals and customs of the good old times are most completely obliterated . . . for Old England itself is unknown to memory'.[3] Dickens, in his portrayal of 'Coketown', carried the image of an atomised environment peopled by almost dehumanised inhabitants even further with his insistence not only on streets 'all very like one another' but on their having been inhabited by persons 'equally like one another'.[4]

Such characterisations raise many problems. What is it that is being argued? That urban industrial settlements are in essence incompatible with the idea of community? or that the early stages of industrialisation represent a time when only skeletal groupings of people came together not having as yet provided themselves with the manifestations of community? The former proposition would seem to be flatly contradicted by the appearance of the recognisable urban working-class community which was to become something of a model for mid-twentieth-century sociologists.[5] Clearly the physical boundaries of a village are likely to have also delineated the frontiers of a local community, but it would seem perfectly possible for urban areas to contain within their environs recognisable 'communities'. These were likely to have been closely linked with occupation. The silk-weavers of Spitalfields or the watchmakers of Clerkenwell perhaps constituted in the 1800s occupational communities as real as those of London's dockland 'discovered' by the sociologists of the mid-twentieth century. It is certain that industrial towns could *produce* their own forms and senses of community, but it is not reasonable to conclude that even the first generation of an urban industrial proletariat was completely uprooted from anything which carried traditional community norms and values. The novels of Mrs Gaskell offer a picture of the social life of the mill town quite different from that of Dickens's Coketown. Her portrayal is bleak indeed in its insistence upon the facts of material deprivation, low life-expectancy and conflict relationships between capital and labour, but offers also a glimpse of a working-class world structured by family, neighbourliness and friendship. Reciprocal relationships, walks and excursions contradict an anatomised presentation of mill town society.[6] In fact, people who came in from the countryside brought with them habits of life and speech and patterns of amusement which formed an intrinsic part of their consciousness. Modified, they nevertheless survived: rural folksong blended into industrial song; field sports into street games; feasts into fairs.

The continuing, and perhaps even increasing, importance of family and kinship networks both within the new towns of the industrial revolution and in linking their populations to their rural origins has been well documented by Professor Anderson. His investigations into propinquity in the working-class neighbourhoods of Preston reveal a strong inclination for offspring when married to settle within 100 yards of one or other parental home (the incidence was 2½ to 3 times larger than that suggested by a random choice prediction). Eighty-six per cent of young householders lived within 400 metres of their parental home. Such a pattern might be explained by factors such as the need to live close to place of work or by the ties of locality and upbringing rather than to kinship *per se*, but Anderson has also noted the sharing of leisure activities, exchange of visits and gathering on family occasions as evidence of the powerful influence of kinship in the new cotton towns. Kinship was very often instrumental in getting a job, and the fresh immigrant from the country often went to lodge with kin already established in the town. Of married couples, 12% of adult immigrants had within their households related persons who had either preceded or joined them.[7]

The new towns' working classes did not constitute as complete and integrated a community as did the smaller agricultural settlement with its intermingling of neighbourhood, friendship and kin links developed over time. But they cannot possibly have been as 'atomised' in their social relations as Engels suggested. In the early days, an especially rapid coming and going meant that neighbours were constantly changing and friendships were not easy to build; perhaps, as Anderson suggests, this made kin more important than friendship and neighbourhood in the establishment of reciprocal and instrumental relationships. Married women especially were not in all cases able to enjoy the social relationships of the workplace and the removal from female networks in the traditional community may have faced them with an increasing sense of isolation and resultant need to draw the maximum reciprocality from kinship connections, but in the event a fairly rapid community building in the urban industrial setting was one of the strongest of working-class responses in this period of upheaval.

OCCUPATION, COMMUNITY AND CLASS

In our present-day world of industrial change and contraction we have become only too familiar with the problem of occupational communities like pit villages, steel towns or fishing quarters where the closing down of an industry produces not just high levels of redundancy but the ending of a way of life for workers and their families. In our period, 1750 to 1850, occupation and community were rather more commonly interwoven than today. With little manufacturing diversification it was country market towns rather than manufacturing ones which presented a varied occupational structure. It has been suggested that this close linking of occupation and community makes it preferable to stress the local rather than the class bases of social and industrial protest before *c.* 1820.[8] Sheffield was a community of cutlers to be placed alongside villages of pitmen, tinners, weavers or nailors. In the grain-growing areas in particular, agricultural villages were effectively villages of farm workers. When such communities mobilised in protest, they commonly did so in defence of traditional or 'customary' rights. This lends credence to suggestions that early protest movements should be regarded as 'populist' rather than class protest. Concepts such as E. P. Thompson's 'moral economy of the English crowd' legitimating action against 'unjustly' high food prices are only sustainable on the assumption of a powerful community consensus:

> During the late eighteenth century and early nineteenth century, a great many public hostilities involved the attempt of local communities to enforce moral obligations with great traditional weight behind them who no longer felt the social pressure of community to be any sanction.[9]

There are, however, problems in asserting community as a populist concept in the stead of class. The two are not necessarily separable and can indeed be different but related facets of the same basis for resistance. Very many occupational communities were also describable as working-class communities in the objective sense of being comprised of persons sharing a common experience of selling their labour power to capitalists who were not of the community. The radicalism of Sheffield commented upon in the jacobin years of the 1790s shows an intermingling of class and community rather than affording evidence for the discarding of the one concept in favour of the latter. The manufacture of cutlery needed little capital and was dominated by small working masters employing two or three journeymen, who received good wages and were devoted worshippers of 'St Monday'. There were no citizens of sufficient weight to carry influence and the magistrates came from outside the town. The cutlers sold their product to 'merchant capitalists' and were 'dependent upon them'; only by organising could they defend their 'prices'. If they were a 'community', they were one with a shared *labour* interest.[10] The trade unionism of weavers, shearmen and combers in the clothing areas of the western counties in the first half of the eighteenth century was, of course, community based. But in so far as it was action against clothiers who did not live within the community, it can also be represented as a struggle of labour against capitalist impositions. Although traditional expectations and customary norms form the basis of action, it was still action against *capitalist* innovation. If a man unsure of whether or not to join in a strike knows that he must live out his life among his fellows, he is indeed constrained in his choice by belonging to a community, but at least part of that constraint depends upon the shared experience and solidarity of a community of workers. Professor Calhoun has suggested that a community populism underlay movements like Luddism. The hosiers who were introducing cheaper methods of production based on the employment of unskilled labour were withdrawing from a 'web of communal relations' which would have guaranteed that entrepreneurial behaviour was in accordance with community norms and the craft traditions which were intermingled with them. Masters who did not employ such methods sided, in opinion at least, with the workmen who broke machines. This does not, however, deny Luddism a place within the *labour* struggle as a movement of protest against the changed conditions in which labour power was to be marketed.

Although there are serious reservations, several of which have been indicated by Professor Neale, Calhoun has made a useful contribution to the study of early movements of labour protest. He seems, however, too quick to overrule the signs of incipient labour consciousness among machine-breakers and early trade unionists. He points out that increasingly the 'fissure of class distinction' allied to the erosion of the face-to-face community by significant demographic increase led to a shift in the identification of the bonds of community and made the self-regulating working-class community a possibility with its friendly societies and trade unions linking workers primarily and laterally to each other. This, together with the development of an elementary concept of a labour theory of value, could lead to the growth of a greater consciousness of commonality within a class, and hence break down localism and displace populism as a basis for action. The difficult point is: when? Most recent specialists accept that class conflict was at least latent in eighteenth-century labour disputes in manufacturing, while it has recently been suggested that in the southern counties and East Anglia a proletarianised agricultural workforce formed a separate 'community of labourers' from the end of the eighteenth century in contradiction to the paternalist model of social harmony. In general, Calhoun's suggested date of 1820 seems late and it is as difficult, as Professor Neale has pointed out, to infer populist consciousness from protest behaviour as it is to infer class-consciousness from it.[11]

COMMUNITY AND SOCIAL ORDER

In one sense the essence of community in the *Gemeinschaft* sense is its predominant degree of self-policing and regulation through communal restraint and legitimation. In so far as horizontal class divisions are not manifestly evident, then within an *accepted* social order, the actions of justices and magistrates speak with a voice of authority the greater because their judgements were in line with community consensus, e.g. in opposing excessive food prices or fixing wages. Where such authority refused to accept such popularly sanctioned activities as smuggling, wrecking or poaching, then the community persisted in them and in regarding its actions as 'legitimate'. Where 'properly constituted' authority offered only inaction in respect of behaviour which the populace regarded as 'immoral', then resort was often had to a range of popular sanctions from food riots through 'charivari' to arson. Such sanctions, involving the ritual humiliation of deviants and the community resistance in defence of custom, were only part of the role of tradition in the maintenance of social cohesion. Local customary calendars not only spaced the year and marked the seasons, but reinforced the identity and solidarity of the community while intermeshing with its economic and social structure. At times, such as at Christmas wassailing or Shrove Tide 'gooding', gift expectations were legitimated and those of the better-off who sought to avoid these expectations exposed: 'When anything is given, a cry of largess is raised, and a dance performed around the plough; but if a refusal to their application for money is made, they not infrequently plough up the pathway, door stone, or any other portion of the premises that happen to be near' runs a description of the keeping of 'Plough Monday' in nineteenth-century Derbyshire. How far the traditions of the countryside survived in the towns is difficult to determine. It is easier to trace equivalent customs to specific occupational groups than to a town or district of a town as such. It would, however, be foolish not to expect that breaking the standards of the community could not be to some degree sanctioned in urban communities, even if ritual was less evident. An observer of Lancashire's mill girls in 1849 remarked the contrast of their talk with the standard of their behaviour. They had a 'saucy prudery' and in fact kept a strict watch upon each other's morals so that fear of scandal was a significant deterrent to deviant behaviour.[12]

Custom and tradition were crucial for social cohesion, and became a matter for conflict as social distancing made 'community' increasingly synonymous with the 'lower classes' and the interests of farmers, employers and proprietors developed in opposition to the normative view of the community held by the labouring people. It was capitalist employers who broke the reciprocating framework of the rural village community – a fact which gives a certain irony to the poorly defined group of ideas, rationalisations and attitudes which can be loosely described as 'paternalist'.[13] Professor Perkin has stressed that the power of the landed interest was such that eighteenth-century England was essentially based on their local position:

> their powers always came back to the social control of the ordinary squire over his tenants and villagers. It manifested itself in the inevitability with which they followed his religion and politics; in the customary treats and charity for the loyal and deserving, and the harsh treatment of poor strangers, vagrants and poachers; and in the continual oversight of the morals and behaviour of all the inhabitants.[14]

The English landed class were remarkably open-ended but whatever the basis of entry into a class, which for all it might affect the style of the patrician had absorbed into its blood the parvenu wealth of the speculator and grocer, the personal face-to-face realities of patronage and deference were essentially those of a society of villages, or at best small towns. Paternalism has served as a 'magical social quantum' but it remains an ill-defined term labelling a concentration of economic and cultural domination which tends to present the notion of a one-class society by viewing social relations as they seem from the top. Of its nature it conceals conflict, blinds those who use its discourse to 'the actual social consciousness of the inarticulate labouring poor' and invites us to accept that until industrialisation, class confrontation was alien to a society of vertical rather than horizontal divisions. It is of value as an approach to eighteenth-century social relations but it presents rather than anatomises social order and questions of power.[15]

E. P. Thompson has pointed out that the term has normative implications suggesting warmth and mutual assent and that, as myth and ideology, paternalism was usually backward-looking. The modes and manners of a previous generation served as a model to set against a subsequent degeneration. Paternalism was always best represented by the good *old* squire and as such the ideal and the real are within its discourse all too often blurred. 'The rural patron is beheld no more . . .' concludes Langhorne's poem *The Country Justice* of 1774, while Richard Polwhele could write of his fellow Cornishman Sir William Lemon: 'In him we justly admire the old country gentleman, faithful to his king without servility, attached to the people without democracy.' Polwhele had only a few years earlier, in 1797, lamented the decline of paternalism and the widening gap between gentry and people in his verse treatise *The Old English Gentleman*, while Lemon affords a clear reminder of the open-ended nature of the gentry class for his grandfather had been a working miner 'without a shilling' who had struck lucky in the copper boom.[16]

By the early Victorian years there was some real applicability in the 'paternalist' stance where it yet fed on long habits of obedience and deference among village populations; but it had become more of a self-deluding representation, an idealisation in which power and wealth could be legitimated against weakness and deprivation. It continued to proclaim the social harmony and unity of all classes, but now in contrast to *urban* class society as well as by reference to a more cohesive past. The Duke of Richmond stated in 1846 the interests of landlords, clergy, farmers and labourers to be 'closely and intimately connected', while Archbishop Manning affected to despise the 'political economists' expression labour market' with its implied casting aside of *duty:* the duty of reciprocating care for honest, sober, diligent and deferential labour. If not largely devoid of meaning by the 1840s, the deluding self-image of the language of paternalism had by then become apparent to a working farmer who scorned the giving of dinners for villagers who had gone *40 years* without resort to parish relief and prizes for huge turnips. Fifty years ago, he said, the squire had resided on his estate, farmers had boarded unmarried labourers in their own houses and there had been a true reciprocation arising from affection and manifesting itself in good cottages, good wages, a cow and a garden. As for now, 'nothing is more meaningless than digging up a retired rustic for a prize at a dinner'. The Duke of Richmond was smug enough to tell an audience that he had never heard a tenant address an angry word to him. Probably had he more sensitive ears he might have caught a complaint or two behind his back. He might well have from workers to whom he paid 10s. or 11s. (50–55p) a week when the local rate was 12s. (60p), and he would have heard nothing to his advantage when none of the schools in parishes which he controlled were judged fit for a government grant although sixty-six other schools in the county were.[17] As we have seen, self-proclaiming paternalists were among those who engaged in cottage removal to rid *their* parishes of the burden of the poor.

The distinction between 'closed' villages where the concentration of landownership gave power to large landowners and 'open' villages where more widely dispersed ownership denied such clear authority is obviously relevant to the discussion of paternalism and squirarchical roles. It is not in all respects a clear distinction. It has been argued, for example, that poor relief could be just as much a discriminating instrument of social control when exercised by a vestry oligarchy as through the agency of a landlord.[18]

RELIGION

What was the role of religion in working-class communities? In the traditional villages of rural England, squire and parson were seen as twin pillars of the establishment. The Anglican church preached contentment and social obedience without being expected to stir up 'enthusiastic religion'. It has been suggested that the squire-parson alliance, as it grew and cemented itself, was a major factor in weakening the moral authority of the Church and the religiosity of the people. Dr Evans has shown how rapidly the rural clergy not only lost much of their spiritual authority, but also earned the hostility of their poorer charges. Non-residence was still a major scandal at the end of the third decade of the nineteenth century; while tithe demands not only alienated farmers, who in their turn stressed to their workers that such burdensome payments lowered their ability to pay proper wages, but fell also upon humble allotment holders – 'Potato Guts', shouted the women and children of Cheadle after their vicar as he passed along the street.[19]

Enclosures had elevated numbers of the rural clergy into prosperous farmers and widened the gap between them and their parishioners by making them more substantial figures in the community. The 22% of magistrates who were clergymen in 1831 was double the figure of 1761, and with this increase the old clerical role as mediator between rich and poor weakened. By 1800 the 'squirson' was common, especially in the Midlands and in East Anglia (47% of Lincolnshire's magistrates in 1847 were clergymen): 'He became an indispensable agent of the new social order which operated to the disadvantage of the labourer.'[20] Small wonder that one recent historian has described 1740–1830 as an 'era of disaster' for the Anglican church, at the end of which period it was in danger of becoming a minority religious establishment. The new urban working classes were hardly within its influence or even concern, while a sample of thirty Oxfordshire rural parishes reveals a 25% decline in communicants between 1738 and 1802. In the 1830s and 1840s the decline was reversed, but the response came too late and was too little to recover the lost ground. Nevertheless the Church finished the period in somewhat better heart and shape: an improvement noted by Charles Kingsley looking back over a dozen years from 1859:

> Every fresh appointment seems to me, on the whole, a better one than the last. They are gaining more and more the love and respect of their flocks, they are becoming more and more centres of civilization and morality to their parishes; they are working, for the most part, very hard.[21]

John Wesley's great Methodist revival began at Bristol in 1739 and by 1840 had reached its all-time peak of membership in relation to population, having outstripped the growth of the latter over the 100 years. Its influence was not, however, evenly spread. Wesley had despaired of success among agricultural populations where he attributed to the 'dullness' of the labouring people what was primarily a result of the scant space afforded him by the rigidities of rural social control exercised by the established church and the gentry. His efforts were especially directed to the 'outcast' communities growing up beyond the writ of the old parochial and patriarchal structures. Hence came the remarkable affinity of Methodism with mining communities: around Newcastle, Kingswood (Bristol) and the tin mining districts of west Cornwall. Methodism also had some impact in manufacturing towns such as those of the West Riding and in the Midlands. It was relatively less successful in some old manufacturing centres such as the clothing towns of the south-west where 'old dissent' was entrenched and where, after scant prosperity before 1770, it thereafter underwent a marked revival, increasing the number of its congregations down to 1840.[22]

What was the nature of Methodism's impact in those settlements where it did take hold? Two areas, popular education and popular recreation, are discussed below, but in general there has been little agreement among historians as to its social and economic effects. It is not surprising that in its early years, Methodism should have been seen as socially dysfunctional and disruptive of the established order, despite Wesley's insistence that he intended no separation from the Anglican church and his own very clear and frequently stated conservative views. A presumption of spiritual equality on the part of a common person with the squire, or for that matter with the parson, is essentially a challenging one; even more so is the 'heresy' of working-class lay preaching. Yet by historians from Halevy to E. P. Thompson, Methodism has been presented not only as a conservative and accommodating influence, but even a counter-revolutionary one. The main body of Wesleyan Methodists had become by the last decade of the eighteenth century an increasingly institutionalised and stabilising force. Its leadership was fundamentally middle class and its ideological identification bourgeois. Officially it was hostile to radical movements like jacobinism or Chartism, and a latent effect of its theodicy of suffering was to turn the experience of exploitation into a vehicle for personal redemption rather than social revolution. Thompson has gone further and presented Methodism as a means of purveying among the new industrial workforce the inner work disciplines demanded by industrial capitalism and its characteristic modes of production.[23]

There is much truth in all this, but there are some aspects of Methodism's contribution to the working-class experience which soften the picture. The opportunity to play a responsible community role as class leader or local preacher enriched the lives and released the talents of many working people. Confidence gained and abilities discovered in, for example, public speaking and organising membership have been shown to have contributed to the making of some at least of the working-class vanguard of the Chartist era and subsequently.[24] This was especially true of the more democratic and revivalist sects like the Primitive Methodists who split from the parent body in 1821. At the same time the very strength of the 'chapel' and its associated activities could in some communities, as we shall see in discussing popular recreation, have a polarising rather than cohesive effect.

Finally, the role of religion in a community cannot be concluded without some consideration of what constituted a plebian 'religious experience' or pattern of beliefs. In recent years several historians, some influenced by anthropology, have revealed the very large gap which could exist between 'official' and 'popular' religious perceptions. Village people lived to a considerable extent outside the culture of literacy, and Dr Obelkevich in a thorough study of Lincolnshire has shown how the 'religious realm' of the labourers reached beyond Christianity to 'encompass an abundance of pagan magic and superstition' and integrated them with conceptions of Christian doctrine which were adapted and transformed as they passed from the church to the cottage. Similar 'accommodations' of religious, especially Methodist, beliefs into folk beliefs and superstitions have been described in the mining and fishing villages of Cornwall. Rural clergymen had to face, with hostility, a 'mass of dimly perceived beliefs that were deviant at best and heathen at worst'. Local preachers and even some of the rusticated clergy might have found themselves being attributed powers which were at least akin to those of the conjurer if not the witch doctor. It is not at all easy to evaluate the impact of religion on a community: it is much more difficult to penetrate the opacity of that oral, largely pre-literate and unrecorded world where the community impacted on religion.[25]

Another institution far exceeded all other social organisations in membership apart from the churches. Friendly societies had a long history, but their growth from the mid-eighteenth century was so rapid that it is surprising only a few historians have taken note of it. Self-help, as Professor Harrison has noted, may have become in its mid-Victorian manifestation an individualistic philosophy to be preached at the working class as an answer to its demands for better conditions, but it was in its original expression a spontaneous response to working-class needs and in the friendly society assumed a collective aspect. The links between the societies amd the early trade unions can be explored elsewhere and the lines of demarcation were often unclear, but generally friendly societies were widespread and most often unconnected with particular trades. They provided a degree of independence from charity and the poor rate for sickness and burial expenses from a mutual insurance; conviviality in their monthly public-house meetings and ceremony in their annual feasts and processions replete with ritual and regalia. Sir Frederick Eden in his famous survey of 1797 noted that no institutions had ever progressed to such an extent in so short a period of time as the friendly societies over the last years of the eighteenth century. In 1801 he estimated there to be 7,200 with 648,000 members; by 1815 the Poor Law overseers estimated a membership of 925,429. Most of these were in local societies averaging 100 members with very few exceeding 200 and there was a disproportionate concentration in the manufacturing districts with Lancashire in

1821 having 17% of the total number of societies while the smallest proportions of populations in societies were to be found in rural counties. By 1870 membership had reached four million, compared with 500,000 in trade unions, in which the influence of the affiliated orders, the Foresters and Oddfellows, had been growing since the 1830s. Where they existed in villages they reinforced community identification; in the towns they helped to build it by providing opportunities for association and belonging which were otherwise scarce in the emerging industrial society.[26]

REFERENCES AND NOTES

1. Quoted in **P. Worsley** (ed.), *Modern Sociology Introductory Readings*, Penguin, 1970, p. 295.
2. This listing is discussed by **Peter Laslett** in his Open University broadcast (available on tape), 'Who were the poor in eighteenth-century England'.
3. Quoted in **J. Lucas**, 'Engels, Mrs Gaskell and Manchester', in *The Literature of Change*, Harvester, 1980, p. 48.
4. **Charles Dickens**, *Hard Times*, 1854, Ch. 5, 'The key-note'.
5. For example, **P. Townsend**, *The Family Life of Old People*, Penguin, 1963; **M. Young** and **P. Willmott**, *Family and Kinship in East London*, Penguin, 1962; and **R. Hoggart**, *The Uses of Literacy*, Penguin, 1958.
6. See the beginning of *Mary Barton*, 1848.
7. **M. Anderson**, *Family Structure in Nineteenth-Century Lancashire*, Cambridge U.P., 1971, pp. 56–67, 119, 152.
8. **C. Calhoun**, *The Question of Class Struggle: Social Foundations of Popular Radicalism during the Industrial Revolution*, Blackwell, 1982.
9. **C. Calhoun**, 'Community: toward a variable conceptualization for comparative research', *Social History*, 5, 1980, p. 112.
10. **A. Aspinall**, *The Early English Trade Unions*, Blatchford, 1949, Doc. 6.
11. **R. S. Neale**, *History and Class. Essential Readings in Theory and Class*, Blackwell, 1983, pp. 286–91.
12. For 'charivari', see **E. P. Thompson**, 'Rough music: le charivari anglais', *Annales*, 27, no. 2, 1972. The account of Plough Monday is quoted by **Bob Bushaway** in his essential book for customary rituals and practices, *By Rite. Custom, Ceremony and Community in England 1700–1880*, Junction Books, 1982, p. 169; **P. E. Razzell** and **R. W. Wainwright** (eds), *The Victorian Working Class: Selections from Letters to the Morning Chronicle*, Cass, 1973, p. 190.
13. For a useful survey, see **D. Roberts**, *Paternalism in Early Victorian England*, Croom Helm, 1979, and for a critique of 'paternalism' as a concept, see **E. P. Thompson**, 'Eighteenth-century English society: class struggle without class', *Social History*, vol. 3, no. 2, 1978, pp. 133–65.
14. **H. Perkin**, *The Origins of Modern English Society 1780–1880*, Routledge & Kegan Paul, 1969, p. 42.
15. Thompson, 'Eighteenth-century English society', p. 134.
16. Ibid., p. 137; **R. Polwhele**, *The Old English Gentleman*, 1979, p. iv; **L.**

Namier and **J. Brooke**, *History of Parliament. The House of Commons*, HMSO, 1964, II, p. 62.

17. Roberts, *Paternalism*, pp. 108–9, 118. For the decline of old paternalism and the coming of a new rhetoric of 'pseudo-gemeinschaft', see **J. Obelkevich**, *Religion and Rural Society. South Lindsey 1825–75*, Oxford U.P., 1976, pp. 23–102.

18. For a recent full discussion of the significance of open and 'closed' parishes, see **D. R. Mills**, *Lord and Peasant in Nineteenth Century Britain*, Croom Helm, 1980, esp. Ch. 4–6; **R. A. E. Wells**, 'Social conflict and protest in the English countryside in the early nineteenth century: a rejoinder', *Journal of Peasant Studies*, vol. 8, pp. 516–23.

19. **A. D. Gilbert**, *Religion and Society in Industrial England. Church, Chapel and Social Change 1740–1914*, Longman, 1976, p. 14; **E. J. Evans**, 'Some reasons for the growth of English rural anti-clericalism c. 1750–c. 1830', *Past & Present*, no. 66, 1975, p. 92.

20. Ibid., pp. 101–4.

21. Gilbert, *Religion and Society*, p. 27; **Charles Kingsley**, Preface to the 4th edn of *Yeast*.

22. Gilbert, *Religion and Society*, pp. 30, 38.

23. **E. P. Thompson**, *The Making of the English Working Class*, Penguin, 1968, Ch. 11, 'The transforming power of the Cross'.

24. This was the argument of **R. F. Wearmouth**, *Methodism and the Working-Class Movements of England, 1800–1850*, Epworth Press, 1945.

25. Obelkevich, *Religion and Rural Society*, pp. 258–62; **J. G. Rule**, 'Methodism, popular beliefs and village culture in Cornwall, 1800–50', in **R. D. Storch** (eds), *Popular Culture and Custom in Nineteenth-Century England*, Croom Helm, 1982, pp. 61–7.

26. **J. F. C. Harrison**, *The Common People. A History from the Norman Conquest to the Present*, Fontana, 1984, pp. 271, 276–7; **P. H. J. H. Gosden**, *Self-Help. Voluntary Associations in Nineteenth-Century Britain*, Batsford, 1973, pp. 9–28. Dr Gosden is one of the few historians to have studied the societies in depth.

Chapter 7

THE FAMILY

The impact on the family of the economic changes of the late eighteenth and early nineteenth centuries, especially the coming of the factory system, was the cause of deep and sustained pessimism among many contemporaries. There were several senses in which the order of the factory was felt to disrupt a more 'natural' one. There was the new machine-dictated rhythm of labour, displacing manual pace and extending a new control over the work process. There was the increasing imposition of night work and, above all, there was the increasing employment of women and children outside the home. William Wordsworth captured these senses of the factory as an 'outrage against nature'. An 'unnatural light' allowed 'never resting labour' to work at night, an outrage emphasised by a summons 'to unceasing toil' from a bell, 'of harsher import than the curfew-knoll/ That spake the Norman Conqueror's stern behest', not only men but 'maidens, youths/Mother and little children, boys and girls'.[1]

Contemporary reactions to the factory employment of women and children in 'unnatural' work could be strong and emotive. Richard Oastler pronounced the 'violation of the sacred nature of the home' to be 'the greatest curse of the factory system', while Lord Shaftesbury viewed it as threatening the very core of society:

> In the male the moral effects of the system are very sad, but in the female they are infinitely worse . . . not alone upon themselves but upon their families, upon society [and] upon the country itself. It is bad enough if you corrupt the man, but if you corrupt the woman you poison the waters of life at the very fountain.

Domestic life and discipline, he argued, would soon be at an end and society come to consist of 'individuals no longer grouped into families; so early is the separation of husband and wife, of parents and children'.[2]

The most startling polemic, and perhaps the most influential, was Peter Gaskell's *Artisans and Machinery* of 1836. To Gaskell the results of the transition from the domestic system to the factory were, for the textile worker's family, simply catastrophic:

> Recklessness, improvidence and unnecessary poverty, starvation, drunken-
> ness, parental cruelty and carelessness, filial disobedience, neglect of
> conjugal rights, absence of maternal love, destruction of brotherly and
> sisterly affection, are often its constituents and the results of such a com-
> bination are moral degradation, ruin of domestic enjoyments, and social
> misery.

Gaskell's strident attack on the factory system clearly influenced
Engels who placed the impact of the new methods of production on
working-class family life in the forefront of his, subsequently, better-
known indictment of 1844: 'The employment of the wife dissolves the
family utterly and of necessity, and this dissolution, in our present
society, which is based upon the family, brings the most demoralising
consequences for parents as well as children.' Neglected by their
working mothers and working themselves for long hours away from
home from an early age, the children had no real experience of family
life and growing up 'like wild weeds' contributed in their turn to the
'general undermining of the family in the working class'. Home
became simply viewed as lodgings, where because of the shift or relay
system, 'family members had minimal weekday contact.'[3]

What were the fundamental grounds for such attacks? Essentially,
antipathetical reaction stemmed from contrast with a stereotyped
image constructed from the presumed features of the weaver's home
and family life during the period of rural industry. Only rarely did the
critics go outside the textile industry in making their comparisons. The
weaver, before the factory, was the head of an integrated family unit of
reproduction, production and consumption. The wife divided her time
between assisting her husband and looking after the home and the
children, who grew gently into work contributing their labour to
age-suited tasks assigned by parents. Sons were thus instructed into
their father's trade while daughters learned both to contribute to the
subsidiary labour needs of the household manufacture and, from their
mothers, the tasks and skills of domestic management and of house-
work. Within the home the child was therefore taught, socialised,
constrained, conditioned and protected from moral contagion.
According to Gaskell, by the time the child became at around the age
of fifteen 'fully useful' by regularly assisting in the family's productive
efforts, it had been taught by 'daily experience, habits of subordination
to its seniors'. Boys came gradually to full earnings at a time when the
'impulses of puberty' needed checking, and work, by keeping the
youths occupied in the home, at the same time kept them away from
bad example. Work at home in the company of sisters, brothers and
parents away from the dangerous 'heat' of the factory was: 'the very
best anodyne for allaying and keeping in due restraint his nascent
passions, whilst his moral and social instincts were under a process of
incessant cultivation'.[4]

The order was unchallenged patriarchy and the sexual division of labour required female members to assist in the making of cloth while also assigning most domestic tasks to them. With 'no separate or distinct interests' acknowledged, all earnings went into a common stock. The father's position as the central breadwinner was dependent upon supplementary labour which commonly received no separate remuneration: in effect there was a family wage.

Although an idealised picture, it is nevertheless one to which weavers themselves could subscribe. One, from Bolton in 1824, testified that in the old days of good prices children had been employed at home where they had been brought up with 'good moral instruction . . . now . . . they send them to the factories, and that is one great grievance to the feelings of a moral man, that he is not able to bring up his children under his own eye'.[5] Of course, families were not guaranteed circles of affection. Sons were often instructed into already overstocked trades, while daughters' choices were even more circumscribed. Yet there is an evident contrast between cottage manufacturing and the factory in which family members worked as individuals, outside the home, from a very young age and for long shifts. A poem on the West Riding *c.*1730 conveys something of the integration of manufacturing and domestic tasks in a weaver's household: tasks involving extra family members in apprentices and living-in servants or journeymen:

> Quoth Maister – 'Lads work hard I pray
> Cloth mun be peark'd next market-day,
> And Tom mun go tomorn to t'spinners;
> And Will mun seek about for t'swingers;
> And go t'sizing mill for sizing,
> And get your web and warping done
> That ye may get into t'loom
> Joe, go give my horse some corn
> For I design for t'Wolds tomorn
> So mind and clean my boots and shoon
> Mary – there's wool take thee and dye it . . .

But Mary, the mistress of the household, has something to say about the allocation of this task on top of a pretty full domestic load:

> So thou's setting me my work,
> I'd think I'd more need mend thy sark,
> 'Prithie, who mun sit at bobbin wheel?
> A ne'er a cake at top o' th'creel.
> And we to bake; and swing and blend
> And milk, and bairns to school to send,
> And dumplings for the lads to make,
> And yeast to seek, and syk as that!
> And washing up, morn, noon and neet,
> And bowls to scald, and milk to fleet,

And bairns to fetch again at neet!

The husband acknowledges some substance to her complaint, but she and the servant lass must just get up 'soon and stir about and get all done',

For all things mun aside be laid –
When we want help about our trade.[6]

It should be noted that weaver households in the West Riding possessed an extra degree of 'independence' compared with the other clothing areas. The contrast use to which the small working master-clothier system of this region was frequently put was a double one. It was used to point out its superiority both over the separation of labour from capital, brought about by the 'putting-out system' in the west, and over the emerging factory system. In the latter case the central issue is the divorce of work from the home and the consequent dis-membering of the family body as a work unit. In this context the advent of the factory affected the lives of both 'dependent' and 'independent' rural workers. In emphasising the domestic skills and functions of the female members, the poem links to a second aspect of contemporary reaction: by working outside the home, the wife, it was argued, was no longer able to see to the provision of domestic comfort and attend adequately to the family's dietary and other needs. Further, because they worked from so early an age in the mills, their daughters were not able to receive the necessary domestic training. Accordingly they were seriously deficient as wives and mothers when, at too young an age thanks to their promiscuous mixing with young men in the factory, they in their turn married.

Other pressures also emanated from the new modes of production. Factories, it was argued, provided work for women and children on a large scale, but proportionately little for men. A scheme of the Poor Law Commissioners in 1835 to encourage the migration of families into the manufacturing districts recommended that widows with large families, or tradesmen such as shoemakers or blacksmiths, would be best suited, as the mills could not train already grown men to become spinners and they would never rise above 'the inferior and worst occupations'.[7]

The pride and status of the breadwinner would be destroyed as he slumped into a position of depending upon the factory earnings of his wife and children. Engels stated this change from super to subordinate position in its clearest form:

this condition which unsexes the man and takes from the woman all woman-liness without being able to bestow upon the man true womanliness or the woman true manliness – this condition which degrades, in the most shameful way, both sexes, and through them, Humanity is the last result of our much-praised civilization.

Marx contrasted the position of the skilled artisan who had stood as an

171

'independent' seller of his own labour power with his reduced condition to that of 'slave-trader' selling the labour of his wife and children. He was not alone in employing the image. 'What', thundered Richard Oastler, the great orator of the factory reform movement, 'is the most debasing principle of human nature, nurtured by African Slavery? That a parent is so dreadfully demoralised as to sell his child for gold.'[8]

THE FAMILY AND THE FACTORY

That the child entering the factory not only worked outside the home but was removed from parental supervision and control has long seemed a self-evident consequence of the new mode of production. It did, however, receive a strong challenge from the socialist N. J. Smelser in an influential book published in 1959. Smelser did not deny the ultimate separation of working children from their parents in the factory, but argued that this separation did not come about from the beginning of the factory system but only from around 1820 when technological developments in spinning and the introduction of steam weaving ended a period during which the adult male mule spinner had recruited his own children to assist him in the cotton mill. The period up to c. 1820 was one of transition for the textile family preceding the changes of 1820–40 which redefined its economic functions and sharply differentiated the roles of its members. The early, usually water-powered and rural-located, cotton mills depended upon the recruitment of 'unfree' child apprentice labour from the workhouses and had little direct impact on the structures of the textile factory. Indeed, in so far as the rural mills did recruit 'free' labour, they favoured the hiring of whole families from the farming rather than the domestic textile areas.

Disruption for the textile family began in the 1820s. Fundamentally its timing was influenced by technological changes. Before then, although with the rapid decline of the pauper apprenticeship system around 1800, free-labour children flocked into the mills, their conditions of recruitment and employment allowed traditional family functions and relationships to continue into the new workplace. Operative spinners hiring their own scavengers and piecers chose relatives; wives and children. Many children, therefore, were taken into the factories by their parents. An eight-year-old entered as a scavenger for his father. If designated for future spinning he became a piecer, mending broken threads, for a further number of years. He was trained to spin until, in his late teens, he became a spinner. The father/son training relationship was codified in many early spinners' trade union rules which tried to prevent spinners from recruiting trainees from outside the narrow classes of own children, brothers, nephews etc. This echoed the recruitment restrictions common to many craft trades where workers sought to protect their trade from the inundation of cheap labour.

The spinner usually paid his assistants from his own earnings, with no direct dealings with the factory master. Employing, instructing and even paying their own or closely related children, the spinners perpetuated traditional family values and authority structures in working with their children. This situation began to end in the 1820s and its disintegration gathered pace in the following decade. Increasing real wages may have led some adult spinners to withdraw or at least delay entering their own children into factory employment while the rapid decline of their trade was increasing the tendency of handloom weavers to send *their* children to the factory. When power-loom weaving developed in this period, it did not reproduce the transition period for the family which early mule spinning had done. Power weaving was overwhelmingly an occupation for young women. Child assistants (dressers) were recruited directly by the factory masters and there was no approximation to a system of parental instruction and supervision.

These pressures, Smelser insists, only became apparent in the 1820s; before then: 'Notwithstanding long hours and other difficult conditions, this transitional system of family-in-factory yielded both higher family income and the maintenance of many traditional values.' Smelser gives his argument an especial importance in explaining why factory reform became so emotive a subject in the 1830s, although conditions had if anything improved since the earlier nineteenth century. Dissatisfactions began when the era of the 'family in the factory ended' and parental responsibility for supervision and safeguarding of their children no longer operated. He points to the complaints that the power-loom weavers, young persons unrelated to their child assistants, overworked children to keep up their own piece-based earnings.[9]

Smelser's arguments have been attacked on several grounds. In particular it has been demonstrated that a regular succession of progeny entering the factory to assist a spinner-father through his working life is demographically improbable. Professor Anderson has pointed out that few mule spinners would at any time of their working life have had enough children of sufficient age to piece for them. More than a third of Preston's spinners in 1851 had *no* co-residing children while a little more than half had none between the age of eight and nineteen. A further 17% had only one child in that age group. In Preston's mills in 1816 only 11.6% of child workers were employed by a parent or sibling (24.5% in the district around the town). Since the demographic facts contradict it, Smelser's 'family in the factory' theory can have only had a limited applicability. Cotton spinners needed more child assistants than they could supply in general, not unusually, children to whom they were unrelated. This must have been as true before 1820 as it was after. More children of increasingly distressed handloom weavers may well have been entering the factories after 1820 and it is also possible that better-paid spinners were not sending their children, but I have seen no substantial evidence to support this latter assertion of Smelser's. Any trend away from working with a parent can only have been insignificant since the proportion who so worked was small in the first place. The idea that there was a crucial change in the nature of industrialisation's impact on the textile family in the years after 1820 hardly seems a valid one.[10]

There are other difficulties with his theory. Some of these are apparent also in the contemporary debate on the factory system's impact on the family. Opposing the factory textile family to an image of the 'undifferentiated' handloom weaver's family has led to many a student to the belief that the early factory labour force was recruited from the declining handloom sector. In fact they were not: only very few handloom weavers entered the factories. Analysis of immigrants into Preston, one of the most rapidly growing of cotton towns, has shown that only 9% came directly from manufacturing villages, and a further 8% from mixed ones. Large numbers of former farm labourers and servants came, as did people from other towns, from already differentiated families who did not work together as a productive unit. They can therefore hardly be expected to have experienced 'dissatisfaction' from the break up of the family as a working unit.[11]

Since only 12% of persons under eighteen in thirteen Preston mills in 1816, and only 25% in eleven recorded cotton mills elsewhere, were employed by parents, brothers or sisters, while in the early 1830s Shuttleworth showed that only 15% of the 3,000 piecers working with 837 fine spinners were relatives, then evidently 1825–30 was not marked by any significant or sudden change in the nature and extent of family-based employment in the mills. The skilled mule spinners did bring their own children to work with them when they were suitably aged. They naturally tried to see that their own sons were instructed to become mule spinners. In attending to this they were acting in the long-established tradition of skilled workers in both ensuring their own sons' future and in limiting an influx to the occupation. Such tradition was codified in trade union practices and sanctions. In this respect, as in so many others, mule spinners should be regarded as 'factory artisans'. Generalising from the experiences of this elite group to that of the factory proletariat in general is unlikely to be profitable.[12]

David Vincent has suggested that the most important legacy which a working-class father could give his male children was instruction in a trade and the 'right' to pursue it with the sense of belonging to a craft. Only rarely could the offspring of a parent not in a position to confer this hope to rise out of the vulnerable ranks of the unskilled. Although insecurity was part of the life of so many in the skilled trades, the gulf between the skilled and the unskilled was a real one. As a child began work in his family economy he also took his place in his father's stratum of society. For the sons of established cotton spinners the old parental role of instruction into an inheritable calling did persist into the factory, but for many families the entry of children into factory employment meant the disruption, or even the abolition, of a parental role of instruction as it both altered the delicate balance between nurturing and exploiting by calling into question the entire relationship between training and child labour. To the extent that the mule spinners avoided this disruption, they avoided sharing in a more general experience.[13]

Similar traditions persisted in mining areas where skilled hewers (or in the case of the Cornish metal mines, tributers) took their own sons, or perhaps nephews, underground, to begin the process of learning by which they would become, at around eighteen, skilled face workers. Such practices were not however universal for in the Midlands coalfields in the mid-nineteenth century the 'butty' system grew up under which middle men made a notoriously exploitative use of pauper apprentices, who were turned away at the end of their time. Angela John has suggested that the exclusion of women from underground employment was not unwelcome in some coalfields as it secured the idea of underground labour as a male preserve and underground tasks previously performed by women and children became part of the 'apprenticeship' period of the male miner.[14]

Kin was certainly important. Anderson has stressed its major role in securing factory employment and its persistent value down to the end of the 1840s both to employee and employer. Within this period the changes of the 1820s and 1830s seem of minimal importance. The main consequence of the 1833 Factory Act was that it forced the children to stay one year longer at home with the mother, but since the father worked away from the home, he had played little part in the socialisation of his children up to eight years of age before 1833, and the extra year can hardly have been significant. Nor should very great importance be attached to the consequence that children from nine to thirteen now had to spend a larger part of their time at home and a very small (and often evaded) part at lessons. Smelser stresses the importance of technological changes in this period which, by increasing the ratio of child to adult labour, forced the spinners to recruit outside the family to a greater extent. This was perhaps happening, though to a lesser extent than he suggests, but even so it did not affect the ability of the spinner to employ his own children: it only forced him to employ more outside children as well. In short, there seems a very weak case for supposing that operative spinners involved themselves in the movement for factory reform because of dissatisfactions brought about by a changing impact of factory employment on their families. Handloom weavers, by contrast, most probably did feel unhappy about sending their children into the factories where they complained they could never secure the better work, or enter on the path of advancement (for males) to mule spinning, because of the spinners' favouring of their own children. Despite the limitations of our knowledge, it seems most likely that it was the children of weavers who went into the factory to assist the first power-loom weavers.

Working-class children had always had to work and this imperative faced their parents with what Dr Vincent has called 'the fundamentally insoluble problem of how to simultaneously nurture their children and exploit them economically'.[15] There need be no supposition that affective relationships could not exist. Children could have entered work in a gradual way, perhaps not in its early stages easily distinguishable from play. In so entering they may have taken some satisfaction of beginning their contribution to the family's efforts and a bond of a kind strengthened. Except for the sons of the elite mule spinners, the early mills allowed fathers to exercise neither socialising authority over their children nor control over their present and future occupation. Child labour was not only intensified but was, in general, emptied of what positive value it had possessed. Handloom weavers sent their children to the factory from necessity during their long and painful decline into extinction and, unlike the spinners and sadly for Professor Smelser's argument, they were not at the forefront of the factory reform agitation.

WOMEN'S WORK OUTSIDE THE HOME

The question of the changing nature of women's work has at least two important dimensions. Firstly we need to assess the extent to which women's work in the factory, by freeing them from the constraints of the family unit of production and wage, was a significant step towards emancipation allowing them into the labour market as *independent* wage earners. Secondly we have to consider arguments that presented such employment as productive of a serious decline in women's proficiency in the 'domestic sphere' and in child rearing, causing the family to suffer both materially and morally.

Marx provided a powerful and much quoted insight:

> However terrible, however repulsive the break up of the old family
> system within the organism of capitalist society may seem; none the less,
> large-scale industry, by assigning to women and to young persons and
> children of both sexes, a decisive role in the socially organised process of
> production, and a role which has to be fulfilled outside the home, is building

the new economic foundation for a higher form of the family and of the relations between the sexes.[16]

The idea of an industrial revolution transforming female employment opportunities was also central to the thesis of Dr Pinchbeck who wrote of a 'tremendous' increase in availability of work outside the home and viewed this as of 'vital importance' to women in its destruction of the family wage, bringing improved status and better conditions. The 'optimist', Hartwell allies himself unusually with Marx in seeing this change as 'the beginning of the most important and most beneficial of all the social revolutions of the last two centuries, the emancipation of women'. Fellow optimist Rhodes Boyson gives a different reaction in suggesting that the 'real advance for wives and families' was that the industrial revolution 'introduced the idea that men's wages should be sufficient to maintain a wife and family and that women should make their contribution by looking after the home'.[17]

Recently Marx's insight has been criticised by historians. Perhaps they have insufficiently noted its date: it is from *Capital*, not from a writing contemporary with the factory debate, and its tense clearly relates to process rather than to achievement. Certainly it has only limited value as a description of early nineteenth-century reality for most working women. Several lines of qualification can be suggested. Did work outside the home free women from the 'constraints' of the family in any very complete sense? Did the industrial revolution in fact increase the opportunities in general for women to work outside the home? Or were the mill girls a special case? Was 'emancipation', if such there was, limited to a short age-defined part of the factory woman's life-cycle?

The notion that the industrial revolution increased the participation of women in general in work outside the home cannot be sustained. Dr Richards, in a widely used study, has shown that female participation rates in the productive economy declined after 1820. Any general increase around the middle years of the nineteenth century would have had to have had a surprising correlation with the highest average family size in British history which imposed upon women the 'tyranny of repeated pregnancy and continuous child rearing'. This must have had some effect in reducing female participation rates, but in general it would seem that 'the unfettered capitalist economy – in the full flood of industrialisation in the mid-nineteenth century utilised a principal supply of labour in a very modest fashion'. The factory girl was exceptional. Richards' conclusions are supported by those of Joan Scott and Louise Tilly who agree that the productive activity of women in manufacturing may well have fallen with the coming of industrialisation. The expansion of opportunities in textiles was numerically more significant in the non-factory needle trades than in the mills. Paradoxically the economic growth of the nineteenth century brought the most noticeable increase in female employment in home sewing and in domestic service: 'traditional sectors in which women worked at jobs similar to household tasks'.[18]

Female participation in the agricultural workforce seems to have decreased in the cereal-producing counties after the mid-eighteenth century. The evidence on seasonal unemployment suggests that their role was moving from harvest labour towards less reliable and well-paid spring-time activities. By the second quarter of the nineteenth century the seasonal pattern of 1690 to 1750 had been reversed, and the sexual division of labour within agriculture had become marked. In the interests of more rapid work, the supplanting of the sickle by the bagging-hook and scythe, never used by women after 1790, had begun in the south around forty years earlier and was one of the innovations working against women's traditional place in high-earning harvest work. These changes had happened by 1830 before 'Victorian' views on women's 'place' gave ideological sanction. The restricted role of women in the cereal regions contrasts by mid-nineteenth century with the much fuller one described by Alice Clark for the seventeenth. They had been reduced to stone-picking or weeding and were 'scarcely, if ever employed in field labour' (Berkshire 1834). 'We have no employment for women and children' (Bedfordshire) and, from Essex: 'There is little employment for women and children.' The reversal of this system in East Anglia, with the growth of the 'gang' system, so offended current conventional morality that it met with ideological opposition. The experience of the pastoral counties was different: there was no decline in women's participation and possibly even rising real wages for female specialisation in livestock, dairying and hay-making.[19]

Whether such emancipation as existed for groups like mill girls did so only for a short defined period of their lives is linked to the question of marriage. Was it usual, even in occupations which were open to women, for wives to work after marriage? If not, then the implication is that a late-teen and early twenties freedom was sandwiched between the period of subordinate dependence in the parental home and that in the husband's home. The much used 'wives and mothers' image perhaps hinders the understanding of the fact that it was above all *daughters* whose employment situations may have changed. The gender truth that the majority of mill operatives were female should not obscure the age truth that an even bigger majority were young persons, and consequently equally preponderantly unmarried. In Preston in 1841 only 26% of female factory workers were living with husbands. In Stockport the percentage was 18% rising to 28% in 1851, and here the early arrival of the power loom had increased female earning opportunities. The same pattern seems to have been true of female surface workers at the tin and copper mines of Cornwall where in 1851 there were practically no 'bal maidens' above the age of 35, 430 between 25 and 30 and more than 3,000 between the ages of 15 and

20.[20] The remarkably consistent figure of around 25% for married women in the female labour force in cotton mills is capable of varying interpretation. The most unlikely presumption is that it represented a permanent fraction of wives working throughout their married lives. Infertile women and women working until their first child arrived may have accounted for some of the 25%. But with brides often pregnant at marriage, the child-free stage of a marriage of normal fertility was very short. Some of the 25% at least must be presumed to have been mothers with children; they could have worked by arranging to have their children minded. Contemporaries made much of this with strident accusations of young babies doped with opium by indifferent minders. Professor Anderson has shown that for Preston, at least, professional baby-minding was used by only a minority (2%) of mothers. Grandmothers and older children are likely to have been more often called into service. Child-minding by whatever arrangement only *allows* a mother to work: it still leaves open the question of in what circumstances she would be likely to do so. A strong argument has been put forward for Stockport that some wives were likely to stay in the mill labour force through the 'crisis' period of the family cycle when the ratio of dependents to earners was so adverse as to create an imperative. In such a situation, mothers would presumably make what arrangements for child-minding they could: favouring kin where such were available, and resorting to paid minding only when it was not. It can, however, be safely concluded that only a minority of children under ten experienced a childhood blighted by the fact of their mother working outside the home. Anderson has suggested for Preston only one-eighth, and of these only half in the factories. Marriage for most women for most of their married life seems to have meant a restriction to the domestic sphere. This does not mean that they did not in some home-based way contribute to the family's income. They may have taken in home sewing, washing or performed other paid services, but emancipation in the sense of independent wage-earning outside the home was, even in the mill towns, largely restricted to the young unmarried women. Older children entering the mill provided earnings which allowed the mother to drop out. Working young mothers before this point did not necessarily see themselves as doing other than contributing to a family wage even if from separate employment. Independent waged work may be a condition for emancipation but it is not a sufficient one. Wives' earnings may well have been regarded as destined for housekeeping; men's as making a discretionary support.[21]

The lasses of the mill towns certainly did impress upon contemporaries a picture of a new 'freedom', casting off traditional restraints of family and home. They secured a reputation for gaudy and flashy dressing (extravagance and vain display) and (undeserved) for sexual promiscuity. The waged young seem in all ages to attract such censure, but what evidence is there that young women did exploit the opportunity of independent earnings to throw off the constraints of the family? Did they tend to refuse a subordinate and deferential position in the household, as Engels suggested, or even leave the family home, the extreme of independence? Certainly mid-century accounts suggested that they did, and in this condemnation included young men as well as women: 'The family income is not earned by a common head, nor does it flow from a common source. The circle becomes a sort of joint stock company, and a law of self preservation takes over from the force of habit and affection.'[22] Self-interest strengthened and, as surely as the young persons saw that they contributed more than they received from the family, so they withdrew from association with it. In contrast this same newspaper carried a description of a family economy still persisting in the silk-weaving village of Middleton where, although the young married early, they commonly took up residence in the home of one of the parents:

> The handloom system here appears, so far as family is concerned to exercise exactly the opposite effect of the factory system. The Middleton weaver keeps not only his sons and daughters but often his sons and daughters in law, long about him; while the children who are too young and sometimes the adults who are too old for the heavy labour of the loom, turn the grinding wheel and prepare the glistening silk for the frame.[23]

The restraints on freedom when working within the household unit of production were real enough. An old farmer/weaver still operating the handloom system of wool manufacture in Saddleworth in 1849 kept several looms and jennies which were worked by his sons. He boarded and clothed them, but paid them no wages. They were allowed *at his discretion* 'anything reasonable' if they wanted to go to a hunt or a fair or 'sooch-loike'.[24] For daughters, the constraints may be presumed to have been greater. What matters, however, is not the fact that an increased opportunity for 'independence' from the family existed for young mill workers, but the extent to which they chose to take advantage of it. On this matter there is reason to doubt the belief of some contemporaries that they commonly did so. Anderson finds little support for the view in Preston. While late-teenagers did earn enough to support themselves, boys around 7s. (35p) in the 1830s at sixteen rising to 13s+ (65p+) by twenty and girls 6s. (30p) rising to 8s. (40p), the contemporary view was based on assertion rather than on fact. In an urban environment, lodgings were certainly available for people unencumbered with children; most of the 10% of the 15–19 age group who lived in them were immigrants or orphans and it seems improbable that more than 2 or 3% of the Preston born left their parental home other than for marriage. Further, of those who did leave home, it seems that factory children were not especially liable. Low-paid parents were the most likely groups to have their children leave, and here they may have been as much 'pushed' as pulled. Individually, cases are as likely to have reflected the treatment which young persons received, its harshness, brutality or repressiveness, as dissatisfaction with contributing to family support. The young could earn sufficiently in mining too, and a collier in 1842 remarked that they generally stayed if the father was in 'middling circumstances', but 'if the father is badly off, and does not do well to them, the children generally take advantage of it and leave him'. The truth is that while teenage and young adult wages were sufficiently high to support independence and created the possibility of leaving home before marriage, family circumstances and relationships determined whether it would happen. Much evidence suggests that good-earning children were in a bargaining position where the disadvantages of the child in a rural industrial or farming family did not exist, for the father of the factory child no longer had complete control over the only viable source of income. Only a tiny minority would seem to have left the parental home, and of these most were probably boys rather than girls.[25]

Some historians are so convinced that the growth of female employment outside the home did free young women from traditional family restraints that they argue for a revolution in behaviour stemming from it. Edward Shorter, in particular, has claimed that a 'new freedom' for young women lay behind the rise in illegitimacy and bridal pregnancy observed to take place in Europe after 1700 which amounted to a 'sexual revolution'. Shorter's thesis has found little support. Apart from the fact that the rise took place equally noticeably in areas where women remained within the domestic economy, and the fact already mentioned that the participation rate of women outside the home did not generally increase, Tilly, Scott and Cohen have amply demonstrated the continuing hold of traditional values even over those young women who did take up work outside the parental home. It is the behaviour of women as daughters rather than as wives which is in question. Daughters were expected to work. If that took place within a family production unit on a farm or in a weaving cottage they were not independently waged. If opportunities existed to 'export' their labour to mine or mill, then the fact that they were independently waged was not a release from the perception of them as contributors to a family income. Indeed, daughters may have worked so that their mothers need not, for as Scott and Tilly point out, they were more expendable than mothers in both rural and urban households.

It can be concluded that there was no widespread or long-lasting emancipation of women from independent waged working in the period of the early industrial revolution. Only exceptional groups like mill girls had the opportunity to earn wages sufficient to support themselves. Women's wages for the most part were at a level which was assumed to be supplementary, a point which Sally Alexander has emphasised in respect of the employment available for women in early nineteenth-century London.[26]

DOMESTIC DEFICIENCIES?

The expectation that daughters would work inside or outside the home was more significant in distinguishing the working from the middle-class family than was the working wife, for it was a general and persistent expectation. Contemporaries certainly loaded blame on to working wives and mothers for a lack of home comforts and failures in domestic management, but equally they emphasised the lack of training in domestic skills for daughters who worked long hours from an early age at mine or mill. This blame, which in effect helped to shift on to the poor the responsibility for their own poverty and squalor, was thus two-pronged in attacking wife and daughter. The attack on the working mother and wife has already been discussed in the context of assumed child neglect and it has been suggested that not only did it have a minority application, but that even where mothers of young children did go out to work there is no reason to assume that the care arrangements which they made were not adequate. The second prong of the attack, that which claimed that young wives came into marriage with sadly deficient housekeeping abilities, was even more commonly made. Even the 'bal-maidens' at the Cornish mines, who in general received a much better press than did the mill girls, did not escape this condemnation: a Wesleyan minister thought them at marriage 'very deficient in domestic work, unable to make and mend'. Another witness bemoaned the fate of girls: 'taken from their hearths at so early an age, and kept at work for ten hours per day they have little opportunity and less inclination to attend to the domestic and matronly duties so necessary to their future culture and well being'. Many miners' cottages were therefore, it was argued, scenes of greater discomfort and squalor than the level of family earnings should have produced. Wages were less the problem than poor budgeting:

> You will find two men, and one who has got a clean, decent, wholesome, industrious wife, and that man's children will be kept as clean and comfortable as possible. You will then see one of the same 'para' (gang) who has got a dirty, careless wife, and that family will be in rags, and yet that man will make the same earnings. One man will be well off and the other always in misery.

One wife was instanced whose husband and several sons brought in £11–14 a month: 'they have not got a chair to sit down upon; there is scarcely a cup or saucer in the place, and as for a bed, what they have would disgrace the poorest persons in the kingdom'. A doctor was prepared to blame the frequency of stomach disorders among men who worked in death-dealing dust and began to cough blood from an early age on crude and coarse preparation of their food by their wives.[27]

Mine girls, mill girls, needle workers in London's increasingly

sweated trades shared in a middle-class con lemnation of their in-
adequacy as wives, mothers, cooks and cleaners. No allowances were
made for the circumstances in which such women had to cope. The
Cornish woman who lacked a chair or a cup lived in a house into which
male workers brought £11–14 a month, but how much of it did they
give to her? The account is silent. If slatternly wives driving husbands
out to pubs is one way of putting the matter, then another, as Dr Hunt
has pointed out, is to suggest that if working-class males had been
obliged to spend more evenings at home, if they had not been favoured
heavily in terms of what food was available, then they might have
shifted a little more of their earnings towards housekeeping. We have
already described the physical conditions in which many of the
labouring people lived. In such poorly constructed, damp, decaying
and overcrowded abodes, 'good housekeeping' by middle-class standards was hardly possible. Occasionally a visitor perceived the real
difficulties. A vicar's wife visiting miners' homes in Cornwall in 1828
noted both the irregularity of the shift system and the problem of
monthly pay and, under the irregular tribute system of pay, the impos-
sibility of knowing what money would be brought home. Wives who
had returned from overseas complained that they had much preferred
the weekly pay there. Miners' tendency to move from one mine to
another meant that investment in improving a temporary home was
not worthwhile. While the shift system was very disruptive:

> The miner neither eats, drinks, sleeps or goes to church with his family,
> insomuch that the wife finds it as hard to regulate the disposition of time as
> of money . . . [she] was in the midst of whitewashing her walls today, when
> word is brought that Tom has changed core and she must instantly 'fit dinner
> for him'.[28]

Similar justifications could be offered for other working-class wives, if
it is needed to combat what, after all, is assertive rather than evi-
dentially supported condemnation. Wives working at home were less a
matter of concern, but their hours with the needle can have left little
time for other domestic tasks, while the space needed for the materials
upon which they worked would have intensified the problems of
clutter. In any event it can hardly be known that mothers did not find
time to instruct their daughters when they returned from the mill or
mine. Perhaps while their brothers played, they were so disadvantaged
as to have been expected to assist their mothers. That is not a situation
which many women even in today's 'symmetrical' families would find
astonishing. Certainly one male mill worker in 1833 had few doubts
about the suitability of mill girls as brides: 'I know to the contrary,
because I married three wives out of the factory, and I take that as
proof. I am certain that as good wives may be had from the factories as
from any other occupation.' A woman witness declared scornfully:
'You think we can do nought but work in factories, neither brew, nor
bake, nor sew.'[29]

CONCLUSION

The idea that the industrial revolution was a step in women's emancipation by creating increased opportunities for waged work outside the home has been criticised on the grounds that the participation level of women in productive labour actually fell with the coming of industrialisation. But Marx was making, perhaps, a qualitative rather than a quantitative point about the significance of the independent wage. That traditional constraints were stronger than has always been supposed and that mill girls were a special case and that most women had to wait much longer for the opportunity of waged work outside the home, qualify but do not remove the underlying importance of his insight. What qualifies it more than anything else were the inter-related points that the level of women's earnings even outside the home was determined by the long-standing assumption that they ought to earn less, and that they would usually work at best only a small part of their married lives. Operating together, these two points ensured that dependence in parental and then in husband's home would be their normal life situation. The idea of increasing opportunities for working-class women would also seem to be contradicted by Judith Walkowitz's demonstration that the typical prostitute of the mid-nineteenth century was a working-class girl of an age with the mill girls, and had entered her trade not as a 'fallen woman' but as a result of rational choice from the limited opportunities available to her.[30]

Contemporary criticism of working women was based less on any real investigation of intolerable conditions than on the image of the nature of the work contrasting with the idealised vision of a proper woman's sphere. Angela John has given good reasons for the pit-brow lasses preferring surface work at the mines to some alternatives, but they afforded such an antipathetic image to domesticated femininity that they could not be left alone, while women who slaved long hours hidden in home-based production or who skivvied in the surrogate home environment of domestic service attracted little attention. Samuel Smiles expressed the view succinctly: 'As surely as you make women day labourers with men, and efface the peculiar modesty and delicacy of the female character so you will produce a ferocious, regardless and desperate population ready for any mischief.' The sooty, betrousered pit-lasses were so evidently degraded womanhood *par excellence* that, forty years after they had ceased to work underground, attempts were made to stop them working at the surface. As Sally Alexander has pointed out, it was not that working-class women were not expected to work, but that they should do so in those sorts of labour which coincided with a woman's natural sphere. Therefore, attacks on particular forms of women's employment had little to do with discriminating against those with exceptional levels of danger or unpleasantness. In London, where women's work took place beneath the surface in the workshop or the home, it passed almost unnoticed to the degree that it was compatible with the deification of the home. Image was important. The Cornish bal-maidens wore long dresses, white head-dresses and aprons; they impressed rather than distressed visitors. Abraham Duncan, a Chartist missionary to Cornwall in 1839, was so impressed that he wondered whether the Convention would allow him anything for a wife. 'We see', wrote one observer, 'the modest, blushing, neatly clad bal maidens.' Yet these girls in breaking and wheeling ores on the surface did work little different from their grimey, be-trousered, northern equivalents the pit-brow lasses. Such was recognised by some who, more closely aware of their tasks, laid upon them the same heavy condemnation.

> . . . too few men being available. Mary and Nancy were called on to assist. The two Amazons rushed forward to the work to move ore in three hundredweight barrows filled with the long-handled 'Cornish Shove' and carry it several yards to the scales, and then onto another heap, a heavy task which few men could sustain for more than an hour or two, cheered on by jokes and coarse remarks.

Although in adverse weather, working outside was unpleasant and, indeed, as with all outside work, health-destroying for the inadequately clad, the physical nature of the work was not extreme; Engels thought it 'comparatively endurable'. Two young women asked by a Commission of 1842 for their opinions seemed to have distinctly preferred it to two alternatives which were not condemned by contemporaries. One had been previously employed in the very female work of straw-bonnet making which she had left because of ill-health. Work at the mines 'agreed with her very well'. The second worked sometimes at the mine and sometimes in domestic service. She did not find much difference in her health, for although work at the mine was harder for the time, when one left it for the day there was nothing more to do.[31]

Women's own evaluation of working outside the home is little recorded. They may have welcomed the companionship and contact with fellow workers, which middle-class moralists saw as a special danger. Gaskell had valued the domestic system for the way in which it guarded the children and women from 'contagion'. Writing on the Cornish mines, Henwood saw this danger as more important than 'mere physical evil' for: 'The indiscriminate association in their employment of the sexes naturally begets a want of modesty and delicacy so important in the formation of character.' Working-class parents could share such views, especially if swayed by Methodism or similar influences. In the 1770s the son of one Cornish Wesleyan mother recalled that although forced to send him to the mines she did so with reluctance:

Associated in this occupation with wicked children, he suffered by the pernicious influence of their conversation and example. While his mother lived she laboured to counteract the moral contagion to which she saw her child thus unavoidably exposed.

When a working miner said in 1842 that if he had fifty daughters he would not send them to the mine to be 'corrupted by bad conversation', he was sharing the sentiment of the better-placed writer who lamented that there was no matron at the mines to see that the 'rules of modesty' were observed, and no 'unbecoming familiarity' between the sexes or foul language 'insulting to female delicacy' were allowed.[32]

The attitudes of labouring men to their wives and children working outside the home were complicated. Engels was surely correct in seeing dissatisfaction in the mill towns arising not from the fact of having children work, but from a situation which made the father the dependent rather than the undisputed breadwinner: 'Thou knows, Joe, its hard for one that was used different.'[33] Where wives could earn as in the mill towns, then they might have to, until the aggregate earnings of children could reserve them once again for the domestic sphere. In cottage industry, women had both productive *and* domestic functions. There is no evidence to suggest that working-class men wanted a share of the latter. In the Cornish mines, adult male wages were sufficiently high to make it very rare for married women to work, but the mines needed the labour of children and young persons and as the family grew children would need to work to maintin a viable ratio between the contributing and dependent members of the household. Since employers expected to recruit their child employees from the miners' families there was, anyway, little choice for parents. One miner complained that he was unable to give up work in a particularly unhealthy part of the mine because if he refused, his children would have been turned away.[34]

What complicates men's attitudes to women's work is the realisation that employers, often with the aid of deskilling machinery, would use the cheaper labour of women to displace men or to force wages down. 'Keep them at home to look after their families', declared the Miners Association of Great Britain and Ireland in 1842, when legislation was restricting women from working underground, 'decrease the pressure on the labour market and there is then some chance of a higher rate of wages being enforced'. The Association employed a lawyer to prosecute employers who continued to ignore the Act, but the attitude of working miners, as distinct from an 'official' union one, might have been more ambivalent. Used to their wives and female children working, they may have opted for necessity over principle, and in Wigan a policeman and a watchman were beaten up for informing on mine-owners who were still employing women.[35]

Skilled artisans were in a better financial position to assert the status claim to a wage which ensured a skilled man could support his wife and family, but even here Mayhew noted that they valued the financial contribution of their womenfolk, while taking care that they were not employed in occupations which would dishonour the status position of the artisan. Sawyers' wives and children did not as a general rule *go out* to work while skilled carpenters' wives did not usually work in the 'slop' tailoring trades: 'We keep our wives too respectable for that', but some of their wives *took in* washing or even kept general shops. Such selectivity was only for the minority of skilled artisans catering for the West End. Mayhew suggested that 10% of the city's artisans were 'society men' combined to preserve their skilled status and remuneration and Edward Thompson that a line of privilege of 30s. (£1.50p) a week ran below only 5–6%.[36] It was the 'dishonourable', warehouse-supplying, labour-sweating East End branches which were expanding in the 1830s. In this sector, women and children had to work. Around the poor tailor or shoemaker, his wife and children sat and stitched and cut and trimmed. The 'new' domestic system, which Marx recognised as growing alongside the factory system, drew the poor more closely together, and on the desperate treadmill of producing in volume sufficient to offset the fall in piece rates which their own expanding numbers aggravated, such sweated workers inverted capitalist development to make the family an economic unit again, but this time in squalid urban tenement rather than rural cottage.

REFERENCES AND NOTES

1. *The Excursion*, 1814.
2. Quoted in **Sally Alexander**, 'Women's work in nineteenth-century London; a study of the years 1820–50', in **J. Mitchell** & **A. Oakley** (eds), *The Rights and Wrongs of Women*, Penguin, 1976, pp. 61–2; **E. Hodder**, *Life of the Seventh Earl of Shaftesbury*, 1886, p. 234.
3. **P. Gaskell**, *Artisans and Machinery. The Moral and Physical Condition of the Manufacturing Population*, 1836, repr. Cass, 1968, p. 89; **Frederick Engels**, *The Condition of the Working Class in England*, 1845, Granada edn, 1969, p. 172.
4. Gaskell, *Artisans and Machinery*, pp. 61–3.
5. *Fifth Report of Select Committee on Artisans and Machinery*, BPP, 1824, v, p. 397.
6. Quoted in **J. G. Rule**, *The Experience of Labour in Eighteenth-Century Industry*, Croom Helm, 1981, pp. 38–9.
7. Quoted in **N. J. Smelser**, *Social Change in the Industrial Revolution. An Application of Theory to the Lancashire Cotton Industry 1770–1840*, Routledge & Kegan Paul, 1959, pp. 202–3.
8. Engels, *Condition of the Working Class*, p. 174; quoted Smelser, *Social Change*, p. 280.
9. Smelser's argument and the supporting evidence can be found in Ch.

9–11 of *Social Change*. The highly theoretical early chapters can be passed over by readers unfamiliar with sociological vocabulary and approaches.

10. **M. S. Anderson**, 'Sociological history and the working-class family: Smelser revisited', *Social History*, 3, Oct. 1976, pp. 317–34 provides a sustained critique, as do **M. M. Edwards** and **R. Lloyd Jones**, 'N. J. Smelser and the cotton factory family: a reassessment', in N. B. Harte & **K. G. Ponting** (eds), *Textile History and Economic History*, Manchester U.P., 1973, pp. 304–19.

11. **M. S. Anderson**, *Family Structure in Nineteenth-Century Lancashire*, Cambridge U.P., 1971, pp. 37–9 for origins of migrants.

12. Anderson, 'Sociological history', p. 324.

13. **D. Vincent**, *Bread, Knowledge and Freedom: A Study of Nineteenth-Century Working-Class Autobiography*, Methuen, 1982, pp. 64–5.

14. **Angela V. John**, *By the Sweat of their Brow. Women Workers at Victorian Coal Mines*, Croom Helm, 1980, p. 23.

15. Vincent, *Bread, Knowledge and Freedom*, p. 85.

16. Karl Marx, *Capital*, Everyman 1930, I, p. 529.

17. **Ivy Pinchbeck**, *Women Workers and the Industrial Revolution 1750–1850*, Cass, 1969, pp. 4, 196; **R. M. Hartwell**, *The Industrial Revolution and Economic Growth*, Methuen, 1971, p. 343; **Rhodes Boyson**, 'Industrialisation and the life of the Lancashire factory worker', in *The Long Debate on Poverty*, Institute of Economic Affairs, 1972, p. 78.

18. **E. Richards**, 'Women in the British economy since about 1700: an interpretation', *History*, vol. 59, no. 197, Oct. 1974, pp. 337–57; **J. W. Scott** and **L. A. Tilly**, 'Women's work and the family in nineteenth-century Europe', repr. in **M. Anderson** (ed.), *Sociology of the Family*, Penguin, 2nd edn, 1980, pp. 125–63.

19. Based on **K. D. M. Snell**, 'Agricultural seasonal unemployment, the standard of living on women's work in the south and east: 1690–1860', *Economic History Review* (2nd series), XXXIV, no.3, Aug. 1981, pp. 425–9.

20. Anderson, *Family Structure*, p. 71; **R. Burr Litchfield**, 'The family and the mill: cotton mill work, family work patterns, and fertility in mid-Victorian Stockport', in **A. S. Wohl** (ed.), *The Victorian Family. Structure and Stresses*, Croom Helm, 1978, p. 182; **J. G. Rule**, 'The labouring miner in Cornwall 1740–1870: a study in social history', Ph.D. thesis, University of Warwick, 1971, graph 3A.

21. Anderson, *Family Structure*, p. 71.

22. **P. E. Razzell** and **R. W. Wainwright** (eds), *The Victorian Working Class: Selections from Letters to the Morning Chronicle*, Cass, 1973, p. 186.

23. Ibid., p. 204.

24. Ibid., p. 206.

25. Anderson, *Family Structure*, pp. 125–32.

26. For Shorter's thesis, see **E. Shorter**, *The Making of the Modern Family*, Fontana, 1977, Ch. 3, 'The two sexual revolutions' and his article 'Illegitimacy, sexual revolution and social change in modern Europe', in **R. I. Rotberg** & **T. K. Rabb** (eds), *Marriage and Fertility*, Princeton University Press, 1980, pp. 85–120. For a major critique, see **L. A. Tilly, J. W. Scott** and **M. Cohen**, 'Women's work and European fertility patterns', Ibid., pp. 219–48. Alexander, 'Women's work', p. 110.

27. *Report of the Royal Commission on Child Employment*, BPP, 1842, xvi, pp. 848, 834; *Report of the Royal Commission on Mines*, BPP, 1864, xxiv, pp. 43, 146.

28. **C. C. Pascoe**, *Walks about St. Hiliary*, 1879, p. 97; **P. Prescott**, *The Case of Cornish Methodism Considered*, 1871, p. 21; **E. H. Hunt**, *British Labour History 1815–1914*, Weidenfeld & Nicolson, 1980, p. 125.

29. **H. Perkin**, *The Origins of Modern English Society 1780–1880*, Routledge & Kegan Paul, 1969, p. 151.

30. See **J. R. Walkowitz**, *Prostitution and Victorian Society: Women, Class and the State*, Cambridge U.P., 1980.

31. John, *Sweat of their Brow*, p. 44; Alexander, 'Women's work', pp. 61–3; quoted Rule, 'Labouring miner in Cornwall', pp. 30, 363; **R. Burt** (ed.), *Cornwall's Mines and Miners: nineteenth-century studies by George Henwood Barton*, Truro, 1972, pp. 10, 118.

32. Burt (ed.), *Mines and Miners*, p. 118; **J. H. Drew**, *Samuel Drew M.A. The Self-Taught Cornishman*, 1861, p. 23; BPP, 1842, *Child Employment*, p. 829; **C. F. Childs**, *The Social and Moral Improvement of the Working Miners of Cornwall and Devon*, Liskeard, 1862, p. 7.

33. Engels, *Condition of the Working Class*, p. 174.

34. BPP, 1842, *Report on Child Employment*, p. 840.

35. John, *Sweat of their Brow*, p. 57.

36. Thompson and Yeo, *Unknown Mayhew*, pp. 394, 454, 407; **E. P. Thompson**, *The Making of the English Working Class*, Penguin, 1968, p. 264 and footnote to p. 277.

Chapter 8

SENTIMENT AND SEX: THE FEELINGS OF THE WORKING CLASSES

The image of the traditional family disrupted and corrupted by factory employment and the environment of the factory town presumed not just the rise of immorality but also the decline of affection. Some historians have supported the contemporary view of the deadening of feeling in the family and its replacement by functional, or even brutalised, relationships between husband and wife and between parents and children. Professor Stone has gone so far as to assert:

> Parental love, which was one of the features of the new family type as it developed in the middle classes, was hardly conducive to early industrial work practices. As Marx and Engels were at pains to document, young children were exploited unmercifully in factories and mines in the early phases of industrialisation. But it was their parents who consented and indeed actively encouraged this exploitation in order to obtain an early economic profit from these otherwise useless mouths that had to be fed.

Professor Anderson's quantitative researches into the family stress 'instrumentality' – the expectation of reciprocation from kin – as the key to understanding the new industrial family, while still allowing considerable scope for sentiment.[1]

COURTSHIP AND SEX

To such questions as: did the working classes fall in love? Or did they choose partners with more material factors in mind – a good provider for a husband, a good housekeeper and hard worker in a wife? – there can be no simple answer. Motives can be mixed and sentiments change. Love can cool after an ardent courtship, but it can also grow into a strong affective bond after a calculative and cold one.

Sam Brook, a miner's son moving into the world of the petty tradesman, recorded in his autobiography: 'I had just started keeping company with a young woman that I thought would make me a good housewife and draper's wife', but the only other reference he makes to his wife is affectionate enough: 'It was the best move that ever I made in all my life, because we were blessed with good health and lived very happy together for forty-three years.'[2] Naturally a serious man would be prudent in choosing a wife, but even after consideration, heart could still overrule head. Thomas Hardy knew that the feet of so solidly-named a yeoman as Gabriel Oak could be lifted from the ground by the lovely Bathsheba even after she had herself put the considerations which ought to have been in his mind:

> I am better educated than you – and I don't love you a bit: that's my side of the case. Now yours: you are a farmer just beginning, and you ought in common prudence, if you marry at all (which you should certainly not think of doing at present) to marry a woman with money, who would stock a larger farm for you than you have now.
> Gabriel looked at her with a little surprise and much admiration.
> 'That's the very thing I had been thinking myself!' he naively said.[3]

Dr Vincent's recent study of 142 autobiographies of nineteenth-century working people is the broadest-based attempt yet to investigate questions of sentiment, but he readily acknowledges the limitations of his material. There are very few autobiographies of working-class women, so we get an essentially male-centred view of courtship, and the male autobiographers did not readily disclose matters which they regarded as either private or as of no relevance to their usual theme of self-improvement. Even if they did have the inclination to report on these parts of their lives, they rarely felt a confident command of the language of emotion. When a farm labourer wrote: 'I was as fond of my wife Has [sic] a Cat is of New Milk', his simplicity does convey real meaning, but more usually love or grief are handled in cliché. By and large, however, Dr Vincent insists that his subjects portray both themselves and their friends as 'falling in love'. Even if that emotion had to be balanced against other considerations and was not a sufficient condition, it was the most important factor leading to and determining the outcome of courtship. Engels after all supposed that because of the absence of property considerations, love under capitalism was only really possible among the proletariat. Dr Vincent concludes that in the end: 'the great majority rested their decision on the state of their affections, and took a chance on the practical consequences'.[4]

Given that many working men did not marry until around their mid or late twenties, they mostly chose their partners at an age of independence from their parents. Parental wishes cannot be reasonably presumed a very significant determinant of choice of marriage partners even if in some cases, especially with regard to daughters, opposition to suitors could be very strong. More generally young working persons made their own choices from within a rather narrow range of possibilities – narrower in the smaller than in the expanding community. Geographers and historians have demonstrated the strong likelihood of marriage being intra-parochial, and Vincent has commented that courting couples most often lived within walking distance of each other. Servant girls leaving their villages for service elsewhere may be presumed to have been widening their marriage choice, but Flora Thompson has noted how many of them kept in touch with and eventually returned to marry their village swains. In the Devon village of Lapford between 1800 and 1827, 65% of all marriages were intra-parochial, while in Widdicombe-in-the Moor in the same county (celebrated in song for its low ratio of horses to inhabitants), the figure in 1813–29 was 70%. For Melbourn in Cambridgeshire between 1780 and 1837 it was 73.3%. A high percentage of the residues would have come from nearby or even adjoining parishes.[5]

Strong community feeling, supported by traditional sanctions, reinforced this tendency, not only in small villages, but within districts of larger communities. In Cornwall young miners trying to pay court to maidens from other mining parishes risked being grabbed by the village lads and run roughly out of the parish in a barrow. Fishing and mining communities in St Ives – 'Up-a-long' and 'Down-a-long' – frowned on inter-marriage, just as their equivalents did in South Shields. In the Yorkshire weaving township of Pudsey in the 1820s and 1830s, since everyone knew each other there was little need to make inquiry in the choosing of a wife: 'Courtship therefore, in this state of things does not consist so much in making each others acquaintance as in keeping each other's company as companions.' Choice was, however, virtually confined not to the town as a whole, but to the district, 'up-town' or 'down-town':

> If a man goes from one part of the village to another to win a girl and make her his wife, he is looked upon as an interloper by the young men there and as a poacher on their preserves, and often badly treated. Many have to give up in despair after being covered with mud, and suffering much bodily harm.[6]

Courtship may sometimes have begun with one of those dazzling moments known as 'love at first sight' (or even 'site'?), but more often it was drifted into. In village and town there was some pattern and rhythm to courtship. There was a seasonal element; with few opportunities for indoor privacy, the coldness of the air and the dampness of the grass had to be taken into account. The fact that contemporaries condemned factories and mines in such round terms for the promiscuous mixing in them of young men and women suggests that traditionally men and women outside the family did not generally work together; a suggestion further supported by the criticisms of the 'gang' system of agricultural labour when it began to spread in the middle years of the nineteenth-century. Harvest time with its jolly romping associations is a proverbial exception:

> Love matches that had populated the adjoining hamlet had been made up there between reaping and carrying. Under the hedge which divided the field from a distant plantation girls had given themselves to lovers who would not turn their heads to look at them by the next harvest; and in that ancient cornfield many a man had made love-promises to a woman at whose voice he had trembled by the next seedtime after fulfilling them in the church adjoining.[7]

Harvest represented much more than simply an occasion in the year when the sexes worked together in the fields. It was a festive highspot of the rural calendar, but only one of a number of occasions when recognised opportunities were presented for young men and women to meet. Both urban and rural calendars allowed them: feast days and fairs, wakes and revels, work's outings, or even the range of activities connected with the chapel ('Love feasts' should not of course be taken as a literal description). Dr Malcolmson has noted that the most active participants on festive occasions were young persons in their teens and early twenties. 'Here meet the village youths on pleasure bent', wrote one poet of a small Cambridgeshire fair in the 1850s, and obviously young persons were especially prevalent at hiring fairs. As Malcolmson remarks, the most important reason for the involvement of young people in recreational events was that they served as courtship and sexual encounters. Pudsey feast was reported a major occasion for matchmaking in the early nineteenth century. The young, if talented, could use the occasion for display:

> In ev'ry Wake his nimble Feats were shown
> When in the Ring the Rustic Routs he threw
> The Damsels' pleasures with his Conquests grew
> Or when aslant the Cudgel threats his Head
> His danger smites the Breast of ev'ry Maid.[8]

Contemporary opinion was that there was altogether too much in the way of impropriety at fairs, feasts and wakes, and especially at May Day celebrations. The antiquary John Brand thought the wakes celebrated in northern villages and towns 'sometimes proved fatal to the morals of our swains, and to the innocence of our rustic maids'. An 1805 description of a Somerset hiring-fair commented: 'many of the fair filles-de-chambre, dairy maids, and even fat cooks and greasy scullion wenches, are so civilly greeted by their amorous swains, that this fair is productive of much business for the country justices and their clerks, parish officers, and midwives, for many miles around'. Working from parish registers, Dennis Mills has suggested a link between the timing of the feast in the Cambridgeshire village of Melbourn and the seasonality of marriages and baptisms, with a notable October 'high' in marriages suggesting the importance of the July feast for summer love-making! The effects of this were by autumn becoming apparent for some of the 40% of the village brides who were pregnant at marriage. Traditional games like 'Kiss in the Ring' were part of ritual procedures of courtship. An old potter recalled how much they were played at the wakes of his youth when the pottery workers made an annual excursion to Trentham Park:

> on no green spot in England have more kissing rings been formed than in Trentham Park . . . Yes, these young folks, without intending it, kissed themselves into courtship and marriage, and the link which widened and brightened out into many a domestic circle was first formed in a kissing-ring under the trees in Trentham Park. For better and for worse this was done, but let us hope that in the simplicity of those days it was mainly for the better.[9]

In the larger more impersonal world of London, the young servants and shop assistants, torn from the calendars of courtship of their rural homes, seem to have contrived to hold such games regularly on suitable spaces in suitable weathers. Lionel Munby described joining in one in 1861 near Crystal Palace. Among the servant girls and shop assistants who were playing, he especially noted one buxom servant from Islington, playing with 'great vigour and abandon':

> It was the satisfaction, in a rude and sensuous kind, of a long repressed and half unconscious desire, to be let loose, from the solitude of her kitchen where no followers are allowed, into a circle of young men prepared for unlimited kissing.

In seeing the game, essentially a marriage one, as the last relic of the 'hearty outdoor merriment of old England' and as proving and maintaining the purity of English working women, he missed its significance. The game may have had 'rustic simplicity' when played by children, but when played by sexually mature young servants it was charged with emotional overtones, and was indeed a rough and ready marriage agency.[10]

Perhaps a man decided that the time had come to 'fall in love' and expected there to be someone available for reciprocation? Certainly the upbringing of women and their expectations conditioned them not to let too many opportunities slip by before attaching themselves to a breadwinner. Lucy Luck, a poor child from a Hertfordshire workhouse, in the mid-nineteenth century went through several employments including one from which she had to flee her master's attempts to 'ruin' her. She ended up working for a couple employed as outworkers in strawplaiting. She was teased about a young man who was a regular caller, but for whom she felt no affection. Her employer advised: 'My girl, you have poor Will; he will make you a good husband, and he will never hit you. Never you mind what Sara or her mother says, you have Will.' She began to think a little better of Will and eventually married him. Autobiographies are more revealing, however, in showing an unashamedly masculine perspective on courtship and marriage. An unskilled labourer had been advised when a teenager by his employer: 'if ever you choose a young woman, look out for one whose hair lies straight on her head, for she'll be sure to have a good temper and be sure you try for a poor servant girl'. As he grew older he 'kept company' with several young women, but when he decided the time for marriage had come, he noted a young girl living opposite his lodgings whom he had never spoken to:

> I used to say to my young landlady, 'That's the girl I'll have for my wife, if I ever have a wife at all; her hair is so nice and straight'
> 'Why, and so would my hair be nice and straight, Bill', says my young landlady, 'if I like to put it so'
> 'Ah but you've got a bad temper', says I, 'I won't have nothing to say to you'.

He spoke only once to the girl, "So you're out for a walk; young woman?" I says to her. "Yes I am", says she, and that was all that pass'd between us.' He went away saved £4.15s. (£4.75p), 'on purpose to marry upon, though I'd never even asked her about it'. Returning, he 'walked out with her' for five weeks before settling on marriage at the next fair day.[11]

Samuel Bamford, the radical weaver, records the stages of relationships with women which preceded his marriage in 1810. He describes how he passed from an emotional one of 'calf love' through a sexual one to the point where he decided it was time to marry:

> I can scarcely recollect a period of my life when the society of females was not very agreeable to me. I was now, however, approaching that age when this general partiality was to become more individualising, and when amongst the mass which I always contemplated with tender regard, some would be found from whom I could not withhold a still warmer sentiment; and instead of repressing or controlling them . . . I abandoned myself to delicious heart-gushings of romantic feeling bowed in silent but earnest regard to female loveliness, and became soul and heart bound – profoundly mute, however, except by sighs and looks – to more than one, in succession, of the young beauties of my acquaintance.

He recalled the 'collier's dark-eyed daughter' of his Sunday school, and the tall fair girl, 'all blush-coloured, and wild as a young roe', with whom he mutually blushed in acknowledgement of a 'sentiment too delicate for oral expression'. They kept 'meeting and blushing, and sighing'. This stage passed into one of Valentines, love letters and kissing games. (Another working-class youth growing up in Cornwall records that because of his ability to write 'tolerably well' he was pressed to write love letters for 'many young neighbours'.) After being frustrated in his courtship of one lass whose mother esteemed him little, Bamford took pique and decided to become 'one of the lads';

> In my intercourse with the fair sex, the emotions of the heart had hitherto been my only offering, and now the unworthy surmise first occurred that

195

the offering had been too pure . . . This notion I found to be the confirmed opinion of some of my more experienced acquaintances . . . So I became a free and easy young fellow . . . my company keeping was more promiscuous; my conversation less modest; and my deportment less reserved. Irreverend thoughts would obtrude whether at church or chapel, and those places became mere rendezvous.

During this period he not only consorted with prostitutes, but became 'amenable to the parish authorities for certain expenses', under which affiliation order he was still paying 5s. (25p) a week six years after his marriage. After a while he met again a sweetheart of long standing, his 'beloved Mimi', at Middleton Wakes and resolved the time had come to change his ways: 'I resolved to marry. This was more likely to be effected without much difficulty, in as much as my courtship had been duly paid, and it was now long since my intended fair had entertained any other expectation than the one I now proposed to accomplish.' It was as well for Mimi that her expectations were realised, for Samuel had indeed 'duly paid' his courtship. On the day after the wedding his wife presented to his view for the first time, 'a sweet infant, just of age to begin noticing things'. 'Bless thee, my dear babe, though my coming has been late', proclaimed the proud father, but his expressions of determination that 'a proud and supercilious world' should not by showing its contempt blight her life and his acknowledgement to his wife that 'the fault was mine, and it shall be my life's endeavour to repair it', would seem intended for the later readership of his autobiography, rather than suggestive of any great moral disparity between his circumstances and what was normal in his community. Bamford was a Lancashire weaver and research on the registers of the weaving community of Culcheth has revealed an illegitimacy ratio of well over 25% in the 1840s and that during the first half of the nineteenth century approximately 90% of first births were conceived outside marriage and two-thirds of them were illegitimate.[12]

Even Gaskell, in his unrestrained attack on the promiscuity of the factory labour force, acknowledged that the old rural community failed to operate a moral check sufficient to prevent 'the indulgence of sexual appetite'. Sex before marriage was, he wrote, 'almost universal in the agricultural districts'. Many of his contemporaries would have agreed. 'Sensual vice abounds', wrote Harriet Martineau from Ambleside in 1846, 'and here is dear good old Wordsworth for ever talking of rural innocence and deprecating any intercourse with towns'. Sometimes, a rural vicar told a French visitor in 1828, villagers on hearing that a girl had got married would remark: 'What! She is getting married and she is not pregnant!' In the western counties it was taken as a matter of course that the brides of labourers would be pregnant: 'young people come to a distinct understanding with each other to cohabit illicitly, until the woman becomes pregnant, the man promising "to make an honest woman of her" as soon as that takes place'.[13]

The clergy had little control over such customs. 'He is very anxious to put to shame all brides who are not virgins', wrote a lady of one vicar, 'I am afraid he will find this sort of reformation a difficult one to effect and it is no new custom – for as long as I can remember hearing about such things, Sussex was very much in that way as well as Cheshire'. Certain groups like the miners of Cornwall were singled out for their pre-marital proclivities. Witnesses before the 1842 inquiry into child labour were convinced that too many of the young women were married 'in a condition in which marriage was the only means of saving their reputation', while mine captains thought more girls were pregnant at marriage than were not. The fisherfolk were similarly inclined; their brides too were said in 1810 to have been 'generally pregnant at marriage'. A check on the parish registers for Camborne in the centre of the mining district (population in 1801, 4,811) reveals that 45.2% of all traceable first baptisms following marriages taking place between 1778 and 1797 were within 8½ months of marriage.[14]

Such a figure confirms the normality of intercourse before marriage in the community and, given the allowance necessary for miscarriage, still birth and 'legitimation' from delayed baptism, the likelihood was of a miner's bride being pregnant as not. However, researches into other parish registers would deny any peculiarity in this respect to Cornish miners. Non-mining parishes in Devon and Cornwall show very similar levels, and a number of scholars following the pioneering investigations of Professor Hair have shown that in the eighteenth and nineteenth centuries bridal-pregnancy levels were much higher than viewing them through the distorting mirror of intervening Victorian Britain might suggest. Hair's researches point out the basis of an 8½-month marriage/baptism gap to a national level after 1700 of around 40%. Later work seems to suggest that there was perhaps a trend from around a third in 1800 to over 40% in the early nineteenth century.[15]

Such evidence strongly suggests that levels of pre-marital sex among lower-class women in the villages and small towns of eighteenth- and nineteenth-century England was rather higher than they were in 1969 when a well-regarded survey of married people under forty-five suggested that 37% of women (75% of men) had had pre-marital sexual intercourse.[16]

Several possible courting practices could have been responsible. Intercourse between 'engaged' couples could have become usual once they had decided upon marriage. This is the explanation favoured by historians of the early modern period who point out that court records show a popular acceptance of marriage being regarded as dating from the point of betrothal rather than the sacrament. Such views did continue into the nineteenth century. Young miners were said to 'keep company' with the girl of their choice until marriage could either be afforded or until 'circumstances of the female made marriage indispensable'. A West Country labourer found it more convenient not to marry his girl at once since she might often have been in service and he working elsewhere: 'They meet occasionally, and are thus relieved at least of the responsibilities and the duties of housekeeping, living better on their separate earnings than they could do in a house of their own. This practice of cohabitation before marriage is almost universal.'[17] It seems reasonable to accept that most bridal pregnancies were indeed the results of anticipated marriage between intending partners. However, there are some qualifications to be made. Young men in having intercourse may well have accepted the need to marry *if* pregnancy resulted, but to have had no such clear intention before intercourse took place. Peter Laslett seems strongly inclined to the belief that pregnancy was a consequence of betrothal rather than vice versa. It was probably both in different cases and in different times. For their part, girls may similarly have expected marriage if intercourse led to pregnancy, without necessarily presuming it otherwise.[18]

In Camborne 1778–97 almost 70% of traced pregnant brides were more than three months pregnant at marriage, and so were probably aware of their condition. It seems likely that while custom tolerated intercourse between engaged couples, this courting practice depended ultimately on strong community sanctions against desertion. As Dr Henriques has suggested, it is perfectly likely that some girls intended to become pregnant to make sure of their partners. They could place some reliance on the strength of community expectation: 'the public opinion of the miners here would be so strong against it [refusal to marry], so as probably to drive a man away from the neighbourhood', said one Cornish witness, while another claimed to have come across only one desertion case in the previous five years. Sanction and custom reinforced each other and sometimes authority, in the shape of the justices, clergy and parish officials, took a hand as well; especially after an Act of 1732/3 obliged the mother to declare a father who had either to marry her, or at least support the child: 'Next at the altar stood a luckless pair/Brought by strong passion and a warrant there', wrote George Crabbe. In 1828 one rural vicar told a visitor that any girl discovered to be pregnant was forced by threat of punishment to name the father 'who is obliged either to marry her or to provide an allowance for the child, who otherwise would be a burden on the parish'.[19]

Gaskell, unlike many critics of the factory system, in being aware that the pregnant bride was a normal feature of rural life, could hardly have accepted George Eliot's Adam Bede as a typical rural lover, in his confrontation with the young squire who had dallied with the affections of his heart's desire: 'And you've been kissing her, and meaning nothing have you? And I never kissed her i' my life, but I'd have worked hard for years for the right to kiss her.'[20] Her urban, middle-class readers would have recognised the steadfast countryman in love and accepted the moral superiority of rustic simplicity over the promiscuity assumed to be the hallmark of emerging industrial Britain. Even if Gaskell accepted the extent of anticipated marriage in the country-side, it was, in his view, quite different from promiscuity and moral decline among the factory population. Here chastity within marriage itself was often disregarded and mill-owners and their sons freely had their lascivious way with female employees, who though thus 'debased' found it easy enough to marry later among their own class and even kept up their relations with their employers up to and after marriage.[21] Engels, too, wrote of the 'jus primae noctis' of a master 'sovereign over the persons and charms of his employees'. He quoted claims that three-quarters of Manchester's female population between the ages of fourteen and twenty were unchaste. The *Morning Chron-icle* quoted a similar view that there was hardly any such thing as 'a chaste factory girl'. The poor lasses could not win. If it was pointed out that illegitimacy statistics did not support the image of a promiscuous factory population, then that was only because the young women were so corrupted as to have the knowledge of avoiding the consequences of their behaviour:

> 'Do you mean that certain books, the disgrace of the age, have been put forth and circulated among the females in factories?'
> 'Yes'
> 'And you attribute the circumstances of there being fewer illegitimate children to that disgusting fact?'
> 'Yes.'[22]

Middle-class moralists, as the reporter of 1849 pointed out, could easily mistake frankness of talk for evidence of promiscuity of deed. It was noted that of fifty-three bastardy warrants issued in Manchester in 1848, thirty-nine were amicably settled. Given that the sexual attitudes of the countryside were not as some critics of the towns assumed them to have been, and that little evidence supports their assertions of a general promiscuity, it is not hard to accept the conclusion of the Factory Commissioners of 1833:

> In regard to morals, we find that though statements and depositions of the different witnesses . . . are to a considerable degree conflicting, yet there is no evidence to show that vice and immorality are more prevalent amongst these people considered as a class than amongst other portions of the community in the same station.[23]

Undoubtedly factory masters and their sons were in a position to sexually exploit their female employees. Novelists like Mrs Gaskell sounded warnings against the fate of the factory girl whose starry-eyed illusions of marriage allowed employers to take liberties. Wherever class and gender power are combined, then sexual exploitation of young women is to some extent likely. But such situations were hardly specific to the factory. Domestic servants were traditionally vulnerable to the advances of their masters and to harassment from male servants in superior positions. Those who supervised the work of women in the fields were as much in a position to force their attentions upon them as were those men who supervised their labour at mine or mill. The author of *My Secret Life* admired some girls at work in a field on his cousin's farm: ' "Why don't you have them?" said Fred . . . "you can always have a field girl; nobody cares – I have had a dozen or two" ', and the text makes clear that the foreman, 'you're a hard man to the women, they all say', exercises such rights as well as the squire. The 'gang masters' hiring out sexually mixed contract labour groups in East Anglia were described as 'ignorant', 'grasping' and tyrannical and were especially suspect.[24] Of course some men took advantage but in general, as Cooke Taylor observed in 1844, seductions when they took place, for the most part did so outside of work and by men of the girl's own class. John Gills has recently suggested that, on the evidence of the unmarried mothers admitted to the foundling hospital in London, servant girls were most likely to have been seduced by fellow servants.[25]

Prostitution is a better illustration of the way in which a socio-economic system pressurises women. In this respect, mill towns were probably superior to most other types of urban settlement. Little is known of eighteenth-century prostitution. What is known is largely concerned with London where prostitution was linked to the destitution of young girls and assumed to merge into the margins of the underworld. It was widespread in the London of Boswell and later of Francis Place, and in a survey of trades in 1746 was associated with the low wages in some female trades: 'Take a survey of all the common women of the town, who take their walks between Charing Cross and Fleet Ditch, and I am persuaded more than half of them have been bred milliners.' This association is interesting in that it makes that link between prostitution and the low-paid female needle trades to which Mayhew was to draw attention in the middle years of the next century: 'They fly to the streets to make their living', said one shirtmaker to him; and he was so often told this that he made a special investigation: 'I've heard of numbers who have gone from slop-work to the streets altogether for a living', said another, 'and I shall be obliged to do the same thing myself unless something better turns up for me.'[26] Modern historians, notably Judith Walkowitz, have confirmed this link. It is because they afforded comparatively better opportunities for female employment that the mill towns had a low incidence of prostitution. Walkowitz has shown that the typical prostitute was a poor working girl whose entry into the profession had been voluntary and gradual. She was, given the courting practices of the working classes, unlikely to be sexually inexperienced, and to have chosen the life from the few employment opportunities open to her in most urban job markets. She was usually young, because prostitution, as William Acton noted in 1857, was likely to be a transitory stage in a woman's life. Difficult to distinguish from the large body of poor women who had to eke out a precarious living in the towns, she was likely to have previously worked in a typical low-paid occupation in laundering, cleaning or as a general servant. After a few years she married back into the unskilled working class from which she had come. Walkowitz emphasises the fluid nature of prostitution before the 1860s: only with the official 'labelling' of women as a result of the Contagious Diseases Acts did a significant separation of prostitutes from the working-class community develop.[27]

Prostitution was largely an urban phenomenon. Most evident in London, it flourished noticeably too in resorts, sea ports and garrison towns. Most large towns had their notorious districts and smaller ones could support a few women selling sex. Village prostitution seems likely to have been of a different nature. The 'parish whore' is a familiar enough figure through the ages, but it is hardly possible to make a firm distinction between a woman who sold her services, one who was generally regarded as 'loose', and one who may have depended upon living with a series of men in short cohabiting relationships.

A report on a small Berkshire township shows this blurring of distinction:

> Chastity is a thing little known in the village and not at all respected. The want of it is regarded as no stain on a woman's character, nor does it mar her prospects in the slightest degree. Herself a prostitute, and the companion of thieves and prostitutes, she is just as likely to marry and get settled as people in her class of life are generally settled – as is the honest and virtuous woman in localities possessing a higher standard of morality. I have found more than one family of children going by different names. The mother was unmarried, and the different names indicated the paternity of the different children. Again a whole family has been known to go by different names at different times. Thus if the mother was living with a man by the name of Smith, the children took his name; but if she changed her paramour, and lived with one called Tomkins, the family would go by the new name.[28]

Historians of the early modern period claim to have uncovered a 'bastardy-prone' sub-stratum within village society. 'Repeaters' who bear a succession of illegitimate children, and who often seem to be following a hereditary trait in so doing, have disclosed themselves to the academic voyeurs of the parish register. Their existence is capable of varying interpretation. If different names of putative fathers are given, then a single 'common law' liaison is ruled out, but not a series of temporary ones. Undoubtedly some such women were the Polly Garters of their day, cheerfully carolling that they served 'men from every parish round . . . good bad boys from the lonely farms' as well as the 'gandering hubbies' of the village wives.[29]

Groups who moved in search of work like navvies, or were highly mobile like sailors, were especially likely to cohabit rather than make formal marriages, but there were also more settled groups who seem to have set little store by the sacrament. Mayhew thought that perhaps only a tenth of London's costermongers who lived together were formally married. At around the age of sixteen, a boy setting up with his own barrow would begin living with a girl of his own age, but such relationships were commonly stable and long lasting:

> 'If I seed my gal a talking to another chap I'd fetch her . . . a punch on the nose', explained one and another, 'the gals . . . it was a rum thing now he came to think on it – axually [sic] liked a feller for walloping them. As long as the bruises hurted, she was always thinking on the cove as gave 'em her'.

A comforting male view expecting female fidelity: a double standard which, as Professor Harrison has remarked, would have been appreciated if not openly approved in more polite Victorian circles. Later in the century Charles Booth, while commenting that legal marriage was the general rule 'even among the roughest class', still found 'un-legalised cohabitation' far from uncommon especially among those who came together in their maturer years. He quoted the view of a clergyman that such relationships were often very stable and affectionate.[30] With divorce unobtainable for the lower ranks of society and desertion common, prior marriage often made legal union impossible. The folk form of 'wife-selling' in rural districts was one way in which second cohabitations could be announced to the community but, and especially in the towns, it seems reasonable to suppose that nothing as formal even as a wife sale took place in other than a minority of cases.[31]

Gaskell's claim that among the factory population there was 'an entire absence of all regard for moral obligations relating to sex' among the married and unmarried alike, not only posed a false antithesis between urban and rural sexual practices, but it cannot be effectively sustained from the evidence. Historians who take a European perspective have commented on the very low illegitimacy rates in English towns compared with continental ones. Nor is there any real evidence to support the claims made by Professor Shorter for a 'sexual revolution' beginning in the mid-eighteenth century and caused by newly 'independent' women being drawn by developing capitalism into the labour market. New opportunities for work outside the home, he argues, led to sexual liberation by revolutionising women's attitudes about themselves. Becoming individualistic and self-seeking, they overthrew traditional constraints and, in the absence of birth control, there was a marked increase in both legitimate and, especially, illegitimate fertility. Shorter has established that a widespread increase in recorded illegitimacy rates in Europe in both rural and urban areas in the second half of the eighteenth century continued until approximately the middle of the nineteenth century. Such an increase, he declares, must have reflected a genuine change in popular sexual behaviour. Economic modernisation had freed sexuality which had previously been 'a great iceberg, frozen by the command of custom' and by the need for community stability. His critics have shown that while remarking the phenomenon, he has misread its causes. As we have seen, it does not appear that there was a significantly larger entry of women into the labour market, and for those that did find employment outside the home, it did not follow that they thereby threw off traditional constraints and expectations. Tilly, Scott and Cohen have suggested that if leaving to work in the towns meant that women lost one family, for most it also meant that they 'sought to create another'. It was their traditional expectations carried into changed circumstances which underlay the increase in illegitimacy. Expecting marriage, they continued traditional courting practices, but in the absence of the constraints of the traditional community their expectations were often disappointed. They became, not more emancipated, but more vulnerable, as lack of money, unemployment and opportunities for work far afield all kept men from fulfilling promises in conditions where there was no power of enforcing them.[32]

There is indeed a link between the astonishingly rapid growth of a capitalist labour market needing propertyless, mobile wage-earners and the rise in illegitimacy which coincided with it. That link, however, lies neither in a sexual liberation of women accompanying a presumed economic one, nor in a new 'urban' promiscuity, for it was emphatically not a uniquely urban phenomenon. The explanation which best suits the evidence is that summed up by David Levine as 'marriage frustrated' rather than 'promiscuity rampant'.[33]

SENTIMENT TOWARDS CHILDREN

In a general survey only a few selected areas of sentiment can be explored and we have concentrated on those where contemporary opinion was apt to assume an absence of feeling and accuse the working people of an instrumental or even exploitative attitude towards members of their family. One such area was the relationship between working-class parents and their children. Contemporaries commented on the eagerness with which parents seized hold of the earliest opportunities to send their children out to work, even to the extent of lying about their age to evade factory legislation, or putting them under overseers they knew to be stern, or even brutal, if that meant higher earnings. These contemporary opinions have been eagerly seized upon by present-day ideological supporters of the market economy, seeking to 'whitewash' the excesses of even the early factory system. We have dealt elsewhere with the problems posed by the institution of child labour. Here we will be concerned with the more general suggestion that in an age of very high infant mortality, parents were conditioned to grieve little over the deaths of their children and were willing to invest little emotional or material capital in their upbringing.

It must be remembered that levels of infant mortality were high at all social levels until late in the nineteenth century and the unfavourable working-class differential was a relative one. Dr Vincent has suggested that evidence from his study of working-class autobiographies does not support generalised accusations of lack of affection towards children. Historians, he remarks, in concentrating attention on the fact that in the 1840s 47% of Preston's children died before their fifth birthday, do not take the point that contemporaries may have been more conscious of the fact that 53% survived. If death was inexplicable, then so too was survival.[34] Diagnosis was rudimentary and the apparently well child suddenly taken had a counterpart in the very ill child who surprisingly recovered, perhaps from the disturbing symptoms which accompany at times short-lived illnesses. There was always hope, and where that was exhausted, then the belief, not confined to the especially religious, that the 'poor mite' had passed on to a better world could be meeting a genuine emotional need. A destitute silk weaver spoke to Mayhew of the death of his two children: 'I thank God for it I am relieved from the burden of maintaining them, and they, poor dear creatures, are relieved from the troubles of this mortal life.' Such a reaction is a mixture of material relief, affectionate remembrance and religious consolation. The death-bed scene was a part of proletarian as well as of middle-class culture.[35]

For many working-class parents, the death of a child perhaps only a matter of days or weeks old, whose expecting and whose birth had already brought anxious anticipation of the problems of supporting yet another dependent family member, was likely to be greeted with an intermingling of grief and relief. If nothing else, it probably meant that the chances of the surviving elder sibling did not deteriorate. Dr Vincent concluded that few of the autobiographies which he studied displayed pure grief: 'Almost always their experiences were controlled by the way in which the strands of their emotional and material lives were woven together.'[36] Contrary to the impression sometimes given by the averaging-out school of quantitative social historians and demographers, life *was* a lottery and the way in which it was cast was bound to affect the responses of working-class families to the death of their children. A family might lose its only child, its only son; it might lose a child so close to birth that bonds had hardly had time to form; it might lose one at an age when it had already absorbed years of emotional and material concern and was perhaps beginning to earn more than its keep.

In his study of Preston, Anderson has found little evidence to support generalised accusations of a callous attitude towards their children by the working class. Their circumstances may have required them to view death with a large degree of equanimity, but an ability to reconcile oneself to the inevitable does not preclude feelings of grief, even if it allows little room for their indulgence. Anderson found as much evidence of sorrow and distress at the death of a child as of indifference. He noted no instance of a sick child being deserted by its parents. His investigation of relationships within the working-class nuclear family pursues the matter at some depth. Accepting some truth in accusations of drunken fathers behaving brutally towards their families, he points out that in the harsh working-class world of the nineteenth century, the perspective on harshness was a relative one. Obviously extreme cases occurred of drunken fathers battering children or of step-parents locking them up or starving them. Drunken mothers overlay small infants and drunken fathers spent money needed for food and clothes. But how is such evidence to be used? If we judged today's family from press reports of court cases and inquests we would obtain a harsh impression indeed. Violence in the family has always stood high among social problems. The anxieties and tensions associated with the uncertainties of working-class life in the nineteenth century might with reason be expected to have increased rather than decreased its incidence compared with more settled times. But there is no need to accept at face value a generally levelled accusation that indifference, brutality and an exploitative attitude towards children were the norms of working-class life.[37]

Anderson has suggested that the experience of suffering from a drunken and brutal father might even have led to a strengthening of the bond of affection between a mother and her children. In the absence of evidence on the attitudes of working-class women towards their children, it is better to at least withhold judgement. While we do not want evidence of some parents seeking, through finding the pennies for schooling or for apprenticeships, to give their children a better chance in life than they had had themselves, those who made no such attempts, or even bitterly resisted attempts to force them to keep their children longer from work, are not to be therefore regarded as wanting in affection towards their children. Individuals may have aspirations for their children, but when expectations of social mobility are low, there is unlikely to be any general encouragement of them. One young man from the rapidly declining trade of handloom weaving recorded his parents' sacrifice to allow his escape: 'I was put to be a mechanic. Perhaps it caused as much remark among our neighbours as it would now if I put a son to be a doctor . . . My parents must have made a costly effort to get me a trade.'[38] He was fortunate, but acceptance of the inevitability of a child remaining in the situation to which he or she had been born need not be equated with a lack of affection, any more than need be the sigh of relief when a young child became of age to earn his own keep, with perhaps a little something over to assist in feeding those still dependent.

REFERENCES AND NOTES

1.   **L. Stone**, *The Family, Society and Marriage in England 1500–1800*, Penguin, 1979, p. 419; **M. Anderson**, *Family Structure in Nineteenth Century Lancashire*, Cambridge U.P., 1971, Ch. 1.

2.   'The Life and Times of Sam Brook and some of the People he has met', Mss. in the possession of his family.

3.   **Thomas Hardy**, *Far From the Madding Crowd*, 1874.

4.   **D. Vincent**, *Bread, Knowledge and Freedom. A Study of Nineteenth-Century Working Class Autobiography*, Methuen, 1982, pp. 39–46.

5.   Ibid., p. 48; **Flora Thompson**, *Larkrise to Candleford*, 1939, Penguin, 1973, p. 166. The data on the two Devonshire parishes was provided by Southampton students working on printed parish registers. For Melbourn, see **D. R. Mills**, *Aspects of Marriage: an example of Applied Historical Studies*, Open University Social Science Publications, 1980, p. 9.

6.   **Joseph Lawson**, *Progress in Pudsey*, 1887, repr. Caliban Books, 1978, pp. 29–30.

7.   **Thomas Hardy**, *Jude the Obscure*, 1895.

8.   **R. W. Malcolmson**, *Popular Recreations in English Society 1700–1850*, Cambridge U.P., 1973, pp. 53–5.

9.   Ibid., pp. 77–8; Mills, *Aspects of Marriage*, p. 16; **Charles Shaw**, *When I Was a Child*, 1903, repr. Caliban, 1977, p. 201.

10. **D. Hudson**, *Munby. Man of Two Worlds*, Abacus, 1974, pp. 103–4.

11. These accounts are from autobiographies reprinted in **J. Burnett** (ed.), *Useful Toil. Autobiographies of Working People from the 1820s to the Nineteen Twenties*, Allen Lane, 1974, pp. 72, 74–5, 57, 61.

12. **Samuel Bamford**, *Early Days*, 1848–9, repr. Cass, 1967, pp. 14–15, 169–78, 215–18, 224, 291, 294. **William Lovett**, *Life and Struggles*, ed. **R. H. Tawney**, MacGibbon & Key, 1967, p. 17; report in *Local Population Studies*, 24, 1980, on the Oxford D.Phil Thesis (1978) of **G. Gandy**.

13. **P. Gaskell**, *Artisans and Machinery*, 1836, repr. Cass, 1968, p. 20; **Harriet Martineau** is quoted in **J. D. Chambers** & **G. E. Mingay**, *The Agricultural Revolution, 1750–1880*, Batsford, 1966, p. 194; **G. D'Eichthal**, *A French Sociologist Looks at Britain*, ed. **W. H. Chaloner**, Manchester U.P., 1977, p. 17; **P. E. Razzell** and **R. W. Wainwright** (eds), *The Victorian Working Class: Selections from Letters to the Morning Chronicle*, Cass, 1973, pp. 31–3.

14. Quoted in **P. Hair** (ed.), *Before the Bawdy Court*, Elek, 1972, pp. 224–5. For Cornish miners, see *Report of the Royal Commission on Employment of Children*, BPP, 1842, vi, pp. 832, 806, 759, 841, 848, 850; the analysis of Camborne is calculated from the printed parish register.

15. The pioneer article by **P. Hair** was 'Bridal pregnancy in rural England in earlier centuries', *Population Studies*, vol. 20, 1967, pp. 233–43. See also Mills, *Aspects of Marriage*, pp. 14–18.

16. Quoted in Mills, *Aspects of Marriage*, p.14.

17. Razzell and Wainwright, *Victorian Working Class*, p. 32.
18. **T. P. R. Laslett**, *The World we have Lost*, Methuen, 2nd edn, 1968, pp. 135–55 for a fuller discussion.
19. **U. R. Q. Henriques**, 'Bastardy and the New Poor Law', *Past and Present*, no. 37, 1967, p. 106; **George Crabb**, *The Parish Register*, 1807; see also references to miners indicated in 14 above. D'Eichthal, *French Sociologist*, p. 17.
20. **George Eliot**, *Adam Bede*, 1859.
21. Gaskell, *Artisans and Machinery*, pp. 88–9, 97–9.
22. **F. Engels**, *The Condition of the Working Class in England*, 1845, Granada edn, 1969, p. 177; Razzell and Wainwright, *Victorian Working Class*, p. 190; quoted in **E. H. Hunt**, *British Labour History 1815–1914*, Weidenfeld & Nicolson, 1980, p. 36.
23. Razzell and Wainwright, *Victorian Working Class*, p. 190; **H. Perkin**, *The Origins of Modern English Society 1780–1880*, Routledge & Kegan Paul, 1969, pp. 152–4.
24. See *Mary Barton*, 1848; quoted in **S. Marcus**, *The Other Victorians. A study of sexuality and pornography in mid-nineteenth-century England*, Corgi Books, 1969, pp. 137–8.
25. Perkin, *Origins*, p. 152; **J. R. Gillis**, 'Servants, sexual relations and the risks of illegitimacy in London, 1801–1900', in **J. L. Newton, M. P. Ryan & J. R. Walkowitz** (eds), *Sex and Class in Women's History*, Routledge & Kegan Paul for *History Workshop*, 1983, pp. 114–45.
26. **R. Campbell**, *The London Tradesman*, 1747, repr. David and Charles, Newton Abbot, 1969, pp. 206–9, 225–8; **E. P. Thompson** and **E. Yeo** (eds), *The Unknown Mayhew*, Penguin, 1973, pp. 175–7.
27. **J. R. Walkowitz**, *Prostitution and Victorian Society: Women, Class and the State*, Cambridge U.P., 1980, p. 22 ff.
28. Razzell and Wainwright, *Victorian Working Class*, p. 33.
29. The reference is, of course, to **Dylan Thomas**, *Under Milkwood*.
30. Quoted in **J. F. C. Harrison**, *The Early Victorians*, Weidenfeld & Nicolson, 1971, pp. 79–80; *Charles Booth's London*, ed. **A. Fried** & **R. Elman**, Penguin, 1971, pp. 247–8.
31. **Jeffrey Weeks**, *Sex, Politics and Society. The Regulation of Sexuality since 1800*, Longman, 1981; cites on wife sales: **E. P. Thompson**, 'Folklore, anthropology, and social history', in *Indian Historical Review*, III, no. 2, 1978, pp. 247–66. Weeks' book is much the best introduction to working-class sexual practices and beliefs.
32. See **E. Shorter**, 'Illegitimacy, sexual revolution, and social change in modern Europe', in **R. I. Rotberg** & **T. K. Rabb** (eds), *Marriage and Fertility*, Princeton U.P., 1980, pp. 86–7; **L. A. Tilly, J. W. Scott** and **M. Cohen**, 'Women's work and European fertility patterns', ibid., p. 235.
33. **D. Levine**, *Family Formation in an age of Nascent Capitalism*, Academic Press, New York, 1977, Ch. 9.
34. Vincent, *Bread, Knowledge and Freedom*, pp. 56–9.
35. Thompson and Yeo, *Unknown Mayhew*, pp. 126–7.
36. Vincent, *Bread Knowledge and Freedom*, p. 59.
37. Anderson, *Family Structure*, pp. 77–8.
38. Ibid., p. 78; Burnett, *Useful Toil*, p. 207.

Chapter 9

POPULAR RECREATION

Two differing approaches to eighteenth-century leisure put forward by Professor Plumb and by E. P. Thompson can serve as convenient approaches to the subject, although neither was intended as a response to the other. We can also look at a third approach by Hans Medick which seems in some respects to suggest interesting links between the other two. Thompson is concerned specifically with the recreational culture of the lower orders, deliberately labelling a distinctive 'plebeian culture'. The pastimes of the 'plebs' included those non-literate 'rude' sports such as wrestling, cudgelling, football, quoits, bell-ringing, bear- and badger-baiting and cockfighting. Such activities revolved around the agricultural calendar, weekly markets and hiring fairs, or in the case of manufacturing workers were associated with 'St Monday'. Thompson presents this culture in the eighteenth century as not only distinctive, but vigorous. Professor Plumb is interested in the commercialisation of leisure, the early development of a leisure industry. This is seen as among the most evident indicators of an eighteenth-century revolution in consumption dependent upon the increase in the number of people having both spare time and some money to indulge recreational pursuits. He is interested in the spread of literature, the arts, theatre and promoted sports like prize fighting and horse racing. All these entertainments involved spending by consumers. He has argued that the late seventeenth and early eighteenth centuries saw a great increase in the provision of such activities as the basis of a leisure culture, which although belonging essentially to the middle class was in the process of downward extension to a significant degree.[1]

These two views, the one emphasising the perpetuation of the traditional and vulgar, and the other commercialisation, are capable of co-existence to the extent that one describes a predominantly rural-based culture while the other relates mostly to towns. The point of conflict is Plumb's assertion that the new bourgeois culture was, from the late seventeenth century, driving both the proletarian vulgar culture and that of the patrician elite into small enclaves, for Thompson asserts that for a variety of reasons the traditional pursuits of the people were especially strong and resilient in the eighteenth century. Not until the nineteenth, and then by identifiable forces, were they weakened. His plebeian culture of the eighteenth century encompasses more than simply popular recreational forms, although these play an important and integrated role in his model of a popular culture which represented a whole way of life in which recreations were a necessary part. He finds for the common people of the eighteenth century a 'comparative freedom' which invigorated popular culture: 'This is the century which sees the erosion of half-free forms of labour, the decline of living-in, the final extinction of labour services and the advance of free, mobile, wage labour.'[2] Capitalism's need for a labour force responsive to the money wage and mobile to follow the needs of the labour market, necessarily meant an interim period in which old forms of control eroded before newer forms of social control and of industrial discipline reformed the basis for hegemony. Henry Fielding saw this with perceptive clarity in 1751, even if medievalists might cavil at his implied dating of the end of feudalism:

> By these and such like means the commonality by degrees shook off their vassalage, and became more and more independent of their superiors. Even servants, in process of time, acquired a state of freedom and independency unknown to this rank in any other nation; and which, as the law now stands, is inconsistent with a servile condition.
> But nothing hath wrought such an alteration in this order of people as the introduction of trade. This hath indeed given a new face to the whole nation, hath in a great measure subverted the former state of affairs, and hath almost totally changed the manners, customs, and habits of the people, more especially of the lower sort.[3]

If we translate Fielding's language into a more modern sociological idiom, then he is evidently describing a social accompaniment of capitalist modes of production. This human dimension of economic transformation presents itself to magistrates like Fielding most evidently as a problem of order. Changes in hiring and in master to man relationships tending towards the wage system in manufacturing and in agriculture resulted in only part of a labourer's life, his working hours, being totally controlled by his employer. Simultaneously, other agencies of control diminished in effectiveness, such as the power of the church through its local clergy, and allowed the people to develop their own culture. Such a freedom did not always manifest itself in ways which implied conflict with ruling patrician society. In fact the country gentry were able to patronise popular leisure pursuits and use them in a paternalist extension of their own authority, since no change to the status system was involved. Thompson does not see only a dominant class resisting a popular culture and attempting to supplant it with a preferred alternative, but rather a willingness not only to acquiesce in its persistence but for involvement in it.[4]

This was not a radical departure in the eighteenth century, as Peter Burke has shown for the early modern period of European history, the gentry had enjoyed participation in many of the recreations of the poor, but in the eighteenth century their role in patronising and encouraging certain popular activities served broader purposes. Through the manipulation of doles in times of dearth, the putting-up of prizes for sports and the supplying of beer for calendrical festivities, together with an elaborate and conscious 'social theatre' of ceremony, the gentry were able to rule *and* to distance themselves from the consequences of their own exploitation. Inherently there is an act of reciprocation in that what is an act of giving from above is one of getting from below. Thus the plebs were not slow to demand, perhaps as a crowd with their own theatrical style and expressive symbols, recognition of what were in their eyes legitimate rights. In such practices are clearly evident the links between direct actions such as food rioting for 'just' prices, and persisting in lighting bonfires on 5 November even if they were regarded as 'nuisances' by authorities.[5]

The pioneering researches of Robert Malcolmson placed eighteenth-century recreational forms sociologically with a thoroughness and insight which cannot be approached in a general text.[6] He describes the vulgar pastimes of football, bear- and bull-baiting, cockfighting and reveals the extent of gentry encouragement and patronage. He also notes the importance of publicans as profit-minded sponsors of plebeian pastimes. How far can their selling of beers and spirits be seen as introducing a commercial element into popular recreations? To an extent it must be so seen, and this is a point to which we must return, but for now we should note that the activities of the drink-sellers took place *within* existing recreational forms. They were an adjunct to and lubricant for existing activities, rather than part of the supplanting of a traditional culture.

In the countryside the timing of feasts, festivals, fairs and wakes was largely determined by the agricultural calendar and there was a degree of integration between the rhythms of work and those of leisure, leading Thompson to suggest some anachronism in the use by historians of the word 'leisure'. Many such observances served to bind communities together by allowing competition with outsiders or even the settlement of internal differences. The wakes and fairs have been shown by Malcolmson to have had a special courtship and sexual significance for the young, as well as allowing those who participated in them the chance of gaining status and prestige among their peers. Although mainly participated in by younger persons, those who watched by that very action attached themselves to and reinforced the validity of the actions of the participants. Above all, traditional games had an element of 'carnival' introducing release into hard lives.[7]

Group solidarity was the cornerstone of plebeian activity. For it was as a group that the poor both sported and, on occasion, demanded their rights, fair prices or customary access. It was as a group that they could in 'counter-theatre' mock, mimic and remind their social superiors of their presence, as well as discipline offenders against their norms by 'charivari' or effigy burning. As a crowd they had power as well as anonymity. In the detailed researches of Malcolmson and others there is ample illustration of the vigour of recreational forms as an integral part of a plebeian culture whose existence is central to an understanding of the social relations of the period.

In his recent writing, Professor Plumb presents a different view of eighteenth-century recreational developments. He sees in the late eighteenth and early nineteenth centuries the emergence of a commercial leisure industry responding to a bourgeois desire to emulate the existing minority culture of the elite. He illustrates the expanding provision of leisure opportunities for a growing middle class and offers a convincing account of, for example, the spread of daily and periodical literature and the complex of activities associated with the remarkable growth and spread of spa towns. Indeed, central to his argument for an expanding leisure industry is that growth of specialised recreational towns which Peter Borsay has described as the essential dynamic in an English 'urban renaissance' between 1680 and 1760. Plumb has noted the importance of bowling greens and race meetings as well as traditional spa activities. Although he points to the participation of better-off tradesmen, he clearly sees the 'leisure industry' as catering for an expanding middle class. Even though race meetings in particular were well-attended and enjoyed by the larger populace, there seems but a poor case for seeing the lower orders as significant participants in new urban recreations, whatever opportunities for employment for them may have been created by the participation of others.[8]

Southampton was briefly a resort. Its history provides examples of plebeian antagonism towards spa users:

> The Long Rooms though more capacious and elegant than their predecessors were not completely satisfactory, being badly situated in a part of the town where there was not sufficient carriage room and the approach to which on foot or by sedan chair lay through dark, dirty and even dangerous lanes where persons dressed for a ball might be exposed at night to insult or attack by the rougher elements of the poor, resentful of the amusements of the well to do and fashionable visitors.

In 1773 a young man going dressed as a shepherd to a ball was set upon by a 'rabble' and 'tossed like a football for some time', while in the following year on the occasion of a masquerade, a mob made it difficult for the would-be participants to get in and out of their carriages, and caused consternation throughout the evening by street disturbances.[9]

How far does the possibility of Plumb's commercial leisure having spread downwards through the eighteenth century, even allowing for a slower percolation than he suggests, point to a need to modify Thompson's presentation of the persistence of a vigorous popular culture on traditional lines, perpetuated and even revived rather than received? Several qualifications do suggest themselves. Plumb, although he includes horse racing and prize fighting, is working from a different and narrower definition of culture than either Thompson or Malcolmson. Literature and the arts figure rather more noticeably than do traditional sports. He would seem to be writing about an added dimension to bourgeois life, through their emulative grasping at a commercial leisure which was derivative from an elite culture. Thompson, on the other hand, is concerned to place plebeian recreational forms into an integrated popular *mentalité* which remained active throughout the eighteenth century. Plumb, and more specifically Borsay, are describing an urban phenomenon at a time when most English people did not live in towns. Urban areas were growing but in the eighteenth century the more general plebeian experience was a rural one. The emergence of an urban middle class to receive and carry a new 'leisure' is plausible but, translated into the countryside where there was no thrusting middle between patrician and pleb to act as the hander down of change, it has little applicability. Without presenting much in the way of evidence, Plumb asserts that his versions of 'high' and 'low' culture were being squeezed out to the extremes by the expanding middle commercial leisure, through the mechanism of social emulation. Thompson, however, draws lines to link the plebs with the patricians through an important deference/patronage model, seeing the eighteenth century as one when the gap between the dependence and subordination of the old paternalist (master/servant) relationship and the coming discipline of the factory economy was filled with a plebeian culture of extraordinary vitality.

Perhaps the 'squeeze' had a varying impact. Much of Plumb's evidence comes from London, a city not only unique in its size. In 1751, Henry Fielding was making claims which suggest a wider extension of leisure provision there: 'What an immense variety of places has this town and its neighbourhood set apart for the amusement of the lowest order of the people.'[10] By the time Francis Place spent (or misspent) his youth as a London apprentice in the 1780s, he and his fellows were clearly avid consumers of commercial leisure. But even in the case of the capital there is need for caution. Dr Corfield has remarked of London's pleasure gardens like Vauxhall, picked out by Fielding, that although the likes of Horace Walpole might remark (in 1744), 'Everybody goes there from his Grace the Duke of Grafton down to children out of the Foundling hospital', in fact with an admission fee of 2s. 6d. (12½p) per head, entry was effectively limited.[11]

Nevertheless in London and to a lesser extent in other urban centres, there is evidence of an increasing leisure *expenditure* from the lower orders. Hans Medick has recently suggested that Thompson's emphasis on a tradition-based resistance to emerging capitalism is concerned with only one dimension of the relationship between plebeian culture and the expansion of capitalist markets. The other dimension, he argues, is found in an everyday life which was to some extent in harmony with the market economy – in consumption, in fashion and especially in the changing forms of plebeian drinking. In this dimension the lower orders did invest *money* as well as 'emotional capital' in leisure. Despite low incomes, they had not switched priority to the long-term needs of their households. Instead, conditioned by the nature of their family economy inherited before the days of wage dependency, they regarded money earnings above those necessary to meet their customary short-term subsistence needs as a surplus which could be expended on the public consumption of festivities and 'luxuries'. This suggests that the constant complaints of social superiors that the poor's expenditure and income were irrationally related were not simply expressions of class prejudice. Medick remarks on the rise of spirit drinking, especially gin, among the plebs and the proletariat. Unlike beer, gin was clearly a 'capitalist' product, linking agrarian capitalism in the form of grain production with 'free market' forms of mercantile capitalism in its distillation and distribution, and through its imposed duties linked to the fiscal interests of the state. Gin consumption and production increased around six times between 1700 and 1743 and indicates that Thompson's 'moral economy' and 'traditional culture' were not only pressurised by external forces such as industrialisation, but were undermined by changes in demand for and taste in leisure – chosen indulgences on the part of the poor themselves.[12]

Medick has certainly posed important questions. Like Plumb, his English examples are, however, narrowly drawn. How representative was London's experience? There seems little doubt, as the growth of smuggling indicates, of a national expansion of spirit consumption, but the 'gin age' was really a label only appropriate to London. Did the drinking culture of the countryside and smaller towns really undergo a significant change? The beer or cider which lubricated the great harvest-following festivities of the rural calendar was not bought, but brewed by the farmers, and it was not sold; it was expected largess.[13] Manufacturing, too, reveals similar expectations from workers. Nevertheless, Medick's linking of new forms of recreation to the early period of adjustment to the money wage and to well-observed rhythms of work and leisure offers more concrete reasons for a downward percolation of commercial leisure forms then the assertions of Professor Plumb. From Medick's approach it is possible to draw important lines between eighteenth-century recreational forms and the revised view of nineteenth-century proletarian leisure recently presented by Dr Cunningham with its greater emphasis on commercial provision for working-class tastes.[14]

POPULAR RECREATIONS IN THE NINETEENTH CENTURY

Rude, rough and ready amusements continued to be characteristic of lower-class life well into the nineteenth century. Historians have begun to discount claims that by the mid-nineteenth century attacks converging from a number of points had brought about a substantially complete 'reformation' of working-class leisure. First the old plebeian pursuits had been tamed by a process of suppression (counteraction) and then had been replaced (counter-attraction) by more acceptable (from the capitalist viewpoint), respectable, less dangerous, 'rational' uses of non-work time. Writings in the 1960s tended towards the establishment of an 'orthodoxy' which used recreational developments almost as much as those in popular education to point out the imposition of a 'social control', more or less as a capitalist imperative, over the lower orders. However overstated such an approach may have become (and even if true about intent, success in implementation cannot be taken for granted), there is no doubt that from the late eighteenth century, with seemingly evident success by the 1840s, popular recreations came under increasing attack from several different, but not unrelated, directions. However successful we judge the attack on traditional recreational forms to have been, there is no doubt at all that attempts to reform popular leisure were a major preoccupation of the first half of the nineteenth century.

Birmingham's workers in the mid-nineteenth century remembered old sports like dog fights, cockfights, bull- and badger-baitings, pugilism and bear-baiting, as being the favoured amusements of the operative class and even of some employers, and as persisting in many cases into the 1820s, especially when associated with the city's wakes. One account suggests that the last bull to be baited was in 1811, while an old man noting that such amusements had largely passed away among the young men by 1849, along with skittle-playing, quoits and football, was not without his regrets: 'There is less fighting now than in my day, for the young men now-a-days have not courage to fight as they used to do.'[15]

In Derby the long-established street football played on Shrove Tuesday with a thousand men and boys contesting for six hours through the streets, in and out of the River Derwent, between goals at opposite ends of the town resisted all attempts at suppression until the mid-1840s. Then the mayor appealed for the ending of

> the assembly of a lawless rabble, suspending business to the loss of the industrious; creating terror and alarm to the timid and peaceable, committing violence on the persons and damage to the properties of the defenceless and poor, and producing in those who play moral degradation and in many extreme poverty, injury to health, fractured limbs and (not infre-

quently) loss of life; rendering their homes desol. te, their wives widowed and their children fatherless.[16]

At Stamford the annual running of a bull through the streets had received the disapprobating attentions of the authorities from the 1780s, but attempted repression had met with determined resistance from the 'bullards' who, in the early nineteenth century, had even had special commemorative mugs printed with the slogan 'Bull for Ever'. They succeeded in holding their annual festival of 'riot, confusion, plunder and bloodshed' until succumbing in 1840 to the combined forces of local government, special constables, the RSPCA, the Home Secretary, a subvention of forces from the Metropolitan Police and a troop of dragoons.[17]

Before analysing the directions from which attacks on popular recreations materialised, it is useful to employ a concept not as much used by English historians as it is on the continent, that of 'carnival'. This pre-Lenten freeing of constraints, temporary reversal of social and sexual order was essentially a festival of release, indulgence and inversion. 'Carnival' allows us to see why it was above all the great public calendar festivals in each locality which were the main and most easily identifiable targets of the spoilsports: Stamford bull running on 13 November, Derby football on Shrove Tuesday, Padstow's Hobby Horse on 1 May and the variously dated wakes and feasts and revels and fairs throughout the country. Such annual releases of constraint were bothersome to the point of being subversive. They could earn the committed opposition of the pleasure-distrusting evangelical; the scorn of the rational; the distaste of the aspiring; the impatience of the business community; and the fear of the magistracy. As public occasions, calendar festivals were striking concentrations of those aspects of rough and disturbing plebeian leisure which were most disliked and most worrying. The more private world of leisure centred on the pub was more resistant and less easy to confront. The pub was accordingly able to serve as the location for the later emergence of a form of popular leisure, which if it had changed its public form, did not necessarily do so into the desired shapes of the recreational reformers.[18]

The carnivalesque feature of revels, feasts, wakes and fairs became a matter of concern. We have already noted the suggestions of sexual licence which attached themselves to the hiring and urban fairs. Portsmouth's great Free Mart Fair, traditionally held on the High Street, was described as a 'disgusting Saturnalia': a source of moral evil such as to make an observer shudder to even allude to the 'monstrosity of the deeds' perpetrated during such a 'licentious period'. Dickens was less emotive and more perceptive of function when he described Greenwich fair as a 'periodical breaking out, we suppose a sort of spring-rash: a three day's fever, which cools the blood for six months afterwards, and at the expiration of which London is restored to its old

215

habits of plodding industry'. *Three Days* – the feature of carnivalesque recreations was not just their calendrical occasioning, but the fact that they extended either side of their central date to form holidays of considerable duration, vastly increasing their nuisance image to their opponents. Three days was modest. At its peak the Portsmouth Free Mart Fair could disturb the quiet of the town for 'fifteen mortal days of each season'. Alun Howkins has written of the traditional jollifications around Whitsuntide in Oxfordshire villages in the early nineteenth century as occasions when rural England played 'carnival' with its maypoles, revelling, sexual relaxation, drinking and fighting. At Woodstock they lasted thirteen days and at Milton ten. Howkins has presented the process of erosion as one of incorporation into a bourgeois-valued world, evident in the change of the week- or fortnight-lasting Whitsuntide of the early nineteenth century into the single ordered day of the 1900s.[19]

THE LOSS OF SPACE AND TIME

Gradually developments in both industry and agriculture encroached upon the space and time available for such recreational activities. Factory discipline (with its regularity of working), urban spread and common-land enclosures were all part of this encroachment. The Hammonds entitled one chapter of their book *The Bleak Age*, 'The loss of the playgrounds'. Malcolmson has argued that enclosure militated against popular recreation since it involved the imposition of absolute rights of property on land which had previously been accessible to the people at large, during at least certain seasons of the year, for the exercise of sports and pastimes. In 1824 Robert Slaney described how in rural areas 'owing to the inclosure of open lands and commons, the poor have no place in which they may amuse themselves in summer evenings, when the labour of the day is over, or when a holiday occurs'.[20]

In the towns the 'street' was to be redefined in business terms rather than as public space. It was not the least of the expectations on the new police of the 1830s that they should keep it clear. Even more fundamental was the pressure of new building under a philosophy which made the provision of leisure space no one's responsibility. A nonogenerian looking back from 1849 at the robust days of his youth in Birmingham remarked sadly that now 'the fellows have no ground to kick upon'.[21] The very real lack of recreational space in urban areas was revealed by the 1833 Select Committee on Public Works, a group which saw that old patterns should not be destroyed in such a manner as to leave a recreational vacuum. Counter-attractions could weaken the hold of the pub, improve health and cleanliness and add to contentment. The common lands which surrounded many towns had been among the early casualties of expansion. By 1844 the Select Committee on Enclosure was noting their loss at Coventry, Nottingham, Oldham, Manchester, Bolton and Blackburn, Birmingham and 'countless other towns' – all of which had literally lost their breathing spaces. In the case of Blackburn, this loss had taken place since 1833. Nationwide, of thirty-four Enclosure Bills passed between 1837 and 1841 covering 41,420 acres, only 22 acres had been set aside for recreation. The Hammonds cited many examples of specific instances of loss. The Select Committee of 1833 had found that, with the exception of London, Liverpool and Preston, none of the towns examined by the committee could point to any recreational provision having been made at a time when urban spread was anyway reducing the distance between the town dweller and the countryside. The General Enclosure Act of 1845 made things worse.[22]

To employers the loss of production time when workers observed traditional holidays was as much a matter of concern as was the lack of regularity in pre-industrial work habits such as St Monday. It was not easy to break down the ingrained habits and anticipations of the labouring people. Even that tireless manager of men, Josiah Wedgwood, could not prevent his potters absenting themselves to attend Burslem wakes. At Portsmouth when the fair came around, it was held 'universally' among the servants as a privilege: 'that they may go . . . if this leave be refused desertion immediately takes place'.[23] There has been no shortage of research by historians demonstrating the impact of new work disciplines upon old recreations. By following through the experiences of a particular labour force, the process of erosion can be revealed. At the beginning of the eighteenth century an historian remarked of the Cornish miners that few labourers worked so little: 'for what between their numerous holidays, holiday eves, feasts, account days (once a month), Yeu Widdens or one way or another they invent to loiter away their time, they do no work one half of their month for the owners and employers. Several gentlemen have endeavoured to break through their customs, but it has hitherto been to little purpose.' These eighteenth-century tinner's holidays were supported rather than attacked by employers. On the day of their patron saint, St Piran, tinners were 'allowed money to make merry withal in honour of St Piran' and account books record such and similar payments towards calendrical merry-making. At the beginning of the nineteenth century a local steward was complaining of 'pay days, taking days and those so-called holidays' which could cost the shareholders in tin and copper mines dearly. Yet by 1817 a change was being recorded:

Desperate wrestling matches, inhuman cockfights, pitched battles and riotous revellings, are happily now of much rarer occurrence than here-

217

tofore; the spirit of sport has evaporated, and that of industry has supplied its place. The occupations in the mining countries fill up the time of these engaged in them too effectively to allow leisure for prolonged revels, or frequent festivities, in the other parts of Cornwall, the constant pursuits of steady labour have nearly banished the traditional seasons of vulgar riot and dissipation.

By 1824 an historian felt that such old holiday practices had declined to the extent that many of the tinners neither knew of or cared about them. The evidence before a parliamentary inquiry of 1842 reveals an astonishingly complete erosion by that date. Then, as a general rule, only Christmas Day and Good Friday were universally observed as holidays in the mining districts, except at the very old Levant Mine where six days a year were still allowed. Some of the evidence suggests a gradual process of erosion. In some areas the parish feast was still allowed, at United Mines, St Austell as a full day (eighteenth-century feasts had lasted for several days.) while at Wheal Vor Mine most of the young surface workers kept the parish feast at the cost of a day's wages: 'They will rather lose than not go if they are allowed.' At the important Consolidated Mines in Gwennap, a huge enterprise by the standards of its time, vestiges of the old pattern persisted and surface workers were allowed half a day at Whitsuntide, two hours at Midsummer, two hours on Christmas Eve as well as all day at Christmas and Good Friday. This increasing control of the miners' holidays was an aspect of the industry's capitalisation which came on top of the increasing discipline of the working day itself and an attack on 'Mazed Monday', the miners' equivalent of St Monday.[24]

Factory capitalists and, as Howkins and Obelkevich have shown, agrarian employers too, showed with mining capitalists a real determination to impose time and work discipline upon workers who presented them with all the inconveniences of traditional rhythms of life and labour. The traditional wakes of south Lancashire came under attack from the cotton magnates and their allies the 'new police' in the second quarter of the nineteenth century and, if their direct attacks were not wholly successful, indirectly the factory's eventual displacement of the handloom weaver removed the essential support of the artisans' rhythm of leisure. Birmingham's wakes underwent similar decline despite some resistant tenacity: by 1842, of twelve children questioned by the factory commissioners, none were allowed a holiday at the time of the wakes. In 1849 a visitor to the old handloom community of Ashton-under-Lyne noted that the 'ancient sporting spirit' of the weavers had been 'utterly extirpated': 'The regularity of hours and discipline preserved seem by rendering any such escapades out of the question, to have at length obliterated everything like a desire for, or idea of, them.'[25]

The decline of at best gentry promotion and at worst gentry toleration of plebeian sports removed what had been a fundamental condition for their existence and was evident from at least the closing years of the eighteenth century:

> The discontinuance in frequency of such sports indeed among the common people, is chiefly to be attributed to a change in the habits and manners of their superiors. In Carew's time [early seventeenth century], gentlemen used to entertain a numerous peasantry at the mansions and castles in celebration of the two great festivals, or the parish feast or harvest home; when at the same time that our halls re-echoed to the voice of festal merriment, our lawns and downs and woodlands were enlivened by the shouts of wrestling and of hurling. Hospitality is now banished from among us: and so are its attendant sports. [26]

Malcolmson has commented on this withdrawal of tolerance by the gentry and better-off farmers as social distance increased and a 'solid barrier developed between the culture of gentility and the culture of the people'. Northamptonshire mumming, Shrovetide football, 'Plough Mondays', all provide instances of a changed gentry attitude towards one which applauded rather than resisted the decline of 'rude diversions' and vulgar games. Gentry magistrates also took their place among the advocates of 'rational' reformed amusements. By the early Victorian years, squires and their ladies as well as parsons and their wives were active promoters of a recreational transformation aimed at 'civilizing' the country labourer. Howkins has shown for rural Oxford-shire an increased gentry concern to 'civilise' the leisure of the poor after 1840 which he suggests paralleled the increased government intervention on more obvious areas of sanitisation. The gentry became guides and mentors in a process of reshaping rather than participants in a 'social theatre' as in the eighteenth century, alongside the clergy, they promoted village benefit clubs and friendly societies with their sober feasts, church parades, dinners and well-ordered marches, perhaps followed by a sedate evening dance, all properly conducted. [27]

Evangelicalism, too, became an especially potent force in the attack on traditional recreations. The distinguishing feature of this onslaught was that condemnation stemmed from a firm belief in the inherent depravity of vulgar pastimes. Such indulgences of time were not just inconvenient and disruptive, but sinful. The evangelical movement within the Church of England, from the royal proclamation of 1787, issued at the instigation of William Wilberforce, aimed at stirring up the vigilant suppression of the 'vice' of popular pastimes, even when not explicitly associated with sabbath breaking. If the committed evangelists were a minority, their influence was nevertheless sufficient to change the way in which a wider section of the ruling classes came to look at the amusements of the poor. Evangelical influences in the countryside and within the rural clergy have been shown to have been important in the taming of Lancashire 'rushbearings', Oxfordshire Whitsuntide festivities and even in driving out the authentic popular musical tradition of the plebeian choirs which had provided the music for Anglican services in rural churches, and replacing them with *Hymns Ancient and Modern* and the organ.[28]

Wherever Methodism took hold, the force of the new 'puritanism' was vastly more effective, not in the least because Methodism anticipated later temperance and teetotal movements in attaching some sections of the working classes to the chapel and thereby creating a recreational polarisation within the community. John Wesley's *Journal* reveals the extent to which Methodism from its earliest days came into conflict with traditional leisure usages. He recorded in 1743 his disgust with 'savage ignorance and wickedness' on the part of colliers near Newcastle who assembled on Sundays to 'dance, fight, curse and swear, and play at chuck ball, span-farthing, or whatever came next to hand'. In the town itself he confronted 'crowds of poor wretches' who passed their Sundays in 'sauntering to and fro on the Sand Hill'. At Otley in 1766 he arrived on feast day and found a town 'gone mad in noise, hurry, drunkenness, rioting, confusion, to the shame of a Christian country'. Charles Wesley recorded his satisfaction on his second visit to Gwennap in Cornwall in 1744 that the miners had, since his visit of the previous year, been unable to get enough men together for a wrestling match: 'all the Gwennap men being struck off the Devil's list, and found wrestling against him not for him'.[29]

By the early nineteenth century even Anglican clergymen were prepared to concede a large measure of credit to the Methodists for the fact that in the mining districts of Cornwall there were no more 'desperate wrestling matches . . . and inhuman cockfights' while 'riotous revellings' were becoming more rare. Methodist condemnation was unequivocal. An advertisement in the *West Briton* in 1821, inserted to dissuade promoters of matches from 'endangering the souls' of miners, claimed that if converted miners were asked why they did not attend wrestlings, they would reply that it was because of the commandment: 'Whether ye eat or drink, or whatsoever ye do, do all to the glory of God.' In 1829 the message was repeated with the insistence that to attend a wrestling was to break no less than eight 'rules of conduct': it wasted time, it wasted money, it meant association with bad company, it encouraged idleness and folly, set a bad example, had been forbidden by God because: 'I must soon die.'[30]

Dr Harrison has remarked that it was over attempts to dominate popular leisure that the churches and the working classes came most frequently into contact in the nineteenth century:

> Nineteenth-century Christians deplored that recreational complex of behaviour which included gambling, adultery, drinking, cruel sports and sabbath breaking and blasphemy – all of which took place together at the race-course, the drinking place, the theatre, the 'feast' and the fair.[31]

In areas like Cornwall, Kingswood, Newcastle and the Black Country,

Methodism provided the clearest instances of confrontation. Dr Stedman Jones has suggested that the impact of religious attacks on popular recreations has been over-stressed by historians who have listened only to 'the case for the prosecution'. Indeed, in some areas 'evangelical' confronters may have been as he suggests 'purveyors of minority causes'; in many places, however, they were large enough to polarise the working classes into 'chapel' and 'pub' and in some few, like Cornwall and Durham, into which Methodism came early and prospered greatly, they could claim majority support in terms of influence if not in terms of membership.[32]

Methodism poses one of the most difficult questions to answer for 'social control' theory in which the forces of pressure are seen as a successful *external* imposition of middle-class values upon the working classes. In fact we have to explain a cultural divide which split the working classes themselves and which was as significant in separating the 'roughs' from the 'respectables' as was the 'imperialism' of other social classes. The polarisation of life after work centred around the 'chapel' with its counter-attractions or around the 'pub' with its associated activities. Movements like temperance or teetotalism when they came into areas where Methodism, especially in its Primitive or Bryanite forms, had already a strong influence over working-class behaviour, did not so much propagate new constraints as reinforce existing ones. The Methodist miner who signed the pledge was more likely to have been re-affirming existing attitudes than undergoing a radical conversion.[33]

For propagators of the culture of the chapel or of the 'pledge', to preach was not enough: counter-attraction was essential. Confrontation, as when Cornish Methodists tried at the end of the eighteenth century to drown by hymn-singing the noise of the revelry at the village feast, or when they held services on a fairground at Camborne in 1840, was perhaps less effective than the counter-attraction of an alternative participation and involvement such as that offered by the St Austell Primitive Methodists, who deliberately held a camp revival meeting on the site of the annual wrestling a week before it took place. Teetotallers were especially active, marching working people around behind bands and banners, sitting them down to monstrous tea-drinkings and moving their emotions with passionate public confessions of struggles in the overcoming of temptation. Teetotallers, according to Dr Harrison, 'transformed temperance meetings from occasional gatherings of influential worthies . . . into counter-attractive functions enabling working men to insulate themselves from public house temptation'.[34] They had to do so, for while the great public calendar festivals offered evident targets for confrontation against which the forces of evangelism, temperance, order and 'serious' business could ally, the pub was a very different world to penetrate. Anthony Delves has pointed out that in Derby the great

221

strength of the pub lay in its inherent suitability for working-class leisure needs. It had no entry fee barrier to participation (unlike the Mechanics Institute), its hours of opening suited the casual leisure needs of workers whose time and income were not only in short, but in irregular supply. In that town, despite successful attempts to discipline the rough street football, the 'problem' of working-class leisure was still being stressed in 1853, when it was estimated that 70% of the working men spent their evenings in pubs.[35] It is observable in Cornwall that after the decline of public festivals and the withdrawing of gentry support for vulgar pastimes, wrestling survived as a traditional sport only because its promotion was taken over by publicans.[36] It needed a powerful magnet to attract working people from their pubs and, especially after the coming of the railway, the organised excursion and the 'field day' were among the most commonly used. Newspapers describing the Whitsun weekend of 1844 in west Cornwall reported a noticeable drop, despite fine weather, in the size of the crowds at the seasonal fairs. They also reported very large attendances at Rechabite and teetotal festivals which, apparently (although one wonders how), were 'celebrated with more than usual gaiety' involving processions and parades, sometimes led by three bands. In 1852 the mineral railway took seventy-six mineral truckloads of abstainers and their families from Camborne to the golden sands of Hayle all singing:

> Steam is up and we are ready;
> See the engine puffing goes!
> Keep your heads cool, and be steady
> Mind your cups and mind your clothes.

Three years earlier the Wesleyan minister had taken the town's Methodist children to the seaside to remove them from the temptation offered by a 'noisy, revelling fair':

> We rejoice, and we have reason,
> Though we don't attend the fair;
> Better spend the happy season
> Breathing in the fresh sea air.
> Happy Children! Happy Children!
> What a number will be there![37]

By mid-century not only Methodists and temperance advocates had come to see the possibilities of the railway excursion. In Birmingham, works outings had become a regular part of the employer-subsidised and approved recreation. Locally known as 'Gipsey parties', these excursions into the countryside were, according to some artisan witnesses in 1849, successfully drawing participants from the wake-observing, rougher pastimes now largely indulged 'on the sly by workmen of the old school'. Gipsey parties had been spreading 'good will and cordiality' for the previous five years. It is not difficult to see why they had won approval and support from the employers as they

were an essentially controllable form of recreation, policed to remove
'carnival'. Workers saved by paying weekly contributions through the
year and the employers topped up the fund. An account of a 'Gipsey
party' arranged by a steel-pin firm survives in some detail. Three
hundred and fifty workers went in forty-five ornamented cars to dine
and dance in tents: 'not teetotal but very temperate'. Beforehand,
each had been given a printed sheet entitled: *Regulations to be
Observed on the Occasion of Messrs Hinckes, Wells and Co. Pleasure
Trip.* Each had his allocated seat number and, if not ready to leave at
6.30 a.m. *precisely*, would be left behind to forfeit his contributions: 'in
getting out of the cars to walk up the hills, you are requested not to mix
with other parties'. Anyone seen in the Park damaging trees or hedges
would be discharged from employment, and the excursionists were to
walk in line four abreast. Once out on the hills: 'You are requested not
to roam in small detached parties, otherwise you will incur the severe
displeasure of your employers.' 'At the sounding of the trumpet, the
whole to return to dinner in the same order.' Returning to Birmingham
at 8.00 p.m., the excursionists were not to sing on their way home
through the streets and it was hoped that 'the greatest order and
propriety' would have been observed throughout the day.[38]

It was not only from the ranks of the religious that a section of the
working class came to oppose the rough and degrading pastimes of the
'roughs'. Men like Francis Place and William Lovett epitomised
changing artisan attitudes in taking a special pride in claiming an
'improvement in manners among the more intelligent workpeople'.
Place warned those who read his recollections of his youth in the
London of the 1780s to prepare themselves:

> The circumstances which it will be seen I have mentioned relative to the
> ignorance, the immorality, the grossness, the obscenity, the drunkenness,
> the dirtiness, and depravity of the middling, and even of a large portion of
> the better sort of tradesmen, the artisans, and the journeymen tradesmen of
> London in the days of my houth, may excite a suspicion that the picture I
> have drawn is a caricature.[39]

William Lovett remarked on a very great improvement in this respect
among working men in London since he had arrived there in 1821.[40]
Such men and other working-class leaders like Thomas Cooper, Henry
Vincent or Robert Applegarth concerned in raising the standing and
self-respect of their class had no liking for the excessive drinking and
rowdyism of much working-class leisure. In Derby they opposed the
bone-breaking, window-smashing and boozing annual indulgence of
street football. During the bitter strike there of 1833/34, the trade
union leaders opposed its holding, seeing in the attempt of some
populist-inclined social superiors adopting a pose of defence of tradition, the wish to strengthen paternalism, or else to discredit the town's
workers: 'Your betters have been foremost in this Fete hallowing you
like brute dogs to the strife. Yes, reverend creatures, full of holiness,

have lent a voice to brutalise the people.' Their decision to boycott the football and organise instead a demonstration of trade union strength was applauded by the Owenite *Pioneer*:

> That glorious shout of moral revolution!
> It spoke a heartful of the kindest things
> It made our souls five Sabbaths better. Let others go who list,
> to be imbruted, but not a Union man – not one.

On the Shrove Tuesday, 2,000 unionists processed the town with bands and banners, singing hymns and popular songs to a rally four miles out, where they were joined by a further 900 unionists from the region. A second rally was held on the Wednesday: 'Give moralists a pill to swallow. Let union do what force nor gospel could achieve.'[41] A rally was also held in 1850 by the shipwrights' unions of South Shields, when around 1,700 went in eight steam boats with bands and banners to Newcastle to attend a mass rally. Two years later a similar number of carpenters held a march through the town.[42]

Those who allied in the fight to repress 'traditional' and implement 'rational' amusements were not always able to avoid rifts in their ranks. The businessmen of Derby grouped around the mayor in the suppression of the football in 1845 wanted to drive its vexatious presence from the streets, but they also wanted to replace it with a race meeting held outside the town, which would lessen nuisance while still being good for traders. Their evangelical allies were not able to approve such a substitution, no matter how strongly they approved the repression of the football. In the case of the working-class trade union leaders, it is perhaps best not to see an alliance with other groups at all. Textual similarities of moral rhetoric hide antipathetical objectives, for what the unionists wanted was a transformed working-class culture not competitive individualism.[43] Indeed, the observable activities of middle-class groups from the late 1830s in the sponsoring of rational recreation were in part at least a cultural counter-offensive in response to fear of the initiative in this respect passing into the hands of the organised working class. This is evident in the strong proscriptions on radical lectures and literature which were usually attached to middle-class provision of libraries and institutes. The Libraries Act of 1849 did not intend as much to encourage a flowering in a literary desert as to repossess a terrain already covered with a lush growth of reading rooms controlled by the working class.[44]

In Sheffield it was not always easy to draw the line between masters and men until the middle years of the nineteenth century and a section of the working class was being integrated, through a 'respectability' already at work within the community, into a common social ideology with the middle class and into tension with a section of its own class, 'the roughs'. The integrating section included the chapel-going, pledge-signing worker, who sent his children to Sunday School and some of his earnings to the savings bank. But between the 'respect-ables' and the 'roughs' was a middle group whose active involvement in trade unionism made them impossible to accommodate despite their general respectability. This group aspired *only* to those middle-class ways which suited them, and their expansion in the later nineteenth century developed into a threat to middle-class cultural hegemony in that they strove for respectability without incorporation into insti-tutions under middle-class leadership.[45] Eileen Yeo has described and documented the achievements and problems of working-class organ-isations and movements in the period 1830–55 in producing what could at times amount to a 'total social world for leisure hours', including recreational educational and (for working-class Methodist and teetotal groups were to be included too) religious activities. The difficulties were great. They had to fight for 'space', as the streets and places of public meeting were outlawed to them; for example the Royal Pro-clamation of 3 May 1839 empowering magistrates to virtually ban Chartist meetings at will provoked the Birmingham Bull Ring riots, and is a clear example of authority confronting working-class move-ments on the fundamental level of limiting their right of public assembly. The meeting halls and lecture rooms set up by working-class movements were more than hopeful symbols of an uplifted culture. They were in themselves independent working-class controlled ter-ritory. If they disputed a frontier with the ubiquitous and hardly-retreating public house, they were even more conscious of a common enemy, and even if the teetotallers would have been embarrassed meeting in a pub, many trade unions, friendly societies and other working-class groups commonly did so. Financing buildings was a major problem, for high entry charges would have denied their acces-sibility to those groups already faced with the 'structured inhospitality' of the fee-charging Mechanics Institutes. As well as operating in this area, working-class movements tried to give a new significance to old holiday dates, holding their activities on Shrove Tuesday, Easter, Whit, Christmas and New Year and, unlike the period since 1850 with its accent on home-based leisure, kept alive the involvement of family in community.[46]

Dr Cunningham has recently opposed the view that the period of the industrial revolution was a 'recreational vacuum' by asserting that it saw a 'vigorous growth of popular leisure and of a commercialisation of it comparable to the commercialisation of leisure for the middle class which Professor Plumb had identified for the eighteenth century'. While not denying that there was a radical curtailment of leisure opportunities and leisure time for the mass of the people, he argues that the context of recreational conflict was one of an *increase* in leisure opportunities of an 'undesirable' kind for the working classes. Some of the people, perhaps most, made their own culture in a way which was different both from that of the 'rational recreationists' and from that of the working-class movements.[47] As Dr Storch suggested, one reason that temperance reformers saw a desperate need for the 'moral improvement' of the masses was the real profusion of pub-centred gambling and sporting activities in early Victorian cities.[48] In the early decades of the industrial revolution, lower-class opportunities for indulgence were growing, for while many traditions survived longer than has usually been assumed, the Lancashire wakes for example, and others learned to survive without patronage, new forms were also being constantly evolved. The outcome was an 'efflorescence' of popular leisure in the later eighteenth and early nineteenth centuries which makes intelligible the virulence of the campaign against it. Travelling showmen, horseriders, circus and menageries add up to a world of professionally supplied entertainment input into a 'closeknit popular culture'. This culture was not on the wane: nor was it a 'survival' for much of it was new and was as suited to the growing towns as to the countryside. If this is what amounted to 'popular culture', it was as innovative as traditional, but its centre, like that of the artisan culture of self-esteem with its debating societies and reading rooms, was located among the people as opposed to those assuming authority over them.[49]

Nevertheless, in opposition from authority lie the ultimate constraints on a people's capacity to make its own culture. What the people preserved, what they innovated and what they substituted, all indicate the weakness of assuming an unqualified success on the part of the middle and upper classes in their confrontation with popular leisure-time usages. There were no constants, but in the making of their own culture the working people were defensive against repression and reactive against restraints. These constraints for the most part came from the imperatives of emerging industrial capitalism. A defensive stance was inevitable. Even if successes in the creating or the maintaining of an independent popular culture were made, the parameters were, as always, defined by the historical moment: that of an emerging entrepreneurial capitalism.

REFERENCES AND NOTES

1.   **E. P. Thompson**, 'Patrician society, plebeian culture', *Journal of Social History*, vol. 7, no. 4, 1974, pp. 382–405; **J. H. Plumb**, 'The commercialisation of leisure', in **N. McKendrick, J. Brewer** & **J. H. Plumb**, *The Birth of a Consumer Society. The Commercialization of Eighteenth-Century England,* Hutchinson, 1983, pp. 265–85; **H. Medick**, 'Plebeian culture in the transition to capitalism', in **R. Samuel** & **G. Stedman Jones** (eds), *Culture, Ideology and Politics,* Routledge & Kegan Paul, 1982, pp. 84–113.

2.   Thompson, 'Patrician society, plebeian culture', p. 382.

3. Henry Fielding, *An Inquiry into the causes of the late increase of Robbers etc.*, 1751, p. xi.

4. Thompson, 'Patrician society, plebeian culture', p. 395.

5. P. Burke, *Popular Culture in Early Modern Europe*, Temple Smith, 1978, p. 25; E. P. Thompson, 'Eighteenth-century English society: class struggle without class', *Social History*, vol. 3, no. 2, 1978, p. 150.

6. R. W. Malcolmson, *Popular Recreations in English Society 1700–1850*, Cambridge U.P., 1973.

7. For calendar festivals and their reinforcement of community solidarity see, as well as Malcolmson, Bob Bushaway, *By Rite. Custom, Ceremony and Community in England, 1700–1880*, Junction Books, 1982. For fairs and young people, see Ch. 9 above, pp.   .

8. Plumb, 'Commercialisation of leisure', p. 284; P. Borsey, 'The English urban renaissance: the development of provincial urban culture c.1680–1760', *Social History*, 5, 1977, pp. 581–603.

9. A. Temple Patterson, *A History of Southampton 1700–1914. Vol. I. An Oligarchy in Decline 1700–1835*, Southampton U.P., 1966, pp. 52–3.

10. Fielding, *Late increase of Robbers*, p. 9.

11. M. Thale, (ed.), *Autobiography of Francis Place*, Cambridge U.P., 1972, p. 73; P. J. Corfield, *The Impact of English Towns 1700–1800*, Oxford U.P., 1982, p. 80.

12. Medick, 'Plebeian culture', pp. 87–96.

13. Bushaway, *By Rite*, pp. 118–25.

14. H. Cunningham, *Leisure in the Industrial Revolution*, Croom Helm, 1980.

15. P. E. Razzell and R. W. Wainwright, *The Victorian Working Class: Selections from Letters to the Morning Chronicle*, Cass, 1973, pp. 303, 309.

16. A. Delves, 'Popular recreation and social conflict in Derby, 1800–1850', in E. & S. Yeo (eds), *Popular Culture and Class Conflict 1590–1914*, Harvester, 1982, pp. 90–2.

17. Malcolmson, *Popular Recreations*, pp. 132–3.

18. See D. A. Reid, 'Interpreting the festival calendar: wakes and fairs as carnivals', in R. D. Storch (ed.), *Popular Culture and Custom in Nineteenth-Century England*, Croom Helm, 1982, pp. 125–53.

19. J. Webb, *Portsmouth Free Mart Fair. The Last Phase*, Portsmouth City Council, 1982, pp. 10–11; H. Cunningham, 'The metropolitan fair: a case study in the social control of leisure', in A. P. Donajgrodski (ed.), *Social Control in Nineteenth Century Britain*, Croom Helm, 1977, p. 164; A. Howkins, 'The taming of Whitsun: the changing face of a nineteenth-century rural holiday', in Yeo and Yeo (eds), *Popular Culture and Class Conflict*, pp. 188–94.

20. J. L. and B. Hammond, *The Bleak Age*, rev. edn, Penguin, 1947, pp. 75–90; Malcolmson, *Popular Recreations*, pp. 107–8.

21. Razzell and Wainwright, *Victorian Working Class*, p. 310.

22. See Hammonds, *Bleak Age*, Ch. 7 for the findings of these enquiries.

23. N. McKendrick, 'Josiah Wedgwood and factory discipline', *Historical Journal*, IV, 1961, p. 46; Webb, *Portsmouth Fair*, p. 11.

24. For holiday erosion among the tinners, see J. G. Rule, 'Some social aspects of the Industrial Revolution in Cornwall', in R. Burt (ed.), *Industry and Society in the South West*, Exeter U.P., 1970, pp. 71–81.

25. Howkins, 'The taming of Whitsun'; **J. Obelkevich**, *Religion and Rural Society. South Lindsey 1825–1875,* Oxford U.P., 1976, pp. 56–61; **J. K. Walton** and **R. Poole**, 'The Lancashire wakes in the nineteenth century', in Storch (ed.), *Popular Culture,* pp. 100–24; Razzell and Wainwright, *Victorian Working Class,* pp. 185, 313–20.

26. **R. Polwhele**, edn of *Lavington's Enthusiasm of Methodists and Papists Compared,* 1833, pp. cxxi-cxxii.

27. Malcolmson, *Popular Recreations,* p. 167; Howkins, 'Taming of Whitsun', pp. 193–4.

28. See **V. Gammon**, 'Babylonian performances: the rise and suppression of popular church music, 1660–1870', in Yeo & Yeo, *Popular Culture and Class Conflict,* pp. 62–82.

29. **John Wesley**, *Journal,* Everyman edn, 1906, vol. I, pp. 420, 425, vol. II, pp. 99, 265. For a fuller discussion of the subject, see **J. G. Rule**, 'Methodism, popular beliefs and village culture in Cornwall, 1800–50', in Storch (ed.), *Popular Culture and Custom,* pp. 48–70.

30. Rule, 'Methodism and village culture', p. 55.

31. **B. Harrison**, 'Religion and recreation in nineteenth-century England', *Papers presented to the Past and Present Conference on Popular Religion,* 7 July 1966, p. 2.

32. **G. Stedman Jones**, 'Class expression versus social control? a critique of recent trends in the social history of leisure', *History Workshop,* no. 4, 1977, p. 165.

33. Rule, 'Methodism and village culture', pp. 50–1.

34. **B. Harrison**, *Drink and the Victorians. The Temperance Question in England 1815–1872,* Faber & Faber, 1971, p. 180.

35. Delves, 'Popular recreation in Derby', pp. 98–103.

36. Rule, 'Methodism and village culture', p. 55.

37. Ibid., pp. 55–9.

38. Razzell and Wainwright, *Victorian Working Class,* pp. 298–9.

39. Place, *Autobiography,* pp. 14–15 and his evidence to *Select Committee on Artisans and Machinery,* BPP, 1824, V, second report, p. 46.

40. **W. Lovett**, *Life and Struggles in Pursuit of Bread, Knowledge and Freedom,* 1876, repr. 1967, MacGibbon & Kee, p. 26. See the discussion of 'respectable' artisans in Rule, *Experience of Labour,* pp. 204–6.

41. Delves, 'Popular recreation in Derby', pp. 104–16.

42. **J. F. Clarke**, 'Workers in the Tyneside shipyards', in **N. McCord** (ed.), *Essays in Tyneside Labour History,* Newcastle upon Tyne Polytechnic, 1977, p. 111.

43. Delves, 'Popular recreation in Derby', pp. 109–13.

44. **E. Yeo**, 'Culture and constraint in working-class movements, 1830–55', in Yeo & Yeo (eds), *Popular Culture and Class Conflict,* p. 179.

45. **Caroline Reid**, 'Middle-class values and working-class culture in nineteenth-century Sheffield – The pursuit of respectability', in **S. Pollard** & **C. Holmes** (eds), *Essays in the Economic and Social History of South Yorkshire,* S. Yorkshire C.C., 1976, pp. 275–8.

46. E. Yeo, 'Culture and constraint', pp. 155–66.

47. Cunningham, *Leisure in the Industrial Revolution,* p. 15.

48. **R. Storch**, 'The problems of working-class leisure. Some roots of middle-

class reform in the industrial north', in Donajgrodski (ed.), *Social Control*, p. 153.

49.   Cunningham, *Leisure in the Industrial Revolution*, pp. 26–27, and Ch. 1 generally.

Chapter 10

EDUCATION FOR THE LABOURING CLASSES

By the mid-nineteenth century the haphazard provision of elementary education for working-class children had given way to a more systematic and general availability, but it had still not become synonymous with the primary instruction of a particular age group. It was, as Dr Sutherland has remarked, 'education for a class, for the labouring poor'.[1] As such it extended to adults at night schools and at Mechanics Institutes and other sources of adult education. This highly-motivated group was, however, small compared to the numbers of the working class who received some form of education during their childhood. Of the measures available to the historian, two, the literacy ratio and the provision of school places, seem to offer the most fruitful resources for the study of the cultural and functional dimensions of popular literacy. The ability to read and write is potentially the most enriching one so far as the quality of life is concerned and there may also be a threshold of literacy which must be crossed in any society before economic modernisation can take place; but this is debatable. Literacy has political implications too. It was apparent to many that the spread of sedition, rebellion or of any 'alternative' ideas on social and economic organisation was to a considerable extent related to the spread of reading ability: a dangerous situation best met by controlling the content and direction of education.

Since schooling was neither compulsory nor universally available free, the decision of a parent to allow children to attend for even a brief period of their young lives was crucial and it had to be taken against the incurrence of an actual cost or, if 'free', at the expense of child labour and earning possibilities. Clearly it was more likely to have been allowed in periods of prosperity for the family than in those of depression.

Historians have much exercised their minds over the measurement of literacy. The most widely used, the ability to sign a register or similar document, is thought flawed by some specialists. On the one hand it does not necessarily imply a wider ability to read and write and, on the other, reading ability on its own might have been rather more wide-spread than the ability to sign. However, it still seems the most useful of the measures available and its changing incidence may be presumed to reveal a good deal about the changing cultural bases of society. School provision and attendance presents problems too, for there is no knowing the numbers who learned to read from parents or friends without ever attending school. In this chapter, literacy will be assumed to be the ability to both read and write and to be indicated by the signing of names and this ability will be presumed to be related in a rather direct way to the availability and take-up of schooling.[2]

EDUCATIONAL PROVISION BEFORE 1815

In the absence of any central directed policy and with provision dependent upon local voluntary initiative, schooling was erratically available for working-class children before the early nineteenth century. Urban districts were in general better supplied than rural ones, but within the same county differences between towns could be very great and, as towards the end of the eighteenth century rapid demographic increase tended to outpace educational provision, the growth in many town populations was such as to cancel out even that which was increasing in absolute terms. Michael Sanderson has argued that this happened in the growing textile towns of Lancashire.[3]

A recent study of Kent schools has demonstrated a marked variation in availability. In 1660 provision for the education of the poor was quite limited, especially in rural districts. By 1811, with the addition of a modest number of new subscription-based schools designed for the poor, things had improved although the geography of provision remained very uneven. Almost half of the county's 172 parishes had a school of some description in 1807, including almost all those with a population in excess of 1,000. In Kent, as elsewhere, there had been a surge in school provision between 1710 and 1725 associated with the so-called charity school movement, but by mid-century this had given way to a pattern of augmentary endowments to already established schools and there was no fresh surge until 1780–90. By 1811 only some rural parishes had no provision, while most could offer improvement over the level of the end of the seventeenth century. Improving rural ratios may have kept the total proportion of Kentish children receiving schooling constant by offsetting a deteriorating situation in the towns. In a few rural parishes, as at Keston and Milsted, in excess of 50% of poor children were enrolled in the non-classical schools. Unless there was a substantial 'school of industry' such as was associated with knitting outworking at Sevenoaks, this level was unlikely to be approached in towns. Normally urban provision was very much less adequate with a rate as low as 5% being common.[4]

Leaving aside for the moment any provided on Sundays, schooling was received by only a minority of labouring-class children, and in some parishes by a very tiny one. The efforts of providers like the Charity School movement have received a larger degree of attention than they perhaps deserve in the educational history of the lower orders. The motives of those who organised and subscribed to provide them are of more interest than the sum total of their efforts or the significance of their impact. The suggestion that there was a 'charity school *movement*' in England between 1710 and 1730 was developed by M. G. Jones in 1938 who argued that this provision of schooling was one of the greatest manifestations of eighteenth-century philanthropic puritanism. Under the guidance and initial leadership of the SPCK, schools affording hundreds of thousands of new places were set up to bring some kind of education to poor children. During its most rapid period, between 1700 and 1730, the movement combined compassion and responsibility in the firm purpose of instilling in the children correct behaviour and moral reformation. The driving purpose reflected fears of a growing 'dangerous class' in the cities, where children were growing up ill-disciplined and ill-exampled by their parents. They could be best kept from crime, prostitution and heathenism by removal from their influence into that of an educational programme designed to educate them into a proper sense of their place and duties in society and into due obedience to the precepts of the established church. Education in the catechism and the Bible in the vital years before the child was apprenticed could capture him from the streets, confirm him in God-fearing ways and inoculate him against those habits of sloth, debauchery and irreligion, which were thought of as increasingly characteristic of the lower orders.[5]

The schools built were distinguished from the free places for the poor in the old endowed grammar schools which had afforded a small measure of social mobility for the bright child. The charity school aimed at something different: an education which, complete in itself, was designed to reconcile the child to his position in society. In conditioning the children to the inevitability of becoming hewers of wood and drawers of water, it could be felt that they were being saved from the alternatives of being hanged for felony, diseased by prostitution or alcohol-debauched into an early grave. Be this as it may, the schools lacked any concept of relating education to social advancement and saw moral reformation as the desperately needed remedy for the social problem of the poor. An ill-regulation of the 'body politic' was not considered. Enough that the poor were there as, on unimpeachable authority, they would always be. Reflecting the growing development of joint stock companies in the world of commerce, the charity schools were not, like the old endowed schools, the results of large bequests, but of collective subscription, drawing in the contributions of trades-men and others so that, in the words of one bishop, 'the bottom of charity is enlarged'.[6]

Charity schools were not for providing a schooling useful in itself: the utilitarian dimension did not assume a popular education as the basis of a common citizenship. Instead, the conviction that the education of the poor was economically unsound and even socially destructive remained entrenched. Instead of the ambitions of the grammar school, curriculum was confined to the 'plain accomplish-ments' which best suited the 'generality of the people'. There was no step to higher things, but a system complete in itself under which the children would receive just that modicum of education needed for them to become useful and content in their inevitable station in life. The movement was certainly the most sustained attempt to reach the children of the poor before the Sunday School movement gained pace in the closing decades of the century but, even so, its extent and consistency have been called into question. By 1730 its momentum had noticeably flagged and even its limited educational objectives had not gone unchallenged. Many saw little utility in teaching reading rather than instilling the discipline of labour more directly. This viewpoint urged instead the workhouse school, the school of industry, where useful accomplishments like spinning would fill up the time. However, in the first half of the century the offerers of the catechism still led the way. Charity schools were inexpensive and could be readily supplied in the boom years, while even such a champion of the bourgeoisie as Defoe approved the attack on sloth and ill-discipline as going to the heart of the problem of the labouring poor. To many it was a crusade: the defence of Anglican protestantism not only against irreligion, but also against popery and the jacobite cause.

Miss Jones argued that there was a *movement*, not only because of the number of schools established, but also because of the co-ordinating activities of the SPCK. This organisation was certainly an initiator and active propagator, and the decline in provision after it turned its priority to foreign missions was in part attributable to its withdrawing. But it did not manage schools and had little strength outside London and several other cities like Bristol. In rural districts and in manufacturing towns it had to compete with the demand for child labour. Complaints of this competition came from clothing, knitting and mining districts. Within a diocese a charity school was always more likely to be evident near or in a cathedral city than in the periphery. Exeter saw a strong movement while in Cornwall it was negligible.[7]

If there are substantial doubts as to whether the provision of charity schools was ever sufficiently widespread, directed or differentiated from earlier efforts to have constituted a 'movement', there is none that provision of schools for the poor in the middle and later years of the century remained haphazard and uneven. A degree of agreement among specialists on literacy suggests a slow rise up to around 1770, but an unclear pattern over the last quarter. The confidence with which Professor Stone saw a rise from c.56% in 1775 to 65% by 1800 as part of an 'upsurge of literacy' after 1780 as 'underlying the process of industrialisation' cannot be really justified. In many places that period saw a swamping of a modest increase in provision by a swelling population as well as a rise in the quantity and intensity of child labour which hindered labouring-class participation. Sanderson has strongly argued for this in Lancashire's cotton districts, while far from the centre of the industrial revolution, the evidence from Kent suggests that only improving rural provision offset deteriorating ratios of school places per head of population in towns. Similar suggestions have been made for Leamington, Cornwall, Devon and the East Riding.[8]

Despite the association of literacy programmes with modernisation in twentieth-century developing economies, there seems no reason to assume that the first industrial revolution necessarily involved an expansion of literacy. This is more especially so because the early factories depended upon the use of unskilled female and child labour. In so far as any agency was to a degree effective in counteracting the anti-literacy effects of industrialisation, it was not schooling provided by a utilitarian concern for a wider literacy and numeracy, but the Sunday School. From slow growth in the later decades of the eighteenth century, these had, according to one historian, by 1851 received attendance from three-quarters of all working-class children between the ages of five and fifteen. Their educational effectiveness can with good reason be doubted. After sabbatarian disputes in the 1790s, many of them discontinued the teaching of writing. The motives of their providers can be disputed, but their important role in working-class schooling is inescapable. By using the only learning time generally made available in a child-employing economy, they at least limited the likelihood of a serious and widespread *decline* in literacy.[9]

The significance of any positive force working against decline is enhanced by the findings of the systematic study of literacy levels in 274 parishes made by Dr Schofield. While he found a slight rise for females from 40% in the mid-eighteenth century to 50% by 1840, he found no overall improvement 1750–1815 for males because any improvement in ratios in rural areas and in towns of stagnant population was being offset by the decline in industrial and populous towns. By the 1830s barely 30% of the workers in south-east Lancashire could write their own names, and the replacement of male handloom weavers by female power-loom weavers, who were only one-third as literate, illustrates a negative link between industrialism and the expansion of literacy.[10]

No sufficiently powerful or large lobby before 1830 spoke out in favour of the expansion of popular schooling. In the Commons, in opposing a Parochial Schools Bill in 1807, Davies Gilbert the scientist spoke for his class and age:

> However specious in theory the project might be of giving education to the labouring classes of the poor, it would in effect be prejudicial to their morals and happiness: it would teach them to despise their lot in life, instead of making them good servants to agriculture and other laborious employments to which their rank in society had destined them: instead of teaching them subordination, it would render them factious and refractory, as was evident in the manufacturing counties: it would enable them to read seditious pamphlets, vicious books and publications against Christianity. It would render them insolent and indolent to their superiors, and in a few years the result would be that the legislature would find it necessary to direct the strong arm of power towards them.[11]

Such views were widely held but, even in the year of his speech, meetings were taking place which led to the creation in 1808 of the British and Foreign School Society, an originally non-sectarian body to promote popular education just as the SPCK had in the previous century sought to reclaim for religion and social peace the children of the labouring poor. The number of pupils was to be maximised by using the monitorial system of Joseph Lancaster under which older pupils passed lessons on to younger ones enabling a teacher-pupil ratio far beyond even those which conservative governments would dare to contemplate today. The 'social question' had by the early nineteenth century much greater force than it had had in the eighteenth. The French Wars were still continuing and radicalism and republicanism were threats in alliance with irreligion – did not Tom Paine combine both? Luddism was on the horizon as the 'machinery question' came to be debated, and the new population of the towns was sprawling beyond the traditional frontiers of constraint. Such concerns were evidently in the minds of the designers of the monitorial system; Lancaster remarked that the effect of building a school would be:

> In a town exposed to all the evils of dissipation and vice, usual in commercial towns where the rising generation are training up in ignorance, wickedness and forgetfulness of God, very large numbers will soon be training in his fear, in the knowledge of his ways; and in the daily remembrance of his commandments.[12]

The BFSS was intended to be non-sectarian, but it is not to be imagined that the 'Tory party at prayer' would have co-operated in an open approach to religious education. The established church set up in 1811 the rival National Society for the Provision of Education of the Poor in the Principles of the Established Church, to promote 'National schools' in rivalry to the 'British' schools, which naturally became as a result more linked to the free churches. The National schools adopted the system of Andrew Bell, a rival claimant to Lancaster for the credit of discovering the monitorial system. It is of small matter who originated it, for the two systems were as alike in operation as they were in social perception. As Bell wrote in 1813 of his system: 'The improvement in the subordination, and orderly conduct, and general behaviour of the children, has been particularly noticed and must be regarded as infinitely the most valuable part of its character.'[13] Especially after 1820 the two providers of the 'voluntary' schools went their intransigent ways, so that a select committee of 1838, though it would have liked to have found otherwise, recognised that to envisage other than paying grants to the two separate and rival societies was impracticable. The government had begun to make public money available from 1833 when it offered a £20,000 subsidy for school building. It was an important beginning, and the amount provided had by 1850 increased to £193,000. By the end of 1838 the government had begun its first tentative moves towards central planning and control by introducing a degree of inspection. In this endeavour it met with the intractable hostility of the established church, opposed to any inspection from outside. The government compromised to the degree of virtually allowing the society to appoint its own inspectors, and this, on top of the hitherto unconditional grants, gave the two societies effective recognition as the approved means of educating the people. This, as Lord John Russell was to admit, restricted the freedom of the government to a degree unknown in other countries, and effectively limited its own schemes. Despite the opposition of the Anglican bishops and the compromises they forced, the setting up in 1839 of the Committee of the Privy Council for Education marks the effective beginning of central involvement in the provision and content of elementary education. Under the leadership of James Kay-Shuttleworth working with a small but growing inspectorate of men like H. S. Tremenheere, this committee began both to investigate existing provision systematically and to formulate policy. Kay-Shuttleworth had come as a doctor in the industrial revolution's hothouse of Manchester to perceive the 'problem' of the lower orders. His intentions stemmed from his fears and historians have been justified in seeing his policy as an advocation of 'social control' through education. Since he was the nearest thing there was to an 'official' spokesman on schooling, he can also be regarded as representative of a broad body of thinking on the subject. It is little more than a truism to suggest that those who rule society will seek to propagate and legitimate their authority through the educational system, once they have decided to provide one. But there remain serious limitations on the extent to which a wholesale adoption of the social control perspective can assist the understanding of the spread of working-class schooling in the early nineteenth century. But before discussing these limitations, we need to estimate the extent and quality of school provision.

PROVISION, ATTENDANCE AND CURRICULUM

Statistics are available from a number of sources to estimate the child school population at a number of points in the early nineteenth century. However, the ratios to the total childhood age cohort which are thus obtained are of limited value for a period when attendance was most often for short periods and even then erratic. Relating to the five to fifteen or sixteen band meaningful for modern times is deceptive in that it specifically assumes schooling to be attached to a particular span of childhood years. In 1841 Henry Tremenheere, one of the best known of the government's inspectors, sampled seven parishes in the mining district of Cornwall and estimated that just over 50% of the age cohort five to fifteen were not receiving daily school instruction (he included dame schools which taught reading and writing). It is a finding of some value for a county which was generally regarded as having a higher literacy than the south-west generally, but it can claim no greater precision than can the versifying historian of one of those Cornish parishes who three years later enumerated:

> 'Tis said, perhaps wisely, that all those between
> Four or five years of age and that of fourteen
> Should be constantly kept to their duty at school
> And if this be allowed as a general rule
> To Gwennap applying, then must we confess,
> The number of pupils, indeed is much less
> Than the case doth demand, for there are no more
> Than eight hundred in all, or eight on a score
> Where two thousand should be.[14]

It was equally true elsewhere that the proportion of any age group attending school at any moment might have been very much smaller than that which had received, or were to receive, some schooling for some portion of their pre-fifteen years. The working-class child attended for perhaps an average of two to four years before working to supplement the family income, but there was considerable variation as to *which* two to four years so that the only safe generalisation is that hardly any were still in attendance beyond the age of ten or eleven.[15]

Rural provision was especially poor. Mid-century investigators found it difficult to overstate the ignorance of the agricultural labourer: 'intellectual darkness enshrouds him'. He lacked the confidence to venture an opinion, and there was little likelihood of his employers wanting it any other way. Although some large landowners made school provision, smaller farmers reacted with resentment and hostility and impeded the spread of an education to the value of which they were themselves frequently insensible. The children of the small 'smock farmers' of the western counties were reported scarcely distinguishable from their labourers in respect of education, while better-off farmers distrusted 'levelling' notions and preferred that the child simply succeeded the father at his toil. Labourers' children were growing up utterly uneducated to be launched into manhood with 'all the stolidity and ignorance of their fathers'.[16]

Even a curtailed attendance could, in so far as it became widespread, provide some basis for a significant expansion of literacy. Those who argue for a decline in literacy in the early industrial revolution accept that it had bottomed by 1820 and that thereafter there was a steady, though geographically uneven, rise through a male ratio of 67.3% in 1841 to 69.3% by 1851, with corresponding female figures of 51.1 and 54.8%.[17] To this growth the school-building activities of the two societies must have contributed a good deal. One historian has attributed the improvement in Nottingham very largely to the educative efforts of the Church of England, but the efforts of the British and National societies are far from being the whole story.[18] Professor West's work on school provision is highly contentious in its suggestion that, even before 1870, educational supply in England and Wales was, according to his market-determined model, at near optimum level, but he has drawn timely attention to schooling provided outside the 'free' schools of the two societies with their government assistance. He has pointed to the large contribution of small schools where working-class pennies purchased education. Often, he argues, parents did so in preference to taking up free places for their children. There were twice as many of these private schools as there were British and National schools, although since the latter were larger they contained two-thirds of the pupils. There are very different opinions as to the real educational contribution of these small fee-paying schools. Many were dame schools or else were school-mastered by crippled or out-of-work men, often only as a temporary resort. Their critics regarded them as little more than creches. West's insistence that they have been over-maligned has been met by the retort that very many of them were as vehicles of literacy, let alone anything else, pretty dreadful. His counter-attack that even baby-minding is educationally important, in that at worst it allows young parents to obtain employment which carried with it both general and specific job training, is really beside the point: in fact child-minding allowed working-class mothers, young and not so young, to work in underpaid, unskilled occupations likely to stifle any wider awareness which they might once have had.[19] West's critics have at least shown that his chosen position, however convenient to his avowed preference for the market allocation of education as a resource, is incapable of statistical confirmation. His emphasis, however, on the small fee-paying working-class school has been a suggestive one. Working-class autobiographies, now recovered in very sizeable numbers, frequently describe such schools and their teachers. In mining districts, crippled miners could thus earn a bare living. The 1807 minute book of a Cornish parish contains an agreement to pay £12 annually to one such unfortunate 'to learn ten or twelve scholars' at the parish's cost and such others at their parents' expense as he could secure. John Harris, growing up the child of a miner in that county in the 1820s, was first taught by such a man: 'In those days any shattered being wrecked in the mill or the mine, if he could read John Bunyan, count fifty backwards, and scribble the squire's name was considered good enough for a pedagogue; and when he could do nothing else was established behind a low desk in a school.' His memory was confirmed by a school inspector in 1841 who to 'crippled miner' added 'failed tradesman'.[20] The son of an East Riding farm labourer, born in 1783, recalled that the salary afforded in his village had been too low to support a single man, let alone one with a family: 'The master must therefore either have property of his own, or connect some other employment with the charge of the school.'[21] William Dodd, crippled in the textile mills and having had exceptional access to books, began in 1836 after twenty-five years in the factory to keep a school, but found that working-class parents were not sufficiently willing to send their children to be taught 'by one who had never been to school himself' and gave up after two years.[22]

Widows who could manage it could, through running a dame school, stay off parish relief or, after 1834, out of the workhouse. Dr Vincent's examination of 142 working-class autobiographies reveals how common attendance at such institutions was. To the unfortunately crippled or bereaved must be added tradesmen, some of whom had 'failed', who sometimes combined school-keeping with, for example, shoemaking. Thomas Cooper, the Chartist, abandoned this trade to embark full time upon school teaching. Between the standards of a Cooper, who possibly lost pupils because of their parents' suspicion that he knew more than was good for them to know, and those of the lowest and most humble of washerwomen-kept dame school there was an enormous gulf, but the best seem to have been no worse than were many of the National or British schools. Thomas Dunning, a shoemaker, records of the National school he attended in Newport Pagnell, that there was opportunity 'to learn but very little': 'The boys who could read moderately well were appointed to teach the younger or lower classes. I was one of these and I had very little time allowed me for either writing or arithmetic, and none for grammar or geography.'[23] Inevitably, monitorial schools were deafeningly noisy with boys of fourteen left in control of large numbers of younger children while it was not unusual for a single master to have responsibility for more than 300 pupils. The findings of inspectors do not testify to an overwhelming educative success. In 1847, out of 12,786 children in inspected National schools in the Midlands, only 2,891 could read in the Bible and a further 651 books 'of general information'. Nottingham could produce only twenty-four fully literate pupils out of 1,109, and half of these came from a single school.[24]

We have already noted that a crucial limitation on the educational potential of a working-class child was the age at which he or she was withdrawn to contribute to the family economy. This was further worsened by an irregular pattern even within such a short period of attendance. For the country child, seasonal labour peaks such as harvest or bird-scaring at sowing time devastated school attendance. John Clare, the poet who grew up a labourer's child in Northampton-shire, thought that of every year that passed until he was eleven or twelve, his parents found 'three months or more' for his 'improve-ment'. Thomas Jackson has described the rhythms of rural attendance in the 1790s:

> When the labourers' children could obtain employment from the farmers, the school was abandoned, and the youthful pupils were sent to cut weeds in the cornfields in the spring; to frighten away the birds from the standing corn; then to assist in harvest operations; and next to glean the fields which had been reaped. In some cases they were employed in tending cattle in the fields during the entire summer.[25]

In the manufacturing towns the trade cycle played a similar role. Brisk trade in lace at Nottingham created opportunities for such good children's earnings that the 'opportunity cost' of keeping them at school was too high: 'If trade is good the number in attendance is considerably diminished', wrote the master of the boys' National school, while the mistress of the girls' school was of similar opinion: 'If it were brisk now, in a fortnight half the school would leave.' A close study of the attendance records of Mitcham National school in the 1830s is revealing: 'If I have 100 children upon the books, I shall not have 30 in regular attendance: but one third of them will come two or three days in a week and then their parents had some little job or other by which they can earn 6d. or 1s. [2½p or 5p].' Girls were especially liable to be kept home if needed for domestic chores. At Mitcham school, monthly attendance could average two-thirds to three-quarters of enrolment over the year but range from almost 100% in January to less than 50% in September, a local speciality being the camomile harvest in that month. Heavy rain reduced attendance from one day to another, especially since the school closed its doors to the children for an hour at lunch time.[26] The constant coming and going of working people also reduced the length of time a pupil could spend at any one school.

There is no way of knowing exactly how many working-class children missed even a brief and spasmodic schooling. But allowing for the fact that some may have been taught at home by parents (mothers not uncommonly appear in this role in autobiographies), the improve-ment in general literacy after 1820 suggests they were a shrinking minority. Possibly this is more true of boys than of girls, for the significantly lower literacy level for women seems to contradict the evidence which suggests that girls were likely to stay longer at school than were boys. Perhaps the more restricted curriculum linked to gender-conditioned expectations explains this. Dr Vincent concludes that by the mid-1840s, if Sunday School attendance is included, then the great majority of working-class children received some education, however notional, or were at least in a position to form some estimation of what they were missing. At the most pessimistic reckoning, two-thirds of working-class children could look back on careers as pupils.[27] Autobiographies can never, especially on this subject, constitute a true sample of working-class people. Men do not typically record their experiences and women provide only six of Vincent's subjects. He defends himself against suggestions of bias by pointing out that the autobiographers came from a very wide section of the working classes, including the poorest and the outcast and, however much a suspicion of bias remains, Vincent is, one suspects, near the truth. More important is his perception of what this experience of schooling amounted to: 'At best . . . a fragmentary experience' capable of imparting to even the most favoured and intelligent working-class child little more than the rudiments of literacy and numeracy. The testimony of his autobiographers is on this point conclusive: they at least mastered the language sufficiently to record the main events of their own lives, but almost without exception had considerably expanded their education after they left school. William Lovett learned to 'write tolerably well, and to know a little arithmetic', while another's accumulation from a Northumberland village school amounted to being able to 'read badly, to write worse, and to cipher, a little further perhaps than the Rule of Three'. John Harris ended his schooling in Cornwall 'barely able to read and write and cast up figures'. From such rudimentary beginnings variously motivated, for preaching in chapel, for understanding the position of labour in relation to capital, or simply to pursue knowledge for its own sake, many nineteenth-century working men erected prodigious structures of self-improvement, but the complete autodidact was rare. A received education of a minimal kind was the common starting point.[28]

Two classes of children were unique in that a generation before schooling became generally compulsory, it had become so for a brief period of each day for them. These were the children who worked in factories covered by the Factory Acts and those who were pauper children in the workhouses after 1834. Even before the first legislative regulation of the conditions of factory apprentices in cotton mills came with the limited Act of 1802, a few paternalist-inclined mill-owners, like Gregg or Entwistle of Ancoats, provided Sunday schooling for their young pauper apprentices, but they were very much exceptions. The Act of 1802 placed a responsibility upon the factory masters for the 'instruction' of every apprentice for some part of the day for the first four years of his or her service to take place within the usual hours of work in reading, writing and arithmetic, by a master paid by the employer in a place especially set aside. The Act was limited to cotton and woollen mills, and the responsibility for inspection was laid upon local magistrates, whose concern with the implementation of legislation, which one of them (at Manchester) confessed in 1816 he had never even read, was lax in the extreme. Nevertheless, Dr Sanderson, in a study of factory education in Lancashire, has suggested that in the years between 1802 and the Factory Act of 1833 considerable advance in the education of factory children did take place. At some mills it was taken seriously and within the factory communities which grew up around rural mills there was an evident inclination to build separate schoolrooms. Yet compliance was still rare: nine mills around Bolton and Bury were employing apprentices in 1819 of which only three gave the required instruction.[29]

The educational provisions of the Factory Act of 1833 retreated somewhat from the stance of 1802 by removing direct responsibility for the elementary education of factory children from the employers. It ruled that all child employees below the age of eleven (to rise to thirteen after two and a half years) were to attend schools for two hours for six days a week as a condition of factory employment. The factory owners were only to employ children who could provide a certificate of satisfactory school attendance for the previous week. These were 'free' children and they were to attend schools agreed by their parents or guardians, or approved by an inspector. Factory masters generally disliked the Act. Traditionally a master might accept the age-old responsibility required of him towards an apprentice, but few welcomed being made even indirectly responsible for seeing that children who lived with their parents received a minimum of schooling. Reliance on external schooling was liable to disrupt the working routines of the mills, and there was little incentive to take any note of the quality of a school so long as a certificate could be produced. The education received was a mockery more often than not, and the tired, alien, factory children, when they took their places in a neighbourhood school alongside the children of artisans and tradesmen, seemed 'as if they didn't belong to it; and had no business there'.[30] Educational provision under the Act in Lancashire did come under the watchful eye of Leonard Horner, the factory inspector for the county, who had a genuine interest in education for the lower orders. His findings are revealing and, given his concern, there seems every reason to suppose that observance in other counties was even worse. Several employers met with his approval, especially those who built schools on factory sites. This method he preferred to sending out the children. At Rochdale the British school seems to have performed satisfactorily from its foundation in 1834 in taking the mill children, but after all it depended upon the contributions of wealthy dissenters and was presumably, in this sense, the mill-owners' school. Horner also strongly favoured the relay system whereby some groups of children would be in school while others were working (usually at a ratio of two groups in the factory for one at school). But few mills adopted it: Bury with 35 out of a total 114 mills and Rochdale with 32 out of 95 were the most receptive, while Manchester used the system in only four out of 163 mills. The lack of seriousness with which the mill-owners took their educational responsibilities is indicated by the number of prosecutions. Horner calculated in 1836 that of a total of 694 factory offences in his area, 148 were for infringement of the educational clauses, the largest single category. There was a definite correlation between mill size and adequacy of education provision. Of the mills which Horner praised, most were large, while small firms working on marginal profits were the most likely to offend.[31]

The 1844 Factory Act contained no specific educational clauses, but the shortening of the hours of work for persons under fifteen was reported in some districts to have made young people much more alert in class and much more willing to attend evening classes. An Act of 1846 contained the interesting requirement that children produce a certificate of *full-time* school attendance for six months previous to their employment, but it was limited to those employed in cotton print works.[32] In 1857 Horner summarised the quality of 427 schools attended by factory children. The results, after more than twenty years, reveal the poverty of the system. Only 76 schools were described as 'good' and a further 26 as tolerably good. 'Inferior' described 146, 'worse than indifferent' 112, while 66 were 'positively mischievous' and represented a fraud upon the poor parents who paid the school fees.[33]

No more effective or encouraging as a model for a more general popular education was the instruction provided by the Poor Law authorities to pauper children after 1834. The begetters of the New Poor Law, Edwin Chadwick and Bassau Senior, had always favoured education as a means of hopefully lowering pauper levels and perhaps even those of crime. Dr Henriques has remarked that the Poor Law Commissioners could speak a language of hope about children, utterly alien to that they employed about adult paupers: 'their opening minds should be richly furnished with all that is useful and exalted'. A well-regulated school could perform a rescue from contamination by association with adult pauper recidivists.[34] At the beginning, principally through its chief architects Edward Tuffnell and James Kay-Shuttleworth, a policy of district schools was advocated. It was felt that these large, separate establishments designed for 400 or 500 pupils would be large enough for the employment of good teachers and distance the child from the adult paupers, as well as remove them from the control of the workhouse master, who was more likely to insist on the priority of the workhouse economy than be at all supportive of 'indulging' the pauper children with an education. Under the district inspectorship of Kay-Shuttleworth, the best Norfolk schools taught history, geography and grammar as well as the fundamentals of literacy, but even in that district he met with the hostility of some guardians who thought that educating pauper children was like 'putting the torch of knowledge into the hands of rick-burners'.[35]

With no willingness on the part of the government to insist, only a few enlightened guardians co-operated. District schools must be counted among the lost educational experiments, being established only in three metropolitan districts and in six smaller rural ones. The pauper child was typically to experience schooling in a small group within the workhouse, and it was not generally a good experience. Neither salary nor environment were likely to attract able or concerned teachers. It is notable that in Charles Shaw's recollections of his workhouse childhood in the Potteries the schoolmaster is simply placed alongside the governor as an insensitive, hard-faced authority figure. The most severe beating described was inflicted by the schoolmaster and for an offence connected with the general discipline of the house, not at all to do with schooling. Even where conscientious schoolteachers tried, they were likely to find their efforts opposed by the workhouse master, as at Blean in 1848 when the master complained that his authority was constantly undermined by the protests of the schoolmaster whenever he took boys out of the classroom to work around the house.[36] In many cases the educational provision remained dismal until the creation in 1846 of a central fund to pay teachers' salaries and a system of inspection to check their quality. Most historians of pauper education seem to accept that it was only after this date that it began to make any significant contribution to the reduction of literacy. The *Morning Chronicle* investigators of 1849/50 in their reports on the rural districts still noted the education of pauper children to be taking place in an atmosphere of indifference to all but its cost or even in one of outright hostility from farmer-guardians who valued education but little, and who resented the teaching of labourers' children. Pauper children were getting too much education; why, they were learning things which even farmers' sons did not know. How could they be properly 'mastered' when they grew up?[37]

EDUCATION AS SOCIAL CONTROL

Only a short while ago in the forefront of historical fashion, the use by historians of the sociological concept of 'social control' has come increasingly under attack. At one level the concept seems little more than a truism: the classes who have power seek both to maintain it and to legitimate their exclusion of others from it while reconciling them to a subordinate social position. Problematical too is the relationship of intent and achievement. Those who established schools might have wished them to become an effective agency of control over the lower orders and a means of inculcating the approved values of the capitalist market economy and work ethic, but there can be no easy presumption that such intentions were fully or even partially realised. Schools for the labouring classes may have been intended as instruments of social control; they may also have been ineffective as such.

It is at the point of intent that the social control argument is most persuasive. Richard Johnson has shown that the purposes of James Kay-Shuttleworth, the central figure of the 1830s and 1840s and as near to an official spokesman for education as there was, were clearly aligned to those of social control in his obsession with the *need*, from authority's point of view, to educate the lower classes. He spoke for many others much less-known like the Birmingham JP who put it starkly enough in 1845: 'I have no conception of any other means of forcing civilization downwards in society, except by education.' It would, however, seem that such perceptions were more likely to be found in manufacturing than in agricultural districts. There is little doubt, nonetheless, that the articulate bourgeois elite who actively promoted education for the poor were in step with the thinking of their class. Increasingly they shared, beyond the compulsion to moralise, an indictment of the patterns of working-class behaviour and a resulting emphasis on the need for a closely controlled form of schooling to fill the vacuum left by the abrogation by working-class parents of their responsibility for instilling social discipline. Alongside physical reforms like sanitation and coercive ones like the new police, people themselves had to be changed, not only through the rigours of the New Poor Law but, especially, by a general and effective system of education which would teach the working man not only occupational skills, but also 'the nature of his domestic and social relations . . . his political position in society, and the moral and religious duties appropriate to it'. Essential to such an education would be the indoctrination of the science of political economy with its validation of profit and its iron explanations of why wages could not be higher. Education was even more essential if hours of work were to be shortened; for otherwise the extra non-work hours would be ones of sloth, dissipation, or worse, listening in 'ignorant wonder' to demagogues and agitators. Kay-Shuttleworth's views were carried into the regions by the inspectors who worked for his department. They readily saw the dangers of a spread of political and economic beliefs based on 'perverted opinion'. H. S. Tremenheere, for example, could note the 'quickness of intellect' among Norwich weavers while fearing the end to which it was being drawn: 'There was hardly a principle of religion, morals, society, trade, commerce, government, which I did not hear perverted.' Ignorance on economic and political matters could be exploited by the disaffected. As Johnson has summed up: 'The ultimate diagnosis was invariably working-class ignorance the solution an authoritative direction of sentiment through education.' What made the task urgent to the point of desperation was the presumed decline of the working-class family as an effective agent of social-isation. In its stead, according to Kay-Shuttleworth, only the school could cope:

> The teacher of the peasant's child occupies, as it were, the father's place, in the performance of duties which the father is separated by his daily toil, and unhappily at present by his want of knowledge and skill. But the school master ought to be prepared in thought and feeling to do the peasant-father's duty.

It is a recurring central idea in his writings. Note the verb in his statement that there ought to be 'school houses with well-trained masters, competent and zealous to *rear* the population'. Or his specific ascription to the *state* of the 'duty of rearing these children in religion and industry, and of imparting such an amount of secular education as may fit them to discharge the duties of their station'. As one of his first inspectors noted, for the children of the middle class a proper education occurred mainly through the 'association of home', while for the child of the labourer it had to be done, if at all, at school. Such a grand design called in practical terms for a 'professionalising' of the teaching profession. In effect this would entail a separation from the ingrained values of the community – not a rooting in them as was the case with the one-legged miners, one-armed factory cripples and destitute widows. To this end, Kay-Shuttleworth inserted teacher training firmly into the governmental area of responsibility (through a Regulation Act of 1846). In the desired outcome: 'Supervised by its trusty teacher, surrounded by its playground wall, the school was to raise a new race of working people – respectful, cheerful, hard-working, loyal, pacific and religious.'[38]

For all its shortcomings, the social control model seems an essential way into the minds of the popular educators of the period. Those historians who have used it have greatly aided our understanding of this dimension, i.e. the growing consensus of a *need* to educate the people. Its assumptions echo from a wide spectrum of sources; from Kay-Shuttleworth and his inspectors to the Cornish vicar who opening a literary institution in 1838, saw safety in education: 'We need not fear one class overtaking and trampling on another – we need not dread the overeducation of the people – the better they are educated, the better men, the better citizens they will become.'[39] The increasing and intensifying educational imperialism of the 1830s and 1840s seems to justify one historian's remark that 'Chartist leaders, albeit unintentionally, were more successful in loosening the purse strings of the charitable than were the incumbents of the throne', and to see the schoolmaster along with the workhouse master as a 'twin agent' through whose activities the labouring classes were to be reconciled to their unfortunate lot in an early industrial capitalist era. Fear of the new self-respect and confidence of self-educated trade union leaders has been shown by Robert Colls to have drawn a new emphasis on providing education from the coal-owners of the north-east in the aftermath of the great strike of 1844. A similar fear has been identified as underlying educational missionary activity in London's silk-weaving district of Spitalfields.[40] The problem remains that it is easier to spot motives than to assess success. Some lack of success is clearly indicated by the problem of attendance which we have already examined. Those who wanted the mind of the child for a sufficient period got it only intermittently for two years. It also suggests a selective response on the part of working-class parents who took the proffered literacy from the shortest possible exposure to moral persuasion. Other evidence points to parental preferences for schools other than those provided by the voluntary societies even where a British or National school was available, and of these latter types increasing the functional literacy and numeracy content of their curricula at the expense of the moral and reformative in order to attract children whose parents could, after all, opt for the simplest alternative of no schooling at all.[41]

More seriously, a rigid social control perspective neglects the agency of the working class itself by presenting it as a passive recipient of proffered education. The persistence of private fee-paying schools taught by working-class teachers denied a monopoly of supply to those who would wish to enforce their values on the working class. Professor Harrison has recently remarked that there is no clearer example of the way in which historians have overlooked the perceptions of the common people than their treatment of the working-class private venture school in the nineteenth century. The denigration of them by the Victorian 'professionalisers' has been simply accepted although, up to 1870, they existed in large numbers because they provided what a large section of the working class wanted and were integrated into their culture. They were far from negligible as providers of basic literacy. Harrison describes them as 'the people's own schools' rather than 'schools for the people'.[42]

Some parents of artisans, like those of Francis Place in an earlier era, associated status with payment, but for most it was a limited choice between education or none at all, or between a free place at a voluntary school or a paid one at a private school, and certainly the more consistent quality of their teaching after the 1840s helps explain the growing inclination to use the British and National schools. By the time, however, proselytising in them had become less strident and utilitarian literacy more evident. As Dr Vincent has remarked of school selection: 'Relative to other important areas of his experience such as employment or housing the working man had a genuine chance to intervene and exercise influence.'[43]

SUNDAY SCHOOLS

This was even more true of the Sunday School. With a more evident moral concern and reformative motive, these institutions have been presented by Dr Laquer in a well-sustained argument as having as much a claim to be regarded as a part of working-class culture as an example of bourgeois educational imperialism. The coincidence of the values of Methodist teaching with the disciplines required by the new industrialism, drawn so sharply by E. P. Thompson, have led historians to expect the Sunday School to have been a prime agent of social discipline, imparting the values of thrift, industry and good time-keeping while through a 'theodicy of suffering' preaching the passive acceptance of this world's trials.[44] In so far as they were, as to a great extent was the case, provided by middle-class benefactions and energies, this was certainly an intent and, as a critic of Laquer has pointed out, often an effect.[45] But it must not be forgotten that many Sunday Schools were taken over by working-class communities from whose ranks their teachers very largely came. Laquer sees them as a creation of a working-class culture of respectability and self-reliance. The values of the Sunday School might well in part coincide with those approved by capitalist society, but this does not preclude the possibility of their arising, like teetotalism, from the labouring poor's own aspirations. In them the line between pupil and teacher was not sharply drawn as the more assiduous of the former provided the recruits for the latter. The secular educational contribution of the Sunday School was limited and in this respect they hardly seem fully deserving of the encomiums heaped upon them by denominational historians. Their deficiencies became more evident after large numbers of them, including the Methodist, ceased teaching writing after the 1790s.[46] Various investigations in the early nineteenth century reveal how little they had to offer in basic elementary education other than as complements to day schooling. In the strongly Methodist mining districts of Cornwall where more than 40,000 attended their Sunday Schools in 1858, the Child Labour Inquiry of 1842 found only one school still teaching writing. Of 33 child witnesses who were questioned on their education, 19 had attended day schools while 10 had or were attending only Sunday Schools. Fifteen of those who had attended day schools had also or were still attending Sunday Schools. None of the ten child labourers who had attended only the latter was able to write and most read very badly. Evidence from Nottingham for the same year points the same way: of 22 children who had attended only Sunday school, 16 could read, 5 read and write, and 1 could do neither. Gaskell in 1836 thought their effect in Lancashire suggested that they had been really effective only in teaching 'moral restraint'.[47]

What working-class parents were given the unwonted privacy to enjoy once they got their children out of the house on Sundays is part of the lore of working-class communities. However, allowing for some hopes of their children acquiring a smattering of useful knowledge, parents, especially in districts of above average religiosity, may have valued the good behaviour, sanctioned by the fear of God, which Sunday Schools inculcated. In such areas similar hopes might well have been entertained of day school teachers. John Harris from Cornwall's mining area was under no illusions in listing the academic deficiencies of the crippled ex-miner who presided over the village school, but he nevertheless saw them as compensated for in other ways:

> But though John Roberts was a stranger to most of the sciences now taught in schools, he possessed what perhaps is better still – a thorough knowledge of the saving powers of the Gospel of Jesus Christ. His daily instruction began and ended with extemporate prayer.[48]

At mid-century, a farmer's son attending a village school, later remembered most vividly the school-mistress's mother, who:

> would often speak to the children on the importance of being truthful, honest and obedient to parents, and to remember that God's eye was always on us and saw all that we did. Amongst other things she showed us a picture of what was said to be the devil – a dreadful looking person with a pitch fork. We were told that he would deal with all wicked children and put them in the fire with this fork.[49]

By 1850, England was without doubt a more literate society than it had been 100 years before. The enormous proliferation of the specialist press and pamphlet literature of popular radicalism testifies to this, as does the outpouring of didactic tracts directed at the working class. As in the case of the improvement in the material standard of living, it is noticeable how much of this advance was concentrated into the years after 1830. There was still a long way to go: provision was far from complete and quality varied in the extreme. Children of the working class attended school for far too short and erratic a time but, increasingly, they *did* attend, and from the standpoint of 1850 it is possible to look forward, over no great distance of time, to universal, required and free elementary education for a regulated period of childhood. In 1750 such a prospect would have seemed remote indeed.

REFERENCES AND NOTES

1. **G. Sutherland**, *Elementary Education in the Nineteenth Century*, Historical Association, 1971, p. 3.
2. For a general survey of these problems, see **R. Houston**, 'Literacy and society in the west, 1500–1850', *Social History*, VIII, no. 3, 1983, pp. 269–93.

3. **M. Sanderson**, 'Literacy and the Industrial Revolution', *Past and Present*, no. 56, 1972, pp. 75–104.

4. This paragraph is based on **R. Hume**, 'Educational provision for the Kentish poor, 1660–1811' *Southern History*, 4, 1982, pp. 123–44 in which the writer's methods of calculation as well as his findings are presented.

5. **M. G. Jones**, *The Charity School Movement. A Study of Eighteenth-Century Puritanism in Action*, Cambridge U.P., 1938.

6. Ibid., pp. 12–13.

7. For a strong critique, see **J. Simon**, 'The charity school movement', a letter in *Bulletin of the Society for the Study of Labour History*, no. 31, 1975, pp. 11–13, a concise statement of the position against Jones adopted by Simon from her research on Leicestershire. For the slight impact in Cornwall, see **F. L. Harris**, 'Education by charity in eighteenth-century Cornwall', *Journal of the Royal Institute of Cornwall*, IX, pt. 1, 1982, pp. 30–52.

8. **L. Stone**, 'Literacy and education in England 1640–1900', *Past and Present*, no. 42, 1969, pp. 69–139; **M. Sanderson**, *Education, Economic Change and Society in England 1780–1870*, Macmillan, 1983, p. 13.

9. Sanderson, *Education*, p. 13.

10. Ibid., pp. 13–14.

11. *Hansard*, 13 July 1807.

12. **J. S. Hurt**, *Education in Evolution 1800–1870*, Paladin, 1972, p. 14.

13. This account is based on Hurt, *Education in Evolution*, pp. 11–38.

14. *Report from the Committee of Council on Education*, BPP, 1841, XX, p. 85; **William Francis**, *Gwennap*, 1845, p. 130.

15. **J. Vincent**, *Bread, Knowledge and Freedom. A Study of Nineteenth-Century Working-Class Autobiography*, Methuen, 1982, pp. 97–8.

16. **P. E. Razzell** and **R. W. Wainwright**, *The Victorian Working Class: Selections from Letters to the Morning Chronicle*, Cass, 1973, pp. 30–2.

17. Sanderson, *Education*, pp. 16–17.

18. **D. Wardle**, *Education and Society in Nineteenth Century Nottingham*, Cambridge U.P., 1971, p. 41.

19. **E. G. West**, 'Resource allocation and growth in early nineteenth-century British education', *Economic History Review*, XXIII, no. 1, 1970, pp. 68–95; **J. S. Hurt**, 'Professor West on early nineteenth-century education, ibid., XXIV, no. 4, 1971, pp. 624–32; **E. G. West**, 'The interpretation of early nineteenth century education statistics', ibid., pp. 633–42. These exchanges have been reprinted in **M. Drake** (ed.), *Applied Historical Studies*, Methuen, 1973. See also **H. J. Kiesling**, 'Nineteenth-century education according to West: a comment', *Economic History Review*, XXXVI, no. 3, 1983, pp. 416–25 and West's rejoinder in the same issue, pp. 426–32.

20. *Breague Vestry Minute Book 1796–1816*, Cornwall County Record Office, D.D.P., 18/8/1; **J. Harris**, *My Autobiography*, 1882, p. 25; *Report of Committee of Council on Education*, BPP, 1841, p. 86.

21. **T. Jackson**, *Recollections of My Own Life and Times*, 1873, p. 18.

22. **W. Dodd**, *The Laboring Classes of England*, 1848, repr. Kelley, 1973, p. 24.

23. Vincent, *Bread, Knowledge and Freedom*, pp. 97, 101–2.

24. Wardle, *Education in Nottingham*, pp. 69–70.

25. Vincent, *Bread, Knowledge and Freedom*, p. 98; Jackson, *Recollections*, p. 19.

26. Wardle, *Education in Nottingham,* p. 57; **B. Madoc-Jones**, 'Patterns of attendance and their social significance: Mitcham National School 1830–39', in **P. McCann** (ed.), *Popular Education and Socialisation in the Nineteenth Century,* Methuen, 1977, pp. 41, 59.
27. Vincent, *Bread, Knowledge and Freedom,* p. 104.
28. Ibid., pp. 99–100.
29. **M. Sanderson**, 'Education and the factory in industrial Lancashire 1780–1840', *Economic History Review,* XX, no. 2, 1967, pp. 267–70.
30. Ibid., pp. 271–8; **U. R. Q. Henriques**, *Before the Welfare State. Social Administration in early Industrial Britain,* Longman, 1979, pp. 216–19.
31. Sanderson, 'Education and the factory', pp. 271–6.
32. Henriques, *Before the Welfare State,* pp. 218–19.
33. Sanderson, 'Education and the factory', p. 218.
34. Henriques, *Before the Welfare State,* p. 211.
35. Ibid., pp. 211–12; see also **F. Duke**, 'Pauper education', in **D. Fraser** (ed.), *The New Poor Law in the Nineteenth Century,* Macmillan, 1976, pp. 67–86; **M. A. Crowther**, *The Workhouse System 1834–1929,* Methuen, 1983, p. 203.
36. **C. Shaw**, *When I was a Child,* Caliban, 1977, p. 112; Crowther, *Workhouse System,* p. 204.
37. Duke, 'Pauper education', p. 74.
38. **R. Johnson**, 'Educational policy and social control in early Victorian England', *Past and Present,* no. 49, 1970, pp. 97, 102, 106, 107, 112, 119.
39. *Cornwall Gazette,* Truro, 23 Sept. 1838.
40. Hurt, *Education in Evolution,* p. 26; **R. Colls**, 'Oh happy English children! Coal, class and education in the north east', *Past and Present,* no. 73, 1976, pp. 75–96; **P. McCann**, 'Popular education, socialisation, and social control: Spitalfields 1812–24', in McCann (ed.), *Popular Education,* pp. 1–29.
41. See the suggestive analysis by Simon Firth, 'Socialization and rational schooling: elementary education in Leeds before 1870', in McCann (ed.), *Popular Education,* pp. 67–77.
42. **J. F. C. Harrison**, *The Common People. A History from the Norman Conquest to the Present,* Fontana, 1984, pp. 288–92.
43. Vincent, *Bread, Knowledge and Freedom,* p. 103.
44. **T. Laquer**, *Religion and Respectability, Sunday Schools and Working Class Culture 1780–1850,* Yale U.P., 1976; **E. P. Thompson**, *The Making of the English Working Class,* Penguin, 1968, pp. 412–16.
45. **M. Dick**, 'The myth of the working class Sunday School', *History of Education,* vol. 9, 1, 1980.
46. Sanderson, *Education,* p. 13; **A. P. Wadsworth**, 'The first Manchester Sunday Schools', in **M. W. Flinn** & **T. C. Smout** (eds), *Essays in Social History,* Oxford U.P., 1974, pp. 110–11.
47. **J. G. Rule**, 'The Labouring miner in Cornwall c.1740–1870: a study in social history', Ph.D. thesis, University of Warwick, 1971, pp. 324–6; Wardle, *Education in Nottingham,* p. 42; **P. Gaskell**, *Artisans and Machinery,* 1836, repr. Cass, 1968, pp. 243–4.
48. Harris, *Autobiography,* p. 25.
49. **C. T. Trevail**, *Life and Reminiscences,* 2nd edn, 1927, pp. 11–12.

Part Four

RESPONSES

Chapter 11

TRADE UNIONISM BEFORE 1825

THE EIGHTEENTH-CENTURY ORIGINS

It has often been suggested that trade unionism developed as a consequence of the industrial revolution: in fact by 1750 it was already well established among many groups of skilled workers. The period prior to the industrial revolution, identified by Marx as the 'period of manufacture' preceding that of 'machinofacture', was already characterised by the separation of labour and capital. The product of the worker was expropriated in the basic sense that he no longer commonly owned the materials upon which he worked nor sold the product of his labour to the customer; he sold 'labour power'. The division of labour was characteristic and manufacturing typically took place either in the workshop – small-scale form of social production until recently much neglected by historians – or in the home under some variant of the putting-out system. Crucially, production in this era, Marx noted, still depended on the skilled labourer. Even where parts of the chain of processes needed, for example, to produce woollen or worsted cloth had become deskilled and overstocked, some groups of workers such as shearmen ('croppers') or combers still controlled strategic steps in the manufacture. Such skilled labourers were both able and inclined to combine in protection of their standing and status and, when circumstances were propitious, even improve them.[1]

James Watt was well aware of the problems which skilled men could present to their employers. He complained in 1786 of a 'rebellion' of his journeymen millwrights and suggested lessening dependence upon them by substituting carpenters wherever possible. He further suggested getting the more tractable hands to sign agreements to neither join the union nor attend its meetings and obtaining advice on prosecuting its leaders for unlawful combination. If all this proved to no avail, then young Scotsmen willing to accept lower rates could be brought down to Birmingham. Essential to skilled labour's power was the control of entry to the trade and to this end the key institution was apprenticeship. Brentano, in relating the rise of trade unions to the need to enforce an apprenticeship only laxly enforced by law, was close to the truth.[2]

Eighteenth-century artisans combined not just to effect a 'closed shop' for 'legal' workmen, but also to resist cuts in their wages and attempts to change their customary ways of working as well as to secure advances in their wages, and, less commonly, shorter hours of work. Defensively they were at a disadvantage since encroachments on their prices and privileges were most often attempted when conditions in the labour market favoured the employer.

In 1776, Adam Smith took the existence of workers' combinations for granted, as he did conflict between labour and capital. Employees were disposed to collective action to raise the price of their labour, while employers combined to lower wages.[3] Recently an historian has enumerated 333 disputes in England (353 in Britain) between 1717 and 1800, a clear indication of the frequency of industrial disputes even if their actual number is beyond computation. Workers included were those in all main branches of the textile trades, seamen, ships' carpenters and shipwrights; and other dockyard workers; tailors, leather breeches makers, hatters and shoemakers, carpenters and other building craftsmen; papermakers, printers and others. In some of these, like woollen weaving, wool-combing and tailoring, organisation went back to the beginning of the eighteenth century or even beyond. The Webbs in their history of the trade union movement narrowed the definition of a trade union to organisations having a *permanent* and continuous existence, i.e. lasting before, through and beyond particular disputes. Few historians would now accept their insistence on 'continuous association', but even within their rigidity of definition, evidence supports the existence of at least fifty trade unions before 1800 among a variety of skilled trades.[4]

In fact in the eighteenth century, and beyond, continuity lay as much in the 'trade' as in organisational forms, and while the surviving documentation might point towards intermittent conflicts and ephemerality, it is clear that continuity essentially rested in the workplace or village club and in the habit of association. It is not useful to insist on a polarisation with organised unions at one end and sporadic industrial protest at the other. Recurrent forms link the two. Groups of workers, although not necessarily keeping an organisation for defence of their craft permanently in being, nevertheless preserved in experience and in tradition the forms of action appropriate to resist employers' impositions at stress points and to push advantages when circumstances in the labour market shifted in their favour.[5]

The degree of organisation varied among different groups of artisans. In the case of such as the London tailors, employers complained in 1810 of a combination which for about a century 'ripened by experience' had been able to impose 'arbitrary and oppressive laws' upon the trade. The union had first come to the public attention in

1720/1 when its activities had led to an Act prohibiting combinations in the tailoring trades of London and Westminster and fixing wages by statute. Conflict over wages was renewed in 1744/5, 1752, 1764, 1768 and 1778. In 1824, despite the Combination Laws having existed for a quarter of a century, Francis Place described their organisation as a 'perfect and perpetual combination' in which orders from an 'executive' reached upwards of twenty delegate-sending 'houses of call'.[6] Among the journeymen hatters, unionism went back as far. Evidence from 1777 testifies to the extent and power of a 'Congress' which made by-laws, exacted fines and prevented masters from taking on too many apprentices. Successful wage demands had been made in 1772 and 1775 and the effect of the union's strength was being felt by master hatters in a dozen English towns from London through the Midlands to Bristol. Evidence also exists of their activities in Manchester in 1780, 1783 and 1785, London again in 1786, Manchester in 1791 and Stockport in 1799. Organisation in London and Lancashire at least continued through the years of the Combination Acts.[7]

In the far south-west the weavers and combers of Devonshire's serge manufacture had developed an effective unionism based on town clubs from the very beginning of the eighteenth century. Complaints by employers in 1717 describe their clubs as having existed 'for some time past'. Conflict came to a head in 1725 when the 'taking of an arbitrary power to ascertain their wages', riots, machine-breaking and rough treatment of blacklegs and recalcitrant employers focused sharp attention on the 'unlawful assemblies' of weavers and combers from Exeter to Bristol. The culmination was a proclamation of 1718 and an Act of 1726 prohibiting combinations among woollen workers.

The country weavers of the clothing districts of Gloucestershire, Wiltshire and parts of Somerset also provide evidence of unionism from at least the 1720s. In this area, where the great broadcloth was produced, conflict centred on attempts by weavers to get employers to pay the rates fixed by local magistrates under wage-fixing clauses which had been included in the Anti-Combination Act of 1726. The issue lay fairly quiescent after the late 1720s through a period of relative prosperity although broken briefly by disturbances in 1738/9. With the return of bad trade and unemployment in 1755/6, weavers' combinations again became active, but the end result of their disturbances was the securing by the employers in 1757 of an Act which ended the principle of wage regulation in this area of manufacture more than fifty years before the general repeal in 1813 of the wage-fixing clauses of the Statute of Artificers (V Elizabeth) after 250 years. Although attention during these disturbances was naturally concentrated on the riotous actions of the weavers, there is good evidence especially in the preparation of articulate and forceful petitions to local justices and to Parliament of the underlying co-ordination of organised trade clubs. Union activity in the area came again forcefully to public notice when attacks and protests against the introduction of shearing frames and gigmills by the shearmen in the 1790s and early 1800s coincided with attempts by the weavers to restrict the introduction of the factory system by reviving apprenticeship restrictions.[8]

Groups like shearmen in the wool cloth districts and combers in the worsted ones were significant in the growth of trade unionism in that they occupied skilled positions essential in the production chains of cloth manufacture. Adam Smith, as well as Karl Marx, recognised the strength of their position:

> Half-a-dozen wool combers, perhaps are necessary to keep a thousand spinners and weavers at work. By combining not to take apprentices they can not only engross the employment, but reduce the whole manufacture into a sort of slavery to themselves, and raise the price of their labour much above what is due to the nature of their work.[9]

Woolcombers' organisations had been noticed in the south-west, Essex, Leicester and Yorkshire by the 1740s, and well before the end of the eighteenth century their societies had linked into a national system: 'They are become one society throughout the kingdom . . . if any of their club is out of work they give them a ticket and money to seek for work at the next town where a box club is.' This was the 'tramping system', a key feature of craft unions in Britain and a fundamental component of the artisan's life experience. It was known in many trades besides woolcombing where the system in 1794 was thought powerful enough to 'counteract all the interests and pursuits of their employers'. Weavers, curriers, hatters, compositors, paper-makers and calico printers all had the system in some form before the end of the eighteenth century, and it seems to have also developed early among tailors, carpenters, shoemakers, metal workers, bakers, plumbers and painters. Linking through 'tramping' was the backbone of communication among trade clubs of skilled workers; without it later federation would have been much more difficult, while in the short term it was a means by which crucial information about prices, conditions and disputes could be spread. Assistance could be sought for localities on strike and activists removed from victimisation.[10]

In the emerging cotton manufacture of Lancashire, organisation among weavers is evident from 1747 and spread rapidly with the object of enforcing apprenticeship. Activities were funded from regular contributions to local 'box clubs' and co-ordinated through delegate meetings with officials being paid for lost time. Attempts in 1758 to break the organisation led to a strike of check-weavers for wage increases, more exact specification of piece sizes and an end to the employment of unapprenticed men.[11] Similar examples of union activity could be presented from other groups like printers with their 'chapels', dockyard workers (especially shipwrights), cutlers, building craftsmen and shoemakers. All had sufficient features in common for historians to accept a general tendency among eighteenth-century skilled workers to combine for defensive and offensive purposes. If so concluding, they would be at one with the assumptions of the *Wealth of Nations*.

But Adam Smith, although noting the widespread existence of craft unions, was dismissive of their effectiveness. It cannot be doubted that the employers' strength was formidable. Smith noted the discrimination of the law in matters of industrial relations; the ability of employers to combine to resist workers' demands or to impose their own, and the imbalance of resources which allowed employers to sit out strikes while hunger drove their workers back. He noted that increasing desperation, if it led to attacks on persons or property or scenes of tumult, would inevitably bring the forces of law and order to the side of the employers. All these were indeed constraints upon union effectiveness, but important qualifications need to be made.[12]

The law was clearly on the employers' side. By the time the general Combination Acts of 1799 and 1800 were passed, there were already more than forty Acts of one kind or another on the statute books which could be used against trade unions, although many of these were confined to specific trades, such as those forbidding combinations in the woollen manufacture (1726), tailors (1721), hatters (1777) and papermakers (1794). Such Acts, as indeed was the general Combination Act which had begun with the petition of millwright employers against the trade union activities of their journeymen, were passed by Parliament in response to employers seeking a speedier and more effective way of combating organisations of journeymen within their trades. Invariably the language of the petitions and of the preamble to the Acts makes it clear that the object was to provide a more effective remedy against a fact of combination which was already presumed illegal. This assumption largely rested upon the common-law concept of conspiracy, under which the fairness or justness of workers' claims was not at issue, only the fact of conspiracy against their employers: 'It is not for refusing to work, but for conspiracy that they are indicted, and a conspiracy of any kind is illegal', ruled the court of King's Bench in 1721 dismissing an appeal against sentence by some Cambridge journeyman tailors who had struck. Through the eighteenth century, conspiracy proceedings against trade unions were of regular occurrence, for example against seven Liverpool tailors in 1783 and in Leicester against hatters and shoemakers in 1777 and 1794. In 1798 the Recorder, summing up against London compositors, put the conspiracy issue with unusual clarity. For men to meet privately to do injury to another (i.e. to harm the business of their employer) had 'at all times been considered by the law of this country, as a very heinous crime'; even had the combination been intended as a 'good and useful act', a strike was clearly a conspiracy. Many cases are presumably 'lost' in local court records, but Dr Dobson's recovery of twenty-nine cases between 1710 and 1800 shows the persistence of conspiracy proceedings as a weapon against trade unionism.[13]

The problem with initiating conspiracy charges from the employers' point of view was that they involved long and costly proceedings. Indictments issued after the calling of a strike gave activists time to flee, while the delay before court hearings could take place sometimes meant that by the time a case was heard, a dispute could well have been over, and the proceedings serve only to re-open old wounds. The passing of specific anti-combination laws by Parliament and the general ones of 1779 and 1800 were designed to provide prompt rather than excessively punitive redress by allowing sentencing summarily before magistrates. Even after the Acts of 1799 and 1800, however, some cases were still brought under the common law of conspiracy. Other powers still resided within statutes such as that of 1384 or some of the clauses of V Elizabeth and, with such powers available, the real question is perhaps why the law was not a more effective inhibitor of eighteenth-century trade unionism than in fact it was. Part of the answer lies in the slowness of proceedings and the disinclination to open old wounds and latent hostilities after strikes had finished. Employers preferred to use the *threat* of legal action and to appear merciful by not proceeding, provided the strikers went back, to the making of martyrs. If strikes took place, as when an advance in wages or an improvement in conditions was sought, they usually did so in times of brisk trade when employers might well prefer to give in and secure uninterrupted production rather than lose the opportunity of a rising market. Their legal advantages did not always coincide with their economic interest, a fact well known to workers. In any case the law was only clearly applicable in cases of attempts to increase wages or shorten hours. Organisations for the purposes of petitioning Parliament for an enforcement of apprenticeship or the regulation of wages were only illegal in so far as they involved strikes or actions of intimidation.[14]

Combinations of employers, as Smith remarked, were as much a feature of the industrial scene as were those of workers. Essentially secretive, they from time to time reveal themselves as behind, for example, the wage-cutting which precipitated the disturbances of 1738/9 in the West Country clothing districts at Taunton and other centres of the serge trade where significantly a strike took place in 1764 when weavers learned that a meeting of masters was *about* to agree to lower prices. Adam Smith suggested that on the upswing of a trade cycle, competition for increasingly scarce workers would naturally break any combination of masters to hold wages below market levels. In fact, employers were able to 'police' themselves in this area. They could by refusing to employ workers unable to present a 'discharge certificate' from their previous employer, or by getting workers to sign agreements to accept proffered wages, limit the extent to which an increased demand for labour would lead to any very quick upward pressure on wages. Faced with the threat or fact of a combination, employers readily formed counter-combinations, sometimes to the extent of using lock-outs to force showdowns with the unions, as in papermaking in 1799. The Worsted Committee formed to suppress the embezzlement of materials in 1791 turned its attention in the 1790s to prosecuting trade unions. While a Sheffield organisation in 1814, calling itself the Sheffield Mercantile and Manufacturing Union, emerged for the specific purpose of resisting extensive unionism among the cutlers which had made 'a progress so alarming as to threaten the most dangerous consequences to the trade'. It aimed at a lock-out and resolved that no member would pay increased wages or employ a cutler who could not produce a discharge certificate. This association was a more formal manifestation of earlier combinations by employers, like that in 1790 when those in scissors-grinding had met to collect funds for the prosecution of strikers and in 1796 when ninety-one out of ninety-six firms jointly resolved to resist the demands of journeymen knife-makers. Francis Place thought the London typefounders so well combined that they had kept unions out of their industry for many years.[15]

The simple but great advantage of being able to hold out longer was the employers' most evident weapon. In 'defensive' strikes designed to resist wage reductions when the market was turning down, then employers having no real interest in maintaining a constant flow of goods already in over-supply could sit out strikes. But to argue that an employer *could* outlast his striking workers is not to say that it was always in his interest to do so. He would not want to forgo the high profits available from expanding output on a rising market. In such conditions it was more rational to concede than to resist demands. From the workers' point of view, choice of the right moment for a withdrawal of labour was crucial: serge weavers chose the spring when the demand for their lighter-weight cloth was at its seasonal high; fellmongers chose the late autumn after the Michaelmass livestock-killing when their employers had large stocks of rapidly deteriorating hides ready for processing. Printworkers working for Hansard turned out in 1805 when there was a backlog of parliamentary bills, coopers took advantage of the rush to provision ships for the war of 1812, while dockyard workers, as at Portsmouth in 1776, took advantage of the fitting out of the fleet. The death of Princess Charlotte in 1817 presented Coventry's weavers of black ribbon with an admirable opportunity to press for higher wages. Given that the statutory regulation of tailors' wages allowed them extra in times of general mourning, one wonders how many church-going tailors prayed with all their heart and soul for the health of the royal family. Place was right to observe that journeymen and their wives dreaded strikes and, apart from cases of defence and desperation, possessed a sense of strategy to make them more effective. Above all, to strike without first building up a support fund was to invite speedy defeat. If the timing was right, and the fund built up, then success was not unobtainable. Box clubs before the passing of the Combination Acts were not always conducted under the disguise of a friendly society or benefit club; in many instances, they openly collected for the 'defence of the trade'. A Huddersfield weaver saw no need for concealment when he stated that besides belonging to a sick club, he belonged to another to secure the better enforcing of apprenticeship. Shoemakers in 1792 expressed their conviction that 'nothing short of a general fund' could provide a foundation for 'lasting union among journeymen of any trade'. There is evidence of long-term financial preparation for strikes from book-binders, printers, breeches-makers, calico printers and others. Various stratagems could eke out a strike fund. Young men could leave the district on the 'tramp'; co-operative workshops could be organised to sell directly to customers, as the Birmingham tailors, among others, did in their strike of 1777. Loans or gifts could be obtained from other trade unions and tactical striking against one employer at a time could enable those in work to support those who had turned out. This last tactic, sometimes known as the 'strike in detail' or the 'rolling strike', was employed before the end of the century by several groups including calico printers, papermakers and compositors. Employers did not always have the support of the wider community and there were several instances when public subscription and even gentry donations as well as favourable treatment from parish Poor Law officials assisted strikers, for example Leicester's framework knitters in 1819. With such possibilities, strikes could last much longer than Adam Smith presumed. At the beginning of the nineteenth century the hatters stayed out for fifteen weeks at a strike pay of 15s. (75p), and although the leather-breeches makers organised by Francis Place in 1793 seemed to have failed after a twelve-week strike, their turn-out sufficiently exhausted their employers for them to concede a wage increase at the mere threat of a strike the following year.[16]

Smith thought that the violence of desperation would usually bring the civil authorities to the aid of employers resisting striking workers: 'The masters upon these occasions are just as clamorous upon the other side, and never cease to call aloud for the assistance of the civil magistrate, and the rigorous execution of those laws which have been enacted with so much severity against the combination of servants, labourers and journeymen.'[17] Much earlier in the century the Wiltshire clothiers were said to have first goaded their weavers into riot, then shouted for the military to put them down.[18]

I have suggested elsewhere that *intimidation* might be a description of workers' actions which although not necessarily conveying approval permits a more positive evaluation of their *motives* than does an insistence on the element of desperation. Historians of the labour movement like the Webbs and the Hammonds found it difficult to reconcile violent action with their gradualist perception of the 'real' labour movement. Violent actions were something apart, the aberrant behaviour of a minority, or a lapse into desperation when 'constitutional' protest met with rebuff. Recent historians tend to reject this view and, following Professor Hobsbawm, emphasise that 'collective bargaining by riot' was a direct method of industrial action whose effectiveness enables its persistence to be viewed as a functional correction to the Webbs' 'episodic' view of eighteenth-century labour disputes. Intimidation could take several forms: sending threatening letters to frighten employers, breaking machines, attacking 'blacklegs', those unwilling to support strikes, or the ritual humiliation of 'unfair' workmen, and at times attacks on recalcitrant employers.[19] Such actions were not always entirely separable: threats could precede action, while the motive in destroying machinery, pit-head lifting-gear for example, could have been to prevent working by strike-breakers. Contrary to the prejudices of the Webbs and Hammonds, such intimidation was quite likely to be found among the tactics of groups of skilled workers who were also in the forefront of organised trade unionism. That the calico printers of Lancashire had sufficient status presumption to have been ironically labelled 'gentlemen journeymen' did not stop them from sending the following letter when printing machinery threatened their craft:

> You must immediately give over any more Mashen Work for we are determined there shall be no more of them made use of in the trade and it will be madness for you to contend with the Trade as we are combined by Oath to fix prices we can afford to pay him [one of their number who had been imprisoned] a Guinea Week and not hurt the fund if you was to keep hime there till Dumsday therefore mind you comply with the above or by God we will keep our Words with you we will make some rare Bunfires in this Countey and at your Peril shake in their Shoes we are determined to destroy all Sorts of Masheens for Printing in the Kingdom for there is more hands then is work for so no more from the ingerd Gurnemen Rember we are a great number sworn nor you must not advertise the Men that you say run away from you when yout il Usage was the Cause of their going we will punish you for that our Meetings are legal for we want nothing but what is honest and to work for selvs and familers and you want to starve us but it is better for you and a few more which we have marked to die then such a Number of Pore Men and there famerles to be starved.[20]

Machine-breaking was often preceded by such letters, notably in the West Country shearmen's campaign of the 1790s and in the better-known Luddite disturbances of the Regency period. Threats of, or actual, violence had the advantage of being usable against those against whom it would have been inappropriate to strike, as in Tiverton in 1738 and 1749 when weavers and combers attacked publicans who made a practice of buying up rejected cloths and spoiling the market by undercutting regular prices. Or at Liverpool in 1792 when carpenters, who had a well-established union, threatened to pull down the houses of abolitionists if the slave trade were abolished, at the same time as they were agitating for a wage increase. Even consumers could be roughly handled as were wearers of calicos by London's silk weavers in 1719 and those of shoelaces by Birmingham's bucklemakers under the Regency. Cornish tin miners, fearing the displacement of pewter, destroyed a consignment of earthenware in 1766.[21]

There is, as Professor Hobsbawm has pointed out, a distinction between action against machinery where the machine itself was presumed to be about to displace labour and action where the machine was not in itself a threat but was simply attacked as the property of a particular employer to bring pressure on him to give in. To give a clear example: miners can hardly have had any quarrel *per se* with the lifting and winding gear which from time to time they destroyed during disputes. Such pressure tactics played a traditional and established role in industrial disputes in the period of domestic manufacture and in the early years of mine and factory development. In many such cases, employers' houses, goods or materials were as likely to suffer as were machines. In their struggle with the clothiers in 1802, Wiltshire shearmen burned hay-ricks, barns and kennels and destroyed cloth as well as frames and gig mills. Cornish miners in dispute in 1795 in removing the shaft ladders were acting as the pitmen were in similar disputes: they were preventing mine-owners from bringing in other workers, or else forcing miners to join the strike. There is no reason at all to suppose, as the Hammonds did, that where both peaceful and violent methods of conducting disputes appear simultaneously, they were the expressions of different groups of workers.[22]

Near ritual forms of deterent intimidation were often used against 'blacklegs', strike-breakers, 'unfair' men or even employers. At Callington in 1725 on the fringes of the serge manufacture a master was 'cool-staffed' – paraded through the town astride a pole – before being dumped in a duck pond, as was a weaver at Tiverton in 1749 who disagreed with his fellow weavers. The cloth weavers of Banbury in 1793, by that year a well-organised group, paraded the streets of the town behind a band of 'rough music' before proceeding to the house of a strike-breaker. They seized the piece from his loom and bore it back to town on an ass, astride which, had he not fled, the weaver was himself intended to have been tied in the manner of the 'Skimmington Ride' or 'charivari'. Pressure was often simply a matter of numbers: workers gathered in hundreds were hardly resistible as they made a tour of mines or factories in a district persuading others to join them. The most extreme forms of treatment were those used against those who informed on their fellows as in the stoning to death of an informer by Spitalfields silk weavers in 1769 when two weavers, arrested on his information, had been executed for cutting cloth from looms during a bitter dispute.[23]

Adam Smith had been concerned to demonstrate that trade unions were ineffective in advancing or in maintaining wages above their market level, but from his comment on the woolcombers it is clear that he accepted that some groups of skilled workers were able through ensuring a strict adherence to apprenticeship to exert some degree of control over the labour supply. Indeed, as E. P. Thompson has pointed out, the unions' demand for a strict observance in this respect made them, rather than their masters, the inheritors of the guild tradition. This was evident in London around 1750. The Masons' Company complained that its journeymen had entered into 'unlawful combination' to prevent an influx of new workers into their trade, while the Company of Painter-Stainers was having trouble with a 'club' of journeymen painters who 'will not work nor let others'. The journeymen brought a case before the Lord Mayor's Court against an employer for taking on someone who was 'not free of the company'. In evidence the masters stressed their need to take on many extra workers in the summer peak in addition to the freemen who were never refused work. The court, however, found for the men. The masters organised themselves to secure a system of licensing for the interlopers and mounted a strong attack on the journeymen's clubs in the press as 'dictators' denying the 'natural right' of Englishmen. Petitions in support of the exclusive right of the 'legal' workman were received from the carpenters, masons and printers as well as the painters. The Court of the Common Council, to whom the appeal of the masters had been addressed, delivered its verdict: the exclusive right of exercising a trade had been a great and valuable franchise, but when journeymen made use of this right they perverted it to promote idleness, destroy subordination and 'raise an intractable spirit in the lower class of freeman'.[24]

This conflict was foreshadowed by the final struggle over the exclusive 'property of skill' which involved so many crafts in London in first seeking to extend and then to preserve the apprenticeship clauses of V Elizabeth before they were repealed in 1814. The employers' attack on statutory apprenticeship was a direct one on the fundamentals of craft unionism. Perhaps even more so than the passing of the Combination Acts, which had attempted to provide effective and speedy sanctions against unions at a time of war, rising prices and fear of popular jacobinism, but the repeal of 1814 was an attempt to remove the very condition by which an established and not wholly ineffective trade unionism existed.

TRADE UNIONS UNDER ATTACK: 1800 TO 1825

During the first quarter of the nineteenth century the notorious Combination Laws were in force. Passed in 1799 and modified in 1800, they have been traditionally represented as the most outstanding example of the repression by the law of the right of working people to combine in their own defence:

> The employers' law was to be the public law. Workmen were to obey their master as they would obey the state, and the state was to enforce the master's commands as it would its own . . . These acts . . . prohibiting all common action in defence of their common interests by workmen, remain the most unqualified surrender of the State to the discretion of a class in the history of England.

So wrote the Hammonds, and concluded that for a quarter of a century 'the workpeople were at the mercy of their masters'.[25] There is now among historians a much more qualified assessment of the effectiveness of the Acts, if not of the intentions of those who secured their passage through Parliament. They were not simply an attempt by an authoritarian government to deal with a *new* threat of trade unionism, although they were clearly intended to provide a speedy and effective remedy against what was perceived as a spreading menace, which under the influence of the French Revolution was seen to be acquiring a political as well as an industrial dimension. The Webbs were correct to see their passing as taking place 'under the shadow of the French Revolution and fear of working class conspiracies' even if they were not correct in seeing them as a 'far reaching change of policy'.[26]

Those who framed the legislation were well aware that in a large number of artisan trades, unionism was not a new, but a well-entrenched presence. Taken together with the repeal of the apprenticeship clauses of V Elizabeth in 1814, the Combination Laws were part of an attack on an existing and effective trade unionism in skilled trades as well as an attempt to stop the habit of association reaching the larger working population. The story is well known of how William Wilberforce, with the encouragement of William Pitt, turned what had been a petition for a Combination Act specific to the millwrights into a general prohibition against 'combinations of all workmen'. Such an Act was bound to assist those employers in trades like engineering who were seeking to break down the defences of skilled men which, as Marx so clearly saw, constrained capitalism's freedom of action in the 'period of manufacture'.[27]

The rapidity with which the Acts were passed seems to have taken workers' organisations by surprise and precluded effective action. Being entirely one-sided, they did not even pretend to sanction combinations of employers in the same way as they did those of workers – even had the former been proceeded against, they did not face imprisonment – they have been fairly described as 'odious class legislation'. So one-sided were they that one cotton weaver on trial could not believe that he was being prosecuted in the name of the King: 'We were told that the King was prosecutor, which is in my opinion, a libel on the King.'[28] It is difficult to judge their effectiveness since the bulk of the evidence on their operation was taken before a select committee and organised through the energies of Francis Place who, seeking their repeal, emphasised that they were not only ineffective, but actually encouraged the forming of workers' combinations and intensified hostility between masters and men. What seems to emerge is a picture of small impact on the well-established organisations of skilled artisans, but a considerably greater one on the attempts to combine by workers in the north and Midlands, the areas of most rapid technological change and most extensive outwork.

In respect of the first group the clerk to the investigating committee of 1824 remarked that the Acts had been 'in general a dead letter upon those artisans upon whom *it was intended to have an effect;* namely the shoemakers, printers, papermakers, ship-builders, tailors, etc., who have had their regular societies and houses of call, as though no such act was in existence'.[29] The historian of the printing workers has commented on the apparent lack of conflict with the law in that trade despite a spreading organisation in London and in the provinces. As well as printers, coopers, shipwrights, hatters, carpenters, sawyers and tailors were among those who had long-lasting and sometimes successful strikes during the years the Acts were in operation. Dr Prothero, the most recent historian of the London artisans during this period, sees them as emerging from the French War years more strongly organised than they had been before, and notices by 1814 in London and among artisans elsewhere a 'new trade union consciousness' linking wages to organisational power. This consciousness was evident in the forging of links both between trade societies in the same craft, as tramping led to confederation, and with other trades for financial assistance in times of difficulty or dispute. Between 1807 and 1811 the iron workers, lock founders, cutlers, papermakers, gold-beaters, pipemakers, cork cutters and brushmakers all received aid from the bookbinders, while the gold-beaters lent aid between 1810 and 1811 to the brushmakers, frizners, silversmiths, pipemakers, leather grounders, tin plate workers, rope-makers, saddlers and mill-wrights. They received aid from the scale-beam makers and musical instrument makers. It has been estimated that whereas in 1800 there was some kind of inter-town contact in seventeen trades, by the mid-1820s it existed in at least twenty-eight. These intra-trade networks could be extensive. The steam engine makers had thirty-seven branches, the mechanics twenty, the shoemakers between seventy and eighty and the papermakers several 'divisions'. It was also in this period too that the first trade union periodical publications appeared in London.[30]

Just how well organised the London tailors were has been described by a provincial journeyman who came to work in the city in 1811 and was swept into their strike of 1812:

> As soon as I was settled in a regular seat of work, it became necessary that I should join the trade or shop meeting, which is a combination for the support of wages. With this end in view, each member pays a certain amount monthly, in order to raise a fund for the support of families when a strike takes place, whether in one shop or more as the case may be, the men being at the same time furnished with 'tramping money' to enable them to go into the country until the dispute betwixt employer and employed is for the time adjusted.

Here was a union of artisans acting in much the same manner as it had done before 1800 and as it would do after 1824. When the strike came in 1812, money was borrowed from other trades, including the carpenters, and meetings at the 'houses of call' were addressed by the 'great orators of the craft'.[31]

There is not space to outline the similar instances of strike action during these years which could be introduced from other crafts and, while it is true that in many of the London trades employers were able to use the fall in food prices in 1816 to bring about a reduction in wages, levels were better maintained than they were in the provinces. There seems much justice for the satisfaction with which London's trade unionists in 1812 boasted to a visitor from the Midlands whose attempts to organise framework knitters effectively were presenting problems of a very different order:

> What would our trade be, if we did not combine together? Perhaps as poor as you are, at this day! Look at other Trades! They all Combine, (the Spitalfields weavers excepted, and what a Miserable Condition are they in). See the Tailors, Shoemakers, Bookbinders, Gold beaters, Printers, Coatmakers, Hatters, Curriers, Masons, Whitesmiths, none of these trades Receive less than 30s. [£1.50] a week, and from that to *five* guineas [£5.25] this is all done by Combination, without it their Trades would be as bad as yours . . .[32]

There is ample evidence of open negotiation over prices between masters and the representatives of organised labour in a number of trades. But there is a qualification to be made to the picture of successful organisation persisting among skilled workers through these years. As we have remarked and will describe below, the artisans lost their struggle to prevent the ending of statutory apprenticeship in 1814, and this accentuated a tendency already at work in a number of trades. The hold of the organised skilled men was becoming confined to a shrinking 'bespoke' end, while unorganised pieceworkers swelled the 'sweated' ranks supplying the ready-made sectors. In such a context, exclusion of many, including women, was an essential part of the skilled man's attempt to protect his status and security, as the Webbs remarked: 'The failure of the Combination Laws to suppress the somewhat dictatorial Trade Unionism of the skilled handicrafts-men and their efficacy in preventing the growth of permanent unions among other sections of the workers, is explained by class distinctions.' More recently an historian has concluded that although the period was a 'dark' one for the skilled worker, it was not a 'blank' one, rather a period of 'chrysalis'. [33]

Although the London bookbinders' union took care not to have its rules *printed* until 1828 and the Loyal Albion Lodge of the button burnishers of Birmingham when it formed in 1810 was careful to present itself as a sick and burial club, 'our only legal hold in those days, but our principal object was to keep up wages', most of the traditions of secret meetings, awesome oaths, concealed records and initiation ceremonies (which the Webbs described as the 'romantic legend') come from the newer industrial areas not from the old artisan trades. One pioneer of the ironfounders was to recall almost sixty years later the founding of the union in 1809 when holes had been dug in the floor to hide books and meetings held on the open moor. This secret unionism has been given especial significance in the writings of Edward Thompson and John Foster. Thompson sees the Combination Acts as forcing trade unions into association with the jacobin re-publican movement, a result their passing had been intended to prevent. According to Foster they served merely to 'clinch the indus-trial control of those who were themselves outlaws, the working-class radicals' in south-west Lancashire where the republicans were reported to have been drinking Mr Pitt's health.

The Acts were as much motivated by hostility as by practicality and symbolised repression more than they enabled it. Nevertheless, most historians accept that attempts to defend their interests by the out-workers of the Midlands and north, the weavers in cotton and in wool and the stockingers met with a much larger degree of hostility from masters and from magistrates than did those of the urban artisans. The first group of factory workers to organise, the cotton spinners, also met with intimidation and deterrence from the law. The actual incidence of prosecutions under the Act of 1800 was low. Foster has pointed out that in Lancashire, excluding Wigan and Liverpool, five years of trade union activity between 1818 and 1822 produced only seven convictions at quarter sessions but, like Thompson, he insists on their general prohibitive influence. Prosecutions may have continued under the older Acts pre-dating 1800, for conspiracy or for leaving work un-finished (V Elizabeth), but to the oppressed workers they were all grouped under the generic 'the laws against combination'. The threat of action under the Act of 1800 was no less potent because the addi-tional opportunities, as Henson complained, were favoured by masters 'to harass and keep down the wages of their work people'. He regarded the existence of the Combination Act as 'a tremendous millstone round the neck of the local artisan, which has depressed and debased him to the earth, every act which he has attempted every measure that he has devised to keep up or raise his wages, he has been told was illegal: the whole force of the civil power and influence of the district has been exerted against him because he was acting illegally'. He complained that the employers would let the framework knitters 'run till they have expended their last farthing' and, when their funds had been exhausted and they had become desperate, prosecute them. Witnesses, several of whom had been themselves prosecuted, spoke feelingly of the dread of the Combination Laws in the East Midlands and how they had been used to cower the knitters into defeat, at a time when wages had sunk to the level of 7s. (35p) a week.[34]

Although cotton spinners can be regarded as the first group of factory workers to organise, they hardly represent a precocious new development, for in most respects other than in their working environment they resembled craft workers and their unionism was much in the traditional style of skilled workers. Above all they were concerned to protect their position as better-paid workers and maintain an effective control over entry to their trade. Where they did differ was in their concentrated numbers, which may explain why their disputes seemed more threatening than did those of scattered rural weavers. The use of the Combination Laws against them both reflects the anxieties of local and national authority and the presumed high level of political consciousness in Lancashire in the Peterloo years. Unions of mule spinners had formed from the early days of the mill era. A friendly society at Stockport in 1785 was already instructing its members not to work below price and seems to have had a continuous existence down to 1802 when imprisonments under the Combination Laws broke it. Manchester spinners conducted two strikes over wages in 1795, the second of which was successful and displayed in a printed address the quality of its leaders. High entry fees in the early nineteenth century reveal the elite nature of spinners' unions. A strike of 1810 centred on Preston and Stalybridge displayed a high level of organisation in that those who turned out to bring country wages up to Manchester levels were supported by those in work. The employers responded with a lock-out and around 10,000 workers were idle for three to four months, including the large numbers of child and women workers dependent on the spinners. The struggle exhausted the union's funds, as the lock-out intended, and the men had to return on the old terms but, in a foretaste of what was to happen in the better-known strike of 1818, the law was used in the later stages of an already doomed dispute to dishearten the spinners and disrupt their leadership.[35]

In 1818 there were four separate strikes among cotton workers: jenny spinners at Stockport; power-loom weavers in the same town; mule spinners at Manchester; and a widespread strike by handloom weavers. The jenny spinners were an isolated group whose action brought no prosecutions, but the law was used against the power-loom weavers who were engaged in their first dispute. The handloom weavers' strike will be discussed below, but the mule spinners' strike of 1818 was one of the major confrontations of the period of the Combination Laws. It began in Manchester in July and 20,000 persons were idle around the 2,000 actual spinners. It was a strike over wages. In common with many other groups of workers, the spinners had in 1816 a year of low food prices and slack trade accepted a wage reduction. The exact extent is disputed: the employers claimed that wages at the time of the strike averaged 30s. (£1.50), while the spinners claimed an average of 24s. (£1.20) reduced in 1816 to 18s. (90p). By 1818, food prices were no longer low and, with trade somewhat more brisk, the spinners expected a restoration of pre-1816 rates as, they claimed, they had been promised. The employers retorted by suggesting that as a group of workers who had had, unlike others, 'constant and uniform employment for the last 28 years', the spinners should count their blessings, and as they did not fully share the risks of capital, why should they expect to immediately participate in its gains? The spinners' organisation was based on delegate meetings, and the distribution of funds and deployment of 'piquets' by an elected twelve-man executive. Contributions to the strike fund were received not only from other cotton towns, but also from other Manchester trades and further afield from, for example, Staffordshire's potters and London's shoemakers. Through its early weeks, good order was preserved as the dispute spread to other cotton towns. To some in authority the very demonstration of disciplined good order was itself a cause for concern. There were a few threats of prosecution but, in general, as in the early stages of 1810, the employers' main reaction was to sit tight while the strike funds were exhausted. Inevitably, with strike pay by then down to 9d. (4p) a week, discipline began to break in late August. It was then that the authorities moved to hasten the disarray by making arrests on conspiracy and similar charges. By early September with the drying up of funds, increasing violence and the arrest of the committee, the strike was over. Men returned not only to the old rates but, in many cases, to sign a document eschewing any further involvement with trade unionism. Around 250 of the most active were blacklisted. There is no doubt the employers would have won without resorting to the law, but it is undeniable that they used it to hasten the end, victimise the leaders and deter a revival of unionism. Later leaders, like John Doherty, himself one of those imprisoned, believed the collapse postponed further strike action for a number of years although, encouraged by a trade revival, Bolton's spinners in 1822 secured a temporary advance.[36]

The handloom weavers were in a different and more difficult position. With the greater availability of mill-spun yarn their trade, entry to which was insufficiently protected by a barrier of skill, had become progressively overstocked and faced low-wage competition from peasant weavers on the continent well before the advent of power weaving. Much has been made of their lack of skill, but their responses and rhetoric illustrate that at least at the core of the trade there remained men clinging to the perceptions of the artisan. Indeed, on the eve of their strike of 1818 they appropriated that very label, describing themselves as 'an immense body of useful artisans', yet the condition implied in the first part of that description denied ultimately the maintenance of the status appropriate to the second part. Around the turn of the century their 'golden age' ended and a long wage decline set in with gathering pace. It has been argued that, even if the millwrights presented the occasion, it was with the immense numbers of handloom weavers in mind that the Combination Acts were passed. Through 1800 and 1801 the weavers sought a state regulation of wages to halt their fall. Instead they got the Arbitration Act which allowed the submission of disputed prices to the decision of local magistrates. It was an Act of limited value and easy for employers to evade. In 1801, a year of very high food prices and of widespread fears of jacobinism, the weavers began to organise for its amendment and found themselves tarred with the brush of revolution: 'This application [to Parliament] . . . certainly originates in the Jacobin Societies and is intended as a means to keep the minds of the weavers in a continual ferment, and as a pretext to raise money from them which will probably be employed in part at least, to seditious purposes.' A minor amendment to the Arbitration Act passed in 1803 changed little and, in 1805, with the assistance of some sympathetic employers who resented the price-cutting of some of their competitors, the weavers commenced a campaign for a minimum wage. Despite this support, which included one employer with an annual wage bill of £40,000, magistrate Fletcher of Bolton still blamed the politically disaffected and employed spies to infiltrate the weavers' meetings. Despite a monster petition, Parliament rejected the minimum wage bill in 1808 which provoked serious rioting, and more positively a strike for an increase of a third in wages. The strike, with the weavers enforcing solidarity by removing shuttles from looms, spread out from Manchester to Stockport, Rochdale, Wigan and beyond. By June, 60,000 looms were idle and the embattled and embittered weavers determined enough to refuse a compromise offer of 20% advance. The outcome is uncertain: no record of the terms upon which they returned to work exists, seemingly they won their rise, but for a very short period before 'it all tumbled to ruins again'. Although only light sentences were pressed for when cases arising out of the dispute were brought at Lancaster assizes, wage reductions were again in process by 1810. The weavers attempted to persuade the employers to keep the old rates and instead reduce the amount of work given out. By enduring a period of privation they hoped the market would recover without painfully won wage increases being forgone. They well knew how very difficult it would be to secure their restoration once cut. Despite this eminently reasonable position their manifesto sufficiently alarmed the Blackburn magistrates into requesting troops. Petitions presented to Parliament in 1811, though couched in terms of a general petition for relief, implied the revival of the old search for a minimum wage. Nothing was forthcoming and the period of petitioning Parliament came to an end. In a dignified pamphlet, weavers recorded their disillusionment: 'We are only mechanics of course, ill acquainted with the reason why the same measures are frequently opposed, at one time, by the same arguments by which at other times they are vindicated and supported . . .' They instanced the areas in which government had interfered: over bread prices; in fixing the wages of the Spitalfields' weavers and those of the London tailors; in augmenting the salaries of judges and clergymen; and in their own case were 'utterly at a loss to conceive on what fair ground legislative interference can be improper under circumstances so necessitous'. In concluding that the House of Commons was 'unfit to manage' industrial despair was linked to the growth of the reform movement in Lancashire in the build-up to Peterloo.[37]

There was a localised strike at Bolton in 1812 to secure wage fixing by magistrates, but in the following year Parliament itself ended all hope of wage regulation by repealing the clauses of V Elizabeth upon which it had been based. The spirits of the petitioners, according to the weavers of Bolton, had been sunk 'beyond description, having no hope left'.[38]

Through 1813 and 1814, relative prosperity dulled protest by temporarily restoring wages to something like old levels. But the end of war in 1815 brought not the anticipated return of prosperity, but an overstocking discharge of soldiers and sailors. By 1818 the widely scattered and hard-to-organise weavers were being praised for their patience in bearing what all agreed was extreme deprivation. Before the year ended their patience broke. Manifestos appeared drawing attention to their desperate situation, and in July a delegate meeting of weavers from all over Lancashire was held at Bury and issued an address to the employers:

> It is from a gulph that absorbs all the faculties of body and mind we address you, supposing you capable of ameliorating the sufferings of an immense body of useful artisans; in this you must admit that we have suspended our exertions in calling upon you, until our vitals are affected, proved by indications in our visage of an untimely approach to nature's messenger.

They wondered why people could not secure the essentials of life in a nation with 'unexampled industry' and commerce. Adam Smith was quoted on the need for a man's wages to support a wife and three children: 'Good God but how they must exist on SIX SHILLINGS per week' (30p), and asked for an advance of 7s. (35p) in the pound: 'within the boundaries of moderation, as several other branches of the trade have called for a greater advance than the whole of our income'.[39]

Some employers gave the advance, more agreed to do so if all the others would. In August it was decided to withdraw labour from those employers who refused. At Bolton, 4,000 to 5,000 were idle. Thousands came in from the country districts to seek the advance, and despite orderly behaviour still met with the disapproval of the authorities: 'It consolidates their power as a body and points out to them a system of co-operation which in future occasions if not in the present may occasion the almost destruction of our commerce.' In the early days of September the weavers marched with banners in the cotton towns, while the authorities responded by banning public meetings. On the 5th in a change of tactics it was agreed to seek the advance in two stages of 4s. (20p) on 7 September and 3s. (15p) on 1 October. Facing tremendous problems of supporting those who were idle, the weavers resorted to billeting them on to those in work and appealing for public support. The Manchester magistrates immediately responded by issuing a notice that subscriptions were illegal under the Combination Laws and three weavers, the president and two secretaries, were committed for conspiracy on 16 September. It was a decisive blow and although small advances were granted for a time, reductions were again the order of the day and had become general by 1819. In February of that year the arrested leaders received two sentences of two years and one of a year. The strike of 1818 was the last desperate throw of the cotton handloom weavers, although some, motivated as much by their hatred of the Combination Laws as anything else, threw themselves into the Reform agitation.[40]

We have dealt at some length upon the trade unionism of cotton spinners and handloom weavers during this period to emphasise the very different situations in which the two groups of workers found themselves. But both the new factory workers and the desperate declining handloom weavers met with the implementation of the Combination Laws used, it seems, with some sense of timing and strategy by employers and their magistrates. Lancashire was arguably the most significant of English manufacturing counties. The tendency of modern historians to play down the effect of the Combination Laws as of little practical consequence gains small support from there.

WOOLLEN AND WORSTED WORKERS

In both the north and in the west, workers in the woollen industry had their confrontations with employers during the period of the Combination Laws. In part, especially in the west, these were connected with the campaign over apprenticeship and will be discussed below. By 1830, spinning of wool had joined that of cotton as a factory operation conducted by male operatives with a larger number of child and female assistants. They seem to have been less involved in industrial disputes than their equivalents in cotton, but did organise to some extent. A union was established at Dewsbury in 1822 which embraced both spinners and weavers in the object of 'equalising wages'. In Leeds in 1819 a strike, again by both groups, had failed after six months to prevent reductions. In the West Country, weavers at Frome struck in 1822/3 demanding the old rates despite the introduction of the spring shuttle. They were unsuccessful, eighteen were gaoled and the rest starved into submission. The structure of the Yorkshire industry built around the small clothiers did not lead as readily to strikes, but there is evidence of a degree of organisation.[41]

The most bitter struggles were those waged by the shearmen and croppers against deskilling machinery in which an exchange of correspondence was kept up between the West Country and the West Riding. That struggle is part of the great Luddite agitation of Regency England and will be examined separately below, but here we must note that during the protest against shearing frames in Wiltshire in 1801–2 the law was used to break the workers' organisations both in the form of conspiracy proceedings and in that of the Combination Act: 'I am bringing forward as many cases as I can under the Combination Act and by forcing some to give evidence against others, I hope to provoke some quarrels amongst them.' Two or more justices were meeting regularly at one or other of the clothing towns and 'as the Combination Act affords a very convenient pretext for summoning and examining upon oath any suspected person, I have continually some before them. It answers the double purpose of keeping the magistrates at their post and of alarming the disaffected, we have six in confinement for offences against the Act and three for refusing to give testimony.' Clearly in the western clothing districts the magistrates were not to know that Dorothy George would one day declare the Combination Acts of little significance.[42]

In Yorkshire the shearmen were more generally known as 'croppers' and those working for Benjamin Gott struck in 1802 against his taking on irregular apprentices. As the strike spread, Gott bitterly complained of the croppers: 'Their power and influence has grown out of their high wages, which enable them to make deposits, that puts them beyond all fear of inconvenience from misconduct.' The croppers held out and the masters gave in. Here, outside of the craft trades, was a union of skilled men again acting as if the Combination Acts had not been passed, and presenting an example of a 'system of combination' to other trades who might follow suit and raise their wages.[43]

Following the petitioning of the West Country shearmen with the support of their Yorkshire fellows, the parliamentary committee which met to consider the various laws regulating the woollen trade reported in 1806 on the side of *laissez-faire* by suspending them. The hope that Parliament might limit the spread of the shearing frames by enforcing old statutes was now gone. The frames came into general use in the west and were then introduced into Yorkshire where they were resisted, in 1812, in the name of 'General Ludd'. Further refinements in 1820 meant that boys could in shearing replace even the decreased number of men necessary. A prophecy which the Lord Lieutenant of Yorkshire had made in 1802 had come about: machinery would defeat the hold of the united shearmen for with its introduction 'their consequence would be lost, their banks [fund] would waste, their combinations would fall to the ground'.[44]

Within the worsted branches the combers, the men who prepared the long staple wools before it could be spun, were a well-organised skilled group occupying a strategic location in the manufacturing process. They kept up their wages and their independence until threatened by machinery. Cartwright's 'Big Ben' was slowly introduced after its invention in 1790, although by 1793 a meeting of combers had already been called at Cullompton in the Devonshire serge district to discuss resistance to the perceived threat and seek parliamentary protection from its introduction. Although these hopes came to nothing, the machine seems to have made only slow progress until after the great strike of the Bradford combers in 1825. While the Combination Acts were in force, the combers seem to have maintained a strong position through effective combination. In 1812 they were even proposing a national congress to be held at Coventry. The law officers in this case seemed less confident: 'These combinations are mischievous and dangerous, but it is very difficult to know how to deal with them.'[45]

TRADE UNIONS, MACHINERY AND THE REPEAL OF APPRENTICESHIP

Of all the events which took place while the Combination Laws were in force, none was more threatening to the effectiveness of skilled worker trade unionism than the repeal in 1814 of the statutory requirement for a seven-year apprenticeship before a skilled craft could be exercised. Adam Smith, as we have noted, was strongly opposed to apprenticeship which, by restricting entry to the skilled trades, could mean combinations of artisans 'reducing the whole manufacture into a sort of slavery to themselves' and raising their wages 'much above what is due to the nature of their work'.[46] If the Act of 1563 (V Elizabeth) had fallen largely into disuetude and had had its effectiveness limited by a series of case law modifications, why did it emerge in the early nine-teenth century as a contested issue between capitalist employers and organised craft labour? The short answer is that the repeal of 1814 came in response to a renewed interest in apprenticeship on the part of skilled workers which amounted to an attempt to revive and even extend the statutory insistence on the institution: the employers silenced a barking dog which they had thought asleep. It was in London that the contest was to climax, but in the provinces that the issue first pushed itself to the forefront of labour consciousness. In the western clothing districts, as we have seen, labour troubles charac-terised the turn of the century. The well-being of both weavers and shearmen was threatened by innovation. The former were resisting the attempts of some entrepreneurs to introduce weaving shops in which grouped looms would remove the work from the home. The weavers hoped that a rigid enforcement of seven-year apprenticeship would prevent the securing of cheap labour for these shops. They employed a lawyer, Jessop, to serve notices of intended prosecution on 'illegal' weavers. The shearmen also hoped that an enforcement of appren-ticeship would prevent the clothiers from working shearing frames with cheap labour and, after an initial period of machine-breaking, fought a legal campaign against infringements of V Elizabeth. But an extremely lengthy parliamentary investigation responded to the clothiers' counter-campaign for the removal of apprenticeship restric-tions by successfully recommending the annual suspension of the apprenticeship regulations in the woollen manufacture before finally abolishing apprenticeship in that industry in 1809, five years before the repeal of statutory apprenticeship became general.[47]

In Lancashire the calico printers were suffering severe unem-ployment as a result of the taking on of large numbers of outdoor apprentices as cheap labour. This trade was too new to have been included in V Elizabeth and the skilled printers were seeking to per-suade Parliament to extend statutory regulation of apprenticeship to them. Well-organised and fiercely status-conscious artisans, they had, before the introduction of roller printing, managed to operate a closed shop through a tight organisation and a carefully built up strike fund. Because of union success in refusing to work with illegal men, the employers had turned both to machinery and to the use of so-called apprentices. Although a parliamentary report found much to sym-pathise with in a trade where one master had fifty-five apprentices to only two fully trained journeymen, it was not prepared to suggest interference beyond hoping that the old 'custom' of two apprentices to a master should be established.[48]

The third area of provincial labour agitation to which the issue of apprenticeship was central was the frame-knitting district of the East Midlands where the outbreak of machine-wrecking in 1811–12 has given the word 'Luddism' to the language. In fact, dislike of machinery *per se* was not an issue in the region. It was the use of unskilled labour to produce inferior products which stirred up the protest and, as with woollen workers and calico printers, petitioning for a parliamentary regulation of the trade preceded the outbreaks of frame destruction.[49]

These three examples serve to show the close connection between apprenticeship agitation and the introduction of machinery in the provinces, but in London the machinery connection was less involved. Here what threatened was the tendency of masters in the craft and building trades to employ at lower wages men who had not served legal apprenticeships and who were accordingly not members of the skilled unions. A combination of London's trades employed the services of a lawyer who from 1809 inaugurated a series of prosecutions against 'illegal' workmen or persons who employed them. There is no direct evidence as to who was actually employing him, but the fact that he brought nineteen cases in three years covering thirteen trades suggested that combined action of the skilled unions was behind the campaign. Even where prosecution was successful, sentences were so light that the artisans began to campaign to have the relevant clauses of V Elizabeth restated and extended. To this end they formed a body calling itself the 'mechanics of the metropolis':

> to devise such measures as may secure the regular bred artisans in future the exclusive enjoyment of the trade he has been brought up to . . . which we consider is our exclusive privilege of following, in so much as it is purchased by large premiums, and other incidental expenses, incurred by our friends, and seven years servitude on our part.

There seems to have been a central co-ordinating group of delegates from the various trades meeting under the name of the Artisans General Committee or the United Artisans' Committee. Attempts were made to involve the craftsmen of the provinces and, in addition to sixty-two London trades, contributions to the fund came in from seventy places in the country, while of 32,735 signatures on a national petition, half came from outside London.[50]

The real nature of the conflict soon became evident. The employers attacked V Elizabeth as affording a 'constant and prosperous rallying point to further the measures of the journeymen against their employers'. The journeymen were building up an enormous phalanx, 'greatly superior to the united energies of the masters'. In a lengthy pamphlet propagating their counter-campaign for the repeal of statutory apprenticeship, the masters not only argued for the free labour market, but consciously sought to break the unionism of skilled workers:

> The mischief . . . is the colour it gives to the combination of workmen for the raising of wages, and the prevention of improvement [i.e. introduction of new machines]. Under the influence of the pretended privileges given by this act, many masters are not permitted to hire their own workmen. No, the

'Shop Committee' must be applied to. They must be assured that all is right – that every workman has, as they pretend, been 'legally apprenticed', that is, in fact, that he belongs to the 'Club'. For they make a distinction if he leagues with them. They choose too what articles shall be made, and impose large fines on whoever disobeys their laws. They fine men also that work for masters who conduct their business in a manner not approved by them.[51]

The fear was echoed elsewhere. Master fellmongers complained that if only 'legal' men could be taken on and then were to combine together, their demands be 'ever so exorbitant', the masters would have to comply. Master printers expressed the view that V Elizabeth was an 'enabling statute' under which unionised compositors could state their own terms. Ten years after the employers saw their counter-case for repeal triumph unsurprisingly in a Parliament as ideologically dominated by *laissez-faire* economic orthodoxy as ever a Parliament has been ideologically dominated, an engineering employer looked back with satisfaction:

> combinations were much more frequent than they are now, and while that law was in existence, every trade was subject to its most mischievous provisions; but after its repeal, when a man was allowed to work at any employment . . . that broke the neck of all combinations, because then the excluding party were so overwhelmed by new men that we could do without them.[52]

In fact, the effect was mixed. Where skill still cornered a vital stage in production and where well-organised artisans could enforce it by their own collective actions, then apprenticeship and with it the closed shop survived. In other trades, less well protected, the repeal of statutory apprenticeship removed the last vestige of legal protection against the employment of the unskilled tide which threatened to engulf them. By 1818, skilled Coventry silk-weavers could only find half-time work as employers resorted to cheap labour, and a parliamentary committee investigating their distress was forced to the conclusion: 'whilst the statute of V Elizabeth was in force . . . the distressing circumstances now complained of, never occurred'.[53]

We have noted that the issue of apprenticeship and that of deskilling machinery were very much bound up in some trades. An element in the great machinery debate of the early nineteenth century, not always as stressed as it should be, is the resort to machinery as a means of breaking the hold of unions able to exploit an essential manual skill. Examples of this can be presented other than those of calico printing machinery, shearing frames and combing machines which have already been mentioned. Andrew Ure in his defence of the factory system of 1835 was emphatic on the significance of machinery in this respect. Indeed, he stressed this aspect more than the more apparent one of increasing productivity: 'The more skilful the workman, the more self-willed and intractable he is apt to become, and . . . the less fit a component of a mechanical system.' In the context of cotton manufacture, he argued that the self-acting mule had been invented to break the power of the adult mule spinners:

> Thus the Iron Man, as the operatives fitly call it, sprung out of the hands of our modern Prometheus at the bidding of Minerva – a creation destined to restore order among the industrious classes, and to confirm to Great Britain the empire of art. The news of this Herculean prodigy spread dismay through the Union, and even before it left its cradle . . . it strangled the Hydra of misrule.[54]

It does seem that the strength of the spinners' unions even during the period of the operation of the Combination Laws was crucial to the speeding up of a search for a self-acting mule which had been going on for some time from 'the enthusiasm of inventive minds'. A modern historian has suggested that 'operative militancy' convinced the group of Manchester owners who approached the engineer Richard Roberts to attack the problem as urgent, and points to the perception too often missed by historians of technology or Ure's maxim: 'The very name of union makes capital restive and puts ingenuity on the alert to defeat its objects.'[55]

That the self-acting mule did not fully achieve this object needs explanation. Despite its invention, the operative spinner retained his skilled status. In part, the explanation was technological as occasional processes of adjustment in resetting and trimming made it impossible to do without the adult supervisory role of the male spinner. Foster has argued that his retention was necessary as a 'pace-setter' for the work group. Nevertheless, something of the employers' objectives was achieved. The physical workload was much lighter and the self-actor could carry significantly more spindles than the manually controlled mule. The price of the spinner's retention of his special status was the acceptance of a greater number of spindles and a higher operating speed.[56]

The engineering industry, too, illustrates the importance of breaking the hold of skilled workers for the pace of technical improvement. Ure reported that one manufacturer of cotton machinery had so thoroughly departed from traditional routines that 'he will employ no man who has learned his craft by regular apprenticeship, but in contempt as it were of the division of labour principle, he sets a plough boy to turn a shaft'. Another employer had apparently postponed making steam engines for the time being as machinery in that branch was not yet available for a movement away from 'the old principle of the division of labour, so fruitful of jealousies and strikes among workmen'.[57]

By 1825, after a quarter of a century's existence under the Combination Laws, unions of skilled artisans would seem, perhaps with the adoption of a lower profile, to have been as capable of defending a labour interest against employers as they had, in many instances, been in the eighteenth century. Marx's insistence on the not inconsiderable ability of *skilled men* to oppose capitalist employers in defence of traditional levels of remuneration, matters of recruitment and customary working practices in the period before the 'industrial revolution' has been vindicated by recent research. Historians sometimes produce findings in proportion to the extent of their searching. Dobson's counting of industrial disputes in the eighteenth century underpins his identification of a 'system of industrial relations' existing between 'masters and journeymen'. For London between 1717 and 1800 he notes 119 labour disputes, whereas Professor Rudé in his pioneering studies of twenty years ago suggested twenty! Nor were journeymen disputes confined to England. Rudé suggested twelve for Paris in the eighteenth century while Sonenscher has since counted 200. German research is even more recent, but a total of 259 disputes in seven cities 1780–1805 has been produced.[58]

On the continent the ability of skilled men depended upon guild or guild-like restriction of entry. In England preserving apprenticeship limitation owed something at least to the legitimating basis provided by the Statute of Artificers. That is why the repeal of 1814 was of more significance for the trade unionism of artisans than were the Combination Acts. However, before 1825 trade unionism showed very few signs of crossing the frontier of skill between the artisan and the larger labour force: we have noted that the cotton spinners were a special case. In so far as the Combination Acts were part of a situation impropitious for the *spread* of trade unionism, then they may have gone at least some way towards meeting the hopes of those who secured their passing.

REFERENCES AND NOTES

1. **Marx**, *Capital*, Everyman edn, I, p. 389.
2. **J. T. Ward** and **W. Hamish Fraser** (eds), *Workers and Employers. Documents on Trade Unions and Industrial Relations in Britain since the Eighteenth Century*, Macmillan, 1980, Doc. no. 9; **L. Brentano**, *On the History and Development of Gilds and the Original Trade Unions*, 1871, p. 104.
3. **Adam Smith**, *The Wealth of Nations*, 1776, ed. E. Cannan, 1904, pbk. edn. 1961, I, pp. 74–5 and see the discussion in **J. Rule**, *The Experience of Labour in Eighteenth-Century Industry*, Croom Helm, 1981, Ch. 6.
4. **C. R. Dobson**, *Masters and Journeymen. A Pre-History of Industrial Relations 1717–1800*, Croom Helm, 1980, pp. 22, 26; Rule, *Experience of Labour*, pp. 149–51; **S.** and **B. Webb**, *The History of Trade Unionism*, Longman, 1911, pp. 1–2.
5. Rule, *Experience of Labour*, p. 151.

6. Ibid., pp. 152–6; Dobson, *Masters and Journeymen*, pp. 39–40, 60, 69–73; see also **F. W. Galton**, *Select Documents Illustrating the History of Trade Unionism: The Tailoring Trade*, 1896, pp. 5–6, 7, 13, 37–9, 47–9, 71–3; *Select Committee on Artisans and Machinery, Second Report*, BPP, 1824, V, p. 45.

7. For hatters, see Rule, *Experience of Labour*, pp. 156–8 and the sources cited therein.

8. For unionism in the south-west and West Country wool districts, see Rule, *Experience of Labour*, pp. 159–64; **W. E. Minchinton**, 'The beginnings of trade unionism in the Gloucestershire woollen industry', *Transactions of the Bristol and Gloucestershire Archaeological Society*, lxx, 1951, pp. 126–41 and the same author's 'The petitions of the weavers and clothiers of Gloucestershire in 1756', ibid., lxxiii, 1954, pp. 218–25.

9. Smith, *Wealth of Nations*, I, p. 141.

10. Rule, *Experience of Labour*, pp. 164–5; **E. J. Hobsbawm**, 'The tramping artisan', in *Labouring Men*, Weidenfeld & Nicolson, 1964, pp. 35, 28, 39–40. The fullest account of the system is **R. A. Leeson**, *Travelling Brothers*, Allen & Unwin, 1979.

11. Rule, *Experience of Labour*, pp. 166–8; and see the relevant pages of **A. P. Wadsworth** and **J. de L. Mann**, *The Cotton Trade and Industrial Lancashire 1600–1780*, Manchester U.P., 1931 and of **H. A. Turner**, *Trade Union Growth, Structure and Policy. A Comparative Study of the Cotton Unions*, Allen & Unwin, 1966.

12. Smith, *Wealth of Nations*, I, pp. 74–7, discussed in Rule, *Experience of Labour*, Ch. 7.

13. Galton, *Tailoring Trade*, p. 81; **G. D. H. Cole** and **A. W. Filson**, *British Working Class Movements: Selected Documents*, Macmillan pbk., 1965, pp. 88–9; Dobson, *Masters and Journeymen*, p. 127.

14. Rule, *Experience of Labour*, pp. 176–8.

15. Ibid., pp. 173–4.

16. Ibid., pp. 178–83 and sources cited therein.

17. Smith, *Wealth of Nations*, I, pp. 75–6.

18. Rule, *Experience of Labour*, p. 184.

19. Ibid., pp. 184–5; **E. J. Hobsbawm**, 'The machine breakers', in *Labouring Men*, pp. 5–22.

20. See **E. P. Thompson**, 'The crime of anonymity', in **D. Hay, P. Linebaugh** & **E. P. Thompson** (eds), *Albion's Fatal Tree. Crime and Society in Eighteenth-Century England*, Penguin edn, 1977, p. 318.

21. Examples cited in Rule, *Experience of Labour*, p. 186; **J. G. Rule**, 'The labouring miner in Cornwall c.1740–1870: a study in social history', University of Warwick, Ph.D., 1971, p. 190; **P. E. Razzell** and **B. W. Wainwright** (eds), *The Victorian Working Class: Selections from Letters to the Morning Chronicle*, Cass, 1973, p. 308.

22. Hobsbawm, 'Machine breakers', p. 7; Rule, 'Labouring miner', p. 382; examples cited in Rule, *Experience of Labour*, pp. 186–7; **J. L.** and **B. Hammond**, *The Skilled Labourer*, new edn, Longman, 1979, ed. J. G. Rule, p. xxii.

23. Examples cited by Rule, *Experience of Labour*, pp. 197–8.

24. **E. P. Thompson**, 'English trade unionism and other labour movements before 1790', *Bulletin of the Society for the Study of Labour History*, no. 17, 1968, pp. 19–24; **J. R. Kellet**, 'The breakdown of guild and corpora-

tion control over the handicraft and retail trade in London', *Economic History Review*, X, 1958, p. 388; Dobson, *Masters and Journeymen*, pp. 50–3.

25. Hammonds, *Skilled Labourer*, pp. 80, 89.

26. **A. E. Musson**, *British Trade Unions 1800–1875*, Macmillan, 1972, p. 23. The orthodox view that the Combination Laws were neither a new departure nor particularly oppressive in operation is that of **M. D. George**, 'The Combination Laws', *Economic History Review*, vi, 1936.

27. The best account of the passage of the Acts is the introduction to **A. Aspinall** (ed.), *The Early English Trade Unions. Documents from the Home Office Papers in the Public Record Office*, pp. ix–xx, 1949. For Marx's discussion of 'the period of manufacture', see *Capital*, Everyman edn, I. pp. 353–90.

28. *S. C. on Artisans and Machinery*, 5th Report, pp. 356–7.

29. Musson, *British Trade Unions*, p. 24.

30. **A. E. Musson**, *The Typographical Association*, Oxford U.P., 1954, pp. 31–2; **I. Prothero**, *Artisans and Politics in Early Nineteenth-Century London. John Gast and his Times*, Dawson, 1979, pp. 41–3; Leeson, *Travelling Brothers*, p. 111.

31. **N. Mansfield**, 'John Brown a shoemaker in Place's London', *History Workshop*, 8, 1979, pp. 130–1.

32. Quoted in **E. P. Thompson**, *The Making of the English Working Class*, Penguin, 1968, pp. 263–4.

33. Webbs, *History of Trade Unionism*, p. 74; Leeson, *Travelling Brothers*, p. 104.

34. **T. J. Dunning**, 'Some account of the London Consolidated Society of Bookbinders', in *Trades' Societies and Strikes*, National Association for the Promotion of Social Science, 1860, repr. Kelley, 1968, p. 98; **C. Behagg**, 'Custom, class and change: the trade societies of Birmingham', *Social History*, vol. 4, no. 3, 1979, p. 460; Webbs, *History of Trade Unionism*, p. 57; **P. S. Bagwell**, *Industrial Relations*, Irish U. P., 1974, p. 10; Thompson, *Making of the English Working Class*, p. 546; **J. Foster**, *Class Struggle and the Industrial Revolution. Earls industrial capitalism in three English towns*, Unwin, 1977, pp. 38, 49–50; Thompson, *Making of the English Working Class*, pp. 551–62; *S.C. on Artisans and Machinery*, 5th Report, pp. 269–74, 265.

35. **A. E. Musson** and **R. G. Kirby**, *The Voice of the People. John Doherty, 1798–1854. Trade Unionist, radical and factory reformer*, Manchester U. P., 1975, p. 13; Hammonds, *Skilled Labourer*, pp. 70–1.

36. Ibid., p. 78; Musson and Kirby, pp. 18–19. The account of strikes in the cotton districts is based on these two works.

37. Hammonds, *Skilled Labourer*, pp. 86, 46, 48, 53–65.

38. Ibid., p. 67.

39. Ibid., pp. 88–9.

40. Ibid., pp. 90–5.

41. Ibid., pp. 124–7.

42. Ibid., pp. 136–40.

43. Ibid., p. 141.

44. Ibid., pp. 147–9.

45. Ibid., pp. 153–7.

46. Smith, *Wealth of Nations*, I, p. 141.

47. For a fuller account of the eighteenth-century background to the apprenticeship issue, see Rule, *Experience of Labour*, Ch. 4. For woollen industry, ibid., pp. 114–15.

48. Ibid., pp. 115–16.

49. Ibid., p. 116.

50. The London-based campaign is described in Rule, *Experience of Labour*, pp. 116–19; Prothero, *Artisans and Politics*, pp. 51–61 and **T. K. Derry**, 'The repeal of the apprenticeship clauses of the Statute of Apprentices', *Economic Histors Review*, iii, 19312, pp. 67–87.

51. *The Origin, Object and Operation of the Apprentice Laws etc*, a pamphlet reprinted in the *Pamphleteer*, III, 1814, pp. 217–42.

52. *Report from Select Committee on the Apprenticeship Laws*, BPP, 1812/13, iv, p. 55; *S.C. on Artisans and Machinery*, 1st Report, p. 27; **J. Child**, *Industrial Relations in the British Printing Industry – The Quest for Security*, Allen & Unwin, 1967, p. 66.

53. *Report of Select Committee on the Silk Ribbon Weavers' Petitions*, BPP, 1818, ix, p. 2.

54. From **M. Berg** (ed.), *Technology and Toil in Nineteenth-Century Britain*, Humanities Press, 1979, pp. 67, 70; **M. Berg**, *The Machinery Question and the Making of Political Economy*, Cambridge U.P., 1980, pp. 200–1.

55. Ibid., p. 200.

56. **H. Catling**, 'The development of the spinning mule', *Textile History*, 9, 1978, pp. 49, 56; Foster, *Class Struggle*, pp. 231–4.

57. Berg, *Technology and Toil*, p. 67.

58. Dobson, *Masters and Journeymen*, p. 22; **G. Rudé**, *Paris and London in the Eighteenth Century*, Fontana, 1970, p. 57; **M. Sonenscher**, 'The sans-culottes of the Year II: rethinking the language of labour in pre-revolutionary France', *Social History*, 9, no. 3, 1984, pp. 312–13; **J. G. Rule**, 'Artisan attitudes: a comparative survey of skilled labour and proletarianisation before 1848', *Bulletin of the Society for the Study of Labour History*, no. 50, 1985.

Chapter 12

THE REPEAL OF THE COMBINATION ACTS AND THE AFTERMATH

Some qualifications have been made of the role of Francis Place in the repeal of the Combination Acts. The reluctance of the skilled unions to give wholehearted support to a man who had not only come to embrace Malthusianism and political economy, but had ten years before actively opposed the campaign over apprenticeship, is understandable. Nevertheless, Place was the main architect of a repeal which not only removed the special sanctions of the Acts, but also allowed protection from prosecution under other statutes and the common law of conspiracy. His campaign was a masterpiece of adroit diplomacy, lobbying and skilled argument. Parliament, already aware that the Acts were ineffective and increasingly accepting that they were unfair, was won over when the growing weight of political economy was thrown into the scale against the Acts. Place, by now a firm supporter of the free labour market, worked closely with economists like Hume and McCulloch, and the *Edinbrough Review* propagated their case. In it the laws were described as 'partial, oppressive and unjust', enforced by magistrates who 'belong to the order of the masters' and imposing differential penalties: imprisonment for men and fines for masters. Violent intimidating combinations had to be punished, but that needed no special law, while voluntary combination was a legitimate and harmless exercise of freedom. Since wages were determined by competition in the labour market, unions could only succeed when wages were below their 'natural' level. Employers did not willingly increase wages so pressure to keep them up to the market level was justified. Strikes which sought to protect or advance wages against the market were futile and this would already have been learned by workers had they not been distracted by the government's imposition of oppressive laws. Distrust, resentment and antipathy towards employers were inevitable from a working class disadvantaged by the law and by their employers' use or threat of using it. It was the crux of Place's argument that repeal would bring about a decrease or even demise in union activity.[1]

Many who had been reassured by the argument soon had cause to rethink. The repeal, coinciding with a boom in trade, released a flood of union activity. Resentful employers and a frightened establishment were quick to react. Subversion of the social and industrial order was described in the conservative *Blackwoods Magazine*:

> No sooner were the Laws repealed, than combinations filled with the worst spirit sprung up in all quarters. These [did] more than exact the highest wages possible; they thought it was in their interest to place the masters under the most grinding tyranny. It was now for the servant to command, and the master to obey. As the former might be pleased to dictate, the latter was to discharge or retain his workmen, to send his goods to market, and to conduct his business generally.

Tyranny over other workmen had been exercised by men who 'murdered and maimed without mercy'. Hostility had replaced the old feeling of reciprocal goodwill and servants cared not what harm or ruin they brought on masters who refused their demands. A working class which would not be governed by its masters would not be governed at all and, in the event of a serious trade depression, their organisations would assume a political character with disastrous consequences for the country.[2]

Making maximum use of a handful of exceptional cases of violence, the employers and their supporters demanded the re-imposition of the Combination Laws and it took all of Place's political skills – this time in co-ordination with a speedily mounted trade union campaign – to prevent this outcome. After a select committee had reported, the new law of 1825 was a compromise. Recognising the right of combination and collective bargaining over wages and hours, it once again made unions subject to the common law of conspiracy as well as allowing the prosecution of individual workers for leaving their work. It also made the law on picketing and intimidation more stringent. Unions had kept the right to exist but had still to operate with powerful legal sanctions against many of the forms of action and organisation which made them effective. Conspiracy proceedings and those under the Master and Servant Act were not even the whole story, for as six unfortunate farm labourers from Dorset were to find in 1834, an ingenious judiciary could banish trade unionists from the country under an obscure Act against oath-taking.

The trade unions which came out in 1825 were a mixture of the old, the new and the newly revealed. For example, the Loyal Albion Lodge of Birmingham's button burnishers had been formed in 1810 after a dispute over prices: 'We had a sick and burial club, our only legal hold in those days, but our principal object was to keep up wages.' They were openly active in industrial matters after the repeal. The seamen of the north-east seem to have formed their first permanent organisation. The Seamen's Loyal Standard Association, in October 1824. Strikes among them in 1792, 1796 and 1815 had been bitter and long lasting but organised on an *ad hoc* basis, showing the reserve power of industrial action which lies within a well-knit occupational community under 'unofficial' leadership. Even after the repeal the seamen still described their combination as a friendly society and stressed its functions in that area, but from the start it was not only taking a lead from the example of combination among the area's shipwrights, but was perceived by the shipowners to be a trade union: 'There is no doubt they are also a very strong combination for the purpose of raising their wages, and, as we have found from their actions, of dictation to the shipowners and commanders of the ships.' It was a justified belief. The SLSA was active in the campaign against the re-imposition of the laws and determined in its efforts to prevent the employment of non-union crewmen.[3] Other groups of skilled men continued collective negotiation with their employers as they had done with a degree of circumspection during the period of the Combination Laws. Prothero has noted that although most public attention in 1825 was attracted by three strikes, the Thames shipwrights, the seamen of the north-east and the woolcombers of Bradford, these were only the best known disputes. In London alone, wage increases were secured by carpenters, carvers, gilders, coopers, twine spinners, rope-makers and upholsterers. New price lists (piece-rate agreements) were successfully negotiated by braziers and sawyers. New unions were formed by bedstead-makers, bricklayers, sawyers, seamen and silk weavers, and strikes organised by carvers and gilders, rope-makers, tin-plate workers, carpenters, cabinet-makers and ladies' shoe-makers.[4]

In many of these cases, attempts were being made to restore reductions which had been made in 1816; in this sense they owed as much to the trade boom as they did to the repeal and exhibited the traditional expectation of a 'customary' reward. However, the number and frequency of disputes is, together with the solidarity-creating effect of resisting the re-imposition of the Combination Laws, evidence of a developing trade union consciousness among artisans and skilled workers. Links were being increasingly sought, for example, between the shipwrights of different ports, the joint campaign of the five London carpenters' societies and the federation of sawyers' attempts to link with provincial societies. More significant was a wider sympathy with non-related trades who were increasingly being seen as facing similar problems, especially where issues of apprenticeship or legal persecution were involving the very right to combine. The Bradford combers in their doomed strike of 1825 received such help from so many trades from all over England that it was proclaimed to be 'all the workers of England against a few masters at Bradford'. In Birmingham too, the processes of economic and social change were creating common areas of complaint and action among the varied artisan trades of the city in the years after 1820 as the 'accepted practices' of work and wages were coming simultaneously under pressure in many workshop trades. The inherent divisiveness of different occupations was weakening as trade unions in their defence of custom against common innovating pressures became reflective of the values and attitudes of the working-class community and their activities connected rather than divorced them from it. The issue of 'work control' and the defence of customary working procedures became as central and as shared an issue as that of apprenticeship had long been.[5]

TRADE UNIONISM 1825 TO 1834

The boom which had combined with the repeal to allow the outburst of union activity of 1824/25 was short-lived. A sharp downturn in mid-1825 returned unions to the defensive. The loss of momentum is unmistakable. Major defeats were sustained, notably by the Bradford woolcombers, and they continued with the depression to 1828. London's tailors in 1827, striking against an influx of cheap female labour, lost for the first time in a generation, and after the repeal of their employment regulating Act in 1824 the silk weavers of Spitalfields were engaged in a desperate struggle in 1827/8 to maintain their piece rates. Other groups like shoemakers, hatters and carpenters were organised effectively only at the shrinking bespoke, quality end of their trades which were now numerically dominated by less-skilled sweated labour. Provincial experience was no happier: the carpet-makers of Kidderminster were defeated in 1828 after resisting a wage reduction of 17% for six months. Negatively it can be concluded that in unfavourable trade conditions the newly emancipated unions were no more able to resist wage reductions than had been the secret and circumspect ones. However, as the Webbs recognised, there was a more positive aspect: the demonstration of the 'futility of mere sectional combination' turned some sections of the working class to wider aims.[6]

Much trade unionism remained small, discrete, sectional and local, but from the late 1820s there is a discernible movement towards federation both vertically in the form of regional or larger groupings within the same trade and horizontally in attempts to set up general unions uniting trades. The latter was more significant for the development of class consciousness and culminated in the spectacular rise and fall of the short-lived Grand National Consolidated Trades Union of Robert Owen.

That a movement towards national or even general unionism was a natural response to repeated experiences of local defeat was clearly perceived by Lord Melbourne. With the first national union of carpenters formed in 1827 and the bricklayers following in 1829, his lordship observed in 1831: 'At present their language is an admission that their partial, and local unions have failed; that in such circumstances the masters are sure to get the better and have done so; that they must have a general and national union.'[7] This process, culminating in the excitement of the years 1829/34, has been characterised by the Webbs as one of growing class consciousness and political awareness. In the press and the speeches of labour and radical organisations was beginning the articulation of an alternative perception of society, economy and ultimately of politics. Fundamental was its emphasis on productive labour as the only true source of wealth. Structural transformation in many trades was giving power not to working masters, but to 'parasitic' capitalists who exploited in the direct sense that they performed no productive labour; indeed, in many cases, having come from merchant rather than manufacturing origins, were unable to perform it. Explicitly they denied to the labourer the full value of his work. The inputs into this emerging labour consciousness were various, coming from Owenism (although departing from Owen's own class-collaborationist views), from the writings of the socialist economists, Hodskin, Bray and Thompson, and incorporating the sense of self-respect and 'improvement' urged by leaders like William Lovett and John Gast. It is too easy to equate 'self-improvement' with aspirations to rise out of the working class. It should not be solely so regarded. What was central to the ideas of such as Lovett was an educative desire to fit the working class to assume a responsible role in a society which at no too distant future must admit it to the political nation. Edward Thompson, using the term in a rather different way from some sociologically-inclined historians, has described the desire as one to achieve for the working classes 'social control' over the conditions of their life and labour. To seek 'improvement' to this end was the antithesis of the educational imperialism of the Mechanics Institutes which aimed to teach the labouring people to accept peacefully the control of others and to acquiesce in the 'imperatives' of the market economy, including those which necessitated the introduction of deskilling technology. The 'swarming variety of journals' which made up the working-class press began to display a new richness of political thought as the discourse of radicalism was forced to stretch its vocabulary to take account of new sources of distress and discontent. Nor was this confined to England: in France, in the United States and, a decade later, in Germany these years were those which saw the development of a new 'language of labour'.[8] The securing of the vote by the middle classes in 1832 meant that the vocabulary of political radicalism had become more and more the property of the working classes. In the language of radicalism as it had developed through the eighteenth century, the 'people' had always embraced the excluded and, as Dr Stedman Jones has put it: 'In radical terms in 1832 the "people" became the working classes.'[9]

Some historians are not willing to attach such significance to the events of the early 1830s, seeing only 'ephemeral excitements'. Professor Musson has been the most persistent spokesman for the view that in highlighting such elements, the Webbs, and left-oriented historians of trade unionism in general, have neglected the true nature of trade unionism, its 'most essential, solid and continuous features', i.e. patient organisation, collective bargaining on wages, hours, apprenticeship, working conditions and the arrangement of benefits for unemployment, sickness and death. Beside such on-going, fundamental trade union concerns, he argues, the effects of ideology and wider perceptions of labour interest were superficial, and the period cannot on the whole be seen as a 'revolutionary' one in trade union history.[10]

This debate is central to recent trade union historiography, and we must return to it later, but first we must resume our description of the main lines of trade union development. The movement towards national unionism can be effectively highlighted through an examination of its progress in two groups of workers: the cotton spinners and the building workers. In 1824 the Manchester spinners involved in several local strikes again took up the object of forming a county union for Lancashire and indicated even wider ambitions by sending delegates to the cotton spinners of Glasgow who were also in dispute. The Glasgow strike collapsed, but attempts to federate the separate Lancashire unions continued. Such a federation was a precondition for the attainment of a major objective, the equalisation of piece rates throughout the county, and would also have enabled more effective resistance to the rate-cutting which was accompanying the introduction of larger spinning mules. There were several strikes, the most serious at Hyde early in 1825 where rates were notoriously low. The masters combined to offer determined resistance and attempted to break the strike by introducing new hands. Attacks on these 'knobsticks' became a recurrent, though occasional, feature of this period of conflict. After expending around £400 of their strike fund, the strikers were defeated, as they were in similar but smaller disputes at Preston, Stockport and Oldham. The wider union movement among the spinners had been confined to Lancashire and adjacent parts of Cheshire and repeated defeats now led to its disintegration. John Doherty, the leader and originating genius, later analysed the failure as stemming from the freedom of the separate localities to turn out as soon as they were faced with a reduction in rates. This produced the situation in which there were 'nearly as many receivers as payers', i.e. insufficient districts in work to support those who had struck. In the disputes which came in the aftermath of the economic slump of late 1825 – years which saw the rioting and machine-breaking by handloom weavers as well as strikes by spinners against reductions at Manchester, Ashton, Stockport, Bolton and Oldham, all of which were defeated – the need for better organisation was again evident. After a period of quiesence, conflict again became serious in 1828. During that year Doherty had the Manchester spinners in a series of 'rolling strikes' against masters who were under-paying. By April 1829 with 2,379 spinners enrolled, the Manchester union had virtually achieved a closed shop. The town's employers, seriously alarmed, followed the example of their Stockport neighbours, whose price reductions in December 1828 had already precipitated a closure of thirty factories, and announced a reduction of fine-spinners' rates of 15%. Clearly the cotton masters were ready for a showdown. At Hyde, Stalybridge and Dukinfield they presented the 'document', meeting especially strong resistance at Hyde. Meanwhile at Stockport the strikers, now many weeks out of work, were becoming increasingly violent. It was, however, a final desperation, for by September they had given in. The Manchester fine-spinners' strike was to last for six months before it too collapsed in the autumn of 1829. To Doherty the lesson was glaringly evident: local unions fighting separately were doomed to failure; but more than that, real prospects of success would be significantly enhanced if the support of other trades could be secured:

> Had the various trades poured in pence in time for their support, a different result must have followed. It is not, however, too late to learn wisdom. It would be absurd to suppose that spinners were the only body that will be reduced, and it is to be feared that unless there be a more general and effective co-operation amongst the working classes themselves, these attempts will be, as in the case of the spinners, but too successful.

Hence the origins of what Doherty was later to try to put into practice in his National Association for the Protection of Labour go back to the failure of the strikes of 1818/9, although the Association is generally regarded as having started in February 1830. Probably this objective did not assist Doherty's more immediate one of once again working towards a federated spinners' union. By keeping both objectives simultaneously in play, he would seem to have lessened his chances of obtaining the more immediately necessary and realistic one. His first concern was the formation of a Grand General Union of Operative Cotton Spinners throughout the whole of Great Britain and Ireland. He wanted a tighter organisation than was prefigured in the loose attempts of 1810, 1818 and 1824/5. The first delegate meeting was held on 29 September 1829 and a national conference convened in December on the Isle of Man. From this, despite regional jealousies between Manchester and Glasgow, emerged agreement on a national strike pay level of 10s. (50p) from a central fund and, more importantly, requirement of the consent of other districts before a turn-out either for an advance or against reductions. The conference also indicated the self-perception of mule-spinners as a restricted, skilled group of workers, for no spinner was to teach anyone to spin other than his son, brother, orphaned nephew, or the poor relative of a mill-owner. No one was to be instructed below eighteen years of age.

Although it would appear to contradict this intention to control recruitment by restricting labour supply, a final resolution shows that it was not thought wholly appropriate to present an 'alternative' ideology of the rights of labour in opposition to the rights of capital:

> It is not the intention of this Association either directly or indirectly to interfere with, or in any way to injure the rights and property of employers or to assume or exercise any control or authority over the management of any mill or mills, but on the contrary will endeavour as far as in us lies to uphold the just rights and reasonable authority of every master.

In fact, by prescribing who could be taught and retaining the manner in which new spinners would be instructed, the union *was* denying to capital one of its fundamental objectives: the control of the labour process. However, the statement has more than rhetorical interest for this was a *factory* occupation in which employment was dependent on capitalist investment. It was artisan groups like tailors, shoemakers or building craftsmen who could envisage the carrying on of their trade in a manner which made large non-productive capitalists unnecessary. The core appeal of Owenism, that through co-operative production working men could re-possess their trades, touched no chord of relevance among the cotton spinners, however much in other respects their status perceptions labelled them 'factory artisans'.

Early blows came from defeats of strikes at Bolton, Chorley and Ashton, but the showdown for the GGU came in December 1830 when fifty-two owners at Ashton and Stalybridge combined to reduce rates provoking a strike of 2,000 spinners. Parades with firearms displayed and tricolours in evidence combined with increasing violence towards 'knobsticks' had already alarmed the authorities when the mill-owner's son Thomas Ashton was shot. Although links with the union were never proved, the incident became central in a growing volume of anti-trade union propaganda. The strike ended in February 1831 in defeat. Its failure seeming to indicate that the GGU had been stronger on words than in deeds. For the men of Stalybridge had received very poor support from the other cotton towns. Strike pay had been only 5s. (25p), half the promised amount, and this had largely come from sums raised in the district itself. The GGU had failed to deliver, and disillusionment was rapid. Expectations had been too high. It was a defensive organisation and in a prolonged trade depression had not succeeded in overcoming difficulties even though it perceived their nature. After January 1831 its decline was rapid. In Manchester, union itself seems to have ceased to exist in a formally constituted way for several years. A further movement towards federation on the part of the Lancashire spinners was to wait until 1842. In the meantime there was no effective counteraction to the increasing deterioration of the spinners' position, in particular to the introduction of the self-acting mule which made the masters to some degree less dependent upon the skills of the spinner.

Doherty had by now shifted his ambitions in the direction of general unionism: to the National Association for the Protection of Labour. The problems so evident in 1829 were the opportunity for him to push ideas which he had already formed. An inaugural meeting on 30 September 1829 was attended by 1,000 workers from twenty trades. A special attempt was made to attract the handloom weavers of places like Bolton whose increasing powerlessness to act independently in their own overstocked trade might have brought them to general unionism as the only way of protesting their destitution. At the beginning, expansion was confined to Lancashire, but the range of trades gathered in was not unimpressive: weavers, calico printers, spindle-makers, basket-makers, jenny-spinners, rope-makers, coalminers and engineers, mule spinners, mechanics and tallow chandlers. Strike support was to be given only for action against reductions. In attempts to spread the movement, 'missioning' took place to the Midlands, Nottinghamshire, Lincolnshire and Derby, Leicestershire, Mansfield and, with mixed results, Birmingham. Reaction in the Potteries was particularly encouraging and perhaps set the groundwork for that area's continued interest in general unionism.

The first seeking of support came from Rochdale, but so early in 1830 that the NAPL was unready and unable to supply it, and this spread a degree of disenchantment. Nevertheless, progress was sufficient for there to be national and local government apprehension before the end of the year, but how significant a movement was the NAPL? At its peak in the autumn it had probably sixty to seventy thousand members overwhelmingly recruited from Lancashire and Cheshire (one-third of its contributing members came from strike-involved Rochdale). Of the constituent trades, four-fifths were connected with textile production (spinners, calico printers and weavers). Further afield some hold had been secured in Nottinghamshire, Lincolnshire and Derby. By 1831 it had recruited some coalminers and spread into Yorkshire, although in this county for the most part general unionism came from a separate local initiative, unconnected with the NAPL. Little is known of this independent 'Trades Union' which was probably formed at Leeds in 1831. A bitterly hostile reaction from employers enforced a heavy cloak of secrecy. It seems to have been behind disputes for several years but to have been defeated by employers. One master dyer at Leeds discharged all of his employees whom he suspected of membership in the summer of 1833. Later in that year a number of employers in the area drew up a 'bond' not to employ any members of a union. The union petered out in a series of failed strikes in that and the succeeding year.[11]

By 1831 too, Doherty had begun to involve the Association in the political reform movement and to use its organ the *Voice of the People* to this end. G. D. H. Cole claimed that by this time Doherty had become an 'ardent Owenite' intent on creating a co-operative commonwealth, a claim repeated by subsequent historians. It probably overstates his pre-occupation in this direction. Professor Musson has suggested that he was a late convert to Owenism and only then in a desperate attempt to breathe some new life into his flagging Association. It may have been so, but the fact that Doherty's 'trade unionist, class outlook' was quite different from Owen's does not mean a great deal. So too was the outlook of those later leaders of the Grand National Consolidated Trade Union who converted Owen, briefly, into an industrial syndicalist. The history of Owenism is precisely one of *its* adoption and adaption by those with a 'trade unionist, class outlook'. Doherty's plans to move the Association's headquarters to London to link up with general movements there suggests his late involvement was neither wholly flirtation nor simply cynical desperation.[12]

There is no doubting the loss of strength and momentum of the NAPL after the autumn of 1831, although it persisted in name until 1833. Musson points out that it had never attracted the most highly skilled workers like engineers and printers who remained aloof in their craft unions. But if these small sectional groups remained outside, then much larger occupational groups had been drawn in: declining handicraft workers like weavers and knitters, as well as the cotton mule spinners, who were, as we have seen, in the depression of 1829/31 at this time in a defensive frame of mind. Beyond the cotton trade, miners and potters had been involved and a tradition of union co-operation had been carried to Derby. Failure was largely consequent on the loss of the short-lived allegiance of the cotton spinners. In a severe depression of trade they were easily disillusioned when the Association failed to mobilise significant support for the spinners of Ashton-under-Lyne whose masters had imposed wage reductions.

Movements towards national and general unionism are also central to the trade unionism of another group, the building craftsmen. Developments towards national organisation began among carpenters and bricklayers in 1827 and towards general unionism soon after. To a unique degree in the building industry, craftsmen of several distinct branches worked together. Carpenters, bricklayers, masons, plumbers, etc. had an obvious motive to cross craft boundaries when faced with common problems, such as the activities of 'general contractors'. Technology was not in the building trades affecting the skills and position of the artisans, but innovations in organisation were. Discontent had arisen because of the increasing practice of 'general contracting'. Individual entrepreneurs had placed themselves between the architect and the master craftsmen. Springing from one or other of the component trades, or even from outside the industry, they were in effect becoming 'builders' and *direct* employers of labour in crafts to which they did not themselves belong. Traditionally, either directly or through architects persons wishing houses built had contracted separately with the master craftsmen in the various branches. Union opposition to the spreading practice of 'general contracting' had brought from some employers, first in Lancashire, the presenting of 'the document' against joining a union to break resistance to 'that baneful, unjust, and ruinous system of monopolising the hard-earned profits of another man's business'. In such a contest, the small employers were in agreement with the craftsmen and, encouraged by their support, the several branches of the building trade in Liverpool sent in, simultaneously, identical claims for a uniform rate of wages for each class of operative to prevent the general contractors from forcing down rates. They also demanded the prohibition of piecework and a limitation on the number of apprentices. To this extent the confrontation was deliberately provoked by the Builders Union; the tone in which the demands were put to employers leaves little doubt of this. Payment was even demanded for any time that might be lost in striking to enforce their 'orders':

> We consider that as you have not treated our rules with that deference you ought to have done, we consider you highly culpable and deserving of being severely chastised . . . each and every one in such strike shall be paid by you the sum of four shillings [20p] per day you refuse to comply.[13]

The confrontation was head-on. In June 1833 the large masters met and combined not only to refuse the demands, but to break the union by a more general issue and enforcement of the 'document'. Events in Manchester followed the pattern of those in Liverpool, and it was in Manchester, at the height of the conflict, that the Builders' Union held a six-day delegate meeting: the Builders' Parliament with 270 delegates representing 30,000 operatives. This was the famous meeting addressed by Robert Owen, which called for the formation of a Grand National Guild of Builders with a membership of 60,000. This new organisation was to provide all the friendly society functions of the traditional craft unions, but would have the resources to enter into competition for contracts with the general contractors; in a word, its principle was co-operative production. Outside of Lancashire the Builders' Union was strongest in Birmingham where it had come under the Owenite leadership of Hanson and Walsh.[14] While the Lancashire strike was under way in August 1833, one of Birmingham's largest contractors precipitated events in that city by discharging all union hands. At Birmingham began the Guild's first attempt at direct contracting with the beginning of a Union Institute or Guildhall. According to Hanson, 'In a confident hope, therefore, of success this work is commenced, being as it is believed, the beginning of a new era in the condition of the whole of the working classes of the world'. This grand vision of a co-operative socialist future was propagated in the *Pioneer* and predicated the industrial syndicalism which was to be the distinctive ideological feature of the general union movement of 1833/4, when both Owen's interest and the *Pioneer* itself moved to London and to the Grand National Consolidated Trade Union. The vision was powerfully persuasive to craftsmen jealous of their status and 'independence'. Through direct contracting by producers' co-operatives, the threat of being exploited and degraded by a ruthlessly competitive capitalism could be combated. As the principle spread from trade to trade, the radical transformation of society would be accomplished, and real power no longer be denied to labour, the only true creator of wealth. The corrupt parliament of privilege and monopoly, no longer sustained by the appropriated product of the working man's labour, would be replaced by a different 'parliament': 'Every trade has its internal government in every town; a certain number of towns comprise a district and delegates from the trades in each town form the Annual Parliament, and the King of England becomes President of the Trades Unions.'[15] It is a sign of the industrial and political ferment of the early thirties that such a vision of an alternative future could have been so enthusiastically received by the building workers. A future of co-operative production was essentially one in which the *artisan* would recover his status, his pride, his well-being and his independence: the just reward of the special property of skilled labour which he possessed. Before Marx the ideology of resistance to the aggrandisement of capitalism was essentially a socialism of skilled workers: of those who considered themselves as such, however labelled by others. 'You have nothing to lose but your chains' proclaimed the *Communist Manifesto* to the 'workers of the world' in 1848, but in that era it was precisely those skilled workers who *did* have something to lose who were in the vanguard of the labour movement. Marx's perception that opposition to capitalism in its formative years was essentially one of *resistance* to a process whose outcome was not perceived as inevitable is a more acute one. In visions of their future, the artisan movements of the 1830s and 1840s were, paradoxically, 'attempting to roll back the wheel of history'.[16] It *was* a labour consciousness but it was one of a particular historical moment.

The position of the unskilled labourer in the building trades was postponed for the future. Quarrymen, brickmakers and tradesmen's labourers were to be granted membership *when* 'they can be prepared with better habits and more knowledge to enable them to act for themselves, assisted by other branches who will have an overwhelming interest to improve the mind, morals and general condition of their families in the shortest time'. Echoes here of John Gast, the shipyard workers' leader exploding suddenly to Francis Place in 1834: 'the only way to an Englishman's brains is through his guts . . . Burke was not much out of the way when he called them the Swinish Multitude; for feed a pig well and you may do anything with him'.[17]

Owen suspected that, underneath, the building craftsmen were really 'rather exclusive' and he meant not only the exclusion of the unskilled, but also an underlying concern with their separate craft interests as carpenters, masons, slaters or whatever. Within each of these, and especially among the masons and carpenters – old-established and tradition-bound trades – a sizeable minority were not ashamed to disassociate themselves from the enthusiasm for general unionism. In London and in Leeds and from the carpenters of Liverpool, motions came proposing the dissolving of the Builders' Union into its component trades. The proposers known as 'the Exclusives' remained for the moment a minority and the *Pioneer* was scathing in its abuse of them: 'We will give them a new name we will call them the Pukes – it is a sickening idea – and will remind us that we are looking upon something which is filthy.'[18]

The practical contribution of the Builders' Union was that it spread trade unionism generally among building craftsmen and increased the number of unionists in each of the component trades. It had been formed from a federation of existing unions, but its impetus carried organisation to more towns and brought in many more recruits. The Manchester plumbers added fifty-eight in six months while the Preston joiners increased thirty-two to seventy-five. The eleven Warrington masons who founded a lodge found themselves 114 strong by the end of 1832. Nationally, the carpenters and joiners increased an 1832 membership of 938 to 6,774 in 1834, at which point the total membership of the Builders' Union stood at more than 40,000. Among the builders, although the carpenters had federated before its formation, general and national unionism came about for the most part together, for national union among groups like masons, plumbers and bricklayers was a product of, not a precondition for, the Builders' Union.[19]

It was a conditioned existence: the 'Exclusives' were always available to lead the regression into sectarian unionism should the Builders' Union over-reach itself, and over-reach itself it did. With strikes and lock-outs to support at Birmingham, Leeds, Worcester, Nottingham, Manchester, Liverpool, Preston and London, it was fatally split between affording the financial support for its members in dispute – which alone could secure their continued attachment – and the cost of initiating and propagating its co-operative schemes. The downfall of the union is often attributed to defeat in the London beer dispute of 1834. Members working for the London building firm of Cubitts combined to boycott beer brewed by a firm which had refused to employ trade unionists. Cubitts stepped in and refused to allow any other brew into their yards. A lock-out of recalcitrant employees broadened to become a virtual showdown between the large London contractors and the union. The union demanded equalisation of pay rates and the dismissal of non-union labour; the employers responded with the 'document' and, after a protracted struggle, their combined strength defeated the union.[20]

In fact the collapse of the Builders' Union had already seemed probable after the failure of the strikes at Liverpool and Manchester at the end of 1833 – which disputes had been the context of its original formation. In Lancashire, section after section gave in and signed the 'document', while joiners and bricklayers from Manchester actively propagated the dissolution of the union. Collapsing in Lancashire, the union was dead in one of its main centres, having been unable to sustain the strikes. Meanwhile in Birmingham serious problems of finance and of organisation had halted work on the Guildhall, the great showpiece of direct contracting. The defeat in London therefore was the occasion rather than the cause of collapse. That strike, already doomed, was struggling into its third month, when the secretary of the Masons' section, George Bevan, absconded with the paltry £36 remaining in its strike fund. The 'Exclusives' time had come. At the next lodge meeting they carried the resolution: 'That this society do come under Exclusive government', and installed their nominee, Angus McGregor, as the new secretary. He was not slow to propagate his triumph to the other sections. 'You', he wrote to Manchester in November, 'will like us be happy to observe the disposition they show to join us and accordingly to separate from the General Union.' Sometime around the New Year of 1835 the Builders' Union passed away. Henceforth the history of unionism in the building industry was once again, for many years, to be the history of its separate trades.[21]

By this time Robert Owen had already turned his volatile attention elsewhere. To him the Builders' Union had always been part of a far grander design, although some members had envisaged a future no less utopian than his, if quite different; one proclaiming:

> The Trades Union will not only strike for less work and more wages, but they will ultimately abolish wages, become their own masters, and work for each other; labour and capital will no longer be separate but they will be indissolubly joined together in the hands of the workmen and work-women.[22]

In 1834, Owen transferred his attention to London and to a new vehicle, the Grand National Consolidated Trades Union. To his chagrin he was unable to carry the builders with him into this most spectacular of all attempts at general union, although the *Pioneer* moved with him to become the journal of the London-based move-ment. Two points need to be made: firstly, the GNCTU was not the capital's first attempt at general unionism, nor were ideas of co-operative production entirely new to it. Secondly, the formation of the GNCTU came in a period of active unionism among the London trades. The city's artisans had shown their inclination and ability to co-ordinate their activities across individual trade frontiers in their campaign of 1814 against the abolition of statutory apprenticeship, and in 1818, the same year as John Doherty had formed his earliest attempt at general union, the 'Philanthropic Society' in Lancashire, some London artisans had come together in the 'Philanthropic Hercules' for 'the mutual support of the labouring mechanic and the maintenance of the independence of their trade against the infringements of avarice and oppression'. This organisation had been inspired by John Gast of the shipwrights, the most influential London leader of his time. The trades sent delegates to a central committee, but retained autonomous committees and the substantial management of their own funds. As Dr Prothero has pointed out, it very much represented the characteristic attitudes of the urban artisans with its aim of maintaining the 'just, legal and customary price' for labour. Francis Place described it as 'John Gast's scheme to keep up wages', and it proclaimed a general union while meaning to preserve the superiority of artisan wages over those of other working men. In reality it amounted to no more than a formalisation of existing practices of inter-trade assistance. Its history is obscure: it was involved in the campaign to have the trial of fifteen arrested cotton spinners moved to London, and quite possibly in the Queen Caroline agitation, but seems to have had only a short-lived existence.[23]

Much of the interest in London artisans in co-operative production, and in the labour exchange movement, was independent of Owen and pre-dated him. Self-employment was a natural activity for many artisans and already a familiar strike tactic. By 1830 a growing interest in co-operative production was shared by even moderate leaders like William Lovett. In 1829 there were six silk-weavers' co-operatives in Bethnal Green and by 1832 two among the tailors and similar activities among the carpenters. These co-operative attempts were, however, limited in ambition and practical in intent.[24]

In the years leading up to 1834 and the GNCTU, three trades were especially active: the carpenters, shoemakers and tailors. The economic upturn of 1833 afforded the opportunity of recovering some of the ground lost in the depression of the late twenties. The pressing problem for the skilled artisan was to avoid being 'sweated' into a proletariat along with the expanding population of the unskilled. By the 1840s only a small proportion of tradesmen at the bespoke end of their craft clung to a position of fair status and well-being, but in the 1830s attempts were still being made to resist the slide into piece-rate poverty by broadening the basis of unionism. The autumn of 1833 saw the formation of an unexclusive Grand Lodge of Operative Tailors of London which attempted to ensure that all work would be done on the employers' premises, not at home; that a limitation on hours of work would share it out more evenly and, recognising that rigid insistence on apprenticeship was a dead issue, insisted on the 'stint', the demonstrated ability of a newcomer to accomplish a given quality and quantity of work in a stated time before he was admitted to work in a shop. Only with the permission of the central committee could older hands and other special cases be allowed to accept work at low rates. Taking advantage of the start of the busy season in April 1834, these demands were put to the employers. Most refused, one emphatically so: 'Sir. I hope the Government will now interfere and transport one half of you blasted thieves, which I think will very shortly take place. If I was on the jury, I should wish it to be done, and promote the sentence.'[25]

The resulting strike was the city's biggest, though only one of several, in that year. Without adequate resources, the strikers were unable to hold out when, after much suffering, the employers presented the 'document'. The shoemakers followed suit in trying to halt the influx of 'sweated workers' by bringing several of their societies together in the United Trade Association in October 1833 and forming a Grand Lodge of Operative Cordwainers after meetings of the whole trade to discuss labour exchanges. The Federated Society of Carpenters grew rapidly in London, in the course of 1833 being in the vanguard of the Builders' Union. In May 1834 it demanded the restoration of the day rate to 5s. (25p) and the ending of task work, sub-contracting and of overtime in order to reduce wage-cutting, overwork and unemployment. Dr Prothero has revealed the extent of industrial action by various groups of workers in London in 1833. There were strikes by plasterers and bricklayers against individual firms, by the sawyers in 1833 and 1834 and in that latter year also by hatters and coopers. Union activity was also evident among groups with little tradition of organisation: gasworkers, washerwomen and stove-makers and bakers, and even female groups like garment dyers, strawplaiters, sewers, bleachers, pressers and bonnet-makers. Several trade unions attended the conference of October 1833 to launch Owen's Grand National Moral Union. The exact sequence and interconnection of events in London in 1833/4 is difficult to reconstruct, but it is abundantly clear that the formation of the GNCTU came in the midst of pre-existing and continuing union activity.[26]

Its catalyst was the Derby lock-out of 1833/4. This dispute, like those of the cotton spinners of 1818 and the wool-combers of Bradford in 1825, attracted widespread support across the country. Derby had been one of the Midland towns where Doherty's efforts at general unionism had had most impact. In November 1833 a turn-out of several trades took place, with the silk weavers the most numerically significant. The *Pioneer* took up the cause in January 1834:

> The master manufacturers of Derby have repeated their firm and inflexible determination not to employ any men who belong to the Trades' Union or to any other Union having similar objects . . . either the men will be forced into tame submission by want, or they will be able, by the assistance of their fellow workmen, and other benevolent persons to establish machinery, etc. of their own . . . Prepare your hands for an united effort and temporary

sacrifice; cease all complaints; use not an angry word; forget all selfishness; and do your best to blast these rich men's hopes, and set the Derby men to work.[27]

The initiative was taken in London by the tailors, and between the 13 and 19 of February the GNCTU was born. Place was later to say that the tailors had become 'Owenised and Union mad', and their leader, James Browne, was in the forefront of the formation. Originally the purpose had been to organise and co-ordinate support for the attempts of the Derby men to hold out against their masters. Here was more than simple sympathy for unionists on strike, something much more positive: an experiment in co-operation. In response to their locking-out, the Derby men had declared their intention to do without their masters and produce for themselves: 'We will be satisfied with the legitimate fruits of our own industry. We have hitherto worked for you . . . We shall henceforth work for ourselves.'[28] By mid-December of 1833 funds had already been coming in for the Derby workers. A Birmingham committee under the Owenite builder, Morrison, had collected £250 in four weeks and similar activities produced results in Wolverhampton, Manchester, Worcester, Huddersfield and Glasgow. Plans for a new factory and purchase of silk machinery were put forward, although ultimately coming to nothing when the men were forced back in April. Support from London had been expressed by the carvers and gilders who saluted the 'pioneers of our social revolution', and the wish to co-ordinate London's support lay behind the founding of the GNCTU. Not all of the thirty original delegates who drew up its manifesto have been identified, but as well as five tailors, at least two other London trades were represented. There were six delegates from Birmingham, and others from Wolverhampton, Derby, Worcester and Bradford. After the return to work at Derby, the movement became increasingly London-centred and oriented. Membership was overwhelmingly dominated by the city's trades, numerically by two, tailoring and shoemaking, but also included representation of more than twenty of the smaller trades.[29]

Certainly, as Prothero has suggested, the main aims represented artisan concerns: mutual support in strikes, provision of sickness and superannuation benefits, employment of members who were on strike and of out of work members, but undeniably there was some reaching out to the unorganised, including women workers. Lodges were formed among various unskilled and female groups: gardeners, coal-whippers, bakers, female shoebinders, two general female lodges, three miscellaneous lodges of shopmen, grocers, porters and clerks. This broader and deeper class consciousness was in fact heightened by resentment of government and employer hostility, and had its symbolic culmination in the marching of 30,000 people on 21 April 1834 in protest at the sentencing of the Dorchester labourers. The central conflict of the GNCTU's brief history was the turn-out of the London tailors in April 1834, and its failure was to precipitate collapse. This meant that although the tailors' strike had much continuity with their past history of unionism going back to the early years of the eighteenth century in terms of objectives and actions, its repercussions reached beyond the trade. In the GNCTU the tailors, to whatever degree they shared utopian visions of the end of competitive capitalism, could see a better means of securing long-held objectives. A year of economic recovery was always the more propitious for union action, and April was the start of the brisk period in what was a highly seasonal trade. To take advantage of such conditions there was now the hope of being able to draw on the funds of a general union: essential to sustain a fresh strike after expensive defeats in 1827 and in 1830. Hopes were rudely shattered. Instead of promised support, the striking tailors received only condemnation from the leaders of the GNCTU. For by now the circle around Owen had become so diverted towards a co-operative vision, it had no patience with the distraction of straightforward industrial action: 'little petty proceedings about strikes for wages' as Owen dismissed them. Even Smith and Morrison, the ideological leaders of the *Pioneer's* war of words against competitive capitalism, saw the strike as 'destructive and unsocial'; only the general strike mattered to them: 'We depend for deliverance entirely upon grand and national movements, and not upon the limited struggles of individual trades.' The executive added its condemnation: 'This association has not been formed to contend with the master producers of wealth and knowledge for some paltry advance in the artificial money price in exchange for their labour, health, liberty, natural enjoyment, and life.'[30]

The total strength of the tailors was estimated at between 9,000 and 13,000 in thirty-one lodges, for the most part in the bespoke West End. As recently as March, one month before they turned out, they had sent £200 from their scarce resources to aid the Derby workers, yet when their struggle began the GNCTU was reluctant and slow to assist, while the shoemakers complained bitterly that they had been promised the first chance to strike and call on funds. In the event the tailors struck despite their limited and uncertain prospect of help. Their chances of success were slight. The press, especially *The Times*, shrieked incontinent abuse, laid wild accusations of tyranny and violence towards non-unionists, and urged the importing of German tailors to break the strike. The organisation of master carpenters announced their support for their fellow employers in the tailoring trade by declining to place fresh orders for clothes while the strike lasted. The only friends were the radical papers the *True Sun* and the *Poor Man's Guardian* whose columns, less esoteric than those of the *Pioneer*, accepted trade unions for what they were: key defensive organisations of the working class. In so doing they showed that divisions in the GNCTU were not only between Owen's increasingly class-collaborationist views, and the syndicalism of the *Pioneer*, but also between the latter and the rank and file unionists who saw blue-prints for total social reorganisation as something of an irrelevance if there was an unwillingness or inability to offer organisational and financial support for individual struggles over wages and working conditions.[31]

In *ad hoc* efforts at co-operative production from hastily acquired workshops, the tailors by the second week of their strike were employing several hundred of their number, but strike pay was below expectations, and a GNCTU executive levy of 1s. 6d. (7½p) on all members met with a very poor response. By mid-May the weakened and disillusioned tailors agreed to negotiate with their masters and, by the end of the month, were apparently ready to return, a thousand of their number having already drifted back. At this point, capital rejected accommodation and went for the throat of labour. At a meeting, by thirty-two votes to eight, they decided to offer the 'document' as a condition for re-employment. Now, at last, the executive of the GNCTU saw the risk it had run by not giving essential support to the tailors: if the move was successful, then the 'document' could be expected to be issued in other trades. It was an awakening which came too late to help the tailors. The suggestion of 2 June that all trade union members should contribute a day's wages a week was in any event poorly supported. The strike was already doomed and towards the end of the month, the bitterly disappointed tailors seceded from the GNCTU. Shortly after the shoemakers, still angry that they had not been the first trade allowed to strike, also withdrew to conduct their own futile turn-out. Such a loss of numbers was beyond the ability of the GNCTU to sustain, although ineffectively it lingered on until the August of 1835.[32]

What had been the significance of it all? Few modern historians would give the events of 1833/4 the importance which the Webbs did. Against their claim of 500,000, the peak subscribing membership of the GNCTU was probably around 16,000, of which 11,000 were from London: 4,000 tailors, 3,000 shoemakers, 1,000 silk weavers and 1,500 from eighteen smaller trades. Outside London, membership was also dominated by tailors and shoemakers and was heaviest in the southern counties. Yet perhaps subscribing membership is not an adequate measure of its provincial potential. Its missionary activities were not without success, especially among handicraft workers, tailors, shoemakers, glovers, weavers and potters. Strikes failed among Banbury weavers, Worcester glovers and, after a long and bitter battle, among the shoemakers of Wellingborough in 1833. Such experiences pointed out the lessons of unsupported action. General union gained considerable support among the shoemakers of Northamptonshire, where during the Wellingborough lock-out of May and early June, in spite of the heavy-handed attentions of the magistrates, an unusual degree of radical class consciousness persisted for several months. It has been shown that during these months of high agitation, the shoemakers did not appear among the accredited members of the GNCTU, although perhaps numbering around 1,300. The point is that paid-up membership is not wholly reliable as a measurement of the influence of the movement for general unionism during these years.[33]

Missionary work had also some effect in the Midlands, Oxford, Coventry, Leamington, Warwick and Birmingham. It had an especial impact in the Potteries and in Cheshire, where London's organisational shortcomings failed to annex a group of lodges centred on Congleton, and a union of 2,000 members was reported among the silk workers of Macclesfield by February 1834. It had little success in the cotton and woollen districts, but here, as we have seen, the tide of general unionism had flowed and ebbed before the advent of the GNCTU. After Doherty's early efforts in Lancashire had faded, attention of the spinners had turned towards factory reform, the trade union implication of which was that control over the working day of child employees would, if achieved, also restrict the hours of work of adult operatives, and thereby reduce unemployment. In Yorkshire the separate 'Trades Union' had persisted in a great degree of secrecy for two years from 1831. Here, too, attention was to be absorbed by the Short Time Committees for factory reform which Richard Oastler was organising. The Builders' Union, as we have seen, had not come across with Owen to the GNCTU and had continued a parallel existence.[34]

Assessing the ideological legacy of general unionism is even more complicated. It is not simply reducible to the grandiose schemes of leaders in contradistinction to the mundane concerns of rank and file trade unionists. In the columns of the *Pioneer*, Smith and Morrison gave to ideas of co-operative production and exchange advanced by Robert Owen, a harder edge of class hostility, which was neither of the great theorist's initiation nor much to his liking. Not in dispute was the conception of labour as the source of all wealth, and its presumed entitlement to enjoy its full product. But identifying the 'producers' involved contentious discussions of class. For Owen, 'productive classes' had an occupational and not a social connotation. He was not class exclusive and was truly utopian in his optimist belief that a millennium was just around the corner if only men would think 'right'. Not for him were theories which saw socialism as developing through an historical process of class struggle. He would seem to have excluded only royalty, clergy and military, legal and medical professions from the ranks of the 'producers of wealth', who most certainly included manufacturers and the buying and selling classes. In the outcry of March 1834 after the sentencing of the Dorchester labourers, he had joined the GNCTU and enjoyed the kudos of riding at the head of the great protest procession through London. In general unionism, he had for a moment perceived a mass movement which could become the agency of the social changes which he desired, but shortly he was to tell the *Pioneer* to stop attacking the employer class and to repudiate the Derby strike and the whole principle of strike action.

The views which Smith and Morrison propagated first to the builders and then to the GNCTU were very different. They issued no clear manifesto, but in the columns of the *Pioneer* presented a clear class analysis of the social problem. Although they presented no rigidly defined concept of a 'capitalist class', they emphasised the contrast between the 'idle class' of which capitalists were a component and a productive class, labour whose condition it was to be exploited. In contrast to Owen, they presented an historical process in which labour from a period of enslaved or compulsory labour was passing through one of hireling or marketable labour into one of 'associated' labour. The transition to this third stage would be a product of the forces unleashed by the factory system, by machinery and by the spread of education. Capitalists dominating the last stages of the period of 'hireling' labour had appropriated 'reserved labour' in the form of capital, but the future would see the social and political supremacy of the productive and labouring classes, and the use of capital to promote general prosperity. In his celebrated study of British socialism, Beer made Morrison the 'originator of the syndicalist conception of class antagonism on the part of the working classes', and in him more than in any other lies the justification for E. P. Thompson's remark: 'When Marx was still in his teens, the battle of English trade unionists between a capitalist and a socialist political economy, had been (at least temporarily) won.' Morrison hoped that ultimately the affairs of the country would be governed by the producers of wealth associated in their crafts and delegating to a 'parliament of trades'. Artisan attitudes still lingered: he thought that the ignorant mass of the un-skilled would be better controlled within a hierarchical union structure than they would be if simply given the vote. (His associate on the *Pioneer*, Smith, was actually in favour of retaining the House of Lords, not only to deal with foreign policy, but also to 'infuse a spirit of refinement and polish into the representatives of the people'.) Hope-fully change could be secured through persuasion (Morrison was still Owenite enough for that), but it might have to come about through force.

As historical analysis and as explanation of the conflict between the unions and the government such views, even when partially adopted and entering only as tiny fragments into consciousness, contribute importantly along with the more intellectual analyses of the socialist economists Thompson and Hodgson to the development of a labour consciousness with a political edge. But although Morrison and Smith rejected the class-collaborationist views of Owen, they shared his failure to attach their analysis to the struggle which had to be waged in the day to day conflicts of labour and capital in the context of the work process if it was to be kept alive and meaningful. Instead, they waited for the grand transformation.[35]

The short-lived GNCTU has, argues Professor Musson, received a disproportionate attention from labour historians. Most 'real' trade unions remained aloof from it; pursuing traditional objectives and maintaining the frontier of skill against the unskilled hordes. On them the practical effects of the new ideologies were minimal and their concern was with patient organisation, collective wage bargaining, hours, apprenticeship and working conditions. They arranged friendly benefits for unemployment, sickness and death. Musson sees the Webbs as having neglected the 'most essential, solid, and continuous features of trade unionism in the nineteenth century', in what was not on the whole a revolutionary period in trade union history.[36] He argues that although there was some degree of broadening of trade union horizons to include political and social ideas, these were never successfully welded together, and in general trade unionists held aloof from radical and socialist movements. Those who spoke and wrote in favour of a general union and of a co-operative socialist millennium were but a small minority. He seems right to stress that for England national and district federations within trades (he instances cotton spinners, letterpress printers, miners, builders and potters) were more the pattern for the future than were 'vast trade federations'.[37] But perhaps a point is being missed here? If we put together the NAPL, the Yorkshire Trades' Union and the Builders' Union (itself a federation of seven crafts) with the GNCTU, then we cannot escape the fact that a significant number of trades were for a period associated with movements for general unionism. These would include not only the tailors and shoemakers of the Consolidated Union and the distressed outworking trades, but also some cotton spinners, miners and potters. Why are these to be regarded as less 'real' trade unionists than were small groups like the printers who, Musson tells us, remained aloof? He has written in depth on the printers, but that does not make them typical. There is some confusion on this matter. In his recent comprehensive textbook on labour history, Dr Hunt, not a representative of the far left, remarks that the GNCTU cannot be dismissed as a temporary aberration by a small part of a labour movement which otherwise remained elitist and conservative. He concludes that the history of the unions in 1829–34 represents 'a move in the direction of working-class consciousness', and even if sections of the labour aristocracy did stand apart, 'it is quite obvious that significant numbers of craftsmen forgot for a time the limitations of their strength and how much it depended upon segregation from the unskilled'. Musson, he suggests, has overdone his corrective. The printers were not unique in their quiet pursuit of their own concerns: the new group of the engineers behaved similarly. It is even more remarkable that John Gast's Thames shipwrights, once in the vanguard of the London trades, went their own way and had little to do with the GNCTU. Yet among the twenty-nine London trades which have been listed as involved are some which certainly were of the skill-protecting, craft kind, for example bookbinders, silk-hatters, jewellers, braziers, gold beaters, carvers and gilders, scale-beam makers and saddlers.[38] Such groups can hardly all be dismissed as unrepresentative of the 'real' trade unionists of the period. There is a kind of 'Whigism' in reading back from the more placid era from the later 'forties on, during which the unions sought 'acceptance' and accommodation within capitalism. Things had not always been so. J. C. Buckmaster, the very experienced secretary of the carpenters and joiners, told a parliamentary committee in 1856 that in the earlier period 'political feeling was certainly an element in all sorts of unions'.[39] Perhaps it was *because* government and employers perceived trade unions as *having changed* that they began to conceive of the possibility of working with them.

It is certainly true of the movements for general unionism that they were very short-lived. In lasting for two years, the NAPL had double the life of the GNCTU. Indeed, no historian seriously suggests that following the events of 1829–34 there issued a permanent, broad-based and continuous class consciousness. Thompson has remarked that what had been found was almost as soon lost in the 'terrible defeats of 1834 and 1835'. In Northampton in the disputes of the depressed shoemakers, an historian has described a 'fleeting' consciousness, which was present in the early 1830s even if it was not evident generally in the first half of the nineteenth century. Working-class political action had complemented and reinforced a desire for a stronger unionism and led to the turn *en masse* of the shoemakers to the GNCTU in the first months of 1834. The special character of the years 1829–34 here as elsewhere was to witness new levels of activity, a new language of class feeling, and the overlapping of forms of activity, all propagated by an extraordinary vibrant and expanding radical press.[40]

But these years did not see the formation of a working class which henceforth endured. Rather they saw the development of a consciousness among skilled artisans and outworkers experiencing or fearing decline into the unskilled proletariat. Historians of western Europe have come to note that the 'rise of the working class' is in effect a way of describing a broadening and deepening of class consciousness among artisans within a rhetoric of a 'labour' interest as opposed to that of 'capital'. Similar concerns and not dissimilar remedies characterise artisan protest in France, Germany and England. The ferment of ideas of 1848 strikes chords for the historian of English artisans of 1834 with their polarisation of labour and capital, even if their terms were not specified according to Marx. Ideas and language both emerged and developed from their relevance to the real situation of skilled workers experiencing structural change in the organisation of capitalist production, and hence expressed a form of consciousness appropriate to their historical moment.[41]

REFERENCES AND NOTES

1. For Place's role and tactics, see **S.** and **B. Webb**, *The History of Trade Unionism*, Longman, 1911, pp. 85–98 and, more critical, **E. P. Thompson**, *The Making of the English Working Class*, Penguin, 1968, pp. 563–9; *Edinburgh Review*, 39, 1823, pp. 315–45.
2. *Blackwoods Magazine*, vol. xviii, 1825, pp. 24–5.
3. **D. J. Rowe**, 'A trade union of the north-east coast seamen in 1825', *Economic History Review*, XXV, no. 1, 1972, p. 82.
4. **I. Prothero**, *Artisans and Politics in Early Nineteenth-Century London. John Gast and his Times*, Dawson, 1979, pp. 59–60.
5. **C. Behagg**, 'Customs, class and change: the trade societies of Birmingham', *Social History*, vol. 4, no. 3, 1979, pp. 456–7.
6. Webbs, *History of Trade Unionism*, pp. 100–1.
7. **W. H. Frazer**, 'Trade unionism', in **J. T. Ward** (ed.), *Popular Movements c1830–1850*, Macmillan, 1970, p. 100.
8. **E. P. Thompson**, *The Making of the English Working Class*, Penguin, 1968, pp. 910–11.
9. **G. Stedman Jones**, 'England's first proletariat', *New Left Review*, 90, 1975, p. 13.
10. **A. E. Musson**, *British Trade Unions 1800–1875*, Macmillan, 1972, p. 29ff. See also his collected essays, *Trade Union and Social History*, Cass, 1974. Musson's pamphlet is the best bibliographical introduction to the subject.
11. For details and chronology of the cotton spinners' strikes and unionism, I have drawn upon **R. G. Kirby** and **A. E. Musson**, *The Voice of the People. John Doherty, 1798–1854, trade unionist, radical and factory reformer*, Manchester U.P., 1975. For mule spinners as 'factory artisans', see Stedman Jones, pp. 50–1; see also **J. L.** and **B. Hammond**, *The Skilled Labourer*, 1919, ed. J. Rule, Longman, 1979, pp. 77–111. For the Yorkshire union, see **H. Pelling**, *A History of British Trade Unionism*, Penguin, 1963, p. 38.
12. Musson, *British Trade Unions*, pp. 31–2.
13. Webbs, *History of Trade Unionism*, p. 115.
14. Ibid., pp. 116–17.
15. **R. W. Postgate**, *The Builders' History*, 1923, pp. 101–2.
16. See **J. Rule**, 'Artisan attitudes: a comparative survey of skilled labour and proletarianisation', *Bulletin of Society for Study of Labour History*, no. 50, 1985.
17. **H. Browne**, *The Rise of British Trade Unions 1825–1914*, Longman, 1979, p. 19; quoted in **E. P. Thompson**, *Education and Experience*, Mansbridge Memorial Lecture, Leeds U.P., 1968, p. 14.
18. Postgate, *Builders' History*, pp. 96–9.
19. Ibid., pp. 56–8.
20. Ibid., p. 110.
21. Ibid., p. 111.
22. Thompson, *Making of the English Working Class*, p. 912.
23. Prothero, *Artisans and Politics*, pp. 68–9, 101, 143.
24. Ibid., pp. 250–3.
25. Ibid., pp. 300–1.

26. Ibid., p. 302.
27. Quoted in **R.** and **E. Frow** and **M. Katanka** (eds), *Strikes. A Documentary History,* Charles Knight, 1971, pp. 22–4.
28. **W. H. Oliver**, 'The Consolidated Trades Union of 1834', *Economic History Review,* XVII, no. 1, 1964, pp. 79–80.
29. Ibid., p. 80.
30. Prothero, *Artisans and Politics,* pp. 302–3; **T. M. Parssinen** and **I. J. Prothero**, 'The London tailors' strike of 1834 and the collapse of the Grand National Consolidated Trades' Union: a police spy's report', *International Review of Social History,* xx, 1977, pp. 71, 74–5.
31. Ibid., pp. 75, 77.
32. Ibid., pp. 78–80; Oliver, 'Consolidated Trades' Union', p. 95.
33. Oliver, 'Consolidated Trades' Union', pp. 85–8; **M. J. Haynes**, 'Class and class conflict in the early nineteenth century: the Northampton shoemakers and the Grand National Consolidated Trades' Union', *Literature and History,* no. 5, 1977, pp. 88–91.
34. Oliver, 'Consolidated Trades' Union', pp. 87–8.
35. For a useful analysis see, Oliver, 'Consolidated Trades' Union', pp. 90–5; Thompson, *Making of the English Working Class,* p. 912.
36. Musson, *British Trade Unions,* p. 29.
37. Ibid., pp. 29–30.
38. **E. H. Hunt**, *British Labour History 1815–1914,* Weidenfeld & Nicolson, 1981, p. 204; Oliver, 'Consolidated Trades' Union', p. 85; Prothero, *Artisans and Politics,* pp. 304–5.
39. Bagwell, *Industrial Relations,* p. 23.
40. Thompson, *Making of the English Working Class,* p. 913; Haynes, 'Class and class conflict', pp. 82–3; Prothero, *Artisans and Politics,* p. 400.
41. See Rule, 'Artisan attitudes'.

Chapter 13

POST-1834: CRAFT UNIONISM, MINERS AND CHARTISM

In May 1834 the manifesto of the Yorkshire Trades Union, the most intensely persecuted and hence the most secretive of the general unions, complained: 'The war cry of the masters has not only been sounded, but the havoc of war; war against freedom; war against opinion; war against justice; and war without justifying cause.' The political divide of 1832 enfranchising the middle class had left a disillusioned working class (including the artisans) as the excluded. The bitter irony was that it was the new reformed Parliament which was now seemingly attempting to crush the trade unions. With appropriate anger, a Leeds trade unionist summed it up:

> It was but the other day that the operatives were led in great numbers to the
> . . . meeting at Wakefield, for the purpose of carrying the Reform Bill. At
> that time, the very individuals who were now [May 1834] attempting to put
> down trade unions, were arraying them to carry by force of number, a
> political reform which . . . could not otherwise have been obtained from the
> aristocracy of this country.[1]

Blackest deed of all, it was the Whig House of Commons which had sanctioned the transportation of the Tolpuddle martyrs. It had also encouraged and backed the employers in their use of the lock-out and 'document' and infiltrated spies into union meetings. Thompson has justly remarked that the intensity of the attack on the trade unions evident by 1834 has been too little appreciated by historians and was as consequential as the radicals and unionists of the time held it to have been.[2]

Appropriately we begin the examination of this persecution with the Tolpuddle martyrs. The story of the sentencing and transportation of the six Dorsetshire farm labourers is well known and need only be repeated in its main lines. The six were unfortunate in the timing of their attempt to form a union for the 'Swing' riots were of recent memory in the rural south. They were unfortunate in living within the magisterial franchise of James Frampton whose whole-hearted zeal to prosecute the six has placed him high on the trade union movement's list of infamy. They were unfortunate in meeting a government which, although it was in the beginning led by the magistracy, was ultimately prepared to allow the stretching of the law to secure an exemplary deterrent against the spread of trade unionism into the countryside. They were unfortunate in a judge who knowing well what was expected of him directed a monstrously unfair trial before passing the most severe of sentences under a desperately searched out law of uncertain applicability. They were truly the *Victims of Whiggery*, as the most articulate of their number, George Loveless, was to entitle his later account of the martyrdom. Already paid as little as 7s. (35p) a week, the labourers were forming a union to resist a reduction to 6s. (30p). They broke no law in forming a union. They had planned no strike; withdrawn no labour; issued no threats; nor carried out any act of intimidation. When, therefore, the malignant squire became aware of their attempt to unionise, on what grounds could he proceed against them? The poor men had administered an oath of secrecy. But this was only a misdemeanour at common law and carried too mild a sentence for the purposes of the magistrate and of the government. However, there existed 32 George III c.104, an Act against unlawful oaths, passed at the time of the naval mutinies of 1797 as part of the machinery to deal with sedition. Although there was *no question* of the six having any such intent, this statute was used to transport them for seven years. Such a monstrous abuse of power and act of class tyranny met with massive protest and a huge campaign for the return of the men who had been despatched with such indecent haste that within a month of the trial the House of Commons was told that they were already in Bombay!

The campaign presents perhaps the moment of greatest unity in the nineteenth-century history of the trade union movement, and its importance in strengthening solidarity and resolve has already been mentioned. These sentiments are simply expressed in broadsheet verse on the occasion of the giant procession led by Robert Owen through London on 21 April:

The gathering of the unions

Base despots! Who deal deadly words
In cunning guise of law
Trust ye to jargon and to swords
Our souls to overawe?

We rend your veil, we scorn your steel;
We shrink not nor dissemble –
By every burning wrong we feel,
Cold tyrants! ye shall tremble

We moved; – a calm majestic mass –
In silence and in power,
And never from men's hearts shall pass
The lesson of that hour.

In our arms that idly hung,
Slumber'd strength that shall not tire –
In our silence was a tongue
Which, though mute, spoke words of fire.[3]

The agitation on behalf of the Dorsetshire labourers was kept up in and out of Parliament by the London Dorchester Committee, which then became a significant trade union co-ordinating body, and the remainder of their sentences was remitted in 1836, although it was to be a further two years before they returned home.

The example of the Dorsetshire gentry was not lost on their fellows in other places where labour conflict was persisting. Eight leaders of the striking Northamptonshire shoemakers were arrested on the same charges in April, but acquitted when the two informers who were to testify to oaths having been administered changed their stories, quite possibly having been effectively intimidated. From Nantwich in Cheshire survives a detailed account of what happened when the authorities moved to break another strike of shoemakers. Learning of the proceedings in Dorset, the magistrates attempted to arrest union members on the evidence of a half-wit informer who would testify to oath-taking. Some of the branch officers fled to Manchester, but two were charged and imprisoned. The strikers secured the help of a sympathetic solicitor and the two were released on bail. In the period before the trial, vital prosecution witnesses were 'persuaded' to remove themselves to Dublin, and after a further postponement the prisoners were discharged. Bringing the case had, however, the desired effect for the expenses of the defence broke the union, while the threat of imprisonment led to a rapid fall-off in membership.[4]

Such prosecutions were potent symbols of the repressive powers which authority could bring to back employers against unions. Far more numerous were less spectacular proceedings under the common law of conspiracy or under the increasingly used Master and Servant Act. In Birmingham alone well over 135 individuals from fifty trades were prosecuted for activities related to industrial disputes, most of these in the latter part of the period and most under the laws of master and servant. Seventy-two men prosecuted between 1833 and 1848 compares with only twenty-seven pre-1820.[5]

Apart from using the law, employers confident of government support and encouraged by the vicious anti-union campaign in the press and in pamphlets – which stressed secrecy, violence and intimidation – made effective use of the 'document'. We have already in a number of instances noted the issuing of these signed renunciations of union membership, but it was following the peaking of the union movement in 1834 that their use became especially widespread. They could be used either to provoke a showdown when it was suspected that a union was preparing to strike, or could be presented to defeated and disillusioned workers as a condition of re-employment. They had been used to break the building workers in 1833/4 in London, Leeds and elsewhere, and in the cotton spinners' strike of 1837. They were to be used in 1851 in an attempt to crush the newly formed Amalgamated Society of Engineers and in the London building strike of 1859.[6]

One group who began to develop a trade union consciousness during this time but who neither fit the usual image of an exclusive craft association nor seem to have had much to do with general unionism were the miners of Northumberland and Durham. Conditions and methods of work on the major English and Welsh coalfields differed so much that any idea of a national union of coal miners was not seriously contemplated until later in the nineteenth century, while the traditional isolation of the mining communities and their mono-occupational nature would not have naturally inclined miners' leaders to think in terms of general unionism.

Some miners from the Lancashire coalfields, from Kingswood (Bristol) and from Yorkshire and the Midlands were involved in local labour disputes during the 1790s and both Lancashire miners and, briefly those from South Wales, had links with Doherty's NAPL. In the case of the Welshmen their union never recovered from the repression following the Merthyr riots in 1831 and thereafter went underground to form the secret organisation, the 'Scotch Cattle', who directed violence against truck shops, workers who accepted lower wages and other offenders. A brief revival of union in 1834 was again beaten by the refusal of the coal-owners to employ any union men, and another phase of 'Scotch Cattle' activity resulted, as it did again in the aftermath of 1842.[7]

Most of the English coalfields outside of the north-east were too small as communities for effective organisation. In the early 1830s, organisations were formed in most of them, but were unsustainable. The south Lancashire colliers, for example, met in March 1830 to form the Friendly Society of Coal Mining but it was defeated in its first strike and had passed away by the summer of 1831. In the north-east the organisation which emerged with the repeal of the Combination Laws in 1824 and by the following year was publicly evident as the United Association of Colliers on the Rivers Tyne and Wear with its own purpose-built union hall came from a 'Brotherhood' which had existed under a friendly society cloak since 1804 and which had clearly led a strike in 1810. It had in 1825 a declared membership of 4,000 hewers. Indeed, it can be regarded as something of a union of skilled men for it was to a large degree an exclusive union of hewers and concerned itself with safeguarding the interests of that elite group of coal winners and would on no account tolerate any 'stranger' who was not a regular bred pitman working at the coalface.[8]

The dispute of 1810 during the time when the Combination Laws were in force was one in which the owners used imprisonment to such effect that the imprisoned leaders overflowed both the available gaol space and the stables of the Bishop of Durham, which his grace had kindly put at the disposal of the authorities. The issue was not wages but, as it had been in a strike in 1765, the attempt of the coal-owners to change the time of the annual 'bond' (hiring) from October to January in order to prevent the men from taking advantage of the pre-winter peak demand for coal to force up the bounty they were paid on accepting their yearly contract. The owners wished the men to bind themselves for only four months in that year and then to renew for a year starting from January. In the event, after negotiation a compromise of binding in April was accepted which remained the date down until the ending of the bond system in 1844. The striking miners, of whom 159 had been imprisoned, seem to have won no significant concessions on other issues such as the truck system and the burden of fines. All of these were to resurface in major strikes in 1831 and 1832.[9]

The United Colliers were well established by February 1826 when the leading coal-owner Lord Londonderry described it as 'entirely established' and if not resisted by the coal-owners, the latter would have to 'surrender at discretion to any laws the Union propose'. In fact the union seems to have lost ground during the next few years and was unable to secure a safeguarding of the hewers' position without open confrontation. In late February 1931, 10,000 pitmen met at Chester-le-Street and a month later a much larger number from forty-seven collieries met at Newcastle and resolved to present a demand for redress of long-felt grievances. Chief among these were the truck ('tommy') shops, the insecurity of their tenure of tied cottages, the punitive system of fines for improperly filled corves and the agreements concerning standby pay to bonded men who were unable to work because of engine failure or similar cause. Apart from meeting a specific grievance that boys were working fourteen hours a day by conceding a twelve-hour day for them, the owners offered no accommodation of these demands. The union struck the pits for several weeks and secured in the end sufficient concessions for the strike to have been regarded as a success for the miners. According to the *Tyne Mercury* it was quite clear that 'the servants have triumphed over their masters in the struggle'. The hero of the contest was Tommy Hepburn, who was a firm upholder of moderation and no violence. Apart from minor and isolated incidents the strike of 1831 with 17,000 men idle was conducted in remarkably good order.[10]

The very success of the union seems to have increased the coal-owners determination to destroy it before its hold on the industry became too complete. In 1832 they provoked a showdown and broke the union. Falling profits since the 1831 strike were being attributed to the success of the union in restricting the hewers to an earnings limit of 4s. (20p) a day. Several owners were bringing in unemployed lead miners from the Pennines to push down wages and break the hold of the union. In March a meeting of owners brought matters to a head by making a point of praising the work of the introduced lead miners and inferring from it that the pitmen were neither overworked nor underpaid. When the April binding came around about half of the pitmen, including those working in the pits of Lords Durham and Londonderry, were able to agree renewal terms, but at the other half the binding was refused.

Eight thousand were holding out. At many pits the insistence of the employers on an explicit renunciation of the union was the issue; at others, other grievances were to the fore, but by mid-May the combined refusal of the coal-owners to bind any man who was a member made union recognition the real issue. The strike of 1832 was for the union a struggle for survival. At first, hopes were high and a weekly contribution of 6s. (30p) (one and a half days' pay) was made by the miners in the half of the pits at work to support the strikers. The owners brought in even more lead miners and incidents of violence against them, and against a magistrate (for which a miner was hanged in chains), meant that the strike failed to keep the good order of 1831. Cottage eviction and the strain of continuing the 6s. contributions eventually brought the strike to an end after five bitter months. On 1 September the men held their last union meeting and offered to change their rules if the masters would allow them to continue in some form. The triumphant coal-owners were adamant: they wanted nothing less than the complete destruction of the union: 'By the introduction of workmen of more upright principles, and with more correct notions of the rights and relative duties of masters and servants.' The union was formally dissolved on 20 September. Hepburn himself, cast aside and supporting himself by hawking tea, had the ultimate humiliation of having eventually to beg work at a colliery and accept the condition that he have no more to do with unions. Perhaps he is better to be remembered for his last speech than for his poignant fate:

> If we have not been successful, at least we, as a body of miners, have been able to bring our grievances before the public; and the time will come when the golden chain which binds the tyrants together will be snapped, when men will be properly organised, when coalowners will only be like ordinary men, and will have to sigh for the days gone by. It only needs time to bring this about.[11]

In taking on the union, the coal-owners had the full backing of government. Lord Melbourne wrote in July to the magistrates of the district to draw their attention to His Majesty's concern at the serious state of affairs in the collieries:

> It appears that, for some time past, extensive and determined combinations and conspiracies have been formed and entered into by the workmen, for the purpose of dictating to their masters the rate of wages at which they shall be employed, the hours during which they shall work, the quantity of labour

which they shall perform, as well as for imposing upon them many other regulations relating to the conduct and management of their trade and concerns.

The letter went on to write of 'unjust demands . . . tumultuous assemblies . . . seditious and inflammatory discourses . . . illegal resolutions . . . menaces and intimidation', and urged on the local magistrates the need for firmness in suppressing all meetings of this 'unlawful combination and conspiracy'. The Hammonds rightly quote this letter as an illustration of the odds which the union faced, but perhaps its deeper and more revealing significance lies in its first part. Why were owners trying so hard to break the union? The answer is that it had come very close to succeeding in wresting for the hewer an effective degree of control over his conditions of hiring and of work. We have already noted that the combined hewers would not allow any 'strangers' to work among them. The fundamental strategy was one shared with many of the craft unions, a self-imposed restriction on work which would not allow the coal-owner to gain from the competition for work among the hewers. Any hewer who set himself to appropriate a greater share of the work available than would earn 4s. 6d. (22½p) a day was to be fined his day's earnings by the union. Against the owners' desire to represent the miners as simply workmen – labourers whose places could be filled by unskilled labour from an overstocked market – the union was asserting the special place and skill of the hewer. The true-bred pitman whose upbringing and acquired ability to select and get good coal made him a far from 'common' labourer and who expected to be accorded that degree of control over his own work processes which was appropriate to his standing and the degree of remuneration appropriate to his well-being. That is why the union had to be confronted and defeated for it was asserting the rights of labour against the ever-increasing presumptions of capital. The 'document' which all had to sign after the collapse of 1832 was extraordinarily explicit:

> I do not belong to the present Pitmen's Union, nor will I become a member of any similar association by the compliance with the fixed rules or regulations or occasional resolutions of which I can be prevented from the strict performance of any contract that I may enter into with my employers.[12]

Edward Thompson has argued that the line from 1832 to Chartism is not a 'haphazard pendulum alternation of "political" and "economic" agitations' but rather a convergence towards a single point, the vote. He has suggested that the anti-political bias of general unionism as it reached to express a syndicalist alternative gave way after the collapses of 1834 to a re-emergence of the view that the parliamentary franchise was 'the more practical key to political power'. This shift gives to Chartism its distinctive pursuit of the vote as a means of securing control over their lives and labour for workers.[13]

We have now in pursuing our analytical narrative to follow two separate streams. One carried the language of radicalism into Chartism, for although the extent of trade union involvement with Chartism is hotly disputed, there can be no doubt that to some Chartists at least the movement was a meshing of industrial with political objectives and actions. The second stream is the one which some historians prefer to see: the continuously flowing current of 'real' trade unionism. In this stream, unions of skilled men keep a profile of respectability and confine themselves to 'compartmentalised' trade union activities, preserving through apprenticeship their limit on entry. They sought to secure the customs of their trade and eschewed the diversion of political action. They displayed the sectional interest of a trade, rather than the wider consciousness of a class.[14]

AN ERA OF 'CAREFUL' UNIONISM?

The Webbs' inflation of the numbers involved in the general unionism of 1833/4 led them to overestimate the extent of the subsequent decline in trade union activity. There was no catastrophic collapse, but there are two ways of viewing the period after 1834 while accepting that the adoption of a low, law-accommodating profile was an evident characteristic of much of its unionism. One, a view found in the Webbs, is to emphasise a decline in confrontation and in the language of overt class consciousness as a reaction to the failures of general unionism. The other is to emphasise, like Professor Musson, the elements of continuity, and to see 1834 as a distortion, an aberration from the usual concerns of craft unions which were hardly different at the end of the 1830s from what they had been at the end of the 1820s. The later thirties would not have been in any circumstances a propitious period for trade unionism since in the trade depression which began after 1836 survival was the priority in the face of a sustained employer offensive; although some groups, such as the declining handloom weavers, in the absence of any effective industrial clout, turned instead to political radicalism in the shape of the Chartist movement.[15]

What were the characteristics of the unions of the period as identified by the Webbs? In their classic history they present an impressive array of evidence in support of the argument for a clear movement away from the confrontation language and behaviour of the early 1830s. A trade union leader recollected in 1841 the excitement of 1833/4 with its 'determination to carry the principles in opposition to every obstacle', but when faced with obstacles 'they chose to turn back, each taking his own path, regardless of the safety or the interests of his neighbour. It was painful to see the deep mortification of the generals and leaders of this quickly inflated army, when left deserted and alone upon the field.'[16]

To the Webbs the retreat was one back to local trade clubs with limited objectives and, by implication, an increasing craft sectarianism. From time to time, especially in the brief interlude of trade recovery in 1835/6, groups like the building workers, often in response to union-breaking attempts by their employers, engaged in aggressive enough strike confrontation to draw loud complaints from the press.[17] But there was little of the grander designs of general unionism in groups like the Operative Society of Stone Masons who concentrated on building up their membership through the country and using local strikes where necessary to keep rates uniform and resist price-cutting. Indeed, a look at the progress of this great union, accepted by the Webbs as one of the strongest of its day, in a remote part of the country not noted for its proclivities towards industrial action is perhaps as relevant for understanding the trade unionism of the day as would be one at its areas of strength. The Society had had a branch in Plymouth in 1834 with seventy-nine members, and it was probably from there that the first branch in Cornwall was established at St Blazey with fifteen members in 1835. In 1836 with an official return of only three paying members it was maintaining the barest of toeholds, but increased again to nineteen in 1837, although falling back to eleven by 1838. After that year the branch disappeared, but the first report of one at Luxillian only a couple of miles away suggests that it had simply changed its headquarters, for this 'new' branch was sufficiently active to send delegates to encourage the opening of further branches at Fowey and Bodmin with six and seven members respectively. Bodmin was to be a bridgehead to take the union into the more densely populated mining districts of the west with branches being opened by 1840 at Truro with nine members and at Penryn with thirty-four. The latter was significant for the town possessed an established granite-quarrying industry. The Penryn branch went rapidly into action: not only did it send delegates to open at Penzance what was certainly the country's most westerly trade union branch, but in the same year, 1840, took on an employer who was attempting to reduce prices below the 'list'. This employer's six employees struck and the branch was strong enough to support them until they were successful. Victory brought the reward of a further increase in membership to forty-six by the end of the year. Nearly fifty members and a successful strike in a small Cornish town to secure the upkeeping of union rates must be accounted an achievement.[18]

If the collapse of the GNCTU and the return of economic depression at the end of 1836 had not been enough to bring about a cautious attitude, then the events of 1837 and 1838 certainly were. The outcome of the bitter Glasgow cotton spinners' strike of 1837 was a sensational trial of five men for violent intimidation and even murder of fellow workers. Yet despite the undoubted violence of this strike, the unions rallied to present a united front of indignation at the prosecutions, not seen since the early days of the Dorchester protests. More significantly, the violence in Scotland coupled with similar evidence from Cork and Dublin re-opened the prospect of government re-introducing laws against trade unions in response to press pressure. Although the outcome of the enquiry of 1838 was not a change in the legal position of the unions, just how seriously the trade unions had taken the threat can be seen in a printed circular sent out by its secretary, William Lovett, to provincial trades societies on behalf of the London's Trades Combination Committee. It was designed to ensure the country societies remained linked with the London-based organisation in order to prevent 'well-organised employers from getting too large an advantage'. Certainly the committee was dominated by London, although twenty-seven provincial committees were listed including ones at Bury, Bolton, Nottingham, Bath, the Potteries and Birmingham and Manchester, where the treasurer had absconded with £3.4s. 3d. (£3.21p). The London Committee suggested that although Lord John Russell had said no further investigations of trade unions were intended, copies of the pamphlet *Combinations Defended* should be retained as a 'memento' of 'one of the most cunning and daring attempts to crush the rights of labour, as well as one of the most successful victories the sons of industry have ever achieved'. The immediate danger having passed, the Committee would not continue to meet, but 'in order that we may be at once prepared to unite as one man against any further infringements of our rights, should it proceed from a corrupt government, a clique of avaricious employers, or the wily tools of either', they had pledged themselves to reassemble promptly if Lovett, who was 'carefully watching the proceedings of government' called them together at a 'critical and important period'. The circular finished by hoping that provincial societies who had at first been reluctant to associate themselves with the London Committee would now perceive the necessity of united action.[19]

Occasions such as that produced by this perception of a threat could bring separate trade societies together just as subscriptions to meet the defence costs of trade unionists under prosecution could reveal that however 'sectarian' craft societies may be presented as having been, they were capable of responding to the needs of those not of their craft who were suffering because they were trade unionists. Subscriptions towards the defence of six Lancashire building workers tried on conspiracy charges at Liverpool assizes in 1837 came in from Birmingham, Crewe, Swindon, Bristol, Brighton, Aberdeen, Southampton, Kidderminster, Dublin and London as well as from Lancashire towns. Occupations represented included smiths, grinders, moulders, brass finishers, mechanics, carpenters, carpet-weavers, bricklayers, papermakers, boilermakers, plumbers, tin plate workers, sawyers, plasterers, stone masons and a donation from the Chartists of South Lambeth.[20] There never was a period during which a union conscious-ness wider than that of the trade did not from time to time manifest itself. The records of the brushmakers record that as well as making a gift to the Glasgow spinners in 1837, they gave or lent to curriers who were supporting 120 men on strike in 1836, the bookbinders in 1839, Manchester hatters in 1841 and the typefounders in 1850. In addition, in 1846 they considered requests from the masons, paper stainers and Manchester builders and 'the Trades Union' but being out of funds themselves were unable to assist.[21]

Despite this, many historians prefer to see the post-1834 era as one whose trade union history is that of a 'real' practical, limited craft unionism. Unions indeed followed a path of caution. In the critical year 1838 the masons had set their house in order by giving up not only secret oaths, but 'all forms of regalia, initiation and pass words'. Down in Cornwall the sale of the regalia of the Luxillian branch raised 4s. (20p). Generally speaking the crisis of 1838 passed because the unions were not in a challenging position of strength. Even those societies of the new skilled crafts in engineering, usually presumed to have been among the industrial revolution's most advantaged groups, were finding that the trade depression through heavy calls by unemployed members was seriously reducing their funds. In part the Webbs and others are correct in seeing too an intellectual change as a new group of workmen not involved in the desperate defence of dying trades, and who had not lived through the years of the Combinaton Acts, were talking less evidently of oppression and becoming instead more recep-tive of some of the economic and political maxims of capitalism: propagated to them through the *Penny Magazine* and lectures at the Mechanics Institutes.[22]

Before, though and beyond the Chartist peaks of 1938 and 1842 major craft unions pursued a careful, gradual extension and refine-ment of their organisations. According to the Webbs they, also in pursuit of more limited aims, substituted 'industrial diplomacy for the ruder methods of the class war'.[23] These aims did, however, go beyond the simple advancement of wages through careful and restrained bar-gaining, for central to craft unionism was the maintenance of entry restriction through apprenticeship. This was in itself a major oppo-sitional position to the capitalist assumption of a free labour market.

The language of the craft unions reveal at least a public presentation of moderation and polite formality evidenced, for example, by the print unions which Musson has studied and whose characteristics he is apt to extend to be those of trade unions in general. In the several trades' journals which appeared the language of accommodation begins to displace the conflict assumptions of the discourse of the early thirties. The *Potters' Examiner* (1843) first appeared only six years after a great strike of the potters and only one after their ruinous involvement in the general strike of 1842; it displayed an approving interest in new technology. In the *Bookbinders Trade Circular*, Thomas Dunning propounded a theory of trade unionism very much in line with the prevailing economic consensus and which would have caused no surprises either if it had appeared in the *Mechanics Magazine* or that of the flint glass makers.[24]

The printers were distancing themselves even further from notions of general unionism for which they have never had any enthusiasm. In 1835 they proclaimed, 'Let the Compositors of London show the Artisans of England a brighter and better example; and casting away the aid to be derived from cunning and brute strength, let us when we contend with our opponents, employ only the irresistible weapons of truth and reason'. Especially after the events of 1842, such attitudes found expression in most of the craft unions in strike-denying ordinances, or rather the relegation of the turn-out to be the weapon of last resort. 'How often', asked the ironfounders rhetorically in 1846, 'have disputes been averted by a few timely words with employers?' The stone masons in 1845 were warning against the dangerous practice of striking: 'keep from it as you would from a ferocious animal that you know would destroy you . . . Remember what it was that made us so insignificant in 1842.' By 1849 the Liverpool branch was ready to propose that the society no longer recognised strikes either as a means of seeking wage increases or of resisting 'infringements', but only after a major building strike for the nine-hour day in 1846 failed to produce results. Its answer was to reduce the supply of labour through assisted emigration. The flint glass makers declared strikes to have been the 'bane' of trade unions and abolished strike pay. But it was hardly possible for any other than a locally based, highly organised body of skilled men to suggest instead that the 'haughty spirit of an oppressive employer' be brought down in a manner so that he 'would feel the power he cannot see' by the simple expedient of withdrawing his men one by one and supplying none to fill their places. Both this union and that of the stone masons were among those to attempt to withdraw the right of calling a strike from local branches.[25]

It was in the engineering industry that the Webbs saw the most evident manifestation of a new kind of unionism, through an amalgamation which, when it reached its culmination in the Amalgamated Society of Engineers of 1851, they christened the 'New Model Unionism' – a label which has ever since caused dissent among labour historians.[26] The old-established society of the millwrights had been the union whose well-organised activities had been the occasion for the passing of the general Combination Act in 1799.

> So regular and connected is their system that their demands are made sometimes by all journeymen within (25 miles of London) . . . at the same time, and at other times at some particular shop and in the case of non-compliance the different workshops (where these demands are resisted) are

wholly deserted by the men and other journeymen are prohibited from applying for work till the Master Millwrights are brought to compliance.[27]

It was fast fading by the 1820s as the engineering trade sub-divided into different branches to which a standard rate would have been inappropriate. Ultimately the further sub-division and the de-skilling implications of the machine tool would, by 1850, substantially reduce the craft element. The engineers are often presented as *the* skilled group called into being by the industrial revolution. In fact, given the increasing technological displacement of their skills, it is doubtful whether their organisations, including at the point of amalgamation into the ASE, were ever again as powerful as the millwrights had been at the close of the eighteenth century. By 1841 a Salford machine-maker could claim: 'most of the tools or machines used in machine-making are self-acting and go on without the aid of man; the man who works the planing machine is a labouring man earning 12 or 14s. a week [60 or 70p]'. Nevertheless the London engineers showed in 1836, when they successfully contested the ten-hour day and overtime payments with their employers in an eight months' strike, what could be established when separate engineering craftsmen were co-ordinated by a joint committee: 'We are determined to make an effort to assimilate the hours of working per day and the rate of paying for overtime in all the shops of the trade in London. As we expected (that the masters) . . . would offer every opposition to salutary measures, we determined to attack them one at a time.' By this policy of striking one shop at a time, the combined unions eventually won despite the employers' use of the 'document'.[28] In fact there was a burst of union formation within the engineering trade from 1833 to 1838 centred on London, Manchester and Yorkshire. The processes by which, with the main impulse coming from the Journeymen Steam-Engine and Machine Makers and Millwrights, the separate engineering unions formed the ASE has been told in sufficient detail by the Webbs and by James Jefferys.[29]

A cornerstone of the new amalgamated union's policy and perhaps the main issue behind its great dispute with the employers in 1852 was the restriction of entry through apprenticeship. No account of the rise of craft unionism in Britain which fails to see that the apprenticeship issue was a fundamental divide between skilled trade unionists and their employers, whatever degree of 'accommodation' to the imperatives of the labour market might have been made, can come close to an understanding of the period. Apprenticeship in effect meant the 'closed shop' crucial for union success. Ever since the repeal of statutory apprenticeship in 1814 only two contexts could preserve it: the genuine barrier of a skill which remained essential to the production process and which could only be acquired through a long apprenticeship, or an effective closing of entry against 'unfair men'. The number of crafts in which a barrier or skill alone could preserve apprenticeship was decreasing with the advance of technology and the growing demand for ready-made goods where mass production of an inferior product suited changing conditions of marketing. There were comparatively few occupations in which the frontier of skill could have held alone without the back-up of a union 'closed shop':'Look to the rule and keep boys back; for this is the foundation of the evil, the secret of our progress, the dial on which our society works, and the hope of future generations' proclaimed the flint glass makers.[30] As Dr Chaloner has pointed out, the struggle for apprenticeship was still vigorously going on in the first half of the nineteenth century, for it represented the most significant of all status lines drawn through the working population: 'The higher order of mechanics, known as "skilled labourers" from their being obliged to pay large fees, and to serve apprentices or seven years to the trade which they follow.'[31] New trades could produce as assertive a defence of the property of skill as ever the old ones had done. The Railway Spring Makers' Society enshrined the principle into their rules:

> Considering that the trade whereby we live is our property, bought by certain years of servitude, which gives us a vested right, and that we have a sole and exclusive claim upon it, as all will have hereafter who purchase it by the same means . . . it is evident that it is every man's duty to protect by all fair and legal means the property whereby he lives, being always equally careful not to trespass on the rights of others.[32]

The continuing importance of apprenticeship to craft unionism is clear. Its survival was a matter of struggle and its preservation a fundamental objective. Professor Pollard has described the restriction of the supply of labour as the main weapon in the armoury of Sheffield's cutlers and grinders. On the whole he sees limitation on the supply of skilled labour as having been successfully exercised through apprenticeship until the mid-Victorian years. It was the extreme form of some of the sanctions used against unfair workmen in the 1860s which were behind the well-known 'Sheffield Outrages' and contributed so largely to the setting up of the parliamentary inquiry into trade union practices in 1867. Possibly some of the less well unionised branches of the trade like razor-grinders were less successful in restricting entry.[33]

Tyneside's shipwrights in 1841 were still managing to hold a ratio of one apprentice to three craftsmen some sixteen years after apprenticeship restriction had been a main issue in the strike of 1824. In 1850, apprenticeship was firmly insisted upon in the union rulebook and no member would work with a non-member. Tyneside's engineers were less successful: an inquiry of 1850 blamed weak unionism both for a disproportionate number of apprentices being admitted and for the employment of a large number of unskilled workers. But as a result of a sharp increase in union membership which began in 1859, apprenticeship limitation seems to have been successfully re-asserted.[34]

This re-assertion of apprenticeship control after a period of reduced ability to keep 'shops' fair was found in other crafts. Professor Musson has noted that compositors were always more likely to retain control in larger centres, like Manchester whose rule for fixing the ratio of apprentices to journeymen was adopted by the Northern Typographical Union and later the National Typographical Association, than in smaller provincial centres where the basic distinction between compositors and pressmen was often blurred and where to find six apprentices to two journeymen was not unusual. The records of the Typographical Union show constant vigilance against what in 1842 was described as the 'malady' of the apprenticeship system, the want of a 'due limitation' which was 'woefully apparent' in many parts of the country. In London the compositors seem to have become more successful in maintaining entry restriction after the re-formation of the London Society of Compositors in 1848.[35]

Among the building craftsmen the stone masons were seeking in 1838 to re-impose their rule of a seven-year apprenticeship after the building boom of the early industrial revolution when the expanding demand for labour had meant the ignoring of the working rules of the trade allowing 'anybody to learn our trade, and to serve what time they pleased'. As in printing, it was a continuing struggle. In 1845, Manchester plumbers and glaziers secured the support of the other building crafts in seeking to secure a limitation on apprenticeship, while in that year and also in Manchester the masons seem to have secured its re-establishment after the great lock-out in south Lancashire. It was to be short-lived for by 1849 the finances of the society were in a grave state and the conditions in the labour market had once again operated against the safeguarding of entry through apprenticeship. There were exceptions. Crossick has noted that although weakening generally in the city, building apprenticeship retained a stronger hold in the artisan community of Kentish London: 'It was easier for an unskilled worker to attain a crisis ridden insecurity, but apparent independence as a small dealer or shopkeeper, than to enter the main crafts of Kentish London.' He points out that virtually none of the workers employed on the building of Greenwich Hospital between 1848 and 1855 were unapprenticed.[36]

Skilled concentrations of craftsmen like Stourbridge's glass-makers seem to have retained an unbroken control over apprenticeship. Their power was complained of to the trade union inquiry of 1867 and the union seems to have maintained its power to supply a man from its national list whenever a vacancy occurred down to a major strike in 1902.[37] The story of apprenticeship control is not one of grand confrontation as much as running skirmish: locally won or held here by this group of craftsmen, lost there by that group. What is to be remarked is that a generation after employers celebrated the repeal of 1814, apprenticeship in defiance of the fundamental capitalist assumptions of a free labour market remained the cornerstone of British craft unionism.

We have seen that there is a strong body of evidence to support the 'received' view of English trade unionism in the post-1835 period as has having renounced the language of class war, concentrated on limited, local and sectional objectives and improved its organisation and public image. There are, however, two qualifications which must be made. In the first place the official disapprobation of strikes does not seem to have prevented a very large number of stoppages, even leaving aside the so-called 'general strike' of 1842, and in the second place it can be contended that unofficial unionism at the workplace displayed a less accommodating attitude towards the capitalist economy than did official discourse.

Officially, branches of the stone masons might, as we have seen, decry the resort to strikes, the Portsmouth branch in 1849 going so far as to propose that the very word strike be abolished, but only a few years before in 1844 the Central Committee had asked:

> When will our caution against strikes have the desired effect? Will our members never be convinced of their destructive tendency, and abandon the thought, or will they continue to cut off every sprout of prosperity as it makes its appearance amongst us? . . . in our present state we have our members striking in places surrounded by hundreds of our fraternity not in Union.

Professor Musson accepts that despite the official policy of the Northern Union to avoid strikes if possible, it was not so possible on frequent even 'innumerable' occasions even if the issues were often 'trivial, frequent and usually small and petty'. Most often the strikes were broken by the introduction of unfair labour. In the first year of the National Typographical Association (1845), fifty-one disputes were reported to the executive, and in that year of good trade many of them were successful, but when bad trade returned in 1846 the success rate in ninety disputes was falling, precipitating the final collapse of the national union in 1848.[38]

It was, as we shall see in the special case of the Miners' Association, all very well to talk of the need for harmony with employers and of prospects of achieving more by peaceful negotiation and conciliation than by strike action, but there was too little reciprocation from employers, who were more likely to respond to trade union weakness with increased attempts to break them. There was no dialogue, for in the employers' conception of the working of the labour market there was no place for combination of labour. Within a year of its formation the 'new model' ASE found itself locked-out in the great national engineering dispute of 1852. Platitudes of conciliation at national level did not change the situation in which workers found themselves in the localities.

In a pioneering study of Birmingham's trade unionism, Clive Behagg has indicated how much of the world of the unions was hidden from outsiders and remains hidden from many historians. It is not simply a matter of the survival of evidence, but of penetrating a world of work relations *meant* to exclude. Behagg has examined the workshops and early factories in Birmingham in which the work group strove to protect its traditional expectations of earnings and traditional methods of working in insisting upon the observance of customary working procedures. To this end it employed various devices including secrecy, ritual, intimidation and even violence in seeking to maintain what Richard Price has called the 'autonomous regulation of work' by the workforce, or what has become more generally known as 'workers' control'.[39] The group was based on some form of trade society and joining it was a condition for joining the work group and we can therefore properly refer to a world of 'unofficial unionism' whereby procedures of work were prescribed which were only rarely contained within formal rulebooks. Outside the workplace the shared values and expectations were reinforced by the pub, forming a symbiosis which underpinned a distinct alternative working-class culture impenetrable to the middle-class reformer. Its members deliberately emphasised its separation. In Birmingham, defence of this culture became particularly vigorous after 1820, when through the two following decades traditional work processes were being attacked by capitalist employers. Of course rituals and customs were traditional in the sense that they linked the worker with an apparently tangible past, but they were more than a survival for many were more elaborately developed after 1820 than they had been before. The carpenters, for example, only *introduced* passwords in 1833.[40]

Secrecy was paramount. Morrison, the Birmingham builders' leader, warned Robert Owen to overcome his distaste for 'relics of barbarism' and introduce initiation rituals for the GNCTU: 'the spirit of the times requires some concessions to popular prejudice and by conceding a little way we may gain much'.[41] The workshop had its own 'theatre' usually, to the chagrin of temperance reformers, involving drinking and treating. Such 'rites de passage' marked the progress of the young entrant from apprentice to journeyman. Treating was expected of newcomers from another works or town, the 'maiden garnish', marriages were so marked and so was the promotion within the shop. Minor breaches of working customs, such as swearing or fighting, were commonly fined, with the money being used to buy drink. William Lovett, after some difficulty in getting into a London carpenters' shop, found that the demands made upon him for drink 'for being shown the manner of doing any particular kind of work' absorbed a fair proportion of his weekly wage. Such customs emphasised conviviality and the sense of belonging. There was, however, no written rule which said that London's coopers were to be provided with as much beer as they wanted during their working day, but should they not be, complained one employer in 1825, within ten minutes 'all the yard is in a ferment'.[42] Outside the workshop, public display in the form of funeral processions and the like gave the wider world a look at the tip of an iceberg of a 'mysterious brotherhood of the trade', but it was within the workshop that the other nine-tenths of the anonymous tradition of early English industrial relations was submerged. In order to change the 'old ways', would-be innovating entrepreneurs found themselves confronting a collective culture whose assumptions they did not share and whose mystifications were a defensive device.

From time to time, for example among the brass-cock founders, there was an attempt at incorporation into formal working rules, but more often as a visitor to Birmingham noted in 1851 there was so much jealousy between masters and men that it was hard to get any information from either on 'any point associated with the trade'. He established that there were cases in which 'by a rule of the union' no journeyman could work with more than one boy under him, but no such *printed* regulations appeared before 1885. In the late-1830s the Britannia metal workers operated a closed shop yet as one member admitted:

> There is no rule of the union which forbids a master to employ other workmen than members of the union, but in an establishment where unionists are employed they do not and will not associate with others except members of their own body which is pretty much the same as forbidding them to work in that establishment.

The button-burnishers had no written regulations to support the expulsion of one of their number for defying 'long-established laws and practices'. The point was that anyone who was a member of the face-to-face relationships of the shopfloor could be expected to *know* how to act. The attempt to systematise in a formal sense would have weakened 'customary practice' both in force and in flexibility. If the formulation was less than precise, obligation was nonetheless exact. Edward Tufnell in 1834, in connection with the Yorkshire Trades Union, remarked: 'A perusal of the rules by which this and other unions profess to be guided will give a very faint and inaccurate idea of their operations'.[43] Sometimes questioning elicited some sense of what actually went on. In 1824 a parliamentary inquiry learned that if a Liverpool shipwright took more than his fair share of available piece-rate work, then he would be 'drilled' by his fellows, that is they would refuse to work with him for a period, perhaps as long as three weeks. The punishment, certainly based on a customary sanction going back much further, was in 1823 being enforced by a union committee, but did not appear as a formal entry in the rulebook. No written regulation of the compositors' unions limited the amount of hours a printer might put in. When someone who described himself as a 'stranger to the customs of the trade' expected on entering a London shop to be able to work overtime he learned that no one was to be allowed to take more than sixty hours a week. Having put in eighty-two hours he expected £2 14s. 8d. (£2.73); instead he got £2, the remaining twenty-two hours he was told had been 'put on the shelf' and he need only work thirty-eight hours the next week: 'you must take what comes and mike [be idle] a bit now and then, if you are such a fast man'. It was an arrangement to which employers had apparently consented, but was not an official rule.[44]

Violence, most often in the form of public ritual humiliation was the ultimate sanction against those who broke the customary practices. It was usually a last resort after disciplines of various kinds from fines, through 'sending to Coventry' to the activities of the 'chapel ghost' transposing and mixing type, or 'Mother Shorney' hiding tools and undoing work in carpenters' shops. Such policies of deliberate and serious annoyance, known as 'rattening' when used in the cutlery trade, were most often used against 'unfair' workmen in 'fair' shops, but could be used against any non-conformist in the workplace.[45]

Hostile critics of trade unions looked upon such practices as 'intimidation' and as evidence of the 'undemocratic' nature of trade unions. As Behagg has shown there was in fact a strong undercurrent of popular democracy in the workplace. Sanctions were rarely imposed without some kind of 'court' in the shop or in the pub used by the trade at which the offender could present his case. William Lovett coming apprenticed into a London carpenter's shop was allowed to do this, while such hearings were part of the accepted procedures of printers' chapels and of the London hatters, among whom if an offender disputed the verdict of the court of his own shop could be taken to a higher court known as a 'dozening' and be heard before delegates from a dozen shops.[46]

The difficulty of finding out the role of officials in early trade unions also reflects this. They were rotated not only to prevent a distancing from the 'shopfloor', but also because the workers did not want a permanent official dialogue through delegates with employers. The anonymity of the workgroup was better preserved in the comparative anonymity of its organisers: 'As long as the workplace retained its enigmatic quality it could be controlled by those whose position within its broadly integrated culture made them privy to its internal complexity.'[47] It is clear that the Webbs and those who have followed them in concentrating on the most formally organised, bureaucratic and permanent unions of a selected group of skilled craftsmen have told only part of the story of English trade unionism; and it is by no means clear that the 'official' has left a more noticeable legacy than the 'unofficial'. Those who fulminated on the undemocratic structures of the early trade societies would have done well to have noted that unless it had been a consensus against which 'deviance' could be judged, 'the trade' could have done little for its members.

CHARTISM AND THE UNIONS

With the drawing up of the six-point Charter in 1838, the London Working Men's Association inaugurated the world's first widely supported movement for universal male suffrage, 'unprecedented in its level of sustained commitment and national organisation and unparalleled anywhere else in Europe'.[48] Historians, especially those who find the 'compartmentalisation' of working-class movements a useful way of denying the development of class consciousness, have tended to present the Chartist movement as having had few points of contact with trade unionism. The Webbs wrote of a movement which, although it played 'the most important part in working-class annals from 1837 to 1842', did not draw in the trade unions to become 'part and parcel' of it as Owenism had done in 1833/4. They accept that unionists furnished some of the movement's most ardent supporters and that individual trades such as the shoemakers were 'permeated' with Chartism and that the strikes of 1842 were 'captured' by the Chartists.[49] There has developed among historians something of a consensus that Chartism attracted a much greater following among the older, depressed trades, such as the urban ones of tailoring and shoemaking and the rural ones of handloom weaving, framework-knitting and nail making. The kind of towns most likely to have had a high level of participation were the smallest ones associated with declining textile crafts like Trowbridge, Bradford, Nottingham or Bolton. Support from the upper trades like engineering and printing was much less evident, and according to some historians practically non-existent. The reaction of the new factory workers is more complex. Asa Briggs suggested that in their case: 'The pendulum swung between economic action through the trade unions and political action through Chartism.'[50] Taken out of context, Briggs' 'pendulum concept' has been treated as if it were intended to describe a movement characteristic of the working class as a whole that they employed well-tried trade union tactics when times were good, and responded politically when they were bad. In fact, for groups like handloom weavers, of whom Nassau Senior remarked that even the Tsar of Russia had not the power sufficient to raise their wages, chronic poverty and under or unemployment were the result of structural factors not cyclical movement and their support for the Charter was not basically dependent upon short-term movements of the trade cycle. However, the factory workers had several options: trade unionism, factory reform movements or Chartism. It seems highly likely that many of them would have preferred to seek concrete advancement of their condition through economic action when times were propitious: after all, however desirable the vote for the working people might be, it was a cause which could be taken up at any time; postponing immediate prospects from industrial action made little sense to those who had some expectation of success from striking.[51]

Generally the pattern of occupational attachment to Chartism is agreed although there are qualifications to be made: for example, the extent to which engineers remained aloof may have been exaggerated by generalisation from London's experience. In Manchester they took the initiative in directing the strikers of 1842 towards the Charter, as well as being strongly involved in Glasgow. Some of the clothing towns of Lancashire too, whose involvement has been attributed to hand-loom weavers, had such shrunken populations of them by 1839 that most of the mass support must have come from the factory workers.[52]

The true complexity of Chartism's relationship with the trade unions can best be understood by concentrating on three specific questions: the nature of its support in London; the 'general strike' of 1842; and the relationship of Chartism to the rise and fall of the Miners' Association.

Most historians now accept that before 1840 London's trade societies showed little enthusiasm for the Charter. It is also generally accepted that the 'aristocracy' within the ranks of skilled labour, engineers, bookbinders and printers for example, remained largely aloof even after 1840. Who then did support the Charter after 1842 among the London trades? Dr Prothero has convincingly demonstrated that its support came strongly from those groups who also showed a readiness to support wider trade movements in general. Tailors, shoemakers, carpenters and stone masons were best represented in numbers. These were all older trades, skilled men not 'common labourers', under pressure from structural changes in economic organisation which were limiting the effectiveness of separate trade union action. The tailors and shoemakers were going under to the 'sweating system' and its increasing use of unskilled labour. The cabinet-makers to an equivalent 'scamping' system whereby cheap furniture was knocked-up for the warehouse trade. The house-carpenters, masons and other building craftsmen were suffering a destruction of their old 'prices' from the activities of 'general contractors'. From such groups came the overlapping involvement of the 'same people in different guises' on which Prothero remarks. In fact these were all groups with long traditions of combination and unless it is linked with the trades in this sense, Chartism could hardly have prospered, for they were the active working class of London. This was recognised in the change of the name of the leading Chartist organ the *Northern Star* in 1844 to the *Northern Star and National Trades' Journal*. The political edge and supra-trade consciousness of this group of trades, more numerous than were the aloof elite, were evident in the most notable new trade organisation formed in the 1840s. This was the National Association of the United Trades for the Protection of Labour, reviving Doherty's title of 1830. The Webbs gave this organisation a fair amount of space but perhaps misplaced it as standing halfway between the 'revolutionary voluntaryism' of 1833/4 and the parliamentary action of 1863–75.[53] Modern historians have not accorded it very much significance, one describing it as a 'modest pressure group seeking better industrial relations through conciliation'.[54] Prothero has shown it to have much more interest. It is true that the upper trades joined it, as they had in the past joined several similar united trades' movements when legal threats were pending and to agitate against the Master and Servant Bill, but left when that danger was past. It is also true that much of the initiative came from Sheffield and that it was a strike by tin plate workers in Wolverhampton which severely weakened it in 1850. However, the real basis of the organisation was in the London trades and their objects went further. Historians have noted the expressed preference for conciliation and negotiation over strike action, but they have failed to emphasise that the fixing of wages through boards of trade modelled on the French *conseills des prud'hommes* which was only defeated by six votes was an advocation of the unthinkable in a *laissez-faire* economy: the binding of employers as well as employees to accept arbitrated rates. There were other policies of interest, noted by Prothero, but in general one remarks the congruence of the objectives of the lower trades in the National Association with the economic objectives of Chartism: 'The artisan mentality was at the heart of the Chartist response to economic movements.' The *Northern Star* was its organ, and it advocated universal suffrage and assumed, like Chartism, a fundamental doctrine of the 'rights of labour'.[55]

THE 'GENERAL STRIKE' OF 1842

The idea of a strike 'for the Charter' was from the very beginning part of the movement's discourse. Deriving from the ideas of William Benbow, it pre-dated the beginnings of Chartist agitation. At the initiation, Chartism was the recipient of evident goodwill from the unions and was able to debate, without an air of total unreality, the question of a political strike at its Convention of 1839, having witnessed, for example, the support of the Manchester trades in attending a rally at Kersal Moor on 24 September 1838. Among those processing behind their banners were a range of trades from the elite engineers through the cotton spinners, wheelwrights, carpenters and shoemakers to the tailors. A conservative estimate puts participation at 50,000.[56] In the event, anxiety and the not unreasonable fear of a debacle was productive of a less than overwhelming response from the established trade societies.

It was not until 1842 that Chartism became sufficiently involved with industrial action for the question of a 'Chartist strike' to be seriously debated by contemporaries and by historians. Few confrontations have received as much recent attention as the wave of strikes and riots which spread across the manufacturing and mining districts at the height of the depression misery of 1842. Popularly known as the 'Plug-plot' risings, these disturbances have been represented by some historians as a spontaneous and simultaneous reaction to wage-cutting which were only belatedly and unsuccessfully 'captured' by the Chartist agitation. But more recent assessments have shown that, especially in south-east Lancashire – their storm centre – the troubles were from a very early stage focused by the Chartists. Their organisations were giving direction to the strikes and injecting them with a measure of political consciousness. From the first week a series of trades conferences assembled in Manchester were passing resolutions calling for a cessation of work until the Charter had been secured,[57] and furthermore attracted some participation from the unions of skilled elites like the engineers. Professor Mather has described the events of 1842 as amounting to a 'semi-revolutionary' strike movement and believes that the two months into which the action was largely squeezed were the most intense threat to order in the early industrial period. He has revealed their geographical spread as extending to fifteen counties in England and Wales and eight in Scotland. In England they were mainly concentrated in a block from the Aire and Ribble in the north to Shropshire, Staffordshire, Warwickshire and Leicestershire in the south, with ripples running into Cumberland and Tyneside. Mather accepts much merit in Challinor and Ripley's claim that 1842 was the first general strike in any capitalist country, for although not completely general in the sense of being nationwide, it involved in many towns an almost complete cessation of labour; for example in Oldham where it brought out together miners, mule spinners and machine-makers as well as surrounding outworkers. It was much more than a strike in the sense that state power, although it was probably never in real danger, was being challenged in a novel way by workers declaring an intention of staying out until the constitution had been overturned in the direction of universal suffrage and who to that end occupied whole towns for hours on end.[58]

Matters commenced with a strike in the North Staffordshire coalfield on 8 July and from there events, as described by Mather, unfolded in four stages. Firstly up to 2 August they were confined to the Staffordshire coalfields and to economic objectives, largely wages and the truck question. Already in the raking of boiler fires and in the pulling of the drain plugs to stop working, they were indicating the peculiar forms of action which characterised the strike and gave them their name. Secondly, from 3–11 August their incidence extended geographically and occupationally. In Lancashire the cotton operatives, whose participation was to have especial significance, commenced their strikes at Stalybridge which soon spread into Manchester and nearby towns. At this point the Charter was not at the centre of the agitation: issues like the need for the Ten Hour Bill and the restoration of wages to their 1840 level were more to the fore. In the third phase from 12–20 August, the height of the strike wave was reached with armies of strikers marching from town to town and mine to mine enforcing a turn-out that became general in the manufacturing districts of Lancashire and Cheshire and the West Riding, and reached into Leicestershire and Nottinghamshire. It was at this point that meetings at Manchester made a specific linking to the cause of the Charter, and open clashes with the military took place at Preston, Blackburn, in the Potteries and in Yorkshire. In the final phase from August to late September, events entered what Mather describes as the 'anticlimacteric'. Violence diminished, although especially in south-east Lancashire cotton workers held out longer, but by then for wage restoration rather than for the Charter: a full circle in that what had begun as a wage struggle ended as one.[59]

In the press and by the government, a view of a concert between Chartists and trade unionists was assumed. Among modern historians some, like Professor Read, have taken the view that the connection was not causal but, rather, economically motivated strikes were briefly taken over and exploited by the Chartists. Mather thinks the truth comes between. Conscious creative leadership was exerted by the Chartists at two successive stages: one was at its inception when the importance of the leaders directing the colliers and cotton workers as to what to demand and where to turn out seems evident. Both from Stalybridge and from Staffordshire there is clear evidence of local trades' committees being crucial to the formulation of these demands, and that the speakers at the open-air mobilisation meetings were mostly Chartists unconnected with local industries. It is unclear why Chartists pushed themselves to the van. There is no more reason to suppose that they did so as part of a plan to take over than as part of a natural attachment to the furtherance of working-class interests, but either way they had a clear influence on tactics and direction.

The second intervention came through the Manchester delegate conferences. There were, as Mather importantly points out, *two* differently convened ones. The National Charter Association held its national conference on 16 and 17 August, and a conference of delegates from the trades of the region met from 11–20 August. The significance of the first which resolved in favour of the strike for the Charter is usually accepted, but Mather stresses the importance of the second for it gave the first general lead to the adoption of the Charter, which may have been less sinister and more spontaneous than the government supposed, and the lead had interestingly come from the mechanics not the cotton workers. Chartist leadership, he concludes, was real and made the outbreak more serious. It failed not because of the quality of their leadership, but because starvation and the determination of the government to restore order were bound to end it.[60]

Subsequent investigations generally accept Professor Mather's account. A count from the *Northern Star* for 1842 has produced 200 meetings in south Lancashire at which the Charter was advocated, and the role of Chartist agitation from the beginning has become even more confirmed.[61] Robert Sykes has been firm in his dismissal of the idea that the connections of Chartism and trade unionism were only a temporary and novel aberration by pointing to both the informal links of shared values and personnel and to formal ones by trade societies acting as such, even if no single society maintaining an existence in an atmosphere repressively hostile towards Chartism gave it wholly continuous open support. The rule so often insisted upon by the 'compartmentalists' that politics were not discussed at union meetings has never been proved as general as they suppose and in any event was often evaded and applied only to *formal* meetings for union business. In south-east Lancashire, distinctions between skilled and unskilled and between factory workers and others seem hardly appropriate as Chartism cut across them, although Prothero's London distinction between the 'upper' and 'lower' ranks of the skilled is more applicable. However, most adult males with some skill were not among the 'aristocrats', and the Charter secured support from cotton spinners, calico printers and dyers as well as from the older craft trades and clothing outworkers. In many cases these trades had a community of interest, facing similar threats to status and well-being from structural reorganisation of their respective manufactures, and they were joined by others of lower status like the power-loom and the handloom weavers. Compared with this support the 'aloof' aristocrats were very restricted in numbers, especially given that the involvement of factory workers in Chartism has been seriously underestimated in cotton and wool towns where the reduction of the numbers of handloom weavers had already proceeded to a point where they were too few to account for the level of support which existed.[62]

Lancashire's cotton workers had, as we have seen, a long tradition of inter-trade action from the days of the Philanthropic Hercules through those of the National Association for the Protection of Labour and the Factory Movement. Mutual strike support was well ingrained in them as it was in building workers. This tradition of co-operation was admittedly strongest among the lower, more insecure trades, but it existed among factory workers and textile outworkers. Most recently, support for the convicted spinners after the Glasgow strike of 1837 had shown the strength of the underlying tradition. The aloofness of the upper ranks of the skilled has received a disproportionate attention from historians because of the permanent nature of their organisations. Chartism had links with less formal associations of 'class, community, neighbourhood workshop and mill', which were also bases for industrial action.[63]

Robert Sykes's warning is very relevant, as indeed it is in other contexts where formal organisation has been held synonymous with unionism and given too great a preponderance in trade union history.

Collective industrial action among groups like handloom and power-loom weavers and among miners did not even by 1842 depend necessarily upon the prior existence of formal organisation: 'Unions' could be temporary creations, or explosive expansions of existing small-scale societies. The earlier peak of Chartist agitation in 1838/9 coincided with a period in which there had been no major mill strike. It was the wage-cutting rounds which began among different groups of workers in 1840 which produced the industrial action which became linked with Chartism's second peak of 1842. Links with the trades, although of a difficult to determine extent, developed with the emergence of the National Charter Association. Sykes concludes that links between Chartism and the trades were of real importance in personnel, leadership and in newspapers. Those who held aloof were the numerically small group of tradesmen loosely correlated to the 30s. (£1.50) a week line, while the numbers of the casualty trades like handloom weaving, though large, have been overstated for in Lancashire Chartism depended as much on artisans and factory workers.[64]

John Foster has given the events of 1842 special importance in his much-discussed argument on the rise and fall of class consciousness in Oldham. Generalisations about cotton mill operatives and their strike for the Charter must be advanced with some caution. Manchester and its district and Ashton certainly declared for it, while Stockport, Macclesfield, Stalybridge, Moseley and Bury were more ambiguous in their support, preferring to emphasise wage issues. In the case of Oldham, Musson has criticised Foster's emphasis on the class-conscious political nature of the strike by pointing out that Oldham's workers seem to have struck their mills only after strikers from Ashton arrived in the town and closed them. In fact the strike did take place within a context of rising political debate and consciousness. At the end of lengthy discussion, the arrival of Ashton's striking operatives on 8 August was perhaps a stimulus rather than a *sine qua non*. Ashton's men brought no arguments with them that had not been passing back and forth in Oldham for several weeks. A Chartist meeting had been attended by more than 1,000 as early as January and one in June by 5,000. In July, Peter McDouall, the member of the Chartist executive most stridently advocating the political strike, was in the town, and it was only by a small vote that the local leadership decided to stick to the line of the majority of the Executive. It was therefore much more the case that when news of the Manchester reversal and call for a strike for the Charter reached the town on 15 August, the workers were ready to respond than that they were nudged into action by the arrival of the Ashton men. All in all it must be accepted that in 1842 there was very considerable, though far from universal, support for the 'political strike' from Lancashire's cotton workers.[65]

The first disturbances took place in Staffordshire, and Robert Fysons has added to our knowledge of its momentum and impact in the Potteries where it climaxed in the riots of 15 and 16 August. Potters were among those most influenced by the wave of general unionism and in fact outlasted the Londoners before going under in a strike in 1837. The rise of a militant Chartism in the area owes something to the aftermath of disillusionment with strike action, but it was with the colliers that the events of 1842 began and it was the resulting stoppage of coal which forced the potteries to close. According to the preconceptions nourished by some historians of trade unionism, this should have set potter against collier. It did not do so. Instead, the potters declared 'a quiet determination to endure anything, so that the rise of wages asked by the colliers may be gained'. Links between the colliers and the Chartists are less clear, although they undoubtedly had some representation on Chartist committees, despite a more general denial that they had any political motives. When Thomas Cooper, the Chartist leader whose speech is generally said to have provoked the riots, arrived in Stoke on 13 August the brink had already been reached: 'I had caught the spirit of the oppressed and discontented thousands, and, by virtue of my nature and constitution, struck the spark which kindled all into combustion.' What really mattered was the news from Manchester that a strike for the Charter had been called, and what followed was an enforcement of it on those at work in collieries and in potteries. Events in the Potteries were less well organised and Chartist leadership less evident than in Lancashire, but once again a moment of economic crisis coincided with spontaneous popular resistance to accept an available politicisation and effect a brief, but definite, challenge to authority. At a basic level the true significance of 1842 is not as a rehearsal for 1926 but as an illustration of close local-level connections between trade unions and political activists from which a recent historian of Chartism has concluded: 'In the depths of misery the fundamental unity of the working-class community was demonstrated, so that reporters with local knowledge could identify . . . the local trades leaders of 1842 as Chartists.'[66]

THE MINERS' ASSOCIATION

The largest single occupational union of the Chartist era was the Miners' Association of Great Britain and Ireland established towards the end of 1842 whose 60,000 members from every major coalfield at its peak in 1844 made it an astonishing national union in an occupation where strong locality orientations made national union in itself a striking achievement. It was, as its modern historians suggest, such an object of awe in its day that contemporaries tended to overstate both its membership and its finances. Its aims were economic: 'to unite all miners to equalise and diminish the hours of labour and to obtain the highest possible amount of wages for the labour of the miner'. In its official discourse in the aftermath of 1842 was a rejection of utopian or political ends. Experience of repression had bestowed a language of caution, but organisationally it intended something more permanent than the coalfields had thus far produced individually. Exact links with Chartism are not clear. Miners in general provided more mass than leadership to Chartism, but among the Association's leaders were several, notably the treasurer Martin Jude, who were Chartists. Thomas Hepburn, the leader banned by his own for swearing from engaging in union activity after leading the defeated strike of 1832, was much in demand as a Chartist speaker and, above all, W. P. Roberts, the lawyer who brought a new dimension to the working-class struggle in the law courts, was a Chartist. So too was Benjamin Embleton whose active role in miners' unions went back to the strike of 1810. With coal-owners only too willing to attribute any manifestation of unrest to Chartist agitation, it is possible, as Challinor and Ripley have suggested, that a 'closet' Chartism only became more open after the great strike in Northumberland and Durham in 1844, when the public image became less important.[67]

The initial impulse in 1842 came from a call at a meeting of York-shire miners at Halifax for a national union for – and here was a touch of recent visions – the establishment of a national fund to support a one-day strike of all the coal miners in England. Contact was made with the north-east in the January of 1843 and the two regions dominated the first conference in the summer which put forward earnings restriction by miners to a maximum of 3s. (15p) a day as its main policy to create more jobs and maintain wages. By August, progress in spreading the idea of a national union had been made in Derby, Staffordshire, Wales, Cumberland and Scotland. Consider-able success was beginning in the Lancashire coalfield, but in north Staffordshire there had been a much greater proportionate success than in the larger south Staffordshire coalfield, where repression in the aftermath of 1842 as well as the failure of local attempts to resist wage reductions in 1843 had crushed the spirit of union.[68]

Crucial figures in the Association's organisation were the itinerant lecturers who, for around 18–21s. (90p–£1.05p) a week and under instruction to stay clear of politics, took the message of union to the coalfields. From them, as from the newspaper *The Miners' Advocate*, a high moral tone was expected and this extended to general conduct at union meetings. Fines for offences such as swearing or being drunk were so high that the *Durham Chronicle* could score points by pointing out that the union was itself fining more heavily than were the hated, exploitative coal-owners.[69]

Much of the union's success was due to the extraordinary, tireless efforts of the Chartist lawyer W. P. Roberts, employed as legal officer first by the Northumberland and Durham miners and then by the Assocation as a whole. His policy was to drag the owners through the courts by contesting every case in the north-east in a war of attrition against the bond; recovering wages, freeing miners imprisoned for breaches of agreement and, later, contesting verdicts on pit deaths:

> Cheer up, my lads, for Roberts's bold;
> And well defends our cause,
> For such a drubbing he's gi'en them
> With their own class-made laws.

The industrial tactic initially preferred by the Association was not the strike but the deliberate restriction of output to an earnings maximum of 3s. (15p) a day. But it was difficult to enforce, and strikes constantly came to the fore in discussion after the national conference of September 1843. Lancashire was the district most in favour and, as we shall see, was the district where a strike was most likely to have met with some success. Official policy was firmly against partial (local) strikes, believing that if the Association could not achieve its objects without striking, then only a national strike could hope to be effective. By the spring of 1844, however, Roberts had engineered a showdown over the bonding system in the north-east and reluctantly, to the anxiety of Jude and his executive associates who feared a major confrontation would break the union, the pitmen of the north-east were given the go-ahead to strike.[70]

The timing was bad: trade was depressed, coal stocks were high and the owners, operating at very low levels of profit, were feeling that they had nothing to give away. The striking pitmen went on week after week solidly and in remarkably good order. The coal-owners brought in 'blacklegs' despite the efforts of the Association to dissuade miners from other districts from coming by sending delegates to inform them of the pitmen's case. Blacklegs were brought from as far away as the tin and copper mines of Cornwall, and from their introduction followed the cottage evictions as miners and their families, young and old, were turned out from their homes. The pitiful scenes and the dignity with which the families bore their affliction are well known. The region's historian Robert Fynes was himself a witness:

> Wholesale turning to the door commenced in almost every colliery village;
> pregnant women, bedridden men, and even children in their cradles, were
> ruthlessly turned out. Age and sex were disregarded, no woman was too
> weak, no child too young, no grandma or grandsire too old; but all must go
> forth.

The coal-owners justified themselves in terms of stern paternalism and
the sacred rights of property, Lord Londonderry supplying a particularly emphatic defence of his savage cruelty: 'I found you dogged,
obstinate and determined – indifferent to my really paternal advice
and kind feelings to the old families of the Vane and Tempest pitmen
. . . I was bound to act up to my word – bound by my duty to my
property, my family and my station.' Roberts appealed for non-
violence – 'Let them *carry* you out' – while tent villages sprung up by
the roadsides. Strike pay of 2s. 6d. (12½p) a week was little enough,
but there were no frontiers to Londonderry's vindictiveness and he
warned off any trader who offered credit and pronounced that any
miner who took it would never be re-employed.[71]

At length the struggle could no longer be borne and by mid-August,
beginning in Durham, with 'blacklegs' increasing in number, the
pitmen started to return. Nothing had been gained by their heroic
stand. Victimisation was widespread and eventually it and the sense of
futility which defeat brings brought about the demise of union in the
north-east.[72]

Defeat in the north-east was a turning point for the Association as a
whole. Avoidance of 'partial' strikes had never been a realistic policy
when in several areas the very right to belong to a union was in dispute
and in most areas statements of a wish to avoid confrontation brought
no reciprocation from the coal-owners. In Derbyshire the owners
responded to a union disclaimer of strike action in favour of 'amicable
adjustment of differences' by refusing to employ union men and
defeating the desperate strike which resulted. In north Staffordshire,
owners with a relatively good reputation as employers did not oppose
the union until it tried to apply the official policy of restricting output,
but then forced a strike in which they comfortably outlasted the
colliers. When the Association met for its conference at Burslem in
July 1844 it had to appraise a situation which had moved far beyond its
intent. In coalfield after coalfield partial strikes had taken place and
were sapping its finances at the very time when the pitmen of the
north-east needed support. There was little to be done and the conference concerned itself largely with matters of relief and with
attempts to unionise the coalfields, especially Wales, from which
'blacklegs' were being recruited.[73]

In Yorkshire, some miners were out for three months. Here, several
of the owners, notably Lord Fitzwilliam, had opposed the union from

the start, dismissing leaders and evicting them from their cottages while declaring that any miner not producing his normal output would be deemed a member of the union and dismissed. They refused to negotiate; to have done so would have been 'an unjust and uncalled for interference with the rights of masters and men'. When a strike began on 12 May, 'blacklegs' were very quickly brought in and mass evictions commenced. The savage indifference to suffering of Fitzwilliam and his ilk brought a flood of sympathy for the strikers not only from trade unionists in the towns, but also in the press, especially the *Leeds Times*, and subscriptions for relief were set up. By October the strike had been defeated although a few of the smaller owners went some way towards meeting the miners' demands.[74]

The year 1844 began with a spate of strikes – nineteen separate ones around St Helens alone – in Lancashire which had always, against national policy, favoured strike action, and in the close-knit industrial area into which the pits were integrated had some success in securing wage advances. In the spring the owners made an attempt to assert control over the labour force by the introduction of a yearly hiring bond on the north-east model and to make it effective by breaking the union through the hire of 'blacklegs'. Amid rioting and the calling in of troops, the strikes spread all over the Lancashire coalfield, but here the unions came through the struggle and even succeeded in obtaining something approaching the 'closed shop'. The market for Lancashire's coal was largely guaranteed by the county's own manufacturing needs and this strong local demand meant that industrial action could have some hope of success, while the tactic of the 'rolling strike' against one mine at a time was well suited to the small-ownership structure of the region.[75]

By 1845 the union had collapsed in the north-east, and although in 1846 there were membership gains in Staffordshire, Derbyshire and in Nottinghamshire, the centre of gravity undoubtedly moved to Lancashire whose members filled all the national offices by the time of the last national conference in 1847. Although, as its historians describe it, the Miners' Association was 'A Trade Union in the Age of the Chartists', the sense in which it was a Chartist union is much more debatable and by some historians, notably Professor Taylor, is largely dismissed. It never at any time seems to have contemplated a strike for other than economic ends, although throughout its existence the inspector of mines in the north-east remained convinced that Chartist agitators lay behind the industrial unrest. There is little doubt that Chartism helped to articulate the grievances of the miners; that many of its leaders, including Roberts, were men of strong Chartist convictions and that the *Northern Star* until it split with the Lancashire union carried support far beyond the reaches of the Miners' Advocate.[76]

When a newspaper correspondent visited the north-east in 1850 he commented that the effects of the defeat of 1844 were apparent in the 'still dissolved' colliers' union, and only in a few pits were there signs of the men restricting their labour. On the Staffordshire field, although restriction seems to have been still practised in 1847, a period of slack trade had finished the union by 1849. Similar reports came from the centre of cotton manufacture, Manchester, where 'unions, trade combinations, and strikes have gone greatly out of fashion'.[77]

In contrast to the decline in the power of the unions in coal mining and in cotton, some groups operating in more specific local labour contexts were still asserting an effective unionism. The shipwrights of Liverpool, for example, having long since realised that they could not control the shipbuilding on the Mersey, had concentrated on controlling the ship-repair yards and were described as 'the most powerful associated body of working men in the town of Liverpool'. Holding regular meetings in rooms which they owned, they had used their 'closed shop' to maintain a position of strength which outlasted the ending in 1832 of their special privilege as freemen voters, when at election time, 'rich merchants' had walked arm in arm with shipwrights. They were still successfully regulating apprenticeship and had through this, and through maintaining the standard work output of 5s. (25p) a day, kept reasonably full employment to ensure to the shipwright an average of four days a week throughout the year. This they had managed to secure by collective pressure, despite not resorting to serious strike action for twenty-three years.[78]

In the mid-century survey of London's trades, Henry Mayhew found similar well-organised groups. The leather curriers had a 'very compact and well regulated trade society' which insisted upon apprenticeship and controlled the numbers admitted and recognised 'fair' masters by their acceptance of a book of rates drawn up in 1812. The 'wet' coopers too exercised a similar degree of control including the 'right' of filling any vacancies which arose. The reforming of unions among groups like tailors, shoemakers and hatters had, however, been much more defensive than assertive. Since the great strike of the 1830s, concern was now to preserve at the small bespoke ends of trades a union presence of skilled workers in the face of the ever-rising tide of the unskilled. Unions of tailors and shoemakers staunchly upheld prices in the West End, but in the former only 3,000 of 20,799 operatives were in the unionised section and in shoemaking only 850 out of 26,478. Clearly the trade unionism had changed from brief but wider visions of the 1830s and was in most trades now reconstituted as protective of the interests of around one in ten of the operatives.[79]

The building unions too had by the late 1840s come through damaging experiences. In London the masons had lost the strike over the building of Parliament when, coming out in protest over the activities of an over-bearing foreman, they had stayed out for six months. At Liverpool and Manchester in 1846, in a contest over the nine-hour day, the employers locked out the building workers. It was a showdown after a long period of contesting the issues of prices, apprenticeship and hours of work – all of which had been brought to the forefront by the growing practice of 'general contracting'. Between 1840 and 1846 the masons alone record forty-four strikes in the northwest of which only twenty-three were over wages issues. Using the building trades as his case study, Dr Price has supplied an important corrective to conventional views of skilled unionists as presenting a less fundamental challenge to capitalist assumptions, not only over the functioning of the labour market (through, as we have seen, insisting on apprenticeship) but also over work control, than they had done in the heady days of Owenism and the political strike episode of 1842. Forms of militancy in 'the age of equipoise', he argues, were not only appropriate but challenging. In a competitive world, building entrepreneurs looked not only to keep labour costs down, but to extract the maximum intensity of labour. To this end 'general contractors' utilised the sub-contract system and 'chasing' foremen who sped up and subverted old working rhythms. In a revealing comment in 1850 a foreman carpenter admitted to Mayhew that never having been formally trained, 'I never could have belonged to our regular trade society'. What building entrepreneurs were seeking was a total freedom to order and organise the labour force as they pleased, to hire and fire at a moment's notice, insist on overtime, and to sub-contract. It was this fundamental struggle for control which underlay the strike of building workers on the new Houses of Parliament and Nelson's column in 1841. The employers made this clear when they pointed out:

> What is called contract work [is] undertaken for specific sums, and for which our calculations have . . . been made on the presumption that a good workman will execute a given quantity of work . . . The position, therefore, in which we must be placed by having the necessary authority of an employer wrested from us . . . by a combination of workmen . . . may easily be imagined.

In opposition to the imperatives of the sub-contracting and piecework systems, the building workers sought to re-assert their traditional 'controls'. Unlike modern historians, the employers did not miss the fundamental nature of the contest, but saw it as a question of whether the 'employers or operatives are to be masters'. The London struggle of 1841 throws a searchlight on to a matter which was more usually less public. The tyranny of George Allen, the foreman, was real enough: he compelled purchases from a relative's pub; he would not allow customary rest breaks; he discharged for borrowing or lending tools; he abused a man who took leave to bury his wife, would not allow another to visit his sick mother and abused a man crippled on a site accident. The separate skilled craft groups who comprised the traditional building industry were not at all used to 'chasing' foremen exerting their authority over the craft concerns of skilled men. Allen was very much a front man for the employers' onslaught on the autonomy of skill; his activities had previously produced a strike on the London–Birmingham railway when he had tried to introduce a piece-rate system in 1837. Shortly before the strike in London began, his 'bell-horse' had been fined by the masons' union for breaking their regulations on work and price. It was unfair 'to get a man of great physical strength and urge him to do a certain quantity of work and then go around to all the men, many of whom had worked for years for the firm, and to tell them "if you do not come up to this standard you will be discharged".' As Price points out, Allen's 'tyranny' was as much a result of the general contracting system and its associated sub-contracting as it was of his horrible personality. From the employer's point of view he was a *good* foreman. He was in fact an unpopular but necessary NCO. The military imagery is appropriate, being consonant with that of the employers:

> that a discipline similar to that maintained in the army or navy should be enforced, and the masons in not quietly submitting to it, must be bent on ruining the firm . . . the competency of the foreman to superintend such work would consist in his being such a man as he was . . . a harsh and severe individual would only answer his purpose.

Had Allen been sacked, the role of foreman as employers' agent would have been seriously undermined. The ultimate question was who was to decide the working arrangements and what constituted a reasonable amount of labour. The issues in the dispute over the length of the day in the north-west in 1846 (resumed in 1859) seem smaller, but in them once again the contesting discourse from the masters' side reveals key 'control' words like 'power' and 'interference'.[80]

The Webbs' chronology, which insisted on the break to the 'new model union' symbolised by the ASE in 1851, has been justly criticised by Musson. Continuities are difficult to deny given that skilled workers remained throughout the vanguard of the trade union movement and had craft interests and standards to protect, but those historians who detect subtle shifts in the meaning of 'elite' unionism at mid-century present cases which are well worth consideration. Prothero has pointed out that although primacy in the trade movement of the 1840s and 1850s may have passed to the upper trades, what was new was precisely this dominance following a period when primacy had belonged to the 'lower' trades like weavers, tailors and shoemakers who, although the future did not belong to them, were distinguished in their period of dominance, the 1830s, by the 'markedly collectivist character of their programmes'.[81] Foster has maintained that the 'aristocracy' of labour as it was constituted by the 1840s had to be funda-mentally different from the 'aristocracies' of elite groups from the traditional artisan ranks, for by the 1840s with the emergence of a factory proletariat and an articulated labour consciousness a wedge *had* to be driven between 'the consciously anti-capitalist elements and labour organisations as such'. The point seems evident: upper ranks within the labour-selling classes had long existed, but only after *c.* 1840 was it necessary for capitalism to seek an accommodation with them. This is the essential assumption for Foster's argument that a 'liberalisation' of a skilled worker vanguard symbolised a sea-change from the radical class confrontation issues of the 1830s.[82] What the student must be cautioned against seeing, however, is in any sense a *complete* accommodation to the values of liberal capitalism for, as we have seen, attempts to effectively close shops by an insistence on apprenticeship and struggles for 'workers' control' over the processes of labour remained important points of conflict between capital and labour. It is sometimes suggested that, in view of the small proportion of the working people who were by the early Victorian years members of trade unions, historians have given to trade unionism a disproportionate amount of attention. There is some truth in this: labour historians themselves sometimes have guilt feelings on the matter, while feminist historians are not slow to point out that by being almost exclusively male, early trade unions excluded half at least of the working people on a gender basis. We are all aware of the dangers of 'Whigism', but there remains a fundamental need to understand the present day in an historical context. Few institutions of modern British society are less intelligibly divorced from their history than the trade union movement. Indeed, journalists are fond of portraying it as a victim of its past. That history is a long one and within it few methods of defending the interests of workers available to modern trade unions have not been prefigured. In fact, since the Webbs completed their celebrated history in 1895 no major synthesis of trade union which gives other than brief coverage to the years before 1850 has appeared. There have been challenging essays, lively debates and significant studies of particular industries or regions. We now need a *new* history of the formative years of the trade union movement which would emphasise much less the institutional history of the unions and search much more for presence in the practices and day-to-day relationships of the shopfloor. It would not ignore the context of politics, society and the labour market in which unions operate, and would remain aware of the relationship of unionism to the working class as a whole.

REFERENCES AND NOTES

1. **E. P. Thompson**, *The Making of the English Working Class*, Penguin, 1968, p. 908.
2. Ibid., pp. 908, 285.
3. **S.** and **B. Webb**, *History of Trade Unionism*, Longman, 1911 edn, p. 131.

The poem is printed in **R.** and **E. Frow** and **N.. Katanka** (eds), *Strikes. A Documentary History*, Charles Knight, 1971, p. 30.

4. **M. J. Haynes**, 'Class and class conflict in the early nineteenth century: Northampton shoemakers and the Grand National Consolidated Trades Union', *Literature and History*, no. 5, 1977, pp. 86–8; 'Reminiscences of Thomas Dunning', in **D. Vincent** (ed.), *Testaments of Radicalism*, Europa, 1977, pp. 126–34.

5. **C. Behagg**, 'Customs, class and change: the trade societies of Birmingham', *Social History*, vol. 4, no. 3, 1979, p. 459.

6. **P. S. Bagwell**, *Industrial Relations*, Irish U.P., 1974, pp. 15–16.

7. Documents on early disputes in coal mining are to be found in **A. Aspinall**, *The Early English Trade Unions*, Batchworth, 1949; for 'Scotch Cattle' see **G. D. H. Cole** and **A. W. Filson** (eds), *British Working Class Movements, Select Documents 1789–1875*, Macmillan, 1951, pp. 260, 15. See also **J. Benson**, *British Coalminers in the Nineteenth Century: A Social History*, Gill & Macmillan, 1980, pp. 189–94 and **J. L.** and **B. Hammond**, *The Skilled Labourer*, ed. J. G. Rule, Longman, 1979, pp. 16, 25.

8. Benson, *Coalminers*, p. 195.

9. Hammonds, *Skilled Labourer*, pp. 16–19.

10. Ibid., p. 21; Benson, *Coalminers*, p. 195. The most detailed account of the strikes of 1831 and 1832 on the Tyne and Wear is Ch. 3 of Hammonds, *Skilled Labourer*.

11. Hammonds, *Skilled Labourer*, p. 35.

12. Ibid., pp. 34–5 for full text of Melbourne's letter.

13. Thompson, *Making of the English Working Class*, pp. 909–10, 913.

14. For a critique of 'compartmentalism', see **F. K. Donnelly**, 'Ideology and early English working-class history: Edward Thompson and his critics', *Social History*, 2, 1976. pp. 224–9.

15. **A. E. Musson**, *British Trade Unions, 1800–1875*, Macmillan, 1972, pp. 29–35.

16. Webbs, *History of Trade Unionism*, p. 137.

17. Ibid., p. 149.

18. Based on the Mss. records of the Operative Stonemasons Society in the Modern Records Centre, University of Warwick.

19. A copy of the circular is in the records of the Operative Stonemasons. See also Webbs, *History of Trade Unionism*, pp. 155–6.

20. Subscription list in the records of Stonemasons Society.

21. **W. Kiddier**, *The Old Trade Unions from unprinted records of the Brushmakers*, Allen and Unwin, 1930, pp. 42–9.

22. Mss. records of Stonemasons; Webbs, *History of Trade Unionism*, p. 161.

23. Ibid., p. 161.

24. Ibid., pp. 179–80.

25. Ibid., pp. 180–2.

26. See Musson, *British Trade Unions*, pp. 49–58.

27. **J. B. Jefferys**, *The Story of the Engineers 1800–1945*, Lawrence and Wishart, 1945, p. 11.

28. Ibid., p. 16; Cole and Filson, *British Working Class Movements*, pp. 290–1.

29. Jefferys, *Engineers,* pp. 18–21; Webbs, *History of Trade Unionism,* pp. 186–94.
30. Ibid., p. 184.
31. **W. H. Chaloner**, *The Skilled Artisan during the Industrial Revolution 1750–1850,* Historical Association, 1969, pp. 5–10.
32. *Trades Societies and Strikes,* National Association for the Promotion of Social Science, 1860, repr. Kelley, 1968, pp. 131–2.
33. **S. Pollard**, *A History of Labour in Sheffield,* Liverpool U.P., 1959, pp. 68, 71, 75.
34. **J. F. Clarke**, 'Workers in Tyneside shipyards' and 'Engineering workers on Tyneside', in **N. McCord** (ed.), *Essays in Tyneside Labour History,* Newcastle upon Tyne Polytechnic, 1976, pp. 109–10, 88.
35. **A. E. Musson**, *The Typographical Association. Origins and History up to 1949,* Oxford U.P., 1954, pp. 19, 28–9, 42–3, 69; Chaloner, *Skilled Artisan,* p. 8.
36. **R. W. Postgate**, *The Builders' History,* Labour Publishing Company Limited, 1923, pp. 27, 29, 31, 131–7, 151; Chaloner, *Skilled Artisan,* p. 9; **G. Crossick**, *An Artisan Elite in Victorian Society,* Croom Helm, 1978, pp. 113–14, 73–4.
37. **E. Hopkins**, 'Working conditions in Victorian Stourbridge', *International Review of Social History,* vol. XIX, 1974, pp. 421–2.
38. Postgate, *Builders' History,* p. 119; Webbs, *History of Trade Unionism,* pp. 80–1; **A. E. Musson**, 'Early trade unionism in the printing industry', in *Trade Union and Social History,* Cass, 1974, pp. 90, 102–4, 119.
39. **C. Behagg**, 'Secrecy, ritual and folk violence: the opacity of the workplace in the first half of the nineteenth century', in **R. D. Storch** (ed.), *Popular Culture and Custom in Nineteenth Century England,* Croom Helm, 1982, pp. 154–79; **R. Price**, *Masters, Unions and Men, Work Control in Building and the Rise of Labour 1830–1914,* Cambridge U.P., 1980.
40. Behagg, 'Secrecy, ritual and folk violence', pp. 157–8.
41. Ibid., p. 158.
42. See **J. Rule**, *The Experience of Labour in Eighteenth-Century Industry,* Croom Helm, 1981, pp. 198–201.
43. Behagg, 'Secrecy, ritual and folk violence', pp. 163–5.
44. Rule, *Experience of Labour,* pp. 195–7.
45. Ibid., pp. 199–200; **S. Pollard**, Introduction to *The Sheffield Outrages,* Bath, Adams & Dart, 1967.
46. Behagg, 'Secrecy, ritual and folk violence', p. 170; Rule, *Experience of Labour,* pp. 200–1.
47. Behagg, 'Secrecy, ritual and folk violence', p. 171.
48. **I. Prothero**, *Artisans and Politics in Early Nineteenth-Century London. John Gast and his Times,* Dawson, 1979, p. 1.
49. Webbs, *History of Trade Unionism,* p. 158.
50. **Asa Briggs**, (ed.), *Chartist Studies,* Macmillan, 1962, p. 6.
51. **D. Jones**, *Chartism and the Chartists,* St Martins Press, 1975, p. 143.
52. **F. C. Mather**, *Chartism and Society. An Anthology of Documents,* Bell & Hyman, 1980, p. 250; **R. Sykes**, 'Early Chartism and trade unionism in south-east Lancashire', in **J. Epstein** & **D. Thompson** (eds), *The Chartist Experience,* Macmillan, 1982, pp. 175, 180, 152.
53. **I. Prothero**, 'London Chartism and the trades', *Economic History*

Review, vol. XXIV, no. 2, 1971, pp. 202–18; Webbs, *History of Trade Unionism*, p. 177.

54. **E. H. Hunt**, *British Labour History 1815–1914*, Weidenfeld & Nicolson, 1981, p. 204.

55. Prothero, 'London Chartism', pp. 213–18; Jones, *Chartism and the Chartists*, p. 142.

56. Mather, *Chartism and Society*, pp. 241–3.

57. Ibid., p. 252.

58. **F. C. Mather**, 'The general strike of 1842: a study of leadership organisation and the threat of revolution during the plug plot disturbances', in **R. Quinault** & **J. Stevenson** (eds), *Popular Protest and Public Order*, Allen & Unwin, 1974, pp. 115–16.

59. Ibid., pp. 117–19.

60. Ibid., pp. 120–35.

61. **B. R. Brown**, 'Industrial capitalism, conflict and working-class contention in Lancashire in 1842', in **L. A.** & **C. Tilly** (eds), *Class Conflict and Collective Action*, Sage, 1981, p. 122.

62. Sykes, 'Early Chartism and trade unionism', pp. 152–3.

63. Ibid., pp. 176–80.

64. Ibid., pp. 184–5.

65. **J. Foster**, *Class Struggle and the Industrial Revolution. Early industrial capitalism in three English towns*, Methuen pbk, 1974, pp. 114–16; **A. E. Musson**, 'Class struggle and the labour aristocracy, 1830–60', *Social History*, 3, 1976, p. 341.

66. **R. Fyson**, 'The crisis of 1842: Chartism, the colliers' strike and the outbreak in the potteries', in Epstein & Thompson (eds), *Chartist Experience*, pp. 195, 197–216; **E. Royle**, *Chartism*, Longman, 1980, p. 30.

67. The fullest account is **R. Challinor** and **B. Ripley**, *The Miners' Association: A Trade Union in the Age of the Chartists*, Lawrence & Wishart, 1968.

68. Ibid., pp. 62–70.

69. Ibid., pp. 75–9.

70. Ibid., pp. 109–25.

71. Ibid., pp. 133–46.

72. Ibid., pp. 141–51.

73. Ibid., pp. 156–61.

74. Ibid., pp. 162–5.

75. Ibid., pp. 167–71.

76. Ibid., pp. 179–97; **A. J. Taylor**, 'The Miners' Association of Great Britain and Ireland, 1842–48', *Economica*, XXII, 1955.

77. **P. E. Razzell** and **R. W. Wainwright** (eds), *The Victorian Working Class: Selections from Letters to the Morning Chronicle*, Cass, 1973, pp. 215–16, 229, 240, 171.

78. Ibid., p. 283.

79. **E. P. Thompson** and **E. Yeo** (eds), *The Unknown Mayhew*, Penguin, 1973, pp. 218, 223, 276–94, 410, 444, 455–6, 500–11, 536–40, 559–60.

80. Price, *Masters, Unions and Men*, pp. 36–8, 41.

81. Prothero, 'London Chartism', pp. 205–6.

82. Foster, *Class Struggle*, Ch. 7, 'Liberalisation' and see his rejoinder to Musson in *Social History*, 3, 1976, p. 359.

Chapter 14

THE PROTESTING CROWD: RIOTS AND DISTURBANCES

THE ENGLISH FOOD RIOTS

Even among miners and manufacturing workers the most frequent form of protest used in the eighteenth century was the food riot, arising not out of industrial grievances but out of food prices. The *Annual Register* for 1766 lists more than forty outbreaks in fifty places, and at least twice that number of incidents have since been noted, and identifies coalminers, tin miners, weavers and bargemen as being involved, although generally referring only to the rioters as the 'mob'. Food riots continued to be the predominant protest form until at least the widespread rioting of 1801. In the early nineteenth century they occurred much less frequently and only in one or two areas. The rioting in the mining districts of Cornwall in 1847 has generally been regarded as the last significant English outbreak, but recently it has been shown that outbreaks in south Devon in 1854 and 1867 were very much in the tradition of the eighteenth-century food riot. Early analyses of the spread of food rioting tended to suggest that from a point of origin in Oxfordshire in the closing years of the seventeenth century they spread over the south and west and into the Midlands, but were uncommon in the northern counties. Recent work has suggested that they were more common in the north-west than has been supposed, probably began in the south-east in the late sixteenth century and also cast doubts on the validity of assuming a geographical pattern from the counting of *documented* incidents.[1]

After the pioneering researches of Rose and Rudé established the forms and functions of the food riot, the most significant contribution to understanding them has come from E. P. Thompson who has written of a 'moral economy' of the English crowd. He has emphasised the sense in which rioters concerned to fix 'just' prices on seized corn saw themselves as acting legitimately in the context both of custom and of paternalist legislation of the Tudor and Stuart periods which restricted the activities of corn dealers (middlemen) in enhancing the price of corn and allowed for the fixing of prices by the local justices.[2] In addition to such 'jobbers', other objects of the righteous displeasure of the rioters included farmers who were suspected of withholding grain from the market in order to push up prices to form an 'artificial scarcity'; merchants who bought up corn for removal from the district in which it was grown when supplies were popularly presumed inadequate for local consumption; and millers who were either thought to be hoarding grain or else charging excessive tolls for grinding it. More rarely, commercial users of grain for other than bread were attacked, for example brewers in Cornwall where barley was the main bread grain, and mills using grain to produce starch.[3] Corn as grain, flour, or in towns as bread was the overwhelmingly preponderant concern of the rioters, but other foods, notably cheese and meat, were seized from time to time and sold at 'just' prices.[4]

Most of the usual and recurrent forms of the riot can be observed in the descriptions of the riots of 1766, although the very many outbreaks of that year, it should be noted, took place in a year when the north of the country had had a good harvest. Cloth workers in Gloucestershire and Wiltshire destroyed mills and distributed their grain among themselves. At Exeter, cheese was seized and sold at a lower price, while in Cornwall farmers and butchers were forced to lower prices, as they were at Wolverhampton. At Derby, cheese was removed from a boat on the Derwent while at Lechdale a wagonload of cheese bound for London was intercepted; in Devon some corn mills were destroyed and wheat removed from the granaries of the farmers and carried 'immediately' to market, 'sold openly from four to five shillings [20–25p] a bushel, and [the rioters] afterwards returned to the several owners, and carried them the money which they had thus raised from the sale of their grain, together with the sacks'. The sense of purpose and confinement to 'legitimate' objects of the crowd are succinctly pointed out in a single sentence description of events at Malmesbury: 'they seized all the corn; sold it at 5s. [25p] a bushel, and gave the money to the right owners'.[5]

By the beginning of the eighteenth century a widespread trade in grain run by middlemen existed and the rise of urban markets spread the demand for food further afield. London, for example, was drawing on corn exported from north- and south-coast Cornish ports by 1727 and by the close of the century the growth of Plymouth as a naval centre was also drawing corn from that county. Given the growth of its non-food-producing mining population, insufficient grain was produced in poor harvest years to feed the local population, in which years the high grain prices were especially likely to increase the activities of the profiteers in sending corn from the ports, while farmers displayed an increasing preference for disposing of their crops in large quantities to selling it piecemeal in local markets:

> We had the devil and all of a riot at Padstow. Some of the people have run to too great lengths in the exporting of corn, it being a great corn country. Seven or eight hundred tinners went thither, who first offered the corn-

factors seventeen shillings for twenty-four gallons of wheat, but being told they should have none, they immediately broke open the cellar doors, and took away all in the place without money or price.[6]

So boasts an account from north Cornwall in 1773. Two things should be noted from it: what the miners considered a fair price was first offered, and the objects of their anger were dealers (factors). There were many incidents in which the crowd clearly discriminated between farmers marketing their own product and factors superimposing a middleman's profit: 'At Nottingham fair the mob seized upon all the cheese the factors had purchased, and distributed the same among them, leaving the farmers' cheese unmolested.'[7] Such selectivity has rightly led to modern historians casting aside the contemporary label of 'mob'. Indeed, there are many instances in which 'demonstration' would have been a better description even than 'riot'. The Cornish miners whose actions were described in the *Annual Register* for 1831 clearly belonged in the former category. Admittedly 1831 was not a year of widespread hunger and no riots were recorded of this kind other than in Cornwall. Presumably, too, some of the 'old, rough ways' of the miners may have been reformed somewhat by the 1830s; after all, very large numbers of them were Methodists and they had already given up wrestling each other in favour of wrestling the devil. Nevertheless the impression of order and seriousness of purpose is emphatic:

> a party of 3,000 miners from the parishes of Breage, Germoe and Wendron, Crowan etc. passed through Helston in the greatest order, (having selected eight men to act as leaders), for the avowed purpose of preventing further shipments of corn from Gweek River. Near Mawgan, they were accidently met by Mr Grylls, who entreated them to return, but to this they would not consent. They said, 'If you, Sir, and Mr Silvester (who had come from Helston) will go with us, we will engage to do no mischief'. Finding that all intreaties to induce them to return were unavailing, Mr Grylls, Rev. Mr Black, and Mr Silvester accompanied them to Geer, where about 100 Cornish bushels of barley were deposited, which Mr Grylls promised should be sent to Helston market.

The party continued to two other places where, having measured the corn stored in barns, they extracted promises that it would be sent to market and then set out for home:

> Near Mawgan Mr Grylls addressed the party and advised them to return peaceably to their homes. This they promised to do, and gave three cheers, they entered the town in good order, some hundreds retiring to their homes, and before eight o'clock scarcely a miner was to be seen. Throughout the day the utmost regularity prevailed; all that the men required being that the corn should be brought to market for which they alleged they could not afford to pay more than 12s. [60p] per bushel.

It was the Cornish miners too who in 1767, after visiting a farmhouse, had flogged one of their number who had crossed the frontiers of legitimacy by pocketing a set of silver spoons.[8]

Bad harvests produced English food riots of some degree of geographical spread in 1709–10, 1727–9, 1739–40, 1748, 1756–7, 1766–7, 1772–3, 1783, 1789, 1795–6, 1799–1801, 1810–13 and 1816–18. In a few places later incidents have been recorded for 1831 (Cornwall), 1847 (West Country) and 1854 and 1867 (South Devon). Within this chronology, some districts showed a greater proclivity to riot than did others. In some towns or districts, rioting took place on perhaps only one or two of these years, but in other areas protest was more frequent. At one extreme the Cornish miners protested to such a degree of regularity that a miner born in 1725 could have remembered from his boyhood the riots of 1729 and 1737, and could have taken part in riots in 1748, 1757, 1766 and 1773. A miner born in 1750 would have had childhood memories of the riots of 1757 and have participated in those of 1773, 1793, 1795, 1796 and 1801; similar results could be calculated from miners born in 1775 and 1800. Without doubt the food riot was a fact of life both to the miners and to those who had dealings with them. Food riots clearly belong to the area of *recurrent* reaction; that is to say that their frequency was such as to impose no strain on the popular memory of the form of protest appropriate to meet pressure situations as they arose.

The geography of food rioting suggests which consuming communities were most vulnerable to the effects of scarcity and high prices in the grain market. Stevenson has noted the importance of transport networks, riots occurring not only in seaports but also where grain might be moved out of a locality among inland waterways like the Trent or Avon.[9] Large industrial or mining populations also increased the regional proclivity to food rioting not only because of the ease with which crowds could be assembled in such areas, but also because they were dependent upon local markets for food. Among such areas were the mining settlements which existed outside the market towns rather than within them. Thus the tinners of Cornwall *came into* Penryn or Penzance, the Kingswood colliers into the markets of Bristol and the Bedworth colliers into those of Coventry.[10] It is this dimension which gives to food riots in many towns the extra element of *invasion*. Apart from miners, groups like rural clothing workers, in the West Country and East Anglia, and dockyard workers were also prominent.[11] Stevenson has noted that increasing urban concentration with industrialisation brought the food riot to places like Halifax, Huddersfield and Rochdale in the 1780s.[12]

Many incidents seem to have arisen spontaneously when consumers, notably women, whose role in this form of protest is well attested, reacted in the market place to rising prices. Other incidents clearly involved prior intent. In 1737 a Falmouth merchant buying up corn for shipping to London received this warning:

> I am told you have brought up a large quantity of corn lately, which has been the means of raising the price of corn to such a degree, as to incense the

tinners so much against you . . . that I am credibly informed no less than a thousand of them will be with you to-morrow early: they are first to assemble at Chacewater and then proceed for Falmouth. This I am told was publicly declared at Redruth market last Friday.[13]

Much in the manner, as we shall see below, of 'Captain Swing', persons who were suspected of hoarding corn or of enhancing its price might receive anonymous warning letters before direct action was instituted:

This is to Latt you to know and the rest of you Justes of the Pace that if Bakers and the Buchers and market peopel if thay do not fall thar Commorits at a reasnabell rate as thay do at other Markets thare will be such Raysen as never was known.

That warning was received by a Norwich magistrate in 1766, while one received by the farmers of the Odiham district of Hampshire in 1800 was even more to the point:

To the Damd Eternal Fire Brands of Hell Belonging to Odiham and its Vicinity. In other Words to the Damd Villans of Farmers that with hold the Corn that please God to send for the People of the Earth away from them.
     This is to inform you all that me and my Companions have Unanamously agreed and likewise made Oath to Each other that if There is not a speedy Altaration made for the Good of the poore that you have corn thinking to make your fortunes of shall have it burnt to the Ground whether it Be in Stacks or Barns for the fire that took Place Last Week was But the begining of your Troble, we know Every Stack of Corn about this Country, and Every Barn that hath Corn concealed in it for the Purpos of starving the Poore But we are Determind if thare is to Be Starvation it shall Be a General thing not a parcial one for Both Gentle, and Simple shall Starve if any Do we dont care a Dam for them fellows that Call Themselves Gentlemen Soldiers But in our opinion the Look moore like Monkeys riding on Bears . . .[14]

Posters appeared in the villages advertising in advance the intent of the populace to take action on the next market day:

This is to give notice that all persons coming to this shop and all other shops in this parish to attend at Church Town Saturday 14 instant. All that have got firelocks are to bring them with them for there we do intend to muster and be independent ourselves and them that have not any firelocks to provide themselves with staffs 9 feet long fix spears in the end of the same and them that refuse to their peril be it.
     So one and all – So one and all

An old miner recollected from his childhood having seen posters calling upon the fathers of starving children 'in the name of God and the King' to prevent vessels laden with corn from leaving Cornish ports.[15]

The size of crowds thus assembled could be formidable, for example where documents refer to Cornish crowds as other than 'a huge multitude' or some similar phrase these estimates can be tabulated:

300	Penzance	1831
400	Padstow	1795
500	Penryn	1795
7–800	Padstow	1773
2,000	Manaccan	1831
2,000	Falmouth	1727
3,000	Truro	1796 [16]

Among food-rioting crowds were to be found most kinds of workers and, especially in the market place, large numbers of women, but only rarely farm labourers, except in East Anglia in 1816. From time to time strong ceremonial, even ritual, elements emphasised the importance of legitimacy and tradition. Fife and drum bands headed processing crowds, banners proclaimed 'Bread or Blood' and loaves draped in crepe were carried on pikes. In Cornwall the 'rope and contract' on visits to hoarding farmers was a motif in 1796, 1801 and 1812: 'If the farmers hesitated to sign this paper [which contained a declaration that they should sell their corn etc. at a reduced price] the rope was fastened about their necks and they were terrified and tortured into compliance.' The rope represented only a formalised threat. It was carried further only in one recorded instance, in 1796, when two farmers were actually suspended, but cut down before they had suffered anything more than a slight choking. In any case the authorities quickly declared any such contracts if signed to be null and void. [17]

In general, violence other than in threat was not a feature of the English food riot, as Dr Stevenson had noted: 'English crowds appear to have killed no one deliberately in the various food disturbances which occurred from the beginning of the eighteenth century to the beginning of the nineteenth.' In this context the often conciliatory responses of the magistrates can be noted. In general they did not seek for harsh retributary sentences once order had been restored and in a surprisingly large number of cases seem actually to have gone some way towards meeting the wishes of the crowd by doing what it was within their power to do in the way of regulating prices. It was with the knowledge that the food riot was not uncommonly effective in securing its short-term objectives that the eighteenth-century crowd resorted so frequently to it. [18]

AGRICULTURAL LABOURERS AND PROTEST

That in the south and in East Anglia the proletarianisation of the farm labourer had already proceeded a long way by 1750 and that thereafter its momentum quickened to become substantially complete by 1830 has been shown above. Yet only recently have historians turned their close attention to the forms of protest which accompanied a transition which was not only a proletarianisation but, especially after 1790, a pauperisation.[19] Conventionally the labourer is presented as severely underemployed and under-nourished yet cowed into dependence for even this poor lot on the 'rulers' of the countryside. Living in physical conditions which brutalised him, he was also de-humanised by being demoralised and broken in spirit. In such circumstances, before the great outburst of 1830, resentment and desperation were evidenced significantly only in crime – not only that related to hunger, poaching, stealing turnips, grain or livestock, but also to crimes such as arson or animal maiming which could reflect individual or community grievances. Historians debate the relative importance of 'social' crime and the problems of definition which it presents.[20] They weigh 'crime as protest' and 'protest crime' against the economically motivated action, but there is no doubt that much rural crime from the late eighteenth century must be considered as part of the protest reaction of the farm labourers of the eastern and southern counties against the increasingly depressed conditions of their existence; some of it, at least, explicitly so. Dr Wells in a challenging article had characterised *covert* protest as the form dictated by the forces of agrarian change which were happening in a local, piecemeal and evolutionary way however significant their aggregate effect may have been on national output and however completely they may in the outcome have transformed the economic structure and the social relations of the countryside. By 1800 this evolution had been so long in train that most quiescent farm labourers were accepting a lot into which they had been bred rather than thrust and from which their expectation was to have work at a living wage. Their superiors, the farmers and the landowners, owed them that, and the frustration of such modest expectations, not the wish to overturn the given order of rural society, moved them into open protest widely in 1830/1 and locally in East Anglia in 1816 and 1822. Reminding their rulers of their minimum obligations was the other side of the coin of paternalism and deference. Although in 1830/1, touched lightly in places and at the edges by the brush strokes of political radicalism, their aspirations were fundamentally limited.

The stability of rural society depended, Wells insists, not just on a sense of a given social order, but on the operation of the old Poor Law. Necessarily so when in the inflationary years of the French Wars, the great grain crises of 1793/6 and 1799/1801, the cost of a basic wheat subsistence could be 6s. (30p) beyond the total earnings of a labouring family. With such a situation the farmers were largely content. Relief from the poor rate relieved them of the obligation of paying a living wage, and social control was greatly enhanced by a system which, of its nature, allowed discrimination in the distribution of a dole upon which nearly all depended. Used against idlers and drinkers, it was equally effective against grumblers or 'troublemakers' and those proud enough to express resentment. Wells has noted an extension of 'public authority' from the 1790s with increasing regulation of such things as the keeping of dogs, gleaning in the post-harvest fields and over village alehouses. The domination of the controlling vestries by squire, parson and farmer led to an increasing class polarisation and, breaking the fragile skin of an organic rural society, came expressions of class antagonism over a hundred bones of contention. On the one side a building up of hatred; on the other a reciprocal feeling of distrust, contempt and, ultimately, fear.[21]

Bitter feelings do not necessarily make for social or political movements and where they do hardly guarantee the success of the outbursts which they fuel. So tight was the repressive power of rural society, Wells argues, that overt protest was not a serious possibility but a rare ephemeral experience: crime was the covert alternative and one which, as he and others have shown, was in rural districts increasing in intensity and in incidence and taking on a more evident protest dimension.[22]

In a critique of Wells's position, Charlesworth has put a different interpretation on the protest implications of the proletarianisation of the farm labourer. To him the polarisation of rural society was crucial in allowing the development of a *separate community* of labourers, sharing a common experience of exploitation and able around the village pub to discuss grievances and, on occasion, mobilise to redress them. The war years were all-important in shaping a new consciousness and their intensified pressures allowed the labourers to look back to the 1770s and 1780s as a 'golden age' though of sufficiency rather than of plenty. In contradistinction to Wells's insistence on the evolutionary and gradual nature of agrarian change, he stresses the consciousness-forming impact of the 1793–1815 war years. He denies that the operation of the old Poor Law provided an overwhelmingly effective instrument of social control and argues that the roles of gentry and clergy should be distinguished from that of the farmers. At a moment when 'developments in agrarian capitalism should have torn down the veil of paternalism', the persistence of the gentry and the clergy in playing time-honoured roles imparted an essential sense of legitimation to actions taken by labourers in defence of *traditional* expectations. (He notes, for example, the effect of the lenient sentences imposed in the early weeks of 'Swing' in allowing that outburst to gather momentum.) For Charlesworth the continuities stressed by Wells are not apparent; the demoralisation and defeat of 1830/1 marks the point at which *overt* forms of protest give way and *covert* forms become the sullen norm. Similarly for him it is the *new* Poor Law of 1834 which is the critical institution in the tightening of social control through the operation of a poor relief system. Much more difficult to sustain is his aggregating of scattered collective protests over wage levels in the south and east 1793–1805 as the overt sign of a growing proletarian protest which was realised in the East Anglian riots of 1816 and 1822 and which, despite the deterioration of the labour market coming with the end of the war in 1814, shaped the labouring community's resolve in a way which makes the sustaining of protest in 1830/1 understandable.[23]

Wells has rejoined that Charlesworth's case is built upon 'uncharacteristic' explosions of overt protest and reflects a concern with historical 'landmarks' rather than with everyday life. He is in line with the findings of historians like E. J. Evans when he insists that the rural clergy were more resented as justices than looked up to as upholders of paternalism and, arguing from the detailed case of Burwash in East Sussex, in the 1820s and 1830s, shows that the vestry even in a so-called 'open' parish was not only as capable of attaching strict rules to the operation of poor relief as ever was the agent of any 'closed-village' squire, but was as often the target of covert protest action. It is a lively debate which is not yet closed. One feels that perhaps Dr Charlesworth claims too much and has as yet too little evidence to support his view of a developing proletarian consciousness feeding an overt collective response. If the outbreaks in East Anglia indicate a growing strength presumably further fulfilled in 1830/1, then one wonders with Dr Wells what one should understand by weakness.[24]

THE EAST ANGLIAN RIOTS OF 1816 AND 1822.

In East Anglia the especially rapid pace of agrarian change produced the only notable instances of open protest before 1830. As Peacock has noted, if one allows a wide definition, then no year in that district in the first half of the nineteenth century was a 'quiet' one; however, overt action was clearly evident only in 1816 and in 1822.[25] In the former outbreak disturbances took several forms. In food riots and attacks on spinning jennies (Bury St Edmunds) agricultural labourers hardly participated, but farming developments on the loams and clays of Essex, Suffolk and Norfolk brought protests not only with the limited wage objective of restoration to the levels of 1793–1805, but which anticipated 'Swing' in attacks on machinery. Mole ploughs and threshing machines were held to threaten the availability of winter employment. Protests against threshing machines in fact began as early as 1815 in Suffolk where given their limited diffusion protest must be seen as against a potential rather than an actual threat. Reactions from the authorities to wage demands varied. At Downham, labourers were angered when they were offered only an increased bread allowance and subsidised flour instead of requested wages for 2s. (10p) a day, but at Ely magistrates agreed to the demand that the farmers pay the labourer 'his full wages'. Disturbances spread into the more varied peasant economy of the Fens where groups other than farm labourers were involved and where a traditional economy was resisting 'improvements' which, culminating in the drainage of the 1820s and 1830s, were destined to destroy it.[26]

The disturbances of 1822 were essentially by agricultural labourers and began in the February with attacks on threshing machines and visits to farmers to either persuade them to give up their machines or, if they would not agree, to destroy them. The almost symbolic attacks of 1816 were replaced by something more like a general protest against the machines, but swift reaction from the authorities seems to have rapidly restored order.[27]

THE AGRICULTURAL LABOURERS' RIOTS OF 1830–1

The agricultural labourers' riots, which began in east Kent with night attacks on threshing machines in the late August of 1830, spread with amazing rapidity through the south of England and reached, significantly, into East Anglia and touched the Midlands and Lincolnshire. Without doubt these disturbances, popularly known as the 'Swing Riots' after the signature of 'Captain Swing' which appeared at the bottom of threatening letters, were 'the most impressive episode in the English farm-labourers' long and doomed struggle against poverty and degradation' and for just wages and the right to work.[28]

From the researches of Professors Hobsbawm and Rudé, supplementing the earlier account of J. L. and Barbara Hammond, we know a great deal about the form, spread and significance of the riots. From their beginning near Canterbury they spread in the course of three months over twenty counties. Passing over Bromley, Sevenoaks and Orpington in a score of incendiary fires, broken threshing machines and demands for increased wages, they had reached west Sussex by mid-November and within days were at the Hampshire border. Almost simultaneously they erupted in Berkshire, Wiltshire and Oxfordshire. They crossed from Wiltshire into parts of Gloucestershire and further west produced scattered outbreaks in Herefordshire, Somerset, Devon, Dorset and Cornwall. In the Home Counties they spread from Berkshire into Buckinghamshire and east into Essex, Bedfordshire, Huntingdonshire, Northamptonshire, Cambridgeshire and into the borders of Lincolnshire. They did not affect all these counties with equal intensity: in Kent, Sussex, Hampshire, Berkshire and Wiltshire there was a fairly 'general social conflagration', and events were also explosive in Norfolk and perhaps Huntingdonshire; elsewhere events were more sporadic. By the time the final acts occurred, again in Kent in late summer of 1831, more than 1,400 incidents had been recorded and there had been 2,000 arrests. At the special commissions which tried them, 500 were imprisoned and nineteen executed.[29]

Hobsbawm and Rudé have noted that a characteristic of the protests was their multiformity. In different places at different times with the pattern varying from county to county they involved the destruction of threshing machines, the firing of ricks, wage demands, protests against rents and tithes, the sending of threatening letters and attacks on Poor Law officials. All in all these grievances were symptomatic of the widespread poverty, low wages and unemployment of the farm labourer in the predominantly cereal-growing southern and eastern parts of the country. Within the frontiers of that particular agrarian economy they were as near a national protest as they could have been.[30]

Events differed between and within the different counties. The early night attacks on threshing machines, whose operation severely diminished one of the few winter employments available to labourers within the cereal economy, were dealt with moderately by a not unsympathetic magistracy but as they broadened into daylight attacks and publicly-issued wage demands, the attitude of the authorities began to harden. By the time they reached west Sussex, 1,000 labourers openly assembled at Chichester market to meet the justices and principal farmers of the district and get their agreement to wage increase from 10s. to 14s. (50p to 70p) a week. As the movement spread into Hampshire and Wiltshire it gained its widest dispersal and greatest momentum. Each of these counties provided more than 300 prisoners in the aftermath compared with only 100 from Kent. In Hampshire and Wiltshire there was less arson than there had been in Kent, but a greater emphasis on machine-breaking, especially in Wiltshire, and on demands for food and 'levies' of money upon local populaces. In Berkshire, wage demands were very much to the fore, one such incident being described in the *Reading Mercury*:

> The labourers of Thatcham parish began to assemble at an early hour, for the purpose of inducing their employers to raise their wages. A sufficient number of them gathered together, they marched off (preceded by one of their company blowing a horn) to visit each of the farms, for the purpose of compelling the labourers to unite with them. By this means their numbers increased, and at noon they amount to two or three hundred. They then marched into the churchyard and, the select vestry being convened, presented to the gentlemen assembled a verbal request that they might be provided with work, and have their wages advanced. To the former of these requests a favourable answer was returned, but no hope was held out of an improvement in the latter. Throughout the whole of these proceedings the men were quite peaceable, excepting forcing some who felt no inclination to join them.[31]

From this time the labourers turned their attention to attacks on machinery. In Bedfordshire, however, although there were threats, wage demands and incendiary fires, no machines were broken. In East Anglia, unlike the southern counties, there had been a previous history of attacks on threshing machines during the disturbances of 1816 and 1822, although when the disturbances reached tentatively into Lincolnshire the incidents were mainly of arson.[32]

The unpopularity of the Poor Law in some districts resulted in attacks on its officials and on workhouses, while in other areas resentment of tithes or of high rents produced alliances between the labourers and some farmers. Bushaway has noted the strong ritual folklore forms of some of the incidents. The demands for 'payment' or for food or beer were in the tradition of the 'doleing' customs of rural England, while the ritual humiliation of officials like the Assistant Overseer at Brede in Sussex (one of ten Sussex villages in which Poor Law officials or tithe-holders were either expelled or threatened) clearly expresses the popular sanction of 'charivari':

> The villagers brought the cart to Abel's door, seized him and placed him in it with a rope round his neck, to which a large stone was tied. Without scarcely an exception, the whole of the inhabitants accompanied the labourers, who thus drew him out of the parish attended by 'rough music'.

Even the popular name for the disturbances, the 'mobbings', has a folk ring to it.[33]

It is this quality of the risings (the sense in which however much the broad structural problems of southern and eastern agriculture forced low wages and severe un- and under-employment on the rapidly rising population of rural labourers, 'Swing' still produces, perhaps more than any other example of widespread disturbance, the telling example of articulation of particular local grievances) which leads the historian to wonder whether the riots made up in any real sense a 'movement'. From Norfolk a Colonel Botherington provided a contemporary misuse of this word when he concluded: 'the insurrectionary movement seems to be directed by no plan or system but merely actuated by the spontaneous feeling of the peasants, and quite at random'.[34]

This is not to suggest a series of coincidental outbreaks entirely unconnected. It would have taken more than the shared experience of poverty and shared feelings of resentment to have spread rioting through twenty counties in a matter of weeks. Of course there was talk of 'strangers' proceeding on paths of agitation through the disturbed regions, but in reality the outbreaks spread by a process of emulation whose symbol was the recurrent appearance of the mythical 'Captain Swing' as the signatory of the threatening letters which preceded disturbances, rick-burnings and machine-breakings in the various counties:

Sir

    This is to acquaint you that if your thrashing machines are not destroyed by you directly we shall commence our labours signed on behalf of the whole

Swing[35]

The extent to which political radicalism played a part is debated. Both Henry Hunt and William Cobbett touch briefly on the events of 1830–1, and nuclei of radicals, shoemakers and the like in the country towns may have been more important than historians have traditionally accepted. One historian has recently suggested that careful mapping of incidents reveals the significance of the 'London highway' for a politicisation of settlements along it by radical propaganda.[36] Certainly the heightened political tension of the peaking of the reform agitation and the revolutions in France and Belgium must have played a part in the spread of the disturbances beyond Kent and Sussex, but the fundamental aims of the labourers remained both economic and *moderate*:

> These are not rural egalitarians, they accept the established order of village society and their expectations are fantastically minimal: a very slightly better wage, the destruction of machines, the opportunity to work while preserving their dignity. They go about their task of riot politely, dressed according to many eyewitnesses' accounts in their best clothes, seldom using threatening language . . . it is the revolt of the proud, conscious of their own rights and aware that they are not doing anything that their fathers would not have done.[37]

In an important sense the objects of the rioters were as much to show resentment against the traditional leaders of the rural community as against grasping farmers. The traditional obligations of the well-off were not being met: 'The riots were in part a protest against the decline of paternalism.'[38]

THE AFTERMATH OF SWING

For the most part historians have emphasised the demoralising aspect of the suppression of the disturbances of 1830/1. Perhaps the best known contemporary description of the southern labourer of this era came from Mrs Gaskell in *North and South* (1854) when the northern factory worker is warned to give up any idea of improving his position by moving to the non-industrialised south:

> You've reckoned on having butchers meat once a day, if you're in work; pay for that out of your ten shillings, and keep these poor children if you can . . . You would not bear the dullness of the life; you don't know what it is; it

would eat you away like rust. Those that have lived there all their lives, are used to soaking in the stagnant waters. They labour on, from day to day, in the great solitude of steaming fields – never speaking or lifting up their poor, bent, downcast heads. The hard spadework robs their brain of life; the sameness of their toil deadens their imagination . . . they go home brutishly tired, poor creatures! caring for nothing but food and rest.[39]

Although as we have seen there is a case for stressing covert protest in the form of crime as a continuing accompaniment of the later stages of the proletarianisation of the agrarian labour force, several historians suggest that arson (especially) and sheep-stealing and maiming became more prevalent and more vengeful after the collapse of 'Swing'. As Hobsbawm and Rudé put it, 'Captain Swing, wrongly cast by public opinion as an incendiary in 1830, triumphed in this role for twenty years thereafter'. Dr Jones has noted the peak of arson in East Anglia between 1844–51 having been only a peripheral accompaniment of 'Swing' in that area. Contemporaries concurred that a new breed of harder farmers confronted a new breed of labourer, sullen to a point unknown to their forefathers. The labourers were largely untouched by education and barely redeemed by religion: of eighty-four persons on arson charges in 1844, forty-five could read only indifferently and twenty-eight not at all, while criticism of the labourers' failure to attend church and bemoaning of the weakening influence of the clergy was common.[40] The condition of the labourer was productive among the propertied of a fear which, following the loaded report of Edwin Chadwick in 1839, meant that the new rural police were unwelcome among the upper classes only to a few traditionalists.

East Anglia has been more closely studied than other areas, but there seems no reason to doubt as Lowerson and others have indicated that its experience was echoed in the south-eastern counties. Although it is difficult to assess how many of more than 500 cases of sheep stealing in Sussex in the bad winter of 1838/9 were motivated other than by simple hunger, the forty committals for arson in Kent between 1842 and 1851 seems to point to the East Anglian experience.[41]

Crime is not the only consideration in assessing the responses of the defeated labourers in the years following Swing. Within a few years, open protest and rioting against implementation of the provisions of the New Poor Law of 1834 was evident. Historians have tended to concentrate study of popular resistance to the New Poor Law on events in the north, but the depth of resistance 1834/6 in the south and in East Anglia should not be underestimated. Apart from what seems to have been a major resistance movement in east Sussex, collective opposition has been recorded from Kent, Wiltshire, Devon and Cornwall as well as from East Anglia with attacks on workhouses and on officials.[42]

In 1834/5 there also seems to have been something of a revival of economic protest of the trade union kind, of which the famous case of Tolpuddle in Dorset was only one and perhaps not the most typical incident. Re-assessing Tolpuddle in the context of a more widespread agrarian unionism has only just begun and it would be premature to project conclusions at this stage. Jones has remarked that unionism appeared in 'various guises' in 1834/5 in East Anglia but very quickly subsided. Hobsbawm and Rudé note reports of farm labourers' unions from Rye, Eastbourne and Winchelsea and from Essex in 1836 and Wiltshire in 1834. Strikes are noted from Goring and from several places in Kent. Especially interesting are the findings of John Lowerson from the south-east. He presents evidence to suggest a serious underestimating of the extent of agrarian trade unionism especially in 1835, but also points to some continuities either side of 1830/1. In the April of 1835 it was being reported from the Kent/Sussex border: 'In the beginning of this year the agricultural labourers were many of them associating in a secret union, the immediate object of which the farmers are unable to ascertain.' The union was to appear as the 'United Brothers of Industry' and march sixty men through the streets of Rye and Winchelsea. It was interchangeable with the 'Agricultural Labourers' Benefit Society' and seems to have spread its branches rapidly and, in the aftermath of Tolpuddle, surprisingly publicly through the district. Its published rules were essentially those of a friendly society but its public utterances spoke a different language. The frightened vicar of Seaford reported:

> Agricultural Trade Unions meet at a public house in this place . . . The ostensible motive for the union is the mutual relief when the members (or Brothers as they term them) are out of work – but their real intention as I know but cannot legally prove it, is intimidation, and they have agreed as soon as they are strong enough to strike simultaneously throughout the country; if possible in harvest – threats are also uttered among them of setting fire to the standing corn . . .[43]

The farmers of the district took the threat sufficiently seriously to present workers with the 'document' before the harvest began, and three men refusing to sign and dismissed as a consequence were supported financially by Brighton's trade unionists. Against the combined and determined opposition of the farmers, the union seems to have faded from the scene by the end of 1835.[44]

The problem awaits further research. How extensive were such organisations? How 'secret'? What links did they have with urban trade unionists (for, as Hobsbawm and Rudé remind us, the men of Tolpuddle were evidently not ignorant of the existence of a trade union movement)? Given the present state of knowledge, it is only cautious to keep in mind the very real difficulties which rural trade unionism faced. Above all before the 1850s regular effective combination to raise wages was structurally impossible not only because of the isolation of the villages and the power of the farmers, but because of the continuing chronic oversupply of labour.[45]

LUDDISM:MACHINE-BREAKING IN THE FRENCH WAR YEARS

Machine-breaking, as we have seen, as a form of industrial action adopted by workers in dispute had a long history whether it was the machine itself which was the direct object of contention, or whether it was attacked as part of a general campaign against employers over issues such as wage-cutting or disregarding of apprenticeship. The word 'Luddite', which has ever since described worker resistance to innovative technologies and work practices, first entered the language in 1811 when letters and proclamations signed 'Ned Ludd', 'Captain Ludd' or even 'General Ludd' preceded and accompanied attacks on machinery in the framework knitting districts of Nottingham conveying a sense of an 'army of redressers' of wrongs suffered by the people further emphasised by some of them bearing the address 'Sherwood Forest'.[46] The study of the 'Luddite' disturbances in their proper historical context reveals, as historical investigations commonly do, how inappropriate has been the adoption of the label for the phenomena it is now used to describe.

The extensive machine-breaking activities of the Luddites ranged through 1811–12 over three main manufacturing districts: the framework knitting areas of Nottingham, Leicestershire and Derby; the woollen districts of the West Riding; and the cotton districts of Lancashire. In the three areas the objectives of the machine-breakers were different, but in all the name of Ludd as the 'captain' of the protesters was invoked. There was a less extensive recurrence in 1814 and 1816 and it is their concentration into such a short period, their geographical extent and their seriousness as a problem of order for the government which gives the machine-breaking activities of Regency England their special place within a longer history of such protest. The more than 12,000 troops which were at the peak stationed in the rioting districts of the north and the Midlands represented a larger military force than that which Wellington took with him on his first expedition to Portugal in 1808.[47]

THE WEST COUNTRY SHEARMEN

There was, however, a prelude to the major machine-breaking activities of 1811–12 which has until recently been rather neglected by historians. Beginning in 1799, but peaking in 1802, the shearmen of Wiltshire vigorously and, as Dr Randall has shown, to a degree successfully fought against two technological innovations which threatened their livelihood. These were gig mills, which raised the nap on the cloth prior to its shearing and enabled a man and two boys to achieve in a much shorter time what had previously taken a man around 100 hours, and shearing frames which by aligning the heavy 40 lb shears reduced the time needed for the shearing of a piece of cloth to a quarter. The main target of the disturbances of 1802 in Wiltshire were the gig mills, but that was because there were very few shearing frames introduced and the general purpose of the shearmen's actions embraced a pre-emptive move against frames as well as a protest against the use of gig mills. As was to be the case in the Luddite districts, protest took 'legitimate' trade union forms and involved the petitioning of Parliament as well as intimidation and attacks on machinery and other forms of property. The use of threatening letters was an integral part of the deterrent intent of the shearmen. Even before the main campaign began in 1802 a Melksham clothier who set up a gig mill in 1796 had his hayricks fired and received this letter: 'Sir – we have just gave you a Caution how we do intend to act as soon as we can make it convenient which we believe that it will be soon . . .'; while clothiers who sent cloth to another gig mill at Twerton in 1799 were warned: 'if you do you own ruen will be for we are determed to go throo with it as nou we be gon it fore next time that we com we will set all the misshenery a fiere . . .'[48] The main period of contention came during the course of a bitter strike in 1802 at Warminster against the gig mill and two other strikes of the same year against attempted wage cuts at Bradford and at Trowbridge. Particular clothiers were the objects of the 'outrages', especially Jones of Trowbridge who added an important dimension to the conflict when, in order to break the strike of shearmen against his gig mills, he had introduced shearing frames. Jones' mill was twice attacked but, effectively garrisoned, beat off both. Two other mills were destroyed, one of them belonging to Thomas Naish, the principal opponent of the shearmen, and subsequently when Naish secured the arrest of an apprentice shearman, his Trowbridge workshops were also burnt down. The Trowbridge clothiers were frightened into accepting an end to the strike on the men's terms, but Jones and two Warminster clothiers refused to be intimidated and virtually turned their mills into forts. By July the violence which had largely begun in April was in any case losing its momentum as workers' energies increasingly turned to petitioning Parliament for an enforcement of statute laws which were presumed to prohibit the use of gig mills.[49] The 'outrages' had been calculated and deliberate and, significantly, they cannot be seen, despite high food prices, as desperate distress riots. Only a handful of machines were in operation in the clothing districts and hardly any shearmen had thus far been displaced. The targets were chosen for what they implied for the shearmen's future status and standing. The victims were those whose innovations, had they been emulated by others, would have destroyed the craft and its traditional culture. This is why Randall is right to stress that they were part of the tactics of a well-organised, strongly unionised group of skilled workers engaged in a conscious pre-emptive action. Effectively they succeeded in postponing the widespread introduction of the machinery for around twenty years.[50]

What is the significance of the West Country machine-breaking for the understanding of the better-known Luddism of 1811–12? In the first place there was a direct link between the Wiltshire outbreak and that of 1811–12 in the West Riding. In effect the struggle of the shearmen of the West Country against deskilling machinery was also the struggle by proxy of their northern comrades the 'croppers' (as shearmen were there known) of the Yorkshire woollen districts. The liaison between these two groups forms one of the most impressive examples of inter-regional communication from early trade union history. The shearmen as skilled workers occupying a strategic place in the chain of production and working in workshops rather than in their own cottages were almost the 'ideal' for the development of effective artisan unionism. Accordingly, in both districts their organised strength revealed itself at several contest points in the eighteenth century. In the closing decade of the century a more significant development came with the founding of the so-called 'Brief Institution' initially in Yorkshire which very soon, building on longer established traditions of mutual support through the tramping system, effectively brought together the two districts in a shared perception of the threat of machinery. Just when the West Countrymen joined the 'Brief Institution' is not certain; it may have been in 1799, but it was fact by the campaign of 1802 when national rules and membership certificates were in evidence as was a direct and regular correspondence link between Leeds and Trowbridge. Financial aid for the Wiltshire strikers was sent and the parliamentary campaign of 1802–6 can properly be regarded as a joint one. The failure of this campaign, which ended in the repeal in 1809 of the innovation-inhibiting statutes which the shearmen had sought to get enforced, not only locates the West Country outbreak at the point where Thompson located the outbreaks of 1811–12, the breakdown of paternalism in the face of emergent *laissez-faire*, but meant that when the northern clothiers started to introduce machinery, the croppers went straight into direct action, the parliamentary campaign having already been fought and lost.[51]

There are, however, several other ways in which consideration of the West Country outbreak raises questions congruent to those raised in the 1811–12 outbreaks. The selectivity of the machine-breakers and their confinement to chosen targets is evident in both outbreaks as is the sympathy and measure of support enjoyed beyond the ranks of the machine-breakers: 'There are a considerable number of persons of respectability in the three counties who . . . still continue to consider the introduction of machinery into the woollen trade as unfriendly to the general interest and particularly injurious to the poor' admitted one of the region's advocates of progress in 1803.[52] Such sympathy was hardly surprising when it is considered how few were the innovators whose activities were so disruptive of the tradition and community-based 'social economy' of a long-established manufacture.

Perhaps even more significant is the scant comfort which a closer look at the West Country campaign affords those who insist on a 'compartmentalist' approach to labour history in which the 'desperate' fellows who resort to breaking machines must be clearly separated from the more serious ones who employ only methods which can be retrospectively viewed as 'proper' trade union ones. Dr Randall has pointed out that the suggestion of a leading proponent of the 'compartmentalist' school, Professor Thomis, that violence occurred 'not through established trade union machinery but in its absence' and that it is possible to separate a 'labour approach' quite different to that of industrial sabotage and direct action is very much at odds with the experience of a region where it was precisely skilled workers with a long tradition of trade union organisation who employed machine-breaking as a tactic. Nor is it possible to avoid the issue by suggesting that different groups among the shearmen acted in different ways: they were too small and compact a craft group for that to have been the case.[53]

THE LUDDITE DISTURBANCES

As a result of the Orders in Council of 1811, part of the economic war against Napoleon, the hosiers of the East Midlands were hit very hard by the closing of their American market. Exports worth £11m in 1810 had been cut to £2m by 1811 and on top of this collapse in trade and bad harvests meant that wheat prices reached a high of 16s. (80p) a quarter in 1812. In such circumstances it was inevitable that within an industry with a long history of disputes over frame rents, truck payments and rate reductions, discontent would manifest itself in some form of protest movement. As the hosiers attempted to cut costs as low as possible, the specific grievance which initiated the Luddite action came to the fore. This was the use of unskilled labour on wider frames to produce 'cut-ups' – inferior stockings woven square and cut-up and stitched at a much lower cost than the traditionally knitted stocking. Under the economic pressures of the French War years a number of larger employers had significantly increased the movement towards these cheaply produced products made by 'colting', i.e. the employment of unapprenticed labour:

> Let the wise and the great lend their aid and advice
> Nor e'er their assistance withdraw
> Till full fashioned work at the old fashioned price
> Is established by custom and law.
> Then the Trade when this ardorous contest is o'er
> Shall raise in full splendour its head,
> And colting and cutting and squaring no more
> Shall deprive honest workmen of bread.[54]

Against these innovating practices the framework knitters in 1811 first devoted their efforts to seeking a parliamentary 'regulation' of the trade. It was to no avail: Parliament was by now more likely to legislate in ways which facilitated rather than hindered the 'iron' laws of the market. In this context of the declining paternalist expectations it is significant that the immediate cause of machine-breaking in the East Midlands was a wage dispute in 1811 when local justices refused to intervene after hosiers reduced prices paid to knitters. As a result sixty frames belonging only to the underpaying hosiers were destroyed. This happened in March, but it was not until November that machine-breaking became widespread and even extended into Leicestershire and Derby. Discrimination was not lost in this expansion; reports from all sources testify to the selectivity of the rioting knitters:

> The guilty may fear, but no vengeance he aims
> At the honest man's life or estate
> His wrath is entirely confined to wide frames
> And to those that old prices abate.
> Those engines of mischief were sentenced to die
> By unanimous vote of the Trade;
> And Ludd who can all opposition defy
> Was the great Executioner made.

In the most active phase from March 1811 to February 1812 around 1,000 frames were destroyed in 100 separate attacks and a worried government made machine-breaking a capital felony and despatched 2,000 troops to Nottingham. Their presence brought this main phase to an end, and the focus of resistance to the intrusion of innovative capitalist practices switched to the attempt by the United Committee of Framework Knitters to secure a parliamentary Bill. With the failure of their campaign and with prosecutions under the Combination Acts in July 1814, frame-breaking resumed again and was an ever-present but spasmodic occurrence until 1816.[55]

By the January of 1812 the first Luddite outbreaks had occurred in the West Riding as the croppers faced the introduction of the shearing frames which had first provoked reaction in the West Country a dozen years before. A Leeds mill was burned down on 19 January and other mills suffered in a series of night attacks around Halifax by croppers with blackened faces. In the threats which preceded the attacks and in the justifications which followed them, the name of 'Ludd' was again evoked; but so too was a new name, 'Enoch', the big hammer of destruction, ironically named for the form of Enoch and James Taylor who made not only the shearing frames but the hammers which broke them:

> Great Enoch still shall lead the van.
> Stop him who dare! Stop him who can!
> Press forward every gallant man
> With hatchet, pike and gun!
> Oh, the cropper lads for me,
> The gallant lads for me,
> Who with lusty stroke
> The shear frames broke,
> The cropper lads for me.[56]

Threats intensified and an organisation capable of attacking larger mills built up. The most serious incident of confrontation came in April 1812 with the attack on the well-guarded mill of William Cartwright, distortingly immortalised by Emily Brontë in *Shirley*, in which two attackers were killed, and after which the vengeful and remorseless inhumanity of the mill-owner and his magisterial friends passed into the local folklore. In the aftermath came the attempted assassination of Cartwright and the actual one of William Horsfall, a mill-owner who had boasted of his intention of riding up to his saddle girths in the blood of Luddites.[57] By this time Yorkshire Luddism entered what Thompson has called its 'crisis' in which machine-breaking became a focus for a 'diffused (and confused) insurrectionary tension' as disturbances spread beyond the clothing districts into Rotherham and Sheffield and as raids for arms, bullets and money marked its closing stages.[58]

In Lancashire and Cheshire the nature of Luddism was considerably more confused than it was in either Nottingham or the West Riding. In so far as there was a machinery issue there, then it lay in attacks by handloom weavers on power looms, but in this disturbed period it was significantly intermingled with food rioting and political agitation. Rumours of contact with Nottingham's Luddites spread in the cotton districts in the winter of 1811–12 and by the February anonymous threatening letters against power looms were signed by 'Ludd'. After several rioters were killed by musket fire during an attack on the power-loom mill of Daniel Burton in Salford in April 1812, the coroner received a letter:

> Beware, Beware! A month's bathing in the Stygian Lake would not wash this sanguinary deed from our minds, it but augments the heritable cause,

that stirs us up in indignation.

Milnes if you really are not a Friend to the great Oppressors, forgive us this – but if you are – the rest remains behind.

Ludd finis est.[59]

An attempt to burn down the warehouse of William Radcliffe at Stockport was followed by widespread rumours of secret gatherings, armings and the swearing of oaths. Towards the end of March and into the following weeks, food riots broke out in several of the towns of Lancashire and Cheshire and on some of these occasions, as at Macclesfield, the crowd went on to attack factories using power looms. By the end of the month, E. P. Thompson has suggested, the machine-breaking phase gave way to 'more serious insurrectionary preparations' as reports of oaths, midnight drillings and the like alarmed the authorities through May and June. Undoubtedly there was at least *talk* at large of a general rising.[60]

INTERPRETING LUDDISM

From the time of the Hammonds' *Skilled Labourer* in 1919 to the appearance of a radical new interpretation in Edward Thompson's *The Making of the English Working Class* in 1963 a particular treatment of Luddism held sway. The detailed description of the disturbances by the Hammonds remains an essential starting point for the student. They disdainfully disposed of the myth that Luddites were no more than simple ignorant men reacting instinctively, but hopelessly, against the march of progress. Specifically they placed Luddism as the resort to violence by traditional workers who had failed in the face of a growing *laissez-faire* ideology to persuade Parliament to protect their interest by invoking old paternalist statutes. Machine-breaking was a final phase in the struggle of workmen for the maintenance or revival of customs and laws from which capitalist employers were seeking to free themselves. In Nottinghamshire, as we have noted, it was not the knitting frames themselves which were the targets, but those masters who used them to produce inferior goods from unskilled labour.

Unlike Professor Hobsbawm who accepted the role of 'collective bargaining by riot' in early trade unionism, the Hammonds were moved by a powerful disposition to push violence to the periphery of trade union history. They were unable to place a movement like Luddism, in which violence was central, into their conception of the long-term evolution of the labour movement. It had to be explained away by insisting that the persons who broke the machines were a group apart from the 'constitutionalists' who concentrated on seeking a parliamentary redress. At the same time, anxious to deny any revolutionary input into the British labour movement, they were at pains to stamp on any suggestion that Luddism could have been to a significant degree a manifestation of an underground revolutionary movement.

This did not preclude their recognising that there was nothing 'blind' about the disturbances of 1811–12 which, although using a long-employed form of protest, were distinguished by an altogether new level of 'well planned and organised policy'. Conceding that it was difficult to assess how far existing trade organisations might have become involved in Luddism, or at least sympathised with it, they nevertheless were at pains to play down any links between machine-breaking and 'legalistic' union activities, even if there was some sympathy: 'It seems probable that most of the members of existing trade societies, without joining in the policy of destruction themselves, were not ill-pleased to have the work done for them.'[61] Directly implicated, however, they could not have been. Gravener Henson, the leader of the Frame-work Knitters' Union, is completely exonerated even from approving Luddite activities. He and his fellow consti-tutionalists were confining themselves to the parliamentary redress campaign which was absorbing the energies and interest of the 'more orderly portion'. In getting arrested, Henson was the victim of poor unfortunates who had sought to save their own lives by falsely informing against him. When the Society for obtaining Parliamentary Relief collapsed in 1816, it was once again only 'a small section' of frame-breakers who revived the attacks on machinery, and the Ham-monds quote as conclusive Henson's retrospective remark of 1824: 'The branch who broke the frames never contemplated any such thing as the combining.'[62]

The parallel existence in the stocking and lace-knitting districts of a movement for parliamentary redress alongside machine-breaking allows some historians to claim that each had been the method of a different group of knitters. In the cases of the cotton weavers of Lancashire and the croppers of the West Riding, it is less easy to discern two distinct strands. However, if in the case of Nottingham the Hammonds were unwilling to accept that frame-breaking could have been done by sound trade unionists, they were equally unwilling to accept that there was any real degree of political revolutionary intent behind the disturbances in the northern counties. Faced with a massive documentation to the contrary, as well as the fact that the government either believed, or at least acted as if it believed, in such a threat, they were forced to emphasise to the extreme the role of government spies and agents provocateurs in the disturbed districts. Spies either invented or exaggerated to the point of distortion, reports of arms, talk of uprisings and plans for insurrection, because it was in their paid interest to do so. When Luddism spread into Yorkshire and Lan-cashire the government itself became the victim of its own played-upon fears. Thus in Lancashire rumours of a general rising were started 'as far as can be gathered solely by spies'. The reports of the spy Bent from Lancashire are especially dismissed as thoroughly untrustworthy and coming from one who specialised in stories of a general rising: 'The Home Office Papers contain numbers of illiterate communications from him, full of lurid hints of the approaching outbursts of the lower orders, encouraged by mysterious beings in high stations.' They suggest that so-called Luddite oaths originated in his fertile brain. They found no evidence to show that Luddite oaths were ever widely administered in the West Riding, except in districts 'where the spies were busy at work'.[63]

The Hammonds' views were echoed in the thorough study of 1934 by F. O. Darvall who also professed to finding no political motivation behind Luddism despite the efforts of spies to suggest them.[64] E. P. Thompson's interpretation of 1963 therefore cut sharply across what had become an orthodoxy and in so doing opened up a vigorous and continuing debate over the nature of Luddism. Thompson saw in the Hammonds a Fabian predisposition to play down to the point of extinction the place of direct action, violence and a revolutionary tradition in the English labour movement: 'The chapters on Luddism read at times like a brief prepared on behalf of the Whig opposition, and intended to discredit the exaggerated claims made by the authorities as to the conspiratorial and revolutionary aspects of the movement.' Other historians too have commented on the Hammonds' reluctance to accept that there was even serious talk of revolution, although they do not go so far as Thompson in seeing that talk as amounting to a serious threat. The problem lies in the interpretation of evidence which consists to a large degree of the reports of spies and informers to receptively panic-stricken magistrates and ministers. Thompson suggests that by their total rejection of all evidence of this kind, the Hammonds put themselves in an unreal position:

> by a special pleading which exaggerates the stupidity, rancour, and provocative role of the authorities to the point of absurdity; or by an academic failure of imagination, which compartmentalises and disregards the whole weight of popular tradition . . . We end in a ridiculous position. We must suppose that the authorities through their agents actually created conspiratorial organisations and then instituted new capital offences (such as that for oath-taking) which existed only in the imagination or as a result of the provocations of their own spies.[65]

In their chapter on Lancashire Luddism, acknowledged by historians to be the region in which it is most difficult to disentangle machine-breaking from other aspirations, the Hammonds' predisposition to believe that 'bona fide insurrectionary schemes on the part of working men were either highly improbable, or, alternatively, wrong and undeserving of sympathy and therefore to be attributed to a lunatic, irresponsible fringe' is most evident. It is perfectly reasonable of Thompson to ask why such a separation of motives should be presumed to have been the case in 1812. War had continued for twenty years. Trade unions were under the interdict of the Combination

Laws. The handloom weavers had suffered a cataclysmic decline in their living standards and high corn prices had produced widespread and severe hunger. Why does it appear improbable that men in such circumstances, who had seen time and time again at the crisis points of their trades the futility of turning to a government increasingly taking the side of capitalist employers, should plot revolution? Perhaps only because the Hammonds and their modern successors have denied close attention and sympathy to movements which were not satisfactory forerunners of the modern labour movement. As Thompson insists, the only reason for believing that reports which spoke of the revolutionary aspects of Lancashire Luddism were false is the presumption that as the evidence of spies they are bound to have been. Reading the evidence without such a presumption, Thompson has produced a very different interpretation suggesting that by 1812 (May) Luddism in both Lancashire and the West Riding had very largely been the supersession of purely economic objectives by political revolutionary ones propagated by a definite underground revolutionary movement. He suggests that an identical form of oath found on an associate of Colonel Despard at the time of the 1802 insurrection is only one of many pieces of evidence which links the revolutionary underground of 1812 to that of 1802. He is, however, disinclined to believe rumours of *national* organisation and of the participation of 'gentlemen' as leaders.[66]

Thompson's account of Luddism is closely related to the thesis advanced in his book that a continuous underground revolutionary tradition linked the jacobins of the 1790s to the radical movements of 1816 to 1820 of which the machine-breaking outbursts were only the most widespread and frightening manifestation. The thesis has been debated by historians at other points as well as the Luddite one, but has been most noticeably challenged in the latter context. Many who accept that the Hammonds were too inclined to reject any suggestion that the workers of England had revolutionaries among their number will still have nothing to do with Thompson's idea of a continuing revolutionary underground tradition or with his view that revolutionary political motives had any significant role in the Luddite disturbances. R. A. Church and S. D. Chapman in a discussion on the role of Gravenor Henson added considerably to our knowledge of this important figure in early trade unionism while disputing Thompson's view of his role in the Nottinghamshire disturbances. The connection between the two wings of the Nottingham movement, the 'constitutionalist' one for parliamentary redress and the machine-breaking one, has always been disputed. Thompson suggested an oscillating pattern with the likelihood that up to 1814 the two strands were directed by the same trade union organisation: 'in which perhaps Luddites and constitutionalists differed in their counsels'. He points out that given that Luddism gave way so quickly to constitutionalism it is difficult to believe in other than a common leadership. The disassociation of Henson himself from machine-breaking is far from being as clear as the Hammonds made out. Church and Chapman, however, follow the Hammonds in insisting on a separation of the two strands, but provide a new twist by suggesting that it followed a line of cleavage between town and country knitters. The former, more skilled and better paid, were 'constitutionalists'; the latter, lower paid and more exploited, were ruder and more desperate fellows, who at the moment that the parliamentary campaign failed took to smashing frames. Such a division is not at all accepted by Thomis, a Nottinghamshire specialist, who has also pointed out that the grounds for supposing that Henson was clear of all involvement with machine-breaking are very tenuous indeed. They amount to the fact that he himself said so, that his colleagues and he were strong in their condemnation of Luddism while engaged in their parliamentary campaign, and that the idea of direct action machine-breaking was alien to Henson's convictions. But he was, after all, unlikely to have admitted guilt to a capital offence; is likely to have distanced himself from Luddism at a time when it was tactically upsetting to his parliamentary agitation; and his preference for legal methods does not preclude a willingness to use other tactics if they seemed to offer better prospects of success. Thomis concludes that Henson's position cannot be proved either way.[67]

Thomis has also criticised Thompson's interpretation of Lancashire and Yorkshire Luddism which he considers 'industrial in its origins and industrial, too, in its aims'. Yorkshire Luddism was an anti-machine movement with shearing frames and gig mills as its targets while in Lancashire steam looms were attacked almost incidentally in what was a more general protest movement arising from low wages, high prices and unemployment, which remained devoid of any tendency to develop into a political revolutionary movement. In Lancashire he acknowledges that the precise industrial aims of the workers are difficult to determine. Their attacks against steam looms had developed out of a background of attempts to secure a minimum wage and a parliamentary regulation of the trade. Such a lack of definition makes it difficult to determine the extent to which there may have been underlying political motivations, as much for contemporaries as for historians. Thomis falls back on the 'spy gambit' suggesting that historians have been right to treat the reports of Bent with scepticism. Bythell, in a detailed study of the handloom weavers, concludes that the debate between Thompson and the Hammonds cannot, given the interpretive problems of the evidence, be finally resolved and while Thomis's work certainly emphasises this difficulty it cannot be said to have disproved Thompson's arguments.[68]

As far as the West Riding is concerned, a different kind of evidence supplements that of spies but, unfortunately, this is just as difficult to evaluate. Thompson insists that an oral tradition records the existence of a revolutionary underground and draws attention to the recording of it by the local historian Frank Peel. His first-hand testimonies strongly point to a revolutionary tradition manifesting itself in the Luddite outbreaks. Difficult as it is to evaluate, this oral evidence was recorded by an historian with no evident motive other than to record honestly a popular tradition. It cannot be simply dismissed because Peel got a date wrong or by disregarding authentic oral traditions as 'legend'.[69]

Thomis's work on Luddism, especially on Nottingham, has served to keep the debate very much alive, but his determination to compartmentalise separate spheres of activity – Luddism, trade unionism, food rioting, political movements – has the air of an artificial academic construct when applied to the actual situations of desperate men in disturbed times. It would seem to represent at least as large a degree of predisposition on the historian's part as the willingness to discover a revolutionary tradition, or the turning of a Fabian blind eye towards manifestations of violence from organised working men. Recently, two other historians have turned their attention to the Thompson thesis of a 'revolutionary' Luddism and found themselves only able to go so far with it. Professor Calhoun has been mainly concerned to stress the importance of community as a basis for 'populist' action rather than social class as a basis for revolutionary action. He accepts that older jacobin radicalism may have been 'recalled' to support what were essentially economic analyses, but insists that since the focus of Luddism remained essentially local, while it was capable of developing an insurrectionary mode of discourse and of action, it was not an 'insurrectionary fury' which could be equated with a stable revolutionary organisation engaged in purposive co-ordination.[70] Dr Dinwiddy has subjected Lancashire and Yorkshire Luddism to a searching examination on the matter of the transference of economic grievance into the language of political protest. He accepts that the extent to which economic grievances could have become politicised is the vital question to be answered. Making interesting use of the reports sent in by Bent before the machine-breaking began, he accepts the pre-existence of a political movement in the northern counties but finds it more difficult to accept definite links between the machine-breakers and the political radicals. The shearmen of the West Riding, the group largely responsible for Luddism there, seem, he suggests, to have little involvement in political radicalism, indeed Sheffield and Barnsley had more evident jacobinical tendencies than did clothing towns like Leeds. Nevertheless he accepts, contra Thomis, that there was a political dimension to northern Luddism and that in at least some places underground groups existed. He doubts, however, whether any revolutionary underground network could have been very extensive; not even extensive enough to link the main industrial centres of the north. He concludes that although there did indeed exist men in the north with revolutionary aims who had begun to mobilise in a rudimentary way, and that they did use Luddite oaths and invoke the name of Ludd, clear links between the machine-breaking and revolutionary groups are not established. Further, although a revolutionary movement may have existed, it was not a formidable one and did not get beyond the formation of a few loosely connected conspiratorial groups or manage to sustain itself effectively beyond the summer of 1812. Luddism, Dinwiddy thinks, was important in the northern counties in the process by which discontent acquired a major political dimension. He suggests that for 'politics' we need not necessarily read 'revolutionary politics', and that the Luddite years were important as a stage in the process 'whereby workingmen came to regard democratic control of the state as an essential means to the improvement of their condition'. As a way towards that democratic control they could become reformist rather than revolutionary.[71]

The interpretation of Luddism suggested by Thompson is difficult to prove. His critics have shown this much. It may even be unprovable, but the student should be warned that this is not the same thing as saying that it has been disproved. It is hardly proper for the author of a textbook who has argued that judgement depends very much upon the evaluation of difficult sources to push his student readers towards a conclusion when they have small opportunity of judging those sources for themselves. Thompson's interpretation of Luddism seems, however, to accord with popular tradition and to stem from the placing of a powerful historical understanding into the situation of the Luddites. The proper exercise of the historical imagination is not to be deliberately confused with the creation of a fantasy. Thompson's version rests no more upon special pleading than do those of some of his critics, and is at least free from the self-imposed blinkers on the subject of collective violence which so limited the insights of the Hammonds, despite the depth of their research.

REFERENCES AND NOTES

1. The *Annual Register* account of the food riots of 1766 is reprinted in **G. D. H. Cole** and **A. W. Filson** (eds), *British Working Class Movements. Select Documents 1789–1875*, Macmillan, 1951, pp. 20–5; **R. Swift**, 'Food riots in mid-Victorian Exeter, 1847–67', *Southern History*, 2, 1980, pp. 101–27; **R. B. Rose**, 'Eighteenth-century price riots and public policy in England', *International Review of Social History*, VI, 1961, pp. 277–92; **A. Booth**, 'Food riots in north-west England, 1790–1801', *Past and Present*, no. 77, 1977, pp. 84–107; **R. Wells**, 'Counting riots in eighteenth-century England', *Bulletin of the Society for the Study of Labour History*, no. 37, 1978, pp. 68–72. For a recent summary of views,

see **J. Stevenson**, *Popular Disturbances in England 1700–1870*, Longman, 1979. Ch. 5.

2.   **G. Rudé**, *The Crowd in History*, Wiley, 1964; **E. P. Thompson**, 'The moral economy of the English crowd in the eighteenth century', *Past and Present*, no. 50, 1971, pp. 76–136. For an important group of studies with a geographical emphasis, see **A. Charlesworth** (ed.), *An Atlas of Rural Protest in Britain 1548–1900*, Croom Helm, 1983.

3.   **J. G. Rule**, 'Some social aspects of the Industrial Revolution in Cornwall', in **R. Burt** (ed.), *Industry and Society in the South West*, Exeter U.P., 1970, p. 87.

4.   For discussion of the range of foodstuffs, see **J. Stevenson**, 'Food riots in England, 1792–1818', in **R. Quinault** & **J. Stevenson** (eds), *Popular Protest and Public Order, Six Studies in British History 1790–1920*, Allen & Unwin, 1974, p. 65.

5.   Cole and Filson, *British Working Class Movements*, pp. 20–5.

6.   Rule, 'Industrial Revolution in Cornwall', p. 88.

7.   Cole and Filson, *British Working Class Movements*, p. 25.

8.   Rule, 'Industrial Revolution in Cornwall', pp. 89–90, 100.

9.   Stevenson, *Popular Disturbances*, p. 94.

10.   For Kingswood colliers, see **R. W. Malcolmson**, 'A set of ungovernable people: the Kingswood colliers in the eighteenth century', in **J. Brewer** & **J. Styles** (eds), *An Ungovernable People, The English and their Law in the seventeenth and eighteenth centuries*, Hutchinson, 1980, pp. 85–127.

11.   Stevenson, *Popular Disturbances*, p. 92; **R. Wells**, 'The revolt of the south-west, 1800–01: a study in English popular protest', *Social History*, 6, 1977, p. 742.

12.   Stevenson, *Popular Disturbances*, p. 99.

13.   Rule, 'Industrial Revolution in Cornwall', p. 88.

14.   **E. P. Thompson**, 'The crime of anonymity: Appendix, A sampler of letters', in **D. Hay, P. Linebaugh** & E. P. Thompson (eds), *Albion's Fatal Tree. Crime and Society in Eighteenth-Century England*, Allen Lane, 1975, pp. 328, 332–3.

15.   Rule, 'Industrial Revolution in Cornwall', pp. 96–7, 102.

16.   **J. G. Rule**, 'The Labouring miner in Cornwall c.1740–1870: a study in social history', Ph.D. thesis, University of Warwick, 1971, p. 157.

17.   Rule, 'Industrial Revolution in Cornwall', pp. 90–1.

18.   Stevenson, *Popular Disturbances*, pp. 105–6.

19.   On proletarianisation, see **R. A. E. Wells**, 'The development of the English rural proletariat and social protest, 1700–1850', *Journal of Peasant Studies*, 6, 1979, pp. 115–39 and Charlesworth (ed.), *Atlas of Rural Protest*, pp. 8–20, 131–9. For a challenging re-assertion of the continuing significance of peasant attitudes in the south, see **M. Reed**, 'The peasantry of nineteenth-century England: a neglected class?', *History Workshop Journal*, 18, 1984, pp. 53–76.

20.   For an attempt at definition, see **J. G. Rule**, 'Social crime in the rural south in the eighteenth and early nineteenth centuries', *Southern History*, I, 1979, pp. 135–53.

21.   Wells, 'Development of the English rural proletariat', pp. 115–26.

22.   Ibid., p. 127.

23.   **A. Charlesworth**, 'The development of the English rural proletariat: a comment', *Journal of Peasant Studies*, vol. 8, no. 1, 1980, pp. 101–11.

24. **R. A. E. Wells**, 'Social conflict and protest in the English countryside in the early nineteenth century: a rejoinder', *Journal of Peasant Studies*, vol. 8, no. 4, 1981, pp. 514–30.

25. **A. J. Peacock**, 'Village radicalism in East Anglia, 1800–50', in **J. P. D. Dunbabin**, *Rural Discontent in Nineteenth Century Britain*, Faber, 1974, p. 39.

26. Charlesworth, *Atlas of Rural Protest*, pp. 146–8.

27. Ibid., pp. 148–51.

28. **E. J. Hobsbawm** and **G. Rudé**, *Captain Swing*, Penguin, 1973, pp. xxi.

29. **J. L.** and **B. Hammond**, *The Village Labourer*, 1911, ed. **G. E. Mingay**, Longman, 1978, Ch. 10 & 11; **E. J. Evans**, *The Forging of the Modern State, Early Industrial Britain*, Longman, 1983, p. 146.

30. Hobsbawm and Rudé, *Captain Swing*, p. xxv.

31. Ibid., p. 105.

32. Ibid., pp. 118, 135–6.

33. **Bob Bushaway**, *By Rite. Custom, Ceremony and Community in England 1700–1880*, Junction Books, 1982, pp. 190–202.

34. Hobsbawm and Rudé, *Captain Swing*, p. 187.

35. Ibid., pp. 201, 172.

36. See **A. Charlesworth**, 'Radicalism, political crisis and the agricultural labourers' protests of 1830', in Charlesworth (ed.), *Rural Society Change and Conflicts since 1500*, Humberside College of Higher Education for C.O.R.A.L., 1982, pp. 42–54.

37. 'A very English rising', *Times Literary Supplement*, 11 Sept. 1969.

38. Evans, *Forging of the Modern State*, p. 146.

39. **Elizabeth Gaskell**, *North and South*, Penguin edn, 1970, p. 382.

40. **D. Jones**, *Crime, protest, community and police in nineteenth-century Britain*, Routledge & Kegan Paul, 1982, pp. 35–6, 39; Hobsbawm and Rudé, *Captain Swing*, p. 244.

41. **J. Lowerson**, 'The aftermath of Swing: anti-Poor Law movements and rural trades unions in the south east of England', in Charlesworth (ed.), *Rural Social Change*, p. 74.

42. Ibid., p. 55; Jones, *Crime, protest, community and police*, p. 45; **Ursula R. Q. Henriques**, *Before the Welfare State. Social Administration in early industrial Britain*, Longman, 1978, pp. 52–4.

43. Jones, *Crime, protest, community and police*, p. 33; Hobsbawm and Rudé, *Captain Swing*, p. 244; Lowerson, 'Aftermath of Swing', pp. 68–70.

44. Lowerson, 'Aftermath of Swing', pp. 72–3.

45. Hobsbawm and Rudé, *Captain Swing*, p. 252.

46. Stevenson, *Popular Disturbances*, p. 155.

47. Ibid., p. 161.

48. **A. J. Randall**, 'The shearmen and the Wiltshire outrages of 1802: trade unionism and industrial violence', *Social History*, vol. 7, no. 3, 1982, p. 293.

49. Ibid., pp. 294–5.

50. Ibid., pp. 296–7.

51. Ibid., pp. 290–1.

52. Ibid., p. 300.

53. Ibid., pp. 283–4.

54. For the full song, see **J. L.** and **B. Hammond**, *The Skilled Labourer*, ed.

J. G. Rule, Longman, 1979, p. 212.

55. The best account of the Luddite disturbances remains the Hammonds', *Skilled Labourer*, Ch. 9, 10, & 11. For a useful shorter account, see Stevenson, *Popular Disturbances*, pp. 155–62.

56. Quoted in Hammonds, *Skilled Labourer*, p. 247.

57. For a discussion of the treatment of the incidents in *Shirley*, see **E. P. Thompson**, *The Making of the English Working Class*, Penguin, 1968, pp. 613–16.

58. Ibid., p. 616.

59. Letter reprinted in **Hay et al**, *Albion's Fatal Tree*, Appendix, p. 323.

60. Thompson, *Making of the English Working Class*, pp. 644–56.

61. The debate over the Hammonds' treatment of Luddism is discussed more fully in my introduction to the 1979 edn of *The Skilled Labourer*, pp. xx–xxvii; see *Skilled Labourer*, pp. 213, 215.

62. Ibid., pp. 190, 194–5, 215–17.

63. Ibid., pp. 225, 273–5.

64. **F. O. Darvall**, *Popular Disturbances and Public Order in Regency England*, 2nd edn, Oxford U.P., 1969.

65. Thompson, *Making of the English Working Class*, pp. 629, 631, 636–7.

66. Ibid., pp. 647–8, 654–6.

67. **R. A. Church** and **S. D. Chapman**, 'Gravener Henson and the making of the English working class', in **E. L. Jones** & **G. E. Mingay** (eds), *Land, Labour and Population in the Industrial Revolution*, Edward Arnold, 1967, pp. 137, 142; Thompson, *Making of the English Working Class*, pp. 585, 608, 916; **M. I. Thomis**, *The Luddites. Machine Breaking in Regency England*, David & Charles, 1970, p. 137 and *Politics and Society in Nottingham 1785–1835*, Oxford, 1969, pp. 86–7.

68. **M. I. Thomis** and **P. Holt**, *Threats of Revolution in Britain*, Macmillan, 1977, pp. 33–4; Thomis, *Luddites*, pp. 90–1; **D. Bythell**, *The Handloom Weavers. A Study in the English Cotton Industry during the Industrial Revolution*, Cambridge U.P., 1969, pp. 209–10.

69. Thomis, *Luddites*, p. 37; see Thompson's introduction to **Frank Peel**, *The Risings of the Luddites, Chartists and Plug-Drawers*, 1895, repr. Cass, 1968.

70. **C. Calhoun**, *The Question of Class Struggle: Social Foundations of Popular Radicalism during the Industrial Revolution*, Blackwell, 1982, p. 61.

71. **J. Dinwiddy**, 'Luddism and politics in the northern counties', *Social History*, vol. 4, no. 1, 1979, pp. 33–63.

CONCLUSION: CLASS AND CLASS CONSCIOUSNESS

It is not only the stubbornness of the protagonists which keeps historical debates alive. From time to time, close studies of restricted communities raise questions about the conclusions of wider ranging ones. The terms in which a problem is stated can change to reflect shifting perspectives and concerns, while new techniques of data gathering and analysis can expand the evidence and test it in new ways. The 'old debate' with which this book opened – that over the standard of living – is one which refuses to lie down. Even though a 'new conservatism' of the 1980s would like to pronounce it settled on the side of the 'optimists', the 'pessimist' case has hardly been weakened by recent developments.

New evidence is being produced from the computer analysis of 200,000 Britons living since 1750. That physical growth in childhood and adolescence is a good indicator of the quality of the environment and the nutritional levels in which young people grow up has long been accepted by biologists and paediatricians. Such measurements can contribute usefully to the standard of living debate. Preliminary findings presented by Professor Floud seem to support the conclusions advanced early in this book that there were major class differentials and that significant improvement in standards cannot be dated much before 1830. Slum boys recruited for the sea service around 1800 were ten inches shorter than London children of today and eight shorter than their upper-class contemporaries. Conclusions are tentative but it seems that the gap did not begin to close until the second quarter of the nineteenth century. Floud also notes that height improvement has been neither smooth nor continuous and has been reversed in periods of depression. This is not only suggestive for the 1840s, but makes it 'not fanciful on the basis of historical evidence, to believe that the present unemployment is affecting the growth and final stature of the British population'.[1]

Professor Floud's researches employ new methods on new data, but re-assessments of existing evidence are also important. The presentation of real wage trends between 1750 and 1850 by Professor Flinn has been discussed in detail above (pp. 33–4) and has become something of an orthodoxy on the subject. Yet a re-assessment of Flinn's evidence by Dr Von Tunzelmann employing a different statistical approach has suggested qualifications to Flinn's conclusions, and suggests that he improperly separated longer-term trends from short-term fluctuations. Serious doubt is also cast upon the choice of the ending of the French Wars in 1815 as a crucial turning point after which real wages 'jumped'. The indices of prices and wages upon which Flinn relied are capable of producing statistically a 'best case' of an overall rise of 2½ times in real wages over those 100 years and a 'worst case' of a fall for sixty years followed by a return to 1750 levels by 1850! The non-mathematical student can do little but wonder if there is ever any certainty in numbers. At the end of his re-assessment, Von Tunzelmann concludes that real wage improvement did not date from the price peak of 1813 which was so stressed by Flinn, for the gains of the ensuing deflation were wiped out by the price rise 1816/18, but from the 1820s and quite possibly only from the end of that decade if a short-term deterioration from 1826–9 is accepted. This conforms to the suggestion that we made in our earlier discussion that 'optimist' cases which claim much improvement before the second quarter of the nineteenth century are not on very strong ground. In general, Von Tunzelmann suggests the proven case for a sustained and significant improvement in real wages is so slight that a plausible case could be made for viewing any rise accompanying industrialisation as no more than sufficient to offset 'a decline in other conditions of life' which it brought about. In particular he suggests that the data on mortality rates in early nineteenth-century cities 'seem damning enough', and certainly recent work in historical demography has much relevance to the standard of living debate.[2]

'Optimists' from Macaulay through Clapham and Ashton to Hartwell have stressed a 'great dip' (Clapham) in the mortality rate as the most difficult fact for the 'pessimists'. After McKeown and Brown had rejected medical improvement as a significant cause of mortality decline, the optimists were able to assert more confidently that it was a reflection of improving economic and social conditions. The appearance of the long-awaited reconstruction of English population from 1541–1871 by Wrigley and Schofield in 1981 has, by emphatically removing the burden of explaining population increase from mortality to fertility, knocked away the main prop of this argument. Dr Armstrong's detailed examination of Carlisle, a town growing with industrialisation, finds an adverse trend in mortality after 1813, the full effect of which was masked by a changing age structure.[3]

A recent examination of London real wage trends by Dr Schwarz suggests a large fall during the second half of the eighteenth century as well as the, by now, widely agreed increase in rates during the 1820s and early 1830s which lifted real wages significantly above the level of the 1790s. Yet because of a growing uncertainty about the eighteenth century the idea of a *long-term* improvement between 1740 and 1820 remains unconvincing.[4]

In 1901, paupers still had a lower life expectation than had the whole population of Stuart times. The Victorian attack on epidemic diseases through sanitation reform had had an effect in lowering mortality. The death rate in 1861 of 20.5 per 1,000 had fallen by 1901 to 16.9, while life expectancy at birth had risen from 40.2 years in 1841 to 51.5 in 1911 (England and Wales). The urban to rural death ratio fell from 124:100 in 1851–61 to 114:100 in 1891–1901. Mortality is not, however, the only valid indicator of health and the new type of Englishman with, according to the social Darwinists, the weaker no longer weeded out by epidemic diseases, was a sickly, stunted, urban type, threatening the national stock. At the time of the Crimean War in 1854, 42% of urban and 17% of rural recruits were rejected and they were from volunteers who had already been pre-selected by local recruiting centres. That poverty was at the root of ill-health was evident in 1864 to Sir John Simon, the greatest of the medical officers of the age: 'the masses will scarcely be healthy unless, to their very base, they be at least moderately prosperous', while twenty-five years later the Reverend Samuel Barnet concluded: 'The poor, by bad air, by dirt, by accident, cannot live out half their days. The good news about health which science preaches to the rich is not preached to them.' Such contemporary verdicts have been amply confirmed by the researches of Professors Wohl and Smith, while careful work on working-class diets by the specialist historian Professor Oddy has cast some doubt on the extent of the assumed improvement, quantitative and qualitative, in working-class food consumption by the late nineteenth century. He considers the consistently high level of infant mortality during the 1890s to be a significant comment on working-class diets.[5]

'Urban disamenities' symbolised by high mortality and poor health are not easily measured yet, as two recent writers who attempt to do so confess, unless ways are devised of 'weighing' such dimensions against material gains, then questions about living standards are not being answered but only those about real earnings. Their attempt to measure by using the wage differential needed to draw workers into the new industrial towns is an interesting one, but their conclusion that it was small enough to suggest that marginal workers put a low implicit value on the sacrifice in quality of life entailed in moving from village to town is hardly surprising. It uses a measure only appropriate if real *choice* had existed and where foreknowledge of awaiting conditions was as widespread and adequate as that of higher wages.[6]

The long-term effect of the industrial revolution in generally raising standards and in decreasing poverty is not in dispute. Primary poverty was almost certainly more widespread and more general in most

381

pre-industrial ages than it was in the early nineteenth century but, as Peter Laslett has concluded in comparing the industrial with the pre-industrial age, Englishmen had to face the 'disconcerting fact that destitution was still an outstanding feature of fully industrial society, a working class perpetually liable to social and material degradation'. The working class remained considerably disadvantaged down at least to 1914 and less, but seriously so, to 1945. In 1901, Seebohm Rowntree discovered 27.84% of the population of York to be living in poverty, 'their total earnings are insufficient to obtain the minimum necessaries for the maintenance of merely physical efficiency'. Charles Booth in 1889 published the results of his inquiries in London revealing that 30.7% of the population lived below his poverty line: 'at all times more or less in want'.[7]

Real wages did rise between 1870 and 1914 and significant gains spread after 1914 to the unskilled working class. By the 1930s, on Rowntree's standard, primary poverty was reduced to around 10% of the population. In that reduction, many things had played a part: not only the growth of the economy; the fall in the prices of imported foodstuffs and the remarkable fall, after 1919, in the size of the working-class family; but also increasing welfare legislation and provision with its recognition of the limitations of market forces in the promotion of general well-being.

Perhaps the whole framework of questioning associated with the debate has, as Stedman Jones has suggested, been focused too much upon real wage and consumption data. Wages alone tell us little about changes in the level of exploitation: they have to be placed in relation to changing hours of work and changing rates of productivity per hour. The latter is hardly an abstraction for it may mean people work harder in each hour, the effect of which may be measurable in industrial disease and death rates, in rising incidence of accidents and changes in the numbers of people dying from premature exhaustion.[8]

Something as difficult to define as the 'quality of life' defies measurement and, because of its subjectivity, is not satisfactorily evaluated through the comparison of literary sources. It became possible in the 1950s for the urban street life of the terraced homes, which had offended so many critics of early industrialisation, to become the object of nostalgia once the building of high-rise flats in new suburbs threatened it. The historian must aim to treat the feelings and reactions of those who experienced the changes he describes without either facile indifference to suffering in the name of the 'greater long-term good' or excessive indignation from twentieth-century expectations and values. What must be avoided is, in E. P. Thompson's memorable phrase, the 'enormous condescension of posterity'.[9]

CLASS FORMATION AND CONSCIOUSNESS

The debate which most persists, which is most likely to continue to do so and which arouses the greatest degree of antagonism among protagonists, is that over class and class concsiousness.

CLASS IN EIGHTEENTH-CENTURY ENGLAND

No serious historian would insist that the lines of social cleavage in the eighteenth century corresponded in any very close sense to the more horizontal class divisions of the nineteenth. Even less applicable would be the suggestion of a formed class consciousness. Although recognising very real inequalities in the eighteenth century, many historians argue that paternalism and deference reciprocated to produce a form of social consensus or at least acceptance in what Professor Perkin has labelled a 'classless hierarchy' which lasted until the advent of industrial society. The sense of a community of shared interests in the rural world has been discussed above, but it also has a manufacturing application. We are urged not to conceive of recognised separate interests of masters and men, capital and labour (although Adam Smith had no doubt of this), but instead of a vertical consciousness of the 'trade' embracing the mutuality of employer and employee. Disputes happened but, like family quarrels, they did not prohibit recognition of an overall common interest. Perhaps like family squabbles they arose because actors at different power levels did not behave according to expectation. *Some* masters in fact acted in an 'unmasterlike' manner and perhaps, as Professor Calhoun has argued, in so doing breached the norms of the occupational community. Even so they were productive of conflict between capital and labour, even if of a temporary kind. Edward Thompson seems inclined to accept the reality of the 'trade' as a consciousness inherited by journeymen from the guilds, and manifested for the most part in a tight organisation of journeymen *within* the boundaries of their occupation. He notes, however, that such an outlook, characteristic of early trade unions, was not always at odds with larger objectives or solidarities, even if it did inhibit economic solidarities between different groups against their employers. Food riots, turnpike riots and other disturbances reveal wide occupational involvement: 'The mob may not have been noted for an impeccable consciousness of class: but the rulers of England were in no doubt at all that it was a horizontal sort of beast.' It has been pointed out by Dr Morris that alongside the eighteenth-century language of ranks and orders existed another which identified the 'mob'. The advocation of a 'classless hierarchy' by Perkin means that he has to employ the uncomfortable concept of 'latent' class feeling when faced with such facts as very frequent industrial disputes which set labour against capital.[10] Nevertheless, articulation of a separate labour interest was most often temporary. Bitter exchanges, sometimes violent strikes and sharply articulated hostility often gave way after settlement to an expressed preference for an ordered world in which masters and men both knew their place and the duties which went with it. The disputes which preceded the parliamentary regulation of the Spitalfields silk manufacture in 1773 were extremely violent, but very soon after a poem was inserted in the new rate book:

> And may no treacherous, base designing men
> E'er make encroachments on our rights again;
> May upright masters still augment their treasure,
> And journeymen pursue their work with pleasure,
> May arts and manufactories still increase,
> And Spitalfields be blest with prosperous peace.[11]

Similar sentiments were recorded by the journeymen papermakers in their rulebook in 1803, again following a period of bitter strikes and a lock-out:

> May masters with their men unite,
> Each other ne'er oppress;
> And their assistance freely give
> When men are in distress.

> We covet not our master's wealth
> Nor crave for nothing more
> But to support our families
> As our fathers have before

> Then may the God that rules above
> Look on our mean endeavour
> And masters with their men unite
> In hand and hand for ever.

Even General Ludd intended no ill will to masters generally but only to those that used wide frames, 'And to those that old prices abate'.[12]

Like the 'old-fashioned squire', the 'old-fashioned master' was always more remembered from the past than found in the present, but he overlay class feeling and allowed only its occasional overt expression. Professor Hobsbawm has suggested that whereas under industrial capitalism, class is an immediate and directly experienced reality, as far as earlier periods go it is more of an analytical construct, hardly recognised by contemporaries, but which allows historians to make sense of a complex of otherwise inexplicable facts and insights.[13]

CLASS IN EARLY INDUSTRIAL ENGLAND

Few linguistic clues are as indicative of the way in which language can reflect changing social realities as the taking over of social description in early nineteenth-century Britain by the 'language of class'. Twenty-five years ago Lord Briggs demonstrated how it displaced the eighteenth-century language of 'orders' and 'degrees'. The labouring people became the 'working classes' and, as their consciousness of a self-interest developed, 'the working class'. The language of class clearly pervades the work of historians on the nineteenth century. Even the least 'Marxist' among them seem to employ it adjectivally: working-class diet, working-class housing, education, protest, etc., etc., while taking pains to suggest that social analysis should not really be based on the 'out-moded' concept of social class.[14]

There are many possible positions on this issue. The *existence* of a working class may be accepted – it is surprising that it could be denied – but the fact of class *conflict* denied. Such a position points to shared outlooks and so far as political action is concerned to collaboration between middle- and working-class radicals. Class can be allowed as a descriptive objective category linking people in terms of their life chances and expectations, mortality, material rewards, way of getting a living, opportunities for education, etc., while *class consciousness* in the sense of (to use Marx's terms) a class *in* itself becoming a class *for* itself can be considered either as something which failed to develop at all in the manner predicted by Marx, or at least only did so after 1850. Marx believed that even by then the English working class, although the most developed in Europe, was only at the beginning of its transition into a conscious class *for* itself. As late as 1870 he wrote: '[England is] the only country in which the material conditions for this revolution have developed up to a *certain degree* of maturity. Therefore to hasten the social revolution in England is the most important object of the International Working Men's Association'.[15]

It is also possible to accept the development of a working-class consciousness as a self-awareness of a separate class identity and interest, without accepting that the consciousness was a 'revolutionary' one aiming at the overthrow of capitalism rather than at accommodation on good terms within the system.

Full discussion of the vast and contentious literature on the subject would fill a book on its own. Here we can consider only the main contributions to the debate over the rise of the English working class. Few books have had a greater or more controversial impact on British postwar historiography than Edward Thompson's *The Making of the English Working Class* first published in 1963, whose title clearly reveals its centrality to the issue we are now discussing. Thompson has been somewhat unfairly criticised by historians of the left for playing down the primacy of changing economic structures and modes of production in class formation. He undoubtedly distances himself from a crude economic determinism in his portrayal of a working class actively participating in its own making and carrying with it into the new industrial world and into its new consciousness, ideas and values from past craft manufacture, from dissenting religion and from traditions of the 'freeborn Englishman' reaching back through the levellers to John Ball. Between 1780 and 1830, he argued, with intensified economic exploitation accompanying political repression and with it its reactions mediated through inherited values, the English working class was 'made'. In the crisis of 1795/6 at the height of the jacobin era, the casting off of the old deferential mode by some sectors of the working class, notably the artisans, can be clearly perceived. By the reform crisis of 1832 the 'making' had been effected and a threshold crossed into a world 'in which the working class presence can be felt in every county in England, and in most fields of life'. Thompson did not suggest, although many of his critics seem to react as if he did, that this point represented the achieving of a fully formed and universally shared class consciousness by the working people at large. There is a sense in which his thesis would have commanded a larger degree of acceptance had he continued his story down to the Chartist years, for most historians would prefer to see the years after 1832, when as Hobsbawm has put it, 'the workers' movement fought and failed alone', as the most formative for working-class consciousness. In fact it is not always easy to see what special meaning Thompson gives to 'making' for he insists: 'The *outcome* of this period of "making" lies . . . in the Chartist years.' But it would presumably be illogical to suppose that working-class consciousness burst from the blue in 1834 with the working-class Owenites and the Grand National Consolidated Trades Union: it is the great merit of *the Making* that it enables us to see how the ideas, associations, programmes and institutions of the 1830s and 1840s could have emerged.[16]

Critics have suggested that his working class is hard to find and that by concentrating on points of conflict he draws general conclusions from the exceptional. In fact it seems to be the nature of working-class consciousness to burst through narrower confines at exceptional 'moments' in history, but it is neither created *ab initio* during those periods nor dies completely when they end. During such periods the essential heterogeneity of the working people, the condition for their sectionalism, is for the time overlaid to a degree far beyond the usual. Contemporaries certainly recognised the broad divisions both material and in terms of consciousness which were to be found among the workers. Henry Mayhew stated it clearly enough in 1849 when he described the great gulf which existed in London between the artisans and the unskilled labourers:

> The artisans are almost to a man red-hot politicians. They are sufficiently educated and thoughtful to have a sense of their importance in the state . . . The unskilled labourers are a different class of people. As yet they are as unpolitical as footmen . . . they appear to have no political opinions whatever; or, if they do possess any, they rather lead towards the maintenance of 'things as they are', than towards the ascendancy of the working people.[17]

The existence of such divisions was recognised by Thompson, who claimed he had tried to distinguish between different group experiences of artisans, outworkers and labourers in showing that they were, to differing degrees and with differing speed, coming 'to act, think and feel, not in the old modes of deference and parochial seclusion, but in class ways'. Since class relations and consciousness were cultural formations and class itself 'a happening not a thing', it is foolish to expect to discover from the application of rigid criteria something equivalent to a 'card-carrying membership'. In fact there was nothing permanent about the consciousness of the 1830s and 1840s and part at least of the collapse of Chartism was due to the tensions within it of different group outlooks which thereafter drew apart once more. Class consciousness cannot be supposed to have happened once and for all and everywhere, but a disposition to *behave* as a class spread during those years among 'a very loosely defined body of people.'[18]

In fact his book is centrally concerned with the politicisation of a section of the proletariat, the urban artisans and the manufacturing outworkers of the countryside. As Dr Prothero has noted of its theme:

The years 1829–34 did not see the formation of a working class that has persisted ever since. That book is mainly about artisans, with whom it deals so sensitively. It is as true of England as elsewhere in Europe that much of what historians mean when they speak of the 'rise of the working class' is artisans becoming politically active.[19]

We have already noted that the trade union movement of the 1830s poses this problem of analysis. Marx and Engels in their early writings placed the artisan along with the lower middle class and the peasantry as those who fight against the bourgeoisie to save their existence as 'fractions of the middle class'. They were conservative or even reactionary in that they sought to 'roll back the wheel of history' and could become revolutionary only if, through perception of an impending transfer into the ranks of the proletariat, they sought to defend their future interest and deserted their standpoint for that of the proletariat. They presumably had in mind artisans more consonant with German than English realities, i.e. sellers of the product of their labour rather than sellers of labour power to merchant capitalists. In England, artisan had an especially wide application and embraced skilled workers in general who, though masters of their trade, were not destined to become masters in any other sense. These constituted the growing class of permanent journeymen in the towns and the outworking proletariat in the villages. Very far from generally did artisans constitute an elite. Machine manufacture triumphed slowly and handworkers, more or less skilled, made up a sizeable, widespread and not shrinking fraction of the English working class. The values they defended may have been traditional, but the defence of custom against an innovative capitalism which has the backing of the state can become an act of rebellion. Further to this, in the 1830s it is evident that old ideas of a 'property of skill' became attached to notions of labour as the source of value. This did not produce a class consciousness in the fully-formed sense; it was too restrictive for that, although its logic pressed awkwardly at times against the walls of its own confinement. It was at very least a labour consciousness appropriate to an historical moment when the triumph of industrial capitalism was not yet seen as inevitable and might yet be halted in its progress. It was bound to have been different from the consciousness of a proletariat under a developed capitalist system. [20]

Two recent books should be noted as being extended critiques of Thompson's book. That by Craig Colhoun stressing community rather than class as the basis for protest which was essentially 'populist' has been discussed above (p. 159). The other, by Robert Glenn, is a close and detailed study of the cotton town of Stockport between 1780 and 1820 made purposely to test Thompson's views on class formation. It is a valuable local study and choosing to entitle it somewhat sweepingly *Urban Workers in the Early Industrial Revolution* should not deceive the student that its conclusions necessarily have a more general applicability. We must await further studies before we can know that. Indeed, further work on Stockport might in itself produce a different emphasis for there is inevitably much that is subjective about judgements on matters of class consciousness. Glenn's conclusion is that during these years the inhabitants of Stockport were not only 'self-effacing' but also '*good natured*' – at last an historian who has found how to apply the felicific calculus! The book deserves attention for its detailed investigation before its conclusion that, although workers' trade organisations did become widespread, evidence of inter-trade solidarity is limited. The different strands of working-class protest trade unions, Luddism, food rioting and political reform movements of varying hues are discussed, but it is contended they never came together to constitute any kind of 'movement'. It must be remarked that linkages of such a kind if they had existed are not noted for leaving documentation which could convince historians with a pre-existing scepticism and it is a little surprising that some reviewers have jumped eagerly to proclaim Glenn's conclusion. The book has been described as yet another contribution to ensure that 'Historiographically . . . the working class has been well and truly un-made', while J. T. Ward congratulates Glenn on driving 'another nail into the coffin of "the working-class movement" theory'. In fact the book has a major weakness and one which is of the author's own choosing. It should be evident to any reader of Thompson that the Reform Bill crisis years are crucial to his thesis, yet Glenn chooses to end his study in 1827 and still manages to conclude that the hostile solidarity of the middle and upper classes towards the workers has been exaggerated. If we are to stop before we reach the great divide of 1832, how can we judge that?

Secondly, we are left in the dark as to what happened in the 1830s and 1840s, and Glenn's explanation that large-scale Irish immigration broke continuity in significantly changing the social structure does more to whet the appetite than turn off the curiosity. Thirdly, one on by the working people. Let, some argue, the warts of early industrial capitalism be painted over, while well-placed historians declare that the history of the 'common people' has no place in the classroom: let the folk make way for the return of the 'great men'! Yet I venture to suggest that this political moment will pass and a proper evaluation of the struggle for the right to work and for a decent existence again become central to the historical curriculum.[30]

Professor Perkin presented the birth of class society in a less combative way than Thompson, but his work has special significance not only for its influential analysis of eighteenth-century society but because it attempts to locate the emergence of a working class within a model of the development, with industrialisation, of other social classes in the formation of a 'viable class society'. Class society appropriate to the new age displaced the 'classless hierarchy' of traditional society and did do within a short and well-defined period of time with the few years after 1815 seeing the birth of the working class. By the third decade of the nineteenth century, English society had come to consist of mutually hostile layers defined by the sources of income: rent, profit and wages. Perkin sees a working-class consciousness as being in part forced by the abdication of traditional social responsibilities by the rulers and by their rejection by the new middle class. To each of four main horizontal groupings he relates consciousness to an 'ideal': aristocratic or paternalistic for the gentry; entrepreneurial for the capitalist middle class; and a weaker brew of co-operation and the labour theory of value for the working class. The fourth class was the professional with an ideal of service and efficiency. Not only was the working-class ideal weakly formulated and shallowly held, but the class suffered from deep and persistent divisions and, although the existence of a working-class oppositional consciousness is accepted, the outcome was the triumph of the bourgeois individualistic ideal of entrepreneurship softened to a degree by something of the professional ideal as the basis of the 'viable class society'.[22]

His stress on the significance for all class society of the strength of the middle class is important. Briggs noted that in the language of class the middle class was the first to describe itself and Thompson saw consciousness as needing to rise in the face of antagonistic ideologies: 'class happens when some men, as a result of common experiences . . . feel and articulate the identity of their interests as between themselves, and as against other men whose interests are different from (and usually opposed to) theirs.'[23] We have already noted the significance of 1832 in severing the political reform alliance between working- and middle-class radicals, for not only were the working class left alone as the excluded, but the measures passed by the post-reform government were hostile to working-class associations and aspirations. No single piece of legislation more clearly reveals the triumph of the middle-class ideology than the Poor Law Amendment Act of 1834. The practical object of the reform was to cut the rising cost of poor relief but, in accordance with the principles of political economy and the creation of the free, low-wage labour market required by the capitalist economy, it administered relief to only the most necessitous of the poor and to them under the most stringently deterrent principles of less eligibility in new workhouses which came more than any other structure to symbolise to the common people their oppression and degeneration. Unlike the old Poor Law it replaced, it had no underlying principle of social welfare and amounted, as Professor Harrison has remarked, to 'the announcement that henceforth the labouring poor must abandon many of their traditional attitudes and expectations and conform to new standards of social and economic rectitude'. It was class legislation of the clearest kind for it oppressed one class of society in the name of the ideology of another. The contribution which hostility to the New Poor Law made to the rhetoric of working-class radicalism was large. Not only did the people in many areas resist it in riot, but it became the grievance most persistently and persuasively articulated by Chartism's orators.[24]

Thompson's book, although written within an important tradition of British Marxist historiography, is rather less schematic in its Marxism than is the third book of influence we have to examine: John Foster's study of Oldham, *Class Struggle and the Industrial Revolution* (1974). Foster's model in his stimulating and amazingly sustained argument owes much to Lenin. For this allegiance he has attracted almost as much criticism from the 'left' as from the 'right'. It has been argued by Dr Stedman Jones that his fallacy lies in carrying back from later *established* capitalism a formulation for the development of a revolutionary consciousness inappropriate for the analysis of the emerging and still unfulfilled industrial capitalism of the English industrial revolution. Foster does not present Oldham as representative of what was happening more generally in England. He rather examines the formation of class and class consciousness among the working class of a cotton town affected by the new factory system. Between 1790 and 1820, influenced by the French Revolution and by English jacobinism, but owing more to the special pressures of what Foster described as the first modern crisis of industrial capitalism (induced by the imbalance of factory yarn so far ahead of power weaving, and by competition from low-wage foreign weavers working on exported yard), there emerged a special form of *trade union* consciousness. This, as in Lenin's model, was limited to economic action and incapable on its own of becoming political. It was hardened by the coercive pressure of the Combination Acts and did achieve an increasing solidarity among the different trades and present, from its illegality, a sporadic challenge to state power.[25]

Class consciousness, Foster argues, came to Oldham's workers in the next period – the step from social being to social consciousness being bridged (again following Lenin) in the role of a revolutionary vanguard more ideologically precocious than the bulk of the working class. From 1830 to 'defeat' in 1848 there was a sustained rejection of bourgeois forms and the presentation of a clear anti-capitalist viewpoint in campaigns for the Short Time Movement and in the achieving of radical control of the vestry and over the police. Working-class consumer power expressed through the tactic of 'exclusive dealing' was used to ensure the election of two MPs emphatically antagonistic to the factory system in its unregulated form, John Fielden and William Cobbett. After mid-century, however, this period ended largely because a new form of the labour aristocracy was accommodated into a liberalised capitalist system. In pointing to the *widespread* nature of class consciousness in Oldham, Foster focuses narrowly upon two major strikes in 1834 and in 1842 which were 'general' across the town's working-class occupations and which produced from the leaders a clear articulation of class consciousness. These he differentiates from the sporadic, 'economic' strikes of the period of trade union consciousness. His critics are less inclined to notice so sharp a difference and remark it a weakness of his position that he does not offer a more continuous and sustained analysis of the 1830s and 1840s.[26]

Crucial to his argument is the insistence that the workers guided by the 'vanguard' gained a new conviction that beyond day-to-day economic struggles the solution to their oppression lay in wholesale change of the social system. This is difficult to sustain. What appears in the speeches of a vanguard cannot be simply presumed to have existed in any widespread form. The week-long strike of 1834 in support of the eight-hour day was an impressive display of shared resentment and solidarity across trades, but it is not easy to prove that it was more. Two of Foster's critics have pointed to the small-scale nature of many of Oldham's enterprises and suggested that rather than representing a classic conflict instance of the polarisation of capital and labour which comes with large-scale industry, the town's structure suggests the likelihood of class collaboration across a narrow social distance between master and man as suggested for Birmingham by Briggs. Leaving aside the qualifications which emerge from the work of Behagg about Briggs's class-collaborationist model for Birmingham, it hardly seems appropriate to discuss Oldham in these terms when its early industrial history is punctuated by bitter strikes. Foster's insistence on a *revolutionary* class consciousness may have found little support, but that does not mean that Oldham does not evidence a significant working-class consciousness in a less specific and more historically appropriate sense.[27]

Recognition of the advent of a new working-class presence was not confined to the speeches and writings of working-class leaders. There was also acknowledgement further up the social scale of the change brought about by the new industrial society. James Kay-Shuttleworth, who as an educationalist was anxious to 'control' the new situation, remarked in 1832:

> Between the manufacturers . . . and the labouring classes subjects of con-
> troversy have arisen, and consequent animosity too generally exists . . .
> bitter debate arises between the manufacturers and those in their employ,
> concerning the proper division of that fund from which (profits and wages)
> . . . are derived. The bargain for the wages of labour develops organized
> associations of the working classes for the purpose of carrying on the contest
> with the capitalist . . . a gloomy spirit of discontent is engendered, and the
> public are not infrequently alarmed, by the wild outbreak of popular
> violence.[28]

When contemporaries noted, as they often did, lines of cleavage across the working class they did not proceed, unlike many historians, from this to deny its existence. Marx was aware of the emergence of sub-classes but this does not imply the elision of meaningful class lines. The two most recognisable sub-groupings to emerge, the 'aristocracy of labour' and the lower middle class, certainly had in common an acceptance of and an accommodation within capitalist society, but in matters of life-styles and values historians have shown them to have been very different. Much conservative historiography seems blind to what was evident to contemporaries, the fact of class-structured industrial society, and insists that social class is too inexact and in-appropriate a tool for the analysis of the subtleties of early nineteenth-century society. It has even been suggested that instead the concept of a 'social spectrum' be employed. It is indeed difficult to imagine how a continuum from the lowest pauper to the richest and grandest duke can much assist in understanding the early industrial era in which material inequalities were so manifest, life chances so sharply differentiated and power so narrowly concentrated. The class conflict which charac-terised the early industrial era was real enough: generations of his-torians have after all struggled to find explanations for the relative quiescence which came with mid-Victorian prosperity and the 'Age of Equipoise'.[29]

The changing occupational structure of twentieth-century Britain, in particular the decline proportionally and in absolute numbers of the manual working class, may have convinced some historians of the inappropriateness of thinking in 'traditional' terms of class society. It is dangerous to carry present-day perspectives back to the nineteenth century. Some historians, who only twenty years ago applied a class model to early industrial Britain and who now reject it, are perhaps falling into this danger.

This book will probably be criticised by some for clinging to outmoded concerns and examining them with out-dated concepts. Certainly it has not offered a picture which would meet with the approval of those who now declare that English history should concentrate on the propagation of our 'national achievements' and wish to consign to dark corners the story of the struggle for dignity and well-being carried on by the working people. Let, some argued, the warts of early industrial capitalism be painted over, while well-placed historians declare that the history of the 'common people' has no place in the classroom: let the folk make way for the return of the 'great men'! Yet I venture to suggest that this political moment will pass and a proper evaluation of the struggle for the right to work and for a decent existence again become central to the historical curriculum.[30]

But, if this book is still looked at, what will date it above all at no great distance of time will have been the continuing development of women's history. Hopefully, soon a history of the working people will be able fully to incorporate working women. So rapid has been the rise of women's history that few of us cast in the traditional mould of social and labour history have been able to absorb more than partially either its findings or its significance. It will not, as Sally Alexander has so cogently pointed out, be enough to write of women's work, to mention the family or note the absence of women from some forms of political life, even though this is a welcome stretching of traditional historical approaches to the working-class experience. The well-tried categories of traditional labour history and of Marxism do not easily accommodate a view of history which places sexual divisions alongside those of class in the discussion of 'exploitation' and power inequalities. As several historians have shown, during the ferment of consciousness of the 1830s and 1840s, the question of the position and role of women forced itself into the political discourse only to be pushed into a separate sphere by a workers' consciousness dominated by traditional male values and anxiously regarding the threat of competition from low-waged female labour. Dorothy Thompson has noted the irony in that the very period during which Chartist leaders were taking part in discussions about European socialism was one in which, except for a very few areas, the women disappeared from working-class politics, and labour's leaders came to accept a version of the Victorian home-centred woman. A period ensued in which the openness and gains in self-awareness of the Owenite and early Chartist years slipped into one of narrowing expectations and demands.[31]

REFERENCES AND NOTES

1. For a brief insight into this investigation whose main results are not yet published, see **R. Floud**, 'The past in the present and future', *The Times Higher Education Supplement*, 6 July 1984, p. 15.
2. **G. N. Von Tunzelmann**, 'Trends in real wages, 1750–1850, revisited', *Economic History Review*, xxxii, no. 1, 1979, pp. 48–9, 39.
3. **E. A. Wrigley** and **R. S. Schofield**, *The Population History of England, 1541–1871*, Arnold, 1981; **W. A. Armstrong**, 'The trend of mortality in Carlisle between the 1780s and the 1840s: a demographic contribution to the standard of living debate', *Economic History Review*, xxxiv, no. 1, 1981, pp. 94–114. It should be noted that Armstrong suggests several qualifications to the use of his findings in support of the 'pessimist' case.
4. **L. D. Schwarz**, 'The standard of living in the long run: London, 1700–1860', *Economic History Review*, xxxviii, no. 1, 1985, pp. 28–9, 34.
5. **A. S. Wohl**, *Endangered Lives. Public Health in Victorian Britain*, Methuen, 1984, pp. 329–41; see also **F. B. Smith**, *The People's Health 1830–1910*, Croom Helm, 1979; **D. J. Oddy**, 'Working-class diets in late nineteenth-century Britain', *Economic History Review*, xxiii, no. 2, 1970, pp. 314–15, 322.
6. **P. H. Lindert** and **J. G. Williamson**, 'English workers' living standards during the industrial revolution: a new look', *Economic History Review*, xxxvi, 1983, pp. 21–3.
7. **B. S. Rowntree**, *Poverty: A Study of Town Life*, 1901. For an application of his poverty line to the period of the industrial revolution, see **J. Foster**, *Class Struggle and the Industrial Revolution*, Methuen, 1974, App. 1. Foster estimates that the cost of the minimum food requirement of 3s. 3d. (16¼p) for an adult per week in 1899 would have been 4s. 3d. (20¼p) in Manchester in 1849, and finds that the majority of Oldham's working families lived below it at any given moment while practically all would have been at times in their life-cycles. For **Charles Booth**, see the convenient selection from his multi-volume work *Charles Booth's London*, ed. **A. Fried** & **R. Elman**, Penguin, 1971. See the effective discussion by **P. Laslett** in *The World we Have Lost – further explored*, Methuen, 1983, pp. 246–56.
8. See the long letter from **G. Stedman Jones** in *History Workshop Journal*, 8, 1979, p. 199.
9. **E. P. Thompson**, *The Making of the English Working Class*, Penguin, 1968, p. 13.
10. See the discussion in **J. Rule**, *The Experience of Labour in Eighteenth-Century Industry*, Croom Helm, 1981, pp. 208–13; **H. J. Perkin**, *The Origins of Modern English Society 1780–1880*, Routledge & Kegan Paul, 1969, Ch. 2, 'The old society'; **C. Calhoun**, *The Question of Class Struggle: Social Foundations of Popular Radicalism, during the Industrial Revolution*, Blackwell, 1982; **E. P. Thompson**, 'Eighteenth-century English society: class struggle without class', *Social History,* vol. 3, no. 2, 1978, p. 145 and 'Patrician society, plebeian culture', *Journal of Social History*, vol. VII, no. 4, 1974, pp. 396–7; **R. J. Morris**, *Class and Class Consciousness in the Industrial Revolution 1780–1850*, Macmillan, 1979, pp. 13, 18.

11. Quoted in Rule, *Experience of Labour*, pp. 209–10.
12. Ibid., p. 210.
13. **E. J. Hobsbawm**, 'Class consciousness in history', in *Worlds of Labour*, Weidenfeld & Nicolson, 1984, p. 18.
14. **A. Briggs**, 'The language of class in early nineteenth-century England', in **A. Briggs** & **J. Saville** (eds), *Essays in Labour History*, Macmillan, rev. 1967, pp. 43–73.
15. For examples of the class collaboration view, see **D. J. Rowe**, 'Class and political radicalism in London, 1831–2', *Historical Journal*, XIII, 1979, pp. 31–47 and **D. S. Gadian**, 'Class consciousness in Oldham and other north-west industrial towns 1830–50', ibid., XXI, 1978, pp. 161–72. Quoted in **G. Stedman Jones**, 'Some notes on Karl Marx and the English labour movement', *History Workshop Journal*, 18, 1984, p. 125. On the dating of '*class* consciousness', see the challenging arguments in **R. S. Neale, Class in English** *History, 1680–1850*, Barnes & Noble, 1981.
16. The 1968 edn by Penguin Books with its important postscript should be used. The quotations are from pp. 887 and 937. **E. J. Hobsbawm**, *Industry and Empire*, Weidenfeld & Nicolson, 1968, p. 59.
17. **E. P. Thompson** and **E. Yeo** (eds), *The Unknown Mayhew*, Penguin, 1973, p. 95.
18. Thompson, *The Making*, pp. 937–9.
19. **I. Prothero**, *Artisans and Politics in Early Nineteenth-Century London. John Gast and his Times*, Dawson, 1979, p. 337.
20. *Communist Manifesto*, Penguin edn, p. 44. For a discussion of artisans arguing for their inclusion in the proletariat, see **J. G. Rule**, 'Artisan attitudes: a comparative survey of skilled labour and proletarianisation in Europe', *Bulletin of Society for the Study of Labour History*, 1985.
21. **R. Glenn**, *Urban Workers in the Early Industrial Revolution*, Croom Helm, 1984, p. 285; reviews by **E. J. Evans** in *Times Higher Education Supplement*, 6 April 1984, p. 21 and by **J. T. Ward** in *Economic History Review*, xxxvii, no. 3, 1984, pp. 440–1.
22. Perkin, *Origins*, esp. Ch. 6–9.
23. Thompson, *The Making*, pp. 9–10.
24. **J. F. C. Harrison**, *The Common People. A History from the Norman Conquest to the Present*, Fontana, 1984, pp. 235–7.
25. Stedman Jones's important review is entitled 'England's first proletariat' in *New Left Review*, 90, 1975, pp. 35–69.
26. For an extended critique from a very different stand than that of Stedman Jones, see **A. E. Musson**, 'Class struggle and the labour aristocracy, 1830–60', *Social History*, no. 3, 1976, pp. 335–56.
27. Ibid., p. 350; Gadian, 'Class consciousness', pp. 163–6; **C. Behagg**, 'An alliance with the middle class: the Birmingham Political Union and early Chartism', in **J. Epstein** & **D. Thompson** (eds), *The Chartism Experience: Studies in Working-Class Radicalism and Culture 1830–60*, Macmillan, 1982, pp. 59–86; **R. A. Sykes**, 'Some aspects of working-class consciousness in Oldham 1830–42', *Historical Journal*, XXIII, 1980, p. 171.
28. Quoted in Morris, *Class and Class Consciousness*, p. 10.
29. See for example, **G. Crossick**, *An Artisan Elite in Victorian Society*, Croom Helm, 1978 and his edited collection *The Lower Middle Class in Britain*, Croom Helm, 1977. See review by **N. McCord** of a recent

textbook in *Times Higher Education Supplement,* 10 February 1984.
30. For a well-argued defence of teaching the history of the working class in schools, see **I. Jones**, 'Whose class is it anyway?', *Teaching History,* 41, 1985, pp. 8–10.
31. **S. Alexander**, 'Women, class and sexual differences in the 1830s and 1840s: some reflections on the writing of a feminist history', *History Workshop Journal,* 17, 1984, pp. 125–49; **B. Taylor**, *Eve and the New Jerusalem,* Virago, 1983, esp. Ch. 4; **D. Thompson**, 'Women and nineteenth-century radical politics: a lost dimension', in **J. Mitchell** & **A. Oakley**, *The Rights and Wrongs of Women,* Penguin, 1976, p. 134. For a rather different view, see **D. Jones**, 'Women and Chartism', *History,* vol. 68, no. 222, 1983, pp. 1–20.

SELECT BIBLIOGRAPHY

CHAPTER 1. INTRODUCTION: PERSPECTIVES AND PROBLEMS

Emsley, C., *British Society and the French Wars 1793–1815*, Macmillan, 1979.
Floud, R. C. and McCoskey, D. N. (eds), *The Economic History of Britain Since 1700*, I, Cambridge U.P., 1981.
Hunt, E. H., *British Labour History 1815–1914*, Weidenfeld & Nicolson, 1981.
Mitchell, B. R. and Deane, P., *Abstract of British Historical Statistics*, Cambridge U.P., 1962.
Musson, A. E., *The Growth of British Industry*, Batsford, 1978.
Thompson, E. P., *The Making of the English Working Class*, Penguin, 1968.

CHAPTER 2. THE STANDARD OF LIVING

Flinn, M. W., 'Trends in real waves, 1750–1850', *Economic History Review* (second series), xxvii, no. 3, 1974, pp. 395–413.
Inglis, B., *Poverty and the Industrial Revolution*, Panther, 1972.
Perkin, H. J., *The Origins of Modern English Society 1780–1880*, Routledge & Kegan Paul, 1969.
Taylor, A. J. (ed.), *The Standard of Living in Britain in the Industrial Revolution*, Methuen, 1975.
Thompson, E. P., *The Making of the English Working Class*, Penguin, 1968.

CHAPTER 3. WORKING-CLASS CONSUMPTION

Burnett, J., *Plenty and Want: a social history of diet in England, 1815 to the present day*, Penguin, 1968.
Rule, J. G., 'Regional variations in food consumption among agricultural labourers, 1790–1860', in Minchinton, W. E. (ed.), *Agricultural Improvement: Medieval and Modern*, Exeter U.P., 1981, pp. 112–37.

Taylor, A. J. (ed.), *The Standard of Living in Britain in the Industrial Revolution*, Methuen, 1975.

CHAPTER 4. HOUSING

Burnett, J., *A Social History of Housing 1815–1970*, Methuen, 1980.
Chapman, S. D. (ed.), *The History of Working-class Housing: a Symposium*, David & Charles, 1971.
Corfield, P. J., *The Impact of English Towns 1700–1800*, Oxford U.P., 1982.
Engels, Frederick, *The Condition of the Working Class in England*, Granada, 1982.
Gauldie, E., *Cruel Habitations. A History of Working-Class Housing 1780–1918*, Unwin, 1974.
Hammond, J. L. and Hammond, B., *The Town Labourer*, Longman, 1979.
Pollard, S., 'The factory village in the industrial revolution', *Economic History Review* (second series), lxxix, 1964, pp. 513–31.
Thomis, M. I., *The Town Labourer and the Industrial Revolution*, Batsford, 1974.

CHAPTER 5. THE WAGE AND ITS FORM

Foster, J., *Class Struggle and the Industrial Revolution. Early Industrial Capitalism in three English Towns*, Methuen, 1974.
Hobsbawm, E. J., *Labouring Men*, Weidenfeld & Nicolson, 1964.
Linebaugh, P., 'Labour history without the power process: a note on John Gast and his times', *Social History*, VII, 3, 1982, pp. 319–28.
Pollard, S., *The Genesis of Modern Management*, Penguin, 1968.
Pollard S., 'Labour in Great Britain', in Mathias, P. & Postan, P. P. (eds), *Cambridge Economic History of Europe, VII. The Industrial Economies: Capital, Labour and Enterprise. Part I, Britain, France, Germany and Scandinavia*, Cambridge U.P., 1978, pp. 97–179.
Rule, J. G., *The Experience of Labour in Eighteenth-Century Industry*, Croom Helm, 1981.

CHAPTER 5. LABOUR INTENSITY, WORK DISCIPLINE AND HEALTH

Henriques, U. R. Q., *Before the Welfare State. Social Administration in early Industrial Britain*, Longman, 1979.
Pollard S., *The Genesis of Modern Management*, Penguin, 1968.
Rule, J. G., *The Experience of Labour in Eighteenth-Century Industry*, Croom Helm, 1981.

Thompson, E. P., *The Making of the English Working Class*, Penguin, 1968.
Thompson, E. P., 'Time, work discipline and industrial capitalism', *Past and Present*, no. 38, 1967, pp. 56–97.

CHAPTER 7. COMMUNITY

Bushaway, R. W., *By Rite. Custom, Ceremony and Community in England 1700–1880*, Junction Books, 1982.
Calhoun, C., *The Question of Class Struggle: Social Foundations of Popular Radicalism during the Industrial Revolution*, Blackwell, 1982.
Gilbert, A. D., *Religion and Society in Industrial England. Church, Chapel and Social Change 1740–1914*, Longman, 1976.
Mills, D. R., *Lord and Peasant in Nineteenth-Century Britain*, Croom Helm, 1980.
Obelkevich, J., *Religion and Rural Society. South Lindsey 1825–75*, Oxford U.P., 1976.
Perkin, H. J., *The Origins of Modern English Society 1780–1880*, Routledge & Kegan Paul, 1969.
Roberts, D., *Paternalism in Early Victorian England*, Croom Helm, 1979.
Storch, R. D. (ed.), *Popular Culture and Custom in Nineteenth-Century England*, Croom Helm, 1982.
Thompson, E. P., 'Eighteenth-century English society: class struggle without class', *Social History*, III, 2, 1978, pp. 133–65.

CHAPTER 8. THE FAMILY

Anderson, M. S., *Family Structure in Nineteenth-Century Lancashire*, Cambridge, U.P., 1971.
John A. V., *By the Sweat of their Brow. Women Workers at Victorian Coal Mines*, Croom Helm, 1980.
Mitchell, J. and **Oakley, A.** (eds), *The Rights and Wrongs of Women*, Penguin, 1976.
Pinchbeck, I., *Women Workers and the Industrial Revolution 1750–1850*, Cass, 1969.
Rotberg, R. I. and **Rabb, T. K.** (eds), *Marriage and Fertility*, Princeton U.P., 1980.
Smelser, N. J., *Social Change in the Industrial Revolution. An application of theory to the Lancashire cotton industry, 1770–1840*, Routledge & Kegan Paul, 1959.
Vincent, D., *Bread, Knowledge and Freedom: A Study of Nineteenth-Century Working-Class Autobiography*, Methuen, 1982.

CHAPTER 9. SENTIMENT AND SEX. THE FEELINGS OF THE WORKING CLASS

Anderson, M. S., *Family Structure in Nineteenth-Century Lancashire,* Cambridge U.P., 1971.

Laslett, T. P. R., *The World We Have Lost,* Methuen, 1968.

Levine, D., *Family Formation in an Age of Nascent Capitalism,* Academic Press, 1977.

Vincent, D., *Bread, Knowledge and Freedom: A Study of Nineteenth-Century Working-Class Autobiography,* Methuen, 1982.

Walkowitz, J. R., *Prostitution and Victorian Society. Women, Class and the State,* Cambridge U.P., 1980.

Weeks, J., *Sex, Politics and Society. The Regulation of Sexuality since 1800,* Longman, 1981.

CHAPTER 10. POPULAR RECREATION

Cunningham, H., *Leisure in the Industrial Revolution,* Croom Helm, 1980.

Malcolmson, R. W., *Popular Recreations in English Society 1700–1850,* Cambridge U.P., 1973.

Medick, H., 'Plebeian culture in the transition to capitalism', in **Samuel, R** & **Stedman Jones, G.** (eds), *Culture, Ideology and Politics,* Routledge, 1982, pp. 84–113.

Plumb, J. H., 'The commercialisation of leisure', in **McKendrick, N., Brewer, J.** & **Plumb, J. H.,** *The Birth of a Consumer Society. The Commercialisation of Eighteenth-century England,* Hutchinson, 1983, pp. 265–85.

Storch, R.D. (ed.), *Popular Culture and Custom in Nineteenth-Century England,* Croom Helm, 1982.

Thompson, E. P., 'Patrician society, plebeian culture', *Journal of Social History,* VII, no. 4, 1974, pp. 382–405.

Yeo, E. and **Yeo, S.** (eds), *Popular Culture and Class Conflict 1590–1914,* Harvester, 1982.

CHAPTER 11. EDUCATION FOR THE LOWER ORDERS

Henriques, U. R. Q., *Before the Welfare State. Social Administration in Early Industrial Britain,* Longman, 1979.

Hurt, J. S., *Education in Evolution 1800–1870,* Paladin, 1972.

Johnson, R., 'Educational policy and social control in early Victorian England', *Past and Present,* 49, 1970, pp. 96–119.

Laquer, T., *Religion and Respectability, Sunday Schools and Working-Class Culture,* Yale U.P., 1976.

McCann, P. (ed.), *Popular Education and Socialization in the Nineteenth Century,* Methuen, 1977.

Sanderson, M., 'Education and the factory in industrial Lancashire 1780–1840', *Economic History Review,* xx, no. 2, 1967, pp. 266–79.

Sanderson, M., 'Literacy and the Industrial Revolution', *Past and Present,* 56, 1972, pp. 75–104.

Sanderson, M., *Education, Economic Change and Society in England 1780–1870,* Macmillan, 1983.

Stone, L., 'Literacy and education in England 1640–1900', *Past and Present,* 42, 1969, pp. 69–139.

Vincent, D., *Bread, Knowledge and Freedom: A Study of Nineteenth-Century Working-Class Autobiography,* Methuen, 1982.

West, E. G., 'Resource allocation and growth in early nineteenth-century British education', *Economic History Review,* xxiii, no. 1, 1970, pp. 68–95.

CHAPTER 12. TRADE UNIONISM BEFORE 1825

Behagg, C., 'Custom, class and change: the trade societies of Birmingham', *Social History,* IV, no. 3, 1979, pp. 455–80.

Berg, M., *Technology and Toil in Nineteenth-Century Britain,* Humanities Press, 1979.

Dobson, C. R., *Masters and Journeymen. A Pre-history of Industrial Relations,* Croom Helm, 1980.

Foster, J., *Class Struggle and the Industrial Revolution. Early Industrial Capitalism in Three English Towns,* Unwin, 1977.

George, M. D., 'The Combination Laws', *Economic History Review,* vi, 1936, pp. 172–8.

Hammond, J. L. and **Hammond, B.,** *The Skilled Labourer,* Longman, 1979.

Hobsbawm, E. J., *Labouring Men,* Weidenfeld & Nicolson, 1964.

Leeson, R. A., *Travelling Brothers,* Unwin, 1979.

Musson, A. E., *British Trade Unions, 1800–875,* Macmillan, 1972.

Musson, A. E. and **Kirby, R. G.,** *The Voice of the People, John Doherty, 1798–1854,* Manchester U.P., 1975.

Prothero, I., *Artisans and Politics in Early Nineteenth-Century London. John Gast and His Times,* Dawson, 1979.

Rule, J. G., *The Experience of Labour in Eighteenth-Century Industry,* Croom Helm, 1981.

Thompson, E. P., *The Making of the English Working Class,* Penguin, 1968.

Webb, S. and **Webb, B.,** *History of Trade Unionism,* Longman, 1911.

CHAPTER 13. THE REPEAL OF THE COMBINATION ACTS AND THE AFTERMATH

Frazer, W. H., 'Trade unionism', in **Ward, J. T.** (ed.), *Popular Movements* *c.1830–1850*, Macmillan, 1970, pp. 95–115.

Hammond, J. L. and **Hammond, B.**, *The Skilled Labourer*, Longman, 1979.

Musson, A. E., *British Trade Unionism 1800–1875*, Macmillan, 1972.

Musson, A. E., *Trade Union and Social History*, Cass, 1974.

Oliver, W. H., 'The Consolidated Trades' Union of 1834', *Economic History Review*, xvii, no. 1, 1964, pp. 77–95.

Prothero, I., *Artisans and Politics in Early Nineteenth-Century London. John Gast and His Times*, Dawson, 1979.

Thompson, E. P., *The Making of the English Working Class*, Penguin, 1968.

Webb, S. and **Webb, B.**, *History of Trade Unionism*, Longman, 1911.

CHAPTER 14. POST-1834: CRAFT UNIONISM, MINERS AND CHARTISM

Behagg, C., 'Secrecy, ritual and folk violence: the opacity of the workplace in the first half of the nineteenth century', in **Storch, R. D.** (ed.), *Popular Culture and Custom in Nineteenth-Century England*, Croom Helm, 1982, pp. 154–79.

Challinor, R. and **Ripley, B.**, *The Miners' Association: a trade union in the age of the Chartists*, Lawrence & Wishart, 1968.

Epstein, J. and **Thompson, D.** (eds), *The Chartist Experience*, Macmillan, 1982.

Foster, J., *Class Struggle and the Industrial Revolution. Early Industrial Capitalism in Three English Towns*, Unwin, 1977.

Hammond, J. L. and **Hammond, B.**, *The Skilled Labourer*, Longman, 1979.

Mather, F. C., 'The general strike of 1842: a study of leadership, organisation and the threat of revolution during the plug plot disturbances', in **Quinault, R.** & **Stevenson, J.** (eds), *Popular Protest and Public Order*, Unwin, 1974, pp. 115–35.

Prothero, I., 'London Chartism and the trades', *Economic History Review*, xxiv, no. 2, 1971, pp. 202–18.

Thompson, E. P., *The Making of the English Working Class*, Penguin, 1968.

Webb, S. and **Webb, B.**, *History of Trade Unionism*, Longman, 1911.

CHAPTER 15. THE PROTESTING CROWD: RIOTS AND DISTURBANCES

Calhoun, C., *The Question of Class Struggle: Social Foundations of Popular Radicalism during the Industrial Revolution*, Blackwell, 1982.

Charlesworth, A. (ed.), *An Atlas of Rural Protest in Britain, 1548–1900*, Croom Helm, 1983.

Hammond, J. L. and **Hammond, B.**, *The Skilled Labourer*, Longman, 1979.

Hobsbawm, E. J. and **Rudé, G.**, *Captain Swing*, Penguin, 1973.

Jones, D. J. V., *Crime, Protest, Community and Police in Nineteenth-Century*

Britain, Routledge, 1982.

Randall, A., 'The shearmen and the Wiltshire outrages of 1802: trade unionism and industrial violence', *Social History,* VII, no. 3, pp. 283–304.

Rudé, G., *The Crowd in History,* Wiley, 1964.

Rule, J. G., 'Social crime in the rural south in the eighteenth and early nineteenth centuries', *Southern History,* I, 1979, pp. 135–53.

Stevenson, J., *Popular Disturbances in England 1700–1870,* Longman, 1979.

Thomis, M. I., *The Luddites. Machine Breaking in Regency England,* David & Charles, 1970.

Thompson, E. P., 'The moral economy of the English crowd in the eighteenth century', *Past and Present,* 50, 1971, pp. 76–136.

Wells, R. A. E., 'The development of the English rural proletariat and social protest, 1700–1850', *Journal of Peasant Studies,* 6, 1979, pp. 115–39.

CHAPTER 16. CONCLUSION: CLASS AND CLASS CONSCIOUSNESS

Alexander, A., 'Women, class and sexual differences in the 1830s and 1840s: some reflections on the writing of a feminist history', *History Workshop Journal,* 17, 1984, pp. 125–49.

Briggs, A., 'The language of class in early nineteenth-century England', in **Briggs, A. & Saville, J.** (eds), *Essays in Labour History,* Macmillan, 1967, pp. 43–63.

Foster, J., *Class Struggle and the Industrial Revolution. Early Industrial Capitalism in Three English Towns,* Unwin, 1977.

Morris, R. J., *Class and Class Consciousness in the Industrial Revolution,* Macmillan, 1979.

Neale, R. S., *Class in English History 1680–1850,* Barnes & Noble, 1981.

Perkin, H. J., *The Origins of Modern English Society 1780–1880,* Routledge & Kegan Paul, 1969.

Rule, J. G., *The Experience of Labour in Eighteenth-Century Industry,* Croom Helm, 1981.

Stedman Jones, G., *The Language of Class,* Cambridge U.P., 1984.

Thompson, E. P., *The Making of the English Working Class,* Penguin, 1968.

Thompson, E. P., 'Eighteenth-century English society: class struggle without class', *Social History,* III, no. 2, 1978, pp. 133–65.

INDEX